# Development and Maintenance of Prosocial Behavior

## International Perspectives on Positive Morality

## CRITICAL ISSUES IN SOCIAL JUSTICE

Series Editor: **MELVIN J. LERNER**
*University of Waterloo*
*Waterloo, Ontario, Canada*

---

THE JUSTICE MOTIVE IN SOCIAL BEHAVIOR
Adapting to Times of Scarcity and Change
Edited by Melvin J. Lerner and Sally C. Lerner

CHILDREN'S COMPETENCE TO CONSENT
Edited by Gary B. Melton, Gerald P. Koocher, and Michael J. Saks

JUSTICE AND THE CRITIQUE OF PURE PSYCHOLOGY
Edward E. Sampson

THE SENSE OF INJUSTICE
Social Psychological Perspectives
Edited by Robert G. Folger

DEVELOPMENT AND MAINTENANCE OF PROSOCIAL BEHAVIOR
International Perspectives on Positive Morality
Edited by Ervin Staub, Daniel Bar-Tal, Jerzy Karylowski, and Janusz Reykowski

---

A Continuation Order Plan is available for this series. A continuation order will bring delivery of each new volume immediately upon publication. Volumes are billed only upon actual shipment. For further information please contact the publisher.

# Development and Maintenance of Prosocial Behavior

## International Perspectives on Positive Morality

Edited by

Ervin Staub
*University of Massachusetts*
*Amherst, Massachusetts*

Daniel Bar-Tal
*Tel-Aviv University*
*Tel-Aviv, Israel*

Jerzy Karylowski
*University of North Florida*
*Jacksonville, Florida*

and

Janusz Reykowski
*Polish Academy of Science*
*Warsaw, Poland*

Plenum Press • New York and London

Library of Congress Cataloging in Publication Data

Main entry under title:

Development and maintenance of prosocial behavior.

(Critical issues in social justice)
Includes bibliographies and indexes.
1. Social ethics—Addresses, essays, lectures. 2. Helping behavior—Addresses, essays, lectures. 3. Cooperation—Addresses, essays, lectures. 4. Altruism—Addresses, essays, lectures. I. Staub, Ervin. II. Series.
HM216.D44 1984 170 84-3355
ISBN 0-306-41299-3


A Division of Plenum Publishing Corporation
233 Spring Street, New York, N.Y. 10013



Printed in the United States of America

# Contributors

DANIEL BAR-TAL, School of Education, Tel Aviv University, Tel Aviv, Israel

LEONARD BICKMAN, Department of Psychology and Human Development, Peabody College of Vanderbilt University, Nashville, Tennessee

HANS WERNER BIERHOFF, Department of Psychology, Philipps-University Marburg, Marburg, West Germany

PETER CALLERO, Department of Sociology, University of California at Riverside, Riverside, California

ELLEN CAMERON, Department of Psychology, Arizona State University, Tempe, Arizona

BELLA M. DEPAULO, Department of Psychology, Gilmer Hall, University of Virginia, Charlottesville, Virginia

W. R. DULL, Department of Psychology, Gilmer Hall, University of Virginia, Charlottesville, Virginia

NANCY EISENBERG, Department of Psychology, Arizona State University, Tempe, Arizona

DORCAS E. EVANS, Stanford Heart Disease Prevention Program, Stanford University, Stanford, California

JEFFREY D. FISHER, Department of Psychology, University of Connecticut, Storrs, Connecticut

JAN HELLER, District Health Service, Heerlen, the Netherlands

RACHEL HERTZ-LAZAROWITZ, School of Education, Haifa University, Haifa, Israel

MARTIN L. HOFFMAN, Department of Psychology, University of Michigan, Ann Arbor, Michigan

JUDITH A. HOWARD, Department of Sociology, University of Washington, Seattle, Washington

JERZY KARYLOWSKI, Department of Psychology, University of North Florida, Jacksonville, Florida

GRAZYNA KOCHANSKA, Laboratory of Developmental Psychology, National Institute of Mental Health, Bethesda, Maryland

MIROSLAW KOFTA, Department of Psychology, University of Warsaw, Warsaw, Poland

CHARLES KORTE, Division of University Studies, North Carolina State University, Raleigh, North Carolina

VICKI LEIPHART, Department of Psychology, Gilmer Hall, University of Virginia, Charlottesville, Virginia

ELIZABETH MIDLARSKY, Department of Psychology, University of Detroit, Detroit, Michigan

ARIE NADLER, Department of Psychology, Tel Aviv University, Ramat-Aviv, Israel

LOUIS OPPENHEIMER, Department of Developmental Psychology, University of Amsterdam, Amsterdam, the Netherlands

JANE ALLYN PILIAVIN, Department of Sociology, University of Wisconsin, Madison, Wisconsin

MARIAN RADKE-YARROW, Laboratory of Developmental Psychology, National Institute of Mental Health, Bethesda, Maryland

JANUSZ REYKOWSKI, Department of Psychology, Polish Academy of Science, Warsaw, Poland

SIDNEY ROSEN, Institute for Behavioral Research and Department of Psychology, University of Georgia, Athens, Georgia

J. PHILIPPE RUSHTON, Department of Psychology, University of Western Ontario, London, Ontario, Canada

SHALOM H. SCHWARTZ, Department of Psychology, Hebrew University, Jerusalem, Israel

RUTH SHARABANY, Department of Psychology, Haifa University, Haifa, Israel

Shlomo Sharan, School of Education, Tel Aviv University, Tel Aviv, Israel

Durganand Sinha, A. N. S. Institute of Social Studies, Patna, India

Ervin Staub, Department of Psychology, University of Massachusetts, Amherst, Massachusetts

Kelly Tryon, Department of Psychology, Arizona State University, Tempe, Arizona

Stephen Worchel, Department of Psychology, Texas A & M University, College Station, Texas

Carolyn Zahn-Waxler, Laboratory of Developmental Psychology, National Institute of Mental Health, Bethesda, Maryland

# Preface

This book was inspired by an intimate, stimulating, intellectually enriching conference that took place in Poland. However, the book is not a conference report. Rather, at the time of the conference, participants agreed that it would be worthwhile to create a volume representing the international state of knowledge in prosocial behavior, and many of them agreed to write chapters. This volume is the outcome.

The book contains chapters by outstanding researchers and scholars who have made substantial contributions to some aspect of scholarship about prosocial behavior—helpfulness, generosity, kindness, cooperation, or other behavior that benefits people. The book concerns itself with how prosocial behavior comes about and what influences contribute to or inhibit it; how prosocial behavior, or values and other personal characteristics that promote prosocial behavior, develop; how socialization, peer interaction, and other experiences contribute to development; and with the cognitive, emotional, and behavioral consequences of receiving help. Some chapters directly, and a number of them implicitly, concern themselves with applications of knowledge about prosocial behavior, particularly with the question of how cooperation and behavior that benefits other people can be promoted.

The purpose of the book is in part to show where the field stands and what knowledge we have accumulated, and in part to suggest future directions and advance the field. It is a truly international book, with contributors from most countries where research on prosocial behavior is being conducted.

I should like to express my gratitude to my coeditors, and to others who importantly contributed to the success of the conference and thereby indirectly to the creation of this book. Daniel Bar-Tal and Janusz Reykowski initiated the idea of the conference and were tireless in organizing it. Martin L. Hoffman, Paul Mussen, Jerzy Karylowski, and I were additional members of its organizing committee. Janusz Reykowski hosted the conference with his enthusiastic and always helpful associates. By their hospitality and grace they laid the groundwork for an atmosphere of camaraderie, warmth, and intellectual excitement. I hope this book embodies the inspiration that arose from this atmosphere.

ERVIN STAUB

# Contents

*Chapter 4*



*Chapter 5*



*Chapter 6*

## PART III DETERMINANTS OF PROSOCIAL BEHAVIOR

*Chapter 20*



## PART V APPLICATIONS OF KNOWLEDGE ABOUT PROSOCIAL BEHAVIOR



*Chapter 21*

# Introduction

## Status of the Field, Trends, Issues, and Tasks[1]

Ervin Staub

During the past decade and a half there has been a revolutionary increase in the amount and variety of research and theorizing about the determinants and development of behaviors that benefit other people—such as helpfulness, kindness, generosity, cooperation—which have been jointly called prosocial behaviors. The study of such behaviors, and of the values and emotional orientations that give rise to them, represents the study of the positive aspects of human morality, the *thou shalts*, the conduct prescribed rather than prohibited by moral rules and principles. On the whole, such behaviors promote human welfare. This book brings together work in this domain by psychologists from around the world.

Lively activity exists and important contributions are being made to this realm of knowledge in Poland and in West Germany, in Holland and in Israel, in the United States and in other countries. This volume is intended to familiarize the reader with the range and variety of research and theorizing in this domain, to summarize existing knowledge, and to advance the field by representing the domain in an interrelated and cumulative fashion.

The initial research on prosocial behavior in both social and developmental psychology consisted mainly of experimental and field studies exploring the influence of specific variables, primarily environmental

[1]This introduction is a brief discussion of issues in the field, and of their representation in this book, rather than a preview of chapters. References to chapters in the book are illustrative, not exhaustive.

conditions or situational influences, on the likelihood of prosocial behavior. This work was of great significance: It called attention to this previously neglected domain of human behavior and accumulated many important findings that received repeated replication. A number of books described and reviewed both the early work and later developments and provided integration (Bar-Tal, 1976; Latané & Darley, 1970; Rushton, 1980; Staub, 1978a, 1979; see Chapter 1).

In the present volume a number of major developments are represented. One of these is the increasing number of interconnected sets of studies, some conducted in real-life settings, that carry us from a bird's-eye view to a closeup or enlargement of parts of the terrain. For example, the studies of Radke-Yarrow and Zahn-Waxler (Chapter 4) represent a careful, finely grained analysis of early socializing influences that contribute to the development of prosocial behavior in children. Schwartz and his associates (Chapter 11) have been engaged in a detailed exploration of how personal norms and some other individual characteristics influence helpful behavior. Their studies contribute to understanding what influences lead to or determine positive, helpful acts.

From the beginning psychologists working in this domain paid attention to the *psychological processes* that lead to helping and not helping, which are the most direct determinants of behavior. They include definitional processes—how events are perceived and what meanings are assigned to them; the experience of responsibility for another person's welfare or for taking action on behalf of another; feelings of empathy; decision making; and others. Latané and Darley (1970), in their influential early work, began to theorize about psychological processes important in leading to (or inhibiting) helpful behavior. Many chapters in this volume describe research and present theory that identify relevant psychological processes, their antecedents and consequences. For example, Hoffman's theorizing (Chapter 6) represents progressive movement toward an extended theory both of psychological processes—empathy and guilt in particular—that lead to prosocial acts and of their developmental antecedents.

In addition to important extensions of early work both through in-depth analyses of specific domains and further exploration of relevant psychological processes, there has been increasing focus on the role of personal characteristics in positive behavior. The general interest in personality and social psychology in interactional approaches (Bowers, 1973; Magnusson & Endler, 1977; Mischel, 1973; Pervin & Lewis, 1978), in the assumption that personality and situations jointly determine behavior, and in attempts to specify how this happens, has gained clear expression in the realm of prosocial behavior (Staub, 1978a,b, 1980; Wilson, 1976). The work of Janusz Reykowski and his colleagues in Poland was probably the earliest serious attempt to consider prosocial behavior as the expression of the individual's personality. This thinking and its developments and extensions are presented in chapters by Reykowski, Karylowski, and Kochanska. My own research and theorizing in the past few years have also been guided by the assumption that prosocial behavior is an expression of the totality of an individual's personality (with some emphasis placed on the motivational aspects of personality) in combination with the environment that an individual encounters, or seeks and creates (Chapter 2). The importance of personality has also been emphasized in Rushton's work (Chapter 13) and in the work of Schwartz (Chapter 11) and others.

The new developments in the field include attempts to create theoretical frameworks to account for all forms of prosocial behavior, and to recognize the coherence of prosocial and other forms of social behavior. This again is characteristic of the approach taken by the Polish group and by my own. In recent European psychology, an action-theoretical approach—essentially a theory of social action—has gained influence. This approach is applied to the domain of prosocial behavior by Oppenheimer and Heller (Chapter 9).

In summary, we are moving toward thorough empirical exploration of the determinants and development of many kinds of prosocial behavior; toward a consideration of personality; toward broader theoretical approaches; and to a recognition of positive behavior being the expression of the totality of a person's personality as it joins with a person's environment. How personality gains expression in interaction with circumstances is beginning to be specified. In the realm of development, also, it is necessary to recognize that the development of positive behavioral tendencies, which necessarily depends on the development of individual characteristics—values, motives, role taking, empathic capacity, a positive self-concept—is part of the development of the totality of the child's personality and social behavior. Moreover, the child's developing personality itself becomes a source of continuing development, affecting the child's interaction with the environment, including socializing agents and peers, and thereby the child's experiences which further shape his or her personality and social behavior.

As Bar-Tal notes in his introduction to Part IV, "to focus only on help giving while studying interactions involving helping behavior can be compared to watching only a half court during a basketball game." This book also explores help seeking, and the consequences of help for recipients—as well as its effects on helpers themselves. Helping behavior under most circumstances is interactive. Would-be recipients can greatly affect whether helping will occur, and are greatly affected not only by the occurrence and nonoccurrence of helping but by the manner in which they are helped. Helping can be of true benefit, material and psychological, or it can deprive recipients of power, status, or for other reasons have negative psychological consequences. Helping can occur on individual or community levels. The opportunity for and experience of cooperation and of helping others can have important psychological consequences, such as increasing self-esteem, improving relationships between children, and increasing their later helpfulness, as the chapter by Hertz-Lazarowitz and Sharan shows. These and other content areas, linked to important theoretical and practical questions—for example, about the best forms of education, about providing welfare and other benefits to people in need in the most positive ways, and about human well-being in general—are explored in a number of contributions.

Also worth noting are some lacunae, the tasks that face us. There has been little attempt to integrate different approaches that, although they have different foci, are connected in substantial ways and thus might greatly enrich each other. For example, although the development of moral reasoning and of prosocial behavior have been jointly considered by researchers who examined the empirical relationship between level of moral reasoning and prosocial behavior (Eisenberg, 1982; Staub, 1978a, 1979), the theoretical linkage received little attention. The same is true of the relation between the conception of a just world and positive behavior (Lerner, 1981). Like relatives, workers in this field have cursory connections, but as in many families, little effort is made to develop real connectedness. The same applies to the connection between the study of altruism and prosocial behavior on the one hand, and of aggression and antisocial behavior on the other. Beginnings are being made in considering relationships, but integration, or broader theory with accompanying research, is yet awaited. Both are important tasks, and thus theoretical attempts that integrate and tie together some of these obviously related phenomena of morality are timely and desirable.

## REFERENCES

Bar-Tal, D. *Prosocial behavior: Theory and research.* Washington, D.C.: Hemisphere, 1976.

Bowers, K. S. Situationism in psychology: An analysis and a critique. *Psychological Review,* 1973, *80,* 307–336.

Eisenberg, N. (Ed.). *The development of prosocial behavior.* New York: Academic Press, 1982.

Latané, B., & Darley, J. M. *The unresponsive bystander: Why doesn't he help?* New York: Appleton-Century-Crofts, 1970.

Lerner, M. J. *The belief in a just world: A fundamental delusion.* New York: Plenum Press, 1981.

Magnusson, D., & Endler, N. S. *Personality at the crossroads: Current issues in international psychology.* Hillsdale, N.J.: Lawrence Erlbaum, 1977.

Mischel, W. Towards a cognitive social learning reconceptualization of personality. *Psychological Review*, 1973, *80*, 242–283.

Pervin, L., & Lewis, M. (Eds.). *Perspectives in international psychology*. New York: Plenum Press, 1978.

Rushton, J. P. *Altruism, socialization and society*. Englewood Cliffs, N.J.: Prentice-Hall, 1980.

Staub, E. *Positive social behavior and morality*. Vol. 1. *Personal and social influences*. New York: Academic Press, 1978. (a)

Staub, E. Predicting social behavior: A model for specifying the nature of personality-situation interaction. In L. A. Pervin & M. Lewis (Eds.), *Perspectives in interactional psychology*. New York: Plenum Press, 1978. (b)

Staub, E. *Positive social behavior and morality*. Vol. 2. *Socialization and development*. New York: Academic Press, 1979.

Staub, E. Social and prosocial behavior: Personal and situational influences and their interactions. In E. Staub (Ed.), *Personality: Basic aspects and current research*. Englewood Cliffs, N.J.: Prentice-Hall, 1980.

Wilson, J. P. Motivation, modeling and altruism: A person × situation analysis. *Journal of Personality and Social Psychology*, 1976, *34*, 1078–1086.

# I
# GENERAL THEORETICAL APPROACHES

# Introduction

Janusz Reykowski

In the mid-1970s, it became obvious that a new, vigorous, and rapidly expanding field of research had appeared in psychology and that new chapters had to be added to textbooks of social and developmental psychology, and even of introductory psychology. As Daniel Bar-Tal argues in Chapter 1, the growth of interest by American psychologists in helping behavior, altruism, and prosocial behavior is clearly related to the social problems of American society. Bar-Tal suggests that this interest stems from the desire to improve the quality of interpersonal life and that it has led to a theoretical attempt to deal with some evils of contemporary urban life in industrial societies. But as this international volume may indicate, the interest in prosocial phenomena is not limited to the American scene. As early as the second half of the 1960s, systematic studies on prosocial behavior began in Poland. In Soviet psychology study of this topic, although under different names, has a long tradition. Apparently, there are different reasons for interest in prosocial behavior, possibly related to the social problems of countries where many conditions necessary for the utilization of individualistic motives for performing social tasks are absent. In effect, there are many factors present that undermine the effectiveness of self-oriented (e.g., consumer-type) motivation for promoting social welfare. In such circumstances the search for alternative sources of human social motivation seems to be, for social scientists, the most relevant issue.

The study of prosocial behavior is still in an early stage. There are still numerous inconsistencies in obtained data and a lack of integration in views of the field. There are, however, growing attempts at achieving such integration. The most advanced recent attempt is presented in the chapter by Ervin Staub. The author, one of those few who have contributed extensively to the development of the field and who published a few years ago two volumes representing a comprehensive review of the field of prosocial studies, offers a model that opens a possibility of integrating a wide body of research conducted until now within separate domains. In fact, Staub's model consists of a set of heuristic principles that can promote integration of variables employed in studies on situational, personality, and developmental determinants of prosocial behavior. Although the author claims that he develops an interactionistic view, it seems to be something more. Using the term "personal prosocial goal" as the key concept of his model, he was able not only to demonstrate the relationship between personality and environmental variables, as it has been done by interactionism, but also to extend it to developmental phenomena. He argues that interaction between "existing personality" and socializing factors contribute to the formation of a prosocial goal—the basic precondition of a prosocial act.

Accepting the assumption that people do have prosocial goals, we must ask: What is the specific nature of the goal? Is it a homogeneous phenomenon or a heterogeneous one? If the latter, we may expect that there are prosocial goals of different kinds and different origin. This is my position in the next chapter, where I argue that prosocial motivation can appear as a result of a specific organization of an individual cognitive system. I present theoretical reasoning, as well as some data from different sources, indicating that the position of representation of a social object in relation to the self-structure has some bearing upon processing information related to the object as well as upon attitudes toward the object. Available facts indicate that value attributed to the object and motivation to act on behalf of it seem to be primarily a function of its location in the subject's cognitive system. This is not the only source of the prosocial goal, but recognition of this specific source of prosocial action points clearly to the inadequacy of the traditional dilemma: Is the prosocial motivation taught by society or does it originate from inborn propensities of the human organism? In fact, it emerges as any other kind of motivation, being to some extent an inevitable consequence of a normal process of personality formation. But its forms and scope vary enormously owing to specific conditions of personality growth and functioning.

# 1

# American Study of Helping Behavior

## What? Why? and Where?

Daniel Bar-Tal

## 1. INTRODUCTION

The last decade has witnessed a rapid expansion in the study of helping behavior[1] within social and developmental psychology. Although the subject itself has preoccupied psychologists in previous decades (e.g., Handlon & Gross, 1959; Hartshorne & May, 1928; Murphy, 1937; Rosenbaum, 1956; Ugurel-Semin, 1952; Wright, 1942), it is only since the end of the 1960s that helping behavior has been extensively and systematically examined (see, e.g., Bar-Tal, 1976; Mussen & Eisenberg-Berg, 1977; Staub, 1978, 1979; Wispé, 1978).

This chapter has three goals. The first is to describe *what* were the origins and directions of the study of helping behavior in the past decade. The second is to explain *why* the study of helping behavior has expanded in the last decade and why it developed along certain direc-

This chapter is based on a presentation at the International Conference on the Development and Maintenance of Prosocial Behavior, Warsaw, June 1980.

[1]*Helping behavior* is a general term referring to acts that benefit others with no external rewards promised *a priori* in return. Cases in which rewards are promised are referred to as *exchange acts*. Helping behavior encompasses a variety of acts such as sharing, aiding, supporting, or donation (Bar-Tal, 1981).

DANIEL BAR-TAL • School of Education, Tel Aviv University, Tel Aviv, Israel.

tions. The last goal is to suggest *where* the study of helping behavior is headed and to propose possible directions for the future.

## 2. HELPING BEHAVIOR: WHAT?

### 2.1. Origins of Helping Behavior Research

The emergence of research into helping behavior can be directly traced to a number of theoretical sources: Gouldner's (1960) proposition regarding the prevalence of the universalistic norm of reciprocity; Leads's (1963) suggestion regarding the prescription of the norm of giving; Piaget's (1932) and Kohlberg's (1958, 1969) theorizing about the development of moral judgment; and Aronfreed's (1968) conceptualization of conscience development. These theories explicitly discuss social conditions for helping behavior, or implicitly offer a cognitive and motivational basis for helping behavior. However, it should be pointed out that most of the helping behavior research has not developed from a particular theory, but has resulted from problem-oriented research questions. Such questions as why people are often apathetic and do not help others, what conditions facilitate helping, or what personal characteristics are associated with the tendency to help have guided the study of helping behavior.

The pioneering systematic studies of helping behavior, which influenced the research of the last decade, were performed in the mid-1960s by Berkowitz and his associates (e.g., Berkowitz & Connor, 1966; Berkowitz & Daniels, 1963, 1964; Daniels & Berkowitz, 1963; Goranson & Berkowitz, 1966). These studies investigated the socially responsible (helping) behavior of individuals toward others who were dependent upon them for their goal attainment. This research grew out of Berkowitz's earlier interest in certain aspects of group behavior (Berkowitz, 1970). In addition to Berkowitz's research, the murder of Kitty Genovese in 1964 (Rosenthal, 1964) can be identified as a key case influencing the emergence of helping behavior research. In this case, 38 individuals who witnessed a murder neither directly intervened nor sought other ways to help the victim. Two social psychologists, John Darley and Bibb Latané, who heard about the Genovese case and were staggered by the human apathy and its tragic consequence, initiated a series of experiments to investigate why bystanders do not help (e.g., Darley & Latané, 1968; Latané & Darley, 1968). These imaginative experiments were influential in stimulating helping behavior research. Finally, one cannot overlook the influence of several comprehensive reviews of the research literature. Reviews conducted by Bryan and London (1970), Krebs

(1970), and Midlarsky (1968) organized the existing studies in accordance with the investigated variables. These works contributed to directing the attention of psychologists to this area, and, since the late sixties, social and developmental psychologists have produced a great volume of studies on helping behavior.

## 2.2. Directions of Study of Helping Behavior

### *2.2.1. Magnitude of Research*

In the last decade the study of helping behavior has become an important focus of social and developmental psychology. This is demonstrated by the fact that textbooks have begun to include a separate chapter devoted to helping behavior (e.g., Baron & Byrne, 1977; Freedman, Sears, & Carlsmith, 1978; Hetherington & Parke, 1975; Meyer & Dusek, 1979; Middlebrook, 1974; Schneider, 1976). In addition, numerous books devoted entirely to this topic have been published (e.g., Bar-Tal, 1976; Hornstein, 1976; Latané & Darley, 1970; Macaulay & Berkowitz, 1970; Mussen & Eisenberg-Berg, 1977; Staub, 1978, 1979; Wispé, 1978). It is a trend that has been clearly documented in social psychology. Hendrick and his colleagues have catalogued social psychological research for each of the past 4 years. In 1975 Capasso and Hendrick (1976) reviewed 530 social psychological journal articles taken from 15 journals for the second half of 1975 and classified them under 34 subject headings. The "Altruism and helping" category ranked third, with 36 articles. A review of 1976 (Capasso, Hendrick, Rahal, & Coleman, 1977) indicated that the "Helping" category, comprising 36 articles, ranked fourth among 38 categories representing 730 articles drawn from 14 journals. In 1977 the "Helping" category ranked sixth among 31 categories (Richardson, Tomarelli, & Hendrick, 1978), and in 1978 it ranked fourth among 33 categories (Reeves, Richardson, & Hendrick, 1979).

Table 1 presents the publication trend over the last decade (1970–1979) in three American social psychological journals, *Journal of Personality and Social Psychology*, *Journal of Experimental Social Psychology*, and *Journal of Applied Social Psychology*, and two American developmental psychological journals, *Developmental Psychology* and *Child Development*. Table 1 indicates that the study of helping behavior received much attention from American social and developmental psychologists in the last decade. At least about 2% of the articles in those journals were devoted to the study of helping behavior. Social psychological journals published more articles about helping behavior than did developmental journals. In the former journals, at least about 5% of the articles focused on helping behavior, and in the *Journal of Applied Social Psychology* this percentage was actually much higher (about 12%).

*Table 1. Percentage of Articles about Helping Behavior in Five Journals, 1970–1979*

| Year | *Journal of Personality and Social Psychology* | *Journal of Experimental Social Psychology* | *Journal of Applied Social Psychology* | *Developmental Psychology* | *Child Development* |
|---|---|---|---|---|---|
| 1970 | 3.9% (7)[a] | 2.5% (1) | — | 1.4% (2) | 3.8% (4) |
| 1971 | 5.3% (11) | 7.4% (4) | 11.5% (3) | 1.1% (2) | 1.4% (3) |
| 1972 | 4.8% (10) | 5.9% (3) | 10.0% (3) | 0.6% (1) | 0.7% (1) |
| 1973 | 5.1% (11) | 10.0% (5) | 11.8% (4) | 2.1% (3) | 2.1% (3) |
| 1974 | 3.4% (7) | 2.0% (1) | 31.0% (9) | 2.9% (4) | 1.4% (2) |
| 1975 | 8.6% (24) | 5.7% (3) | 13.3% (4) | 1.7% (3) | 1.9% (3) |
| 1976 | 4.4% (11) | 4.0% (2) | 11.8% (4) | 2.8% (3) | 2.8% (5) |
| 1977 | 0.7% (1) | 4.2% (2) | 9.7% (3) | 1.6% (2) | 1.2% (3) |
| 1978 | 5.0% (7) | 5.7% (3) | 6.7% (2) | 1.8% (2) | 1.1% (2) |
| 1979 | 3.3% (6) | 2.3% (1) | 9.3% (4) | 7.8% (8) | 2.9% (5) |
| Total | 4.7% (95) | 5.1% (25) | 12.5% (36) | 2.2% (30) | 1.8% (31) |

[a]In parentheses are numbers of helping behavior articles.

It should be noted that, in general, in European journals the study of helping behavior has received only minor attention. For example, in the *British Journal of Social and Clinical Psychology* only five articles about helping behavior were published from 1970 to 1979, and in the *European Journal of Social Psychology* only five articles pertaining to helping behavior appeared from 1971 to 1979. In the *International Journal of Behavioral Development,* which has appeared only since 1978, there were two articles about the development of helping behavior. Polish and West German journals, however, are exceptions to this trend.

### 2.2.2. *Directions and Methods of Research*

Although this review indicates the volume of research, it does not indicate the directions of helping behavior study. To facilitate such analysis, nine categories of subject matter have been selected and the published research has been classified along them. Table 2 shows the classification of helping behavior research in five journals. This table shows that the great majority of studies investigated situational and personal variables affecting helping behavior. More than 50% of the articles in the *Journal of Personality and Social Psychology* and more than 70% in the *Journal of Experimental Social Psychology* and the *Journal of Applied Social Psychology* were devoted to the investigation of situational variables. In the *Journal of Personality and Social Psychology* a number of articles were devoted to the investigation of personal variables (9.5%), mediating factors (8.4%), process of helping (6.3%), and cultural variables (5.3%). In the developmental journals, over 40% of the articles were devoted to the investigation of either situational variables or social learning conditions. In addition, at least 15% of the articles focused on cognitive developmental processes.

Examination of the studies reveals that helping behavior researchers investigated a number of different situational and personal variables. Among the situational variables most investigated were types of verbal requests, prior helping, observation of helping behavior, observation of harm doing, presence of other individuals, ambiguity of the situation, outcome of a performance on a task, size of the request, degree of the dependency of the person in need, characteristics of the person in need, and physical distance between the potential helper and the person in need. Among the most frequently investigated personal variables were age, sex, race, socioeconomic status, birth order, social approval, mood, justice motive, level of moral development, level of cognitive development, locus of control, and social responsibility.

In spite of the large quantity of research, it is difficult to draw unequivocal conclusions about helping behavior processes. The attempt

*Table 2. Classification of Articles about Helping Behavior According to Subject Matter in Five Journals, 1970–1979*

| Subject matter | *Journal of Personality and Social Psychology* | | *Journal of Experimental Social Psychology* | | *Journal of Applied Social Psychology* | | *Developmental Psychology* | | *Child Development* | |
|---|---|---|---|---|---|---|---|---|---|---|
| | Articles | | Articles | | Articles | | Articles | | Articles | |
| | Number | Percentage | Number | Percentage | Number | Percentage | Number | Percentage | Number | Percentage |
| Personal variables[a] | 9 | 9.5% | 3 | 12% | 3 | 8.3% | 2 | 6.7% | 5 | 16.6% |
| Situational variables | 53 | 55.8% | 19 | 76% | 27 | 75.0% | 5 | 16.7% | 5 | 16.1% |
| Personal and situational variables | 8 | 8.4% | 1 | 4% | 4 | 11.1% | 2 | 6.7% | 2 | 6.5% |
| Cultural variables | 5 | 5.3% | — | — | 1 | 2.8% | — | — | 1 | 3.2% |
| Process of helping[b] | 6 | 6.3% | 1 | 4% | — | — | — | — | 1 | 3.2% |
| Mediating factors | 8 | 8.4% | — | — | 1 | 2.8% | 3 | 10.0% | — | — |
| Parents' socialization practices | 2 | 2.1% | — | — | — | — | 3 | 10.0% | 1 | 3.2% |
| Social learning conditions | 4 | 4.2% | 1 | 4% | — | — | 8 | 26.6% | 11 | 35.5% |
| Cognitive developmental processes | — | — | — | — | — | — | 7 | 23.3% | 5 | 16.2% |
| Total | 95 | 100.0% | 25 | 100% | 36 | 100.0% | 30 | 100.0% | 31 | 100.0% |

[a]Personal variables include personality and demographic studies.
[b]Process of helping includes studies that focused on the general question of how a person decides to perform a helping act.

to induce general principles of helping behavior is often hampered by contradictory results, especially in the domain of situational and personal variables. The fact that individuals encounter many different situations to which they might react differentially makes it difficult to predict helping behavior, without knowing the meaning of the specific situation for the specific individual with the particular characteristics. Findings with regard to situational variables have shown high inconsistency: Whereas in several studies the results showed that the observation of helping behavior increases the likelihood that the observer will subsequently help another (e.g., Bryan & Test, 1967), a study by Willis and Goethals (1973) demonstrated that under certain conditions the helping model might have a negative effect on the observer's behavior; whereas Konečni, Libuser, Morton, and Ebbesen (1975) found that subjects exposed to invasions of personal space offered less help to the invader than those not exposed to such intrusions, Baron (1978) obtained opposite results.

Similar inconsistent results can be found with regard to personal variables: Whereas some studies have shown that males are more likely to help than females (e.g., Bryan & Test, 1967; Latané & Dabbs, 1975; Piliavin, Rodin, & Piliavin, 1969), other studies have found opposite results (e.g., O'Bryant & Brophy, 1976; Schopler, 1967) and still other studies found no differences (e.g., Gruder & Cook, 1971; Thayer, 1973); whereas Wispé and Freshley (1971) found no racial differences in helping behavior, other studies (e.g., Thayer, 1973) found that the race of the helper interacted with the characteristics of the person in need; and whereas Schwartz (1974) was unable to find a relation between locus of control and helping, Lerner and Reavy (1975) found that there is a relationship, and that it depends on a situation.

More consistent findings have been obtained with regard to studies that investigated the socialization process for helping behavior and factors that mediate helping behavior. Socialization studies have found, in general, that nurturance of parents, prescriptive orientation of parents, moral values of parents, and use of induction are important determinants of children's acquisition of helping behavior (e.g., Bar-Tal, Nadler, & Blechman, 1980; Hoffman, 1975; London, 1979; Mussen, Harris, Rutherford, & Keasey, 1970). With regard to factors mediating helping behavior, research has shown that experience of empathy (e.g., Aderman & Berkowitz, 1979; Krebs 1975) and of attention (e.g., Underwood, Froming, & Moore, 1977) are important preconditions for performing helping behavior.

Table 3 shows the types of methods used in the reviewed studies in the five journals over the last decade. This table indicates that the overwhelming majority of the researchers used experimental methods to

*Table 3. Classification of Articles about Helping Behavior According to Method Used in Five Journals, 1970–1979*

| Method | *Journal of Personality and Social Psychology* | | *Journal of Experimental Social Psychology* | | *Journal of Applied Social Psychology* | | *Developmental Psychology* | | *Child Development* | |
|---|---|---|---|---|---|---|---|---|---|---|
| | Articles | | Articles | | Articles | | Articles | | Articles | |
| | Number | Percentage | Number | Percentage | Number | Percentage | Number | Percentage | Number | Percentage |
| Laboratory experiment | 63 | 67.7% | 18 | 72% | 19 | 54.3% | 21 | 72.4% | 25 | 80.7% |
| Field experiment | 24 | 25.8% | 6 | 24% | 13 | 37.1% | 1 | 3.5% | 0 | — |
| Questionnaire | 4 | 4.3% | 1 | 4% | 2 | 5.7% | 4 | 13.8% | 5 | 16.1% |
| Observation | 2 | 2.2% | — | — | 1 | 2.9% | 3 | 10.3% | 1 | 3.2% |
| Content analysis | — | — | — | — | — | — | — | — | — | — |
| Total | 93 | 100.0% | 25 | 100% | 35 | 100.0% | 29 | 100.0% | 31 | 100.0% |
| Theoretical or review papers | 2 | | | | 1 | | 1 | | | |

investigate helping behavior. In social psychology over 90% of the studies were experiments; in developmental psychology the percentage was lower. Most of these studies were carried out in laboratories, although it can be observed that social psychologists performed a not inconsiderable number of experiments in the field. Developmental psychologists also used, to some extent, questionnaire and observation research methods. In the empirical helping behavior literature is general, the great majority of research has investigated situations in which subjects had an opportunity to help strangers with a single act. In laboratory situations, subjects often knew nothing about each other, the act of helping was isolated from a naturalistic sequence of interaction, and a very specific time constraint was imposed on the encounter. Moreover, the episode was often detached from all other events in the course of the subject's everyday life and took place in an unfamiliar setting and context.

### 2.2.3. *Theoretical Developments*

Two major theoretical directions have been developed in the study of helping behavior to answer different questions. One direction has led to attempts to explain the development of helping behavior; the other has involved attempts to explain how helping behavior is maintained in a society and how individuals decide to carry it out.

The development of helping behavior has been explained within at least four theoretical frameworks: sociobiology, psychoanalysis, social learning, and cognitive development (see reviews in Bar-Tal, 1976; Bryan & London, 1970; Mussen & Eisenberg-Berg, 1977; Rushton, 1976; Sharabany & Bar-Tal, 1982; Staub, 1979; Wispé, 1972, 1978), though only the latter three focus on development on the individual level. The sociobiological approach looks for the biological and societal conditions that facilitate the development of helping behavior. This approach incorporates two views: The first assumes that helping behavior has been developed through sociobiological evolution—that is, through selective accumulation of behavior transmitted genetically, the second postulates that helping behavior has been developed through sociocultural evolution, that is, through selective accumulation of behavior retained via purely social modes of transmission. The psychoanalytic approach emphasizes the enduring effects of early experiences, especially the experiences of the child with its parents, as determinants of helping behavior development. The experiences are subjectively interpreted and the behavior often reflects the unconscious motives of the individual. The social learning approach assumes that helping behavior is learned via interaction with the social environment, mainly through principles of reinforcement and modeling. The cognitive development approach emphasizes transformations of cognitive structures and experiential role-taking opportunities as determinants of helping behavior development.

It should be noted that only the latter two approaches, social learning and cognitive development, have stimulated much research on the development of helping behavior (see Table 3). Research derived from the social learning approach has focused on the effect of learning conditions and mechanisms in the social environment (e.g., exhortation, conditioning, reinforcement, and modeling) that foster the development of helping behavior. In contrast, research derived from the cognitive development approach has focused on the relationship between the development of helping behavior on the one hand, and cognitive, role-taking, and moral development on the other hand.

Two theoretical frameworks have been offered to explain why individuals perform helping acts. The first framework, the exchange approach, suggests that the individual's behavior is guided by the principle of maximizing rewards and minimizing costs, in order to obtain the most profitable outcomes in any human interaction. Thus, according to exchange theory, helping behavior is instrumental in acquiring rewards that can take materialistic, social, or even self-reinforcing forms, (see Blau, 1964; Cialdini & Kendrick, 1976; Homans, 1961; Lerner, 1977; R. F. Weiss, Buchanan, Altstatt, & Lombardo, 1971). The second framework suggests that helping behavior is regulated by societal norms. According to this approach, individuals help because they conform to norms which prescribe helping. They follow the prescription of helping norms not only because of external pressure but also because they internalize them. Three norms have been proposed: the norm of giving, which prescribes giving for its own value (Leeds, 1963); the norm of social responsibility, which prescribes helping dependent others (Berkowitz & Daniels, 1963); and the norm of reciprocity, which prescribes that individuals should help those who have helped them (Gouldner, 1960).

Finally, several attempts have been made to explain how individuals decide on and perform helping acts. These attempts were influenced by exchange and normative theory. Latané and Darley (1970) proposed a decision-making model of the helping process, specifically for cases of emergency situations. Their model consists of five sequential decisions, beginning with the decision as to whether something is happening and ending with the decision of how to implement a decision to help. Piliavin and Piliavin (1972), also dealing with emergency situations, suggested a decision-making model that focuses on the calculation of costs and rewards involved in helping and not helping. In earlier work, I (1976) suggested a model that extends the cost–reward calculation and adds the consideration of attribution of responsibility—the decision why the other person is in need. In addition, I suggested four types of variables that affect the judgmental process: personal, situational, and cultural variables, and characteristics of the person in need. Another relatively elaborate model was proposed by Schwartz (1977) and is presented in Chapter 11. Recently, Staub (1978) proposed a model that specifies the manner in which situational and personality factors jointly affect helping behavior. According to Staub, helping behavior occurs as a function of personal goals (motives); however, the activation of the behavior depends on the importance of the goal relative to other goals, the characteristics of the situation, and the existence of conflict between goals. It should be noted that all of these models seek to explain the processes through which personal and situational variables join together to influence the individual's helping behavior.

## 3. HELPING BEHAVIOR: WHY?

It is no accident that interest has increasingly focused on the study of helping behavior and that the direction of research has gone the way it has. Rather, the study of helping seems to have emerged as a consequence of a social *Zeitgeist*, and the directions and methods of helping behavior research merely reflect the underlying influential basis of social and developmental psychology. As Crutchfield and Krech (1966) suggest,

> The effect of the Zeitgeist on science is most obviously felt through the general ideological climate of the times. The effect is not only from the more formal philosophical thinking, but also from the values and outlook that characterize the popular beliefs of the literate people of the culture. (p. 12)

Since most helping behavior research has been performed by American psychologists, the reasons for how it developed as an area of study should be sought in the social problems confronting American society, in the values guiding Americans, and in the scientific-philosophical premises that influence American psychologists.

### 3.1. Emergence of Helping Behavior Research

Neither the murder of Kitty Genovese nor the studies of Darley, Latané, or Berkowitz could have stimulated so much interest in helping behavior among the social and developmental psychologist unless the *Zeitgeist* supported it. Interest in the study of helping behavior has developed not only because of the scientific merit of the problem, but mainly as a consequence of the nature of the social problems that have preoccupied American society in the last decade. In the way that the rise of facism influenced the study of authoritarian personality, the events of the Second World War stimulated research into aggression, and the pressures of McCarthyism provoked the study of conformity, so the interest in helping behavior in a period when American society was looking for a better way of life—for ways of improving the quality of interpersonal relations.

In the late sixties the burden of social problems, as demonstrated by the increased sense of alienation and the increase in violence, led Americans to look for new ways of life (e.g., Gerson, 1971; Harrington, 1972; Hoult, 1975). Humanistic concern for all members of society was advanced as one way of improving the quality of life. This way stressed education toward empathy, cooperation, helping, and trust. This search for a new quality of life was reflected especially in the values adopted by the students who created a counterculture in the 1960s. Among these values, a special place was given to the humanistic-moral values that prescribed compassion, sympathy for other people, cooperation and helping, openness and trust (see Flacks, 1967; Laufer & Bengtson, 1974; Lauter & Howe, 1970; Lewis & Kraut, 1972; Reich, 1971; Starr, 1974). These values spread during the 1960s and early 1970s to the majority of the American young generation (Yankelovich, 1974). Hence it is not surprising that parallel to the growing interest of American society in improving the quality of interpersonal relations, helping behavior study has become one of the central research areas in social and developmental psychology.

## 3.2. Nature of Helping Behavior Research

Important factors in the development of helping behavior research have been the American value of individualism, as well as the influence of positivistic philosophy on American psychology.

### 3.2.1. *Individualism*

A dominant value of American society is self-sufficient individualism (see, e.g., Diamond, 1976; Slater, 1970; Williams, 1970). This value emphasizes the responsibility and the right of each individual to pursue personal goals in as much freedom as possible from restraints. As Slater (1970) writes:

> It is easy to produce examples of the many ways in which Americans attempt to minimize, circumvent or deny the interdependence upon which all human societies are based. We seek a private house, a private means of transportation, a private garden. . . . Even within the family Americans are unique in their feeling that each member should have a separate room, and even a separate telephone, television, and car, when economically possible. (p. 7)

Such individualistic values, however, lead to limitations of the social nature of behavior by deemphasizing the functionality and importance of interdependent relationships. Thus Sampson (1977) suggests that

> excessive individualism leads to alienation and estrangement; it isolates person from person; it separates us from the very nutrient soil out of which we cast in the first place. Interdependence is inbred early as we form our basic attachments to parents and others; yet we see the breakdown of those attachments espoused as an ideal in the island-like ethos of our contemporary culture. (1977, p. 780)

The influence of individualism upon psychology has been noted by a number of writers (see Hogan & Emler, 1978; Moscovici, 1972; Riegel, 1972; Sampson, 1977). They have pointed out that social and developmental psychology have disregarded the social context of human behavior. As Huston-Stein and Baltes (1976) observe, "most of the available research on children's social development is focused on individual experiences with other people, primarily the parents" (p. 174). With regard to social psychology, Hogan and Emler (1978) note that "one of the most remarkable features of current social psychology is its systematic denial of man's social nature" (p. 487).

As a result of this individualism, helping behavior has mostly been investigated in a social vacuum with the focus on a helper who must decide whether to help a stranger in need. The laboratory studies even limit the social content of the behavior by constructing formal situations between strangers that require a ritualistic interaction. Such themes as mutual obligations and expectations, the climate of a group, differential status of group members, communication, the nature of ongoing interactions, and the nature of interpersonal relationships have received relatively little attention from researchers of helping behavior. The accumulated findings about helping behavior are based on studies of individualistic behavior. In these studies the major effort has been directed to understanding the situational variables that inhibit or facilitate the *individual's* helping behavior and the *personal tendencies* that increase or decrease the willingness to help.

### 3.2.2. *Positivism*

In an attempt to become a respected scientific discipline, psychology has absorbed the principles of positivistic philosophy, which limits knowledge to the facts of experience and refuses to embark on speculation regarding the nature of behaviors. One consequence of this approach has been great reliance in psychology on empiricism, reflected in the predominant use of experimental method to obtain data (see Kantor, 1969; Levine, 1974; Petrinovich, 1979).

Asch (1959) points out that "although social psychology was partly a revolt against the existing order, it nevertheless grew up in the shadow of general psychology, from which it borrowed its concepts and procedures" (p. 366). Indeed, the positivistic philosophy has been adopted to a large extent by social and developmental psychologists through embracing methodological positivism (see Armistead, 1974; Buss, 1975; Harré & Secord, 1972; McCall, 1978; Samelson, 1974). This approach is reflected in research practices—the formulation of specific predictions about behavior that are empirically falsifiable, operationalization of the concepts as measurable variables, and then usually the inclusion of these variables in an experimental design. In other words, social and developmental psychologists, like other psychologists, have translated the positivistic position into experimental methods of investigation in their research. The predominant use of experiment has been noted by numerous social and developmental psychologists who critically assessed this trend (e.g., Bronfenbrenner, 1977; Gergen, 1978; Hendrick, 1977; Kruglanski, 1975; McCall, 1978; Sherif, 1963). McCall (1978), for example, notes that

> most modern psychologists have been taught that it is only by the experimental method that direct cause-effect conclusions can be specified with confidence and that such statements constitute the principal goal of our discipline. The axioms of experimental method have served general psychology well, and they have provided developmentalists with much useful information. Certainly no one would want to exclude this approach from our discipline. But developmental psychology has embraced this attitude so completely that the experimental method now dictates rather than serves the research questions we value, fund, and pursue. (pp. 4–5)

Thus, in view of the dominance of the positivistic position among psychologists, it is not surprising that most of the research into helping behavior has been performed by means of experiments (see Table 3).

Another consequence of this positivistic influence, expressed through behavioristic approach, is the frequent investigation of the effect of environmental variables on human behavior. The assumptions guiding the use of environmental variables are that it makes truly causal relationship observable and ensures the objectivity of psychological research (Bowers, 1973). Although since the 1950s social and developmental psychology have become more cognitive, the preoccupation with the effects of different situational stimuli on social behavior indicates that these two subdisciplines are susceptible to various behavioristic influences (see Charles, 1970; Hendrick, 1977). Helping behavior research can be characterized as situationistic in its nature. As shown in Table 2, this characteristic appears especially in social psychological journals. The articles in the developmental journals were also devoted to the study of cognitive developmental processes.

## 4. HELPING BEHAVIOR: WHERE?

Although the study of helping behavior has expanded in recent years and has contributed to the understanding of human social behavior, analysis of the present state of the art of helping behavior research and theory has revealed a need for liberation from some dominating assumptions and habits in order to open new avenues of development.

### 4.1. Research Derived from a Theory

Although several theoretical frameworks have been offered for the study of helping behavior, with few exceptions the research on helping behavior focuses on the collection of empirical facts in a sporadic and fragmented way. At present, much of the research is a cluster of disorganized and disconnected pieces of knowledge. Without a theory,

> the experiments and empirical studies are not really capable of confrontation in a common framework; the contradictory results published about the same phenomenon rarely lead to a conceptual analysis which could provide a decision and transform our knowledge. (Moscovici, 1972, p. 44)

A theory might direct the research questions and prevent a chaotic investigation of variables. It might filter out certain facts and organize those that remain in an interrelated manner. A theory with collected findings can make the desired contribution toward an understanding of helping behavior. Therefore, we need to increase research that derives from theoretical frameworks.

### 4.2. Methods of Research

The predominant use of experimental methods in the laboratory in the study of helping behavior has limited the scope of investigated problems, and has often restricted the examined social reality. Although it is beyond the scope of this chapter to point out the shortcomings of experimentation (and there is no intention to disregard the importance of experimental method), it seems clear that experimental method alone should not be relied upon and that a variety of research techniques should be used. Studying helping behavior through observations, interviews, surveys, or content analysis can provide an opportunity to examine aspects that are difficult to investigate in experiments, enable a naturalistic and realistic investigation of helping behavior, and validate experimental results. It is disappointing that psychologists, for example, with few exceptions, have not observed helping behavior in groups in such naturalistic settings as schools, factories, or an army; have not interviewed individuals regarding their expectations, feelings of obligation, or perceptions of helping behavior in interpersonal and group situations; nor have they utilized archives relating to philanthropy, volunteering for public service, or performing sacrificing acts in wars to save the lives of other people.

### 4.3. Social Context

It should be remembered that much of helping behavior takes place between persons who know each other and/or in the context of social groups, as part of ongoing interactions. Social and developmental psychology have disregarded the social nature of helping behavior, focusing on helping behavior between strangers. As Bronfenbrenner (1977) states, "developmental psychology is the science of the strange behavior of children in strange situations with strange adults for the briefest possible periods of time" (p. 513). The study of helping behavior should also be performed within the framework of the social context as reflected in interpersonal, intragroup, and intergroup relationships. Such study should take into account such social variables as group structure, group climate, interpersonal obligations, mutual expectation, nature of interactions, or conformity, in order to understand the dynamics of helping behavior in groups. Helping behavior should be viewed as part of sequential interactions in which there has been a past and will be a future.

### 4.4. Interdisciplinary Approach

The social and developmental study of helping behavior has become encapsulated within the discipline of psychology. The study of helping behavior, however, has bearing upon many aspects of human life, starting with international relationships, through medical or welfare help, and ending with informal help between friends. Such disciplines as medicine, nursing, political science, or social work have developed theories and performed research on the specific problems of helping behavior that interest them. It is regrettable that social and developmental psychologists have disregarded the literature pertaining to helping behavior in other disciplines (see, e.g., Arrow & Scitovsky, 1969; Beveridge, 1948; Bracht, 1978; Burnand, 1969; Combs, Avila, & Purkey, 1971; Fellner & Marshall, 197O; Haveman, 1977; Healey, 1971; Keenleyside, 1966; Pappenfort, Kilpatrick, & Roberts, 1973; Rogers, 1958; Routh, 1970; Stubbins, 1977; Weiss, 1973). It seems clear that the social and developmental psychology of helping behavior could benefit from other disciplines in its attempt to understand the phenomenon of helping behavior. Whereas social and developmental psychology focus on general principles of helping behavior, other disciplines focus on its specific aspects in specific contexts. Thus, whereas psychology may know a little about a wide spectrum of helping behaviors, other disciplines may know much about a narrow spectrum of helping behaviors. The knowledge collected by other disciplines could stimulate the study of helping behavior by psychologists. It could also facilitate the construction of a theory, validate obtained psychological findings, or open new directions of research.

### 4.5. Relevance

No one can deny the importance of helping behavior for the individual, group, or society. The existence of helping behavior indicates adaptation of people to the social environment. Helping behavior can facilitate human living and improve human relations. It can occur in an interpersonal, informal context, as well as within formal societal institutions and in the framework of international relations. It is surprising that social and developmental researchers of helping behavior have investigated often meaningless situations and have isolated the study of helping behavior from individual and societal needs. In these times, when psychology, in general, has been called upon to improve the conditions of mankind (Tyler, 1973), to provide intellectual leadership in the search for new and better personal and social arrangements (Miller, 1969), and to improve the quality of life (Varela, 1977)—times when social and developmental psychology are urged to be useful, relevant, and applied (e.g, Deutsch, 1975; Gergen, 1973; Helmreich, 1975; Sanford, 1970; Saxe & Fine, 1980; Yarrow-Radke, 1974)—the study of helping behavior should take a different course. Without neglecting pure scientific research, the study of helping behavior should also focus on those issues that have direct bearing upon the needs of the individual, of groups, and of society. The applied problems of helping behavior provide a sophisticated and complex issue that should challenge social and developmental psychologists to utilize the most adequate theories and methods. The applied problems should encourage psychologists to test hypotheses derived from their theories in the field and should induce them to develop new approaches in order to understand helping phenomena in real-life situations. The accumulated findings could serve as bases for making proposals and for formulating policies that refer to helping behavior in different social contexts.

### Acknowledgments

The author would like to express great indebtedness to Arie Kruglanski, Leonard Saxe, Shalom Schwartz, Ruth Sharabany, and

Sidney Strauss for their helpful comments on the earlier version of this chapter.

## 5. REFERENCES


Aderman, D., & Berkowitz, L. Observational set, empathy and helping. *Journal of Personality and Social Psychology*, 1970, *14*, 141–148.

Armistead, N. Introduction. In N. Armistead (Ed.), *Reconstructing social psychology*. Harmondsworth, V.K.: Penguin Books, 1974.

Aronfreed, J. *Conduct and conscience*. New York: Academic Press, 1968.

Arrow, K. J., & Scitovsky, T. (eds.). *Readings in welfare economics*. London: Allen & Unwin, 1969.

Asch, S. E. A perspective on social psychology. In S. Koch (Ed.), *Psychology: A study of a science* (Vol. 3). New York: McGraw-Hill, 1959.

Baron, R. A. Invasions of personal space and helping: Mediating effects of invader's apparent need. *Journal of Experimental Social Psychology*, 1978, *14*, 304–312.

Baron, R. A., & Byrne, D. *Social psychology* (2nd ed.). Boston: Allyn & Bacon, 1977.

Bar-Tal, D. *Prosocial behavior: Theory and research*. New York: Halsted Press, 1976.

Bar-Tal, D. *Sequential development of helping behavior: A cognitive-learning model*. Developmental Review, 1982, 2, 101–124.

Bar-Tal, D., Nadler, A., & Blechman, N. The relationship between Israeli children's helping behavior and their perception of parents' socialization practices. *Journal of Social Psychology*, 1980, *111*, 159–167.

Berkowitz, L. Theoretical and research approaches in experimental social psychology. In A. R. Gilgen (Ed.), *Contemporary scientific psychology*. New York: Academic Press, 1970.

Berkowitz, L., & Connor, W. H. Success, failure and social responsibility. *Journal of Personality and Social Psychology*, 1966, *4*, 664–669.

Berkowitz, L., & Daniels, L. R. Responsibility and dependency. *Journal of Abnormal and Social Psychology*, 1963, *66*, 429–436.

Berkowitz, L., & Daniels, L. R. Affecting the salience of the social responsibility norm: Effect of past help on the response to dependency relationships. *Journal of Abnormal and Social Psychology*, 1964, *68*, 275–281.

Beveridge, L. *Voluntary action*. London: Allen & Unwin, 1948.

Blau, P. M. *Exchange and power in social life*. New York: Wiley, 1964.

Bowers, K. S. Situationism in psychology: An analysis and a critique. *Psychological Review*, 1973, *80*, 307–336.

Bracht, N. F. (Ed.). *Social work in health care*. New York: Haworth Press, 1978.

Bronfenbrenner, Y. Toward an experimental ecology of human development. *American Psychologist*, 1977, *32*, 513–531.

Bryan, J. H., & London, P. Altruistic behavior by children. *Psychological Bulletin*, 1970, *73*, 200–211.

Bryan, J. H., & Test, M. A. Models and helping: Naturalistic studies in aiding behavior. *Journal of Personality and Social Psychology*, 1967, *6*, 400–407.

Burnand, G. The nature of emotional support. *British Journal of Psychiatry*, 1969, *115*, 139–148.

Buss, A. R. The emerging field of the sociology of psychological knowledge. *American Psychologist*, 1975, *30*, 988–1002.

Capasso, D. R., & Hendrick, C. Bibliography of journal articles in social psychology: Second half 1975. *Personality and Social Psychology Bulletin*, 1976, *2*, 191–206.

Capasso, D. R., Hendrick, C., Rahal, L., & Coleman, J. Bibliography of journal articles in personality and social psychology, 1976. *Personality and Social Psychology Bulletin*, 1977, *3*, 307–327.

Charles, D. C. Historical antecedents of life-span developmental psychology. In L. R. Goulet & P. B. Baltes (Eds.), *Life-span developmental psychology: Research and theory*. New York: Academic Press, 1970.

Cialdini, R. B., & Kenrick, D. T. Altruism as hedonism: A social development perspective on the relationship of negative mood state and helping. *Journal of Personality and Social Psychology*, 1976, *34*, 907–914.

Combs, A. W., Avila, D. L., & Purkey, W. W. *Helping Relationships: Basic concepts for the helping professions*. Boston: Allyn & Bacon, 1971.

Crutchfield, R. S., & Krech, D. Some guides to the understanding of the history of psychology. In L. Postman (Ed.), *Psychology in the making*. New York: Alfred A. Knopf, 1966.

Daniels, L., & Berkowitz, L. Liking and response to dependency relationships. *Human Relations*, 1963, *16*, 141–148.

Darley, J. M., & Latané, B. Bystander intervention in emergencies: Diffusion of responsibility. *Journal of Personality and Social Psychology*, 1968, *8*, 377–383.

Deutsch, M. Introduction. In M. Deutsch & H. A. Hornstein (Eds.), *Applying social psychology: Implications for research, practice and training*. Hillsdale, N.J.: Lawrence Erlbaum, 1975.

Diamond, M. The American idea of man: The view from the founding. In I. Kristol & P. Weaver (Eds.), *The Americans: 1976* (Vol. 2). Lexington, Mass.: Lexington Books, 1976.

Fellner, C. H., & Marshall, J. R. Kidney donors: The myth of informed consent. *American Journal of Psychiatry*, 1970, *126*, 79–85.

Flacks, R. The liberated generation: An exploration of the roots of student protest. *Journal of Social Issues*, 1967, *23*(3), 52–75.

Freedman, J. L., Sears, D. O., & Carlsmith, J. M. Social psychology (3rd ed.). Englewood Cliffs, N.J.: Prentice-Hall, 1978.

Gergen, K. J. Social psychology as history. *Journal of Personality and Social Psychology*, 1973, *26*, 309–320.

Gergen, K. J. Experimentation in social psychology: A reappraisal. *European Journal of Social Psychology*, 1978, *8*, 507–527.

Gerson, W. M. Alienation in mass society: Some causes and responses. In C. D. Bryant (Ed.), *Social problems today*. Philadelphia: J. B. Lippincott, 1971.

Goranson, R. E., & Berkowitz, L. Reciprocity and responsibility reactions to prior help. *Journal of Personality and Social Psychology*, 1966, *3*, 227–232.

Gouldner, A. W. The norm of reciprocity: A preliminary statement. *American Sociological Review*, 1960, *25*, 161–178.

Gruder, C. L., & Cook, T. D. Sex, dependency and helping. *Journal of Personality and Social Psychology*, 1971, *19*, 290–294.

Handlon, B. J., & Gross, P. The development of sharing behavior. *Journal of Abnormal and Social psychology*, 1959, *59*, 425–428.

Harré, R., & Secord, P. F. *The explanation of social behavior*. Oxford: Basil Blackwell, 1972.

Harrington, M. American society. Burdens, problems, solutions. In I. Howe & M. Harrington (Eds.), *The seventies: Problems and proposals*. New York: Harper & Row, 1972.

Hartshorne, H., & May, M. A. *Studies in the nature of character*. Vol. 1. *Studies in deceit*. New York: Macmillan, 1928.

Haveman, R. H. (Ed.). *A decade of federal antipoverty programs*. New York: Academic Press, 1977.

Healey, J. M. *The economics of aid*. London: Routledge & Kegan Paul, 1971.

Helmreich, R. Applied social psychology: The unfulfilled promise. *Personality and Social Psychology Bulletin*, 1975, *1*, 548–560.

Hendrick, C. Social psychology as an experimental science. In C. Hendrick (Ed.), *Perspective on social psychology*. Hillsdale, N.J.: Lawrence Erlbaum, 1977.

Hetherington, E. M., & Parke, R. D. *Child development: A contemporary viewpoint*. New York: McGraw-Hill, 1975.

Hoffman, M. L. Altruistic behavior and the parent-child relationship. *Journal of Personality and Social Psychology*, 1975, *31*, 937–943.

Hogan, R. T., & Emler, N. P. The biases in contemporary social psychology. *Social Research*, 1978, *45*, 478–534.

Homans, G. C. *Social behavior: Its elementary forms*. New York: Harcourt, Brace & World, 1961.

Hornstein, H. A. *Cruelty and kindness: A new look at aggression and altruism*. Englewood Cliffs, N.J.: Prentice-Hall, 1976.

Hoult, T. F. *Social justice and its enemies*. New York: Schenkman, 1975.

Huston-Stein, A., & Baltes, P. B. Theory and method in life-span developmental psychology: Implications for child development. In H. W. Reese (Ed.), *Advances in child development and behavior*. (Vol. 2). New York: Academic Press, 1976.

Kantor, J. R. *The scientific evolution of psychology* (Vol. 2). Chicago: Principia Press, 1969.

Keenleyside, H. L. *International aid*. New York: James H. Heineman, 1966.

Kohlberg, L. *The development of modes of moral thinking in the years ten to sixteen*. Unpublished doctoral dissertation, University of Chicago, 1958.

Kohlberg, L. Stage and sequence: The cognitive-developmental approach to socialization. In D. Goslin (Ed.), *Handbook of socialization theory and research*. Chicago: Rand McNally, 1969.

Konečni, F. J., Libuser, L., Morton, H., & Ebbesen, E. B. Effects of a violation of personal space on escape and helping responses. *Journal of Experimental Social Psychology*, 1975, *11*, 288–299.

Krebs, D. L. Altruism: An examination of the concept and a review of the literature. *Psychological Bulletin*, 1970, *73*, 258–303.

Krebs, D. L. Empathy and altruism. *Journal of Personality and Social Psychology*, 1975, *32*, 1134–1146.

Kruglanski, A. Theory, experiment and the shifting publication scene in personality and social psychology. *Personality and Social Psychology Bulletin*, 1975, *1*, 489–492.

Latané, B., & Dabbs, J. M. Sex, group size and helping in three cities. *Sociometry*, 1975, *38*, 180–194.

Latané, B., & Darley, J. M. Group inhibition of bystander intervention in emergencies. *Journal of Personality and Social Psychology*, 1968, *10*, 215–221.

Latané, B., & Darley, J. M. *The unresponsive bystander: Why doesn't he help?* New York: Appleton-Century-Crofts, 1970.

Laufer, R. S., & Bengtson, V. L. Generations, aging and social stratification: On the development of generational units. *Journal of Social Issues*, 1974, *30*, 181–205.

Lauter, P., & Howe, F. *The conspiracy of the young*. New York: Meridian Books, 1970.

Leeds, R. Altruism and the norm of giving. *Merrill-Palmer Quarterly*, 1963, *9*, 229–240.

Lerner, M. J. The justice motive: Some hypotheses as to its origin and forms. *Journal of Personality*, 1977, *45*, 1–53.

Lerner, M. J., & Reavy, P. Locus of control, perceived responsibility for prior help, and helping behavior. *Journal of Research in Personality*, 1975, *9*, 1–20.

Levine, M. Scientific method and the adversary model: Some preliminary thoughts. *American Psychologist*, 1974, *29*, 661–667.

Lewis, S. H., & Kraut, R. E. Correlates of student political activism and ideology. *Journal of Social Issues*, 1972, *28*(4), 131–150.

London, P. The rescuers: Motivational hypotheses about Christians who saved Jews from the Nazis. In J. Macaulay & L. Berkowitz (Eds.), *Altrusim and helping behavior*. New York: Academic Press, 1970.

Macaulay, J., & Berkowitz, L. (Eds.). *Altruism and helping behavior*. New York: Academic Press, 1970.

McCall, R. B. Challenges to a science of developmental psychology. In S. Chess & A. Thomas (Eds.), *Annual progress in child psychiatry and child development*. New York: Brunner/Mazel, 1978.

Meyer, W. J., & Dusek, J. B. *Child development: A developmental perspective*. Lexington, Mass.: D. C. Heath, 1979.

Middlebrook, P. N. *Social psychology and modern life*. New York: Alfred A. Knopf, 1974.

Midlarsky, E. Aiding responses: An analysis and review. *Merrill-Palmer Quarterly*, 1968, *14*, 229–260.

Miller, G. S. Psychology as a means of promoting human welfare. *American Psychologist*, 1969, *24*, 1063–1075.

Moscovici, S. Society and theory in social psychology. In J. Israel & H. Tajfel (Eds.), *The context of social psychology: A critical assessment*. New York: Academic Press, 1972.

Murphy, L. B. *Social behaviour and child personality: An exploratory study of some roots of sympathy*. New York: Columbia University Press, 1937.

Mussen, P. H., & Eisenberg-Berg, N. *Roots of caring, sharing and helping*. San Francisco: W. H. Freeman, 1977.

Mussen, P. H., Harris, S., Rutherford, E., & Keasey, C. B. Honesty and altruism among preadolescents. *Developmental Psychology*, 1970, *3*, 169–194.

O'Bryant, S. L., & Brophy, J. E. Sex differences in altruistic behavior. *Developmental Psychology*, 1976, *12*, 554–555.

Pappenfort, D. M., Kilpatrick, D. M., & Roberts, R. W. *Child caring:* Chicago: Aldine, 1973.

Petrinovich, L. Probabilistic functionalism: A conception of research method. *American Psychologist*, 1979, *34*, 373–390.

Piaget, J. *The moral judgment of the child*. London: Routledge & Kegan Paul, 1932.

Piliavin, I., Rodin, J., Piliavin, J. Good samaritanism: An underground phenomenon? *Journal of Personality and Social Psychology*, 1969, *13*, 289–299.

Piliavin, J., & Piliavin, I. Effects of blood on reactions to a victim. *Journal of Personality and Social Psychology*, 1972 *23*, 353–361.

Reeves, R. A., Richardson, D. C., & Hendrick, C. Bibliography of journal articles in personality and social psychology, 1978. *Personality and Social Psychology Bulletin*, 1979, *5*, 524–542.

Reich, C. A. *The greening of America*. London: Allen Lane, Penguin Press, 1971.

Richardson, D. C., Tomarelli, M. M., & Hendrick, C. Bibliography of journal articles in personality and social psychology, 1977. *Personality and Social Psychology Bulletin*, 1978, *4*, 638–652.

Riegel, K. F. Influence of economic and political ideologies on the development of developmental psychology. *Psychological Bulletin*, 1972, *78*, 129–141.

Rogers, C. R. The characteristics of a helping relationship. *Personnel and Guidance Journal*, 1958, *37*, 6–16.

Rosenbaum, M. The effects of stimulus and background factors on the volunteering response. *Journal of Abnormal and Social Psychology*, 1956, *53*, 118–121.

Rosenthal, A. M. *Thirty-eight witnesses*. New York: McGraw-Hill, 1964.

Routh, T. A. *Rehabilitation counseling of the blind*. Springfield, Ill.: Charles C Thomas, 1970.

Rushton, J. P. Socialization and the altrusitic behaviour of children. *Psychological Bulletin,* 1976, *83,* 898–913.

Samelson, F. History, origin, myth and ideology: Comte's discovery of social psychology. *Journal for the Theory of Social Behaviour,* 1974, *4,* 217–231.

Sampson, E. E. Psychology and the American Ideal. *Journal of Personality and Social Psychology,* 1977, *35,* 767–782.

Sanford, N. Whatever happened to action research. *Journal of Social Issues,* 1970, *26*(4), 3–23.

Saxe, L., & Fine, M. Reorienting social psychology toward application: A methodological analysis. In L. Bickman (Ed.), *Applied social psychology annual* (Vol. 1). Beverly Hills, Calif.: Sage, 1980.

Schneider, D. J. *Social psychology.* Reading, Mass.: Addison-Wesley, 1976.

Schopler, J. An investigation of sex differences on the influence of dependence. *Sociometry,* 1967, *30,* 50–63.

Schwartz, S. H. Awareness of interpersonal consequences, responsibility denial, and volunteering. *Journal of Personality and Social Psychology,* 1974, *30,* 57–63.

Schwartz, S. H. Normative influences on altruism. In L. Berkowitz (Ed.), *Advances in experimental social psychology* (Vol. 10). New York: Academic Press, 1977.

Sharabany, R., & Bar-Tal, D. Theories of the development of altruism: Review, comparison, and integration. *International Journal of Behavioral Development,* 1982, *5,* 49–80.

Sherif, M. Social psychology: Problems and trends in interdisciplinary relationships. In S. Koch (Ed.), *Psychology: A study of science* (Vol. 6). New York: McGraw-Hill, 1963.

Slater, P. E. *The pursuit of loneliness.* Harmondsworth, V.K.: Penguin Books, 1970.

Starr, J. M. The peace and love generation: Changing attitudes toward sex and violence among college youth. *Journal of Social Issues,* 1974, *30*(2), 73–106.

Staub, E. *Positive social behavior and morality.* Vol. 1. *Personal and social influences.* New York: Academic Press, 1978.

Staub, E. *Positive social behavior and morality.* Vol. 2. *Socialization and development.* New York: Academic Press, 1979.

Stubbins, J. (Ed.). *Social and psychological aspects of disability: A handbook for practitioners.* Baltimore: University Park Press, 1977.

Thayer, S. Lend me your ears: Racial and sexual factors in helping the deaf. *Journal of Personality and Social Psychology,* 1973, *28,* 8–11.

Tyler, L. A. Design for a hopeful psychology. *American Psychologist,* 1973, *28,* 1021–1029.

Ugurel-Semin, R. Moral behaviour and moral judgment of children. *Journal of Abnormal and Social Psychology,* 1952, *47,* 463–474.

Underwood, B., Froming, W. J., & Moore, B. S. Mood, attention and altruism: A search for mediating variables. *Developmental Psychology,* 1977, *13,* 541–542.

Varela, J. A. Social technology. *American Psychologist,* 1977, *2,* 914–923.

Weiss, R. F., Buchanan, W., Altstatt, L., & Lombardo, J. B. Altruism is rewarding. *Science,* 1971, *171,* 1262–1263.

Weiss, R. S. Helping relationships: Relationships of clients with physicians, social workers, priests and others. *Social Problems,* 1973, *20,* 319–328.

Williams, R. M. *American society* (3rd ed.). New York: Alfred A. Knopf, 1970.

Willis, J. A., & Goethals, G. R. Social responsibility and threat to behavioral freedom as determinants of altruistic behavior. *Journal of Personality,* 1973, *41,* 376–384.

Wispé, L. G. (Ed.). Positive forms of social behavior. *Journal of Social Issues,* 1972, *28*(3), 1–19.

Wispé, L. G. (Ed.). *Altruism, sympathy and helping.* New York: Academic Press, 1978.

Wispé, L. G., & Freshley, H. B. Race, sex and sympathetic helping behavior: The broken bag caper. *Journal of Personality and Social Psychology,* 1971, *17,* 59–65.

Wright, B. Altruism in children and perceived conduct of others. *Journal of Abnormal and Social Psychology*, 1942, *37*, 218–233.

Yankelovich, D. *The new morality: A profile of American youth in the 70's*. New York: McGraw-Hill, 1974.

Yarrow-Radke, M. Research on child rearing as a basis for practice. In S. Chess & A. Thomas (Eds.), *Annual progress in child psychiatry and child development*. New York: Brunner/Mazel, 1974.

# 2

# Notes toward an Interactionist-Motivational Theory of the Determinants and Development of (Pro)Social Behavior

Ervin Staub

## 1. INTRODUCTION

The determinants of certain kinds of behavior, such as positive conduct, can be understood only in the framework of a more general theory of social behavior. We cannot simply ask whether people will or will not behave positively. We have to concern ourselves with conditions and influences that lead to positive, in *contrast* to other types of, behavior. When will people respond to others' need, or take action to benefit others, in contrast to engaging in behavior for the sake of self-related outcomes?

Recently the question of how personal characteristics and the nature of the environment jointly determine social behavior has received extensive attention. This represents a return to the earlier focus of Murray (1938), Lewin (1938), and others. These early thoughtful advocates of interactionism began to specify *how* the environment and individual characteristics join in influencing action. Developing a theoretical model

---

ERVIN STAUB • Department of Psychology, University of Massachusetts, Amherst, Massachusetts 01003. The preparation of this chapter was facilitated and some of the research reported here was supported by NIMH Grant MH-23886 to the author.

that specifies theoretical terms for personality characteristics and for the classification of the environment (or situations) that match with each other, so that they can be conceptualized and measured in relation to each other, is an important task (Murray, 1938; Staub, 1980). An approach to this task will be described below.

A basic question for a theory of social behavior is that of motivational base. Is there some unified way to consider motivational bases of positive and other kinds of conduct? In this chapter a theory will be briefly presented that focuses on motivation and on the role of the environment in activating motives and affecting their expression. The development of the type of motivation that is the focus of attention here—the development of personal goals—will also be discussed.

So far interactionist approaches have focused on the determination of social behavior in adults. A personality–environment interaction approach can be extended to children, however, in two senses. First, it can be applied to the study of how children's social behavior is determined. More important, it can be employed in a truly developmental fashion to understand how the already existing personality of children, at any point, joins with socializing influences and experiences in affecting further learning or development. The extension of the interactionist approach to developmental psychology in the latter sense is profoundly needed for further progress. Cognitive developmental psychologists have used such an approach in the specific domains of their interest. Piaget and Kohlberg both postulated that the level of an individual's cognitive development or moral reasoning determines whether particular events or aspects of the environment will be processed, how they will be processed, and what effects this will have on a person. A person's level of development and environment jointly affect change.

The same joint influences of the characteristics of a child or person and of the environment must operate to determine learning or change in many or all dimensions of children's and adults' personality and social behavior. Although in principle developmental psychologists share this view, in practice—in theory and research—they have neglected the consideration of how already existing characteristics modify the meaning and impact of further experiences, and thereby affect the degree and direction of change. Recent work on how differences in the quality of infants' attachment to the mother relate to their later social experiences and later characteristics is relevant (Sroufe, 1979), although the focus of this work has been more on continuity than on the specification of how individual characteristics and social influence join in affecting development. Children with different characteristics, for example, with differences in their already existing motives or goals, will both process events differently, and by what they do shape their environment and create different experiences for themselves, which in turn affect the further development of their goals (Rausch, 1965; Toda, Shinotsuka, McClintock, & Stech, 1978).

In the following a model will be briefly described for specifying the nature of personality–situation interaction in determining social behavior. Then ways for extending this model to encompass development will be proposed. The illustrations of the model will focus on positive social behavior: helpful, kind, generous action. However, the general form of the model should be applicable to most forms of social behavior.

## 2. CONCEPTUALIZING PERSONS: FOCUS ON MOTIVATION

To successfully specify a model that will increase our understanding of how personality and situations jointly determine (positive) behavior, and to predict behavior, it is necessary to find a limited number of personal characteristics that account for a substantial amount of variance, to define the nature of relevant situational influences, and to provide a specification of their joint influence. The concepts or variables ought to be sufficiently small in number that measurement and testing is possible (and that we are able to comprehend their relationship to each other, given limitations on our human capacities) and sufficiently central that they enable us to make accurate predictions of behavior. The major concepts would ideally have universal applicability, rather than being completely bound by cultural and historical relativity.

Long ago McDougall (1908) proposed that human behavior can be understood by the goals people pursue—in contrast, for example, to the means by which they pursue their goals. Other writers echoed this belief (Lewin, 1938, 1948; Murray, 1938). Some stressed the subjective value of outcomes (reward value) as an important determinant of behavior (Mischel, 1966; Rotter, 1954). A primary characteristic of human behavior seems to purposefulness. Even infants appear to engage in intense, purposeful action, in the course of manipulating objects and interaction with people, behavior that is now regarded by many as intrinsically motivated.

In recognition of the purposeful nature of human conduct, the motivational construct "personal goal" will be used to denote individual motivational orientations. The word *goal* implies preference for certain outcomes or end states, or an aversion for certain outcomes and the desire to avoid them (a negative goal). Different people have different goals and even if people in the same culture share many of the same goals, the organization of goals within persons, their hierarchy or relative importance, varies. Furthermore, goals can have a special, personal quality, because of differences in cognitive elaboration and in ranges of applicability. Nevertheless, enough similarity is assumed (and so far in our research has been found) among particular goals of different individuals that people can be grouped on the basis of their goals.

The nature of personal goals will vary across cultures, as a function of socialization in specific families, as the result of personal experiences in life, and perhaps even because of heredity. In a monolithic society, where social life and institutions (Garbarino & Bronfenbrenner, 1976) are organized around the same goals, many people should acquire these goals. In pluralistic cultures, where individuals are exposed to varied and contrasting influences and examples, and can enter varied roles, greater variation in goals should be evident. Different prevalent goals can be expected in different cultures and in different historical periods in the same culture. Although the outcomes that motivate people will differ, the existence of motivation is certainly universal (Mead, 1937) and its form and nature are such that it allows a conceptualization focusing on purposefulness and goallike character.

What are some of the characteristics of personal goals? One that I already noted is the desirability or value of certain outcomes, a class of similar or interrelated outcomes. Another is a network of cognitions that is usually associated with a goal. It does happen, of course, that the inclination to reach some goal—or the desire to avoid an outcome, a negative goal—is primarily emotional, that a person has few conscious thoughts, beliefs, or values that are associated with or embodied in a goal. Usually, however, we have varied thoughts, beliefs, and values that are associated with or specify outcomes that are desirable (or aversive) to us. These cognitions function, in part, to tune us perceptually to the kinds of circumstances that make it possible to satisfy our goal.[1]

The primary defining characteristics of (positive) goals are the desire for valued outcomes and the expectation of satisfaction in reaching them. Although positive evaluation of and desire for outcomes can exist without much cognitive elaboration, usually a related cognitive network is present. The focus in the subsequent discussion will be on goals with associated cognitive networks, goals characterized and/or defined by a cognitive goal orientation. The cognitive network is involved in interpreting circumstances as relevant to the desired outcomes and frequently in giving rise to related emotions, particularly when the relevance of circumstances, of stimuli in the environment, is not evident on the basis of past experience, so that affects related to the desired outcomes or the possibility of pursuing them will not be directly aroused.

[1]In the case of unconscious motivation the outcome that is valued would not be conscious, but a relevant cognitive network may exist, with conflicting and/or contradictory elements.

The emotions that arise from the interpretations (Arnold, 1960; Averill, 1980; Lazarus, 1966; Leventhal, 1974) give rise to the experience of desire for outcomes related to the goal and motivate attempts to reach the goal. As suggested above, some circumstances may have direct associations to relevant outcomes or may have acquired well-developed meanings and give rise to strong emotions without much cognitive elaboration. Seeing a child standing in the path of an onrushing car will give rise to strong emotion, in most people, with little or no thinking about, or cognitive work involved in determining, the meaning of the event.

A third assumed characteristic of personal goals is the arousal of tension upon the activation of the goal, which continues to exist until either the goal has been reached or it has been deactivated in some manner. The notion that tension is aroused and maintained by the activation of a goal has been proposed by Lewin (1948; see also Deutsch, 1968) and currently extended to the realm of prosocial behavior by Hornstein (1976). The limited evidence that is available about tension systems and their properties supports the concept. An example is the well-known Zeigarnick (1927) effect. Consistent with Lewinian assumptions, Zeigarnick found that interrupted tasks are remembered better than completed ones. Tasks that are interrupted nearer their completion—nearer to reaching the outcome—are remembered better than tasks interrupted further from completion (Deutsch, 1968). The latter finding provides support for another Lewinian concept relevant to the model described here, that of a goal gradient.

Some further specifications of the nature of goals (see Staub, 1978, 1980) are in order. First, goals are similar to values, which also specify what is important for people, but values embody less the quality of purposefulness, the motivation that is implied by goals. Second, goals as motivational orientations are usually delimited for specific individuals by their norms and standards, which guide how the goals are applied. Third, in this and in other ways the *range or circumstances of applicability of goals* may be different for different people. For example, a prosocial goal, when combined with a belief that the world is a just place where people get what they deserve (Lerner & Simmons, 1966; Rubin & Peplau, 1975) may lead people not to react to others' deprivation or need when circumstances allow them or lead them to view the need as deserved or just.

## 3. CONCEPTUALIZING ENVIRONMENTS

Personal goals represent potentials. In any given moment the *desire* for outcomes or end states embodied in a goal may be active or dormant.

Sometimes internal stimuli, thoughts, images, or feelings can activate a goal, or lead people to seek or create environments in which the goal can be pursued and satisfied; at other times aspects of the environment might do so. The following analysis will focus on external activation. Even when activation is internal, being in a particular environment, such as a student at a university, or on vacation at a beach, may strongly contribute to thoughts that give rise to a high level of activation of goals such as an achievement goal, or of finding sexual companions. For different persons the same environment may have activating potential for different goals. Whether a goal is activated or not will depend both on the nature of the situation, its *activating potential,* and on the characteristics of the person, the degree to which the person possesses the personal goal that might be activated in that situation.[2] Thus goals and activation potential of situations are related or matching concepts, similar to Murray's (1938) conception of need and environmental press, which influenced this model.

The importance of a personal goal (which is a function of the desirability or value of related outcomes and of cognitive elaboration) and the intensity of the activating potential of the environment for the goal are the primary influences that determine whether a personal goal will be activated. Frequently, circumstances have the potential to activate several goals. The extent to which particular persons possess these goals may determine whether one, another, or several goals will be activated. When more than one goal is active, they may sometimes conflict, in that only one or another can be pursued. Other times they may join and support each other, in that the same action may lead to the satisfaction of each goal. Sometimes the same goal may be activated by two different stimuli, requiring different actions. Feinberg (1977) found that individuals with a high achievement goal both tried to work hard on a task, and tried to respond to a confederate who either engaged them in conversation or expressed psychological distress. The press of fulfilling their achievement need through both task-related work and verbal responsiveness to the distressed confederate apparently made the situation aversive to these subjects, who disliked several aspects of the situation, particularly the distressed confederate.

The reasoning described so far implies a *relational classification* of the environment. Following the recognition that we need to conceptualize, classify, categorize characteristics of the environment, just as we classify personal characteristics (Frederiksen, 1972; Mischel, 1976; Moos, 1974),

[2]Theoretically, the activating potential of situations can be quite idiosyncratic. In practice, for many individuals in the same culture, having had somewhat comparable socializing experiences, particular settings, environments, or situations are likely to have comparable meanings, to represent potentials for the satisfaction of comparable personal goals.

environments have been classified in varied ways: as "behavioral settings" such as school, church, or home; by the characteristics of inhabitants, their age, status, and occupation; by perceived social climate, such as the "nature and intensity of personal relations"; and by such functional properties as the "reinforcement consequences for particular behaviors in that situation" (Mischel, 1976, p. 496). The conception of the activating potential of the environment implies that a meaningful classification of the environment is in terms of its relevance for or relationship to personal goals, hence a relational classification.

When we identify dimensions of situations relevant to personal goals, as an application of a relational classification, we would best regard these as general or conceptual dimensions. That is, many different actual characteristics of stimuli can specify their location on the conceptual dimensions. For example, the degree of someone's need for help is a primary dimension of the activating potential of a situation for a prosocial goal. But many different kinds of actual stimuli can define degree of need, such as different types and degrees of physical distress or different types and degrees of psychological distress, and so on.

Since most life situations embody activating potentials for more than one goal, what determines which personal goal will exert dominant influence in a particular situation? The strength of an activated personal goal must be a joint function of the importance of the personal goal to the individual and the intensity of the activating potential of the environment for that goal. First, most likely, a rough assessment of circumstances and their relationship to one's goals is made, before the actual process of activation. In other words, goal activation is not a passive process, but arises out of a true interaction between person and environment. As an initial assumption, I shall suggest that the strength of the activated goal will be a function of the multiplicative relationship between the importance of the personal goal and the intensity of the activating potential. The amount that results from this multiplication will determine both whether a goal is activated and which goal will be dominant. When the resulting amount is similar for two or more goals, both or all may be activated. If the goals are in conflict (if they require different courses of action), goal-directed behavior required to pursue any of them may be inhibited, and/or various processes may be involved in conflict resolution.

## 4. SELF-CONCEPT, OTHER PERSONAL CHARACTERISTICS, AND THE DETERMINATION OF BEHAVIOR

No single type of characteristic of persons, such as their motivation, as expressed in their personal goals, is likely to determine how they behave. Personal goals may be central organizers: When activated, they may guide attention and interpretation of events, and determine the relevance of other personal characteristics. *Perceptual tendencies, the self-concept and self-esteem, competencies* (general subjective competence, such as differences in locus of control; knowledge and/or the capacity to generate plans of action; and specific skills and competencies demanded for action), as well as some other characteristics may be involved in determining both whether goals will be activated, and whether they will be expressed in action.

These characteristics have been discussed elsewhere (Staub, 1978, 1980). Here it may be briefly noted that a person's self-concept and self-esteem are especially important with regard to prosocial behavior, which is strongly affected by the nature of self–other connections (Reykowski, 1975; Staub, 1978). Human beings tend to make self–other comparisons. The research findings on the effects of positive and negative experiences and positive and negative affects on prosocial behavior may be explained in terms of self–other connections, self–other comparisons, and the need to maintain a positive self-concept. When experiences result in positive mood or increased self-esteem, a state of positive hedonic balance exists (for a detailed discussion see Staub, 1978): One's state of welfare is perceived as better than that of another person, both in comparison to one's usual state of well-being and the other person's current state of well-being, and this perception increases prosocial action. (Furthermore, a positive mood and/or enhanced level of self-esteem satisfy the personal goal of enhancing the self, which may otherwise be high in a person's hierarchy of goals.)

How do personal goals, environmental (stimulus) conditions and associated activation potentials, competencies, and other relevant personal characteristics jointly affect behavior? A precise formulation of the interrelationship among these determinants of behavior may be premature. As noted above, an initial assumption may be that the importance of a personal goal and the intensity of the activating potential of the situation join in a multiplicative fashion to determine the strength of an activated goal. Competencies may affect expectancies that one can or cannot successfully pursue an outcome that would satisfy the goal. Such expectancies may arise (may be constructed) on specific occasions following the activation of a goal, and may inhibit or promote the active pursuit of goal satisfaction. This may be one primary effect of individual differences in competencies. However, differences in competence may also give rise to firmly established expectancies about the success of goal-directed behavior, which in turn may affect the probability of goal activation. In the initial stages of testing the theory, it is sufficient to assume that strong competencies for pursuing some outcomes will promote and weak ones will inhibit of the expression of a personal goal in behavior.

It is important to consider the specific ways in which self-regulation takes place. However, space limitation does not allow a detailed discussion here (but see Staub, 1978, 1980). Self-reactions accompanying a flow of events—which include self-rewards and self-punishments for having already taken specific steps of action; different kinds of thoughts that accompany events, which are likely to promote or inhibit different kinds of actions (such as persistence on tasks—Masters & Santrock, 1976); decisions that are made as a function of specific beliefs and values and their applications to events—all enter into self-regulation.

According to the theoretical model presented here, consistency in behavior could range from very low to relatively high, depending on individual characteristics. We might expect a relatively high degree of cross-situational consistency if a person possesses a strong personal goal (a goal high in the hierarchy of his or her goals), with a wide range of applicability to situations, and such supporting characteristics as relevant competencies. Given these conditions, it is likely that in many situations this goal would be activated, that even when several goals are activated it would be dominant, and that it would lead to goal-directed behavior.

## 5. RESEARCH SUPPORTING AND TESTING THE THEORETICAL MODEL

In several studies an attempt was made to test both the desirability of outcomes and the cognitive network of participants in the prosocial domain, using already existing tests. In one study (Staub, Erkut, & Jaquette, as described in Staub, 1974) these tests included measures of responsibility (social responsibility, Berkowitz & Lutterman, 1968; responsibility for others' welfare, Schwartz, 1970), of orientation toward other people as measured by the Machiavellian test (Christie & Geis, 1968), certain values on the Rokeach values scale, and Kohlberg's measure of moral reasoning. These measures (a) provide an evaluation (positive or negative) of human beings and human nature (a positive evaluation probably a precondition for valuing human welfare); (b) assess the importance or value placed on other people's welfare, and provide an indication of the desire for human welfare as an outcome, or end state; and (c) assess a feeling of personal responsibility for others' welfare. Jointly these tests have the potential of assessing a prosocial goal.

Analysis of variance that examined the interaction between situational influences (whether persons received permission to enter an adjoining room from which they later heard distress sounds, were prohibited from entering, or received no information) and the division of subjects into high and low on some of the specific personality measures that were described above showed a joint influence of personality and situation in several instances. On the whole, subjects who scored on the prosocial end of the specific measures helped more, in response to another person's distress, but only when they received permission to enter the adjoining room. This greater help was demonstrated either by actually entering, or, whether they entered or not—in the latter case the distressed person entered their room—by attempting to fill a prescription for him.

The scores of subjects on the various measures of values and prosocial thinking had high loading on a single factor (whereas other measures, related to action tendency, did not load on this factor). High scores on this factor, suggesting a general "prosocial orientation"—a well-developed and important prosocial goal—were related to attempts to help regardless of situational influences. This index of a personal orientation predicted prosocial behavior across the different experimental conditions that varied the permissibility of entering the adjoining room.

In other studies (Feinberg, 1977; Grodman, 1978) prosocial orientation was measured in a similar fashion, and the participant's response to a person's psychological distress was established. The exact tests that were used varied somewhat. For example, Kohlberg's test was not used, and a measure of orientation toward others' psychological needs, developed by Feinberg and Staub, was added. This measure included direct questions about how a person felt about other people's psychological needs, their degree of concern, and ease or difficulty in responding. The tests were always administered several weeks before the experimental sessions.[3]

In Feinberg's study, the female subject and the female confederate were both working on a task. The confederate, in response to a paragraph from a study they both had to read, either expressed strong distress that resulted from an experience the day before, her boyfriend breaking up a long-term relationship that was serious enough to discuss marriage (high need), or described the same experience as having occurred a year earlier (low need). High and low need were seen as representing high and low activating potentials for a prosocial goal. The

[3]The tests that remained in use in the different studies had surprisingly similar loadings on the factor that emerged in all the studies, in spite of variations in some of the other tests, in the subjects' sex (males in Staub, Erkut, and Jaquette's study, females in other studies) and in the universities where subjects were students.

subjects were supposed to work on a task when exposed to the confederate's need, this representing an activating potential for an achievement goal.

The subjects were divided into high and low groups on both prosocial orientation (or goal) and achievement orientation (or goal). The latter was also measured using a number of tests, and deriving factor scores for subjects. Subjects high on the prosocial goal orientation responded more nonverbally in the high need condition, by looking at and attending to the confederate rather than the task, than did subjects in any other condition. Subjects high on the achievement goal orientation but low on the prosocial orientation responded substantially more verbally, talked more to confederate, *both in high and low need,* than did subjects in other treatment groups. These subjects—as subjects high in achievement in general—also worked more on the task and, perhaps because of the combined pressure of the task and the confederate's need on them, they expressed some dislike of the confederate in high need. It seems that prosocial orientation was activated in high need and expressed primarily through nonverbal responsiveness, but achievement orientation was also activated by the confederate's actions, both in high and low need. Seemingly, high achievement individuals wanted to "respond well" to the initiative of the confederate, perhaps because among females achievement orientation is activated by situations that provide opportunity for effective social interaction (Stein, 1973).

Grodman (1978) used Feinberg's high need condition, but also varied the cost of helping the confederate. In the high cost group, if they completed less of their task, subjects were providing less information as a basis for feedback about their personality, which they were to receive afterward. As a postexperimental questionnaire indicated, more prosocial subjects valued such feedback more. In this study high prosocial orientation, as indicated by factor scores, was strongly associated with more helpful responding to the confederate, both verbally and nonverbally. High cost reduced the responsiveness of high prosocial subjects to the level of low prosocial subjects on some measures, but not on other ones. For example, on judgments of overall helpfulness by naïve judges who listened to the tape recording of the interaction, regardless of cost, high prosocial subjects were more helpful.

In a further study, Godfrey-Pinn (1979) explored the interaction of levels of prosocial orientation, measured as before, and perceptual sets, on observers' responses to two films of child abuse. The films varied in the severity of abuse they portrayed. The perceptual sets were experimentally induced, following procedures of previous studies (Regan & Totten, 1975; Stotland, 1969). The observational sets included an "imagine the child" set, an "imagine the parent" set, a witness set, and an observer set that was intended to lead subjects to see events in an objective, noninvolved manner. Subjects' reactions were evaluated by extensive ratings they were asked to make after the film. Since perception of and emotional reactions to events affect action, it was of interest to see whether subjects with a strong prosocial goal would be less affected by perceptual sets that might diminish concern for and empathy with an abused child.

Females with a high prosocial goal orientation, in comparison to those with a low one, experienced more helplessness, particularly in the imagine-parent and imagine-witness conditions. Subjects with a high prosocial orientation who saw severe child abuse experienced much more anger in the imagine-parent perceptual set condition than those with low prosocial orientation. Being directed to take the perspective of the abusive mother did not deflect high prosocial subjects from responding to the child's fate. Low prosocial subjects who saw severe abuse believed that the child felt less unloved after the abuse than low prosocial subjects who saw moderate abuse, or high prosocial subjects who saw either kind of abuse. Seemingly low prosocial subjects had a defensive reaction to the severe abuse of the child. There were no differences in subjects' reported willingness to intervene as a function of prosocial orientation. However, in explaining the ratings of their willingness to intervene, high prosocial subjects expressed the desire not to interfere with others' business more than low prosocial subjects.

These findings, though complex, suggest that subjects who differ in their prosocial orientation or goal process relevant events somewhat differently. They tend to be more concerned and affected by the fate of an abused child, when an externally imposed perspective might diminish such concern. They are also concerned, however, about their role in relation to the other people in the situation.

A substantial amount of existing research can be used to provide additional support for the model presented here, both with regard to the demonstration of the relationship between personal goals and action under activating conditions, and with regard to the role of other characteristics, such as competencies, that modify the influence of personal goals (see Staub, 1978, 1980). The testing of the model can be extended in many ways (and we are in the process of doing some of these extensions). For example, activating potentials of situations can be measured, rather than assumed, and in combination with indexes of goals can provide more accurate predictions of behavior. The extent to which the combination of an intense activation level and an important personal goal produces thoughts and feelings either about desired outcomes or expressive of the related cognitive network in one group of subjects, and corresponding action in another group, would attest to the type of cognitive-affective mediation of action that is suggested by the model. The extent to which the inclusion of additional characteristics improves prediction of behavior, and the existence of consistency in behavior across situations that have an intense activating potential for a goal, by subjects for whom the goal is important, can be studied.

## 6. THE DEVELOPMENT OF SOCIAL BEHAVIOR AND PERSONAL GOALS

To understand the development of any type of behavioral tendency, such as prosocial behavior, aggression, or achievement-related actions, we have to concern ourselves with the development of the child's personality in general. The preceding section suggests that a primary determinant of whether children or adults behave one way or another is the relative strength of the personal goals they possess. Thus we need to understand how such goals develop. As already noted, there are a number of characteristics that affect the likelihood that a particular goal will be activated and will gain expression in action—somewhat different characteristics depending on the type of goal in question. If we are to understand the development of a certain behavioral orientation, we have to come to understand the development of the various characteristics that affect such behavior.

### 6.1. The Development of Specific Goals in Children

An important area in which our knowledge is limited is the development of individual motives. There is continuing discussion as to what motives are and the nature of linkage among cognition, affect, incentive, and motive (Izard, 1978; Kagan, 1978). It is assumed here that motivation as embodied in personal goals involves outcomes (objects, events, or behaviors) that have incentive value; the expectation or fulfillment of outcomes is associated with positive affect (or, in the case of negative goals, with relief from negative affect); the outcomes usually have cognitive networks associated with them; and when the goal is in an active state tension is maintained until the satisfaction of the goal or its deactivation.

Specific goals, as they are conceptualized, develop as a function of socialization and experience. There are several basic motivational systems in the human organism that can be the source of such goals that, in a sense, represent second-order motivation. The basic motivational systems include: primary (survival) needs; other stimuli that have biological meaning (contact comfort and other sensory experiences); interest in external stimuli, in acting on the world—intrinsic motivation; the capacity for the development and the existence of attachment; developing a positive self-concept and protecting the existing self-concept; and identification with other people (which might have several sources). Some of these motivational systems are themselves the result of development, and depending on their nature they represent bridges to specific social (and nonsocial) personal goals. Secure attachment and identification are, presumably, precursors for a strong affiliation goal and perhaps for the goal of developing intimate relationships. The opportunity for developing and expanding intrinsic motivation, the availability of varied stimulation and the manipulation of objects, can lead to the development of a sense of agency and, in combination with other elements, to a strong achievement goal.

How do specific social goals develop out of basic motivational systems? Let us briefly examine the achievement motive (which in the present conceptualization is goallike in character). It is usually defined as a desire to do well in comparison to standards of excellence. It is contrasted with fear of failure as a motivation, which is regarded as a desire to avoid failure, rather than to gain success. For achievement motivation, as discussed and explored in past theory and research, to exist, an individual has to value success; has to set reasonably high standards of accomplishment for him or herself; and has to have a sense of his or her agency or capacity to do well. In part, achievement motivation is likely to be an outgrowth of opportunities for the optimal evolution of intrinsic motivation. But that is probably not enough. The definition of the motive implies more than a desire to engage in activities that are challenging or difficult for their own sake, because the activities are intrinsically satisfying. The definition suggests that a person adopts standards that define excellence. Parents who set standards for the child and push the child to work hard to achieve these standards appear important. Such behavior is characteristic both of parents who have children with high self-esteem, and of parents whose children have a high need for achievement (Coopersmith, 1967; Rosen & D'Andrade, 1959). Identification with such parents—perhaps a result of their affection or their interest in the welfare of the child—may also contribute to children's accepting these standards as their own.

### 6.2. Prosocial Goal Orientation

The development of a prosocial goal would mean the development of affective-cognitive orientations that make others' welfare valued, a desirable outcome of behavior. The development of positive attachment is a natural contributor to such a goal, since through generalization it can result in positive affects toward people in general. This seems a basic component of the type of prosocial goal that was discussed earlier. There is some evidence, in fact, suggesting that children with a secure attachment to their mothers are more comfortable with their peers, move more easily toward them (Sroufe, 1979). Developmental (love-based) identification with caretakers, the desire to be like them, should further extend a positive affective orientation toward other people. If the caretakers are concerned about others' welfare, and express their emotions in words, feelings, and actions, the child is likely to develop similar concern for others. Rosenhan (1970) reports that many of the civil rights workers who traveled South to participate in desegregation efforts, and were in other ways "fully committed" to civil rights activities, described their parents' examples. One remembered being carried on his father's shoulders to protest Sacco and Vanzetti trials; another's father went off to fight on the Republican side in the Spanish Civil War.

The warmth and affection that are preconditions for developmental identification can have the effects noted above. By promoting positive feelings toward other people, they can contribute to a sense of connectedness to others. They can also affect the child's experience of self, the value the child places on the self, that is, his or her self-esteem.

Parents talk to children to different extents, saying different things. A substantial amount of research suggests that verbal communications have important consequences, depending on what is said, how, and in what context. Clearly, what parents say can affect what children come to value, how they come to interpret the world, and the kind of understanding they have of the world. Induction, for example, the explanation to the child of how his or her actual or potential behavior affects other people, is likely both to serve motivational functions and to enhance the capacity for role taking.

The standards that parents set for children are also likely to be importantly involved in the development of prosocial goal orientation. As in the development of self-esteem, or in an achievement goal, a personal, in contrast to abstract, valuing of others' welfare will come only if children act on standards of kindness and helpfulness, if they actually do act to enhance others' welfare. For cognitive-affective orientations to further develop, they have to be connected to action in the individual's experience. Learning by doing, by engaging in prosocial behavior, is likely to be important both in the development of the motive and in its connection to or expression in action (Staub, 1979). With the development of personal standards for prosocial action, a positive self-esteem comes to be associated with behaving according to those standards. The motivation may be to benefit others, but nevertheless the prosocial goal comes to be intrinsically connected to the self.

A number of writers have differentiated between two kinds of prosocial motivation, which have been described in varied ways but may best be summarized as other-oriented and self-oriented motivation. For example, I discussed one prosocial goal based on a prosocial value orientation, on concern about others' welfare and the desire to benefit them, and another one based on feelings of duty or obligation to help others under certain conditions. The focus in the first case is on benefiting another, and feelings both of empathy and of responsibility appear essential components of the motivation (see Staub, 1979, 1980). It also seems inevitable that a connection between responding to others and feelings about the self would exist. With regard to motivation that is focused on duty and obligation, norms and standards that specify both the conditions under which action should be taken, and the kind of action that is to be taken, are regarded as central and predominant over concern about others' welfare. We are probably dealing with a continuum that has two motivational poles, one focusing on others' welfare but also involving the relationship between oneself and others' welfare, the other focusing on the relationship between oneself and internalized norms and rules (see also Chapter 7; Hoffman, 1970).

## 7. THE EFFECTS OF EXISTING PERSONALITY ON FURTHER DEVELOPMENT

### 7.1. Children Shaping Their Own Environment

There is substantial evidence that children shape their environment and thereby their experiences. The interaction between children and their environment is transactional. This begins early in life: In the first day, depending on individual differences in infants' visual or auditory orientation, differences have been found in maternal behavior. As their motives develop, the manner in which children shape their environment is likely to take different directions or forms. Children who initiate competition receive competitive reactions (Toda *et al.*, 1978), as do adults (Kelly & Stahleski, 1970). Aggression by children induces aggressive responses to them (Rausch, 1965). Children who vary in the kinds of attachment they form to their mothers show differences in social behavior with other children (Sroufe , 1979). Reasons for this may include differences in affiliative and other directed goals, and differences in orientation toward the self, with different strategies for enhancing or maintaining the self and self-esteem.

Social interaction, and peer interaction in particular, appears reciprocal in nature. Although reciprocity is far from complete, children who behave positively tend to be recipients of positive behaviors, whereas those who behave negatively tend to be recipients of negative behaviors (Staub & Feinberg, 1980). Different behavioral tendencies, which express different motives, self-concepts, and social skills, influence the child's further experience and thereby shape the child's personality.

In one study (Staub & Feinberg, 1980) we found that boys who tend to engage in "negative" behaviors, which include aggression, instrumental aggression, aggressive self-defense, and submission to others—behaviors that are interrelated—were the objects of the same kinds of behavior from others, and had relatively little positive behavior directed at them. In contrast, boys who engaged in predominantly positive behaviors—cooperation, expression of positive emotions, sharing—were the recipients of primarily positive behaviors from others and had relatively little aggression directed at them. Similarly, reciprocity existed between girls' positive and sociable behaviors and such behaviors directed at them by their peers. However, among girls aggression was infrequent, its varied forms were not interrelated, and it did not evoke primarily aggressive behavior from others. Different patterns of behaviors by children and directed at children should give rise to different conceptions of other people and the self, and give rise to or maintain differences in interpersonal strategies and skills.

In our study, girls' capacity to infer others' feelings, and to respond sympathetically to those feelings, was associated with positive behaviors directed at them by their peers. Inferential capacity and/or empathy may give rise to sensitivity to others; through their expression in interpersonal behavior, and through the responses they generate, they further shape the child's personality and social behavior.

Usually, the differences in young children's behaviors are seen as the result of different social skills or others self-related characteristics. At an early age, however, differences in interpersonal goals may exist, in what children would like to happen in their interactions with other people. This may partly explain individual differences in social interactions.

### 7.2. Socialization, Existing Personality, and Principles of Change

The reasoning in this chapter implies that the socialization that children experience will be a function, in part, of their existing personality. Although the view of transactional influence among children and their socializers has replaced the earlier emphasis on unidirectional influence by parents (Bell, 1968), only limited relevant research exists, particularly in the realm of prosocial behavior (but see Bell & Harper, 1977).

Dlugokinski and Firestone (1974) found that children who experienced induction at home responded more to an inductive statement, whereas those who were used to power assertion at home responded more to a power assertive statement, when these statements attempted to induce them to share. This finding shows personality–situation interaction in affecting behavior, but not in inducing change or development. Radke-Yarrow and Scott (1972) report that in experimental groups where experimenters were supposed to behave either in a warm or in an indifferent manner toward children, the behavior of individual children resulted in differences in experimenter behaviors. Moreover, the frequency with which children experienced certain interactions differed as a function of their own initiative. Dependent children experienced more warmth in the warm adult treatment and more rejection in the indifferent adult treatment. Basic questions such as the stability of personality are involved here. Given certain characteristics of children at a given point, for example, aggression or dependency in kindergarten, the nature of the environment will interact with these existing characteristics to determine how much stability, how much change, and what kind of change will occur. Included and perhaps of substantial importance among these characteristics are the already existing goals of the children and their expression in behavior.

An important consideration in the realm of acquisition may be that personality–environment interaction can affect not only *what* is learned, but also *how* learning takes place. That is, the principles by which learning takes place may be affected, which in turn may affect what is learned. As an example, consider that in research on forbidden toys, principles of cognitive dissonance and dissonance reduction appear to operate when there is mild threat used to prohibit children from playing with toys. Mild threat results in devaluing the toys. Severe threat may have a different set of consequences: It may evoke a different principle by which learning takes place, that of fear of punishment, with a possible external (in contrast to internal) orientation toward rules as a result. In considering these different levels of threat, which are aspects of the situation, one must consider that what is a mild threat or a severe threat to a child is certainly a function of the past experience of the child. Both variation in an accustomed level of threat, and the extent to which a child already possesses an external or internal orientation to rules, can affect how a given threat is perceived, processed, and what learning follows.

In summary, the child's existing personality not only affects current behavior, in interaction with environmental conditions, but also affects what the child learns from experiences or events, and even the principles by which learning, change, or development occurs. Already existing goals may result in children exposing themselves to different experiences, shaping others' behavior toward themselves, or experiencing the same events in different ways.

## 8. REFERENCES


Arnold, M. *Emotion and personality*. New York: Columbia University Press, 1960.

Averill, J. R. The emotions. In E. Staub (Ed.), *Personality: Basic aspects and current research.* Englewood Cliffs, N.J.: Prentice-Hall, 1980.

Bell, R. Q. A reinterpretation of the direction of effects in studies of socialization. *Psychological Review,* 1968, *75,* 81–95.

Bell, R. Q., & Harper, L. V. *Child effects on adults.* Hillsdale, N.J.: Lawrence Erlbaum, 1977.

Berkowitz, L., & Lutterman, K. G. The traditional socially responsible personality. *Public Opinion Quarterly,* 1968, *32,* 169–185.

Christie, R., & Geis, F. (Eds.). *Studies in Machiavellianism.* New York: Academic Press, 1968.

Coopersmith, S. *Antecedents of self-esteem.* San Francisco: Fremont, 1967.

Deutsch, M. Field theory in social psychology. In G. Lindsey & E. Aronson (Eds.), *Handbook of social psychology* (Vol. 1). Reading, Mass.: Addison-Wesley, 1968.

Dlugokinski, E. L., & Firestone, I. J. Other centeredness and susceptibility to charitable appeals: Effects of perceived discipline. *Developmental Psychology,* 1974, *10,* 21–28.

Feinberg, H. K. *Anatomy of a helping situation: Some personality and situational determinants of helping in a conflict situation involving another's psychological distress.* Unpublished doctoral dissertation, University of Massachusetts, Amherst, 1977.

Frederiksen, N. Toward a taxonomy of situations. *American Psychologist,* 1972, *27,* 114–124.

Garbarino, J., & Bronfenbrenner, U. The socialization of moral judgment and behavior in cross-cultural perspective. In T. Lickona (Ed.), *Moral development and behavior.* New York: Holt, 1976.

Godfrey-Pinn, D. *Empathic responses to child-abusive behaviors: The influence of observational set and personality.* Unpublished master's thesis, University of Massachusetts, Amherst, 1979.

Grodman, S. M. *The role of personality and situational variables in responding to and helping an individual in psychological distress.* Unpublished doctoral thesis, University of Massachusetts, Amherst, 1978.

Hoffman, M. L. Conscience, personality, and socialization techniques. *Human Development,* 1970, *13,* 90–126.

Hornstein, H. A. *Cruelty and kindness: A new look at aggression and altruism.* Englewood Cliffs, N.J.: Prentice-Hall, 1976.

Izard, C. E. On the ontogenesis of emotions: Cognition relationships in infancy. In M. Lewis & L. A. Rosenblum (Eds.), *The development of affect.* New York: Plenum Press, 1978.

Kagan, J. On emotion and its development: A working paper. In M. Lewis & L. A. Rosenblum (Eds.). *The development of affect.* New York: Plenum Press, 1978.

Kelly, H. H., & Stahleski, A. J. Social interaction basis of cooperators' and competitors' beliefs about others. *Journal of Personality and Social Psychology,* 1970, *16,* 66–91.

Lazarus, R. S. *Psychological stress and the coping process.* New York: McGraw-Hill, 1966.

Lerner, M. J., & Simmons, C. H. Observer's reaction to the "innocent victim": Compassion or rejection? *Journal of Personality and Social Psychology,* 1966, *4,* 203–210.

Leventhal, H. Emotions: A basic problem for social psychology. In C. Nemeth (Ed.), *Social psychology: Classic and contemporary integrations.* Chicago: Rand McNally, 1974.

Lewin, K. The conceptual representation and measurement of psychological forces. *Contributions to Psychological Theory,* 1938, *1,* 247.

Lewin, K. *Resolving social conflicts.* New York: Harper, 1948.

Masters, J. C., & Santrock, J. W. Studies in the self-regulation of behavior: Effects of verbal and cognitive self-reinforcement. *Developmental Psychology,* 1976, *12,* 334–348.

McDougall, W. *Social Psychology.* London: Methuen, 1908.

Mead, M. *Cooperation and competition among primitive peoples.* New York: McGraw-Hill, 1937.

Mischel, W. Theory and research on the antecedents of self-imposed delay of reward. In B. A. Maher (Ed.), *Progress in experimental personality research* (Vol. 3), New York: Academic Press, 1966.

Mischel, W. *Introduction to personality (2nd ed.). New York: Holt, Rinehart & Winston, 1976.*

*Moos, R. H. Systems for the assessment and classification of human environments. In R. H. Moos & P. M. Insel (Eds.), Issues in social ecology.* Palo, Alto, Calif.: National Press Books, 1974.

Murray, H. A. *Explorations in personality.* New York: Oxford University Press, 1938.

Rausch, H. Interaction sequences. *Journal of Personality and Social Psychology,* 1965, *2,* 487–499.

Regan, D., & Totten, J. Empathy and attribution: Turning observers into actors. *Journal of Personality and Social Psychology,* 1975, *32,* 850–856.

Reykowski, J. Introduction. In J. Reykowski (Ed.), *Studies in the mechanisms of prosocial behavior.* Warszawskiego: Wydaevnictiva Universyteter, 1975.

Rosen, B. D., & D'Andrade, R. The psychological origins of achievement motivation. *Sociometry,* 1969, *22,* 185–218.

Rosenhan, D. The natural socialization of altruistic autonomy. In J. Macauley & L. Berkowitz (Eds.), *Altruism and helping.* New York: Academic Press, 1970.

Rotter, J. B. *Social learning and clinical psychology.* Englewood Cliffs, N.J.: Prentice-Hall, 1954.

Rubin, Z., & Peplau, L. A. Who believes in a just world? *Journal of Social Issues,* 1975, *31,* 65–89.

Schwartz, S. H. Moral decision-making and behavior. In J. Macauley & L. Berkowitz (Eds.), *Altruism and helping behavior.* New York: Academic Press, 1970.

Sroufe, L. A. The coherence of individual development: Early care, attachment, and subsequent developmental issues. *American Psychologist,* 1979, *34,* 834–842.

Staub, E. Helping a distressed person: Social, personality, and stimulus determinants. In L. Berkowitz (Ed.), *Advances in experimental social psychology* (Vol. 7). New York: Academic Press, 1974.

Staub, E. *Positive social behavior and morality.* Vol. 1. *Personal and social influences.* New York: Academic Press, 1978.

Staub, E. *Positive social behavior and morality.* Vol. 2. *Socialization and development.* New York: Academic Press, 1979.

Staub, E. Social and prosocial behavior: Personal and situational influences and their interactions. In E. Staub (Ed.), *Personality: Basic aspects and current research.* Englewood Cliffs, N.J.: Prentice-Hall, 1980.

Staub, E., & Feinberg, H. *Regularities in peer interaction, empathy, and sensitivity to others.* Paper presented at the meeting of the American Psychological Association, Montreal, August 1980.

Stein, A. H. The socialization of achievement orientation in females. *Psychological Bulletin,* 1973, *80,* 345–366.

Stotland, E. Exploratory studies in empathy. In L. Berkowitz (Ed.), *Advances in experimental social psychology* (Vol. 4). New York: Academic Press, 1969.

Toda, M., Shinotsuka, H., McClintock, C. G., & Stech, F. J. Development of competitive behavior as a function of culture, age, and social comparison. *Journal of Personality and Social Psychology*, 1978, *36*, 825–839.

Yarrow, M. R., & Scott, P. M. Imitation of nurturant and nonnurturant models. *Journal of Personality and Social Psychology*, 1972, *23*, 259–270.

Zeigarnick, B. Über das Behalten von erledigten und unerledigten Handlungen. *Psychologische Forschungen*, 1927, *9*, 1–85.

# 3

# Spatial Organization of a Cognitive System and Intrinsic Prosocial Motivation

Janusz Reykowski

## 1. INTRODUCTION

For students of prosocial behavior, the crucial issue, as Lauren Wispé put it some time ago, is: Why would anyone do it?

According to the dominant approach, a human being is an individualist by nature and would pursue his or her own happiness if not curbed by a society. A society can organize conditions in such a way that a cost–reward calculation makes a prosocial behavior profitable; it can also install in personality special mechanisms (superego, conscience, personal standards) that impel people to action on behalf of others.

There are those who argue against this hedonistic view, claiming that man is by nature prosocial; in other words, all (or a majority of) people have some inborn qualities such as empathy that make them sensitive to the fate of others and are the source of inclination to positive social behavior. These qualities may be enhanced or suppressed by some factors, and an empirical identification of these factors can be one of the possible goals of prosocial research.[1]

[1]For a more detailed discussion of contemporary approaches, see Chapter 1 in the present volume.

JANUSZ REYKOWSKI • Department of Psychology, Polish Academy of Science, 00-063 Warsaw, Poland.

I should like to argue with both positions since both, in my view, fail to give a fair account of the mechanisms involved. But instead of trying to point out what seems doubtful in these two approaches, I shall propound an alternative one. I shall try to suggest that there exists an intrinsic prosocial motivation that emerges as the result of development of personality. The motivation is not predetermined by our genes, but it is likely to appear as a "natural" consequence of formation of personality.

## 2. INITIAL ASSUMPTIONS

I shall start by making some clarifications concerning the term *prosocial,* since the term has been used with different meanings. For the present purpose the term is used in a descriptive sense; it describes an action oriented toward protection, maintenance, or enhancement of the well-being of an external[2] social object, that is, a concrete person, a group, a society as a whole, a social institution, and so on.

It should be stressed that the concept "prosocial" as defined here does not include any assumptions concerning motivation of the act. The act is classified as prosocial according to its social meaning. That is, it can be called "prosocial" if its organization indicates that valuable consequences for someone other than the subject are likely to occur and action is aimed at those consequences (they cannot be regarded as an unexpected by-product of the given act).[3] There is, however a difficult question: valuable from whose point of view? In many cases, it is a point of view common to the recipient and the donor (and the observer as well). There are other times, however, when it is only the donor who believes that consequences of his or her action are valuable for the recipient.

Our main postulate is that prerequisites of prosocial behavior can be found in the intrinsic characteristics of the "mental apparatus" as much as can prerequisites of many other forms of goal-oriented activity. Thus the nature of the mental apparatus is a critical focus here.

In fact, we are assuming that the mental apparatus can be regarded as a highly organized system developing in a brain. It is on the one side a representation of an external reality, and on the other a mechanism with productive capabilities, that is, having a potential for generating new organizations.

[2]The term *external* means different from the subject him or herself.

[3]Such terms as *helping, sharing,* and *cooperating* are usually defined in the same way, that is, according to the social meaning of the acts—the motivation for such acts is a separate issue. The term *prosocial* is simply more general than any of the above-mentioned terms.

This way of thinking about the nature of the mental apparatus is quite common in contemporary psychology, although in different psychological schools and in different countries a different terminology has been used. For example, Soviet psychologists use the term *consciousness* to refer to these phenomena; in France, some authors use the term *social representation;* in Poland, the term *regulatory mechanisms* is popular; and in American psychology the term *cognitive system* seems to convey a similar meaning.

In our further discussion the term *cognitive system* will be used with, however, one reservation. Many if not most authors use the term *cognitive* to suggest information-processing phenomena only. However, it was demonstrated some time ago that information processing has emotional and motivational consequences. Hebb (1949), Hunt (1963), and recently Zajonc (1980) have argued that our relationship with the world is regulated by two different although interconnected systems, one based on "discriminanda" (purely "cognitive") and another on "preferenda" (i.e., affective processing).[4] Taking this into consideration, we regard the cognitive system as an organization where cognitive *and* affective processes are generated.

We assume that the cognitive system consists of a number of cognitive structures (concepts, schemata, scripts) that represent objects and their relations, as well as operations that make possible symbolic transformations of them. The content and organization of those structures (schemata) and the characteristics of available operations determine how the system performs its regulatory functions. In this chapter, I shall discuss some implications of the hypothesis that relations among the cognitive structures can be described in spatial terms; that is, I shall try to present a model of a cognitive system as a multidimensional space. We believe that a spatial model of the cognitive system has important bearing upon a theory of prosocial behavior.

## 3. A MODEL OF A COGNITIVE SYSTEM: MULTIDIMENSIONAL SPACE

The attempt to construct a spatial model of the mind is not at all a new one. Models of this kind were developed by Pavlov, Freud, Lewin,

[4]In our theory of personality we have postulated that the regulatory (cognitive) system has two modes of functioning: operational (descriptive) and evaluative (affective) (Reykowski, 1974; Reykowski & Kochanska, 1980; Chapter 8, present volume). Some differences between those two modes have been demonstrated experimentally by Lewicka (1979).

and Osgood, to mention just a few of the best known. And recently the spatial interpretation of data based on Kelly's (1955) Reptest, measuring personal constructs, has been applied to a variety of cases (Slater, 1976).

A new inspiration for such thinking comes from studies on semantic organization developed within the framework of research on long-term memory, artificial intelligence, and psycholinguistics. Two phenomena especially should be mentioned here. The first one has been observed in studies on "natural concepts." It has been shown that category membership is a matter of degree (see Mervis & Rosch, 1981; Rips, Shoben, & Smith, 1973; Trzebiński, 1980). The second phenomenon concerns the relationship between concepts. On the basis of studies applying a multidimensional scaling method for a domain of concepts, it has been shown that spatial relations between concepts (obtained by means of this procedure) are not merely a convenient way of representing data but have an explanatory value. Rumelhart and Abrahamson demonstrated that knowing the spatial relations between concepts (i.e., their semantic distances), one is able to predict results of information processing within the given domain such as classification, solution of analogy problems, and so on (see Sternberg, Tourangeau, & Nigro, 1978).

The predictions are possible because attributes of the given structures are "carried on" other objects that have their representations in a cognitive space. Applicability of the specific attribute to an object is a decreasing function (probably an exponential one) of its distance from the source (Sternberg *et al.*, 1978). We can speak here about the gradient of application (or applicability).

In cognitive studies these structures are described from a purely cognitive point of view (i.e., only their information-processing functions are taken into consideration). But it does not give a full account of their functions.

Many structures comprise schemata concerning actions that can or should be taken with an object. More often than not, possible actions are socially regulated in a form of normative standards concerning an object (or situations). Norms prescribe or recommend certain forms of action with the given object and prohibit other forms. Acquisition of concepts includes a process of learning normative standards related to given objects. It can be said that an object's representation comprises normative (or prescriptive) standards.

Cognitive structures also have some affective characteristics; hence, an object identified by the given concept evokes some affective states.

This reasoning leads us to the following conclusions:

1. Cognitive structures are a source of judgments of three kinds: descriptive, normative (prescriptive), and affective.[5]
2. The judgment can be applied to objects depending upon their semantic distance from a given concept: The closer the given object is located in a semantic network to a specific structure, the greater the probability and the greater the certainty of application of this judgment.

There are some data that seem to support these conclusions. In a study by Andrzej Nowak of our laboratory, subjects (high school students) were requested to perform a series of paired comparisons of 30 names belonging to a specific domain; the three domains chosen were animals, vehicles, and social roles. The data were analyzed by means of a multidimensional scaling method.[6] As a result three spatial solutions, for the three different domains, respectively, were obtained. The second group of subjects was asked to compose sentences that describe objects represented in the domains (descriptive statements), evaluate them (affective statements), and form postulates concerning those objects (normative statements). The third group of subjects received the sentences concerning a few of the objects (two from each domain); they were asked to assess, by means of a 7-point scale, the applicability of the given sentence to 15 objects belonging to the domain.

Figure 1 illustrates the relationship between semantic distance of the object (as measured on the basis of the multidimensional scaling) from the original and degree of applicability of sentences containing the descriptive, affective, and normative judgments. It can be seen that there is a negative relationship between semantic distance and degree of applicability of all three kinds of judgments.

These results are not at all surprising. They correspond with earlier findings concerning generalization of affect. It has been known for several decades that affect spreads in the semantic network and that its strength depends upon the semantic distance between the sources of affect and examined stimuli (e.g., Iwanov-Smolenski, 1954; Krasnogorski, 1954; Razran, 1949). Although there are no directly comparable data concerning normative statements, there are some that have important bearing on the issue. Kurcz (1963) has demonstrated that behavioral acts can be generalized on the basis of their semantic distance.

We can now extend the model of a semantic space into the area of social behavior.

[5]The term *affective judgment* has been used by Zajonc (1980).

[6]The comparisons were made within each domain separately by the Shepard-Kruskal method—MD scale Osiris III.

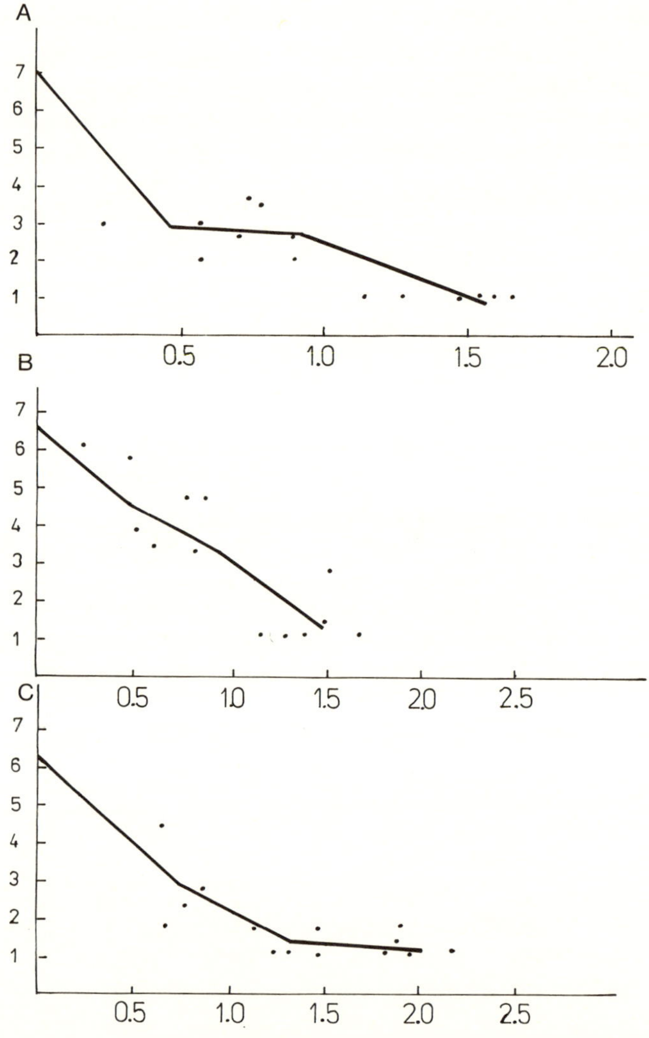


Figure 1. Semantic distance and judgment applicability. Subjects were asked to evaluate on a 7-point scale the appropriateness of the sentence for each of the 14 words representing a given domain (i.e., whether the sentence is correct when the first word is replaced with another vehicle's name). (A) *Airplanes* can be used for fast transportation (descriptive statement). (B) *Cars* are awful because they kill people and spoil the environment (affective statement). (C) *Airplanes* should be used for peaceful purposes (normative statement).

## 4. REPRESENTATION OF SOCIAL OBJECTS IN A COGNITIVE SYSTEM

It is a rather obvious fact that a cognitive system represents not only lexical symbols but consists of much more complex structures representing objects (as individuals and as categories). We have not only a vocabulary of words but also a vocabulary of things, and not only a grammar of speech but also a grammar of actions. Representations of words and things are not the same, to be sure. The relationship between them might be described, in Chomsky's terms, as the relationship between surface structures and deep structures. We usually need many words and sentences for the description of any well-known object, or category of objects, and in most if not all cases there remains some content that is not covered by the words used for description. More often than not, those "remnants" seem to be quite sizable, hiding the gist of the thing. It probably would not be too far from the truth to say that the more extensive and the deeper the acquaintance with an object, the greater the portion of experience related to the object remains beyond the range of verbal interpretation. The organization of deep structures seems to be the real base or core of personality.

But the main point of this reasoning is that the same basic rules are governing the organization of surface and deep structures; the relationship that we have observed with words can also be observed with representations of things. It can especially be assumed that representations of objects are located in multidimensional space and that the closer they are located to one another, the greater is the tendency to apply to them the same descriptive, normative, and affective judgments.

Let us analyze more thoroughly a specific instance of this reasoning, namely, the relationship between the self-structure and structures representing other social objects. We assume that the self-structure can be interpreted as a representation of one's own person in the cognitive system. It should be stressed that the term *self-structure* is reserved here for some parts of a cognitive system and should not be used interchangeably with such words as "I," "me," and "mine." Whereas the word "I" (and "me") refers to the person as a whole, the term *self-structure* refers to the part of the cognitive system of an individual that represents his or her own person as different from those parts that represent other objects. In fact, one could say that, "In my cognitive system there are representations of the self (of myself) and other social objects—my brother, my wife, my country, my institute," and so on. To avoid confusion we shall hereafter use the term *self-structure;* its meaning is similar to that of the term *self-schemata* (Markus, 1977, 1980).

On the basis of our previous argument, we may formulate the following hypotheses:

1. The closer the given object is located with respect to the self, the greater is the tendency to apply to him or her the same characteristics that are being applied to the self (application of descriptive judgments).
2. The closer the given object is located with respect to the self, the greater is the tendency to apply to him or her the same rules (norms, principles) that are applied to the self (application of normative judgments).
3. The closer the given object is located with respect to the self, the greater is the tendency to evaluate him or her as one evaluates oneself (application of affective judgments).

It should be noted that these hypotheses can be reversed because we can also say that descriptive, normative, or affective judgments can be transferred from a social object onto the self. It seems quite probable, though, that not always is it equally easy to move from object to self as from self to object. We suspect that this asymmetry is a function of a difference in regulatory potential of the given structures. An example of such asymmetry would be the phenomenon of projective assimilation—the phenomenon seems to be related to the dominant position of the self in the cognitive system (Lewicki, 1977).

The three hypotheses imply that psychological distance between the self and a social object has bearing upon the interpretation of an object. The term *psychological distance* describes the subjective representation of the degree of separation of two or more elements in time, in physical space, in social position, or in a semantic system. Thus, whereas the degree of separation is a function of the objective position of the given element with respect to other elements, the psychological distance is the subjective representation of such a separation.

In two separate studies we obtained data concerning the relationship between psychological distance of a social object from the self and descriptive judgments regarding the object. Andrzejczyk, who studied delinquent boys' ability to recognize the needs of others, found that her subjects required less information for identification of the needs of a target person if he was described by the experimenter as someone from reformatory school (see Reykowski, 1979). Korzeniowski (1980), who measured psychological distance from the self by means of a special graphic technique, found that subjects who located other persons further away from the self had a lower ability for perspective taking, as assessed by Feffer's Role Taking Test (RTT). We believe that in some cases, though not all, seeing the situation through the other person's eyes requires attributing to him or her some characteristics that are attributed to oneself. Apparently, when people are located at a greater distance from the self the ability for such attribution diminishes.

The hypothesis concerning the application of affective judgments implies that liking someone should be a function of (1) the psychological distance of a person from the self, and (2) the affective characteristics of the self. The first statement is supported by data that show a positive relationship between the similarity of a person to oneself and liking a person (Byrne, 1971). The relationship is explained very often in terms of the greater reinforcing value of people whose views support our belief system. This interpretation, however, overlooks the fact that the relationship is not being held in cases of negative self-evaluation: People who ascribe to themselves negative characteristics tend to have negative evaluations of others (Leonard, 1974).

In fact, the relationship seems to be even more complicated. Karylowski (1975, 1976) found that there is a positive relationship between self-evaluation and liking another person, but that it holds only for persons whose semantic distance from the self is rather small ($r = .51$, $p < .001$); for remote persons (dissimilar) this relationship tends to disappear ($r = .11$). Smoleńska (1979), in a separate study, obtained the same pattern of results (see Table 1).

A similarity to the self is not, to be sure, the only source of liking. But for similar persons, that is, persons whose psychological distance from the self is small, there is a clear-cut relationship between self-evaluation and liking; and this finding supports the idea that affective judgments are being spread from the self to other social objects psychologically close to the self.

Our model suggests that not only semantic, but also other forms of proximity, should have the same effects. Thus we expect that physical distance has an impact upon liking. It should be recalled that the hypothesis concerning a positive attitude for people who are physically close is a rather old one (e.g., Bossard, 1932, and Kipnis *et al.*—see Schneider, 1976). Festinger, Schachter, and Back found that there was a

*Table 1. Self-Evaluation, Liking, and Psychological Distance*[a]

Relationship between self-evaluation and liking of close and remote persons

| | Partner | |
|---|---|---|
| | Close | Remote |
| High self-evaluation | .32 | .05 |
| Low self-evaluation | .03 | .15 |

[a] $p < .05$.

relationship between the proximity of an apartment in a dormitory and a sociometric choice; respective probabilities of choices were: for a next-door apartment, .412; for two apartments away, .225; for three, −.162; and for four, −.103 (cf. Schneider, 1976).

As for the hypothesis concerning application of normative statements, the anthropologist Sahlins observed that the application of rules of an equal exchange depends upon social distance; he classified social distance into such sectors as home, lineage, village, tribal, and intertribal, concluding that as the distance increases (from home sector to intertribal sector), reciprocity decreases and cheating increases (see Alexander, 1975). And Bar-Tal, Bar-Zohar, Greenberg, and Hermon (1977) obtained data that can be interpreted to suggest that the norm of helping has a decreasing legitimacy as the social distance increases.

In summary, there are good reasons to believe that a meaning ascribed to a social object, that is, descriptive and affective judgments applied to him or her as well as the rules of interaction with him or her, depend upon the psychological distance of the social object from the self.[7]

But now the crucial question arises: How can this reasoning be applied to the main issue of this chapter—that is, to the regulation of prosocial behavior?

## 5. PERSONAL INVOLVEMENT AS A FUNCTION OF PSYCHOLOGICAL DISTANCE

According to the argument presented above, our judgments concerning social objects are affected by their psychological distance from the self . This phenomenon can have an impact upon prosocial behavior since it is related to such processes as recognition of needs and emotional states of another person, liking or disliking him or her, recognition of his or her rights, and so on. The argument is based upon the hypothesis of spatial organization of a cognitive system.

We now can apply the same hypothesis to the investigation of motivational processes. To do so, we shall assume that motives are aroused whenever a person is confronted with events that concern his or her well-being (for our discussion, it does not make a difference if the events have already taken place or have been imagined); such events lead to an

[7]It should be stressed, however, that for the sake of the clarity of our argument we have concentrated on the relation between a social object and the self, not taking into consideration relations to representations of other social objects. We shall come back to this problem at the end of the chapter.

involvement of the self-structure. The degree of involvement depends, to some extent, upon the characteristics of an event. One of the characteristics that is of main concern for us here is the psychological distance of an event from the cognitive structure (in this case, from a self-structure). As an extension of our previous reasoning, we can formulate a hypothesis that the degree of involvement of the self is a function of the psychological distance of the event from the self.

This hypothesis finds support from various sources. It has been shown in two Swedish studies that the degree of involvement in events occurring in remote places (various European cities) depends upon their distance from the place where the subjects were living (Stockholm). The involvement was an exponential function of the distance when the size of the city and its familiarity were kept constant (Bratfish, 1966; Ekman & Bratfish, 1965). The same relationship has been observed with respect to the temporal and semantic distances. Two Finnish researchers (von Wright & Kinnunen, 1977) as well as two Swedish (Lundberg & Ellonen, 1977) found that the degree of involvement in future events is an exponential function of time. Epstein (1962) has shown that parachuters examined on the day of the jump reacted emotionally when exposed to words having some relation to parachuting: the greater the semantic proximity of the stimulus word to the situation of a jump, the stronger the emotional reaction that was manifested by the parachuter.

We can now apply the same principle to events that do not directly affect the subject him or herself, but somebody else—for example, to a case of someone who does not perform a parachuting jump but is aware that another person is making one. We predict that the degree of involvement in such an event will depend upon the *psychological distance of the person with respect to whom this event takes place.* In other words, the greater the proximity of the person affected by an event, the greater the involvement. As a consequence, the subject may react to the situation as if he or she were affected. Events that affect one's well-being are likely to evoke self-protective tendencies. We expect, therefore, that such protective tendencies are aroused when a person located sufficiently close to the self is involved.

It should be acknowledged that so far as everyday life is concerned, such a statement is hardly surprising. As a matter of fact, one of the most common phenomena of individual experience is one person worrying about the fate of another close to him or her. But it should be borne in mind that we are dealing here not with the fact itself but with its mechanisms. I am postulating that observed phenomena can be explained as a result of the spreading of effects in the cognitive system from the place where they originated to other representations including the self-structure.

It is possible to point to various data that apparently support this line of reasoning. The main evidence comes from studies showing that emotional reactions to the fate of someone else and protective tendencies concerning him or her (helping) can be affected by operations that modify his or her psychological distance from the subject, not changing other possible factors that allegedly could account for observed results, such as expected reciprocity, external reward, and so on.

With respect to emotional reactions, one can mention the results of Stotland's experiment, which demonstrated that the greater the similarity (semantic proximity) of a person who is getting a painful treatment to the female observer, the greater the emotional reaction of the observer (as measured by vasoconstriction) (Stotland, 1969).[8] The same has been observed by Krebs (1975), who found that subjects who observed a performer ostensibly experiencing pain reacted more strongly if they believed that the performer was similar to them. Emotional reaction to a similar person was also observed in the case of a positive treatment of the performer.

In this context one can interpret the well-known observations concerning traumatic reactions of wartime pilots who witnessed a midair destruction of their colleagues' plane (Grinker & Spiegel, 1945). It should be noted that it was not the destruction itself that produced those reactions, since no such effect was observed in the case of the destruction of an enemy's plane; it seems, instead, that psychological proximity of the event was the main factor.

It has also been demonstrated that the strength of tendencies to protective behavior concerning an object is a function of psychological proximity of that object. Various forms of proximity can have an impact. The most important one seems to be the semantic proximity, that is, similarity.[9] We can expect, therefore, that a similar person would obtain more help than dissimilar ones; this, in fact, can be shown.

Karylowski (1975), who measured an amount of work on behalf of an unknown partner, found that subjects increased their output when they learned that their partner had interests similar to theirs.

Smoleńska (1979), using a similar procedure, obtained evidence that subjects offered more help to a person if they believed that the person

[8]Stotland found that this relationship held only for some of his experimental groups.

[9]It should be borne in mind that although the semantic distance can be described as similarity, the term *similarity* is very often applied to rather trivial phenomena (e.g., having the same hair color). People sometimes say that "in spite of our dissimilarity we are very close to each other," pointing to an opposition between similarity and psychological proximity. From our point of view there are different levels of semantic distance (i.e., similarity): namely, surface and deep levels. Thus we shall say that those people are dissimilar on the surface level but similar on a deep level, that is, on dimensions that are important for self-identity.

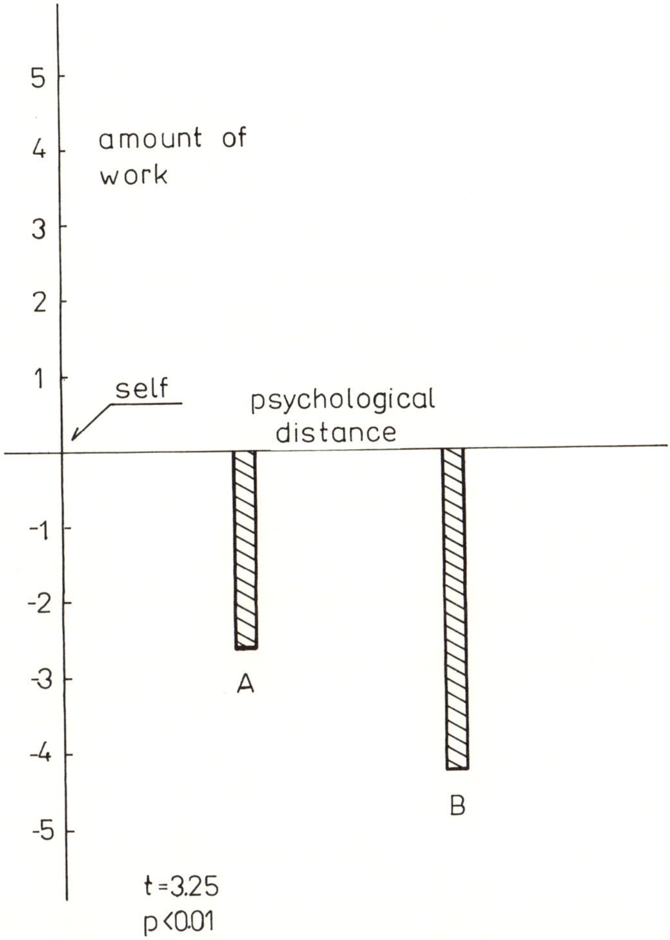


Figure 2. Amount of helping and psychological distance of a partner. Partner A was described by experimenter as a person attending the same type of school as the subject; Partner B was described as attending a different type of school. The figure illustrates the psychological distance (means) of Partners A and B as perceived by subjects; and the amount of work on behalf of both partners. Subjects worked for the partner less than for themselves (baseline indicates the amount of work for the self) but still more for a close than for a remote partner.

belonged to a similar social group. They also located such a person as closer to themselves (on a specially designed graphic scale) than another one who allegedly belonged to a different social group (see Figure 2).

The connection between similarity of a subject to the needy person and willingness to help has been observed in several studies. For example, Batson, Duncan, Ackerman, Buckley, and Birch (in press) found

*Table 2. Distance of the Victim and Helping*[a]

| | Accident occurred: | |
|---|---|---|
| | On same side of the street | On different side of the street |
| Number of witnesses | 32 | 26 |
| Number of subjects who approached the victim | 23 | 7 |
| Number of subjects who made a phone call | 16 (3/4)[b] | 2 (1/4) |

[a]Data are from Staub and Baer (1974).
[b]Proportion of those who approached the victim.

that the subject's willingness to take electric shocks to relieve someone from distress was greater if the victim was perceived as similar to the subject. (For a review of other studies see Bar-Tal, 1976; Staub, 1978.)

There are some hints that physical proximity affects helping as well. Piliavin (n.d.) asked a group of students for financial help for unmarried women living in an unknown town and observed that the proportion of positive responses depended upon the location of the town. Subjects who were led to believe that the town was in the same state were more willing to help than subjects who were told that the town was located in a more remote state. Staub and Baer (1974) report a puzzling fact that seems, however, to fit our model: They found that a passerby who witnessed a street accident and was asked by the victim to call his home did it more frequently if the accident occurred on the same side of the street than if it occurred on the other side (see Table 2). It should be stressed that we are dealing here only with those subjects who reacted to the accident by approaching the victim. One suspects that the "other side of the street" victim was originally located at a greater distance from the self than the "same side of the street" victim.

In both studies, the differences in helping offered to physically closer and more remote persons cannot be explained either by the difference in the costs of helping or by the difference in an anticipated profit.

On the basis of the argument I have presented, we come to the conclusion that emotional involvement in the fate of another person is a natural consequence of the fact that representations of the self and another social object are interconnected and the objects that are located at close psychological distance to the self can be a source of strong impact upon the self. The emotional involvement seems to result from the fact that events that affect a given representation produce an effect that spreads in a cognitive system and evokes an involvement of other structures including the self. The involvement is a decreasing function of the psychological distance; we can thus speak of the *gradient of involvement*.

## 6. WHOM SHALL WE HELP?

The model that has been presented implies that prosocial behavior on behalf of a specific person (or other social object) is a function of the psychological distance of the representation of that person from the self-structure. It is a result of the facts that (1) normative and affective judgments that the subject generates with respect to him or herself are carried onto another social object located at not too great a psychological distance from the self, and (2) events that affect the social objects produce an involvement of the self.

Such reasoning leads to some important questions: What factors determine the psychological distances of social objects? How can we measure these distances? What is the relationship between the psychological distance and the degree of personal involvement?

The limited scope of this chapter will permit only some general formulations on these issues.

As for factors that determine psychological distance of social objects, it seems that the distance depends on objective relations existing in the physical and social world but that its specific characteristics are mediated by culture and personal experience. For example, the psychological distances between some geographical locations are determined by a mapping of these locations as developed by a given culture and by personal experience with these locations (Milgram, 1977). The role of the latter factor is illustrated in an Italian study of the representation of a working environment, which has shown that the personal map of a factory is dependent upon the job range and the number of years spent there (Dobrowolny, Misiti, & Secchiaroli, 1980). Other examples of culturally determined subjective "maps" are the networks of social roles, of social positions, kinships, political organizations, and so on. We must, however, be aware that there is always some discrepancy between the content of culture and the content of an individual mind. One of the factors that contributes to this difference can be found in the intrinsic characteristics of the cognitive system and individual differences with respect to the course of its development (Witkin, 1964). In general, individuals differ with respect to their "internal maps" of the social world, and, accordingly, with respect to the distances between the self and social objects. Some systematic differences are determined by culture.

The problem of the measurement of psychological distance is a difficult one since there is no universal unit of such measurement. We operate on the assumption that the units are specific for a dimension, that is, for different dimensions there are different units. In many practical cases the units are implicit in the construction of an instrument that is being used in research. Still, it is possible to seek the real units. For example, if one were studying the distance within the network of family relationships, one would want to find out what the elements of the network are and how many intermediary steps (in terms of the elements of the network) separate the given social object from the self.

It should not be ruled out, however, that different kinds of distances are reducible to one common measure of "psychological proximity." The fact that multidimensional scaling methods based upon comparisons of similarities or factor analysis of semantic differential data give results that are meaningful suggests that such a supposition should be treated seriously. The whole problem, to be sure, requires much more research.

The third problem, namely, the relationship between psychological distance and the degree of involvement, needs some clarification. A physical analogy may be helpful: If we want to predict whether a specific signal will produce an effect in a receiver, we must know the distance between the transmitter and the receiver as well as the range of the signal. Since the effectiveness of the signal is usually a decreasing function of the distance, we must take into consideration the gradient of effectiveness of the signal as a function of the distance. Applying this analogy to our problem, we assume that there are two factors affecting the relationship between psychological distance and the degree of involvement: the length of the distance betweeen two representations—in psychological units—and the shape of a gradient of transmission of psychological processes.[10]

Presumably, there are different gradients for different dimensions. It should especially be noted that the steepness of the gradient seems to increase along with the importance of the dimension: For dimensions that deal with an issue of high importance, the gradient becomes, quite likely, very steep.

This conjecture is based upon the theory of assimilation and contrast in attitudes (Sherif & Hovland, 1961). According to this theory, as the importance of the dimension increases, the "range of acceptance" and "range of indifference" become more narrow. The reasoning can be applied to prosocial behavior. We can predict that in the case of important dimensions, a social object is recognized as similar[11] and evokes

[10]There is the question whether the gradient of judgment's application and gradient of involvement are identical (or very similar). This question cannot be answered as yet.

[11]Recognition of similarity is connected to the fact that the descriptive judgments are applied to the object.

involvement only if its distance is rather small. In other words, the range of judgment application and range of involvement are rather short.

Such a conjecture is supported by empirical data. Hornstein (1978) has shown that although willingness to help is dependent on the degree of attitude similarity between the subject and the person to whom help was offered, the gradient of willingness is steeper in the case of more important attitudes.

If one accepts the hypothesis that the application of judgment operates within a certain range, one is led to conclude that there are social objects that are located beyond such a range and are perceived as dissimilar. This means that descriptive judgments related to the self are not applied to them, norms that stand for the self and similar others are no longer operating, affect is not transferred from the self to them. The same can be said about the limits of the gradient of involvement: Objects that are located beyond those limits will not evoke sympathy and their fate does not evoke any involvement.

Such a position of an object in the system may be a prerequisite of dehumanization. Dehumanization can take various forms, depending upon the region in which the object is located. In regions with a highly positive valence, heroes, celebrities, saints, divine persons, kings, and presidents are represented. In regions with a strong negative valence, beasts, insects, and outcasts are situated. Some objects may be located in rather neutral regions and be treated indifferently.

A strong emotional reaction can be provoked if the physical distance between the self and a dehumanized object decreases: in the case of a positive object there will be a feeling of awe, in the case of negative objects feelings of fear, disgust, hate are likely to appear. In the latter case a tendency to destroy and to exterminate may arise. Phenomena of discrimination and persecution can be interpreted in this framework.[12]

## 7. SOME COMPLICATIONS OF THE THEORY OF PSYCHOLOGICAL DISTANCE

I have argued that prosocial behavior stems from the fact that the self-structure is involved in events affecting objects located at not too great a psychological distance from the self. This apparently implies that (1) the self is the only source of motivation, and (2) the closer the given object is located to the self, the stronger the tendency to convey to it judgments attributed to the self and the stronger the tendency to act on

[12]A dramatic example of the "gradient of dehumanization" comes from recent history: the ordering of persecutions by the Nazis that consisted of Jews, Slavic people, West Europeans, German antifascists, and German criminals.

behalf of the object. Both formulations require, however, some reservations.

With respect to the first one, it should be noted that our analysis of consequences of different locations of representations of objects with respect to the self is a special instance of a more general principle. Namely, we are assuming that the self is a value object but *not the only value object*. In most cases there are, in a cognitive system, some other structures that possess characteristics of value, and are a source of motivation (Reykowski, 1982a). There are cases where such a value (a concrete person as an ideal, or some abstract concept—e.g., "good Christian") achieves a dominant position in a system. A person may evaluate him or herself on the basis of his or her distance from the value and may treat him or herself better or worse depending upon this distance (believing that he or she deserves or does not deserve some benefits). It seems feasible to assume that for most people living in contemporary cultures there is more than one source of value.

Such an assumption has important bearing upon a theory of prosocial behavior. It implies that the well-being of another person can evoke serious concern if this person is represented as located close to the value object. Thus we expect that for people for whom the concept "president of my country" describes a value object, persons who are located close to the president will be treated as deserving special care and protection (see Reykowski, 1982a,b). Still, it should be emphasized that even those people who feel that the self is the most important object (being self-professed egoists) are not completely lacking in interest in the fate of others, provided that "others" are perceived as similar to the self. Also, as long as the self is the main source of prosocial motivation, everything that affects the self, that is, whatever produces changes in "hedonic balance," should have an impact on prosocial behavior. This phenomenon has been identified and described by Staub (1978).

The second issue concerning the linear relationship between the distance of an object and gradients of judgment application and involvement is a more complicated one. Our reasoning was based upon an assumption of continuity in the cognitive system, but this assumption is not always met; representations of objects form a kind of "gestalt" and tend to preserve their identity as separate organizations. One of the possible effects of such tendencies would be a motivation to preserve some degree of differentiation from others. By the same token, a situation of too great a similarity would be avoided.

Codol (1977) describes the so-called PIP effect (*Primus inter Pares*), that is, a pervasive tendency to perceive oneself as somewhat different in a positive direction from one's own group (i.e., slightly better on those dimensions that are important for self-identity). Jarymowicz and

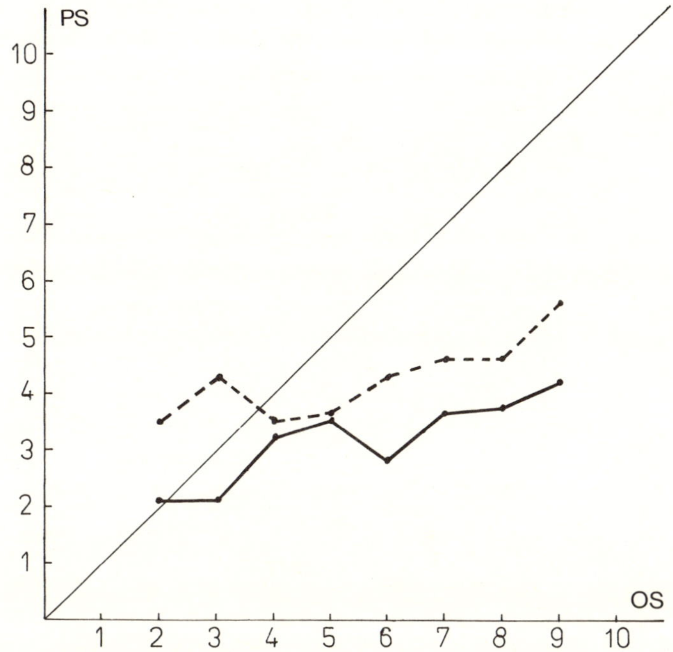


Figure 3. Objective similarity (OS) and perceived similarity (PS). Subjects received information about the target person; degree of similarity between the target person and the self-description of the subject was varying. Subjects tend to overestimate their similarity to a target person on dimensions where objective similarity was low (Points 1 and 2) and to underestimate the similarity on dimensions where similarity was high (Points 6 to 9). The former phenomenon is observed only for traits important for self-description (dashed line).

Codol (1979) found that their subjects consistently underestimated their similarity to other persons if the similarity was very great (but also misperceived similarity as greater when it was very low) (see Figure 3). Jarymowicz (in press) also found that the attractiveness of people very similar to the self is somewhat lower than that of people whose similarity is lesser. Other results show that the gradient of application and involvement is not a monotonic function of distance. In a study in our laboratory by Nowak and Wisniewski, the interpersonal space of individual subjects was plotted (by means of factor analysis) and attitudes toward social objects located at different distances from the self were measured. As can be seen in Figure 4, there is a "bending effect" at the initial part of the curves. Apparently, at a very close distance to the self there are some "forces" that counteract the tendency to treat a social object the same as the self. The nature of those forces as well as factors that determine their strength have yet to be studied.

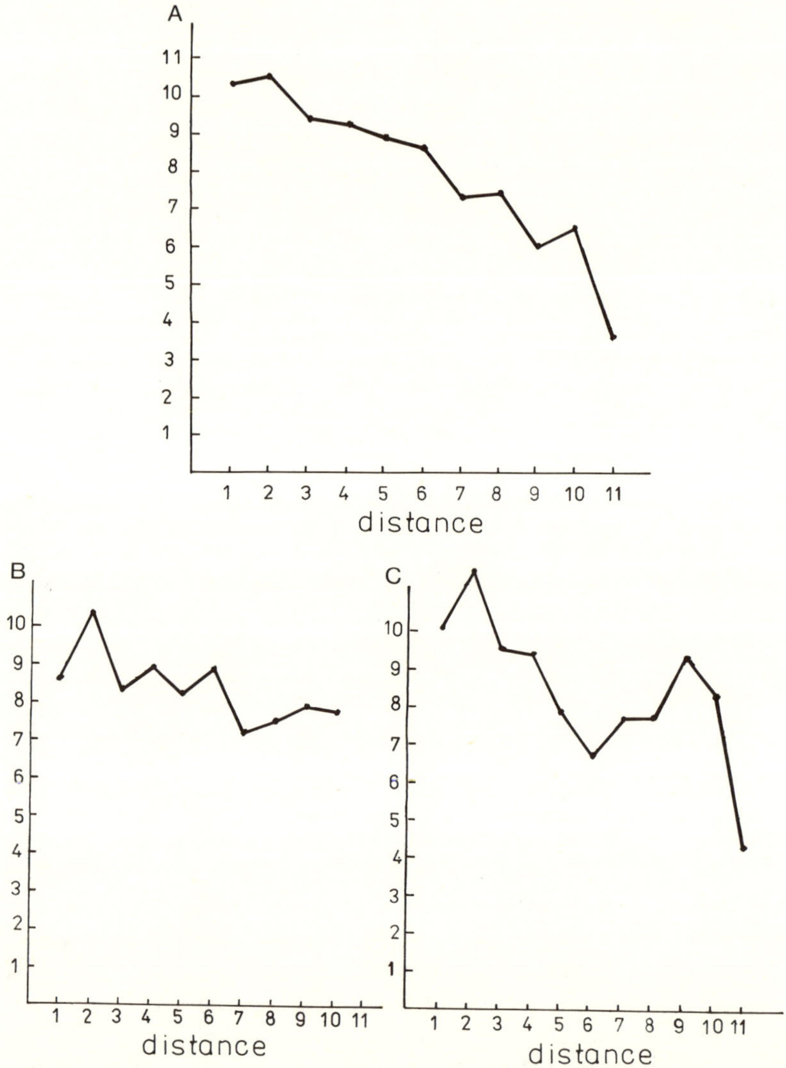


Figure 4. Psychological distance and attitudes: (A) tendency to help; (B) emotional involvement; (C) liking. Intensity of attitude is a decreasing function of the psychological distance from the self. The relationship does not hold, however, for very close objects. (The data concern positive attitudes only.)

## 8. CONCLUDING REMARKS

It appears, in conclusion, that the widespread individualistic assumption that the self is a sharply differentiated and isolated organization, a kind of monad, is not generally true, although, to be sure, there are some cases that seem to fit such a model. More often than not, however, self-structure is interwoven with other representations—primarily with representations of social objects, and that is why the well-being of others becomes more or less a personal issue for most people. Of course, concern for other people depends upon the location of the cognitive structures representing those people in the cognitive system of an individual.[13]

If the self-structure develops as an isolated organization while other social objects are located at remote distances from the self, a helping motivation based upon involvement of the self is unlikely. It should be considered, however, that the same object is located on many dimensions and its distance with respect to the self may vary depending upon the dimension that is applied at a given moment. Factors that have an impact upon the salience of a dimension may influence prosocial behavior.

The salience of a dimension is modified by situational factors, such as figure–ground relationships. This is why the same person can be perceived as close to a subject in one context and remote in another. Nationality can be a good example: In a foreign country, nationality is a salient dimension and people of the same nationality are perceived very often as close to the subject; but the same people may seem quite remote when nationality becomes an irrelevant dimension.

The gist of my argument is the idea that intrinsic prosocial motivation develops as a natural consequence of the formation of personality—more specifically, as a result of the organization of deep structures within the cognitive system. In this framework the development of prosocial behavior can be described as a function of those factors that determine the content of the self-structure and the content of schemata representing other social beings as well as their location in the system. Such factors should be sought:

1. In the content of culture, which supplies basic categories and dimensions for the organization of the individual's experience
2. In the individual history, which determines the amount of "common content" in the structures (schemata) representing self and others as well as influences an affective meaning of such content
3. In the characteristics of the cognitive system as a self-organizing whole; characteristics of this kind having been described by theories of cognitive development (e.g., Piaget, 1965, 1967)

[13]I must acknowledge that this idea was suggested to me for the first time by Professor Donald Hebb during a discussion with him in 1968. Some of his ideas were presented in his manuscript that I had an opportunity to read then; I have recently learned that a book based upon this manuscript was published in 1980.

It should be stressed, however, that the argument concerning the role of spatial organization of the cognitive system in the regulation of prosocial behavior does not preclude the existence of other sources of intrinsic prosocial motivation: Autonomous values (Reykowski, 1982a,b) and empathic sensitivity mediate a pro-social behavior having mechanisms different from the one described above (see, e.g., the analysis of impulsive helping by Piliavin, Dovidio, Gaertner, & Clark, 1981).

We cannot, of course, presume to encompass the mechanisms of prosocial behavior on the basis of a few simple principles.

## 9. REFERENCES

Alexander, R. D. The search for a general theory of behavior. *Behavioral Science,* 1975, *20,* 77–99.

Bar-Tal, D. *Prosocial behavior: Theory and research.* Washington, D.C.: Hemisphere, 1976.

Bar-Tal, D., Bar-Zohar, Y., Greenberg, M. S., & Hermon, M. Reciprocity behavior in the relationship between donor and recipient and between harm-doer and victim. *Sociometry,* 1977, *40,* 293–299.

Batson, C. D., Duncan, B. D., Ackerman, P., Buckley, T., & Birch, K. Is empathic emotion a source of altruistic motivation? *Journal of Personality and Social Psychology,* in press.

Bratfish, O. Further study of the relation between subjective distance and emotional involvement. *Reports from Psychological Laboratories* (University of Stockholm), 1966, No. 208.

Byrne, D. *The attraction paradigm.* New York: Academic Press, 1971.

Codol, J. P. Porównanie ja-inni a normy spoleczne: Zjawisko P.I.P. *Studia Psychologiczne,* 1977, *16*(2), 5–25.

Dobrowolny, M. B., Misiti, R., & Secchiaroli, G. Spatial cognitive representation of the working environment and working experience in the factory. *Italian Journal of Psychology,* 1980, *7*(1), 1–13.

Ekman, G., & Bratfish, O. Subjective geographic distance and emotional involvement. *Reports from Psychological Laboratories* (University of Stockholm), 1965, No. 189.

Epstein, S. Measurement of drive and conflict in humans. In M. Jones (Ed.), *Nebraska Symposium on Motivation* (Vol. 10). Lincoln: University of Nebraska Press, 1962.

Grinker, R. R., & Spiegel, J. *Men under stress.* Philadelphia: Blakiston, 1945.

Hebb, D. O. *The organization of behavior.* New York: Wiley, 1949.

Hornstein, H. Promotive tension and prosocial behavior: A Levinian analysis. In L. Wispé (Ed.), *Altruism, sympathy and helping.* New York: Academic Press, 1978.

Hunt, J. M. Motivation inherent in information processing and action. In O. J. Harvey (Ed.), *Motivation and social interaction: Cognitive determinants.* New York: Ronald Press, 1963.

Iwanov-Smolenski, A. G. O badaniu wspóldzialania I i II ukladu syngnalów. In A. G. Iwanow-Smolenski (Ed.), *Zagadnienia wyzszych czynności nerwowych.* Warsaw: PZWL, 1954.

Jarymowicz, M. Atrakcyjnosc i awersyjnosc podobienstwa "ja"-"inni." *Przeglad Psychologiczny,* 1982, *1,* 61–73.

Jarymowicz, M., & Codol, J. P. Perception of similarity between self and other: A search for uniqueness of the self. *Studia Psychologiczne,* 1979, *18*(2), 41–57.

Karylowski, J. *Z badań nad mechanizmani pozytywnych ustosunkowań interpersonalnych.* Wroclaw: Ossolineaum, 1975.

Karylowski, J. Self-esteem, similarity, liking and helping. *Personality and Social Psychology Bulletin*, 1976, *2*, 71–74.

Korzeniowski, K. Samoakceptacja i izolacja struktury "ja" a sympatia w stosunka do innych i decentracja interpersonalna. *Studia Psychologiczne*, 1980, *19*(1), 33–47.

Krasnogorski, I. N. *Studies of higher nervous activities* (Vol. 1). Moskwa: Medgiz, 1954.

Krebs, D. Empathy and altruism. *Journal of Personality and Social Psychology*, 1975, *32*, 1134–1146.

Kurcz, I. Generalizacja semantyczna ruchów dowolnych. *Studia Psychologiczne*, 1963, *5*, 35–74.

Leonard, R. L. Self-concept and attraction for similar and dissimilar other. *Journal of Personality and Social Psychology*, 1974, *31*, 926–929.

Lewicka, M. Wplyw nastawienia poznawczego na kszaltowanie i modyfikacje sadów o drugiej osobie. *Studia Psychologiczne*, 1979, *18*(1), 21–36.

Lewicki, P. *Przedmiotowy i podmiotowy mechanizm percepcji spolecznej*. Unpublished doctoral dissertation, University of Warsaw, 1977.

Lundberg, U., & Ellonen, E. Involvement in potential future events estimated by males and females. *Scandanavian Journal of Psychology*, 1977, *18*.

Markus, H. Self-schemata and processing information about the self. *Journal of Personality and Social Psychology*, 1977, *35*, 63–78.

Markus, H. The self in thought and memory. In D. M. Wegner & R. R. Vallacher (Eds.), *The self in social psychology*. Oxford: Oxford University Press, 1980.

Mervis, C. B., & Rosch, E. Categorization of natural objects. *Annual Review of Psychology*, 1981, *32*, 89–115.

Milgram, S. *The individual in a social world*. Reading, Mass.: Addison-Wesley, 1977.

Nowak, A., & Wisniewski, A. *Psychological distance between concepts and generalization of judgments*. Unpublished report, n.d.

Piaget, J. *The moral judgment of a child*. New York: Free Press, 1965.

Piaget, J. *Six psychological studies*. New York: Vintage Books, 1967.

Piliavin, J. A., & Piliavin, J. M. *The good Samaritan: Why does he help?* Unpublished manuscript, n.d.

Piliavin, J. A., Dovidio, J. F., Gaertner, S. L., & Clark, R. D. *Emergency intervention*. New York: Academic Press, 1981.

Razran, G. Sentential and propositional generalization of salivary conditioning to verbal stimuli. *Science*, 1949, *109*, 447.

Reykowski, J. *Teoria osobowosci: Tezy*. Unpublished manuscript, University of Warsaw, 1974.

Reykowski, J. *Motywacja, postawy prospoleczne a osobowość*. Warsaw: PWN, 1979.

Reykowski, J. Motivation of prosocial behavior. In V. D. Derlega & J. Grzelak (Eds.), *Living with other people*. New York: Academic Press, 1982. (a)

Reykowski, J. Social motivation. *Annual Review of Psychology*, 1982, *33*, 123–155. (b)

Reykowski, J., & Kochanska, G. *Szkice z teorii osobowosci*. Warsaw: Wiedza Powszechna, 1980.

Rips, L., Shoben, E., & Smith, E. Semantic distance and verification of semantic relations. *Journal of Verbal Learning*, 1973, *12*.

Schneider, D. J. *Social psychology*. Reading, Mass.: Addison-Wesley, 1976.

Sherif, M., & Hovland, C. I. *Social judgment: Assimilation and contrast effects in communication and attitude change*. New Haven: Yale University Press, 1961.

Slater, P. (Ed.). *Exploration of interpersonal space*. New York: Wiley, 1976.

Smoleńska, M. Z. *Dystans psychologiczny partnera a dzialanie na jego rzecz*. Unpublished doctoral dissertation, University of Warsaw, 1979.

Staub, E. *Positive social behavior and morality*. Vol. 1. *Social and personal influences*. New York: Academic Press, 1978.

Staub, E., & Baer, R. J. Stimulus characteristics of sufferer and difficulty of escape as determinants of helping. *Journal of Personality and Social Psychology*, 1974, *30*, 279–284.

Sternberg, R. J., Tourangeau, R., & Nigro, G. *Metaphor, induction and social policy: The convergence of macroscopic and microscopic views*. Unpublished manuscript, Yale University, 1978.

Stotland, E. Exploratory investigation of empathy. In L. Berkowitz (Ed.), *Advances in experimental social psychology* (Vol. 4). New York: Academic Press, 1969.

Trzebiński, J. Natural concepts and creativity. *Polish Psychological Bulletin*, 1980, *11*, 45–51.

von Wright, J., & Kinnunen, R. Scaling of involvement in personal and global future events. *Scandinavian Journal of Psychology*, 1977, *18*.

Witkin, A. A. Origins of cognitive style. In C. Sheerer (Ed.), *Cognition: Theory, research, promise*. New York: Harper, 1964.

Zajonc, R. B. Feeling and thinking: Preferences need no inferences. *American Psychologist*, 1980, *35*, 151–175.

# II
# DEVELOPMENTAL ASPECTS

# Introduction

Ervin Staub

It may seem presumptuous to announce that an outstanding group of papers is gathered here. But they are outstanding in quality, in content, and in what they together accomplish. The purpose of the following comments is not simply to preview the chapters in this section of the book, but rather to connect them to important issues in the study of the development of prosocial behavior; to give a bird's-eye view of the field and locate these chapters in it; and to identify both accomplishments and the need for new directions.

One important task is to gather thorough empirical knowledge about the development of prosocial behavior. What influences on the child, what experiences of children, contribute to it? A related task, inseparable from the first, is to develop theoretical conceptions that account for how the child becomes—or does not become—an individual with a tendency to respond to others' needs, to help others, or to engage in cooperative interactions. A number of chapters in this section make important empirical contributions. Radke-Yarrow and Zahn-Waxler identify very early modes of responding by children to others' distress, including individual differences—for example, more affective, or more controlled and cognitive, or more avoidant modes of responding—and changes in responding in the first few years of life. They also identify important socializing antecedents of prosocial responding. Reassuringly, their findings support earlier research that showed that affection or nurturance, induction, and effective control by parents are important contributors to prosocial behavior (Eisenberg, 1982; Staub, 1979; Yarrow, Zahn-Waxler, & Chapman, in press). They also show that effective induction is "hot" rather than cold, the verbal communication by parents affectively charged.

Parents are not the only socializers of children. Peers are both important socializers (Hartup, 1978; Staub, 1979), and elicitors of prosocial behavior. Eisenberg-Berg, Cameron, and Tryon explore some aspects of prosocial behaviors in peer interaction. They make an important distinction between positive behaviors that are spontaneous, self-initiated, and those that are responses to others' requests or demands. Such behaviors have different meanings, are likely to result from different motives, and have different correlates or consequences for the child's relationship to others. Both positive and negative behaviors tend to be reciprocal among peers (Staub & Feinberg, 1981). Children who initiate prosocial acts provide themselves with different further socializing experiences, and thereby affect the course of their own further development differently, than children who do not initiate such acts (or initiate negative acts). How existing personality and social behavior of children shape further socializing experiences and affect the course of the child's development is important to ascertain.

The above chapters provide empirical findings about the two primary domains of the socialization of prosocial behavior, parental and peer, with important theoretical implications. The subsequent chapters increasingly focus on theory, drawing on research they also describe and/or on existing research findings. Martin Hoffman adds to his well-known and highly influential theorizing on the development of empathy. Empathy is regarded by him, and is generally seen, as one of the primary motivators of prosocial responding. In this chapter the role of guilt as a motivator of prosocial behavior is examined. Guilt arises out of internalized values and standards. The childrearing contexts in which internalization is likely to take place, and the processes of internalization, are both explored by Hoffman. For example, self-attribution, apparently one of the important sources of the development of prosocial behavior (Grusec, 1981; Staub, 1979), is examined as a process of internalization.

One question for future research and theorizing is the relationship of empathic motivation and internalized values and norms as sources of motivation. The two may be related under certain circumstances: When socialization practices focus on the child's concern about others' welfare, so that values that the child acquires embody such concern, they can give rise to feelings of empathy. Thus an affective base, which is elaborated through a developing cognitive sense of others—Hoffman's view of the development of empathy—can join with a learned appreciation of other human beings and concern about their welfare into a value orientation that partly represents an outcome of internalization and is also a source of empathy. Varied value orientations or standards may be acquired, however, which motivate prosocial acts in different ways. In his chapter, Karylowski suggests the possibility of concern about other people and their welfare as one type of prosocial motivation, with the desire to live up to internalized standards a different kind, the two having different consequences.

A further issue is how the developing motivation gains expression in action. A joint theory of development and determinants will have to evolve for a complete account. Motivation is expressed partly as a function of other individual characteristics, such as self-esteem and role-taking capacity (Staub, 1978). We need to identify these characteristics and concern ourselves with their development if we are to understand the origins of a prosocial behavioral orientation.

The next two chapters move toward a general theory of prosocial development and conduct, arising out of the work of an important group of investigators in Poland. As noted, Karylowski differentiates between two types of motivation for prosocial behavior. In one (exocentric), the actor's focus is on the welfare of the recipient; in the other (endocentric), on the self, in the sense that the actor is motivated to live up to internalized standards. This is a potentially highly important distinction, since different types of motivations can give rise to prosocial conduct of different types and/or under different circumstances. Karylowski presents research that explores and demonstrates differences in such motives and their antecedents in socialization. Kochanska's chapter goes a step further in a direction that, as already noted, I consider a primary goal. She presents a theory that denotes how personal characteristics enter as determinants of prosocial action. She then discusses the development of these characteristics, or systems—such as the self-system, the operational system, and others. A theory of prosocial conduct that helps identify important individual characteristics can serve as the best guide to what aspects of development ought to be the focus of research and theorizing.

In the next chapter Oppenheimer and Heller apply action theory—a theory of social behavior widely used and highly regarded in Europe (similar in some respects to my own theory, described in Chapter 2 in that both focus on the purposive, goallike nature of behavior)—to the realm of prosocial behavior. They then describe research about one aspect of the theory, the development of role taking in children, important for the recognition of and concern with others' needs.

The last chapter of this part approaches the development of positive connectedness to other human beings and altruism from another important perspective. Partly guided by object relations theory, Sharabany focuses on the role of important human relationships in the life of individuals. In addition to the quality of relationship to parents and peers in general, the importance of friendship and of cross-sex relations is discussed. In essence, all significant human relationships in the life of children, adolescents, and adults are seen as important developmental influences. Their existence, nature, and quality determine the inclination for altruism.

The chapters in this part address many important issues. One significant issue they do not attend to, however, is how the larger social system—the nature of a culture, the social organization, the institutions, including schools—exerts influence. The culture and social organization can make the presence of some of the "direct" (parental and peer) influences that contribute to the development of prosocial behavior more or less likely, and can exert a biasing effect by modifying the impact of direct influences that are present. (One aspect of the potential influence of the school—the effect of cooperative learning on children—is discussed in Hertz-Lazarowitz and Sharan's chapter in Part V.) The exploration of the influence of the larger social system both in the development of prosocial behavioral tendencies and in directly influencing prosocial acts is a major task for the future.

## REFERENCES


Eisenberg, N. (Ed.). *The development of prosocial behavior.* New York: Academic Press, 1982.

Grusec, J. E. Socialization processes and the development of altruism. In J. P. Rushton & R. M. Sorrentino (Eds.), *Altruism and helping behavior.* Hillsdale, N.J.: Lawrence Erlbaum, 1981.

Hartup, W. H. Children and their friends. In McGurk, H. (Ed.), *Issues in childhood social development.* London: Methuen, 1978.

Staub, E. *Positive social behavior and morality.* Vol. 1. *Personal and social influences.* New York: Academic Press, 1978.

Staub, E. *Positive social behavior and morality.* Vol. 2. *Socialization and development.* New York: Academic Press, 1979.

Staub, E., & Feinberg, H. *Regularities in peer interaction, empathy, and sensitivity to others.* Paper presented at the meeting of the American Psychological Association, Montreal, August 1980. (Revised version, 1981).

Yarrow, M. R., Zahn-Waxler, C., & Chapman, M. Prosocial dispositions and behavior. In D. Mussen (Ed.), *Manual of child psychology* (Volume on personality and social development). New York: Wiley, in press.

# 4

# Roots, Motives, and Patterns in Children's Prosocial Behavior

Marian Radke-Yarrow and Carolyn Zahn-Waxler

## 1. INTRODUCTION

Prosocial behavior is a matter of ancient as well as modern interest. The long history of philosophy and social thought about the "goodness" of human nature makes us aware that current empirical research and the theories upon which it is based are not fashioned *de novo* but have their origins in these predecessors. Human nature has been variously regarded. It has been viewed as innately endowed with feelings of compassion in Confucian philosophy (Chan, 1963), as naturally virtuous and with a communal sense of self (Rousseau, 1755/1952), as waging a war of all against all and as based on rational self-interest (Hobbes, 1651/1952). Accordingly, children have been variously regarded and reared, and, perhaps, as a result, they have been variously prosocial.

The basic issues of human nature have not been settled. The contributions of empirical studies of prosocial behavior to an understanding of these issues can only be relative to the time and culture in which the studies are done, for the implicit or explicit philosophies of the investigators enter into the questions, methods, and findings of the research. Moreover, the human subjects in the research are also, to some degree, products of prevailing social thought concerning motives of self-interest and altruism.

When psychologists inquire into the issue of "nurture"—how chil-

---

MARIAN RADKE-YARROW and CAROLYN ZAHN-WAXLER • Laboratory of Developmental Psychology, National Institute of Mental Health, Bethesda, Maryland 20205.

dren's prosocial behaviors can be facilitated or inhibited by experience—what philosophical grounding underlies the research? When investigators devise conditions to promote helpful, generous, or compassionate behavior by children, are they assuming that these behaviors are "natural" to the child, intrinsically rewarding, aversive, or neutral? What overarching philosophies and conditions of time and culture influence the answers and determine research findings.

The research we are reporting is neither culture free nor value free. It was carried out in a period of American society that social critics (Lasch, 1978; Slater, 1970) have characterized as excessively and aggressively preoccupied with self. There is reason to believe that there are also sounds of societal alarm regarding the extreme to which this situation has gone. Certainly altruism has gained increased consideration in the science and the popular media.

The organizing questions of our research concern the development of prosocial behaviors in young children. We are interested in children's empathic responses and attempts to care for others who are in distress or need. How do children (developmentally considered) respond when confronted with the distress of others? What are the underlying processes? We have focused on "distress" with a clear tone of affect as an essential component of the phenomena we are studying. Expressions of need (e.g., sadness, pain, anger, fear, despair) by persons in the child's environment are stimuli that are present in every child's life, beginning in infancy. Such affective events result in reactions at many levels: physiological, perceptual and cognitive, affective, and interactive. Prosocial responding is one class of reactions to such events, with any or all of these components involved in responding. Our research strategy has been (1) to give *development* major consideration, that is, to look for prosocial behavior as it emerges in children's earliest behavioral repertoires; (2) to investigate how prosocial feelings and interactions are patterned and organized into the broader domain of children's concepts of self and "other" and into their social interactions; and (3) to examine experiential (i.e., rearing) influences on the form and course of prosocial responding.

Until recently, research into children's prosocial behaviors has to a remarkable degree been without major reference to the affective properties of either the stimulus conditions eliciting prosocial behavior or the prosocial response to these conditions. Research with children has been situational more than developmental in orientation. It has not been interactional in ways that permit examination of reciprocal influences between the person in distress and the person responding prosocially. Generally, small fragments of a child's behavior are the basis of assessments of his or her altruism. Little attention has been given to conceptualizing the kinds of responses made by the child. Other kinds of research evidence are needed, particularly information that tells us considerably more about prosocial behavior in the total behavior repertoire of the individual child. To arrive at such information one needs to invest in data of substantial volume and depth about each child and about the range and quality of his or her prosocial behavior.

In bringing empirical data to the questions we have stated, we are drawing upon research carried out in our laboratory over the past dozen years. We are reporting on studies that are closely interlocking in their questions. These studies involve more than 300 children from 10 months to 8 years old. They are urban American children; most are from intact families, residents of the Washington area. About 90% are Caucasian, 10% black. Parents are mostly high school or college graduates. The families are predominantly in comfortable socioeconomic circumstances; parents' jobs range from clerical to professional. There is a small sample of low income families; parents' jobs are mainly unskilled. An overview of the children who have been our subjects and the methods by which they have been studied will give some notion of the research sources on which we are drawing for our findings on prosocial development.

## 2. SUBJECTS

The following is a description of the children who were the participants in these studies.

*Sample 1* is 24 children who were studied in three age cohorts, beginning at 10, 15, and 20 months and followed for 9 months. These children were also studied for a 3-month period when they were from 6 to 7 years old (Cummings, Zahn-Waxler, & Radke-Yarrow, 1981; Radke-Yarrow & King, 1977, 1979; Radke-Yarrow, Zahn-Waxler, & Chapman, 1983; Yarrow & Waxler, 1976; Zahn-Waxler & Radke-Yarrow, 1981).

*Sample 2* is a replication sample of 10 children, beginning at 10 months and studied for a year.

*Sample 3* is 7 1-year-old boys from families in which one parent is manic-depressive and is undergoing treatment, and a matched control group of 14 boys from normal families. These children were studied for 1 year (Zahn-Waxler, 1981).

*Sample 4* is 128 children from 3½ to 5½ years old who were observed in nursery school over a 6-week period (Yarrow, Scott, & Waxler, 1973).

*Sample 5* is 108 children who were observed and tested over a nursery school summer session (Yarrow & Waxler, 1976a; Zahn-Waxler & Radke-Yarrow, 1977).

*Sample 6* is 79 children, 5 to 8 years old, who were observed and tested during a 4-week summer day camp session (Barrett & Yarrow, 1977).

Approximately equal numbers of boys and girls were in all samples except Sample 3.

## 3. PROCEDURES

The main methodological features for all of the studies will be presented so that we can report findings across studies integratively. Studies 1, 2, and 3 are longitudinal in design and share a common method. The primary data on children's behavior come from mothers' systematic observations. This method was devised to overcome what, in our opinion, are serious weaknesses in most methods used in studying children's prosocial responding; namely, innocuous or trivial stimuli represent distress, and "just noticeable" prosocial responses by children provide the very limited raw material on altruism. Sampling of behavior tends to be brief and in staged circumstances. We have developed a method by which it is possible to study compelling distress situations and children's responses to them, a technique that lends itself to both naturalistic and experimental approaches.

Mothers were trained as "research assistants," to make systematic observations and to record them. Their observations were directed to events of affective distress (pain, sadness, fear, physical distress, anger, and fatigue) occurring in the immediate environment of the child. Mothers were instructed to try to report every relevant emotional incident and to record it as soon as possible. They had available portable tape recorders and they dictated their observations in narrative style, progressing through the episode sequentially: the distress stimulus and circumstances, the child's reactions and interactions, and the mother's own behavior to the distressed person and/or to the child. Mothers' training involved individual instruction as well as demonstrations and discussions in small groups. Mothers were also monitored throughout the months of data gathering. A staff member visited the home every third week. One function of these visits was to keep the mothers optimally tuned to the observing–reporting task.

In addition to the mothers' reports of naturally occurring events, standard stimulated emotional incidents were introduced in two ways. Mothers were instructed to simulate pain (e.g., hurting ankle), acute physical discomfort (choking cough), fatigue, anger (on the telephone), and crying. The simulated incidents were scheduled in a predetermined order, one occurring each week. On the home visits, the investigator also simulated an emotional incident (pain, discomfort, anger). Both investigator and mother reported on these investigator incidents, thus supplying one estimate of mother's reporting reliability (average agreement, 80%). Furthermore, on each home visit (28 hours of observing) the investigator rated the mother on empathic caring for the child.

In a follow-up Sample 1, mothers' reporting was resumed for 3 months when the children were 6 to 7 years old. Laboratory tests of prosocial behavior and tests of social cognition and reasoning were administered at this time.

Because observations of child behavior via mothers' records constitute a major data source and because this is not a familiar procedure, we shall identify the properties of these data. The following is one sample protocol from a mother's record on her 20-month-old son.

> A visiting baby cries. "Danny went into the kitchen, picked up the baby's bottle, went into his room where the little girl was crying, and put the bottle into her mouth. He didn't even take a sample himself. I always keep thinking that when he sees someone else's bottle he's going to want to try it. He has been off the bottle himself for about two weeks. He held the bottle in her mouth. When she moved her head, it would slip out and he'd try readjusting it and holding it back in there again correctly. It then slipped out and fell on the floor and she started to cry again. Danny looked at me and back down at her, picked up the bottle and put it in her mouth again. I said, 'I'll fix it, Danny, that's okay' and he watched while I stopped her crying by just patting her on the back. Then Danny went into the living room."

These naturalistic reports brought the researcher into close range of intimate, infrequent, sometimes very traumatic, as well as tender human interactions and provided literally thousands of descriptions of children's responses to distress in another person. (For a detailed description of the method, including details of parental training and assessments of reliability and validity of the mothers' observations, see Zahn-Waxler & Radke-Yarrow, 1981.) The training of the mothers, the short time lag in reporting, the reporting in specific terms, and the continued monitoring contributed to quality of the data.

The data permit the categorizing of children's immediate responses to the emotions of others. There are many kinds of reactions: pleasure, aggression, avoidance, crying, fearful or anxious expressions, positive interventions of helping, sympathizing, and no affective response. In addition to the coding of discrete responses, the data also provide possibilities of coding *process*. By "process" we are referring to mechanisms that can be inferred from the sequence of the child's behaviors in a given incident, and from the child's successive behaviors over time. Because there are many data points on the child over the 9 months of reporting, it is possible to observe change (development) in responding rather than merely to compare behavior at two time points. It has been possible to observe the child's behavior before a prosocial response occurs, at its first appearance, and as it continues or changes over time.

This method of mothers' observations and reporting also provides fine details of certain maternal socialization practices. As she describes how she handles distress incidents, especially incidents in which her child has caused harm to someone, the mother gives concrete accounts of interactions with the child.

There may be prejudices about data obtained from trained mothers, the much maligned agents of children's problems, as compared with data from graduate students, "unbiased" by extensive experience with children. We have, therefore, acquired several kinds of evidence on the data themselves: (1) We have replicated the findings of our original study on a second normal sample. (2) We have carried out simulations by the investigator, with paler but similar findings. (3) We have videotaped simulated distresses in the home (Zahn-Waxler, 1980); these visual data compellingly document the detailed narrative records from the mothers. (4) We have compared children's responses to contrived emotional distress in the laboratory and to responses reported by mothers.

In Samples 2 and 3, data were also obtained on the infants and toddlers in laboratory procedures: These included tests of cognitive capabilities (self-awareness for the very young child, perspective taking, and inferential abilities) and behavioral responses to interactive (contrived) situations of distress. Studies 5 and 6 are naturalistic observational studies of prosocial behavior among peers in play settings (nursery school and day camp). In both studies there were also standard laboratory measures of prosocial behavior.

Sample 4 is an extensive experimental study of rearing conditions and prosocial learning. Four environments were developed, representing configurations of rearing that differed in the adult's nurturant relationship with the child and in how she conveyed her own prosocial principles, feelings, and behavior. Children were assigned to nursery school groups in which an adult provided either highly nurturant or relatively aloof, matter-of-fact care, for 30-minute sessions over a period of 2 weeks. *Following* these histories of rearing, the adult provided one of two kinds of programmed experiences that dealt with prosocial content. In Condition A she expressed prosocial principles and values in relation to incidents of distress presented in pictures and in miniature play materials (dioramas depicting a child, an adult, or an animal in some kind of situation in which help was needed). The adult's reactions to these symbolized distresses combined inductive reasoning and positive affective involvement. ("Look, this little bunny is caught in the bush and can't get out. Poor bunny must be scared. I am going to help it out of the bush so it can get back to its mother. There, that makes the bunny feel better.") Condition B included the preceding procedures, with the important addition of the adult's responding similarly to programmed distresses that involved interaction with real people and animals. These training conditions took place in a series of sessions over several weeks.

Both procedures provided information intended to help the child to recognize cues of distress and feelings of the victim, to demonstrate ways of helping, and to indicate the consequences for the victim. Conditions A and B differed in two important respects: (1) Principles expressed by the adult in A were only at the level of the hypothetical or abstract; in B, principles were put into practice with real consequences for the distressed persons. (2) Prosocial modeling by the adult in B involved interaction with the distressed person, which gave the adult the direct experience of the consequences of her prosocial interventions. High and low nurturant histories were used with each training type.

This is not a design intended to pinpoint the separate socialization effects of nurturance, modeling, "preaching," and "practice" of altruism. It was intended as a study of configurations of rearing conditions as they are practiced by parents and experienced by children.

## 4. FINDINGS

From the preceding series of studies we shall bring together findings on the development of prosocial behavior.

### 4.1. Early Development

The first question is a developmental one. It concerns the emergence of behavior that unambiguously involves the child in a positive approach to a distressed person, behavior that is, in some preliminary way, a form of helping behavior. We are not so much interested in pinning an emergent date on such behavior as in tracing the transformations that take place in early development.

We have examined the successive characteristics of children's responding to expressive signals of distress (pain, sadness, fear, anger, fatigue) in the natural environment. Such signals rarely come in single modalities; crying, facial expressions of worry, verbal exclamations, bodily positions, and gestures, often in combination, convey the distress. Likewise, children's responses are very often a compound or a series of behaviors. For each incident, each discrete response was coded (e.g., no reaction, stops ongoing activity, stares, tears come, face puckers, pats "victim," hits other person). Responses were also coded

*Table 1. Reactions to Affective Distress in Others: Average Ratio Scores*[a]

| Week ages | 38–61<br>A[b]<br>T1[c], % | 62–85<br>A<br>T2, % | 62–85<br>B<br>T1, % | 86–109<br>B<br>T2, % | 88–109<br>C<br>T1, % | 110–134<br>C<br>T2, % |
|---|---|---|---|---|---|---|
| No response | 10 | 11 | 7 | 7 | 11 | 10 |
| Attending only | 26 | 33 | 21 | 16 | 8 | 5 |
| Crying | 28 | 14 | 16 | 12 | 5 | 10 |
| Seeking caregiver | 20 | 10 | 26 | 25 | 11 | 18 |
| Laughing, smiling | 7 | 5 | 9 | 5 | 5 | 4 |
| Aggression | 4 | 10 | 12 | 11 | 8 | 13 |
| Imitation | 4 | 14 | 16 | 19 | 14 | 12 |
| Prosocial intervention | 11 | 11 | 16 | 30 | 39 | 32 |

[a]$N = 8$ children in Cohort A; 9 in Cohort B; 7 in Cohort C.
[b]Similarity in ages in the two cohorts provides a replication.
[c]T1 refers to the first 4½ months of reporting, and T2, to the second 4½ months.

in terms of *process* (e.g., imitates mother's behavior, refers other person's experience to own body, shows approach–avoidance actions). For the analyses reported here, all incidents of negative affect (sadness, hurt, fear, etc.) have been combined. To construct a developmental profile of the individual child, coded responses have been ordered by time. For age group analyses, coded responses were considered in blocks of time. For each time period, each kind of response was given a ratio score. Thus the total number of affective incidents to which the child was exposed in a given time period is used as the denominator and the number of incidents in which a given type of response appears is the numerator. Group age trends have been analyzed using multivariate analyses of variance (see Tables 1 and 2).

Developmental changes are documented both in the individual profiles and in the group analyses. Children's earliest reactions in the presence of another person's expression of distress are agitation and general disturbance (crying, whimpering, silent tense attending). These reactions predominate approximately from 10 to 14 months. Whimpering and crying occur not only on hearing cries of another person but in response to the spectrum of distress signs. These reactions continue in later months but gradually lose centrality.

In this early period children do not engage the "victim." They generally do not look so much for specific cues or locations of distress as to the distressed person as a whole. They may also seek out the mother through visual contact or reaching. In the samples studied, there is little deviation from this central tendency. An excerpt from a protocol at 11 months gives the prototype:

> Sari (on witnessing physical pain) looked sad, puckered up and burst out crying. She continued to cry intensely. She crawled over to her mother to be picked up.

At 14 months, another child is responding in an almost identical manner:

> Jenny observed a crying 6-month-old baby. She watched; tears welled in her eyes; she began to cry.

In succeeding months as distress crying wanes (a statistically significant decrease to 2 years), more controlled and positive actions to the victim appear (a significant increase). Again, almost uniformly among all of the children, first tentative positive physical contacts of patting or touching the victim occur. (For a detailed statistical analyses see Zahn-Waxler & Radke-Yarrow, 1981). By the middle or end of the second year, these contacts develop into more differentiated positive interventions. Jenny, described above, is observed in a similar situation at 18 months, to which she responds in new ways:

> A neighbor's baby cries. Jenny looked startled, her body stiffened. She approached and tried to give the baby cookies. She followed him around and began to whimper herself. She then tried to stroke his hair, but he pulled away. Later, she approached her mother, led her to the baby, and tried to put mother's hand on the baby's head. He calmed down a little, but Jenny still looked worried. She continued to bring him toys and to pat his head and shoulders.

*Table 2. Characteristics of Prosocial Responses at Each Age Level*

| Week ages | 38–61 ($N$ = 8) %[a] | 62–85 ($N$ = 17) % | 86–109 ($N$ = 16) % | 110–133 ($N$ = 7) % |
|---|---|---|---|---|
| Positive physical contact | | | | |
| Pats, rubs | 75 | 59 | 81 | 86 |
| Hugs, kisses | 25 | 59 | 88 | 86 |
| Instrumental acts | | | | |
| Gives an object | 25 | 70 | 81 | 71 |
| Gives physical help | 12 | 12 | 50 | 14 |
| Involves aid from a third person | 00 | 24 | 56 | 28 |
| Protects or defends victim | 12 | 35 | 31 | 43 |
| Verbal concern | | | | |
| Concerned question | 00 | 12 | 69 | 100 |
| Advice to victim | 00 | 00 | 44 | 86 |
| Sympathetic reassurance | 00 | 12 | 75 | 86 |
| Ritualistic, sympathetic reassurance | 12 | 24 | 62 | 57 |

[a]The percentage represents the number of children at a given age level who made the given response.

Other changes in reactions to distress occur during the second year. There are increases in imitation of the other's emotion, and increases in negative behaviors directed toward the victim. The negatives are of very low absolute frequencies. Laughter and smiling are never frequent. No sex differences were found in these developmental progressions or in the frequencies of specific kinds of responses.

In the latter half of the second year, children initiate contacts with the persons in distress. They embrace the victim, enlist help from a third person, "inspect" the distresses (tears, hurts, facial expressions) in ways quite uncharacteristic of their earlier approaches. The children give things to the victim. This is a particularly interesting action, since to choose something to give to someone who is hurting or sad or angry or tired is a complex response. What children choose to give is not random; the objects are, by and large, out of the child's own experiences of comfort—a toy, a cookie, a bottle, a blanket, a teddy bear. The choice of gift is at times a good one that indeed serves well to comfort the other person; at other times the offering is more appropriate to the giver than the receiver:

> Mary at 15 months watches a visiting baby who is crying: She watched him carefully. She followed him around, and kept handing him toys and also other items that were valuable to her, like her bottle or this string of beads which she's so fond of.

Although developmental progression in some respects is orderly and stagelike, it must be emphasized that different children progress through the various response patterns at different ages; that is, there are early and late maturers in responding to emotional stimuli, as there are early and late maturers in most behaviors. Moreover, reactions that are characteristic of early ages do not disappear. It is important to note that developmental progression is also very individualistic in the paths or processes by which children move from general disturbances to cognitively more sophisticated and emotionally more differentiated social interaction. To investigate this progression further we (1) examined the *processes* involved in the developmental changes, and (2) analyzed the patterned prosocial responding within the individual children. To do so, we reexamined the responses we have just described.

In these early behaviors, imitation appears to be one important vehicle of developmental change. Imitation is of many kinds, however, and functions in very different ways that are not necessarily developmentally ordered. At times imitation is fragmented or is a relatively simple "trying on" of the other's affect. This is seen when the child echoes the victim's sob or gesture without apparent affect of his or her own, but perhaps learning something in the process. On other occasions, or in other children, imitation is serious and with deliberate concentration. "Studied" imitation appears at times to be the overt expression of the child's attempts to deal with a self–other differentiation, where the child is attempting to locate the other person's emotions—is it inside or outside the self? Consider the child of 21 months who, while seriously contemplating his crying mother, wipes his own eyes though they have no tears. Or another child of 21 months who, upon observing a person bump her elbow, utter "ouch," and grimace, looks pained too, rubs his own elbow, says "ow" and then rubs the victim's elbow. The reactions here involve new discriminations that the child is mastering by very active investigative problem solving. The imitation that is manifested in these sequences may well be important in the child's discriminations and comprehension of the affective signals from others. Imitation with this function is not an early response; it is more evident in the later months.

Imitative learning is apparent, too, in the specific emergent skills of being prosocial. The child has learned what to do when someone is hurt or tired or sad (get a bandaid, smooth someone's hair, say "I'll kiss the hurt," etc.) by having observed the mother's or father's prosocial acts in similar circumstances. Such specific memories and delayed reproductions are often described by the mothers.

An entirely different process which seems to be important in many responses is sheer affective arousal when the child is confronted with someone's distress. The child is clearly feeling emotion, perhaps empathically experiencing the emotions of the other person in distress. This kind of responding continues throughout the developmental course that we have observed.

Language is an important part of the developmental progression in responses to distress. Almost as soon as children were using language, mothers reported their labeling of emotions ("cry"), making evaluative expressions ("oh-oh!" "hurting"), questioning, expressing remorse, sympathy ("Mommy okay. I sorry"), and condemnation ("bad"). Their language provides us with a sense of how the children are processing distress; it also provides the children with a self-educative medium by building up a reference repertoire for beginning to categorize social-emotional experience.

In summary, the findings are empathic in pointing to multiple routes in the development of "caring" behavior toward persons. At the same time, the data reflect development change and characterize prosocial responses at successive age levels. The individual developmental pathways that have been described can be read into the group trends presented in Tables 1 and 2.

### 4.2. Individuality in Development

The data available on children in our studies permitted us to investigate issues of individual consistency and continuity on the basis of a substantial sampling of behavior on each child. Since the method of data gathering based on mothers' observations of naturally occurring events does not provide absolute frequency measures that can be compared across children, analyses have been focused on the kinds of behavior represented in a child's repertoire, and on the relative emphasis on differing kinds of reactions.

Patterned individuality in the quality of responding to the distress of others becomes evident very early. Thus certain children, as their reactions are plotted over time, stand out as affectively prosocial. Their prosocial responding has a large component of emotional arousal. They are seldom described in ways that suggest careful cognitive processing, reflection, or problem solving. In contrast, other children who progress equally in complex and effective prosocial intervention manifest prosocial behavior that is without apparent strong emotional underpinnings. They appear to be approaching the distress "cognitively"—by inspecting, exploring, asking questions. Other children have an aggressive component in their prosocial interactions (hitting the person who made the baby cry; hitting at one of the parents in the midst of the parents' quarrel; tearing up the newspaper that made his mother cry). Others shut out signals of distress and turn or run away.

It would be misleading to oversimplify individuality in prosocial behavior; or to suggest that children are so stereotyped in responding as to conform to a single invariant response pattern. Nevertheless, there are clearly distinguishable tendencies and profiles for individual children—in the mode of approach, the complexity, and the intensity of responding. This individuality becomes especially noteworthy when viewed over time. It will be recalled that the 24 children in the initial longitudinal study were followed up at 7 years. In addition to the maturational changes (much more sophisticated inferences and greater skill in helping), there are unsubtle individual stabilities over time in the qualitative terms just described. In about two-thirds of the children, the differentiating dimensions so apparent at the 1½- to 2½-year level reappeared at the later period. That is, the pattern of intense empathic, affective prosocial attempts by certain toddlers was in evidence in these children 5 years later. Likewise evident were the patterns initially described as the combative responding, the cognitive or problem-solving approach, and the anxious "guilty" reaction pattern. The imperviousness and the intolerance of children of early years were also echoed in the assessments in the later period. Continuity was, of course, in degree. There were untypeable children, and children for whom development meant change. We offer these data somewhat tentatively and as preliminaries to further systematic study.

Data on individual consistency, that is, cross-situational consistency, were also obtained in our studies. In most research concerned with consistency in prosocial responding, rates of behavior in different situations are compared. The samples of behavior are generally quite brief. In such comparisons, correspondence is generally in the +.30 range of correlations. (See Radke-Yarrow *et al.*, 1983). Our data on 3- to 7-year-old children (Sample 5) are based on similar brief sampling of behavior, and show consistency of the same magnitude (Yarrow & Waxler, 1976). The data on continuity and those on situational consistency are not incompatible. The behavior samplings are very different and the dimensions used in analyses are different. Therefore, the findings need to be kept distinct and the conclusions properly confined. Further investigation is needed before we are in a position to arrive at conclusions about the organization of prosocial behavior within the individual children.

Quite obviously, issues of consistency and continuity in children's prosocial behavior are not settled. On the one hand, there is support for the idea of situational specificity and inconsistency in behavior. On the other hand, investigators are deeply invested in the kinds of research problems in which there are theoretical expectations of some significant degree of generality and developmental continuity. Such is the research on personality variables in relation to prosocial behavior, as well as the research on socialization influences on prosocial development. In both of these areas, research questions are ones concerning generalizable relationships between prosocial behavior and personality variables (aggression, ego strength, locus of control, etc.) or socialization variables (various control techniques). Given the differences that we have indicated in the ways in which individual children's prosocial responding develops or is learned, in the styles of responding to distress, and (implicitly) in the functions of prosocial behavior, one would not necessarily expect to see uniform associations with personality variables or with specific rearing techniques. For example, a child in our sample whom we described as having an aggressive component in his altruism (protecting the victim by punishing the aggressor), and another child who responded helpfully after having just aggressed against another child, would be expressing behavior patterns that are consistent with the sometimes positive correlations reported in the literature between aggression and prosocial behavior (see Radke-Yarrow *et al.*, 1983). On the other hand, for children whose prosocial interventions express warm positive affect, and for those who anxiously provide for others out of feelings of guilt, one might hypothesize different kinds of behavioral organization, and, therefore, different relationships with personality and socialization variables.

These speculations are consistent with our findings from two studies (Samples 5 and 6). In one naturalistic study of aggressive and prosocial interactions in preschool children, we found that the relationship between these variables depended on numerous personal factors (Yarrow & Waxler, 1976). There is virtually no association between prosocial and aggressive interaction for the sample as a whole. When many modifiers are introduced (sex of child, absolute level of aggression, amount of aggression received from others, and kind of prosocial behavior), associations were positive, negative, or nonexistent, depending on the specific factors.

In a second study of 5- to 8-year-olds (Barrett & Yarrow, 1977), there is further evidence suggesting the futility of a single personality variable approach. Prosocial actions and social assertiveness were measured naturalistically. Children's inferential abilities were measured (their interpretations of standard video vignettes of social interaction). Neither assertiveness nor inferential ability showed promise as a predictor of prosocial behavior when considered alone. However, viewing them in combination was informative. Assertiveness was significantly positively related to prosocial behavior in children with good inferential abilities, but was unrelated in children with poor inferential abilities. Thus, among children who were "sensitive" to interpersonal factors, assertiveness made it more likely that they would intervene prosocially. These findings coupling inferential ability and assertiveness in 5- to 8-year-olds remind one of the 2-year-olds (Sample 1) whose approach was described as inspecting the "hurts," questioning, and examining the victim; in other words, children whose prosocial interventions appeared to depend on having cognitively solved the problem of "what was the matter" before acting on the problem prosocially.

### 4.3. Rearing Influences on Prosocial Behavior

The need for conceptualizations and strategies in research that recognize the multidimensional character of behaviors that result in caring for others, and the diversity of mechanisms involved in the development of these behaviors (Reykowski, 1977), is our recurrent theme. Differences in children's responsiveness to others' needs, well before school age, in our studies and those of other investigators (e.g., Murphy, 1937; Sawin, 1980) lead inevitably to questions of the influences of varied learning conditions (especially rearing conditions) on prosocial behavior. One study involved mothers and the 1½- to 2½-year-olds whose development we have described. The other study is the experimental design (Sample 4) involving 3½- to 5½-year-olds. The two studies provide multimethod and multiage data.

Of the four experimental rearing environments (described in Section 3), one produced a significantly higher frequency of helping behavior from the children and more verbal expressions of sympathetic feelings than the others. It was the condition in which there was a history of a nurturant relationship between experimenter and child, and in which the adult provided the child with the model of her own "caring" behavior for others in real interaction with those in need. The adult's prosocial interactions involved child, adult, and animal "victims" of distress; her behavior was accompanied by clear cognitive and positive affective cues. She provided the child with information about the victim's experience, her own feelings, and the consequences of her prosocial intervention. The adult model *and* the recipients of her help provided this information. Exposing the child to hypothetical or vicarious experiences of these kinds was not, in itself, effective. Although the described rearing environment was superior to the other environments, it is important to note that not all children were materially influenced in prosocial responding. (Perhaps the real rearing histories of these children tempered or limited the effects of the experimental conditions.) This again shows that there is not one royal set of conditions that eventuates in children's learning of prosocial behavior.

In many ways the data from mothers' reports on the 1½ to 2½-year-olds (Samples 1 and 2) confirm the conclusions from the experiment. These reports focus on a situation in which the mother's behavior is likely to have special influences on the child's prosocial learning, namely, when the child causes injury to someone. In these circumstances mothers were emotionally aroused and intervened with heavy rearing commitments. Their techniques were significantly associated with child behavior outcomes. The approach that was positively associated with children's altruism was one in which the mothers convey a clear cognitive message (an explanation or demonstration) of the consequences of the child's behavior (for the victim) and the message is accompanied by an intensity of feeling and an expression of principles and expectations for child behavior. The compound of cognitive and affective components is essential. Plain explanation (induction) was not effective; nor was plain prohibition (power).

The maternal pattern that was found to be positively related to children's altruism includes differently motivated and affectively toned behavior from different mothers, ranging from a punitive and negative quality to one that is stern but more positive in affect. The resulting behavior in the children reflects these differences. Just how the differences relate to the mother's actions we are not prepared to say; we can only be anecdotal on this point. One set of anecdotes concerns children's hyperconcern about their own responsibility. After a child has hurt someone, there is sometimes evident ambivalence: Child alternates aggressive and comforting responses to the victim. On occasion there is aggression toward the self. A child at 16 months, who has made his sibling cry, kisses her and then hits his own head. Children sometimes express anxious concern about the consequences of their acts: For example, when Bobby bites his mother and she expresses pain, he repeats the bite then hugs her and says, "I love Mommy. Mommy love me?" A 2-year-old child hurts a peer's head accidentally, says, "I hurt your hair; please don't cry," and then kisses the peer. Other instances are reported in which children as innocent bystanders respond as if they were responsible and guilty. "Sorry, I be nice." "Did I make you cry?"

As the young child struggles with the locus of "cause" and attempts to repair the feelings of the other, one sees, perhaps, the precursors of early guilt-bases for prosocial action. Rearing methods are undoubtedly critical—when does the child learn prosocial responding out of guilt, and when out of an understanding empathic response?

The parallel findings from our experimental and our naturalistic studies are encouraging. The studies are in agreement on the importance of a nurturant rearing figure who is explicit in his or her prosocial training, using inductive and affective communications. There is agreement despite the fact that the experimental study dealt with prescriptive techniques in influencing the child toward prosocial behavior, whereas the disciplinary stiuations on which the mothers were reporting dealt with proscriptions about hurting someone and prescriptions about caring for someone. Again, these findings cannot be construed as identifying the only kinds of rearing influences on prosocial behavior. A strongly contrasting rearing condition provides an example of very different roots of children's prosocial behavior. We have studied young children of severely depressed parents. In a few instances, children in these circumstances manifest sensitive "caring" behavior toward their parent. Such early development of altruism under stressful conditions has been reported elsewhere in the research literature. The accounts by Freud and Dann (1951) of the war-orphaned German Jewish preschool children brought to English hostels provide a dramatic example of extremely sympathetic and altruistic peer behaviors among these children. Since the development of altruism under conditions of adversity does not conform to familiar theories of rearing influences on children's behavior, one is made very aware of the incompleteness of our understanding of the roots of prosocial behavior.

## 5. CONCLUDING COMMENTS

We have brought together evidence from a number of studies in our laboratory on the development of children's prosocial motivations and behaviors. Two perspectives that often take independent courses in research have been interwoven in these studies: development as maturation, and development as rearing (learning). No one assumes that they are unrelated, but very often theories as well as research designs and methods deal exclusively with one or the other.

In dealing with maturation we have been serious about investigating the emergence of complex social responses toward other persons when those persons are giving signals of distress. The monitoring of behavior of the individual child over time has been used as the method of tracing development. Behavior that is observed in the first years of life compels new views of children's interpersonal sensitivities. It also necessitates interpretations of developing prosocial behavior in terms other than social norms, peer influences, norms of reciprocity, or histories of punishment or reward.

We have observed children's responses to distress of many types. As we have seen, there are distinct, patterned, and in many ways predictable reactions within the individual child. Complex prosocial responses occur long before there is a high level of cognitive development. The developing cognitive capacities bring changes in the child's sensitivities, reasoning, and conceptualizing; however, the cognitive changes do not necessarily bring changes in the various kinds of affective arousal and affective messages from the child to the "victim."

Developmental theorists and practitioners have placed great stress on the child's attachments to caregiver(s), and children are reared and provided for accordingly. Our data suggest that there is a need to enlarge the concept of attachments to include infants' and children's "attachment" to others as evidenced by their many attempts at caring for the victimized other.

These data on the origins of prosocial responding have implications for socialization. (1) The assumptions that caregivers make about children influence the treatment and behavior settings that they provide for children; this includes the opportunities they give to young children for prosocial behavior and their reactions to children for such prosocial behavior. These positive, other-oriented, affective, and instrumental capabilities of children have not been part of professional education for parents and other caregivers. (2) Questions about rearing and prosocial behavior would appear to need some reformulation and refinement: How are the child's positive tendencies that are observed in the first few years modulated, altered, extinguished, supported, and developed into the variously motivated prosocial behaviors (or into the variously motivated reluctance to act prosocially) that are seen in older children?

In summary, although certain uniform developmental progressions are evident very early in childhood, and certain conditions of rearing contribute predictably to prosocial development, there is not one single course for the development of children's caring behaviors; there are many different processes and lines of development that contribute to the evolution of children's motivations and capabilities for prosocial behavior.

## 6. REFERENCES


Barrett, D. E., & Yarrow, M. R. Prosocial behavior, social inferential ability and assertiveness in children. *Child Development*, 1977, *48*, 475–481.

Chan, W. *A source book in Chinese Philosophy*. Princeton: Princeton University Press, 1963.

Cummings, E. M., Zahn-Waxler, C., & Radke-Yarrow, M. R. Children's responses to expressions of anger and affection by and between family members. *Child Development*, 1981, *52*, 1274–1282.

Freud, A., & Dann, S. An experiment in group upbringing. *Psychoanalytic Study of the Child*, 1951, *6*, 127–168.

Hobbes, T. *Leviathan*. In R. M. Hutchins (Ed.), *Great books of the western world* (Vol. 23). Chicago: Encyclopedia Britannica, 1952. (Originally published, 1651).

Lasch, C. *The culture of narcissism*. New York: W. W. Norton, 1978.

Murphy, L. B. *Social behavior and child personality*. New York: Columbia University Press, 1937.

Radke-Yarrow, M. R., Zahn-Waxler, C. J., & Chapman, M. Children's prosocial dispositions and behavior. In P. H. Mussen (Ed.), *Carmichael's manual of child psychology* (Vol. 4). New York: Wiley, 1983.

Reykowski, J. Cognitive development and prosocial behavior. *Polish Psychological Bulletin*, 1977, *8*, 35–45.

Rousseau, J. J. On the origin of inequality. In R. M. Hutchins (Ed.), *Great books of the western world* (Vol. 23). Chicago: Encyclopedia Britannica, 1952. (Originally published, 1755.)

Sawin, D. B. *A field study of children's reactions to distress in their peers*. Unpublished manuscript, University of Texas, Austin, 1980.

Slater, P. *The pursuit of loneliness*. Boston: Beacon Press, 1970.

Yarrow, M. R., & Waxler, C. J. Dimensions and correlates of prosocial behavior in young children. *Child Development*, 1976, *47*, 118–125. (a)

Yarrow, M. R., & Waxler, C. Z. Emergences and functions of prosocial behaviors in young children. In M. S. Smart & R. C. Smart (Eds.), *Infants: Development and relationships*. New York: Macmillan, 1978.

Yarrow, M. R., Scott, P. M., & Waxler, C. J. Learning concern for others. *Developmental Psychology*, 1973, *8*, 248–260.

Zahn-Waxler, C. J. *Young children's responses to the emotions of others. Paper, presented at the meeting of the International Conference on Infant Studies, New Haven, Connecticut, April 1980.*

*Zahn-Waxler, C. J. The social-emotional development of young children with a manic-depressive parent.* Paper presented at the meeting of the Board of Scientific Counselors, National Institutes of Mental Health, Bethesda, Maryland, May 1981.

Zahn-Waxler, C. J., & Radke-Yarrow, M. R. Perspective-taking and prosocial behavior. *Journal of Developmental Psychology,* 1977, *13,* 87–88.

Zahn-Waxler, C. J., & Radke-Yarrow, M. R. The development of prosocial behavior: Alternative research strategies. In N. Eisenberg-Berg (Ed.), *The development of prosocial behavior.* New York: Academic Press, 1981.

Zahn-Waxler, C. J., Radke-Yarrow, M. R., & King, R. A. The impact of affective environment on young children. Paper presented at the meeting of the Society for Research in Child Development, New Orleans, March 1977.

Zahn-Waxler, C. J., Radke-Yarrow, M. R., & King, R. A. Child rearing and children's prosocial initiations toward victims of distress. *Child Development,* 1979, *50,* 319–330.

# 5

# Prosocial Behavior in the Preschool Years

## Methodological and Conceptual Issues

Nancy Eisenberg, Ellen Cameron, and Kelly Tryon

## 1. INTRODUCTION

In the past few years interest in the development of prosocial behavior has increased dramatically. Numerous researchers have examined the socialization antecedents and situational determinants of prosocial behaviors, as well as the personality characteristics of those most likely to engage in prosocial action (Bar-Tal, 1976; Mussen & Eisenberg-Berg, 1977; Rushton, 1976, 1980; Staub, 1978, 1979). As this research has accumulated, it has become increasingly clear that the prosocial domain of behavior (as any other domain of social behavior) can be best understood from an interactional perspective, that is, with an approach that neglects neither the role of the individual's personal characteristics nor situational determinants.

The need to consider one side of the coin—the role of personal variables—becomes apparent as soon as one attempts to define prosocial behavior. Although definitions of prosocial behavior and altruism vary, prosocial behavior is frequently defined as behavior that benefits an-

NANCY EISENBERG, ELLEN CAMERON, and KELLY TRYON • Department of Psychology, Arizona State University, Tempe, Arizona 85287.

other and is intended to do so (Staub, 1978). Many theorists also assume that prosocial actions (particularly the subtype of prosocial behavior called altruism) must not only be intended to benefit a recipient, but also should not be motivated by the expectation of external rewards—if one benefits another accidently or in an attempt to enhance one's own well-being, the action frequently is not considered altruistic (Mussen & Eisenberg-Berg, 1977; Rushton, 1976). Thus the mere act of defining which behaviors are prosocial and which are not forces the researcher to attend to such personal characteristics of an individual as values, goals, and motives.

In a complementary fashion, the need to consider situational factors is apparent from the ways in which the term *prosocial behavior* is operationalized in research. In various studies the term is used to encompass a variety of different positive behaviors, including sharing, helping, and comforting. Since it is clear that situations that elicit one prosocial behavior (e.g., the provision of assistance with a difficult task) frequently differ in certain stimulus characteristics from situations that tend to elicit other behaviors (e.g., comforting in psychological distress), current operational definitions of prosocial behavior implicitly refer to a broad range of situational variables.

The purpose of this chapter is to consider both personal and contextual contributions to the young child's prosocial behavior. In doing so, two related issues will be addressed: (1) the ways in which various types of prosocial behavior frequently reflect both different stimulus conditions and variations in individuals' personal characteristics; and, more importantly, (2) the significance of differentiating between prosocial behaviors initiated in different ways, that is, between spontaneous and "asked for" (complaint) prosocial behaviors. It will be argued that the spontaneous–"asked for" differentiation is crucial to the understanding and prediction of prosocial behavior. This is because the two modes of behavior are embedded in different circumstances and should be more attractive to, as well as more characteristic of, some individuals than others. Since one can best understand the role of environmental and personal variables by studying children in real-life settings, data from naturalistic studies will be viewed as especially pertinent.

## 2. THE CLASSIFICATION OF TYPES OF PROSOCIAL RESPONSES

One of the most obvious and common differentiations in the literature on prosocial behavior is among various modes of prosocial responding. Thus prosocial behavior is frequently classified into a variety of categories of behavioral response, including helping, sharing, and comforting. Since each type of behavior involves and/or is related to a different configuration of costs, benefits, and competencies, the meanings of these behaviors to the young child are probably quite different. By considering the complex interplay of situational and personal factors connected with each mode of prosocial behavior, one can better understand the development and meaning of children's prosocial behaviors.

Let us first consider the cost of various modes of prosocial behavior. Sharing is generally defined as the giving up of an object (or work space, Barrett & Yarrow, 1977) in the child's possession (Eisenberg-Berg & Hand, 1979; Hansen, Goldman, & Baldwin, 1975; Iannotti, 1981; F. F. Strayer, Wareing, & Rushton, 1979; Tonick, Gelfand, Hartmann, Cromer, & Millsapp, 1977). In instances of sharing, the cost is concrete (temporary or permanent loss of an object—a loss that may or may not be anticipated by the young child). Furthermore, little loss of time is generally required. In contrast, helping is usually defined as attempts to alleviate another's nonemotional (nondistress related) needs, including assisting another to achieve a goal (Eisenberg-Berg & Hand, 1979; Hansen *et al.*, 1975; Yarrow & Waxler, 1976), giving information, or offering an object not previously in the child's possession (Eisenberg-Berg & Hand, 1979; Hansen *et al.*, 1975). Such behavior does not involve the loss of an object previously possessed but may cost the individual time and effort. Finally, comforting, or attempts to alleviate another's emotional distress (Eisenberg-Berg & Hand, 1979; Hansen *et al.*, 1975), involves time and attention, but seldom the loss of possessions or physical exertion. Thus each mode of response, by definition, typically entails somewhat different objective costs.

It is important to consider the subjective as well as the objective cost of a given prosocial response for a particular individual. The subjective cost is determined by the individual's personal goals (individual motives and cognitions relating to these motives, Staub, 1978), and the configuration of the child's various personal goals and competencies (see Chapter 2, this volume).

Both the strength of an individual's personal goals and their position in an individual's hierarchy of goals are important in determining the subjective costs of a particular behavior to a specific individual. Consider, for example, the role of strength of personal goals and needs in determining the cost of sharing and helping behaviors. The cost of sharing an object in relation to the cost of providing help with a simple task will vary depending, in part, on how much the individual values both material possessions (and, in particular, the possession to be shared) and his or her time. The individual who values material objects more than time should be less likely to share than to provide time-consuming help.

Furthermore, consider two individuals who both strongly value possession of material objects (including the particular object to be shared), one of whom is even more concerned both with others' emotional states and with personal achievement. In general, the individual concerned with people's emotional states should be more likely to share than the other person. This is because his or her concern with material possessions is lower on a hierarchy of goals than another goal (concern with another's well-being) that is salient in many sharing situations. However, in a helping situation that requires extended disruption of achievement-related activities, the same individual may be less likely to help, especially if the other's need is not great. In brief, although various modes of prosocial responding may differ systematically in objective costs, the relation of these costs to an individual's behavior will be clearer if one considers the mediating role of the individual's subjective personal goals.

It is also useful to consider the role of an individual's personal competencies when calculating the subjective costs of various prosocial behaviors. For example, the cost in time for helping with a particular task is less if the helper has the skills required to perform the task. Similarly, sharing of an object may seem less costly if the individual has the means or ability to easily replace the lost object, or is too young to anticipate the potential cost of losing possession of an object. Thus the subjective costs of various prosocial responses are, in part, a function of how well the individual's abilities mesh with the specific requirements of the situation.

Various modes of prosocial responding differ in potential benefits to the actor, as well as in costs. However, differences in benefits for sharing, helping, and comforting are not as clear as differences in costs, perhaps because the costs of a prosocial behavior are more inherent to the mode of prosocial behavior than are the benefits. Nevertheless, some potential differences in benefits are evident. For example, helping behaviors provide an opportunity for praise and admiration of the skills that are required for helping, whereas sharing provides little opportunity for recognition of individual skills (since relinquishing an object requires little skill). Furthermore, one could hypothesize that helping behaviors, which would tend to require more time than relinquishing an object, should generally result in more prolonged positive social interaction than should sharing, an act that is usually quickly accomplished.

Subjective benefits (and costs) of various modes of prosocial responding frequently may be mediated by individual differences in personality characteristics such as tempo, temperament, interest, and sociability. For a nonassertive, passive child, relinquishing an object may be less costly (e.g., easier or less intimidating) than providing extensive physical or verbal assistance. In contrast, for an active, assertive, and/or social child, the opportunity to help or share may provide desired activity or social interaction, and/or may be relatively easy and nonthreatening (Barrett & Yarrow, 1977). In other words, individual differences on a variety of characteristics will determine which prosocial act a person might prefer to perform (Gergen, Gergen, & Meter, 1972), and how likely the individual is to perform prosocial acts that he or she desires to perform (Suda & Fouts, 1980).

### 2.1. The Research

Thus far we have been primarily theorizing regarding the differences among various modes of prosocial behavior. Unfortunately, there are few studies dealing directly with the role of environmental and personal factors in the elicitation and performance of various modes of young children's prosocial responding. Nevertheless, the limited data are suggestive.

If different modes of prosocial behavior reflect similar environmental conditions and/or are equivalent in meaning to most people, one would expect an association between these behaviors in the child's natural environment. Frequently, however, this is not the case for young children (although there is some consistency across modes of prosocial behavior when composites of behaviors are computed, Rushton, 1980; F. F. Strayer *et al.*, 1979). For example, measures of sharing and helping (when not broken down into various subcategories such as spontaneous and asked-for sharing and helping) tend to be unrelated in the preschool environment (Eisenberg, Cameron, Tryon, & Dodez, 1981; Iannotti, 1981; Staub & Feinberg, 1977, cited by Staub, 1979; Yarrow & Waxler, 1976). Similarly, preschoolers' cooperation appears to be unrelated to their sharing and helping in the classroom (Iannotti, 1981). Moreover, Krebs and Sturrup (1974), in a naturalistic study with second and third graders, found no relationship between offering help and offering support.

The fact that patterns of personal characteristics relate differently to helping and sharing behaviors is also consistent with the conclusion that various modes of prosocial behavior are not equivalent. For example, Yarrow and Waxler (1976) noted a complex relationship between aggression and sharing/comforting behavior but not helping. Similarly, Eisenberg-Berg and Hand (1979) found that helping (but not sharing) was associated with a number of social contacts; in contrast, sharing (but not helping) was related to level of moral judgment. In yet another study, Staub and Feinberg (1977, cited by Staub, 1979) found that sharing in response to others' requests was associated with girls' positive responsivity to others (positive emotional responsivity toward others, positive physical context), but this responsive pattern of behavior did not include the tendency to help.

It is also likely that the normal eliciting conditions for helping and sharing frequently differ. For example, Hansen *et al.* (1975) found that among 4-year-olds in the preschool classroom, the need for sharing was less frequently indicated by situational cues (the behavior of the needy child in the situation rather than an explicit or implicit request from the child) than was the need for helping. Similarly, Iannotti (1981) found that preschoolers' sharing but not helping was usually initiated by a verbal or nonverbal request from the potential recipient. Finally, it appears that some types of prosocial behaviors are more likely than others to be elicited by peers' affective displays. For example, J. Strayer (1980) found that preschool children reassured a peer who displayed a hurt facial expression 19% of the time, but never shared with an injured peer.

In summary, according to the limited data, different modes of prosocial responding seem to represent somewhat different patterns of behavior that reflect varying configurations of situational and personal determinants. By attending carefully to these differences, researchers should be better able to understand the development, elicitation, and maintenance of prosocial behavior.

## 2.2. Methodological Issues

As yet, empirical data regarding the differences among the major modes of prosocial responding are piecemeal and not entirely consistent. This is attributable to at least three factors. First, data concerning environmental and personal determinants of early prosocial behaviors are limited in quantity and scope. Second, investigators have frequently defined helping behavior in somewhat different ways. For example, Yarrow and Waxler (1976) defined helping as "helping someone attain a goal," regardless of whether the goal is mutual or not. In contrast, Eisenberg-Berg and Hand (1979) and Eisenberg-Berg and Lennon (1980) defined helping thusly:

> the child attempts to alleviate another's emotional needs, e.g., assists another by giving information, helps another with a task, or offers another an object not previously in the giver's possession. These behaviors were not coded as helping if they occurred as part of cooperative play *and* involved completion of a mutual goal.

Thus Eisenberg-Berg and her colleagues have used a stricter definition of helping than Yarrow and Waxler, and were examining a somewhat different set of prosocial behaviors. Since operational definitions of the various prosocial behaviors are not standardized, differences in researchers' data may be attributable to differences in the behaviors sampled.

Finally, it will be very difficult to determine the various factors influencing different modes of prosocial behavior until critical distinctions among the various subtypes of helping, sharing, comforting, and so on are made.

## 3. SPONTANEOUS VERSUS "ASKED-FOR" PROSOCIAL BEHAVIORS

According to recent research, there is a distinction among prosocial behaviors that may be as important as the differentiation among the various modes of prosocial responding. This distinction, which refers to the source of initiation of a prosocial act rather than to the individual's mode of response, is between "asked for" and "spontaneous" prosocial behaviors. Spontaneous prosocial behaviors are those prosocial behaviors initiated by the actor without the potential recipient (or anyone else) requesting (verbally or nonverbally) assistance. In contrast, asked-for behaviors are prosocial behaviors in response to either a verbal or a nonverbal request for aid from the potential recipient (or, perhaps, a third party). Thus spontaneous acts are self-initiated (although they are often in response to situational cues that clearly indicate another's need), whereas asked-for prosocial behaviors are other-initiated and involve compliance with a needy other's (or a third party's) request.

These two types of prosocial behaviors are responses to very different environmental cues and frequently involve quite different configurations of costs and benefits. Thus asked-for and spontaneous behaviors may be performed by somewhat different types of people who are different in their personal goals and attributes.

How, specifically, do the costs and benefits of spontaneous and asked-for behaviors differ? Let us consider, first, the type of situations in which asked-for behaviors are embedded. In these situations, the individual is directly requested to provide assistance. Once the child is explicitly asked to comply with a request, not doing so constitutes an act of noncompliance. Thus among the most obvious potential benefits of responding to a request for assistance are (1) avoidance of interpersonal conflict resulting from a noncompliant response, and (2) concrete or interpersonal rewards (e.g., approval) from the recipient who explicitly requested the prosocial behavior (but only if the child is not seen as a compliant "sucker"). Furthermore, if the cost of an asked-for prosocial behavior is low, responding to a direct request may be the easiest thing to do; for example, not sharing a toy when requested to do so may result in further requests, negative sanctions, and/or a prolonged social exchange that would disrupt the potential benefactor's ongoing activities. Finally, although the costs of an asked-for prosocial behavior obviously include the time, effort, or loss of a possession required by the actor's assistance, an additional cost may involve the child's being labeled as an easy, compliant target for future requests.

In contrast to asked-for behaviors, spontaneous prosocial actions do not involve explicit compliance. Thus performance of spontaneous prosocial behaviors would not seem to indicate an especially compliant nature, and failure to provide assistance should be less likely to result in a negative interpersonal reaction than should refusal to respond to a request for assistance. More simply, the child's motive for acting spontaneously is unlikely to be mere compliance or the avoidance of negative sanctions for noncompliance. Thus the eliciting circumstances for spontaneous prosocial acts (including potential costs and benefits) will tend to be associated with different personal goals and personality characteristics than will the eliciting circumstances for asked-for prosocial behaviors.

### 3.1. The Research

There are data consistent with many of the above suppositions. First, according to naturalistic data, the dimension of source of initiation tends to be an efficacious one for conceptualizing consistencies in prosocial behavior. Although the two types of helping or sharing behavior (asked-for and spontaneous sharing, and asked-for and spontaneous helping) are frequently unrelated (Eisenberg-Berg & Hand, 1979; Eisenberg-Berg & Lennon, 1980; Marcus & Jenny, 1977), asked-for sharing and helping tend to be intercorrelated and/or to cluster together in factor analyses, as do spontaneous sharing and spontaneous helping (Eisenberg-Berg & Lennon, 1980; Eisenberg, *et al.*, 1981, unpublished data). For example, in a naturalistic study of 33 preschool children, spontaneous sharing was unrelated to asked-for sharing ($r = .03$), and spontaneous helping was not correlated with asked-for helping ($r = -.04$). However, spontaneous helping and sharing were marginally related ($r = .32$, $p < .07$), and asked-for sharing and helping were nonsignificantly, positively associated ($r = .27$, $p < .13$). Furthermore, when the four types of prosocial behavior were subjected to a factor analysis with a varimax rotation, asked-for behaviors loaded on one of the two factors whereas spontaneous behaviors clustered on the other.

One way to test the hypothesis that spontaneous and asked-for prosocial behaviors differ in many fundamental aspects is to examine the correlates of these two types of prosocial behavior, including the personality characteristics of individuals who tend to perform one or the other type of behavior. This has been done in several studies. In one study, asked-for and spontaneous prosocial behaviors were differentially related to an empathy measure somewhat similar in form to the Feshbach and Roe (1968) Affective Situation Test (which may have measured compliance rather than empathy). Spontaneous prosocial responding was significantly, negatively related to the empathy measure, whereas frequency of asked-for sharing and helping tended to be positively related. Furthermore, spontaneous but not asked-for behaviors were related to sociability (Eisenberg-Berg & Lennon, 1980). In another study, Eisenberg-Berg and Hand (1979) examined the relationship between preschoolers' sharing in their classroom and their moral reasoning about prosocial moral dilemmas (dilemmas in which the needs or wants of one individual conflict with those of another in a context in which the role of authorities, prohibitions, and punishment is minimal or irrelevant). According to their data, spontaneous sharing (but not asked-for sharing or either type of helping/comforting behavior) was positively related to higher level, needs-oriented reasoning and negatively related to hedonistic reasoning, a developmentally immature type of reasoning. Although the relationship between moral judgment and the combined spontaneous prosocial behaviors (or combined asked-for behaviors) was not significant (unpublished data), the results of this study are consistent with the conclusion that spontaneous sharing is different from either asked-for sharing or helping.

If, as suggested previously, asked-for prosocial behavior frequently represent compliant behavior, then one would expect the tendency to perform asked-for behaviors (but not necessarily spontaneous behaviors) to be negatively related to dominance. This prediction has received some empirical support. In a study involving 2½- to 5-year-olds, Eisenberg and Giallanza (in press) found that less dominant preschoolers were more likely than dominant children to comply with a request for sharing behavior. The procedure of the study involved taking the children into a playroom in triads (22 triads in all) and leaving them alone with a desirable toy. Their subsequent object-related behaviors (taking the toy, defense of the toy, requests for the toy, and sharing of the toy) were coded from videotapes that were made through a one-way mirror. The child in each triad who maintained possession of the toy for the longest amount of time (when at least one other child was attending to the toy) was labeled as the dominant child; the child who possessed the toy the least time when at least one other child was attending to the toy was designated as being low in dominance. (High and low dominance, as determined in this manner, also related to teachers' ratings of dominance.) Next, the object-related behaviors of the high and low dominance children (controlled for opportunities to share or defend and/or for amount of time possessing the toy) were compared. Although the high and low dominance children did not differ in attempts to spontaneously share, the low dominance children were significantly more likely to share in response to a verbal or nonverbal request for sharing (number of sharings/number of times the child was verbally or nonverbally requested to share or the other child attempted to handle the toy). The dominant children were also significantly more likely than the low dominance children to try physically (but not verbally) to take the toy from a peer. These data are consistent with the conclusion that spontaneous and asked-for sharing behaviors are functionally different patterns of behavior, and that asked-for sharing is frequently a compliant or submissive behavior.

Other research is consistent with the conclusion that children who perform much asked-for prosocial behavior (1) elicit different responses from peers and teachers than children high in spontaneous prosocial behavior, and (2) differ somewhat in patterns of social behavior from children who are high in spontaneous prosocial behavior. In a recent study, 33 children's naturally occurring behavior was videotaped in their respective classrooms through a one-way mirror for 15 minutes a session (two or three times a week) for approximately 9 weeks. The children's prosocial behaviors, reactions of others to these behaviors, and a variety of other social behaviors (number of social contacts with peers and teachers, requests for help from peers and teachers, attempts to physically or verbally take another's objects [impinges], and physical or verbal attempts to defend an object) were coded. The children were also administered the Mischel, Zeiss, and Zeiss (1974) test for internal versus external locus of control (Eisenberg *et al.*, 1981). According to the data, children who performed high levels of asked-for acts (per time period observed) received a significantly higher proportion of neutral feedback (primarily passive acceptance of the prosocial behavior by the recipient) and less positive feedback (smiling, initiation or sustaining of social interaction, a thank you) from peers than children displaying fewer asked-for prosocial behaviors. Except for a marginally significant relationship between frequency of spontaneous prosocial responding and positive feedback for girls only, level of spontaneous prosocial behavior was unrelated to amount of positive or neutral feedback from peers. Furthermore, children who exhibited high frequencies of asked-for behavior, in comparison to children who exhibited high levels of spontaneous behavior, received significantly more negative and neutral feedback, and less positive feedback from peers for their asked-for behaviors.

Since there were sex differences in the frequency of emitting spontaneous prosocial behavior and in sociability (males were higher on both measures), the correlations between frequency of prosocial behavior and peers' reactions were recomputed partialing out the effects of sex and sociability (number of social interactions). When this was done, the pattern of results described above was essentially retained; that is, the pattern of peer feedback was quite different for spontaneous and asked-for prosocial behaviors.

According to additional analyses in which opportunities to do an asked-for prosocial behavior were controlled, children who performed asked-for behaviors a relatively large percentage of the time they were requested to do so received peer feedback similar to children who performed asked-for behaviors a smaller percentage of the time they were asked. Thus it appears that valence of peer feedback was not a function of how likely a child was to grant any single request for assistance or sharing. Rather, type of peer feedback seemed to be related to frequency of asked-for responding irrespective of the proportion of times children refused to help or share. Children who performed many asked-for behaviors were those whom peers were most likely to ask for help (the correlation between frequency of performing asked-for behaviors and frequency of requests directed at a given child was .95). This suggests that these children had been singled out by peers as targets for requests for assistance and that being singled out in this manner was not viewed as especially desirable (since the children who performed high levels of asked-for behaviors received less positive feedback from peers than other children).

High frequencies of asked-for and spontaneous behaviors were also associated with different reactions from teachers. Although children who exhibited high quantities of asked-for behaviors received positive feedback (primarily in the form of social interaction) for these behaviors, teachers did not respond differentially to the spontaneous prosocial behaviors of children who exhibited high and low frequencies of spontaneous behavior. The correlation between proportion of positive teacher feedback and the tendency to display high rates of asked-for prosocial behavior was higher than the correlation between the proportion of positive feedback for asked-for behaviors and the tendency to exhibit spontaneous prosocial behavior. That is, children exhibiting much spontaneous behavior were less likely to receive positive reactions from teachers for asked-for behaviors than were children who exhibited high levels of asked-for prosocial behavior. Teachers did, however, react positively to twice as many spontaneous behaviors (4.8%) as asked-for (2.3%) behaviors, although they reacted to only a small percentage of prosocial actions.

Not only did peers and teachers respond somewhat differently to children exhibiting high frequencies of spontaneous and asked-for behaviors, high frequencies of the two types of prosocial responding were also associated with different behavioral correlates. Children who exhibited much spontaneous behavior, in contrast to those relatively low on spontaneous prosocial behavior, engaged in more positive peer interactions, were unlikely to ask teachers for assistance, and tended ($p < .10$) not to ask peers for help and to respond positively rather than neutrally to others' asked-for prosocial behaviors. Children high on asked-for prosocial behaviors, in contrast to those exhibiting few asked-for prosocial behaviors, tended ($p < .10$) to ask teachers for help, were significantly less likely to verbally or physically attempt to defend an object, were external in their locus of control, and were more likely to give bland, nonresponsive, neutral feedback rather than positive feedback to others' asked-for prosocial behaviors, and neutral feedback to others' spontaneous prosocial behaviors. When the effects of sex were partialed out of the above correlations, they were essentially unchanged with the exception of the correlations relating to children's reactions to others' asked-for behaviors (which became nonsignificant). Furthermore, according to tests for differences between correlations from correlated samples, the relationships between high levels of prosocial behavior and (1) sociability (number of social contacts, $p < .01$), (2) negative and neutral responding to peers' spontaneous prosocial behaviors ($p$'s $< .10$ and .01, respectively), (3) neutral and positive responses to peers' asked-for behaviors ($p$'s $< .01$), (4) asking peers or teachers for help ($p$'s $< .10$ and .01, respectively), and (5) frequency of physical or verbal defense of reactions ($p < .01$) were different for spontaneous and asked-for behaviors. Finally, teachers' ratings of the children's "compliance" were significantly, positively related to frequency of performing asked-for (but not spontaneous) prosocial behaviors ($r = -.32$).

## 4. IMPLICATIONS OF THE RESEARCH ON SPONTANEOUS AND "ASKED-FOR" BEHAVIORS

The tendency to perform asked-for rather than spontaneous prosocial behaviors may have long-term consequences for the young child. Since asked-for behaviors are externally initiated and frequently may constitute little more than acts of compliance, these behaviors may often be based upon extrinsic rather than intrinsic motivations (Deci, 1975). Consequently, because people seem to be less likely to voluntarily perform extrinsically motivated than intrinsically motivated behaviors, the tendency to act in a prosocial manner actually may be decreased or undermined for children who tend to enact many asked-for behaviors.

This suggestion is consistent with the findings that people are sometimes less likely to perform a second prosocial behavior if they have previously received external concrete rewards for a prosocial act (Batson, Coke, Jasnoski, & Hanson, 1978; cf. Schwartz & Howard, 1980), or have been induced to attribute their prior prosocial behavior to external rather than internal causes (Batson, Harris, McCaul, Davis, & Schmidt, 1979; Grusec & Redler, 1980; Grusec, Kuczynski, Rushton, & Simutis, 1978). Of course, it is also possible that children who exhibit much asked-for prosocial behavior do so because they are already externally oriented (recall the positive correlation between asked-for behaviors and external locus of control) and, therefore, tend to assist primarily when external rewards or pressures are evident.

To summarize, the limited research is consistent with the hypothesis that different types of children are likely to display high frequencies of asked-for and spontaneous prosocial behaviors. Although the groups of children who exhibit these two types of behaviors may overlap in membership to some degree, correlations between frequencies of spontaneous and asked-for prosocial behaviors are generally nonsignificant. Overall, children who comply with others' requests for help seem to be relatively dependent, submissive, and external in locus of control whereas children who display high levels of spontaneous behavior are relatively sociable and are low in dependence on adults. These patterns are consistent with the conclusion that children who display much asked-for behavior tend to be somewhat submissive and compliant (and, perhaps, are seen as compliant targets by their peers), whereas children who exhibit spontaneous behavior are socially responsive. Thus it seems likely that asked-for and spontaneous prosocial behaviors are reactions to different stimulus situations, and that different types of children with different personal goals and/or attributes are likely to react to the stimulus cues that are associated with the two types of prosocial behaviors.

The limited data are certainly compelling enough to merit further attention to the differentiation between asked-for and spontaneous behavior. This differentiation could be studied in at least three ways. First, one could obtain measures of various relevant personality dimensions (via sociometric measures, personality tests, etc.) and then relate these dimensions to frequency of asked-for or spontaneous sharing in the natural setting. Alternatively, personality measures (or observations of such relevant dimensions as submissiveness) could be related to prosocial behavior in contrived situations in which the child is either requested to help (or share), or allowed to help spontaneously. Finally, in order better to understand the dynamics of various types of sharing, researchers could carefully catalog the types of situations in which asked-for and spontaneous prosocial behaviors are most likely to occur (see Iannotti, 1981). Such a procedure could aid in determining the situational antecedents and correlates of spontaneous and asked-for prosocial behaviors, for example, the role of potential adult or peer approval in the instigation of various modes of prosocial behavior.

## 5. CONCLUSION

There is much diversity in the realm of prosocial behavior. People can assist one another in a variety of ways. Some people prefer to perform certain modes of prosocial action; others are more likely to choose other forms (Hampson, 1979). The factors determining an individual's choice of prosocial behavor are both internal and external; the individual's preferences, personal characteristics, and values as well as situational contingencies and cues are potentially important determinants of whether or not an individual assists in a specific situation. Furthermore, internal and external factors interact; people with different characteristics interpret and respond differently to various situations. Thus, given the complex nature of prosocial responding, it is essential that researchers examine both the varieties of prosocial responding and the meaning of various types of prosocial behavior for different people. Helping versus sharing, spontaneous versus requested prosocial behavior, and intrinsically versus extrinsically motivated prosocial acts are all important distinctions. Other relevant distinctions have yet to be delineated. To do so is one of the major challenges facing theorists and researchers concerned with prosocial behavior.

## 6. REFERENCES

Barrett, D. E., & Yarrow, M. R. Prosocial behavior, social inferential ability, and assertiveness in children. *Child Development*, 1977, *48*, 475–481.

Bar-Tal, D. *Prosocial behavior: Theory and research.* New York: Halsted Press, 1976.

Batson, C. D., Coke, J. S., Jasnoski, M. L., & Hanson, M. Buying kindness: Effects of an extrinsic incentive for helping on perceived altruism. *Personality and Social Psychology Bulletin*, 1978, *4*, 86–91.

Batson, C. D., Harris, A. C., McCaul, K. D., Davis, M., & Schmidt, T. Compassion or compliance: Alternative dispositional attributions for one's helping behavior. *Social Psychology Quarterly*, 1979, *42*, 405–409.

Deci, E. L. *Intrinsic motivation.* New York: Plenum Press, 1975.

Eisenberg, N., & Giallanza, S. J. Components of successful proprietary behavior among preschool children. *Child Study Journal*, in press.

Eisenberg-Berg, N., & Hand, M. The relationship of preschoolers' reasoning about prosocial moral conflicts to prosocial behavior. *Child Development*, 1979, *50*, 356–363.

Eisenberg-Berg, N., & Lennon, R. Altruism and the assessment of empathy in the preschool years. *Child Development*, 1980, *51*, 552–557.

Eisenberg, N., Cameron, E., Tryon, K., & Dodez, R. Socialization of prosocial behavior in the preschool classroom. *Developmental Psychology*, 1981, *17*, 773–782.

Feshbach, N. D., & Roe, K. Empathy in six and seven year olds. *Child Development*, 1968, *39*, 133–145.

Gergen, K. G., Gergen, M. M., & Meter, K. Individual orientations to prosocial behavior. *Journal of Social Issues*, 1972, *28*, 105–130.

Grusec, J. E., & Redler, E. Attribution, reinforcement, and altruism: A developmental analysis. *Developmental Psychology*, 1980, *16*, 525–534.

Grusec, J. E., Kuczynski, L., Rushton, J. P., & Simutis, Z. Modeling, direct instruction, and attributions: Effects on altruism. *Developmental Psychology*, 1978, *14*, 51–57.

Hampson, R. B. *Peers, pathology, and helping: Some kids are more helpful than others.* Paper presented at the meeting of the society for Research in Child Development, San Francisco, March 1979.

Hansen, R., Goldman, B. D., & Baldwin, M. *Towards a taxonomy of altruism: An observational study of spontaneous prosocial behavior among young children.* Paper presented at the meeting of the Canadian Psychological Association, Quebec City, June 1975.

Iannotti, R. J. *Prosocial behavior, perspective taking, and empathy in preschool children: An evaluation of naturalistic and structured settings.* Paper presented at the meeting of the Society for Research in Child Development, Boston, April 1981.

Krebs, D., & Sturrup, B. Role-taking ability and altruistic behavior in elementary school children. *Personality and Social Psychology Bulletin*, 1974, *1*, 407–409.

Marcus, R. F., & Jenny, B. A naturalistic study of reciprocity in the helping behavior of young children. *Alberta Journal of Educational Research*, 1977, *23*, 195–206.

Mischel, W., Zeiss, R., & Zeiss, A. R. Internal-external control and persistence: Validation and implication of the Stanford Preschool Internal-External Scale (SPIES). *Journal of Personality and Social Psychology*, 1974, *29*, 265–278.

Mussen, P., & Eisenberg-Berg, N. *The roots of caring, sharing, and helping.* San Francisco: Freeman, 1977.

Rushton, J. P. Socialization and the altruistic behavior of children. *Psychological Bulletin*, 1976, *83*, 898–913.

Rushton, J. P. *Altruism, socialization, and society.* Englewood Cliffs, N.J.: Prentice-Hall, 1980.

Schwartz, S. H., & Howard, J. A. *Internalized values as motivators of altruism.* Paper presented at the International Conference on the Development and Maintenance of Prosocial Behavior, Warsaw, June–July, 1980.

Staub, E. *Positive social behavior and morality.* Vol. 1. *Social and personal influences.* New York: Academic Press, 1978.

Staub, E. *Positive social behavior and morality.* Vol. 2. *Socialization and development.* New York: Academic Press, 1979.

Strayer, F. F., Wareing, S., & Rushton, J. P. Social constraints on naturally occurring preschool altruism. *Ethology and Sociobiology*, 1979, *1*, 3–11.

Strayer, J. A naturalistic study of empathic behaviors and their relation to affective states and perspective-taking skills in preschool children. *Child Development*, 1980, *51*, 815–822.

Suda, E., & Fouts, G. Effects of peer presence on helping in introverted and extroverted children. *Child Development*, 1980, *51*, 1272–1275.

Tonick, I. J., Gelfand, D. M., Hartmann, D. P., Cromer, C. C., & Millsapp, R. *A naturalistic study of children's prosocial behavior.* Paper presented at the meeting of the American Psychological Association, San Francisco, August 1977.

Yarrow, M. R., & Waxler, C. Z. Dimensions and correlates of prosocial behavior in young children. *Child Development*, 1976, *47*, 118–125.

# 6

# Parent Discipline, Moral Internalization, and Development of Prosocial Motivation

Martin L. Hoffman

## 1. INTRODUCTION

In most research on prosocial behavior the actor is an innocent bystander. Of equal importance are situations in which the actor is the cause of the other's distress. I have for some time been dealing with both contexts. Regarding the first, I have put together a theory of the development of empathy (see Hoffman, 1982, for the most recent version) that includes several modes of empathic affect arousal and several stages of social-cognitive development. The empathic arousal modes combine with the social-cognitive stages, and the result is four developmental levels of empathic distress that I believe may account for the individual's motivation to help in the innocent-bystander context. Regarding situations in which the actor is the cause of the other's misfortune, I use as a framework the development of an internal moral orientation in which guilt is the major moral motive.

Psychologists have long been intrigued with moral internalization, probably because it epitomizes a central problem of human existence—

MARTIN L. HOFFMAN • Department of Psychology, University of Michigan, Ann Arbor, Michigan 48109.

that of how individuals come to manage the inevitable conflict between their own personal needs and social obligations. The legacy of Freud and Durkheim is the agreement among social scientists that most people do not go through life viewing society's moral norms as external, coercively imposed pressures to which they must submit. Although the norms may initially be external to the individual and often in conflict with his desires, they may eventually to some extent become part of the person's motive system and guide his behavior even in the absence of external authority.

Previous theories of how moral internalization develops appear to have certain limitations (see Hoffman, 1983), although some of the concepts do bear on important aspects of moral internalization, and modified versions of these concepts are included in my own theoretical formulation. In this formulation I attempt to identify a particular norm and to pin down the socialization setting and the child's experience in that setting that may be necessary for internalization of that norm. The current version, still incomplete, which I shall summarize here, is a focused and systematic information-processing analysis that highlights the affects and cognitions generated in discipline encounters, speculates about how these affects and cognitions are organized and retained in memory, and suggests the implications for moral motivation and moral action.

Before presenting the theory, I shall briefly define what I mean by moral internalization, explain why I think discipline is especially important in its development, and summarize the pertinent research.

## 2. MORAL INTERNALIZATION AND MORAL MOTIVATION

The moral norm at issue here is simply that people should act out of consideration for the needs of others, as well as their own needs. Examples of morally prescribed acts are telling the truth, keeping a promise, and helping. Examples of proscribed acts are deceiving others, lying, stealing, betraying a trust, inflicting physical harm, or hurting another's feelings. A moral norm is usually viewed as internalized when the person feels an obligation to act in accord with it even in the absence of any concern about being caught and punished for doing otherwise. This formulation may obscure the fact that in most moral encounters or temptation situations a motive to behave in an egoistic, self-serving way is also present (e.g., one is excited about going to a new movie but then remembers one's promise to visit a sick friend). For the moral norm to have an effect, it must be able to compete with the egoistic motive, which means that the norm, too, must have motive force. The activation of a moral norm or motive does not guarantee moral action, since the egoistic motive may be more powerful, but it does assure the existence of a moral conflict, and if the egoistic motive prevails the person may be expected to pay the price of feeling guilty.

Moral norms also have a cognitive component that becomes increasingly complex with age. Included are a person's representations of the consequences that his actual or anticipated behavior may have for someone else, his awareness of prohibitions against acting in ways that may harm others, his judgments about the rightness or wrongness of particular acts and the reasons underlying these judgments. Also included are cognitive elaborations, such as the idea that it is especially wrong to harm someone smaller, weaker, and more helpless than oneself; or to harm someone without any provocation or justification; or to retaliate for a hurt if the other person was only trying to help; or to retaliate excessively.

If a person has internalized a moral norm, then when it is activated it is usually experienced as deriving autonomously from within the self. That is, the cognitive dimensions of the norm, the associated affect (guilt), and the disposition to act in accord with the norm are experienced as self-generated. The original source of the norm, for example, the parent, has lost most or all of its motive force and may be forgotten. The question for development psychology is: What prior socialization experiences are central in the development of an internalized, autonomous moral norm or motive? The answer, I believe, lies in the child's experiences in discipline encounters with parents.

## 2.1. Why Is Discipline Important?

The special importance of discipline, as compared to other parent behaviors, can be grasped by considering what people who have internalized the norm of considering others do when the moral requirements of a situation are in conflict with their desires of the moment. To the degree that a person has internalized the norm he will weigh his desires in relation to the welfare of others, without regard to external sanctions. And when he violates the norm he will have the unpleasant affective reaction of guilt. The central conflict in the moral encounter, then, is between the person's desires and the moral norm applicable in the situation. Consider, for example, what happens when a person who is tempted to see a movie is reminded of his promise to visit a sick friend. To the extent that he is internalized he will not only want to see the movie but will also feel an urge to visit the friend. He may feel some anticipatory guilt as he contemplates going to the movie. And if he does go, he will almost certainly feel guilty.

The developmental question is: What past experiences make a person vulnerable to such a conflict? One obvious answer lies in the kind of experiences he had as a child when faced with a similar conflict—that between his desires of the moment and the requirements of the norm. The norm was then, of course, external to him, embedded in many of the physical and verbal messages from the parent regarding how the child should act—that is, in the parent's discipline techniques. Information pertinent to the cognitive dimensions of moral norms is also communicated to children outside discipline encounters, and this information may contribute to the child's moral-cognitive structure. Only in discipline encounters, however, are connections often made among the norm, the child's egoistic desires, and his behavior. Furthermore, it is only in discipline encounters that the child may have the earliest experience of being expected to control his deviant actions for reasons that derive from his own active consideration of these norms.

It is important to note here the evidence that discipline is a recurrent salient feature in the child's life. Although parents rarely discipline children in the first year (Moss, 1967; Tulkin & Kagan, 1972), by age 2 about two-thirds of parent–child interactions have been found to involve an attempt by the parent to change the child's behavior against his will (Minton, Kagan, & Levine, 1971). And in over 60% of these instances the children obeyed or were compelled by the parent to obey. Comparable data have been obtained with preschool-age children and with children up to 10 years old (Lytton, 1979; Schoggen, 1963; Simmons & Schoggen, 1963). Stated differently, young children appear to experience pressures from parents to change their behavior on the average of once every 6 to 7 minutes throughout their waking hours, and in most of these instances they end up complying.

In summary, in the pertinent discipline encounters the child acts or is tempted to act in a way that will have an adverse effect on someone else. The parent intervenes to change the child's behavior in accordance with the other person's needs. In moral encounters, too, the child acts or is tempted to act in a way that will adversely affect another. The similarity is obvious; the difference, of course, is that intervention is not necessary in the moral encounter if the child has internalized the norm, that is, if he is internally motivated to take the other's welfare into account. The processes mediating the shift from the discipline encounter, in which intervention is necessary, to the moral encounter, in which intervention is not necessary, are what the present theory attempts to explain.

### 2.2. Generalizations from Research

There is a rather large body of research indicating that (1) a moral orientation characterized by independence of external sanctions and by high guilt is associated with the frequent use of inductions (Hoffman, 1970a), discipline techniques that point up the effects of the child's behavior on others. (2) A moral orientation based on fear of external detection and punishment, on the other hand, is associated with the frequent use of power-assertive discipline—which includes physical force, deprivation of possessions or privileges, direct commands, or threats. There is evidence, however, (3) that the occasional use of power assertion to let the child know that the parent feels strongly about a particular act or value, or to control the behavior of a child who is acting in an openly defiant manner—by parents who usually employ inductions—may make a positive contribution to moral internalization (Hoffman, 1970b; Zahn-Waxler, Radke-Yarrow, & King, 1979). Finally, (4) there appears to be no relationship between moral internalization and love withdrawal—techniques in which the parent simply gives direct but nonphysical expression to his anger or disapproval of the child for engaging in some undesirable behavior (e.g., ignores the child, turns his back on him, refuses to speak or listen to him, explicitly states a dislike for the child, isolates or threatens to leave him). The bulk of this research was done with children from about 4 to 12 years old. There is recent evidence, however, that the generalization also holds up for children as young as 2 (Zahn-Waxler *et al.*, 1979).

## 3. AN INFORMATION-PROCESSING APPROACH TO DISCIPLINE AND MORAL INTERNALIZATION

There are two parts to my current theoretical analysis of how inductive discipline contributes to moral internalization. One deals with the child's affective and cognitive processes in discipline encounters especially when inductions are used. The other deals with what happens between discipline encounters, in which the parent intervenes, and later moral encounters or temptation situations, in which moral motives are aroused in the internalized child in the absence of an authority figure.

### 3.1. The Child's Affective and Cognitive Responses in Discipline Encounters

The speculations that follow are derived from Hoffman (1970a, 1977a, 1983).

#### *3.1.1. Optimal Level of Arousal*

Although the research describes discipline techniques in terms of the three categories mentioned earlier, the techniques actually used by parents are usually multidimensional. Thus all techniques are apt to have some power-assertive and love-withdrawal properties, since they all interrupt the child's ongoing act and communicate both a dissatisfaction with it and a desire that he do something else. Furthermore, even if power assertion and love withdrawal are not explicit in a particular discipline technique, the technique may nevertheless have an implicit power-assertive or love-withdrawal component owing to past discipline encounters in which the parent has made his or her displeasure more apparent. And some techniques also contain the informational content characteristic of inductions.

The multidimensionality of discipline techniques is also attributable to the fact that they usually have a nonverbal, emotional as well as a physical and verbal dimension. The parent can communicate anger, disapproval, hurt, or disappointment, for example, by changes in volume or tone of voice, facial expression, gaze, or posture. He can also communicate concern for the victim of the child's action by comforting the victim. These expressions of feeling interact with the verbal message and add another dimension to it; a raised voice may add a note of urgency—and perhaps a power-assertive overtone—to a verbal induction, and a hurt look may add an inductive dimension to a demand. Conversely, the emotion communicated to the child may be influenced by the verbal component. For example, an expression of moral outrage by the parent is more apt to be received as hostility toward the child's act rather than rejection of the child if it is accompanied by an explanation of what aspect of the child's behavior is being criticized.

The power assertion and love withdrawal together comprise what I call the *motive-arousal* component of the technique, which may often be necessary to get the child to change his behavior and, more important for present purposes, to pay attention to the parent. Having attended, the child will often be influenced cognitively and affectively by the information contained in the inductive component that may also be present, in a manner that I shall soon describe. First, it must be noted that if there is too little arousal, the child may simply ignore the parent. With too much arousal, that is, if the love withdrawal or power assertion is salient, several things may happen.

1. If power assertion is salient, the child may perceive a clear threat to his freedom of action, which may arouse the motive to restore freedom, or "reactance" (Brehm, 1972), as well as anger. Fears of punishment may also be aroused, however, and the child may therefore comply reluctantly and displace his anger toward less powerful figures outside the home (Bandura & Walters, 1959; Hoffman, 1960).

2. If love withdrawal is salient, this may not arouse reactance and anger but it does appear to arouse anxiety over the possible loss of the

parent's love. This anxiety may serve as a powerful motive for the child to comply in order to avoid that loss and restore harmony with the parent. Techniques with pronounced love-withdrawal components are often used when the child expresses anger toward the parent (Hoffman, 1970b), which may explain why love withdrawal appears to contribute to the inhibition of anger, if not to moral internalization (Hoffman, 1963; Hoffman & Saltzstein, 1967).

3. In either case the child's attention is directed to the consequences of his behavior for himself. Whether he complies or not, he is compelled to weigh the importance of his desired behavior against the anticipated punitive reaction of the parent. This should intensify any feeling of opposition between the child's desires and the moral standards reflected in the parent's demands, and thus accentuate his view of these standards as external to himself. More important for present purposes, the combination of reactance, anger, fear, and anxiety—which may be called "deviation anxiety"—that is aroused may prevent the child from effectively processing the information in any inductive component that may also be present in the technique. This is in keeping with the research on attention showing that high emotional arousal generally disrupts cognitive processing in such complex tasks as deriving meaning from verbal and other cues (Kahneman, 1973), and, more specifically, that it directs a person's attention to the physical features of verbal communications, with a relative neglect of semantic content (Mueller, 1979).

Thus there may be an optimal range of arousal for processing the information in the inductive component of a technique. Techniques with salient power-assertive and love-withdrawal properties will, for the reasons just mentioned, often exceed the optimal level. What happens when the inductive component predominates? First, the child's attention is directed to the consequences of his action for someone else rather than for himself. Second, the explanation given by the parent may lessen the arbitrary quality of the demand, hence diminish the likelihood of a reactance response by the child. Third, the punitive element is diminished considerably, since the explanation communicates that the parent is criticizing the child's act rather than rejecting the child, which should reduce the likelihood of an intense anxiety response. In short, techniques with pronounced inductive components focus on the child's action and its consequences, and allow the pressure put on the child and the source of the pressure to be low in salience. Although these techniques may arouse some concern over punishment and approval, it is apt to be far less intense than the deviation anxiety aroused by predominantly power-assertive and love-withdrawal techniques. Indeed, inductions may sometimes fall short of the optimal arousal level, although in general they should not since, as noted, virtually all discipline techniques are motive arousing to some extent. All things considered, the optimal level of arousal for processing information is more apt to be achieved by inductions than by other discipline techniques.

In some instances, such as emotionally charged situations and emergencies, excessive arousal may be avoided and the optimal arousal level achieved by delaying the inductive component of the discipline technique. For example, the parent may be highly power assertive because there is no time to do otherwise; afterward, when the situation has calmed, he may bring the matter up again and add an explanation. The child may process the information at that time, or later when he is alone. Thus the cognitive and affective responses to inductions may be part of the child's reaction during the discipline encounter, or may occur later.

### 3.1.2. *Cognitive Response to Induction*

Given an optimal level of arousal, the child may be expected to attend and process the information contained in the inductive portion of the discipline technique. He will as a result be more likely than with other techniques to perceive the causal connection between his action and the physical or psychological state of the victim, and, depending on the content of the induction, he may gain information about other dimensions of the norm against harming others. This information may be totally new to the child, or it may be a reminder of something he previously knew but overlooked in the situation.

It is necessary, of course, if the child is to have these responses, that the inductions are cast in terms that are within the child's cognitive and linguistic capabilities. Common sense tells us that parents would tend to do so, and there is some evidence that parents use more inductions and fewer power assertions as children get older (Chapman, 1979).

### 3.1.3. *Affective Response*

For a norm to have an internal obligatory quality, it must have affect associated with it—not the fear associated with the motive-arousal component of the discipline technique, which, as I noted, concerns the well-being of the self, but an affect that derives from the induction component and concerns the well-being of the victim of the child's actions. Since inductions direct the child's attention to the victim's pain or distress, they may frequently enlist just such an affect—a motivational resource that exists in the child from an early age, namely, the child's capacity for empathy, defined as a vicarious affective response to others. There is abundant evidence that when children as well as adults are witness to another's pain or discomfort they typically react with empathic distress. And, furthermore, the arousal of empathic distress operates like a positive social motive, that is, it predisposes the observer to help the victim (Hoffman, 1977a). (This is the point of connection between the present theory and my formulation about the development of empathy.)

Inductions also indicate that the child's action caused the other's pain or discomfort. This is important because young, even highly empathic children might simply empathize and cry along with the victim without realizing that they caused the victim's distress; or they may not be empathically aroused in certain contexts because their attention is directed toward other aspects of the situation such as competitive task demands (Levine & Hoffman, 1975). Older children may often not see their own causal role in another's distress for a different reason: Most of the situations in which they harm others are ambiguous as regards who is to blame, as in accidents and even in fights where it may seem as reasonable to blame the other as the self. Because of such ambiguity, it is easy for the child to project, rationalize, or use other cognitive strategies that facilitate blaming the other, or such perceptual strategies as turning away from the other.

Inductions are thus the techniques most likely to arouse both empathic distress and the awareness of being the causal agent of the other's plight. I have suggested elsewhere that the integration of empathic distress and awareness of being the causal agent produces a feeling of guilt. This is not the Freudian guilt based on repression of unacceptable impulses and transformation of the anxiety over loss of parental love associated with them. Rather, it is a feeling based on the awareness of actually harming someone in the present and the realization that this is wrong (Hoffman, 1976, 1982). I am suggesting further that this integration may not occur spontaneously in the young child and that intervention in the form of inductive discipline may usually be necessary. (This analysis is most applicable to those instances in which the victim of the child's act exhibits clear signs of being sad and downcast, hurt, or otherwise distressed. If the victim is angry and retaliates, the child may feel anger or fear rather than empathic distress and guilt.)

Suggestive evidence for the hypothesized contribution of empathy to guilt arousal was obtained by Thompson and Hoffman (1980). The subjects, first-, third-, and fifth-grade children, were shown stories on slides, which were also narrated by the experimenter, in which a story character does harm to another person. For example, a boy who accidentally bumps into another boy, scattering his newspapers, does not stop to help because he is in a hurry. Two guilt measures were used: (1) The subject was asked how he would feel if he were the story character who committed the transgression; and (2) the subject completed the story, and guilt scores were derived from the amount of guilt attributed to the culprit. Before administering the guilt measures, half the subjects were asked to tell how the *victim* in each story felt. The subjects in this empathy-arousing condition produced higher guilt scores than a control group who were not asked to think about the victim.

I have elsewhere presented in detail the evidence regarding the motivational property of guilt (Hoffman, 1976, 1980, 1982). Briefly, there is considerable experimental research showing that the arousal of guilt in adults leads to altruistic or reparative action, not only to the victim but to others as well. Furthermore, in the research involving story completion and guilt and in interview studies with 1960s social activists, there is evidence for long-range effects of guilt arousal in children and adolescents. That is, guilt arousal not only appears to contribute to future moral action but also at times seems to lead to a self-examination and reordering of one's priorities, including a resolution to act less selfishly and to consider the needs of others more often.

To summarize thus far, all discipline techniques arouse some concern about punishment and parental approval. If there is a pronounced power-assertive or love-withdrawal component, this concern is heightened and the child may feel intense fear or anxiety. His attention will in any case be directed to the consequences of his action for himself and he will have to consider whether to comply with the parent's wishes or risk the consequences of noncompliance. When techniques that have salient inductive components are used, these concerns are allowed to be less salient and, together with the child's desire to maintain harmony and good feeling with the parent, they may help ensure that the child acquires cognitions about the effects of his behavior on others, including causal connections between his actions and the physical and psychological state of others, and an increased awareness of various dimensions of the moral norm against harming others. These cognitions (together with any direct cues of distress from the victim) may trigger feelings of empathy and empathy-based guilt that give them a motivational quality.

It is worth noting that when the child changes his behavior in response to inductions, this is not so much compliance in the sense of submitting to someone, but rather a change in perspective resulting from the semantic processing of information.

### 3.2. What Happens between Discipline Encounters and Moral Encounters?

The child's affective and cognitive responses to inductions that I just described may be necessary for the development of an internalized moral orientation, but they are not sufficient. We must also explain how, from countless and varied discipline encounters, children acquire a fairly coherent set of cognitions that make up the norm of considering others and an internal, autonomous motive to act in accordance with the norm. How do children's cognitive and affective responses to the parent's inductions in early discipline encounters become transformed into internally generated moral motives that operate in later discipline encounters, and eventually in temptation situations and moral encounters when the parent is absent? How do children come to respond to distress cues (actual or anticipated) from victims or potential victims of their actions by generating their own guilt feelings and cognitive awareness of the norm they are violating? How do these affective and cognitive responses become integrated, and dissociated enough from the discipline encounters to be experienced by children as their own?

Some time ago I suggested casting this problem in memory terms (Hoffman, 1970a), and recent developments in memory research are in keeping with that idea, notably Tulving's (1972) distinction between semantic and episodic memory and Craik and Lockhart's (1972) depth-of-processing approach. According to Craik and Lockhart, the extent to which a stimulus persists in memory depends on the level at which it was processed when initially presented. There are basically three levels of processing that operate successively. First, there is a simple level of sensory registration of the stimulus. This is followed by a perceptual level involving matching or pattern recognition of the stimulus, and finally by a deep, semantic level in which the stimulus is enriched by being associated with past images and cognitive structures. This deep semantic level is more apt to be called forth by relatively complex, information-containing communications than by simple stimuli (although if the subject is given a semantic-organizational set it may be applied even to simple stimuli).

Craik and Lockhart argue that since organisms are normally concerned primarily with the extraction of meaning from stimulu it is advantageous to store the products of deep semantic analysis, whereas there is usually little or no need to store the products of the relatively shallow sensory and perceptual analyses. It follows that stimuli that require the semantic level of analysis will ordinarily be remembered far longer than stimuli that require only the shallower levels. The informational content of a communication that requires the semantic level should then be retained longer than other aspects of the communication that do not. The implications of this formulation for our purposes are obvious, since inductions should provide more appropriate arousal conditions and stimuli that require a deeper level of processing than other types of discipline. It thus seems reasonable to assume that the informational content of inductions, which corresponds to the cognitive dimensions of the moral norm described earlier, is ordinarily processed semantically. Over time, in numerous discipline encounters, the cognitive dimensions are presumably organized cumulatively by the child and integrated in an increasingly complex structure—possibly but not necessarily hierarchically organized—that comprises his emerging moral norm regarding how one should, and should not, act toward others.

Those other aspects of inductions that contribute little to their meaning, such as the exact words and sentence structure employed, the fact that they originated with the parent, and the physical setting in which they occurred, will be processed in a relatively shallow manner. Consequently, they may provide little or no interference with the cumulative organization of the child's cognitive-normative structure, and, furthermore, as this cognitive-normative structure develops it may become increasingly dissociated in the child's mind from its origins in discipline encounters. The result is that in future situations in which the child harms another or contemplates acting in ways that might harm another, he or she may be reminded of the norm whether or not the parent or anyone else is present to point it out.

Craik and Lockhart also introduce another concept useful for our purposes, namely, the "awareness of potential for interpretation." According to Craik and Lockhart, a person may, when exposed to a verbal message, defer interpreting it although he recognizes that it has meaning. This concept is in keeping with my earlier suggestion that the child may at times process the information contained in inductions retrospectively, after the discipline encounter has ended.

### 3.2.1. *Processing Guilt*

The analysis thus far has been confined to the child's processing of the cognitive dimensions of his experience in discipline encounters, which is in keeping with the neglect of affect in the memory research. Also important is how the child's affective responses in the discipline encounter—especially guilt feelings—are encoded in memory and evoked in moral encounters or temptation situations that occur later on. There are several possibilities, all of which are compatible with the hypothesis that the guilt feeling derives from the moral cognitions produced by the child's processing of inductive information. These speculations will be brief since there is very little in the literature on which to draw.

One possibility is that the guilt feeling is encoded in memory in the discipline encounter together with the moral cognitions that gave rise to it. Later on, in situations in which the child harms another or contemplates acting in ways that may harm another, these moral cognitions are evoked and they then trigger the guilt feelings more or less in the same manner that they did in the discipline encounter. This sequence suggests a general model in which the memory for an effect is tied to the cognition that gives rise to it—a model that gives primacy to cognition.

Another possibility is that although guilt feelings may derive from a cognitive product of the child's information processing in the discipline encounter (from the child's awareness that his or her actions have harmed someone), the guilt feelings may not be *encoded* together with that cognitive product. Although evoked as the result of cognitive processing, once evoked the guilt feeling may have a life of its own so far as how it is stored and remembered is concerned. For example, the guilt feelings may be associated, hence encoded, not with the words and ideas that gave rise to them but with the kinesthetic cues associated with the child's deviant act or with a visual image of the event—perhaps the distress cues from the victim made salient by the parent's induction. Future moral encounters or temptation situations in which the child's action produces the same kinesthetic cues or that contain similar picture images (e.g., anticipated crying by a potential victim of one's actions) may then evoke the guilt feeling. The guilt feeling may then in turn contribute to "recall" of the associated moral cognitions. This might occur, for example, if the encoding and retrieval of kinesthetic cues or picture images are especially swift, as seems possible.

This second model, which implies an affective rather than a cognitive primacy, is in keeping with Zajonc's (1980) conclusion, based on a review of the adult memory research, that affect is encoded more quickly and efficiently, stored separately, and retained in memory longer than cognition. The model is also in keeping with Bower's (1981) finding that the subject's mood in recall situations serves as a cue that facilitates retrieval of cognitions acquired when the subject was in the same mood and that are pertinent to that mood. If we think of guilt as a mood state, then the guilt evoked in the moral encounter should bring to mind the cognitions that were pertinent to the guilt aroused in discipline encounters.

A third possibility is that the guilt feeling and moral cognitions are not encoded separately. Instead, once guilt feelings are aroused in discipline encounters the accompanying moral cognitions are suffused with guilty affect and become "hot cognitions" whose affective and cognitive features are inseparable. These hot cognitions are then encoded in memory and eventually experienced in temptation situations as an affective-cognitive unity.

These three models of how moral affects and cognition are encoded in discipline encounters and retrieved and utilized in moral encounters may not exhaust the possibilities, but they do suggest directions for research. It may turn out that only one model applies or that they all operate, with individuals differing as to which is predominant. It is also possible that the processes described in all three models are employed by everyone, with situational factors determining which one or more are called into play at any given time. For example, if distress cues from the victim are salient, then guilt may be the first thing to be evoked. If, on the other hand, the moral conflict is articulated verbally, the pertinent moral cognitions may be evoked first. Clearly, more research is needed before we can speak with authority on this topic.

### *3.2.2. Moral Internalization and "Self-Attribution"*

Owing to the power of semantic organization in memory, children may not only be reminded of the moral norm and feel some compulsion to act in accordance with it when they act in a potentially harmful way even in the parent's absence, but they may also forget the many discipline-encounter settings in which they were first exposed to the norm. We may ask whether similar processes can explain the fact noted earlier that children are often unaware that their parents rather than themselves are the source of the norms they internalize. It may seem strange that children often do forget this, since parents are probably the major invariants across discipline encounters as well as being so affectively important to the child. We might therefore expect the image of the parents to be permanently connected to the induction content in the child's memory.

It must be noted, however, that the relation between parent image and induction content is a simple associationistic one. The parent's image is not *semantically* related to the induction content, which pertains to the causal relation between the child's action and the well-being of others. Although the parent provides the information and the motivation for the child to process it, as noted in our earlier discussion, when inductions are used it is typically the induction content that is made salient, not the parent. The parent's image may therefore not ordinarily be part of what the child semantically organizes in discipline encounters.

The parent's affective value to the child is high in all interactions, not just discipline encounters, so it should not contribute to making discipline encounters particularly salient and memorable especially when inductions are used. The child's image of the parent may therefore not only lack a semantically meaningful connection to the moral ideas, it may also lack a distinctive affective tie to the discipline encounters in which the moral ideas were generated. Consequently, although the child may remain fully aware of the parent's existence, there may eventually be little or no connection in the child's mind between the parent and the induction or moral-norm content, and, increasingly as the child gets older, he or she may thus lack an external referent to the norm.

Having no external agent to whom to attribute the norm, to whom should the child be expected to attribute it? One possibility is that children, who are known to have a tendency to externalize (they often externalize blame, for example), will show great ingenuity in coming up with some other external agent to account for the norm. As already noted, however, a characteristic of internalized norms is that they are often experienced as emanating from the self. Self-attribution theory suggests a reason for this: If the external sources of one's actions and thoughts are salient, unambiguous, and sufficient to explain them, then the person attributes them to these external agencies. But if the external sources are not perceived, or if they are unclear or invisible, it is assumed that children as well as adults will attribute their actions and thoughts to themselves (e.g., Lepper & Greene, 1975). Similarly, without an external agent to whom to attribute the moral norm, the child may then be expected to experience it as originating from within the self.

There is another, perhaps more compelling, reason for expecting the child to attribute the norm to the self. The child's mental activity—semantically organizing the induction content—is apt to make his or her own internal processes highly salient. The mental activity is also semantically related to the induction content (the child is thinking about the connection between his act and the victim's condition, or the way in which his act relates to some cognitive dimension of the moral norm). Under these conditions it seems reasonable to expect the child over time not only to loosen the connection between the parent's image and the induction content but also eventually to perceive himself, rather than the parent, as the source of the information in inductions, hence as the source of the norm. I do not mean here that the child consciously attributes the origin of the norm to the self. Metacognitive operations such as these apparently come fairly late in development, at around 6 years. Even after that, however, the child may not think about where the cognitions came from, but simply experience them as thoughts that occur spontaneously.

### 3.3. Introduction of the Moral Dimension in Early Discipline Encounters

Thus far I have been describing what goes on in discipline encounters and afterward as a continuous process, without inquiring into the origins, that is, the earliest instances in which children are exposed to inductions, before they can be said to have internalized any moral norm.

To speculate about origins intelligently, we need to know the cognitive and affective capabilities that young children bring to discipline encounters. At what age is the child capable of processing and storing information in the manner I described? When does the child possess the necessary developmental prerequisites of guilt—the capacity for empathy, the sense of the other as distinct from the self, the causal schemata—and how does the parent relate the induction information to them?

The research suggests that by age 2 the child has an empathic capability, an awareness of others as physical entities distinct from the self, and an emerging awareness that they have inner states (thoughts, feelings, perceptions) independent of one's own (Hoffman, 1977b). As for the necessary causal schemata, Piaget's work (1976) suggests that just a few months after birth children discover simple causal connections through their own physical action. Gunnar (1980) found evidence that 1-year-old children respond to objects with different emotions depending on whether or not they can control the movement of the object. This indicates that they have some sense of having an impact on the physical environment. And I have elsewhere presented anecdotal evidence that children under age 2, when in natural settings and properly motivated, are clearly aware of the impact of their actions on others and can use this awareness in helping or manipulating others (Hoffman, 1975). Although these findings are not definitive, it does appear reasonable to conclude tentatively that children do have the requisite schemata for processing the information in simple inductions and responding cognitively and affectively, as I hypothesized earlier, by about the same time that parents begin to discipline their children in earnest, which, as noted, is sometime in the second year. Perhaps this explains the finding of Zahn-Waxler *et al.* (1979) that the use of inductions relates positively to consideration for others in children under 2 years.

We can now speculate about those early discipline encounters. First, it seems safe to assume that for an induction to be effective at that early age it must be very simple, perhaps doing nothing more than to point up the harmful physical effects of the child's behavior on someone. If the explanation is something the child can comprehend, and assuming of course that the child is properly aroused and attends, we may then expect him to integrate its content (e.g., the cause–effect relation between his act and the well-being of another person) with his own causal schema. The result is that the newly enriched schema has the beginnings of a moral-cognitive dimension that it previously lacked. The child may also be expected to react with feelings of empathy and empathy-based guilt. (These feelings may sometimes be further enhanced by exposure to direct distress cues from the victim.) As a result, the newly emerging, rudimentary moral schema is infused with these moral affects. They are then presumably encoded in memory and activated in the next discipline encounter, and the process is repeated. In this way children's simple, at first nonmoral, cognitive structures may be gradually transformed, through their experience in countless discipline encounters, into structures that have the moral-cognitive dimensions and affective-motivational quality that characterize internalized moral norms.

### 3.4. Relation to Development of Empathy

There are some connections between the position developed thus far and my notions about empathic development. First, in early discipline encounters in which the parent uses inductions, empathic distress is aroused in the child, and the combination of empathic distress and awareness of being the cause of the other's plight produces a guilt feeling. It is the guilt feeling that provides the motive base for prosocial action when one is *not* an innocent bystander. Second, the level of empathic distress aroused in the discipline encounter corresponds to the four levels of empathic distress I have outlined elsewhere. The levels of guilt aroused in the discipline encounter should also correspond to these four levels, which I shall summarize briefly here.

First, before the child is aware of others as separate physical entities, he responds to simple expressions of pain by others with a confused empathic distress. He also responds at times with a rudimentary guilt feeling, even though he may lack a keen sense of being the causal agent (e.g., Zahn-Waxler *et al.*, 1979). Second, once he knows that others are separate entities, he experiences empathic distress when observing someone who is physically hurt; and his empathic distress may be transformed into guilt if his own actions were responsible for the hurt. Third, once the child is aware that others have inner states, the empathic distress he experiences in the presence of someone having painful or unhappy feelings may be transformed into guilt if his actions were responsible for those feelings. Fourth, once the child is aware of the identity of others beyond the immediate situation, his empathic response to their general plight may be transformed into guilt if he feels responsible for their plight.

Although empathic distress is here viewed as a prerequisite for the development of guilt, it seems likely that guilt may eventually become largely independent of its empathic origin. In some situations, for example, those in which the victim is visibly sad or hurt, guilt may continue to be accompanied by empathic distress. In others, however, this may not be so. At some point in development, the awareness of being the causal agent of another's misfortune may be enough to trigger guilt feelings without empathy. Thus, although empathic distress may be a necessary factor in the *development* of guilt, it may not always be an inevitable accompaniment of guilt.

It seems likely, moreover, that once the capacity for guilt is attained, especially guilt over inaction (e.g., over not helping someone in need), the main influence may occur conversely. That is, guilt may become a part of all subsequent responses to another's distress, at least in situations in which one might have helped but did not. From then on, even as an innocent bystander, one may rarely experience empathic distress without some guilt. The line between empathic distress and guilt thus becomes very fine, and being an innocent bystander is a matter of degree. To the degree that one realizes that one could have acted to help but did not, one may never feel totally innocent. This is another way of saying that empathy and guilt may be the quintessential social motives, since they may transform another's pain into one's own discomfort and make one feel partly responsible for the other's plight whether or not one has actually done anything to cause it.

## 4. SUMMARY AND CONCLUDING REMARKS

Here is a summary of my analysis of what happens in discipline encounters and afterward: (1) Most discipline techniques have power-assertive and love-withdrawal properties, which comprise the motive-arousal component needed to get the child to stop what he or she is doing and pay attention to the inductive component that may also be present. (2) Too little arousal and the child may ignore the parent; too much arousal and the resulting fear, anxiety, or resentment may prevent effective processing of the inductive component of the technique, as well as direct the child's attention to the consequences of his action for the self. Techniques that have a salient inductive component should ordinarily achieve the best balance and direct the child's attention to the consequences of his action for the victim. (3) The child may then process the information in the inductive component. The cognitive products of this processing constitute knowledge about the cognitive dimensions of the moral norm against harming others. (4) Processing the information in the inductive component should also often arouse empathy and empathy-based guilt—affects known to have prosocial motivational properties. (5) The cognitive products of the information processing are hypothesized as being semantically organized and encoded in memory, and activated, modified, and integrated with similar information provided by inductions in countless discipline encounters over time. The source of the information—the discipline-encounter setting—is organized separately in a shallower mode. It interferes minimally with the semantic organization and may be soon forgotten. (6) The prosocial affects that continue to be associated with the cognitive products in one or more ways are seen as providing the necessary internal motive base. (7) Owing to the child's active role in processing the information, as well as the differential memory for idea content and setting, the child may eventually experience the moral cognitions and affects generated in discipline encounters as deriving from the self. I have also suggested how the young child's simple, initially nonmoral cognitive structures and causal schemata may be gradually transformed through the processing of information in many discipline encounters into structures that have the moral-cognitive and affective-motivational properties of internal moral motives.

It should be clear that this formulation does not deal with the totality of morality but with the early development of an internalized motive to consider the needs of others. Although the entire focus of my analysis has been on parental discipline, I believe that other experiences of the child outside the discipline encounter are also important. For example, given the early motivational base discussed here, the child is apt to be receptive to inductionlike communications from authority figures and from peers outside the home. These communications should help expand the domain in which the child's motive is applicable. This domain may also be expanded as the child acquires language and social-cognitive (e.g., role taking) skills of increasing sohpistication, so that he can comprehend the effects of his actions on others beyond and long after the immediate situation, or anticipate the effects ahead of time. It is true that social cognition and language are neutral skills that bear more directly on moral competence than on moral motivation; these skills can be useful in manipulating as well as benefiting others. But if the child has developed an early motive to consider others, he may be expected to employ these skills more often in the service of benefiting others. The same may be true of children's increasing ability to learn by observing others. If children are motivated to consider others, they should be selective in their observational learning, more apt to pick up ways of acting morally than immorally.

Finally, insofar as the motive to consider others persists into adolescence, the individual may be more receptive to certain moral as well as political and economic ideologies—perhaps those pertaining to victims and other distressed people. In adopting these ideologies, another, as yet unmentioned, internalized mechanism may come into play. According to Erikson (1970) and other contemporary psychoanalytic writers (see review in Hoffman, 1980), some adolescents may, in the face of overwhelming evidence from the adult world, become disillusioned with the moral beliefs and values acquired in childhood. They may then become strongly motivated to search for moral concepts or an ideology that resolves the conflict. I would suggest that to the extent that a person is morally motivated and actively involved in constructing such an ideology, he or she may be expected to feel personally bound to it and try to act in accordance with it, and thus to internalize it. The individual's new moral viewpoint may be considered an advancement because it incorporates certain social realities previously ignored. These ideologies that the individual constructs thus become part of his or her moral motive system, rather than being adopted as abstract modes of thought lacking a motive base. In other words, the simple moral motive discussed in this chapter may provide a motive base for ideological commitment (see Hoffman, 1980, for an extended discussion of this point).

I have suggested the antecedent factors that may lead to the development of an early moral motive to consider others. Later experiences of various kinds may expand this motive to other areas of life, provide skills and competences that serve the motive, and built upon it to create complex moral ideational structures.

## 5. REFERENCES

Bandura, A., & Walters, R. H. *Adolescent aggression.* New York: Ronald Press, 1959.

Bower, G. H. Mood and memory. *American Psychologist,* 1981, *36,* 129–148.

Brehm, J. W. *Responses to loss of freedom: A theory of psychological reactance.* Morristown, N.J.: General Learning, 1972.

Chapman, M. Listening to reason: Children's attentiveness and parental discipline. *Merrill-Palmer Quarterly,* 1979, *25,* 251–263.

Craik, F. I. M., & Lockhart, R. R. Levels of processing: A framework for memory research. *Journal of Verbal Learning and Verbal Behavior,* 1972, *11,* 671–684.

Erikson, E. H. Reflections on the dissent of contemporary youth. *International Journal of Psychoanalysis,* 1970, *51,* 11–22.

Gunnar. M. R. Control, warning signals, and distress in infancy. *Developmental Psychology,* 1980, *16,* 281–289.

Hoffman, M. L. Power assertion by the parent and its impact on the child. *Child Development,* 1960, *31,* 129–143.

Hoffman, M. L. Parent discipline and the child's consideration for others. *Child Development,* 1963, *34,* 573–588.

Hoffman, M. L. Moral development. In P. H. Mussen (Ed.), *Carmichael's handbook of child psychology* (Vol. 2). New York: Wiley, 1970. (a)

Hoffman, M. L. Conscience, personality, and socialization techniques. *Human Development,* 1970, *13,* 90–126. (b)

Hoffman, M. L. Developmental synthesis of affect and cognition and its implications for altruistic motivation. *Developmental Psychology,* 1975, *11,* 607–622.

Hoffman, M. L. Empathy, role-taking, guilt and development of altruistic motives. In T. Likona (Ed.), *Moral Development: Current theory and research.* New York: Holt, Rinehart & Winston, 1976.

Hoffman, M. L. Moral internalization: Current theory and research. In L. Berkowitz (Ed.), *Advances in experimental social psychology* (Vol. 10), New York: Academic Press, 1977. (a)

Hoffman, M. L. Empathy, its development and prosocial implications. In C. Keasey (Ed.), *Nebraska Symposium on Motivation* (Vol. 25). Lincoln: University of Nebraska Press, 1977. (b)

Hoffman, M. L. Moral development in adolescence. In J. Adelson (Ed.), *Handbook of adolescent psychology*. New York: Wiley-Interscience, 1980.

Hoffman, M. L. Is altruism part of human nature? *Journal of Personality and Social Psychology*, 1981, *40*, 121–137.

Hoffman, M. L. Development of prosocial motivation: Empathy and guilt. In N. Eisenberg-Berg (Ed.), *Development of prosocial behavior*. New York: Academic Press, 1982.

Hoffman, M. L. Affective and cognitive processes in moral internalization: An information processing approach. In E. T. Higgins, D. Ruble, & W. Hartup (Eds.) *Social cognition and social development: A socio-cultural perspective*. New York: Cambridge University Press, 1983.

Hoffman, M. L., & Saltzstein, H. D. Parental discipline and the child's moral development. *Journal of Personality and Social Psychology*, 1967, *5*, 45–57.

Kahneman, D. *Attention and effort*. Englewood Cliffs, N.J.: Prentice-Hall, 1973.

Lepper, M. R., & Greene, D. Turning work into play: Effects of adult surveillance and extrinsic rewards on children's intrinsic motivation. *Journal of Personality and Social Psychology*, 1975, *28*, 129–137.

Levine, L. E., & Hoffman, M. L. Empathy and cooperation in four-year-olds. *Developmental Psychology*, 1975, *11*, 533–534.

Lytton, H. Disciplinary encounters between young boys and their mothers and fathers: Is there a contingency system? *Developmental Psychology*, 1979, *15*, 256–268.

Minton, C., Kagan, J., & Levine, J. Maternal control and obedience in the two-year-old. *Child Development*, 1971, *42*, 1873–1894.

Moss, H. Sex, age, and state as determinants of mother–infant interaction. *Merrill-Palmer Quarterly*, 1967, *13*, 19–26.

Mueller, J. H. Anxiety and encoding processing in memory. *Personality and Social Psychology Bulletin*, 1979, *5*, 288–294.

Piaget, J. *The grasp of consciousness*. Cambridge: Harvard University Press, 1976.

Schoggen, P. Environmental forces in the everyday lives of children. In R. G. Barker (Ed.), *The stream of behavior: Explorations of its structure and content*. New York: Appleton-Century-Crofts, 1963.

Simmons, H., & Schoggen, P. Mothers and fathers as sources of environmental pressure on children. In R. G. Barker (Ed.), *The stream of behavior: Exploration of its structure and content*. New York: Appleton-Century-Crofts, 1963.

Thompson, R., & Hoffman, M. L. Empathy and the development of guilt in children. *Developmental Psychology*, 1980, *16*, 155–156.

Tulkin, S. R., & Kagan, J. Mother–infant interaction in the first year of life. *Child Development*, 1972, *43*, 31–42.

Tulving, E. Episodic and semantic memory. In E. Tulving & W. Donaldson (Eds.), *Organization of memory*. New York: Academic Press, 1972.

Zahn-Waxler, C. J., Radke-Yarrow, M. R., & King, R. M. Childrearing and children's prosocial initiations toward victims of distress. *Child Development*, 1979, *50*, 319–330.

Zajonc, R. B. Feeling and thinking: Preferences need no inferences. *American Psychologist*, 1980, *35*, 151–175.

# 7

# Focus of Attention and Altruism

## Endocentric and Exocentric Sources of Altruistic Behavior

Jerzy Karylowski

### 1. INTRODUCTION

In recent years several attempts have been made to describe motivational mechanisms underlying altruistic behavior and various mechanisms have been proposed (see Karylowski, 1977, 1982a, for a review). There now seems to be an emerging consensus that altruism is a polimotivated phenomenon and that one-factor theories are insufficient (cf. Bar-Tal, 1976; Piliavin, Dovidio, Gaertner, & Clark, 1981; Reykowski, 1975, 1979; Rushton, 1980; Staub, 1978).

The multiplicity of the suggested mechanisms makes searching for the determinants of altruism a complex task. The most obvious strategy might be to acknowledge those altruistic behaviors that are motivated by different mechanisms as separate, only spuriously similar phenomena, and to study them separately. This strategy, however, would be very difficult to apply. Our ability to distinguish between various altruistic motivations on the empirical level is very weak, not only because a single act of altruistic behavior may be motivated simultaneously from

---

JERZY KARYLOWSKI • Department of Psychology, University of North Florida, Jacksonville, Florida 32216. Research reported in this chapter was done at the University of Warsaw as part of Project 11.8 sponsored by the Polish Academy of Sciences.

various sources (by various mechanisms), but also because of insufficient understanding of the differences between motivational mechanisms in question even at the theoretical level (cf. Karylowski, 1977, 1982a).

Faced with such a difficulty, most researchers tend to accept an oversimplified model of altruistic behavior that takes no account of the multiplicity of the underlying motivational mechanisms. Yet, strangely enough, such a global approach might be quite effective. Let us assume that a researcher attempts to study the origins of a tendency for altruistic behavior (e.g., a tendency to share) using a global approach. He may select a group of particularly generous subjects and compare them (e.g., with respect to various childhood data) to a group consisting of subjects low in generosity. Although the generous group will probably be highly heterogeneous with respect to underlying motivations for altruism (generosity), the study may nevertheless be successful. If it includes a sufficiently large sample and if sufficiently precise techniques of data collection and data analysis are applied, then, at least theoretically, the researcher has a chance to find out something about correlates of each kind of motivation for altruism that was overrepresented in his generous group (as compared to the group low in generosity).

The global strategy has its shortcomings, however. Although by using his theoretical thinking a researcher may *ex post facto* try to figure out which of the discovered factors are correlates (or determinants) of which of the potential motivational sources of altruism, his task would be a hazardous one. In fact, he can do little more than make a guess (and quite often he does not even attempt that much).

By using the global strategy it might also be difficult to discover those factors that, though facilitating certain motivational types of altruistic behavior (e.g., based on anticipatory guilt), do not facilitate and possibly even hinder other types (e.g., based on empathy). Depending on the kind of population from which our subjects are drawn, experimental settings, operationalization of altruistic behavior, and so on, a factor of that kind will be found to be positively related, not related at all, or even inversely related to altruism. Such inconsistent patterns of findings do in fact exist with respect to both developmental antecedences (e.g., the effect of love withdrawal on various indexes of altruism and moral development; see Hoffman, 1970a) and situational factors (e.g., the effect of negative affect on altruism; see Rosenhan, Karylowski, Salovey, & Hargis, 1981). This fosters doubts as to the comparability of results from different studies and considerably hinders the accumulation of knowledge in this respect.

But is there not the possibility of a compromise between the theoreticaly ideal but unrealistic strategy of studying each motivational kind of altruistic behavior independently, and the global strategy just described? I believe the possibility consists in assuming some, even rough, classification of the hypothetical motivational mechanisms underlying altruistic behavior and accepting such a classification as a starting point in both theoretical considerations and empirical research. The classification must fulfill certain conditions: First, it should concern the theoretically meaningful properties of mechanisms of interest, and second, it should be possible to apply it in empirical studies. As I have suggested elsewhere (Karylowski, 1975, 1977, 1982a), such a classification might be based on our knowledge of sources of gratification for altruistic behavior. It seems that once we exclude from analysis pseudoaltruistic behaviors that are controlled either by anticipations of external reinforcement (in the form of material rewards, material punishments, or social approval) or by nonspecific sources of motivation for helping (e.g., need for stimulation), only two kinds of sources of gratification are plausible. Thus "truly" altruistic helping behavior might be classified into two motivational types. *Endocentric* altruism refers to helping that derives from considerations concerning one's own self-image. That is, we help someone in order to feel better about ourselves or to avoid guilty feelings and other kinds of self-concept distress. One's altruistic behavior is endocentrically motivated to the extent it is controlled by anticipations of desirable changes or avoidance of undesirable changes in one's self-image. In *exocentric* altruism, on the other hand, the source of gratification lies only in the improvement of the conditions of another person in need. One's altruistic behavior is exocentrically motivated to the extent it is controlled by expectations of desirable changes or avoidance of undesirable changes in another person's situation.

The differences between endocentric and exocentric sources of altruism are further explained by the following example. Two hypothetical individuals, A and B, can both be considered highly altruistic persons, but A has a capacity for endocentric altruism only, B for exocentric altruism only. Let us further assume that each of these altruistic individuals meets another person, C, who is in need, but whose situation now improves. For A, such a change in the situation of C is rewarding only to the extent that A perceives that the change has been caused by his own helping action. For B, however, it hardly matters who or what has caused a desirable change to occur. What matters is his perception of the external situation and not of his own behavior in that situation.

I do not mean to suggest that purely endocentric or exocentric individuals in fact exist. But perhaps some individuals in their altruistic motivations are more endocentric, others more exocentric. Similarly, the chances are that a given act of altruistic behavior is usually motivated partly endocentrically and partly exocentrically (not to mention pseudo-altruistic components usually present); still, the proportional contribution of the two sources may vary. Moreover, the classification forms a convenient theoretical framework that easily incorporates the "clear-cut" mechanisms of altruistic behavior considered in different theories (cf. Karylowski, 1977, 1982a).

## 2. ENDOCENTRIC VERSUS EXOCENTRIC SOURCES OF ALTRUISM: THE MEASUREMENT OF INDIVIDUAL DIFFERENCES

I shall now present a psychometric technique (Karylowski, 1982b) that has been developed for measuring individual differences with respect to the altruistic motives in question.[1]

We considered those aspects of endocentric and exocentric motivations that should be reflected in consciousness. We assumed that activation of exocentric motivation is normally accompanied by conscious focusing on the partner, his states, needs, and feelings both present and anticipated. The decision to help in this case is controlled by the imagined partner's gratification or avoidance of loss. The case is different in endocentrism, where the whole situation is perceived first of all as a challenge to the self and an opportunity to verify one's moral assets, with the decision to help being controlled by thoughts and imaginations of future moral satisfaction (or by avoidance of guilt feelings and other forms of self-concept distress).

We decided to design our technique so that it would measure one bipolar variable (a tendency for endo- vs. exocentric altruism) rather than two separate unipolar variables (tendency for endocentric altruism and tendency for exocentric altruism). We suspected that the measurement of two separate variables would be largely contaminated by social approval, and that such a problem may be overcome with a single-dimension technique since both poles would then be loaded with social approval. We reasoned that in decision situations, both alternative choices—focusing on one's own moral standards and focusing on a partner's needs—would be socially approved. Using a single dimension has its disadvantages, however, as this technique can be reasonably used only with those subjects who are otherwise known as capable of altruistic behavior.

The technique, called the Prosocial Motivation Inventory (PMI), has a semiprojective character. It consists of seven short stories. In each case the hero is a girl student (a different one in each story). Each of the

[1]This measure was developed in collaboration with Hanna Gorska and Maria Wasiak.

stories describes a situation in which the girl is faced with a moral dilemma forcing her to decide whether or not to help another person. In each case helping would involve some psychological and/or material costs and there are no clear prospects for any external rewards. Each story is followed by a list of 24 items that enumerate various pros and cons of helping the person. The prohelping items are always listed in the

*Table 1. Sample Story Followed by a List of Items*[a]

Olga spent all afternoon clearing up the cellar. She was very surprised to find an old bicycle she had used when she was a child. It seemed that its condition wasn't too bad. It could still be used perfectly well. While looking at the bicycle, Olga wondered whether she could sell it. It seemed there were always a lot of people ready to buy such things. And some money would be very handy.

But then, Olga recalled the announcement she saw in yesterday's paper. For Child's Day, the Local Council had appealed for presents for children in its care—abandoned children from so-called problem families. Olga wondered what to do.

| I think I'll give the bicycle to those kids: | I think I won't give the bicycle to those kids: |
|---|---|
| ● I can imagine how they need to feel loved and remembered. | — If I were one of those kids I'd feel bad getting an old bicycle. |
| ● My bicycle will certainly give the kids a lot of fun. | — I'm sure a lot of people are going to respond to the appeal; my bicycle would get lost in the crowd. |
| ■ I wouldn't feel at peace with myself if I didn't do so. | — There's no other way I can get some cash and the money would be very handy. |
| ■ I'd feel terribly bad if I wasn't able to give up a bicycle. | — It's such a pain taking a bicycle to a collection; I'm too lazy. |
| ● They'll be happy to see that someone cares about them. | — Why should I be the only person to respond to the appeal. |
| ■ It wouldn't say much for me if I couldn't make some sacrifice for others. | — I really do need the money. |
| ■ If I didn't do so, I'd prove to be selfish; that would bother me for a long time. | — I hate all this charitable business. |
| ● I can imagine how sad those kids' life must be and how great any gift must seem to them. | — Everyone cares so much about money, why should I be different? |
| ■ I must learn to overcome my materialist attitude toward life. | — Nobody would ever recognize my good deed. |
| ■ I'll feel better about it if I take the bicycle to the collection. | — Their parents will take the gifts away from them and sell them, anyway. |
| ● I'm so sorry for those kids. | — I'd regret not getting the money. |
| ● Almost all kids dream of having a bicycle; I can imagine their fun. | — I hate such forced goodness. |

[a](●) exocentric; (■) endocentric.

left column of the answer form, and half of them are considered to be indicative of endocentric altruism and the other half of exocentric altruism. Both kinds of items have been arranged in random order. The items in the right column are all arguments against helping and serve as fillers.[2] A sample story followed by a list of items may be found in Table 1. Subjects are told to identify with the hero of the story and to choose in each story 5 to 10 items that they consider the most representative of the hero's thoughts and feelings in that situation. An index of the relative predominance of endocentric versus exocentric sources of altruism (a tendency to focus on the moral aspect of the self vs. on a partner) is the difference between the number of endocentric choices and the number of exocentric choices made by a given subject. The index is based on standardized frequencies.

The split-half reliability of the PMI is .65 ($n = 120$), which shows its moderate internal consistency. However, its stability over time is relatively high; the test–retest correlation after 2 years was $r = .61$ ($n = 41$).

The correlation with the Marlowe and Crowne Scale of Social Approval is nonsignificant; for two independent samples of $n = 133$ and $n = 56$ the correlations were $r = .14$ and $r = -.11$, respectively.[3] The correlation with the lie scale of Eysenck's Maundsley Personality Inventory MPI is also insignificant ($r = .13$; $n = 133$). On the other hand, moderate correlation with Szustrowa's (1976) scale measuring a generalized tendency for self-focused attention ($r = .37$; $n = 53$; $p = .01$) might be interpreted in terms of both discriminant and convergent validity.

## 3. CHILDREARING ANTECEDENCES OF ENDOCENTRIC AND EXOCENTRIC ALTRUISM

The development of endocentric and exocentric sources of altruistic behavior may be promoted by different socialization techniques. It even seems likely that certain childrearing techniques that make a child focus his attention on himself might promote the development of endocentric sources but inhibit the exocentric ones (see Karylowski, 1982a, for a detailed discussion). This could perhaps clarify some previous inconsistent findings on childrearing antecedences of moral behavior, especially

[2]There were two reasons for including fillers of this kind: (1) It was shown in the pilot studies that such fillers made the subject's task look more natural; and (2) as the pro- versus antihelping dichotomy is strongly loaded with social desirability, inclusion of antihelping fillers decreases the effect of social desirability upon choice of items from the prohelping list.

[3]In the case of the first sample we were also looking for a curvilinear correlation; however, no significant correlation was found.

concerning the effects of frequent use of love withdrawal (cf. Hoffman, 1970a).

In order to demonstrate some usefulness of the suggested approach and the theoretical validity of the PMI, I shall turn now to a study (Karylowski, 1982b) in which we attempted to find some childrearing antecedences of endocentric and exocentric altruism.[4]

The study was conducted in five stages. In the first stage, 235 high school girls age 16 to 19 were rated by their classmates on a trait defined as "nonprofit-making action on behalf of others." One hundred twenty girls who received at least average ratings passed to further selection, which had been made on the basis of the PMI scores. Two altruistic groups were finally selected, one endocentric ($n$ = 20) and one exocentric ($n$ = 18). The groups were equal with respect to age, socioeconomic status, birth order, and school grades.

In order to widen the interpretation of possible differences between the two types of altruism, a third group ($n$ = 20) was added that consisted of subjects rated by their peers as the least altruistic ones. (There was a slight although insignificant tendency for this group to score lower than the other two in school grades.)

In order to gather from subjects' mothers some retrospective data on the most frequently used childrearing techniques, a highly structured interview was used. The interviewers were not told which group the child belonged to. Data obtained during the interviews were rated by two independent judges.[5] In cases of disagreement a third judge was added who made the final decision. All ratings were blind.

In presenting the results it will help to focus first on the differences between the two altruistic groups on the one hand and the nonaltruistic group on the other. (Note that this resembles the global approach in which the multimotivational nature of altruism is totally ignored.) Here the findings are far from spectacular. Out of 14 socialization techniques analyzed, only in one case was the difference found significant. Mothers of altruistic girls reported a more frequent use than mothers of nonaltruistic girls of a rearing technique that consisted of suggesting to the child the possibility of a compromise between her interest and the interest of her partner (e.g., by suggesting that instead of fighting for an attractive toy they could play together or take turns). It seems that a systematic pointing to the possibility of such solutions decreases the perceived (as well as real) costs of altruistic acts. The child's own interest is not then set in clear opposition to the interest of the partner. This

[4]The study was conducted in collaboration with Anna Szuster and Lena Wojdan.

[5]The correlations between ratings given by the two judges ranged from $r = .76$ to $r = .96$ depending on the variable being rated.

strengthens the tendency to display altruistic behavior, independent of the underlying motivational mechanisms.

Results of comparisons between the two altruistic groups were much more pronounced. In line with our expectations, the mothers of endocentric girls scored higher in general than mothers of exocentric girls in the reported frequency of using those socialization techniques that focus the child's attention on herself (particularly on the moral aspect of the self). Significant differences were found for the following techniques: (1) love withdrawal[6] (e.g., refusal to talk to the child or remarks such as "I can't love you when you behave like this"); (2) labeling, especially in its open, indefinite form (e.g., "You behave so that one could think that you are a hooligan," "Only thieves take things that are not theirs");[7] (3) focusing the child's attention on inconsistencies between her behavior and demands of her social role (e.g., "Don't do it, as a girl you should be more understanding," "You are 6 already, but you behave like a little baby"); and (4) demanding that a child apologize. On the other hand, mothers of exocentric girls scored higher than mothers of endocentric girls in the reported frequency of using other-oriented induction, that is, indicating the consequences the child's behavior may have for her partner (e.g., "Look, the boy is sad and cries because you have taken his toy").

## 4. ENDOCENTRIC VERSUS EXOCENTRIC SOURCES OF ALTRUISM: AN EXPERIMENTAL APPROACH

The last two sections suggest that the relative predominance of endocentric versus exocentric sources of altruism may be treated as a trait variable that has its own childrearing antecedences. I shall now present a different approach and shall consider the relative predominance of endocentric versus exocentric sources as a state variable that can be experimentally manipulated.

[6]The more frequent use of love withdrawal by mothers of endocentric girls is in accordance with the results of a previous study by Hoffman (1970b). He has found that children whose moral judgment responses show rigid adherence to conventional norms report more frequent use of love withdrawal by their mothers than do (presumably more exocentric) children whose responses show more concern for the human consequences of behavior.

[7]Although mothers of endocentrics also scored higher than mothers of exocentrics in the reported frequency of using a definite form of labeling (e.g., "You are a bad kid," "You are an awful egoist"), the difference was insignificant. Perhaps an indefinite, open form of labeling may promote the development of endocentric altruism more effectively than a definite form simply because it suggests to the child that the negative evaluation she receives may easily change if only she changes her behavior.

Although in designing the technique for measuring the individual differences in relative predominance of endocentric versus exocentric sources (PMI) it was sufficient to assume that the focus of attention may be treated as an index of the relative predominance of these two sources, in experimental manipulation a more far-reaching assumption was needed. Such an assumption is that when manipulating the direction of attention we can modify the relative intensity of both kinds of motivational sources. More specifically, we assume that by focusing the subject's attention on the moral aspect of the self we will increase the relative predominance of the endocentric motivation.

The assumption is justified by the research findings that show that the prior activation of certain cognitions ("priming") increases the regulatory potential of those very structures that incorporate the cognitions. This results in increasing the role of these structures in the organization of perception and in information processing and, in consequence, in the regulation of other aspects of behavior (cf. Taylor & Fiske, 1978; Wyer & Srul, 1981).

Focusing attention on the moral aspect of the self is a form of what Duval and Wicklund (1972; Wicklund, 1975) call objective self-awareness or self-focused attention, and Berkowitz (1970, 1972) calls self-concern. According to Wicklund (1975), the state of self-focused attention tends to lead to spontaneous shifts from one aspect of the self to other situation-relevant aspects. Thus in a situation of conflict between one's own interest and the interest of the partner, producing self-focused attention with such nonspecific means as mirrors, listening to tape recordings of one's own voice, or television cameras (see Wicklund, 1975) may promote activation of endocentric sources of altruism.

Interestingly enough, more than a decade ago Berkowitz (1970) proposed that self-focused attention (self-concern) has a debilitating effect on altruism, mainly because it interferes with empathy. Empirical evidence, however, is scarce. The previous research by Berkowitz and his colleagues (cf. Berkowitz, 1970, 1972) and by Gibbons and his colleagues (Gibbons & Wicklund, 1982, Study 1, 2) in which such a help-decreasing effect of self-focused attention was found, leaves open the question of the specificity of the response decrement. What these studies have shown is a debilitating effect of the self-focused attention manipulation upon the amount of work done for a dependent partner. It is not clear, however, whether such a decrement is true only of altruistic behavior or of responding in general (e.g., owing to distractive aspects of self-focused attention manipulation or to the effects it has on subjective costs of working).

My point is that self-focused attention might well operate in two different directions. It may cause inhibition of exocentric sources of altruism but promote endocentric ones. Insofar as altruistic self-expectations are components of one's self-concept (real self or ideal self), they will have a stronger guiding effect upon behavior if the individual is in a state of self-focused attention.[8] Even if, in general, self-focused attention inhibits altruism, this effect should be weaker (or even reversed) the more important the relevant altruistic standards (self-expectations) are for one's self-concept.

An experimental study (Karylowski, 1979) was designed to test the above prediction. The study consisted of two ostensibly unrelated sessions. During the first preliminary session subjects were presented with a list of 20 desirable traits and asked to order them according to "how much you care to have this trait regardless of how strongly you have already developed it." Rank ascribed to the trait "not being an egoist, being helpful" was used as an index of subjective importance of altruistic standards (with respect to self-concept). In the second session, experimental in character, the experimental design was 2 × 2. The two independent variables were self-focused attention and level of the partner's dependency. The dependent measures were work for the partner's benefit and work on one's own behalf.

The experimental task required a special apparatus. When working on it each subject had an equal chance to earn money for himself and for a partner (a confederate). Thus it was possible to test which person (self, other, or both) was to lose or gain as a result of self-focused attention.

Actual trials were divided into two consecutive stages. At the outset of the trials the dependency manipulation was introduced. It was said that the other's earnings would be determined either by how much the subject scored for him (high dependency condition) or by a complex function of the performance of the given subject for his partner and the performance of several other subjects for their respective partners (low dependency condition). In order to introduce the self-focused attention variable, half of the subjects were exposed to a mirror image of themselves through the second stage of work (mirror condition) and the other half were not (no mirror condition).

The subjects were 112 high school boys, age 16 to 18. Their participation in the experiment was anonymous. The results can be summarized as follows:

1. A significant help-decreasing effect of self-focused attention was found. The effect was a specific one since no similar effect was obtained for self-helping (in fact, there was even a slight tendency to the op-

[8]This seems to be in line with Berkowitz's (1970) comment that self-focused attention (self-concern) may sometimes lead to greater helpfulness because "if [an individual] thinks of himself as a helpful person, he might act in a helpful manner in order to conform to his ideals and his self-conception" (p. 150).

posite, i.e., toward an increase in self-helping in consequence of self-focused attention).[9]

2. For low dependency conditions the help-decreasing effect was significantly related to the position ascribed to the standard of "not being an egoist, being helpful." The lower the help-decreasing effect of self-focused attention, the higher was the position of this standard. In the case of subjects who ascribed to this standard a position no lower than 5, there was even a tendency toward help-increasing effect of self-focused attention.

3. For high dependency conditions, the help-decreasing effect of self-focused attention was not related to the position of the standard in question.

The first result is in accordance with Berkowitz's (1970) claim. A possible interpretation is that it results from inhibition of exocentric (but not endocentric) sources of altruism. I would, therefore, expect this help-decreasing effect of self-focused attention to be rather unreliable across different populations and different experimental settings. The second result already points to one such limitation that does not, however, seem to be the only one. Another limitation may concern the problem of how salient in particular settings are those normative aspects of the situation that might be expected to promote the shift of self-focused attention to altruistic self-expectation (Berkowitz, 1972; Gibbons & Wicklund, 1982).[10]

The second result also corroborates our predictions as to the relationship between self-focused attention and endocentric sources of altruism, though for the low dependency condition only. The next section will seek to explain why the predictions were not met in the high dependency condition.

## 5. ENDOCENTRIC VERSUS EXOCENTRIC MOTIVATION AND PSYCHOLOGICAL REACTANCE

Lack of corroboration of our predictions in the high dependency condition made us suppose that activation of endocentric sources of

[9]Interestingly, the number of points scored for oneself was on average almost two times higher than number of points scored for a partner. This seems to corroborate the effectiveness of the safeguards used in the experiment against expectations of social approval as a motive for helping.

[10]Recent studies by Berkowitz and Miller (1980) and Rosenhan, Salovey, and Hargis (cited in Rosenhan *et al.*, 1981) suggest that still another limitation may concern affect. Self-focused attention seems to enhance altruism if an individual is in a positive affective state.

altruism does not always lead to an increase in consistency between altruistic self-expectations and overt altruistic behavior, simply because any form of self-focused attention may promote the occurrence of psychological reactance.

Being spontaneous and free of various "oughts" has become a crucial value of contemporary culture both in Europe and in North America (Jawlowska, 1975; Kohlberg, 1976). This value, when internalized, may take a form of specific self-expectations concerning personal freedom. As the self-focused attention tends to shift from one aspect of the self to other aspects (Wicklund, 1975), previous activation of self-expectations of any kind (including the altrustic ones) will make the activation of self-expectations of personal freedom more likely. When activated, they will counteract the "ought" feelings resulting from activation of altruistic self-expectations and will prevent these feelings from being actualized in the form of appropriate overt behavior. This seems to explain our third result in the preceding section quite well. In the high dependency condition (higher demand for help) rather than in the low dependency condition (lower demand for help), the subjective importance of being helpful may have different effects on the altruistic behavior of self-focusing individuals depending on the subjective importance of reactance-facilitating self-expectations. It may increase altruism in some individuals (those for whom the reactance-facilitating self-expectations play only a small role); in others (for whom such self-expectations play an important role) the resulting self-imposed threat to freedom (see Wicklund, 1974) may cause reactance and we may find an opposite relationship, namely, the higher the importance of altrustic standards the lower the altruism. A possible overall effect may be a total absence of correlation.

If the suggested interpretation is valid, then focusing attention on the moral aspect of the self (rather than on a partner) should result in an increase in consistency between self-expectations and overt altruistic behavior, but only in those individuals for whom the reactance-facilitating self-expectations are of relatively little importance. These implications were tested in a separate sutdy (Karylowski, 1979) that was of a pencil-and-paper character.

First, a relative predominance of endocentric versus exocentric sources of altruism was measured with the PMI.[11] Then, the subjective importance of the reactance-facilitating self-expectations was assessed by asking subjects to rank 20 descriptions of various desirable traits. As in the previous study, those traits were to be ranked in the order of "how much do you care to have this trait, regardless of how strongly you have already developed it." This time, however, two of the traits

[11]An earlier version of the PMI was used (see Karylowski, 1979, for details).

referred directly to personal freedom. One ("independence—not letting other people or external conditions control my behavior") emphasized independence from externally imposed threats to freedom; the other ("freedom—being somebody who always behaves as he wants to and not as he thinks he should") stressed independence from self-imposed threats to freedom. Ranks ascribed to these traits were considered measures of subjective importance of reactance-facilitating self-expectations.

Finally, each subject was asked to rate (on a 7-point scale) his sense of moral obligation to help a dependent other in 12 different situations. The situations were described in detail and formed a representative sample of different help-requiring situations in a student environment. At the same time the real behavior of the subject in each situation was rated on a 7-point scale by six or seven peers who were best acquainted with the given subject. The raters were asked to base their estimations on their knowledge of the typical behavior of the rated subject in similar situations. Thus information on the consistency between subject's altruistic self-expectations and her overt behavior was obtained by comparing her declarations as to how she felt she should behave in various help-provoking situations with peers' ratings of her actual behavior in such situations. A global index of consistency based on 12 different situations was used in the analysis.

The study included 110 female students age 18 to 22. The final analysis, however, was performed on 52 subjects only who were rated by their peers as at least moderately altruistic.

No overall relationship was found between the tendency to focus attention on the moral aspect of the self versus on a partner (predominance of endo- vs. exocentric sources) on the one hand and our index of consistency between altruistic self-expectations and overt behavior on the other. Such a significant relationship was found, however, for a subsample consisting of those who declared both reactance-facilitating standards as having only a minimal importance for them. A parallel analysis has also revealed that for the subsample consisting of those showing a tendency to focus on the moral aspect of the self (predominance of endocentric sources), the reactance-facilitating self-expectations were inversely related to our index of consistency. This was not the case, however, for the subsample consisting of those showing a tendency to focus on a partner (predominance of exocentric sources).

These results, when taken together with the results of the previously discussed experimental study, strongly indicate that focusing attention on the moral aspect of the self (predominance of endocentric sources of altruism) may facilitate reactance and, therefore, does not necessarily result in an increase of consistency between altruistic self-expectations and overt behavior. In those cases, however, where there is little chance for the occurrence of psychological reactance, owing either to situational factors (low situational pressure) or to personal ones (low subjective importance of reactance-facilitating self-expectations), focusing attention on the moral aspect of the self rather than on a partner (relative predominance of endocentric sources) does increase the impact of altruistic self-expectations upon overt behavior.

## 6. CONCLUSIONS

In this chapter I have argued that in studying altruism "global" research strategies that take no account of the multiplicity of potential motivational sources underlying altruistic behavior, although widely used, have serious shortcomings. A researcher using such a strategy hardly knows the determinants of which motivational type(s) of altruism he is studying. This must arouse doubts as to the comparability of results from different studies and considerably hinders the accumulation of knowledge. At the same time a seemingly ideal strategy for studying the differently motivated kinds of altruism independently is simply unrealistic, mainly because of our inability to differentiate among them at the empirical level. Given these circumstances, a rough classification of motivational sources underlying altruism may be a useful starting point for research. I have argued that it may be fruitful to distinguish two motivational types of altruism, endocentric and exocentric, and that focus of attention (focusing attention on the moral aspect of the self vs. on a partner in need) seems to be a crucial factor in differentiating between the two at the empirical level. The results of the empirical studies presented in which a relative predominance of endocentric versus exocentric sources of altruism has been either measured or experimentally manipulated seem to bear out the usefulness of the proposed approach.

The main focus of this chapter has been on differentiating between endocentric and exocentric sources of altruism at both the theoretical and the empirical level. Although I believe this might be an important first step, I realize that to treat the two systems as if they were independent of each other is an oversimplification. The (at least) two-factor theory of altruism still needs to be developed.

### Acknowledgments

Preparation of the chapter was greatly facilitated by help and encouragement from Barbara Arska-Karylowska. I am also grateful to Janusz Reykowski for his continuous inspiration, insights, and support and to Shalom Schwartz for his helpful comments on the previous presentations of some of the research and ideas included in the chapter.

## 7. REFERENCES

Bar-Tal, D. *Prosocial behavior: Theory and research.* Washington, D.C.: Hemisphere, 1976.

Berkowitz, L. The self, selfishness and altruism. In J. Macauley & L. Berkowitz (Eds.), *Altruism and helping behavior.* New York: Academic Press, 1970.

Berkowitz, L. Social norms, feelings, and other factors affecting helping and altruism. In L. Berkowitz (Ed.), *Advances in experimental social psychology* (Vol. 6). New York: Academic Press, 1972.

Berkowitz, L., & Miller, L. *The interaction of mood and self-awareness on helpfulness.* Paper presented at the Conference on the Development and Maintenance of Prosocial Behavior, Jablonna, Poland, September 1980.

Dubal, S., & Wicklund, R. A. *A theory of objective self-awareness.* New York: Academic Press, 1972.

Gibbons, F. X., & Wicklund, R. A. Self-focused attention and helping behavior. *Journal of Personality and Social Psychology,* 1982, *43,* 462–474.

Hoffman, M. L. Moral development. In P. H. Mussen (Ed.), *Carmichael's manual of child development* (Vol. 2) New York: Wiley, 1970. (a)

Hoffman, M. L. Conscience, personality, and socialization techniques. *Human Development,* 1970, *13,* 90–120. (b)

Jawlowska, A. [The roads of counter-culture.] Warsaw: PIW, 1975.

Karylowski, J. *Objective self-awareness and altruism: Some hypotheses.* Unpublished manuscript, University of Warsaw, 1975.

Karylowski, J. Explaining altruistic behavior: A review. *Polish Psychological Bulletin,* 1977, *8,* 27–34.

Karylowski, J. Prosocial norms, self-focused attention and prosocial behavior. *Polish Psychological Bulletin,* 1979, *10,* 57–66.

Karylowski, J. Two types of altruistic behavior: Doing good to feel good or to make others feel good. In V. Derlega & J. L. Grzelak (Eds.), *Cooperation and helping behavior: Theory and research.* New York: Academic Press, 1982. (a)

Karylowski, J. [*On the two types of altruism: Studies on endocentric and exocentric sources of altruistic behavior.*] Wroclaw: Ossolineum, 1982. (b)

Kohlberg, L. Children's perception of contemporary value system. In L. B. Talbot (Ed.), *Raising Children in modern America.* New York: Little, Brown, 1976.

Piliavin, J. A., Dovidio, J. F., Gaertner, S. L., & Clark, R. D. *Emergency intervention.* New York: Academic Press, 1981.

Reykowski, J. [Introduction.] In J. Reykowski (Ed.), [*Studies in the mechanisms of prosocial behavior.*] Warsaw: Wydawnictwa Uniwersytetu Warszawskiego, 1975.

Reykowski, J. [*Prosocial motivation, prosocial attitudes and personality.*] Warsaw: PWN, 1979.

Reykowski, J. Prosocial motivations. In V. Derlega & J. L. Grzelak (Eds.), *Cooperation and helping behavior: Theory and research.* New York: Academic Press, 1982.

Rosenhan, D. L., Karylowski, J., Salovey, P., & Hargis, K. Emotion and altruism. In J. P. Rushton & R. M. Sorrentino (Eds.), *Altruism and helping behavior.* Hillsdale, N.J.: Lawrence Erlbaum, 1981.

Rushton, P. J. *Altruism, socialization and society.* Englewood Cliffs, N.J.: Prentice-Hall, 1980.

Staub, E. *Positive social behavior and morality.* Vol. 1. *Personal and social influences.* New York: Academic Press, 1978.

Szustrowa, T. Test of egocentric associations (TES). *Polish Psychological Bulletin*, 1976, *7*, 263–267.

Taylor, S. E., & Fiske, S. T. Salience, attention, and attribution: Top of the head phenomena. In L. Berkowitz (Ed.), *Advances in experimental social psychology* (Vol. 11). New York: Academic Press, 1978.

Wicklund, R. A. *Freedom and reactance*. Hillsdale, N.J.: Lawrence Erlbaum, 1974.

Wicklund, R. A. Objective self-awareness. In L. Berkowitz (Ed.), *Advances in experimental social psychology* (Vol. 7). New York: Academic Press, 1975.

Wyer, R. S., & Srul, T. K. Category accessibility: Some theoretical and empirical issues concerning the processing of social stimulus information. In E. T. Higgins, C. P. Herman, & M. P. Zanna (Ed.), *Social cognition: The Ontario Symposium on Personality and Social Psychology*. Hillsdale, N.J.: Lawrence Erlbaum, 1981.

# 8

# Regulatory Theory of Personality and the Development of Prosocial Behaviors

Grazyna Kochanska

## 1. INTRODUCTION

Many types of approaches exist to the problem of the description and explanation of prosocial behavior. Moreover, there are still many inconsistent findings and difficulties in interpretation. The difficulties encountered in the analysis of the phenomena itself also imply the difficulties in explaining the maintenance, development, and formation of prosocial behavior within a unified theoretical framework.

This chapter is an attempt to explain prosocial behavior within a broader theoretical model of human personality. The model, called the *regulatory theory of personality*, has been developed by Janusz Reykowski and his colleagues (Reykowski & Kochanska, 1980). After presenting the

---

GRAZYNA KOCHANSKA • Laboratory of Developmental Psychology, National Institute of Mental Health, Bethesda, Maryland 20205. Work on the paper was facilitated by a grant from the nodal project of the Polish government (11.8) when the author was at the Department of Psychology of Polish Academy of Sciences and in part by the American Association of University Women fellowship for the academic year 1981–82, when the author was a visiting scholar at the Department of Psychology of the University of Massachusetts in Amherst.

general assumptions of this model, I shall attempt to demonstrate its applicability to prosocial behavior and also to integrate some of the existing research within this framework.

## 2. THE REGULATORY THEORY OF PERSONALITY: GENERAL MODEL

The regulatory theory of personality regards the personality as a complex, multifunctional system, acting as a whole to regulate bilateral relations between the individual and the social and physical environment. In spite of the holistic nature of its functioning, some subsystems of regulatory organization may be distinguished within the personality system, namely, emotional-drive mechanisms, the self-structure, the value system, and the operational system.

### 2.1. Emotional-Drive Mechanisms

The most basic level of regulatory organization are the *emotional-drive mechanisms*. A newborn is already equipped with some rudimentary properties that become the basis for the subsequent formation of various drives or emotional needs. These properties include sensitivity to changes within the organism, for example, sensitivity to the changes of the chemical composition of blood resulting in the increase of emotional tension; and sensitivity to some external stimuli, resulting either in negative emotional reactions as in the case of pain, sudden noises, and so on or in positive emotional reactions as in the case of some visual stimuli, fondling, gentle touching, and so on. Another inborn primary characteristic is the capacity for rudimentary learning, which consists in associating the signals of pleasant and unpleasant events with subsequent emotions. Also related is the capacity for the formation of rudimentary behaviors, that is, the organization of actions that are aimed at avoiding unpleasant events and at seeking pleasant ones.

Complex emotional regulatory organizations, including the representation of emotional cues of gratifying objects or persons and of consummatory techniques, are formed on the basis of these primitive regulatory properties. Established emotional mechanisms are sometimes referred to as drives, emotional needs, and so on.

Purely emotional-drive regulation, however, is most uncommon in humans. Even in the early phases of development, emotional-drive mechanisms become integrated within a broader regulatory system—the conceptual space. The process of the formation of conceptual space (also called cognitive network, cognitive map, cognitive structures) begins in the early phases of development. It may be considered a process of creating the representation of the child's world. The representation of the experience connected with our own self plays a particular part in the process of behavior regulation. That area of conceptual space that represents experience connected with the self is called in our model the *self-structure*.

## 2.2. The Self-Structure

The self-structure is formed as a result of the process of gathering and transformation of experience connected with the self. Primary differentiation in psychological space between the self and the area beyond the self is one of the first steps in self-structure formation. In the course of this process, the emotional-drive mechanisms become integrated under one central "administration." The sense of identity, the sense of practical and symbolic control over the environment, all develop as the self-structure establishes itself in conceptual space. In the later phase, the ideal self is formed as the cognitive representation of the desired state of self.

But the self-structure is only one of the elements in conceptual space, in which the whole diversity of human experience is stored. The self-structure is embedded in the more general level of regulatory organization (Reykowski, 1980).

## 2.3. The Value System and the Operational System: The Twofold Nature of the Cognitive System

What is crucial in this model of personality is the assumption that human experience is stored according to two different classes of rules: evaluative, affective rules; and rules of value, as well as descriptive, informational rules.

These two classes refer to two types of rules they may be employed in information processing. People may process experience according to its affective value, and therefore try to separate "good" from "bad", try to maintain affective consistency, evaluate events and things as desirable or nondesirable. In other words, they try to establish and arrange their affective world. They may also process information according to its logical and descriptive content, logical consistency and accuracy. The product of this type of information processing results in "knowledge"—the representation of the descriptive qualities of the world. Similar ideas have been expressed by Abelson *et al.* (1982), Peabody (1970), and Zajonc (1980). The system of cognitive representations, organized according to value rules, is called in our framework the *value system*. It may bethought of as the affective map of man's experience. The self, other people, events, things, and an almost infinite number of the elements of one's world are stored here according to evaluative rules, that is, rules of "good" and "bad." Characteristics for the value system is the presence of standards, or representations of the desired states of objects. For example, the ideal self may be considered a standard for the self-structure.

The same reality that is stored according to evaluative rules may also be organized according to descriptive, informational rules. Children do not merely represent the elements of reality as possessing "good" or "bad" qualities. They also act in reality; they have to consider its "objective" characteristics; they gather purely cognitive information about the world; they learn what things are and what their transformations can be. This process results in the descriptive map of experience that is called in our model the *operational system*. It is derived from the objective characteristics of the world and from a child's actions, as Piaget puts it. Evaluative rules of organization are here replaced by logical, descriptive rules.

This twofold nature of cognitive representation is also discussed by Peabody (1970) with reference to interpersonal reality. Peabody introduces the term *evaluative* and *descriptive* to describe two classes of rules that may be used in organizing one's interpersonal experience. Similar ideas are expressed by Zajonc (1980), who points to the informational and affective regulatory systems. These two classes of rules are, according to Zajonc, based on two classes of properties of things: discriminanda and preferenda. In Poland the same point has been discussed by Reykowski and Kochanska (1980) and Lewicka (1977).

## 3. MOTIVATIONAL ROLE OF THE PERSONALITY ORGANIZATIONS

Each of the personality organizations outlined above plays an important role in the process of regulation of bilateral relations between the individual and the world. Emotions and motivation are generated by all the subsystems—emotional-drive mechanisms, the self-structure, the value system, and the operational system. However, the personality acts as a whole; the impulses originating in a particular subsystem are usually controlled by the more general organization at an integrated level. Nevertheless, there exists some specificity of the motives arising in various suborganizations.

### 3.1. The Emotional-Drive Mechanisms

The emotional-drive mechanisms are the source of such biological or almost biological needs as hunger, sex, and early attachment. They may also play a part in some early sensitivity to the distress of others.

### 3.2. The Self-Structure

The self-structure is the source of various motives. It requires information confirming its identity, its ability to control the environment, and its value. Thus there are needs of identity; motives of dominance and achievement, of approval and failure avoidance; needs to be loved and recognized, and so on. The self-structure also underlies motives of shame and guilt avoidance on the one hand, and of self-acceptance and self-esteem maintenance on the other. The last motives are implied by the possible discrepancies between the actual and the desired self-state. The self-structure also mediates behaviors directed toward increasing our own welfare.

### 3.3. The Value System

The value system mediates behaviors which confirm the affective and evaluative order of experience. People display positive behaviors towards positively valued objects and aversive behaviors toward the ones which have negative value. But, what is even more important, it generates motivation to act for the benefit of an object, in case when there is a discrepancy between its actual and desired standard as represented in the value system.

Do all the objects represented there have this motivational quality?

In order to evoke this kind of motivation, as argued in the works of Reykowski (1975, 1982b), the objects have to possess well-established representations in the cognitive system. Such representations acquire their own inherent value as cognitive entities; motivation is then directed not only to the mere sustaining of objects but also to improving their condition in the case of discrepancy between the actual and the desired state. The value system is also the source of tendencies toward evaluative consistency of judgments and attitudes. This phenomenon has been clearly described by Peabody (1970) and also in the framework of cognitive dissonance theory. People tend to keep characteristics together with respect to their value. "Bad" qualities and "good" ones are usually stored together, but separately from each other (as in the case of prejudices, stereotypes, etc.).

### 3.4. The Operational System

Motivational properties of the operational system have been discussed in the theories of cognitive curiosity and exploration. Cognitive curiosity theorists have developed a framework in which they describe various forms of motivation to explore, to gain new information, to extend one's knowledge. Hunt, Berlyne, and other representatives of this approach broadly explain how this kind of motivation is instigated and developed. Informational discrepancy, inconsistency, and lack of information seem to be the most important conditions for motivational arousal. We may say that whereas the regulatory task of the value system is to evaluate the world, that of the operational system is to understand and explain it; such motives as knowledge extension, informational-discrepancies reduction, and exploration belong here.

## 4. REGULATORY THEORY OF PERSONALITY AND THE REGULATION OF PROSOCIAL BEHAVIOR

Although each of the outlined regulatory organizations may mediate prosocial behavior, the underlying mechanism of such behavior is different in each case. Thus prosocial actions are regarded as manifestations not of an inner "disposition" or "trait," but of various internal regulatory subsystems in action. This type of approach has some important implications. The developmental history, the promoting and inhibiting factors, and the action characteristics of such behavior may all differ depending upon the internal mechanism actually involved. Let us now consider various mechanisms underlying prosocial behavior within the model of personality that has been presented.

### 4.1. Emotional-Drive Mechanisms and Prosocial Behaviors

Emotional-drive mechanisms play an important role in the regulation of prosocial behavior. Beginning from a very early level of development, an infant reacts to crying and other distress cues from other infants. Emotional tuning or syntony takes place (Simner, 1971). This early emotional response to others' distress occurs because of the lack of differentiation (fusion) between self and the area beyond the self; it is a kind of unspecific sensitivity to one's own and others' distress. Hoffman (1975) argues that in very early stages of development humans are capable of experiencing empathic distress long before acquiring a cognitive sense of the other. Distress cues from other people elicit a global empathic distress response that Hoffman ascribes to a tension of unpleasant feelings and stimuli from the infant's own body, the dimly perceived "other," and the situation. The cues associated with another person's distress evoke an upset state in the infant himself.

Human sensitivity to "infancy scheme" features (big head, big eyes, characteristic figure) may also be ascribed to the early roots of empathy. Cues of this kind release tenderness, protectiveness, and approaching behavior. This phenomenon has often been described by animal psychologists; it is a type of readiness to act for the benefit of others that also belongs to the basic emotional equipment of man.

However, a child's development leads to very extensive transformations of both the mechanism of early unspecific sensitivity to others' distress and the mechanism linked with the infancy scheme. In the course of development, other, empathylike emotional mechanisms become linked with or integrated within cognitive regulators of behavior. Moreover, other mechanisms of prosocial behavior begin to play their role—mechanisms implied by the formation of more complex regulatory organizations.

### 4.2. Self-Structure and Prosocial Behaviors

A particularly marked role in the process of prosocial behavior regulation is played by the self-structure. As has been mentioned, the self-structure is the source of motives responsible for actions directed toward one's own well-being. This motivation increases as the concentration upon the self increases. Thus the question arises: How does the self-structure mediate prosocial behaviors, when common sense suggests that self-structure involvement should instead exert an inhibiting influence in this case?

In fact, not only common sense, but also experimental evidence illustrates the inhibiting influence of the self-structure on prosocial behavior (Berkowitz, 1970). The experimental results are supported by theoretical reasoning. Thus it is assumed that when the regulatory potential of the self-structure is particularly high, it begins to play a competitive role in relation to objects from the area beyond the self. Indeed, it is possible that most of the actions of some people are regulated by the self-structure, and when this is the case, other objects hardly have any opportunity to become the regulators of behavior. This high regulatory potential of the self-structure may arise from various factors. It may, for example, be because the self-structure has a particularly favored position in the conceptual space. This phenomenon was found in persons with exceptionally high self-esteem, who were less prosocial than persons with average self-esteem (Kowalczewska, 1972; Szustrowa, 1972).

When there exists a permanent or situational tension connected with the self-structure, this may also lead to an increase in the regulatory potential of the self-structure and therefore to domination of the self-structure over other structures including the representations of other people. This may be the case when a person has very low self-esteem or other serious problems with the self, or in situations that evoke tension connected with the self. Some experimental data are cited in Berkowitz (1970).

Jarymowicz (1979) subjected a group of young boys with serious self-esteem problems to experimental treatment aimed at increasing their self-esteem (experience of success, approval, praise). The treatment significantly increased the boys' readiness to help and their sensitivity to others' problems. Jarymowicz attributes the effect to the self-tension reduction.

Another form of permanent self-involvement, need for approval, may also have negative impact on prosocial behavior. Staub and Sherk (1970) found that the higher the child's need for approval, the lower his level of prosocial behavior (sharing). This relationship held in the situation where helping or refusal to help would not be discovered by the experimenter. When helping or not helping could be discovered, the negative relationship between need for approval and helping was no longer present.

Situational concentration on the self also increases the regulatory potential of the self-structure, and thus decreases helping behavior. Karylowski (1977) increased concentration on the self in boys by placing a mirror in front of them. In general, this led to a significant decrease in prosocial behavior as measured by the amount of work sacrificed to help a partner. Although these and other experimental data indicate that the self-structure may have an inhibiting impact on prosocial behavior, it may also be the source of specific prosocial behavior mechanisms, for example:

- When helping is a means of improving the subject's own well-being (instrumental mechanism)
- When helping enhances the feeling of self-esteem, ideal-self achievement, or guilt avoidance (endocentric mechanism)
- When helping is implied by the generalization of positive feeling from the self onto other people, whose cognitive representations are encoded in the conceptual space at a short distance from the self (similarity mechanism)

#### 4.2.1. *Instrumental Mechanism*

Altruism motivated by the will to gain a reward for oneself is quite common. Investigators such as Homans have even considered it a universal mechanism. Although this claim no longer seems to hold up, there is no doubt that helping is sometimes controlled by the anticipation of approval or other rewards. Staub (1978) argues that self-interest not only makes people adhere to others' expectations, which often prescribe prosocial behavior, but also makes them help others in the hope of being rewarded with others' positive feelings or with the return of benefits.

If so, then high need for approval does not necessarily lead to a decrease in helping. Staub and Sherk (1970) give an interesting illustration of this point. Although children with high need for approval shared less than children with low need for approval, this relationship disappeared when circumstances implied to the children that helping was expected by the experimenter and that it would be discovered whether they had helped or not; in other words, when helping became the means of gaining approval. "External orientation" (Hoffman, 1970) may be regarded in including strong components of altruism mediated by this instrumental mechanism.

Using the concepts of our model, it may be stated that the instrumental mechanism functions because in the subject's conceptual space other people are represented in instrumental relation to the self-structure. Acting for their benefit is nothing more than an element of a more general action for the subject's own benefit. It is very likely that instrumental altruism has its specific characteristics. It should be accompanied by a lack of interest in the recipient and low accuracy of offered help.

### 4.2.2. *Endocentric Mechanism*

This mechanism has been introduced and analyzed in our laboratory by Jerzy Karylowski (1977, 1979; see also Chapter 7, this volume). In this case helping is controlled by the expectation of the feeling of ideal-self approximation. A similar line of reasoning is presented by Schwartz (1977), who assumes that helping may be mediated by "personal norms"; these are norms of helping that are incorporated into a person's feeling of self-worth. Adherence to personal norms is a source of internal satisfaction with one's own self.

In the course of development the ideal self is formed, that is, the representation of the desired state of the self. The ideal self is a powerful source of human motivation. It generates satisfaction as a result of adherence to personal norms, or dissatisfaction (guilt) when personal norms are violated. In cases where the norm of helping has been actualized, the endocentric mechanism of helping is activated. Karylowski (1979) found that although self-concentration generally decreased helping, the more important the norm of helping was for the subject the weaker was the relationship. If the norm was of particular importance for self-esteem, an opposite tendency arose: Self-concentration increased altruism. A similar phenomenon is described by Hamer (1978), who evoked helping in girls by means of specific concentration on the prosocial elements in their self-images.

### 4.2.3. *Similarity Mechanism*[1]

In psychological space, representations of persons and events are not isolated structures but elements of a broader organization. This is also true for the self-structure. As has been found in the generalization studies, actualization of one cognitive structure also evokes actualization of other structures, which are located at close psychological distance on various dimensions (semantic, temporal, physical, etc.; this point is developed in Chapter 3 of this volume).

Thus it is possible to generalize positive attitudes from the self to other persons located at a close distance. For example, Karylowski (1976) found that girls who had been made to believe that their partner in an experimental task was similar to themselves helped the partner more than did the girls who had not been informed of such a similarity.

Smolenska (1971) found that young people who attended highly competitive art schools and because of that perceived themselves as very different from their peers (ascribing this to their exceptional intelligence) were less prosocial than their colleagues who considered themselves more similar to their peers.

## 4.3. Value System and Prosocial Behaviors

As has already been mentioned, the value system is not just another distinct organization within personality but is a more general level of personality organization. This level of generality is evident in the fact that the self-structure and, in a sense, the emotional-drive mechanisms are embedded and integrated within this system.

Prosocial behavior mechanisms that may be described with reference to the value system belong to one of two categories. They both arise from the twofold nature of storage in the value system: representations of the actual state of the world, and of its desired state.

The discrepancy between the actual and the desired state of another person may lead to prosocial behavior (directed toward discrepancy reduction).[2]

In this framework, it is assumed that the motivating potential of this discrepancy is implied by the existence of a well-established representa-

[1]Some authors, such as Hoffman, have expressed opinion that the similarity mechanism has a different theoretical status than other mechanisms. He claims that it is implied by the features of the conceptual space as a whole and may therefore interact with other mechanisms, for example, with the normative one. In other words, similarity may define the objects to which the norms are applied (Hoffman, personal communication).

[2]It may also lead to discrepancy reduction through symbolical transformation, for example, the distortion of incoming information.

tion of another person in the value system (Czapinski, 1976; Reykowski, 1975, 1982a,b). A representation of this kind acquires inherent value in the cognitive system. This mechanism was introduced by Reykowski (1975, 1982a,b) and is defined as the autonomous mechanism of helping in order to stress its relative independence from other elements in psychological space, particularly the self-structure.[3]

The phenomenon defined as autonomous altruism has also been analyzed by other authors. Hoffman's description of a humanistic-flexible group includes many elements that are typical for this mechanism. Similar differentiation may also be found in the works of Staub (1978, 1980). Karylowski designed a special questionnaire to measure the relative domination of autonomous altruism over endocentric altruism and vice versa. It appeared that the tendency to behave according to the former or to the latter may be a rather stable characteristic of a person (see Chapter 7, this volume).

Another category of mechanisms, also derived from the twofold nature of the value system, includes normative mechanisms of helping. Space will not permit an analysis of all the relevant literature on normative regulation. Extensive reviews, dealing with prosocial behavior may be found in Schwartz (1977) or Staub (1978). From our point of view, norms may also be regarded as standards that function in the value system; they refer to human behaviors in interpersonal and social life, rules of social organization, and so on. Norms may become articulated in the value system through various processes. They are often incorporated as the result of the influence of social groups and socializers. On more mature developmental levels, norms may be self-produced. Norms have been extensively studied by many investigators; it is important to stress that according to the regulatory theory of personality, normative mechanisms may be linked with the self-structure, for example, the conceptualization of Schwartz or Karylowski, or may be independent of self. They may thus be referred to as extrapersonal norms.

Extrapersonal norms have also been studied in our laboratory by Kaminska-Feldman (1980), who increased some aspects of the readiness for prosocial behavior in boys. They were presented with some egocentric statements. They then had to invent counterarguments and reasoning that would justify prosocial attitudes. No self-involvement was introduced; the task was presented as a game. Kaminska-Feldman argues that what was actualized were the extrapersonal norms independent of the subjects' self-images. This treatment led to an increase in the readiness for prosocial behavior.

[3]Karylowski cites this mechanism as a specific example of exocentric mechanisms (see chapter 7 in this volume).

### 4.4. Operational System and Prosocial Behaviors

As I have suggested, man's experience is organized not only according to affective, evaluative rules, but according to descriptive rules as well. The operational system, constructed in this way, is the motivational basis of such phenomena as cognitive curiosity, exploration, the tendency to explain, understand, and cognitively master the reality. This personality organization may also participate in the process of prosocial behavior regulation; however, its impact is indirect in nature. The operational system plays an important role in the process of regulation of actions that require cognitive, informational processing of another person's state. Role taking, cognitive empathy, understanding other people, and interpersonal curiosity are examples of the regulatory tasks that require descriptive social representations to be activated.

## 5. SOME GENERAL CONCLUSIONS: THE MULTIMOTIVATIONAL NATURE OF PROSOCIAL BEHAVIORS

It is therefore assumed in the outlined model that various internal regulatory organizations of personality and their appropriate mechanisms may underlie prosocial behaviors. Similar ideas suggesting the diversity of prosocial behavior mechanisms have lately been put forth by Bar-Tal (1982) and Eisenberg-Berg (1979). They both suggest that prosocial behavior may be mediated by various internal mechanisms, some of them analogous to the mechanisms distinguished in the present framework.

In the existing literature, many authors pay attention to the distinction between helping another person in order to increase his welfare on the one hand, and helping another person in order to obey one's own moral rules, to fulfill one's duties and obligations, on the other. The differentiation is discussed by Staub (1980), who speaks of prosocial orientation as person centered and duty orientations as based on norms and principles. He regards these orientations as two types of prosocial goals.

Hoffman (1970) suggests a similar distinction between an external orientation, in which children are concerned with external rewards or punishment (this corresponds to our instrumental mechanism), and two internal orientations: the humanistic-flexible one, in which a child is concerned with another person's welfare (corresponding to our autonomous mechanism), and the conventional-rigid one, in which a child is concerned with obeying moral rules and principles (corresponding to our endocentric mechanism).

Some implications can also be derived from this model for the analysis of the developmental and childrearing aspects. Within the framework presented, these problems become much more complex than when prosocial behaviors are considered the manifestation of one, relatively homogeneous, internal disposition or trait. It is assumed that the development of each of the outlined mechanisms is closely linked with the development of the relevant internal regulatory organization. For example, if we consider endocentric prosocial behavior, that is, helping aimed at the increase of our own self-worth, it is obvious that self-structure has to be developed enough to become a source of this kind of motivation. Simple differentiation between self and the area beyond self will not be sufficient to make endocentric function possible; what is necessary is the ideal self, which contains personal norms and standards of conduct.

Particular mechanisms may also be shaped and influenced by the treatment addressed to the relevant internal organization. The problems are even more complicated by the fact that each of the regulatory organizations mentioned (emotional-drive mechanisms, the self-structure, the value system, and the operational system) may be a potential source of factors either promoting or inhibiting prosocial behavior. The dialectic of regulation is very complex: In the same regulatory subsystem there may arise conflicting tendencies as a result of the same external influence. For example, the cues of others' pain and distress are strong emotional factors evoking empathy; but they may at the same time elicit disgust that evokes avoidance behavior. Self-concentration may increase endocentric helping; but at the same time it may activate norms of personal freedom, also encoded in the self-structure, conflicting with norms of helping (such a result was actually observed by Karylowski). Moreover, the same factors that increase one form of prosocial behavior may at the same time decrease another form, because of the antagonistic relationships that exist between some of the regulatory organizations. For example, self-structure involvement may decrease the involvement of the representations of other people (Reykowski, 1982a).

The following summary illustrates the differences in prosocial behavior mechanisms, their developmental history, childrearing antecedents, and action characteristics. Some of the elements presented in the summary are the result of research carried out in our laboratory; some are the result of the analysis, interpretation, or reinterpretation of other investigators' studies; some still have the status of hypotheses or theoretical implications of the model that need empirical examination. Only some of the mechanisms are included; normative mechanisms have been omitted because there is an extensive literature on this type of regulation. The operational-system mechanisms are omitted because the problem is still in the initial phase of investigation.

1. *Personality organization involved:*
Emotional-drive mechanisms

*Mechanism of prosocial behavior:*
Empathic mechanism

*Developmental history:*
The roots of this mechanism lie in the baby's reactions to others' distress (Simner, 1971). It is attributable to the fusion between self and others. As a result of early conditioning the cues of others' distress become associated with that of the subject (Hoffman, 1975).

*Childrearing antecedents:*

*Promoting factors*

It may be assumed on the basis of the Aronfreed study (1970) that conditioning processes are responsible for empathic mechanism formation. In the study, empathy formation was achieved making children experience the experimenter's emotions and linking them with their own emotions. Subsequently, the subjects were more willing to benefit the experimenter than to benefit themselves (in comparison with subjects whose emotions had not been linked with those of the experimenter).

It is sometimes suggested that one's own experience of distress may be an important condition of subsequent empathy. Hoffman (1975) argues that the distress a child experiences when it encounters another's distress is a form of remembrance "of [the child's] previous suffering; the cues of another's emotions are then linked with its own."

*Inhibiting factors*

Some relationships found in research studies illustrate the complex and almost paradoxical regulation of empathy. It appears that the same factors (experiences of other's distress) may inhibit empathy. This may happen when other's distress also evokes another response at the emotional-drive level, namely, disgust. In the Piliavin, Piliavin, and Rodin study (1975), a stigmatized victim received less help. It may also happen that another's distress becomes a factor evoking aggression ("adding oil to the flames"). In a study by Hartman (1969) and also in one by Eliasz (1980) it was found that although another's distress generally evoked empathy, under some conditions it exasperated the subject and, instead of increasing empathy increased aggression. Eliasz had girls punish their partners by means of electric shocks. Some girls (the ones with great need for stimulation) were more aggressive in the situation where they were made to concentrate on the partner's suffering.

It also seems probable that frequent experience of self-involvement such as physical punishment or material rewards, can decrease empathic ability.

*Action characteristics*

Although there is not enough evidence, it seems very likely that the impulsive nature of action is characteristic of behaviors motivated by emotional empathy.

2. *Personality organization involved:*
Self-structure

*Mechanism of prosocial behavior:*
Instrumental mechanism

*Developmental history:*

This mechanism is characteristic of the early phases of development (e.g., Eisenberg-Berg, 1979). In the course of development it is gradually replaced by other, more complex mechanisms of helping. However, it is often present even in adults.

*Childrearing antecedents:*

*Promoting factors*

Instrumental helping is established as a result of experiences that bind an altruistic act with extrinsic reinforcement. In a group of 9-year-old girls, Kochanska (1980) succeeded in shaping instrumental helping through an experimental procedure consisting of reinforcement of altruistic acts with material rewards.

Experiences of helping a person who does not need help may also increase the probability of subsequent occurrence of instrumental altruism. In the Masters and Pisarowicz study (1975), the authors had children help either people who needed help ("remedial altruism") or people who did not really need help ("simple altruism"). The subjects then self-rewarded themselves. It turned out that after simple altruism they rewarded themselves more than after remedial altruism. One might argue, then, that if the hope for external rewards is one of the crucial characteristics of instrumental helping, then the described procedure has indeed fostered this mechanism. The finding, if confirmed in other studies, may have serious childrearing implications. The educators and parents, while assigning children prosocial tasks, should probably make sure that the recipients of help really do have a need for it.

Some other forms of self-involvement (not only through material rewards) may also foster instrumental altruism. Staub and Sherk (1970) showed that need for approval may mediate prosocial behaviors if the behaviors increase the subject's well-being, that is, when they were the means to gain social approval. Interestingly, altruistic motivation does not seem to decrease as a result of being "instrumental" to another goal (Kruglanski 1975), as it is the case with other forms of motivation (Greene, Lepper 1977), although there is some evidence that it might happen (Garbarino 1975). However, as it is argued here, the subsequent helping has different characteristics than when it is motivated by genuine desire to improve someone else's well-being.

*Inhibiting factors*

Factors that undermine instrumental altruism may be other-oriented techniques, for example, induction. Staub (1971) found that induction decreased helping the adult experimenter. This unexpected finding may be interpreted as follows: Induction, according to Staub, Hoffman, and many others, is a technique that concentrates subjects on other people. It has often been found an effective technique to increase helping. In this case it may have undermined helping the adult because adults are often perceived as people who control and distribute approval and other external rewards; thus it is probable that if they do receive children's help, it may be a case of instrumentally motivated behavior (at least more so than the other children are the recipients). And in this case the other technique concentrated on others undermined this kind of help, that is to say, undermined the instrumental helping behavior. Thus, on the theoretical level, we can probably assume that activation of the representation of other people may diminish the regulatory role of self-structure. It may elicit autonomous altruism, but supress the instrumental one.

*Action characteristics*

Low interest in the recipient is the typical feature of instrumental helping. In Kochanska (1980), the group of children in whom instrumental altruism had been shaped were extremely uninterested in the children they helped in comparison to all the remaining experimental groups. It is also probable that instrumental helping is accompanied by low accuracy of perceiving others' needs. This trend was also found in the "instrumental" group.

3. *Personality organization involved:*
   Self-structure

*Mechanism of prosocial behavior:*
   Endocentric mechanism

*Developmental history:*

This mechanism is hardly possible in early development. It appears along with ideal-self formation. It should increase during adolescence because of the increment in self-concentration and self-awareness typical for this period. The "imaginary audience" phenomenon described by Elkind (1967) seems relevant here, as responsible for the growth in self-concentration. Adolescents tend to believe they are the constant focus of attention of other people.

*Childrearing antecedents:*

*Promoting factors*

According to the theory presented above, appeals to self-esteem and inducement of guilt feelings are the crucial factors in the formation of the endocentric mechanism. Childrearing practices that concentrate children on themselves and make them concerned about what they are or should be like, for example, conditional acceptance, are likely to increase the regulatory role of the ideal self and, thus, endocentric helping. Instilling prosocial norms in children's self-structure and associating them with self-esteem are also important for the formation of endocentric mechanisms (see Chapter 7). Actualizing prosocial personal norms and ascribing them to the subject's self-image was also found to promote endocentric helping (Hamer, 1978). Hamer concentrated her female subjects on this particular component, bound up with prosocial behavior, of their self-images. Subsequently, they were more willing to help than the subjects who had not been given such treatment.

*Inhibiting factors*

The endocentric mechanism may be impaired if, in the course of development, prosocial norms are not encoded in the child's ideal self. It may happen that the ideal self's content is other than prosocial, even quite antisocial. Aggressive features, strong norms of dominance, or inconsideration for others may become elements of self-image. Also, very strong norms of personal freedom were found to inhibit the endocentric mechanism (Karylowski, 1977).

*Action characteristics*

Endocentrically motivated helping should be characterized by low interest in the recipient and low accuracy of offered help. On the other hand, however, endocentric helping should be very resistant to diffusion of responsibility, for there would be no satisfaction for the subject if help was offered by someone else. The same reasoning leads to the expectation that even high personal sacrifice should not be a discouraging factor for an endocentric helper. These predictions have been formulated by Karylowski, but not yet empirically tested.

4. *Personality organization involved:*
   Self-structure

*Mechanism of prosocial behavior:*
Similarity mechanism

*Developmental history:*

The developmental history of the similarity mechanism has been investigated by Zwolinski (1974) in a study using projection doll play. Children faced distribution problems in an imaginary interpersonal situation. Dolls represented the self, a similar other, and a dissimilar other; some attractive goods were to be distributed. Children age 4 to 5 were typically egocentric: They would choose the "self" doll. Children 5 to 6 favored the "similar other" doll. Older children tended to coordinate the needs of all the dolls. Interestingly, helping mediated by similarity did not require understanding of the self–other similarity notion and appeared even earlier. (Understanding of the self–other similarity notion was measured independently in cognitive tasks.) Therefore, helping mediated by similarity may be based on the generalization of feeling toward the self. In adolescence a decrease in perceived similarity may be expected, because of the phenomenon described by Elkind (1967) as the "personal fable," that is, the adolescent's belief in his own exceptionality and the uniqueness of his feelings.

*Childrearing antecedents:*

*Promoting factors*

Techniques directed at showing a similarity between the self and other people should create facilitating conditions for the formation of the similarity mechanism. This was confirmed empirically. Karylowski (1975) made his subjects believe that their partners were similar to them in some important respects. This procedure significantly increased the amount of work subjects did for the benefit of their partners.

*Inhibiting factors*

It is not surprising that the experience of subjective uniqueness undermines the formation of the similarity mechanism. This was confirmed by Smolenska (1971), who found that exceptionally intelligent children felt less similar to others in comparison with their peers of average intelligence, and consequently were also less prosocial. The results may be generalized: All kinds of experiences that create strict borders in conceptual space between the self and others, all kinds of dichotomization of the social world (us vs. them), can impair generalization of attitudes from the self to others. This was impressively illustrated by Zimbardo's "prison study" (1975); arbitrary assignation of attributes to the subjects introduced a sharp distinction between the two groups that made all feelings of sympathy or community diminish (see also Reykowski, 1982b).

*Action characteristics*

Low accuracy of offered help should be typical for helping mediated by similarity, because of the generalization of the subject's own standards and the ascription of his own needs or emotions to other people. This expectation is confirmed by Lewicki's study (Lewicki, 1979). Young girls in whom the similarity mechanism seemed to be operating made more deformations in a task that required description of other people. The mistakes consisted in generalization of one's own characteristics.

5. *Personality organization involved:*
Value system

*Mechanism of prosocial behavior:*
Autonomous mechanism

*Developmental history:*

Autonomous altruism is implied by the appearance and stabilization of well-established representations of other people in the child's cognitive system. However, not much is known about the developmental history of this mechanism. It certainly requires some level of cognitive development. Acquiring new information about other people and storing it in the child's conceptual space seems to be the crucial factor in the process of development. As we have seen, representations of other people are developed and established in the value system of a child. In the process of development the representations become more elaborated, involving more and more elements. First other people have to be perceived as separate entities; then they become perceived as possessing their own internal features and identity (the developmental steps are discussed in Hoffman, 1975, and Flavell *et al.*, 1975). Gradually, according to our theory, like other representations in the value system, the representations of other people also begin to possess standards of desired conditions for them. A discrepancy between the standard and the actual state of another person can then elicit prosocial motivation directed at discrepancy reduction. The motivation can be quite independent of the subject's own actual state, and is not linked with personal gain. That is why we call the mechanism an autonomous one. Of course, there are some prerequisites for the autonomous mechanism to arise; at this point we do not have enough evidence to describe them sufficiently. But it seems that not only should the cognitive representations of others be elaborated and developed, they must also possess positive value. The processes of acquiring such value may vary. In general, positive evaluation and complex representation of other people in a child's cognitive system deserve more attention.

Also important for the formation of the autonomous mechanism are cognitive stages in child development. It seems reasonable to expect qualitative changes in the representations of other people as formal operations develop. This should affect the child's capacity to formulate ideal standards for other people and to consider subtle psychological cues that may be signals of the discrepancy between the actual and desired state of others.

*Childrearing antecedents:*

*Promoting factors*

Factors fostering the development of the autonomous mechanism include all the other-oriented techniques that point to the consequences of one's own behavior for other people, for example, induction. Hoffman's results concerning the role of induction in the formation of a humanistic-flexible orientation may be regarded as an example of this relationship. It has been also recognized by Staub (1979). Karylowski also found induction, applied in preschool years, to increase subsequent exocentric helping. The role of induction may be to provide information about the recipient's needs and likely reactions; the information is stored in the child's cognitive system and thus extends the representations of others.

Involvement in prosocial behavior leading to salient outcomes for the recipient also plays a similar role. Kochanska (1980) shaped autonomous altruism in boys as the result of prior helping followed by observation of the recipients' reactions to this help. This experimental procedure led to significant increase in helping that was described as autonomous helping on the basis of some other indexes.

*Inhibiting factors*

The antagonistic relationship between the self-structure and the representations of other people leads to the expectation that all kinds of personal involvement (extrinsic endocentric appeals, tensions in the self-structure) may impair the development of autonomous mechanism.

*Action characteristics*

Kochanska (1980) found that autonomous altruism is accompanied by high interest in the recipient. High accuracy of perceiving the other's needs may also be expected. However, Karylowski predicts that autonomous altruism may be strongly affected by diffusion of responsibility. If the change in another person is the controlling factor in the regulation of behavior, then it makes no difference who helps; thus the phenomenon of the diffusion of responsibility should occur.

ACKNOWLEDGMENTS

I would like to express my gratitude to Janusz Reykowski and Ervin Staub for their help and comments.

## 6. REFERENCES


Abelson, R. P., Kinder, D. R., Peters, M. D., & Fiske, S. T. Affective and semantic components in political person perception. *Journal of Personality and Social Psychology,* 1982, *42,* 619–630.

Aronfreed, J. The socialization of altruistic and sympathetic behavior: Some theoretical and experimental analyses. In J. Macaulay & L. Berkowitz (Eds.), *Altruism and helping behavior.* New York: Academic Press, 1970.

Bar-Tal, D., & Raviv, A. A cognitive-learning model of helping behavior development: Possible implications and applications. In N. Eisenberg (Ed.), *The development of prosocial behavior.* New York: Academic Press, 1982.

Berkowitz, L. The self, selfishness and altruism. In J. Macaulay & L. Berkowitz (Eds.), *Altruism and helping behavior.* New York: Academic Press, 1970.

Czapinski, J. Structural features of cognitive representations of social objects and the readiness to act for the benefit of these objects. *Studia Psychologiczne,* 1976, *15,* 83–99.

Eisenberg-Berg, N. Development of children's prosocial moral judgement. *Developmental Psychology,* 1979, *15,* 87–89.

Eliasz, H. The role of empathy, activity and anxiety on interpersonal aggression. *Polish Psychological Bulletin,* 1980, *3,* 169–178.

Elkind, L. D. Egocentrism in adolescence. *Child Development,* 1967, *38,* 1025–1034.

Flavell, J., Botkin, T. P., Fry, C. L., Wright, J. W., & Jarvis, P. E. The development of role-taking and communication skills in children. New York: Krieger, 1975.

Garbarino, J. The impact of anticipated rewards on cross-age tutoring. *Journal of Personality and Social Psychology,* 1975, *32,* 421–428.

Greene, D., & Lepper, M. R. (Eds.). *The hidden costs of reward.* Hillsdale, N.J.: Lawrence Erlbaum, 1977.

Hamer, H. Prosocial motivation evoking in actively egocentric women. In J. Reykowski (Ed), *Theory of personality and prosocial behavior* Warsaw: Polska Akedemia Nauk, 1978.

Hartman, R. Influence of symbolically modeled aggression and pain on aggressive behavior. *Journal of Personality and Social Psychology,* 1969, *11,* 280–288.

Hoffman, M. L. Moral development. In P. H. Mussen (Ed), *Carmichael's manual of child development.* New York: Wiley, 1970

Hoffman, M. L. Developmental synthesis of affect and cognition and its implications for altruistic motivation. *Developmental Psychology,* 1975, *11,* 607–622.

Jarymowicz, M. *Modification of "self" cognitions for the increase of the readiness for prosocial behaviors.*Wroclaw: Ossolineum, 1979.

Kaminska-Feldman, M. Extrapersonal norms actualization and sensitivity to other people's problems. *Psychologia Wychowawcza,* 1980, *2.*

Karylowski, J. Self-esteem, similarity, liking and helping. *Personality and Social Psychology Bulletin,* 1976, *2,* 71–74.

Karylowski, J. Explaining altruistic behavior: A review. *Polish Psychological Bulletin,* 1977, *8,* 27–34.

Karylowski, J. Self-focused attention, prosocial norms and prosocial behavior. *Polish Psychological Bulletin,* 1979, *10,* 57–66.

Karylowski, J. On the two types of altruistic behavior: Doing good to feel good versus to make others feel good. In V. Derlega & J. Grzelak (Eds.), *Living with other people: Theory and research on cooperation and prosocial behavior.* New York: Academic Press, in press.

Kochanska, G. Experimental formation of cognitive and helping social motivation in children. *Polish Psychological Bulletin,* 1980, *11,* 75–87.

Kowalczewska, J. Relationship between attitudes towards self and others and the tendency to allocentric behaviors. Unpublished master's thesis, University of Warsaw, 1972.

Kruglanski, A. W. The endogenous–exogenous partition in attribution theory. *Psychological Review,* 1975, *82,* 387–406.

Lewicka, M. Evaluative and descriptive aspects of organization of cognitive structures. *Polish Psychological Bulletin,* 1977, *8,* 3–12.

Lewicki, P. Self-image and trait inferences. *Polish Psychological Bulletin,* 1979, *10,* 15–20.

Masters, J. & Pisarowicz, P. Self-reinforcement and generosity following two types of altruistic behavior. *Child Development,* 1975, *46,* 313–318.

Peabody, D. Evaluative and descriptive aspects in personality perception: A reappraisal. *Journal of Personality and Social Psychology,* 1970, *16,* 639–646.

Piliavin, I., Piliavin, J., Rodin J. Costs, diffusion and the stigmatized victim. *Journal of Personality and Social Psychology,* 1975, *32,* 429–438.

Reykowski, J. Zadanie Pozaosobiste jako regulator czynnosci. In I. Kurcz & J. Reykowski (Eds), *Studia nad teoria czynnosci ludzkich* [Studies in the theory of human actions]. Warsaw: Panstwowe Wydawnictwo Naukowe, 1975.

Reykowski, J. Development of prosocial motivation: A dialectic process. In N. Eisenberg (Ed.), *The development of prosocial behavior.* Academic Press, 1982. (a)

Reykowski, J. Social motivation. *Annual Review of Psychology,* 1982, *33,* 123–154. (b)

Reykowski, J., & Kochanska, G. Szkice z teori osobowoŝci [Essays in the theory of personality]. Warsaw: Wiedza Powszechna, 1980.

Schwartz, S. Normative influences on altruism. In L. Berkowitz (Ed), *Advances in experimental social psychology.* New York: Academic Press, 1977.

Simner, M. L. Newborn's response to the cry of another infant. *Developmental Psychology,* 1971, *5,* 136–150.

Smolenska, M. *Perceived similarity and allocentric and egocentric behaviors in exceptionally talented youth.* Unpublished master's thesis, University of Warsaw, 1971.

Staub, E. The use of role-playing and induction in children's learning of helping and sharing behavior. *Child Development,* 1971, *42,* 805–816.

Staub, E. *Positive social behavior and morality: Social and personal influences* (Vol. 1). New York: Academic Press, 1978.

Staub, E. *Positive social behavior and morality: Socialization and development* (Vol. 2). New York: Academic Press, 1979.

Staub, E. Social and prosocial behavior: Personal and situational influences and their interactions. In E. Staub (Ed.), *Personality. Basic aspects and current research.* Englewood Cliffs, N.J.: Prentice Hall, 1980.

Staub, E., & Sherk, L. Need for approval, children's sharing behavior and reciprocity in sharing. *Child Development,* 1970, *41,* 243–252.

Szustrowa, T. *Ability to act for extrapersonal goals and some characteristics of family training.* Warsaw: Zeszyty Naukowe Uniwersytetu Warszawskiego, 1972.

Zajonc, R. B. Feeling and thinking: Preferences need no inferences. *American Psychologist,* 1980, *35,* 151–175.

Zimbardo, P., & Ruch F. *Psychology and life.* Glenview, Ill.: Scott, Foresman, 1975.

Zwolinski, M. *The relationship between the development of concept constancy and the development of distributional justice.* Unpublished master's thesis, University of Warsaw, 1974.

# 9

# Development of Cooperation and Help-Seeking Activities

## An Action Theoretical Approach

Louis Oppenheimer and Jan Heller

## 1. INTRODUCTION

Within the large literature dealing with prosocial behavior in children and adults the same few key concepts are often employed in radically different ways. The term *prosocial behavior* is sometimes meant in a narrow or restricted sense to include only such behaviors as helping and/or altruistic behavior (cf. Bar-Tal, Raviv, & Leiser, 1980), being kind or helpful or reacting empathically (cf. Chandler & Helm, 1980), and also in a much wider sense that includes such behaviors as "sharing, helping, defending, sympathy, rescuing, cooperation, and others" (Yarrow & Waxler, 1976, p. 118). The range of subtopics treated within this literature is equally wide and, among other things, deals with (1) the development of prosocial behavior (cf. Bar-Tal *et al.*, 1980; Mussen & Eisenberg-Berg, 1977); (2) the conditions under which it is evidenced (cf. Pearl, 1979; Yarrow & Waxler, 1976); (3) the types of helping behavior judged to be required by the situation (Chandler & Helm, 1980); and (4) even

---

LOUIS OPPENHEIMER • Department of Developmental Psychology, University of Amsterdam, Amsterdam, the Netherlands. JAN HELLER • District Health Service, Heerlen, the Netherlands.

with whether altruism is an integral part of human nature (Hoffman, 1981).

Despite research results from these and many other fronts, few authors have directed attention to the fact that prosocial behavior cannot be exclusively defined in terms of subject variables, but is dependent upon an interactive dialogue with those others whose actions in some way elicit or evoke prosocial responses. As Nelson-Le Gall (1981) notes, "very little is known about helping from the perspective of the helpee" (p. 2; Gergen, 1974). Any complete account of prosocial behavior will require a filling in of the details of this other half of the dialogue.

In keeping with the perceived need, the purposes of this chapter will be to provide some insight into the conditions under which cooperation, as a form of prosocial behavior, will occur; to examine what subject and object variables are related to cooperative behavior, especially in order to illuminate some variables related to help-seeking behavior and how the latter is related to cooperative behavior; and finally to present a theoretical framework that informed two illustrative studies of help seeking.

### 1.1. Cognition and Social Behavior

In addition to the general lack of information regarding the situations and variables that elicit or evoke prosocial behavior, there is also little clarity about the more general relationship between social cognition and social behavior or action. One dimension of study that has examined this relationship in some detail concerns the ability to infer the inner psychological processes of others (i.e., role taking or perspective taking). More than a decade ago Hartup (1970) argued that "role-taking would appear to be one prerequisite for the emergence of many . . . social behaviors. . . . It is inherent, for example, in cooperation and altruistic interaction" (p. 368). On the strength of this assumption a whole research literature on the relationship of role taking to prosocial behavior has developed. Several years later, however, in summarizing this literature, Shantz (1975) concludes that "the hypothesis of substantial relationship between role-taking ability and social behavior has not been strongly supported to date, but neither, certainly has it been refuted" (p. 308). Similarly, Light (1979) has recently concluded that the data with regard to the relationship between social cognition (i.e., perspective taking) and social behavior are both conflicting and confusing.

A similar lack of apparent correspondence between social thought and social action has been observed in the area of moral development (cf. Eckensberger, 1977). As Flavell (1977) has indicated, we are, despite considerable research devoted to the problem, still quite unsure what the relation is, if any, "between a person's assessed moral reasoning stage and his level of moral behavior in real situations" (p. 143). Emmerich, Cocking, and Sigel (1979), studying the relationship between cognitive and social-cognitive functioning, have also concluded that there is little clearly demonstrated reciprocity between the cognitive and social domains. In their own research they found that "certain cognitive processes facilitated social adaptation, but social adaptation did not influence cognitive growth" (p. 495).

Another group of studies have suggested that such discrepancies between cognitive levels of competence and concrete social behavior may in fact be the result of specific social situations in which the problems are experienced (Butter & Seidenberg, 1973; Haan, 1969), or that some conditions allow behavior to be directed by cognitive structures whereas others do not (Burton, 1978).

It appears that there is no easy, one-to-one relationship between (social) cognitive variables and social behavior, and that this relationship appears to depend on a number of variables within the interaction between individuals and their environments. What seems required, then, is some theoretical framework representing the interaction between the *external* social world and the *internal* or perceived social world, in which subjects are seen as active constructors of their own social knowledge (cf. Oppenheimer, 1979).

### 1.2. The Individual–Environment Relationship

According to Pervin (1978), we are in need of "a conceptualization of the process of interaction with an emphasis on the point of engagement between the organism and the environment" (p. 83). Two aspects of this moment of engagement are important. The first is that in any social interaction different events or processes occur simultaneously both in the organism and in the environment. Second, it is clear that particular or isolated events can only be understood fully within the context of a longer sequence of such events.

Whereas Pervin emphasizes the interaction between the individual and the environment, Riegel and Meacham (1978; Riegel, 1975) propose a dialectical or transactional model stressing the necessity to focus on the reciprocal relationship between the "individual-psychological dimension and the cultural-sociological context" (p. 44) as the interactional account of development. Such an approach coincides with other theories and with the ecological approaches in particular (cf. Bronfenbrenner, 1977; Wohlwill, 1980).

## 2. THE ACTION THEORETICAL APPROACH

Action theory, as described by Hollis (1977), Von Wright (1976), and Boesch (1976), explicitly takes the position that human action can only be explained by the interaction or transaction between and among systems, both within the individual and within the environment. The basic postulate of this action theoretical position is that "human action is purposive, intentional and subject to rules" (Hollis, 1977, p. 10). That is, people act with respect to goals; they attempt to reach these goals by intended actions, and the latter are either facilitated or restricted in their scope by rules and norms imposed by the environment (i.e., society).

For an action to be purposive, it has to be explained by reference to goals and is consequently based to a greater or lesser extent on the agent's own wants and interests (Von Wright, 1976). This implies that the meaning of an action lies within the actor and not in his environment (cf. Mead, 1934), that it has a purpose and is motivated: The action finds its grounds in an epistemic attitude and intentions (Von Wright, 1976). Motives to reach a goal are then regarded as a "desire defined in terms of its object [and] can be treated . . . as the actor's real reason defined in terms of his interests" (Hollis, 1977, p. 132). Intentions, then, can be determined by two types of internal determinants: Besides the actor's own interests (i.e., "wants," Von Wright, 1976), the actor also has "duties." Wants, like interests, refer to intrinsic values of actions; duties refer to explicit and implicit rules set by, for instance, the social role of an actor (i.e., "role-holder duties," Von Wright, 1976, p. 429). Duties can overrule wants, however, and in this case the actor becomes a slave of his roles and has no time left to attend to his wants.

Both Von Wright and Hollis note that caution is needed in the application of such views in that too often a direct link is postulated between the intention and the resulting action. As Hollis (1977, p. 115) remarks:

> a causal law is a contingent connection between contingent events (or facts). [However,] firstly, . . . the *explanans* (i.e., the intention) is not a distinct antecedent; secondly, it is not contingently connected to the *explanandum* (i.e., the action; cf. also Louch, 1966); thirdly, since the agent knows what he is doing without having to know that he is an instance of a class, the connection is not general.

In other words, "to talk of intentions is . . . to answer the question *what*, not *why*" (Louch, 1966, p. 106).

Hollis (1977) ascribes still another characteristic to intentions; namely, that they are related to criteria by means of which one selects the methods to reach a goal. Such a selection of methods must take account of the situation in which the action will be executed. It is the situation—

be it a clearly defined laboratory setting, the family, the peer group, the society, or a culture—that provides opportunities to act and that also restricts the possibilities of action by its rules (norms, moral standards, etc.), that is, exerts the "normative pressure" (Von Wright, 1976). Human action in social context is consequently always subject to rules and is dependent upon the opportunities to act provided for by the situations. In addition, the abilities, either mentally or physically, to execute an action limit the actor's choice of possible actions. An important notion offered by Von Wright (1976, p. 432) is that "every action by any man creates and destroys opportunities for action," emphasizing the dynamic character of any act within contexts.

In summary, the theoretical and conceptual model that emerges from these action theoretical accounts is one in which the goals of action are regarded as the basic element in explaining human action.[1] Such intentions are not the causes of actions in that they do not logically lead to an action, but are conceptually related to action. Two internal determinants of actions can consequently be distinguished: first, the motivation to reach a goal (divided into wants and duties), and second, the intentions. Whereas wants seem to be equivalent to the actor's own interests and determine his reasons for a choice from possible methods (i.e., actions) to attain a goal, the duties are an additional factor in the explanation of that category of actions appropriate to the social roles of the actor. The prediction of action in the latter case may thus be more accurate than the prediction of action based on the personal interests and wants of the actor. The intentions together with the rules or normative pressure determine the class of methods most suited to attain the desired goal. In addition, the personal factor of abilities (mental and physical) is included because it restricts the choice of actions to be taken. Similarly, the external features of the situation, that is, its opportunities, further narrow down the number of possible actions. The resulting picture is then one of individuals with their personal wants, interests, and limitations; society with its rules and normative pressure; the situation with its opportunities; and the relations and interactions between these elements.

### 2.1. The Plan of Action

The actions that finally ensue from this complex, multidimensional system are the intentional actions, or "reason-actions" (cf. Enç, 1975). However, the fact that an action is decided to be the best overall method

[1]For an elaborate discussion of the various related philosophical, sociological, and psychological arguments, see Oppenheimer (1979).

(i.e., within the context of the specific situation) in order to reach the desired goal does not tell us anything about the processes of action execution, regulation, and goal attainment—in other words, the *plan of action* (cf. Kreitler & Kreitler, 1976; Miller, Galanter, & Pribram, 1960). According to Louch (1966), one of the grounds on which an intention can be attributed to individuals is the "intensity or elaboration of planing, which appears to have an action of a certain sort as a consequence" (p. 116), or, as Rubinstein (1977) remarks, that are such intentional actions that possess a mental component (cf. Parsons, 1959; Shutz, 1967; Thomas, 1931; Von Wright, 1976; Weber, 1966). The intermediate stage between the "intent to act" and the "execution of the act" is referred to by most action theorists as the "plan of action." Thus Reinshagen (1977) notes that

> the constituting factor of an action is not the real execution, acting itself, but the conscious anticipation of the action in a plan-of-action, that is, the final relation of a positively evaluated goal-of-action with possible methods [to reach it] and their causally determined effects. (p. 135)

As such, the plan of action includes the relationships among the goal, the methods to reach the goal, the anticipated effects of the methods, possible obstacles, and alternative courses of action. The plan of action refers to a conceptual relationship among the goal, methods, and effects.

The plan of action can also be regarded as a regulating principle, that is, referring to three different stages inherent in action: the begin-stage, the course of action, and the end-stage (cf. Boesch, 1976), or the triggering of output programming, regulation of the course of action, and completion of action (cf. Kreitler & Kreitler, 1976). According to the latter authors the plan of action constitutes the programming of the action; it provides the details of the *how:* "the processing of programming and elicitation of output programs fill in the gap between the decision to act for a specific goal and the actual action" (p. 143). In short, the plan of action refers to an imagined general outline, scheme, or blueprint of the total sequence of action(s) to reach a desired goal. It includes the relationships among the goal, method(s), and effects, the potential obstacles, and alternative courses of action. The degree of sophistication or elaboration of the plan of action may then depend on: (1) one's anticipatory abilities and their levels of development; (2) the development of the ability to generate methods to reach goals; (3) the comprehension of the rules set by the (social) environment; and (4) evaluative processes with regard to the situation (cf. Shure & Spivack, 1972).

In another sense, the plan of action refers to a frame of reference for the regulation of the course of action. As such the plan of action has to be flexible and accessible to changes. The assumption that the plan of action should be open to accommodation and assimilation (Kreitler & Kreitler, 1976) places the plan of action under the direct control of the intellectual (i.e., operational) system. Each act within the sequence of actions leading to goal attainment will change the environment, that is, will have certain effects as consequences. If all the effects caused by the actions are anticipated and taken account of in the plan of action, no changes in the overall plan of action will be necessary; that is, the goal will be attained without any direct problems for the agent. The processes taking place can be described as matching procedures between the real events and anticipated events in the plan of action based on feedback processes. If, however, effects or events occur that were not anticipated or taken account of, that is, nonpredicted effects either intended or not intended, the plan of action will have to be changed. Such unanticipated effects may then be the source of new conflicts whenever they prevent goal attainment. In the latter instance, two individuals, simultaneously present in the same situation, may have incompatible plans of action. Miller *et al.* (1960) again stress the role of the intellectual system by noting that the "the discovery that two plans-of-action are incompatible may require great intelligence" (p. 97). The awareness that two plans of action are conflicting may result in either (1) the abandonment of the goal and subsequent plan of action, or the construction of a new plan of action based on changes in the internal representation of the external environment while the original goal is maintained; (2) the modification of the plan of action so as to reduce the conflict to a minimum or to avoid it; or (3) maintenance and execution of the plan of action in its original form even, if necessary, with force (cf. Oppenheimer, 1977). The extrapolation of such *intrapersonal* conflicts between a single individual's competing plans of action (Miller *et al.*, 1960) to conflicts between incompatible plans of action or goals of two or more different individuals makes feasible the study of *interpersonal* conflicts within this same theoretical framework.

### 2.2. Help-Seeking Activities and the Action Theoretical Approach

In reviewing the available literature on help-seeking activities it becomes clear that help seeking must be considered one of the classes of actions taken by individuals in order to reach their goals. "Children must," according to Nelson-Le Gall (1981), "learn to associate others with the achievement of their goals and must learn various means of inducing others to help attain these goals" (p. 3). Help seeking, then, is a process by means of which one finds the right person to aid in solving a problem and as such can be seen as an independent method to attain a goal.

Within this context help seeking is not simply equated with dependency, but is instead thought to be a characteristic of autonomous behavior, reflecting a high degree of internal rather than external locus of control (Murphy, 1962). In addition, it is suggested that the process of help seeking also consists of the inclusion of others as resources in goal attainment. As such, help seeking was found to be related to general cognitive functioning (Enright & Sutterfield, 1980; Wright, 1980) and social perspective taking (Wilson & Shantz, 1977). In summary, then, the available literature dealing with help-seeking activities suggests that help seeking will be positively related to (1) cognitive functioning, (2) social-cognitive development, and (3) autonomy.

## 3. RESEARCH FROM AN ACTION THEORETICAL PERSPECTIVE

On the basis of the preceding account and the literature that has been reviewed, it is possible to differentiate two separable but interrelated research questions concerning plans of action. The first concerns the process by means of which such plans of action are generated and elaborated. The second deals with the ways in which goals are integrated with alternative plans of action of one's own or of others.

We shall first report a study in which the several aspects of the plan of action were explored (Oppenheimer & Veerman, 1980). Second, we shall describe a further study in which an attempt was made to relate personal, cognitive, social-cognitive, experiental, and situational variables to concrete behavior (cf. also Oppenheimer, 1981).

### 3.1. Research on Components of the Plan of Action

The first study represents an attempt to operationalize several different components of overall plans of action. These include efforts to measure the ability of children (1) to generate methods to reach stated goals; (2) to judge whether such methods are effective or ineffective; and (3) to infer the goals of other people (this inferential ability will be referred to as "goal taking"; cf. Eckensberger, 1977; Oppenheimer & Veerman, 1980). Goal-taking ability was thought to be of central importance in allowing children to anticipate potential obstacles to their own goal attainments, and in permitting them to generate alternative courses of action that take such obstacles into account.

This study was primarily descriptive rather than predictive and sought only to develop means of documentation rather than to assess the behavioral consequences of such plans of action. The methodology adopted roughly corresponded to that employed by Shure and Spivack (1972), who also stress method–goal thinking. According to these authors the development of a plan of action can be defined as "an ability to carefully plan, step by step, means to reach a stated goal," and includes reference to the forethought that is required to forestall and develop alternative routes that circumvent potential obstacles to one's goals.

In order to gain some insight into ways in which children of various ages develop and employ such plans of action, 105 children from the first, third, and fifth grades (mean ages 6.9, 9.0, and 11.1, respectively) of an elementary school were presented with six short social episodes, illustrated by pictures, about which they were asked three major questions pertaining to (1) their preferred methods for reaching the stated goals, (2) the effectiveness or ineffectiveness of such methods, and (3) the anticipated goals of the other people depicted in the episode. Each child was asked only one of these questions about any particular episode, but questions of all types were asked of each subject. As a result of this counterbalanced design it was possible to analyze the relation among method generation, goal taking, and the judgments of the effectiveness and ineffectiveness of the methods within each age group, as well as to compare over age groups in regard to developmental differences.

### 3.1.1. *Results*

For our present purposes only the results with regard to the method-generation component will be discussed in detail. These results indicated that there was a significant difference among the first, third, and fifth graders in the level of effectiveness of the methods produced to reach the stated goals, $F(2,16) = 7.08$, $p < .01$. The significance of this age trend was, however, largely due to the inferior performance of the youngest subjects and no significant difference was found between the oldest age groups. After an obstacle was introduced to the first method, a second method was obtained. An examination of these methods revealed that the first method was significantly more effective, $F(1,24) = 9.58$, $p < .01$, than the second, alternative method. Newman-Keuls analyses revealed that the first method given by the first and third graders was significantly more effective ($p < .05$) than the alternative method, whereas for the fifth graders no such difference was found. In short, the older subjects but not the first and third graders seemed to have more than one trick up their sleeves. Furthermore, the methods produced showed an increase in the number of steps (i.e., subgoals) as a function of age which was most salient for the two-, three-, and more-steps answers combined, $\chi^2(2) = 6.2$, $p < .05$.

Of particular interest here was the question whether children would include other individuals in their methods for achieving their goals. A detailed examination of the methods offered by the children demonstrated that "depending on the situation presented, use was made of other persons, not present in the described situations, in order to reach the goal" (Oppenheimer & Verrman, 1980, p. 66). The frequencies of occasions in which another person was introduced in the methods tended to significance ($p < .10$). This result suggests that, on the one hand, use will be made of other persons whenever the situation requires or allows it, whereas, on the other hand, the use of another person as resource to attain a goal increased rather than decreased with age.

In brief, the remaining data indicated that the ability to infer the goals of other people was linearly related to age. Although the ability to judge the effectiveness of methods showed a progressive development with age, all age groups did equally well in judging the lack of effectiveness of badly conceived methods. Correlation computations among these abilities and a factor analysis revealed that, with no control for the effects of age, all variables were related to one another and loaded on one factor, suggesting the existence of one structure: the plan of action. With the effects of age controlled, however, the four abilities appeared to be divided over two structures or factors dealing with the method generation and the judgments of effectiveness and ineffectiveness on the one hand, and with the ability for goal inference or goal taking on the other hand (cf. Oppenheimer & Veerman, 1980).

### 3.2. Methods of Goal Attainment

The results of the foregoing study formed the basis for the study to which we now turn. In the previous study the introduction of a hypothetical obstacle to reaching a "given goal" was shown to produce different reactions in the three age groups. In that study, however, subjects were not required to carry out their plans of action and no attempt was made to measure actual behavior. The next study to be reported went beyond this "as if" approach and sought to investigate plans of action in a concrete behavioral context. The study is further based on the following additional assumptions derived from the action theoretical perspective: first, that in order to reach "stated goals" children will use particular methods, and second, that the opportunities provided by the situation will affect the method and modes of implementation employed in reaching such goals. In order to test these assumptions a task was developed that permitted subjects a diversity of methods to reach the stated goal, and would enable an examination of the effects of an experimental restriction imposed on the opportunities of the subjects to carry out their plans of action.

### 3.2.1. *The Tower Task*

A very common toy in the Netherlands is "Lego," plastic building blocks, from which children can build structures of varying complexity. From these blocks a "model" tower was constructed that consisted of a *double* row 20 blocks high, such that the tower consisted of a total of 40 blocks. The children were asked to build a tower *"as high as* the model tower" from a supply of additional blocks.

In a pilot study it was found that for most children building a tower *as high as* the model tower meant building a tower *identical to* the model tower. In others words, children started directly with a base consisting of two blocks leading to a tower of a double row of blocks. The experimental manipulation consisted of varying the number of building blocks provided.

This pilot datum led to the development of an individual and a dyadic block-building task. In the individual task, with only 20 blocks the only solution to the problem would be to build a tower of a single row of blocks. If the child's initial interpretation of the task was to build a tower identical to the model, then in the course of the implementation of this approach he or she would be confronted by a clear "shortage of means." If, however, the child correctly evaluated the opportunities provided, he or she would realize that the former method could not be implemented and that another method was called for.

In the dyadic building task, two subjects were provided a common supply of 40 blocks and each was instructed to build a tower as high as the model. In this condition the shortage of means (i.e., the blocks) that previously constituted a physical obstacle now became a potential interpersonal, social obstacle as well (cf. Reinshagen, 1977). That is, in this situation each subject could assume that "the other child has the blocks I need." If the children decided *a priori* upon a strategy of each individually building a single-row tower, no conflict needed to occur. If, however, either child decided upon the method of building a tower identical to the model, the shortage of means would necessarily become an interpersonal conflict between incompatible plans of action, or methods of reaching a stated goal. The obstacle in this case would not be an absolute shortage of means but a conflict over the ownership of the necessary blocks. This conflict, as implied above, can be solved in three ways: (1) Both children can settle upon the method of the single-row tower (i.e., methods are changed, the goal is maintained); (2) they can decide to cooperate (actually representing a change in the goal), that is, reinterpret the task as a joint project in which *together* they create a tower as high as the model tower (here the method is maintained, but the goal is slightly changed); and (3) a competitive situation can emerge in which one or both of the children may attempt to take away the blocks of the other.

### 3.2.2. *Cognitive and Social-Cognitive Correlates of Action*

In addition to developing a descriptive account of how children of different ages approached the tower problem, an attempt was made to situate their performances in a broader context of cognitive and social-cognitive abilities, personality variables, and behavioral measures.

First, the behavior of children in earlier pilot studies suggested that the solution of the tower task that involved the building of a single-row tower probably required a considerable amount of decentration; that is, decentration from the visual aspects of the model tower and understanding that its height and breadth were different and separable dimensions. In other words, identical height could be attained by a reduction in breadth, that is, compensation. Consequently, this form of problem solution was hypothesized to rely to a large extent on cognitive abilities in general and conservation in particular. Consequently, all children were assessed as to their levels of conservation for discrete quantity, length, weight, and volume. All of these measures were combined into one score for conservation ability. It was hypothesized that only subjects with the necessary cognitive prerequisites could attempt to solve the tower problem in this fashion, which we shall refer to as the *cognitive method*.

The cooperative and competitive methods, on the other hand, were hypothesized to be a function of social-cognitive abilities rather than of cognitive abilities as such. Hence these methods will be referred to as the *interactional methods.* Although the exact relationship between social-cognitive abilities and cooperative behavior (here defined as sharing means to reach identical goals) is unclear (cf. Light, 1979; Shantz, 1975), it was hypothesized that affective and conceptual perspective taking would be related to cooperative behavior (cf. Hartup, 1970; Johnson, 1975; Marcus, Telleen, & Roke, 1979). Consequently, all children were presented with an affective and a conceptual perspective-taking task (Oppenheimer, 1978) to assess their levels of development. The competitive method, which may be regarded as a form of non- or antisocial behavior, is assumed to have a negative relationship with levels of perspective taking (cf. Chandler, 1972, 1973; Light, 1979; Neale, 1966).

### 3.2.3. *Autonomy*

In addition to the previously mentioned variables of cognitive and sociocognitive level, it was also hypothesized that children's plans of action in solving the tower problem would vary as a function of their degree of autonomy or locus of control (cf. Milgram & Milgram, 1975). It can be argued within the action theoretical context that the way in which children react to physical and/or social obstacles may reflect their feelings of control, independence, or autonomy. For physical obstacles this should pertain to the control over objects, for social obstacles (i.e., in the dyadic condition) to their independence from peers. Shouval, Zakay, and Halfon (1977) described an "autonomy multiple choice–3" measure that distinguishes between object, parent, and peer pressure and traumatic situations. This scale was validated with children averaging 12 years. For the present purpose—the exploration of the relationship between autonomy measures and social action in the tower problem—a selection of items most suited for translation into the Dutch language and for adaptation to a younger age group (approximately 5 to 10) for object-press and peer-press was administered to all children. (Because of the younger age groups this scale was verbally presented to each child individually).

### 3.2.4. *Aspects of Social Behavior*

In addition to the assessment of developmental levels for conservation, affective and conceptual perspective taking, and autonomy, an observational scheme was also developed in order to rate more directly the behavior of the subjects in the tower-building task.

Our concerns included (1) whether children would anticipate the shortage of means during the execution of the incorrect method, or only after no means were left (*anticipation*). The scoring was dichotomous, that is, the anticipation of the shortage *before* the last two blocks was assigned a score of 1, and *after* the last two blocks a score of 0. We were interested (2) in how the children would expressively react to the perception of the shortage (*perception*). Thus the realization could be expressed either verbally or nonverbally; in both the latter cases a score of 1 was given, and no expressive reaction to the perception was scored as 0. We were concerned (3) with how the children would react to the realization of the shortage (*react*), that is, whether they would abandon their attempt for goal attainment (0 score) or continue to search for another method (1 score). We wanted to know (4) when the children would develop a new method (*procedure*)—directly after the decision to continue their attempts to reach the stated goal (1 score), or after some period of experimenting (0 score), that is, the followed procedures after the reaction. Our next questions were (5) whether the children would *request help from one another* (*help;* 1 score) or not (0 score); and (6) whether they would check their progress, that is, compare the progress of their course of action with the model tower (the goal to be reached; *comparison*). The comparison could be made either visually or manually; in both cases a score of 1 was given. If no comparisons were made a score of 0 was given.

Finally, we were interested in some other personal and task-specific variables not assessed by any of the above instruments. After the children completed the tower task (no time limits were used) they were presented with four additional questions. The first referred to whether they had previous experience in playing with the Lego blocks and, if so, how much they played with them (i.e., once weekly, twice weekly, etc.). The second question dealt with the explanation of the shortage of means. Could the children give an adequate explanation why there were too few blocks? This explanation should then make reference to the comprehension that to build a tower "as high as" the model tower does not necessarily imply that the tower should also be identical in breadth; that is, reference should be made to compensatory aspects of the problem. We also asked the children whether they still remembered the instructions, and, finally, to what extent they applied the instructions during their activities.

### 3.3. Procedure and Subjects

The assessment instruments for conservation, perspective taking, and autonomy were presented in one session. The tower task and the questionnaire were presented in a second session separated from the first by an interval of approximately 1 week.

In the present study 72 children participated from a kindergarten and elementary school divided over three age groups with mean ages 5.7 years for the kindergarten, 7.3 years for the first grade, and 9.1 years for the third grade. Each age group of 24 children was randomly divided into one group of 8 children that was assigned to the individual condition and one group of 16 children assigned to the dyadic condition (i.e., eight dyads). Although all children knew one another, the formation of the dyads was such that no regular friends were present in one dyad. No restrictions were made in regard to sex, although there were approximately equal numbers of boys and girls in each age group and condition.

### 3.4. Results

The results will be discussed on two levels: first, with regard to the general research question by the comparison between the individual

*Table 1. The Frequency and Types of Methods Selected by the Three Age Groups in the Individual and Dyadic Conditions*

| | Individual condition | | Dyadic condition | | | |
|---|---|---|---|---|---|---|
| | *n* | Cognitive | *n* | Cognitive | Cooperative | Total |
| Kindergarten | 8 | 1 | 8 | 0 | 3 | 3 |
| First grade | 8 | 2 | 8 | 1 | 3 | 4 |
| Third grade | 8 | 7 | 8 | 2 | 5 | 7 |
| Total | | 10 | | 3 | 11 | 14 |

and dyadic conditions; and second, with regard to the help-seeking processes.

A first analysis of the data aimed at verifying whether the children in the dyadic and individual conditions were comparable in regard to their developmental levels on the various covariables (conservation, perspective taking, autonomy, and experience). A 3 × 2 × 6 (age × condition × task) analysis of variance with repeated measures on the last factor showed no effect for the condition, nor for the condition × task, nor for the age × condition × task interactions. From this result it could be concluded that the children in each condition did not significantly differ from one another on the respective cognitive, social-cognitive, personality, and experiential variables.

The next step concerned the types of solutions (i.e., methods), their frequency and relations to the conditions. Each occurrence of a method leading to goal attainment, independent of the type of method, obtained a score of 1. In Table 1 the main results concerning the types of methods selected by the children are given. It is striking that in none of the dyadic groups, at any age, there was any evidence that subjects adopted the competitive method. Either the cognitive or the cooperative method was decided upon in every case. A first 3 × 2 (age × condition) analysis of variance on the total number of methods leading to goal attainment revealed that with increasing age progressively more children reached goal attainment in both the individual and the dyadic conditions, $F\,(2, 42) = 6.62$, $p < .05$; neither the effect for the condition nor the age × condition interaction was significant. A second 3 × 2 (age × condition) analysis of variance on the cognitive method revealed a significant effect for age, $F(2,42) = 8.13$, $p < .01$ but also a significant effect for the condition, $F(1,42) = 7.85$, $p < .01$, indicating that the number of children who opted for the cognitive method in the individual condition was significantly greater than in the dyadic condition. Again the age × condition interactions was not significant. The final 3 × 2 (age × type of method) analysis of variance within the dyadic condition showed that, although there was significantly more use of the cooperative than the cognitive method, $F(1,21) = 4.96$, $p < .05$, neither method was related to age, nor was the age × type of method interaction significant.

These results suggest, first, that cooperative behavior, that is, the successful implementation of the cooperative method, does not represent an age-related development. Second, whenever it was possible the cooperative method appeared to be preferred to individual and competitive methods, in this respective order of decreasing occurrence. It should be noted, however, that there is a nonsignificant trend toward an increase in the successful implementation of the cooperative method from ages 7 to 9.

### 3.4.1. *The Methods and the Cognitive and Social-Cognitive Abilities*

The abilities of conservation and perspective taking as well as the personality characteristic of object-press were all significantly correlated with age ($p < .05$). The Pearson product–moment correlation coefficients ranged from .32 for object-press to .89 for affective perspective taking. Only peer press was not significantly related with age. Also, the amount of experience the children had with the play materials was related to age ($r = .49$, $p < .05$). Within the dyadic condition, none of these variables was related to either the cognitive or the cooperative method. When, however, the cognitive method was the only possible method to attain the stated goal (i.e., in the individual condition), the abilities of conservation, affective perspective taking, as well as the experience with the materials were found to be related to the adoption of this method (the respective correlation coefficients were .35, .35, and .54).

The result that the development of the conservation ability is related to the cognitive method confirmed the expectation that the latter method could be adopted only by subjects who possessed a degree of decentration competence.

### 3.4.2. *The Observation System*

In the preceding sections the final method, that is, the method finally leading to goal attainment, was taken as point of departure. It has to be noted, however, that like in the pilot study all children in both conditions started directly with the method of building the tower identical to the model tower. Only after the shortage of means was anticipated or encountered was a new method developed.

The average reliability for the six observation categories used in the present study was .95. Again, all six categories (anticipation, perception, reaction, procedure, help, comparison) were significantly related

*Table 2. The Pearson Product–Moment Correlation Coefficients Among the Various Variables Employed in the Dyadic Condition*

| | Anticipation | Perception | Reaction | Procedure | Help | Comparison | Explanation | Memory | Application |
|---|---|---|---|---|---|---|---|---|---|
| Cognitive method | — | −.56 | — | −.43 | — | — | — | — | — |
| Cooperative method | — | — | — | — | — | .54 | — | — | .43 |
| Conservation | .43 | — | — | — | .50 | — | .38 | .45 | .67 |
| Affective p. t.[a] | .37 | — | — | — | .68 | — | .39 | .53 | .55 |
| Conceptual p. t. | — | — | — | — | .68 | — | .35 | .55 | .51 |
| Experience | — | — | — | — | — | — | — | .39 | — |
| Object-press | — | — | .41 | — | — | — | .42 | — | — |
| Peer-press | — | −.38 | — | — | −.46 | — | — | — | — |
| Anticipation | | — | — | .42 | — | — | — | — | — |
| Perception | | | — | — | .43 | — | — | — | — |
| Reaction | | | | — | — | — | — | — | — |
| Procedure | | | | | .35 | — | — | — | .50 |
| Help | | | | | | — | — | — | — |
| Comparison | | | | | | | — | — | — |
| Explanation | | | | | | | | — | — |
| Memory | | | | | | | | | .52 |

[a]p. t. = perspective taking; all correlation coefficients are significant on the $p < .05$ level.

to age (the *r* values ranged from .38 for perception to .56 for help). The three remaining aspects of "explanation" for the shortage of means, "memory" of the instructions, and the "application" of the instructions during their activities, obtained by the questionnaire, were also related to age (the *r* values were .37, .50, and .55, respectively).

Because, among others, the help processes (i.e., the help-seeking activities) are not applicable in the individual condition, we shall make no further reference to this condition (see Oppenheimer, 1979).

In Table 2 the Pearson product–moment correlation coefficients are represented between the assessed abilities, personality characteristics, the six observation categories, the questionnaire items, and the methods used in the dyadic condition. As can be observed from the correlation matrix, almost none of the behavioral processes was related to either the cognitive or the cooperative method in the dyadic condition. Although the (social) cognitive abilities are related to the anticipation of the shortage of means, it is important to note that conservation and the perspective-taking abilities are related (1) to the help processes, and (2) to the explanation of the shortage. The latter relationship can be understood in terms of the type of explanation used. Instead of grounding the shortage of means on the realization that "as high as" does not mean "identical to," the shortage was explained by the fact that two children were working simultaneously with only one pile of blocks: If they had been working alone (as in the individual condition) no shortage would have occurred. In other words, the physical obstacle of a shortage of means that could be solved by compensatory abilities became an interpersonal conflict in which the obstacle was the other child. Both the cognitive and social-cognitive abilities are related to the process of "asking help." This result suggests that the ability to convey a message of distress may depend on social-cognitive abilities, as, in all likelihood, does the interpretation of such a message and the subsequent altruistic or helping behavior (cf. Iannotti, 1978; Rushton, 1976).

Experience with the materials was found to play no role in the dyadic condition; object-press, on the other hand, was positively related to the reaction. The relation between object-press and explanation of the shortage illustrates the children's realization that the shortage could have been solved had they been working alone. The level of autonomy with regard to peers was shown to be relevant only in interactional situations. The negative correlations between peer-press and the expressive reaction (*perception*) to the shortage of means as well as asking for help indicate that the higher the level of social autonomy, the lower will be the amount of overt reactions or expressions and requests for help.

The lower part of the correlation matrix shows the interrelationships between the behavioral processes and between the latter and memory of the instructions and its application. In the dyadic condition the application as well as the memory of the instructions are nearly unrelated to any of the behavioral processes. This result may be based on the change of instructions that took place in the dyadic condition. Although each child started with the initial implicit goal "to build individually a tower as high as the model tower," this goal was changed after the occurrence of the shortage of means in the new explicit goal "to build *together* a tower as high as the model tower."

### 3.5. Discussion

The guiding assumption of the present study was that children's goals and methods of goal attainment would utilize the materials (i.e., the opportunities) provided by the situation. The manipulation of the materials (in the present study, the amount of blocks) lead to a conflict between the anticipated effects of a selected method and the real effect—the shortage of means.

The reconstruction or construction of a new method to overcome the shortage and reach the stated goal was naturally situation dependent. If no choice was present between methods, then subjects evidenced a significant increase in the adoption of the suitable methods to reach their goal (i.e., the cognitive method). In addition, only in the restricted-choice situation was the adoption of this latter method found to be related to cognitive, social-cognitive, and experiential variables as well as to age. If, however, the child is given a free choice to select a method, whether cooperative, cognitive, or competitive, quite a different picture emerges. Although the children appeared quite able to make use of the cognitive method (see the individual condition), they rarely adopted this method in the dyadic condition. Instead they preferred to change their original goal and adopt an analogous, but not identical, cooperative goal.

According to action theory (Hollis, 1977; Von Wright, 1976), the selection of methods to reach a goal will be based on the actor's own subjective reasons, wants, and the affective loadings for these wants and goals. The frequency of occurrence of the methods, that is, the cooperative method (11), the cognitive method (3), and the competitive method (0), may then reflect subjective wants. There is then a clear preference for the cooperative method, a method that can be characterized as interactional or "fundamentally" (pro)social. The cognitive method is obviously individualistic, whereas the competitive method could be described as non- or antisocial. This line of thinking coincides first with previous empirical data (cf. Crockenberg, Bryant & Wilce, 1976) suggesting that young children prefer cooperatively structured environments to competitive ones, "implying a greater personal satisfaction with the cooperative experience" (p. 387), and second with a theoretical line of thought assuming that children are "naturally" social (cf. Mead, 1934; Wallon, 1947). Individualism them emerges from social interaction, or, as Harré and Secord (1972, p. 8) note, "unless we can see that other individuals see us as a person we cannot see ourselves as such." A direct derivative from such an argument predicts that social action will precede individual action, whereas competitive action, as a form of non- or antisocial action, should be a last-resort solution to problem situations. The results of the present study tend to confirm the latter sequence.

The total absence of the competitive method might also be explained by the low level of incentive attached to goal attainment. It can be argued that the level of incentive affects the level of motivation to reach the stated goal, that is, the affective loading attached to the goal (cf. Brady, Newcomb, & Hartup, 1979). In the present study the children did not fear a reduction of incentive, for none was given when they modified the original goal. The promise of an incentive—often a characteristic of our Western society—could have resulted in the occurrence of the competitive method.

The results also indicate that the method selected does regulate behavioral processes (i.e., specific actions), although only indirectly. In the restricted-choice situation (the individual condition), however, the actions were directly related to the selected method (see Oppenheimer, 1981). The cognitive and social-cognitive abilities were found to be related to a number of behavioral processes rather than to the methods in the dyadic condition.

## 4. GENERAL DISCUSSION AND CONCLUSIONS

In contrast to previous results (cf. Bar-Tal *et al.*, 1980; Yarrow & Waxler, 1976) showing no effect for age in the amount and/or frequency of helping behavior but only in the motives for (Bar-Tal *et al.*, 1980) and quality of help giving (Bar-Tal, Raviv, & Goldberg, 1983), help-seeking activities were found to increase with age. In addition, the older the children, the more they tended to make use of other persons in their methods to attain their goal (see Section 3.1.1.; Oppenheimer & Veerman, 1980). Combined with the result that children's methods to attain goals become more effective with increasing age, help-seeking activities and the inclusion of other resources in the methods can indeed be regarded as "a class of instrumental social-cognitive responses that function to assist the child's goal attainment and adaptation to the environment" (Nelson-Le Gall, 1981, p. 4) and that increase as the child grows older.

Help seeking hence becomes a method in its own right, independent from other (pro)social activities. Although help-seeking activities were found to be part of the social repertoire of children in cooperatively attaining a goal, they were *not* related to the cooperative method. The latter method was also not related to cognitive and social-cognitive abilities but appeared to be based on other determinants, possibly to subjective feelings of well-being. Help-seeking activities, on the other hand, were related to cognitive and social-cognitive abilities, thereby adding support to the claim that help seeking may be a social-cognitive ability (Nelson-Le Gall, 1981). It appears as if children become increasingly able to infer that another person will pay attention to requests for help. In addition, the results confirm previous findings showing help seeking to be related to cognitive functioning (Enright & Sutterfield, 1980; Wright, 1980) and social perspective taking (Wilson & Shantz, 1977).

In the dyadic condition the object obstacle was transformed to an interpersonal obstacle. Consequently, the absence of any relationship between help-seeking activities and self-reliance with regard to object obstacles is clear. The relationship observed between self-reliance with regard to peers and help-seeking activities was contrary to expectation, that is, the higher the level of self-reliance with regard to peers, the less help-seeking activity was evident. In addition, fewer overt reactions, either verbal or nonverbal, to the shortage of means were given with higher levels of autonomy with regard to peers. The latter type of autonomy, in contrast to autonomy with regard to objects, was not age related, which suggests that self-reliance with regard to peers may be a developed personality characteristic at the age of 5½. This type of autonomy was not found to be an indicator for help-seeking activity (cf. Murphy, 1962).

Even more interesting, however, is that the individual cognitive solution in the dyadic condition was inversely related to the frequency of overt reactions to the shortage. In other words, overt reactions are apparently intended as a form of help-seeking activity (see the positive relationship between the reaction and help processes) and apparently lead to communication and to the cooperative method to attain the goal. Help-seeking activities also increased the probability that an alternative method to attain the goal would be directly found after the encounter with the obstacle. This may illustrate another aspect of the help-seeking activity as an apparent goal-oriented activity. Again there is some support here for the argument that help seeking may be considered as an independent method for goal attainment. The helpee then appears to be goal oriented, which confirms an earlier finding showing that teachers judge elementary school children who seek help as more goal oriented than those who give up easily or passively wait for help (cf. Nelson-Le Gall, 1981).

In conclusion, besides providing interesting data on cooperative action and help-seeking activities, our research illustrates several action theoretical concepts. Our greatest concern was with the validity and operationalizability of several aspects of the models, constructs, and ideas discussed in action theory. In addition, we were interested in the extent to which these ideas could provide insight into the relationships between covert psychological processes and concrete actions of individuals, and whether these relationships could be explored from a developmental point of view. Although the above-discussed studies are exploratory in nature, incomplete, and in need of elaborate replication, it can at least be concluded that the results are promising and that the hypotheses generated within the action theoretical framework warrant additional investigation.

### Acknowledgments

We wish to express our gratitude to Michael Chandler for his comments on earlier drafts of this chapter.

## 5. REFERENCES

Bar-Tal, D., Raviv, A., & Leiser, T. The development of altruistic behavior: Empirical evidence. *Developmental Psychology*, 1980, *16*, 516–524.

Bar-Tal, D., Raviv, A., & Goldberg, M. *Helping behavior in kindergartens: An observational study*. Manuscript submitted for publication, 1983.

Boesch, E. E. *Psychopathologie des alltags*. Bern: Huber, 1976.

Brady, J. E., Newcomb, A. F., & Hartup, W. W. *Incentive condition and the companion's behavior as determinants of cooperation and competition in children*. Paper presented at the meeting of the Society for Research in Child Development, San Francisco, March 1979.

Bronfenbrenner, U. Toward an experimental ecology of human development. *American Psychologist*, 1977, *32*, 513–532.

Burton, R. V. Interface between the behavioral and cognitive developmental approaches to research in morality. In B. Z. Presseisen, D. Goldstein, & M. H. Appel (Eds.), *Topics in cognitive development* (Vol. 2). New York: Plenum Press, 1978.

Butter, E. J., & Seidenberg, B. Manifestations of moral development in concrete situations. *Social Behavior and Personality*, 1973, *1*, 64–70.

Chandler, M. J. Egocentrism in normal and pathological child development. In F. J. Mönks, W. W. Hartup, & J. de Wit (Eds.), *Determinants of behavioral development*. New York: Academic Press, 1972.

Chandler, M. J. Egocentrism and antisocial behavior: The assessment and training of social perspective-taking skills. *Developmental Psychology*, 1973, *9*, 326–332.

Chandler, M. J., & Helm, D. *Knowing the sort of help that is really wanted*. Paper presented at the International Conference on the Development and Maintenance of Prosocial Behavior, Warsaw, June–July 1980.

Crockenberg, S. B., Bryant, B. K., & Wilce, L. S. The effects of cooperatively and competitively structured learning environments on inter- and intrapersonal behavior. *Child Development*, 1976, *47*, 386–396.

Eckensberger, L. H. "Soziale Kognition" und "Sozial orientiertes Verhalten": Versuch einer Integration durch das Konzept "Handlung." *Newsletter Soziale Kognition*, 1977, *1*, C68–90.

Emmerich, W., Cocking, R. R., & Sigel, I. E. Relationship between cognitive and social functioning in preschool children. *Developmental Psychology*, 1979, *15*, 495–504.

Enç, B. On the theory of action. *Journal for the Theory of Social Behavior*, 1975, *5*, 145–167.

Enright, R., & Sutterfield, S. An ecological validation of social cognitive development. *Child Development*, 1980, *51*, 156–161.

Flavell, J. H. *Cognitive development*. Englewood Cliffs, N.J.: Prentice-Hall, 1977.

Gergen, K. J. Toward a psychology of receiving help. *Journal of Applied Psychology*, 1974, *44*, 187–294.

Haan, N. *Equivalences and differences in moral judgments about hypothetical dilemmas and a situation where students made a choice concerning civil disobedience*. Paper presented at the meeting of the Society for Research in Child Development, Santa Monica, California, 1969.

Harré, R., & Secord, P. F. *The explanation of social behaviour*. Oxford: Basil Blackwell, 1972.

Hartup, W. W. Peer interaction and social organization. In P. Mussen (Ed.), *Carmichael's manual of child psychology* (Vol. 2). New York: Wiley, 1970.

Hoffman, M. L. Is altruism part of human nature? *Journal of Personality and Social Psychology*, 1981, *40*, 121–137.

Hollis, M. *Models of man: Philosophical thoughts on social action*. Cambridge: Cambridge University Press, 1977.

Iannotti, R. J. Effect of role-taking experience on role taking, empathy, altruism, and aggression. *Developmental Psychology*, 1978, *14*, 119–124.

Johnson, D. Affective perspective-taking and cooperative predisposition. *Developmental Psychology*, 1975, *11*, 869–870.

Kreitler, H., & Kreitler, S. *Cognitive orientation and behavior*. New York: Springer, 1976.

Light, P. *The development of social sensitivity*. Cambridge: Cambridge University Press, 1979.

Louch, A. R. *Explanation of human action*. Berkeley: University of California Press, 1966.

Marcus, R. F., Telleen, S., & Roke, E. J. Relation between cooperation and empathy in young children. *Developmental Psychology*, 1979, *15*, 346–347.

Mead, G. H. *Mind, self, and society*. Chicago: University of Chicago Press, 1934.

Milgram, N. A., & Milgram, R. M. Dimensions of locus of control in children. *Psychological Reports*, 1975, *37*, 523–538.

Miller, G. A., Galanter, E., & Pribram, K. H. *Plans and the structure of behavior*. New York: Holt, 1960.

Murphy, L. *The widening world of childhood*. New York: Basic Books, 1962.

Neale, J. Egocentrism in institutionalized and non-institutionalized children. *Child Development*, 1966, *37*, 97–101.

Nelson-Le Gall, S. Help-seeking: An understudied problem-solving skill in children. *Developmental Review*, 1981, *1*.

Oppenheimer, L. Moral judgment: The investigation of a unidimensional or multidimensional construct. In L. H. Eckensberger (Ed.), *Entwicklung des moralischen Urteilens: Theorie; Methoden; Praxis*. Saarbrücken: Universitätsdruck, University of Saarland, 1977.

Oppenheimer, L. *Social cognitive development*. Unpublished doctoral dissertation, Nijmegen: Universiteit van Nijmegen, 1978.

Oppenheimer, L. *On action theory.* Unpublished manuscript, Nijmegen: Universiteit van Nijmegen, Department of Developmental Psychology, 1979.

Oppenheimer, L. *(Social) cognitive development and social action: An action theoretical approach.* Paper presented at the meeting of the International Society for the Study of Behavioural Development, Toronto, August 1981.

Oppenheimer, L., & Veerman, H. The plan-of-action: Exploration of several of its components. *Newsletter Soziale Kognition,* 1980, *3,* 53–71.

Parsons, T. The general theory of action. In T. Parsons & E. A. Shils (Eds.), *Toward a general theory of action.* Cambridge: Harvard University Press, 1959.

Pearl, R. A. *Developmental and situational influences on children's understanding of prosocial behavior.* Paper presented at the meeting of the Society for Research in Child Development, San Francisco, March 1979.

Pervin, L. A. Theoretical approaches to the analysis of individual-environment interaction. In L. A. Pervin & M. Lewis (Eds.), *Perspectives in interactional psychology.* New York: Plenum Press, 1978.

Reinshagen, H. Handlungsvortstellungen als konstituierende Kategorie sozial-kognitiver Prozesse. *Newsletter Soziale Kognition,* 1977, *1,* C128–141.

Riegel, K. F. Toward a dialectical theory of development. *Human Development,* 1975, *18,* 50–64.

Riegel, K. F., & Meacham, J. A. Dialectics, transaction, and Piaget's theory. In L. A. Pervin & M. Lewis (Eds.), *Perspectives in interactional psychology.* New York: Plenum Press, 1978.

Rubinstein, D. The concept of action in the social sciences. *Journal for the Theory of Social Behavior,* 1977, *7,* 209–236.

Rushton, J. P. Socialization and the altruistic behavior of children. *Psychological Bulletin,* 1976, *83,* 898–913.

Shantz, C. U. The development of social cognition. In E. M. Hetherington (Ed.), *Review of child development research* (Vol. 5). Chicago: University of Chicago Press, 1975.

Shouval, R., Zakay, D., & Halfon, Y. Autonomy or the autonomies?: Trait consistency and situation specificity. *Multivariate Behavioral Research,* 1977, *12,* 143–158.

Shure, M. B., & Spivack, G. Means-end thinking, adjustment, and social class among elementary-school-aged children. *Journal of Consulting and Clinical Psychology,* 1972, *38,* 348–353.

Shutz, A. *The phenomenology of the social world.* Chicago: Northwestern University Press, 1967.

Thomas, W. I. *The unadjusted girl.* Boston: Little, Brown, 1931.

Von Wright, G. H. Determinism and study of man. In J. Manninen & R. Tuomela (Eds.), *Essays on explanation and understanding.* Dordrecht: Reidel, 1976.

Wallon, H. *Les origines de la pensée chez l'enfant.* Paris: Presses Universitaires de France, 1947.

Weber, M. *The theory of social and economic organization.* New York: Free Press, 1966.

Wilson, K., & Shantz, C. Perceptual role-taking and dependency behavior in preschool children. *Merrill-Palmer Quarterly,* 1977, *23,* 207–211.

Wohlwill, J. F. The confluence of environmental and developmental psychology: Signpost to an ecology of development. *Human Development,* 1980 *23,* 354–358.

Wright, M. J. Measuring the social competence of preschool children. *Canadian Journal of Behavioral Science,* 1980, *12,* 17–32.

Yarrow, M. R., & Waxler, C. Z. Dimensions and correlates of prosocial behavior in young children. *Child Development,* 1976, *47,* 118–125.

10

# The Development of Capacity for Altruism as a Function of Object Relations Development and Vicissitudes

Ruth Sharabany

## 1. INTRODUCTION

The aim of this chapter is to explore the potential contribution of significant others to altruism in the course of development. Examination of definitions of altruism demonstrates a feature common to most of them, namely, a reference to an interpersonal event, taking place between an actor and another person. For example: Altruism "refers to a regard for the interest of others without concern for one's self-interest" (Wispé, 1978). Another recent example: "Altruism may be defined as social behavior carried out to achieve positive outcomes for another rather than for the self" (Rushton, 1980, p. 10). Such definitions lead us to examine the relations of person to other as a basis for the development of in altruism. Thus in this chapter I shall discuss the origin of altruistic motivation based on self–other relations. In discussing self–other relations,

---

RUTH SHARABANY • Department of Psychology, Haifa University, Haifa, Israel. Part of this chapter was presented at the International Conference on the Development and Maintenance of Prosocial Behavior, Warsaw, June 1980.

the term *object* will be borrowed from the psychoanalytic literature. The object (or love object) is a significant other (mother, spouse, etc.), either a real one or an internalized one. I shall attempt to delineate milestones in the development of object relations and their reflection in the development of altruism. Individual differences in the quality of altruistic behavior will be presented in light of quality and level of object relations achieved in adulthood.

## 2. MOTIVATION FOR ALTRUISM

Theories of altruistic motivation differ vastly along lines of degree of emphasis on self-gain versus concern for the other. For example, learning theories emphasize the role of reinforcement and modeling as examples of mechanisms through which altruism is acquired (Bar-Tal, 1976; Staub, 1978). A common feature of these mechanisms is some form of reinforcement, direct or vicarious, internal or external. Thus it has been aptly pointed out that there is a paradox (Rosenhan, 1978; Rushton, 1980) in defining altruism. Altruism is an act that supposedly benefits only another person, yet there are embedded various levels of reward, at least emotional and vicarious, for the doer. It seems a fair conclusion that these theories are built on the assumption that altruism is basically a behavior motivated by the same forces as any other behaviors; namely, self-gain or reduction of discomfort.

Several cognitive developmental theories avoid this paradox altogether by emphasizing the increase of potential for altruism as a function of more refined cognitive abilities related to understanding the other. An exception is Hoffman's (1975) attempt to integrate development of concepts of the other with basic altruistic motivation. He suggests a model based on the assumption that there is an altruistic motive independent of the selfish one, which so far has received greater recognition than this other motive. Although I accept the formulation that an altruistic motive exists independently of the selfish one, I suggest that the former motive should be regarded as *one* of the derivatives of a basic object-seeking (person-seeking) motivation in human nature. As such, the altruistic motive is influenced by very early psychic structures and continues to develop and change throughout the life span. This chapter is an attempt to carry further the suggested model.

The traditional psychoanalytic approach, like most traditional learning theories, has viewed all human acts as resulting from self-seeking, pleasure-seeking motivation. It regards altruistic behavior as resulting from socialization processes that at best channel and transform the basic selfish motivation (A. Freud, 1937, 1966; S. Freud, 1953). In contrast, new developments in psychoanalytic thinking have brought about a conception of object relations motivation. Some proponents of this approach have gone to the extent of rejecting Freud's dual instinctive theory (Fairbairn, 1952, 1963). According to this approach a primary objective of the development of the psychic apparatus is the establishment of relations with other human beings. Thus even sexual interest in objects later in life (which was a cornerstone motivation in traditional psychoanalysis) derive from the basic need of establishing loving relationships with others (Kernberg, 1979). This places the object relations approach, derived from psychoanalytic theories, at the far end of the continuum of self versus other. Interest in the other, in this view, is as primary as self-interest.

## 3. THE DEVELOPMENT OF ALTRUISM

There are several theoretical formulations contributed by the object relations approach that are related to the development of altruism. First, there is the assumption that object relations development is primary and is the basis for development of other psychological functions (regulation and control of drives, thought processes, etc., see Horner, 1980). The object relations approach assumes that the child has his own psychological and physiological "givens" (heredity, constitution, etc.). This initial endowment determines the extent to which the child can use his first significant object (usually the caregiver, i.e., the mother) to develop his psychological functions (Mahler, Pine, & Bergman, 1975). Thus the process of development is composed of two aspects: first, the inborn dispositions and abilities; and second, the experience that the mother provides by performing for the child various caretaking functions. The relations with the mother consist of two related processes: (1) the actual behavior of the mother, namely, the relation with her as real external object; and (2) the mother as internalized object, which is a synthesis and outcome of the experience with the mother in reality through the filter of the child's internal processes. What the child can take from whatever the mother offers is determined by the remaining two aspects (his endowment and internalized object). Thus the child reaches each phase of development with inner objects based on previous relations. Growth and transition from one developmental phase to the next is a two-way process. Experiences with new significant objects at a new phase of development are influenced by the inner objects. (For example, the new experiences are interpreted by the individual according to the inner objects, in congruence with them. Simultaneously, the inner objects are modified by the internalization of the new relations.)

The traditional psychoanalytic approach has become known for stressing the internalized relations w1th parental figures as most significant objects who have long-term influence on altruistic potential (Staub, 1979). In this chapter the emphasis is on several significant objects throughout the life span, thus perhaps implying greater modifiability of the altruistic potential. It is assumed that the quality of the relations with significant others selected on the basis of developmental change provides the basis for potential altruism, and that the potential of altruism is composed of such complex processes as empathy, perception of others, and personal identity (Hoffman, 1975). There are cognitive and emotional processes that through motivation and development contribute their share to the development of altruism (Bar-Tal, Sharabany, & Raviv, 1982). It is the thesis of this chapter that the relations with a significant other in each developmental phase are the *laboratory* in which empathy, perception of other, and identity crystallize. We shall examine each phase in the relations to a significant other.

## 4. INFANCY

Relations to parents, particularly to a caregiver, are considered an important antecedent of altruistic behavior. In infancy, altruism is restricted to *fantasy* and attachment behavior, which express processes through which the infant cherishes the relations with the mother (Bowlby, 1969). The cycles of frustrations and pleasures (corroborating underlying drives) produce in the infant parallel fantasies of aggression and guilt for the object-mother (Klein, 1937/1975; Winnicott, 1963/1974). These internal processes in the infant are the elements of concern and altruism. Or, more specifically, the rudiments of the need "to do good" appear before social pressures and develop very early in infancy (Klein & Riviere, 1967).

Klein contributes elaborate descriptions of the intrapsychic dynam1cs of the child during infancy (Klein, 1970). According to her theory the infant has fantasies that are images derived from the two instincts: love-libido and aggression-death. These fantasies are mingled with the respective real experiences. Gratifying fantasies are mingled with pleasant experiences (such as being fed), whereas aggression and death fantasies are fused with frustrations (such as feeling hunger). The unpleasant fantasies and experiences create anxiety, whereas a positive libidinal relationship with the mother provides the child with positive experiences of "repairing" or "undoing the bad" that the child "did" in his fantasy when he/she was angry and frightened. Thus in fantasy the infant has wishes to retain the good object (breast, or later the mother) and reduce the anxiety by undoing the fantasized harm. The infant attributes to his/her own doing both the positive experiences (such as the appearance of the good-object, the mother) and the negative ones (such as injuring the bad-object by being aggressive). This is the beginning of *guilt* feelings as well as *concern* for others (who are gratifying objects for the child) which Klein (1970) attributes to infants.

Winnicott (1974), in basic agreement with Klein, describes the transformation of the infant's feelings from anxiety and aggression to guilt and concern. He adds that although the origin of the anxiety and aggression is inherent in the mother–infant relationship, it is up to the "environment-mother" to provide "good-enough-mothering" in which the positive experiences will prevail.

> In favorable circumstances there builds up a technique for the solution of this complex form of ambivalence. The infant experiences anxiety, because if he consumes the mother he will lose her, but this anxiety becomes modified by the fact that the baby has a contribution to make to the environment-mother. There is growing confidence that there will be opportunity for contributing-in, for giving to the environment-mother. The anxiety held in this way becomes altered in quality and becomes a sense of guilt.
>
> Instinct-drives lead to ruthless usage of objects, and then to a guilt-sense which is held, and is allayed by the contribution to the environment-mother that the infant can make in the course of a few hours. (pp. 76–77)

> When confidence in this benign cycle and in the expectation of opportunity is established, the sense of guilt in relation to the id-drives becomes further modified, and we then need a more positive term, such as "concern." (p. 77)

> Briefly, failure of . . . the environment-mother to provide reliable opportunity for reparation leads to a loss of the capacity for concern and to its replacement by crude anxieties. (p. 78)

According to the object relations approach, then, the experience of being able to "undo" bad things and thus to save or rescue the beloved object is couched in very early mother–infant relations. Moreover, the greater the weight of the positive experiences (being fed, being held, etc.) over the bad ones (being deprived, abandoned, etc.), the more likely is the infant to allow himself to experience concern and guilt. It is assumed that the infant does not escape from these negative feelings but learns to deal with them. Thus there are parameters that are likely to provide the infant with the experience of concern and guilt. For example, *continuity* of the relations provides the experience of "undoing" or "repairing" the same object. The feelings of concern and guilt are likely to lead to altruistic behavior (Hoffman, 1975).

It may seem that the traditional psychoanalytic approach emphasized just as much as the new object relations school the significance of early relations with parents. However, traditional psychoanalysis did not see the roots of altruism in early infancy, nor did it recognize an internal, inherent tendency for altruism.

> Psychoanalytic studies have shown that automatic patterns of moral behavior are developed, not out of the theoretical and philosophical systems . . . but rather out of the deeply buried residues of our earliest emotional relationships to our parents or to other important figures. It is what we are toward our children in the nursery and not what we preach to them that makes them good or bad, because ultimately what they unconsciously feel toward us will determine automatically how they feel unconsciously toward others. (Kubie, 1975, p. 231)

The following three hypotheses have been relatively prominent in the literature on altruism and stem from both traditional psychoanalytic theories and object relations theories.

*Hypothesis 1.* More altruistic behavior will be expressed by children who were "well taken care of" (greater degree of need satisfaction compared with amount of frustrations).

*Hypothesis 2.* Children who grow up in an intense-attachment social structure will show more altruistic behavior.

*Hypothesis 3.* An intolerable amount of frustration during infancy will bring about reduced potential for altruism.

There is no specific evidence that demonstrates the contribution of caregiver–infant relations to altruistic behavior, but there is related evidence based on the more general concept of parent–child relations. For example, Rutherford and Mussen (1968) found that generosity of 4-year-old boys was related to perception of their father as warm, nurturant, and affectionate. The father becomes a model of kind behavior, and the child experiences the significant other as positive and need satisfying. Evidence for the relation of parental behavior and child's altruism is reviewed by Rushton (1980), Staub (1979), and others. For example, Hoffman (1963) found that maternal affection had an effect on 10-year-old boys' altruism, although not on that of same-age girls (see Rushton, 1980). These findings support object relations theory that altruism increase when there is enough positive experience with a significant figure to counterbalance frustration. However, most claims about the contribution of positive parent–child relations to development of altruistic behavior are based on self-reported socialization behavior of parents by children (Bar-Tal, Nadler, & Blechman, 1981). Thus, the positive report may be the result of other antecedents, which are common both to altruism and to positive perception of the parents.

The object relations approach implies very specific caregiver behaviors that are likely to increase concern, guilt, and thus empathy and altruism. Generally speaking, the following are caregiver behaviors that would increase the experience of "reparation" (Klein, 1970) and "undoing of harm'' (Winnicott, 1974) done in fantasy by the infant: (1) continuity in relations to the caregiver, (2) sameness of the caregiver, and (3) keeping contact with the infant while he/she is frustrated. These behaviors by the caregiver enable the child to experience, following the natural frustrations, a relief and, thus, concern. To put it in hypothesis form:

*Hypothesis 4.* Mother–infant interactions that increase the likelihood of experiences of ''reparation'' increase the tendency for altruistic behavior.

Rosenhan (1970) reports findings that civil right workers who showed strong involvement and commitment (altruistic social involvement) were also likely to maintain relationships with their parents characterized by strong positive affect. This evidence supports both the positive experience with parents and the continuity aspect of the relations. In this study, of course, the subjects are adults and thus the evidence is very indirect. I know of no studies that assess aspects of infant attachment patterns or mother–child interaction and their relations to altruism.

The prediction that the early attachment pattern to the parental figure(s) is predictive of differences in altruism (via changes in patterns of emotion and empathy) is supported by cross-cultural anthropological studies and comparisons:

> Our traditional and still predominant family pattern is one of intensive, frequent, and durable relations among members, especially when the children are small. Under such conditions affective responses develop and indeed are fostered so that deep emotional attachments can be part of social relations between persons who are ''close to'' each other. (Cohen, 1978, p. 89)
>
> Highly developed emotional capacities as parts of interpersonal relationships are, I contend, limited to nuclear family systems in which there are long-term nonrejecting stable relationships with parents who do not share the household with any other adults. This welds emotional qualities to interpersonal relations in a very intense way. And it is under these conditions that empathy and sympathy necessary for altruism can develop. (pp. 91–92)

*Hypothesis 5.* Children growing up in *troubled* backgrounds who had *warm* parents would be altruistic (assuming that the cycles of frustration-guilt-reparation were more intense for them).

Young adolescents who considered themselves to be highly deprived helped more on two separate occasions than subjects who regarded themselves as not deprived (Yinon, 1979). In the same study, material deprivation combined with positive regard by parent led to a higher level of altruism than the reverse combination. ''When a person is deprived of material rewards but enjoys nonmaterial rewards, he is going to be more altruistic than a person whose situation is reversed'' (Yinon, 1979, p. 294).

Parental influence, of course, does not cease with infancy, neither as internalized objects nor as in reality close objects (see Aronfreed, 1969). Moreover, the caregiver has been the focus of our discussion and further elaboration is needed to specify the role of additional significant figures during infancy. With these limitations in mind, we proceed next to examine childhood with focus on friends as significant objects.

## 5. CHILDHOOD: THE CRIB OF FRIENDSHIP

Childhood brings about changes that occur with *objects* in reality. The experience with *peers* (in addition to parents) often evolves into meaningful relations with a *close friend*. There is also a change in the *mode* of giving: The *act* of altruism takes the place of (or is added to) fantasy activity. There is a change in the balance between giving and taking from the significant object: from taking, toward more mutuality in giving.

Changes occur in object relations and altruistic behavior as a result of maturational processes, the nature of the inner objects (carried on from infancy), and new environmental experiences. Importantly, the inner objects provide the mental structures (to borrow a Piagetian term) that enable or inhibit utilization of experiences provided by the environment.

### 5.1. Contribution of Inner Objects

Childhood is marked by broadening social relations: In addition to parents, peers become significant others. Reaching childhood with "good" inner objects gives the child a better chance to experience good relations with his peers. Positive experiences with peers are likely to be amplified and incorporated into the positive experience with parents (Staub, 1979). Likewise, assuming that the inner "bad objects" are relatively minor in salience, the corresponding negative experiences encountered with peers receive less internal amplification. Also, developed and familiar cycles of frustration-guilt-reparation produced altruistic fantasy toward parents are likely to impel the child to begin cycles of interactions with his peers. In contrast, a child whose "bad" inner objects are more salient is likely to follow an opposite course of experience. One way of formalizing the hypothesis is to expect children who are well-adjusted socially (thus showing evidence of emerging adjusted from the previous phase) also to show more prosocial and altruistic behavior.

*Hypothesis 6.* Positive social relations with peers enhance altruism.

The expectation that good object relations contribute to altruism is borne out by studies that show that in general, social skills and emotional stability are related to greater altruism (Turner, 1948). Also, after a review of the literature Krebs (1970) concludes:

> On the basis of the available evidence, altruistic children seem to be better adjusted socially than others—and they are more emotionally stable. (p. 285)

Kohlberg (1964), citing evidence from both his own work and Dilling's (1967) work, concludes:

> Being attractive as a friend, and high on sociability and ingroup involvement was found positively related to level of moral judgment.

However, there is an exception to the finding of positive relations of popularity and moral judgment (Porteus & Johnson, 1965). Popularity as measured in these studies may or may not have reflected a high degree of close friendship. This exception suggests that finer distinctions in manifestations of positive peer relations are necessary.

## 5.2. Contribution of New Objects

The great influence of the nature of inner objects emerging from infancy on altruism in childhood emphasizes the expected congruence between experiences in infancy and childhood. However, this does not mean that the early effects are irreversible.

*Hypothesis 7.* Children who had highly frustrating relations with their parents would nevertheless exhibit a considerable degree of altruism if they have close peer relations.

The example is the classic study by Freud and Dann (1951) in which there was a great degree of sharing, helping, and so on among a close group of children who were refugees. They enjoyed continuity and sameness in their peer relations, which seemed to have a rehabilitating effect. However, a known shortcoming of this study is that there was no control group, since it was based on adversary war circumstances. Likewise, there have been several references in the literature to peers, particularly friends, as "therapists" (Hartup, 1979; Reisman, 1979; Suomi, 1979).

In line with object relations theory, a more specific hypothesis about relations to peers and altruism can be examined. Close friendship, such as reciprocal friendship, provides a chance for role taking, mutual validation that increases self-esteem, exchange of empathy and sympathy. Thus, extrapolating from object relations theory, dyadic friendship is a central experience during childhood. Such friendship can be viewed as an intensive "laboratory." Within this laboratory, which is parallel to the caregiver–child relations in infancy, processes that contribute to the development and learning of altruism are enhanced.

*Hypothesis 8a.* Mutual close friendships enhance altruistic behavior.

> The satisfactions and the security which are being experienced by someone else, some particular other person, begin to be as significant to the person as are his own satisfactions and security. (Sullivan, 1953, p. 43)

A study (Mannarino, 1980) that attended to variables that were specified in the previous section as relevant to the assessment of quality of object relations (continuity, sameness of object, etc.) provides some evidence about the relation of mutual friendship to altruism. In this study sixth-grade boys, each with a mutual best friend ("chum" relations), exhibited a greater level of altruism toward an unknown peer. Friendship relations in the study, it should be stressed, were clearly distinct from popularity; in the comparison of the two groups the author controlled for the latter.

*Hypothesis 8b.* Friends engage in activities that foster altruistic behavior (role taking, sharing, etc.) more than nonfriends.

There is evidence for the relation between role-taking ability and altruism. For example, following role-taking play, girls helped a distressed child significantly more than the control subjects. Boys, following a similar experience, shared more than did the controls (Staub, 1971). Role taking, which is related to altruism on the one hand, is also related to improved social relations on the other. Thus there is evidence that children who were "coached" and trained in role-taking improved their social relations with their peers (Oden & Asher, 1977). There is, however, no evidence yet that demonstrates the links of friendship and altruism *through* role-taking activity.

Sharabany (1974, 1980), in studies of intimate friendship, found that mutual friends ("reciprocating" friends) were higher than nonmutual friends on intimacy as well as on reported help toward their friend (one subscale of the intimacy measurement was helping).

There are indications that Hypothesis 9 needs further elaboration and perhaps modifications. So far we have assumed a degree of generalization of altruistic behavior from within the dyadic relations to other relations. This was well supported by Mannarino (1980), who found that children who have best friends ("chums") are more altruistic to a fictitious peer. However, helping behavior toward a more distant friend (sixth on the list of friends) showed less help and less intimacy than toward the best friend (Sharabany, 1973, 1974). There are also studies that show that in laboratory settings dyads of kindergarten and first-grade friends actually shared less between themselves than did nonfriends from the same class (Sharabany & Hertz-Lazarowitz, 1981).

Without going into in-depth discussion, it can be pointed out that prosocial interactions within dyadic relations do vary (as a function of duration of relations setting, tasks presented, etc.), and need further study.

## 6. ADOLESCENCE: OPPOSITE-SEX FRIEND

In discussions of childhood friendship, the object of friendship is almost exclusively a same-sex friend (Sharabany, Gershoni, & Hofman, 1981). Adolescence, however, is marked by changes along both dimensions of *self* and *other*. The object relations theory provides the theoretical bridge between these two aspects. Internal objects are to some extent components of the internal reality, thus of the self. For example, aspects of ego-ideal and superego are often described in the developmental literature as reflecting past parental socialization practices (Aronfreed, 1979; Staub, 1979). On the other hand, internal objects may determine the selection of external objects as well as the nature of relations toward them. For example, identifying with a "Machiavellian" parent may lead to relations based on manipulation-exploitation rather than trust and altruism (Bar-Tal, 1976; Rushton, 1980; Staub, 1979).

In adolescence, there is a transition in the selection of the external object from a same-sex to an opposite-sex object. This transition reflects the ability and interest to meet someone different from the self. In a parallel way, the adolescent focuses on the developmental task of crystallizing his or her identity.

### 6.1. Broadening Concept of the Other

The transition toward the inclusion of an opposite-sex friend occurs concomitantly with the growing cognitive ability to view dyadic relations from a "third person's point of view" by the age of 10, and to move on to a "generalized other" and a "social system view" in adolescence (Selman, 1976), as well as to pay more attention to the motives of the other person (Hill & Palmquist, 1978). The needs to explore the other and to disclose oneself are shown in findings of the dimensions of intimate friendship, which increase in adolescence—specifically, such dimensions as mutual frankness and spontaneity, sensitivity and knowing, and so on (Sharabany *et al.*, 1981). The particular change toward increased intimacy with an opposite-sex friend is shown by the finding that by eleventh grade, the discrepancy between intimate friendships with same-sex friends, and those with opposite-sex friends is reduced (Lev-Ran & Sharabany, 1981; Sharabany *et al.*, 1981). This is in accordance with findings of a marked change from seventh to tenth grade, when adolescents show a greater tendency to integrate, for example, both the positive and negative perceptions of a person (Hill & Palmquist, 1978).

Early adolescence is marked by a particular type of "adolescent egocentrism" (Elkind, 1967). On the one hand, the adolescent makes an extreme assumption that he or she is the center of the observation of others ("imaginary audience"); on the other hand, there is an assumption of his or her uniqueness of experience ("personal fable"). Both these extreme assumptions are gradually tested against reality. "Once the young person sees himself in a more realistic light . . . he can establish true rather than self-interested interpersonal relations" (Elkind, 1967, p. 1,032). One of the avenues that enables the adolescent to test these extreme assumptions is via mutual self-disclosure and feedback from an intimate friend. In turn, the more realistic the adolescent's view of him or herself, the less self-centered are his or her relations. These changes in the view of the self and others affect the altruistic potential of the individual in several ways. The processes of feedback operating among intimate adolescent friends enable more accurate assessment of the other person's needs. The interest in opposite-sex friends broadens the circles of empathy to persons whose needs may be different from one's own.

*Hypothesis 9.* In comparison to younger children, adolescents who are able to relate to others different from themselves (i.e., those who have an opposite-sex friend) are likely to be altruistic toward people who are not similar to themselves.

*Hypothesis 10.* Adolescents who have an opposite-sex friend are likely to respond to the needs of others when the needs are not similar to their own, more so than adolescents who do not have an opposite-sex friend.

### 6.2. A Model That Emphasizes Intimacy

According to this model friends are necessary in order to form and clarify one's identity. Thus this model assumes that there can be found adolescents who have intimate friends at the same time that these adolescents' identity is still in flux.

*Hypothesis 11.* Adolescents who have intimate friendships are likely to have a clearer identity than adolescents who do not have intimate friends.

We have found support for this hypothesis based on the interpretation of data collected mainly on adolescent girls. According to these data, friends are necessary for establishing and clarifying one's identity (Douvan & Adelson, 1966). The impression of Douvan and Adelson was that girls need a same-sex friend for the task of mutual clarification of identity. However, some theoretical formulations stress that early intimate relations with opposite-sex friends also serve the same function.

> Falling in love, which is a common occurrence at this stage is not so much of a sexual nature as it will be at a later age; but it is an attempt to project and test one's own diffused and still undifferentiated ego through the eyes of a loved person in order to clarify and reflect one's one self-concept and one's ego identity. (Muuss, 1975, p. 65)

However, several writers have emphasized the achievement of an integrated identity as a necessary step toward full intimacy. Intimacy may be viewed as the ultimately close and altruistic relation.

## 6.3. A Model That Emphasizes Identity

According to Erikson, the adolescent is thrown into a phase of rapid changes. The aspects of sameness and continuity in identity and in object relations that were established earlier have to be rediscovered and redefined. Erikson describes the phase of intimacy:

> The young adult, emerging from the search for and the insistence on identity, is eager and willing to fuse his identity with that of others. He is ready for intimacy, that is, the capacity to commit himself to concrete affiliations and partnerships and to develop the ethical strength to abide by such commitments, even though they may call for significant sacrifices and compromises. (Erikson, 1950, p. 27)

Or, as Constantinople (quoted in Muuss, 1975, p. 67) puts it: "The giving of oneself to another, which is the mark of true intimacy cannot occur until one has a self to give."

Hoffman (1975) describes steps in the development of "a sense of the other" as one of three main elements in the development of altruism. According to Hoffman, aspects of personal identity seem to accumulate all through the child's development. Hoffman cites the fact that constancy of gender identity is not formed before age 6. We may also add that gender constancy of the *other* is likewise not achieved before age 6 (Emmerich, Goldman, Kirsh, & Sharabany, 1977; Sharabany, 1982a,b; Sharabany & Eitan, 1983). These additional findings also support the notion of correspondence between the concepts of self-identity and of the other person's identity.

A model that emphasizes the acquisition of identity as a prerequisite for intimacy with another person seems to contradict the previous one, which emphasizes intimacy as a prerequisite. However, this may perhaps be resolved by differentiating between two phases: (A) The first phase is characterized by the search for an identity and the beginning of intimacy (the "falling in love" phase [Kernberg, 1979]); (B) the second, characterized by a more clearly defined identity and the attainment of stable and integrated relations, of increased ability "to remain in love" (Kernberg, 1979).

Apparently, there is need for further theoretical clarification of the relation among altruistic capacity, intimate relations, and identity formation. For our purposes, we may observe that normal adolescence seems to manifest itself by advances along all three developmental lines (altruism, intimacy, identity). Having had mostly positive experiences in previous stages, the adolescent fortifies his or her positive internal objects. This enables him or her to choose an opposite-sex friend and thus to enlarge the circle of experience with others different from the self, and to exercise and expand altruistic potential.

A conservative postulate for this chapter might be that the three elements (altruism, intimacy, identity) are related. Each is a necessary condition for the other two; thus the change in one would be expected to affect the other two, and the change in two (e.g., both in intimacy and identity) would be expected to have a still stronger effect.

*Hypothesis 12.* In adolescence, a more clearly defined identity (i.e., integrated self-concept) is likely to contribute to altruistic potential.

*Hypothesis 13.* In adolescence, having a close opposite-sex friend as well as a clearer identity would enable greater altruistic potential.

*Hypothesis 14.* In adolescence, having a more integrated identity would lead to having a close friend, and thus would increase (indirectly) altruistic potential.

The three hypotheses are interrelated, and a positive correlation among the three elements is assumed.

According to Kernberg (1979), adolescence is marked by a phase of crisis of ego identity, the resolution of which depends upon earlier stages.

> The following characteristics are particularly helpful in differentiating relatively benign emotional turmoil from the syndrome of identity diffusion: (1) the capacity for experiencing guilt and concern, and the genuine wish to repair aggressive behavior, which is recognized as such after an emotional outburst; (2) the capacity for establishing lasting, non-exploitative relations with friends, teachers, or other grownups, as well as a relatively realistic assessment of such persons in depth; (3) a consistently expanding and deepening set of values. . . . The absence of these capacities reflects a lack of integration of the self-concept, a lack of understanding in depth of others . . . all characteristics of identity diffusion. (p. 225)

Elements that are related to altruistic behavior are present in the normal adolescent: object relations, guilt, concern, nonexploitative relations with significant others, and a set of clear and developing values.

## 7. ADULTHOOD: INDIVIDUAL DIFFERENCES

There is a large body of research on various aspects of altruistic behavior. In this chapter we have been particularly interested in aspects of altruism that are relevant to object relations theory. The central aspect is internal motivation and the meaning of the altruistic act (see Sharabany & Bar-Tal, 1982). The same observed act can stem from various motivations. It could be the result of a psychic defense mechanism such as reaction formation; it could be an act resulting from the infantile needs of an immature personality; it may also be a manifestation of a mature personality with mature object relations.

In adulthood, another developmental milestone is achieved: Durable love relations are, again, the dyadic laboratory for both expressing the achieved level of altruism as well as developing and enhancing altruism.

*Hypothesis 15.* Mature love relations (compared with immature relations) are more altruistic and involve a higher level of altruism (such as more appropriate to the other's need, and greater sacrifice).

Kernberg (1979), citing works by Balint, Freud, May, and Bak, describes mature love as composed of recognition of the other; a higher level of identification with the pain or joy of the other; guilt, pity, and so on. Love is an emotional state based on achieving separation from the mother, which follows a positive symbiotic experience. There are several levels and cycles of separation in the life of the individual that are steps toward individuation, each phase on a more mature level.

According to Gilligan (1976), love is the highest level in which the interest and benefit of each member of the dyad are mutual. In other words, within loving relations the interest and the satisfactions are not one versus the other but are simultaneous and the same. The more one gives the more one receives in return. Gilligan uses satisfaction in sexual relations as an example for the overlap between altruistically satisfying the other and at the same time being selfishly satisfied. According to Gilligan (1976) the selfish versus altruistic choice, is an artificial cognitive invention.

*Hypothesis 16.* There is correspondence between the developmental level of object relations and the qualitative level of altruism the person can reach.

This hypothesis attempts to account for individual differences in the quality of close relations and the quality of altruism. Implied here is the assumption that achieving a higher level of interpersonal relations increases the potential for altruism. Also implied is the idea that meaningful relations provide the basis for the further development of altruism.

The two themes that we have been trying to analyze emerge on

Loevinger's (1966) description of the stages of development of interpersonal relations, incorporating some of Sullivan's as well as others' work. One theme is the changing quality of relations to a significant other, the second is the changing balance of give-and-take in these relations, which to some extent also defines these significant relations. The first two developmental stages in the list that follows concern mainly with relations to parents.

1. *Presocial-symbiotic* (autistic, symbiotic). This first stage is divided into two substages: (1) the presocial substage in which the infant does not distinguish animate from inanimate objects; and (2) the symbiotic substage, in which specific attachment is formed to the mother and self is not clearly distinguished from the mother.
2. *Impulse ridden.* In this stage the interpersonal relations are exploitative and dependent, and people are seen as sources of supply. However, the dependence is not recognized as such by the child.
3. *Opportunistic.* In this stage, which may reflect early peer relations, the morality is purely expedient. Interpersonal relations are manipulative and exploitative but less dependent. Life is treated as a zero-sum game: What you win, I lose.
4. *Conformist.* This stage is characterized by genuine interpersonal reciprocity; mutual trust is extended to a narrowly conceived ingroup. There may be strong prejudice against various outgroups conceived in stereotyped terms. However, interpersonal relations are superficial (seen primarily in terms of actions rather than of feelings and motives). Inner feelings are expressed in a stereotyped, banal, and often moralistic fashion.
5. *Consciousness* (intensive, responsible). In this stage there is also access to introspection and self-consciousness. Interpersonal relations are seen in terms of feelings and traits rather than actions. Inner moral imperatives take precedence over group-sanctioned rules. Conscious preoccupation is with obligations, ideals, and so on.
6. *Autonomous.* Concern for autonomy is central to this stage. Interpersonal relations remain intense; they involve the recognition of inevitable mutual interdependence and—a crucial addition—the recognition of other people's need for autonomy.
7. *Integrated.* Individual differences are not only tolerated at this stage, but cherished. At this stage the individual achieves a sense of integrated identity beyond role differentiation. Few adults in any society achieve this stage of ego development. It is emphasized in Loevinger's model that there is no specific age correspondence. The levels of ego development represent a model where each level is higher than the previous one. In addi-

tion, this model attempts to specify milestones that could serve as indicators to predict a person's level of development. For example, the role and nature of relations with a significant other at each stage are indicators of the level of potential for altruism, as well as maturational level.

Whereas Loevinger described stages of interpersonal development, Kernberg (1979) explicitly points to the give-and-take correlates of broad clinical diagnostic categories. One may generalize as follows:

*Hypothesis 17.* The more deeply disturbed a person is (disturbed interpersonal and object relations), the less likely is this person to be altruistic.

*Hypothesis 18.* The normal person (normal interpersonal relations and normal object relations) has both the capacity to be altruistic and the capacity for taking.

Kernberg (1979) provides examples, using diagnostic categories, from which the following are drawn.

1. *Severe narcissistic personality structure* implies total incapacity to establish genital and tender relations with any other human being.
2. *Sexual promiscuity* refers to a moderately ill narcissistic personality.
3. *Borderline* primitive idealization of love object is accompanied by clinging infantile dependence upon it and some capacity for genital gratification.
4. *Neurosis* refers to the capacity for establishing deep object relations without the capacity for full sexual relations.
5. *Normal* integrations of genitality are accompanied by the capacity for tenderness and a stable, deep object relation. Kernberg (1979) includes in these diagnostic categories: (1) Capacity to give or take is lacking; (2) exploitation and inability to give—love and hate relations are split; (3) beginning of give-and-take; (4) dependency on taking and guilt feelings; and (5) full capacity for give-and-take.

According to object relations theory, the balance between the experiences of satisfaction versus frustration is important. Thus, for example, an adult who has memories of hardship embedded in a context of warm, loving relations with his significant objects (parents) is one most likely to have altruistic potential. In contrast, perhaps, are adults who remember unrelieved hardship or a continuous, uninterrupted positive experience; these persons are, perhaps, less likely to become altruistic.

## 8. CONCLUSION

The aim of this chapter has been to add a new dimension to the study of altruistic behavior. The pivotal theoretical assertion is that relations with a close and significant object (person) are the laboratory for the development and exercise of altruistic relations. The mutual experience of cycles of frustration and satisfaction, in which the latter prevail, provides the potential for the growth of altruism. The elements that constitute this theoretical assertion (object, satisfactions, mutuality, etc.) vary developmentally on the basis of maturation, environmental influence (i.e., parental behavior), and their interaction. Specifically, the significant *object* changes from a parent to a spouse via close same-sex and opposite-sex friendships. The nature of *satisfaction* changes, for example, from being fed in a responsive way in infancy to being sexually gratified; or from physical care to symbolic care, that is, being understood psychologically. The degree of *mutuality* changes from a dissimilar mode to a similar one. For example, the mother–infant mutuality is based on the mother's action and the infant's fantasy. Adulthood is marked by a greater similarity in the contribution of the partners (integration of fantasy and action; integration of give-and-take).

I have limited my focus to dyadic relations throughout life. By this I am assuming that the dyad is the atomic unit for the experience and development of the capacity for altruism. I recognize the need to expand this model to include the third-party direct and indirect contribution to dyadic relations—for example, the contribution of altruism between the parents to altruism of the child. For an in-depth discussion of this model, see Bronfenbrenner (1979). The central question is whether the model of relations with several others is an extension of the model presented here, or a totally different matter. In other words, are the more complex relations an extension and generalization of the nuclear, dyadic relations?

This chapter reflects the belief that healthy and optimal lines of development produce altruistic potential. This happens both by the *specific* experiences of give-and-take with the significant object throughout life, which are relevant to altruism, as well as through personality structure and traits that are conducive to altruism. This underlying assumption should be investigated. Such figures as Joan of Arc and Don Quixote who may be regarded as fighters for a positive cause may deviate from such standard clinical terms as "balanced" and "healthy." Moreover, it could conceivably be that the more satisfied and content a person is in his/her intimate personal relations, the less he/she would seek to help needy others. The specific hypothesis that emerges here (which has already received some support from Yinon, 1979) is that the *combination* of memories and experiences of deprivation with positive supportive experiences with a significant object (i.e., love) is most conducive to altruism in its full meaning.

I have suggested that there are relations to internal objects that are continuous from each developmental phase to the successive one. Simultaneously, each phase is characterized by *changes* in the choice and relations to significant objects (parents, same-sex friend, opposite-sex friend, etc). We need to investigate in more depth the relation of these internal and external object relations to altruism. To what extent can an experience in a late developmental phase modify behavior? Does earlier experience account for more generalized altruistic potential?

The present model has expanded Hoffman's model (1975) of the development of altruistic motivation. One of the limitations of that model is pointed out by Staub (1979), who notes that it stresses the *cognitive* developmental aspects of the sense of other and the sense of self (person permanence, role taking, personal identity), combined with early primitive empathic responsiveness. Staub claims, however, that the quality and content of relations with others are overlooked (i.e., the positive or negative valence attached to both self and other). In addition, Staub points out the lack of emphasis on the contribution of the actual experience of the child (socialization) to the shaping of these dimensions of self-perception and the perception of others. This chapter complements Hoffman's article in assuming an innate object-seeking motivation, and in emphasizing the affective-experiential aspect of the development of altruistic motivation.

The model put forth here also complements another model that stresses the cognitive aspects of the development of altruistic behavior (Bar-Tal *et al.*, 1982). This cognitive model emphasizes the changes in quality of altruistic *acts* as a function of two dimensions: (1) the mode of reinforcement that is effective at different developmental levels, and (2) the origin of the act (from external authority which is complied to, to self-initiated act). Whereas Bar-Tal *et al.* (1982) present conditions that are likely to elicit *behaviors*, this chapter has focused on the potential for meaningful altruism and has stressed the *quality* of the motivation.

## Acknowledgments

Thanks are due Rachel Hertz-Lazarowitz and Ervin Staub for discussion of some of the early ideas; Lee B. Gaber for critical reading of a previous draft and his very useful suggestions; Daniel Bar-Tal for his help and for editing the chapter; and Urie Zaliuk for encouraging and helping in many ways.

## 9. REFERENCES

Aronfreed, J. The concept of internalization. In D. Goslin (Ed.), *Handbook of socialization theory and research*. Chicago: Rand McNally, 1969.

Bar-Tal, D. *Prosocial behavior: Theory and practice.* New York: Wiley, 1976.

Bar-Tal, D., Nadler, A., & Blechman, N. The relationship between Israeli children's helping behavior and their perception of parents' socialization practices. *Journal of Social Psychology,* 1981, *111,* 159–167.

Bar-Tal, D., Sharabany, R., & Raviv, A. Cognitive basis of the development of altruistic behavior. In V. J. Derlega & J. Grzelak (Eds.), *Cooperation and helping behavior.* New York: Academic Press, 1982.

Bowlby, J. *Attachment and loss.* Vol. 1. *Attachment.* New York: Basic Books, 1969.

Bronfenbrenner, U. *The ecology of human development: Experiments by nature and design.* Cambridge: Harvard University Press, 1979.

Cohen, R. Altruism: Human, cultural or what? In L. Wispé (Ed.), *Altruism, sympathy and helping.* New York: Academic Press, 1978.

Dilling, C. A. *A study of moral orientation in relation to Piagetian concepts of egocentrism.* Unpublished doctoral dissertation, Michigan State University, 1967.

Douvan, E., & Adelson, J. *The adolescent experience.* New York: Wiley, 1966.

Elkind, D. Egocentrism in adolescence. *Child Development,* 1967, *38,* 1025–1034.

Emmerich, W., Goldman, K. S., Kirsh, B., & Sharabany, R. Evidence for a transitional phase in the development of gender constancy. *Child Development,* 1977, *48,* 930–938.

Erikson, E. H. Eight ages of man. In C. Stendler-Lavatelli & F. Stendler, *Readings in child behavior and development.* New York: Harcourt, Brace, Jovanovich, 1972.

Erikson, E. H. Growth and crisis of the healthy personality. *Psychological Issues,* 1959, *1,* 50–100.

Fairbairn, W. D. *On object–relations theory of the personality.* New York: Basic Books, 1952.

Fairbairn, W. D. Synopsis of an object–relations theory of the personality. *International Journal of Psychoanalysis,* 1963, *4,* 224–225.

Freud, A. *The ego and the mechanisms of defence.* London: Hogarth Press, 1937.

Freud, A. *Normality and pathology in childhood.* London: Hogarth Press, 1966.

Freud, A., & Dann, S. An experiment in group upbringing. In R. Eissler, A. Freud, H. Hartman, & E. Kris (Eds.), *The psychoanalytic study of the child* (Vol. 6). New York: International Universities Press, 1951.

Freud, S. Beyond the pleasure principle. In I. Strachey (Ed.), *The standard edition of the complete psychological works of Sigmund Freud* (Vol. 18). London: Hogarth Press, 1953.

Gilligan, J. Beyond morality: Psychoanalytic reflections on shame, guilt and love. In T. Lickona (Ed.), *Moral development and behavior: Theory, research and social issues.* New York: Holt, Rinehart & Winston, 1976.

Hartup, W. W. The social words of childhood. *American Psychologist,* 1979, *34,* 944–950.

Hill, J., & Palmquist, W. J. Social cognition and social relations in early adolescence. *International Journal of Behavioral Development,* 1978, *1,* 1–36.

Hoffman, M. L. Parent discipline and the child's consideration for others. *Child Development,* 1963, *34,* 573–588.

Hoffman, M. L. Developmental synthesis of affect and cognition and its implication for altruistic motivation. *Developmental Psychology,* 1975, *11,* 607–622.

Hoffman, M. L. Development of moral thought, feeling, and behavior. *American Psychologist,* 1979, *34,* 958–966.

Horner, A. J. *Object relations and the developing ego in therapy.* New York: Jason Aronson, 1980.

Kernberg, O. F. *Object relations theory and clinical psychoanalysis.* New York: Jason Aronson, 1979.

Klein, M. On observing the behavior of young infants: On the theory of anxiety and guilt. In J. Riviere (Ed.), *Developments in psychoanalysis.* London: Hogarth Press, 1970.

Klein, M. Love, guilt and reparation. In M. Klein, *Lover guilt and reparation and other works 1921–1945.* New York: Dell, 1975. (Article published, 1937.)

Klein, M., & Riviere J. *Love, hate and reparation.* London: Hogarth Press, 1967.

Kohlberg, L. Development of moral character and ideology. In M. L. Hoffman &. L. W. Hoffman (Eds.), *Review of child development research* (Vol. 1). New York: Russell Sage Foundation, 1964.

Krebs, D. R. Altruism: An examination of the concept and a review of the literature. *Psychological Bulletin,* 1970, *73,* 258–302.

Kubie, L. S. *Practical and theoretical aspects of psychoanalysis.* New York: International Universities Press, 1975.

Lev-Ran, A., & Sharabany, R. *The development of intimate friendship among kibbutz children: A longitudinal study.* Paper presented at the meeting of the International Society for the Study of Behavioral Development, Toronto, August 1981.

Loevinger, J. The meaning and measurement of ego development. *American Psychologist,* 1966, *21,* 195–206.

Mahler, M., Pine, F., & Bergman, A. *The psychological birth of the human infant.* New York: Basic Books, 1975.

Mannarino, A. P. The development of children's friendships. In H. C. Foot, A. J. Chapman, & J. R. Smith (Eds.), *Friendship and social relations in children.* New York: Wiley, 1980.

Muuss, R. E. *Theories of adolescence.* New York: Random House, 1975.

Oden, S., & Asher, S. R. Coaching children in social skills for friendship making. *Child Development,* 48, *2,* 495–506.

Porteus, B., & Johnson, R. C. Children's responses to two measures of conscience development and their relations to sociometric nomination. *Child Development,* 1965, *36,* 703–711.

Reisman, J. M. *Anatomy of friendship.* New York: Irvington, 1979.

Rosenhan, D. The nature of socialization of altruistic autonomy. In J. Macaulay & L. Berkowitz (Eds.), *Altruism and helping behavior.* New York: Academic Press, 1970.

Rosenhan, D. L. Toward resolving the altruism paradox: Affect, self-reinforcement and cognition. In L. Wispé (Ed.), *Altruism, sympathy and helping.* New York: Academic Press, 1978.

Rushton, J. P. *Altruism, socialization and society.* Englewood Cliffs, N.J.: Prentice-Hall, 1980.

Rutherford, E., & Mussen, P. Generosity in nursery school boys. *Child Development,* 1968, *39,* 765–775.

Selman, R. L. Social-cognitive understanding: A guide to educational and clinical practice. In T. Lickone (Ed.), *Moral development and behavior.* New York: Holt, Rinehart & Winston, 1976.

Sharabany, R. *Development of intimacy in the kibbutz.* Paper presented at the meeting of the International Society for the Study of Behavioral Development, Ann Arbor, Michigan, August 1973.

Sharabany, R. *Intimate friendship among kibbutz and city children and its measurement.* Ann Arbor, Mich.: University Microfilms International, 1974.

Sharabany, R. *Friendship: A developmental and cultural perspective.* Unpublished manuscript, 1980.

Sharabany, R. Comradeship: Peer group relations among preadolescents in kibbutz vs. city. *Personality and Social Psychology Bulletin,* 1982, *18*(2), 302–309. (a)

Sharabany, R. The gender constancy issue revisited: A discussion of W. Emmerich's paper "The transitional phase in the development of gender-constancy." In S. Strauss (Ed.), *The U-shaped behavioral growth.* Cambridge: M.I.T. Press, 1982. (b)

Sharabany, R., & Bar-Tal, D. Theories of the development of altruism: Review, comparison and integration. *International Journal of Behavioral Development,* 1982, *5,* 49–80.

Sharabany, R., & Eitan, T. *Gender constancy in cross-cultural perspective.* Unpublished manuscript, University of Haifa, 1983.

Sharabany, R., & Hertz-Lazarowitz, R. Sharing among friends and non-friends, in kindergarten and first-grade. *International Journal of Behavioral Development*, 1981, *4*, 45–59.

Sharabany, R., Gershoni, R., & Hofman, J. Girl-friend, boy-friend: Age and sex differences in intimate friendship. *Developmental Psychology*, 1981, *17*, 800–808.

Staub, E. The use of role playing and induction in children's learning and helping and sharing behavior. *Child Development*, 1971, *42*, 805–816.

Staub, E. *Positive social behavior and morality*. Vol. 1. *Personal and social influences*. New York: Academic Press, 1978.

Staub, E. *Positive social behavior and morality*. Vol. 2. *Socialization and development*. New York: Academic Press, 1979.

Sullivan, H. S. *The interpersonal theory of psychiatry*. New York: W. W. Norton, 1953.

Suomi, S. J. Peers, play, and primary prevention in primates. In M. Kent & J. Rolf (Eds.), *Primary prevention of psychopathology* (Vol. 3). Hanover, N.H.: New England University Press, 1979.

Turner, W. D. Altruism and its measurement in children. *Journal of Abnormal and Social Psychology*, 1948, *43*, 502–516.

Winnicott, D. W. The development of the capacity for concern. In D. W. Winnicott (Ed.), *The maturational processes and the facilitating environment: Studies in the Theory of Emotional Development*. New York: International Universities Press, 1974.

Wispé, L. G. (Ed.). *Altruism, sympathy and helping*. New York: Academic Press, 1978.

Yinon, Y. Perceived deprivation of material and non-material rewards as related to altruistic behavior among young adolescents. *International Journal of Behavioral Development*, 1979, *2*, 287–295.

# III

# DETERMINANTS OF PROSOCIAL BEHAVIOR

# Introduction

Janusz Reykowski and Jerzy Karylowski

One of the main aims of the research on prosocial behavior from its very beginning was to find out what the determinants of such a behavior might be. In fact, during the past 15 years a great body of evidence concerning the variety of possible determinants has been accumulated. An extensive review of such evidence by Bar-Tal (1976) indicates that a large number of factors can play a role in promoting (or inhibiting) prosocial behavior.

While new research was extending the list of factors that allegedly influence prosocial behavior, there were also attempts to achieve some order in this otherwise rather chaotic picture and to account for interrelations between various determinants. One of the earliest attempts of this kind was made by Schwartz (1970), who proposed a comprehensive model of determinants of prosocial behavior. A more advanced and elaborated version of the model was published in 1977 (Schwartz, 1977). In the present volume the most recent version of the model is presented by Schwartz and Howard (Chapter 11).

The model assumes that prosocial behavior can be a result of a complex decisional process. The crucial role in that process is played by a motivational component: Personal standards originating in the value system of an individual are activated. Schwartz and Howard concentrate on the role of personal standards and their relation to the value system. This analysis offers a new contribution to the theory of determinants of prosocial behavior.

A noteworthy addition to the theory of the functioning of personal standards is proposed by Kofta (Chapter 12). His data seem to indicate that the controlling function of standards depends upon perceived freedom of choice. The condition "freedom of choice" may pertain to different aspects of the stimulus situation: Kofta shows that it may be the freedom of the choice of the person to whom the behavior is directed or a choice of activity.

Is freedom of choice the necessary condition for the operation of standards of value? Kofta emphasizes that it plays a regulatory role if an expectancy of choice has been created. In such a situation the denial of freedom decreases the regulatory power of standards. This formulation seems consonant with the results of some earlier studies on the role of psychological reactance in prosocial behavior (cf. Berkowitz, 1968; Horowitz, 1968; Karylowski, 1979; Schwartz, 1977).

Rushton's chapter deals with the issue of cross-situational consistency among various forms of prosocial behavior. He argues that there is, in fact, a remarkable consistency in this respect and that it is fully justified to treat the tendency for prosocial behavior as a trait variable ("trait of altruism"). Surprisingly enough, Rushton's most persuasive arguments are based on a reanalysis of the famous character–education inquiry (Hartshorne & May, 1928–1930)—the classic source of evidence against the idea of personality traits. Rushton claims that the two useful constructs with which to understand individual differences in altruism are personal norms and empathy.

It should be noted that this argument does not at all contradict Schwartz's model. In fact, Schwartz assumes that although (prosocial) personal standards might be of a rather specific character, the extent to which such standards are expressed in overt (prosocial) behavior depends on two relatively general and stable characteristics of an individual: (low) responsibility denial and (high) awareness of consequences. Although a low tendency for responsibility denial might be of a normative character itself, the concept of awareness of consequences bears a close resemblance to the concept of empathy (at least the cognitive aspect of empathy).

Both personal normative standards and empathy can be regarded as fairly specific personality determinants of prosocial behavior. But there are others, less specific, that also play an important role. One of them is discussed by Midlarsky (Chapter 14). She presents an elaborate analysis of the relationship between competence and prosocial behavior and argues that competence (both perceived and actual) might not only be a direct consequence of one's previous experience with prosocial behavior, but will promote subsequent prosocial behavior as well.

Interestingly enough, the importance of competence is assumed by the Schwartz model as well. He postulates that the recognition of one's ability to deal with the problem of a person in need is a precondition of prosocial action.

Such a recognition might certainly be a function of social (and environmental) conditions. This brings us (skipping over one chapter) to Korte's contribution. He shows that the occurrence of prosocial behavior might be facilitated by certain characteristics of urban neighborhoods. The setting that seems to make this kind of behavior more likely is described as urban village quality. It is characterized by *both* an active street life and the residential character of the area.

One may note that such an urban village quality is precisely the sort of social setting that might be expected to promote both the feeling of personal competence and the feeling of responsibility toward local events that require help. Thus, we are back to the Schwartz model again.

Korte's attempt to study the determinants of prosocial behavior within a broader social context is very much in accordance with a recent tendency in European psychology to abandon the individualistic perspective in social psychology and to replace it with a more social one (Eiser, 1980; Mummendey, Bornewasser, Löschiper, & Linneweber, in press; Stroebe, 1979; Tajfel, 1979). A strong plea for this kind of approach to the problems of the determinants of prosocial behavior is presented by Bierhoff in Chapter 15.

Bierhoff argues that prosocial behavior always implies an interaction and that it should be understood in the context of social interactions in general. He applies to the prosocial area the classification of social interactions into pseudocontingency, assymmetrical contingency, reactive contingency, and mutual contingency (Jones & Gerard, 1967) and shows that prosocial behavior might be determined by different factors depending on the particular pattern of interactions involved.

## REFERENCES


Bar-Tal, D. *Prosocial behavior: Theory and research.* New York: Wiley, 1976.

Berkowitz, L. Responsibility, reciprocity and social distance in help-giving. *Journal of Experimental Social Psychology,* 1968, *4,* 46–63.

Eiser, J. R. *Cognitive social psychology.* New York: McGraw-Hill, 1980.

Hartshorne, H., & May, M. A. *Studies in the nature of character.* New York: Macmillan, 1928–1930.

Horowitz, I. A. Effects of choice and locus of dependence on helping behavior. *Journal of Personality and Social Psychology,* 1968, *8,* 373–376.

Jones, E. E., & Gerard, H. B. *Foundations of social psychology.* New York: Wiley, 1967.

Karylowski, J. Self-focused attention, prosocial norms and prosocial behavior. *Polish Psychological Bulletin,* 1979, *10,* 57–66.

Mummendey, A., Bornewasser, M., Löschper, G., & Linneweber, V. "Aggresiv sind immer die Andern": Für eine sozial-psychologische Perspective in der Aggressions Forschung. *Zeitschrift für Sozialpsychologie,* in press.

Schwartz, S. H. Moral decision making and behavior. In J. Macaulay & L. Berkowitz (Eds.), *Altruism and helping behavior*. New York: Academic Press, 1970.

Schwartz, S. H. Normative influences on altruism. In L. Berkowitz (Ed.), *Advances in experimental social psychology* (Vol. 10). New York: Academic Press, 1977.

Stroebe, W. The level of social psychological analysis: The plea for a more social social psychology. In R. H. Strickland (Ed.), *Soviet and Western perspectives in social psychology*. Oxford: Pergamon Press, 1979.

Tajfel, H. Individuals and groups in social psychology. *British Journal of Clinical and Social Psychology*, 1979, *18*, 183–190.

# 11
# Internalized Values as Motivators of Altruism

Shalom H. Schwartz and Judith A. Howard

## 1. INTRODUCTION

For us, altruism refers to self-sacrificial acts intended to benefit others regardless of material or social outcomes for the actor. Crucial to this definition is an emphasis on the actor's motivation: An act is altruistic only to the extent that it is motivated by concern for the welfare of others. In other words, altruistic behavior is motivated by the desire to affirm one's own moral values (Schwartz & Howard, 1981). The more general notion of *prosocial* behavior points to the outcomes of action rather than to the intentions that underlie action (Wispé, 1972). Prosocial behavior usually entails a mixture of altruistic and other types of motivation. An adult may stop children who are fighting, for instance, both because of her own value-based concern for their welfare and because this act may elicit social approval and enhance her sense of competence.

Since the crucial concern in this chapter is motivation, we begin by

This is a revised version of a paper delivered at the International Conference on the Development and Maintenance of Prosocial Behavior, Warsaw, June–July 1980.

SHALOM H. SCHWARTZ • Department of Psychology, Hebrew University, Jerusalem, Israel. JUDITH A. HOWARD • Department of Sociology, University of Washington, Seattle, Washington 98195. The writing of this chapter was supported by NSF Grant BNS 77-23287 to the first author.

briefly describing our conception of motivational processes. In line with the converging ideas of cognitive psychology (e.g., Birch, Atkinson, & Bongort, 1974; Mischel, 1973) and symbolic interactionism (e.g., Blumer, 1969; Mead, 1934; Stryker & Gottlieb, 1981), we view people as information seekers and processors who actively pursue goals in an ongoing stream of behavior. People modify their behavior as various goals shift in their relative importance to them. Three sources of inputs influence the importance of goals: inputs from our external environment, from our own physiology, and from our cognitive memory processes. For example, the importance of help giving as a goal may increase in response to the salience of another's need (environment), to our empathically induced physical distress (physiology), or to our memory of a request (cognition).

Regardless of the source of an input, we process it cognitively, though not necessarily consciously. Each input suggests potential actions we might take and possible outcomes associated with these actions. We compare the potential outcomes available to us with our enduring expectations and preferences. In this way, we set goals. When we perceive an undesirable discrepancy between the situation we experience and the situation we expect or prefer, we are motivated to perform behaviors that might reduce this discrepancy. Thus, like other cognitive discrepancy models of motivation (e.g., Deci, 1975; Reykowski, 1975), our model locates the "motor" for behavioral change in a need to reduce perceived discrepancies between present and desired conditions. In our view, for example, bystanders are motivated to help a heart attack victim when they perceive a discrepancy between the victim's endangered state and their own preference for his good health.

Most often, people generate specific conceptions of desirable conditions in response to each new situation. This is because conceptions of ideal or preferred states drawn from past experience seldom match current perceptions precisely. Where do these new, situation-specific conceptions of what is desirable come from? We suggest that people generate them from their individual values, that is, from their relatively enduring beliefs that certain general modes of conduct or end states of being are preferable to their opposites (Rokeach, 1973). Values are organized hierarchically according to their importance as behavioral guides. They encompass the full range of a person's goals—social (e.g., esteem), material (e.g., a comfortable life), psychological (e.g., competence), and moral (e.g., compassion).

We generate our conceptions of what actions and outcomes are more or less desirable in a given situation by assessing their implications for our values. The potential actions and outcomes we evaluate are those suggested by immediate inputs from our environment, physiology, and memory. The assessment process produces specific goals and plans of action.[1] Moral values are especially likely to be an important basis for assessment when inputs in a situation suggest actions that entail self-sacrifice for another's benefit. But other values may also play a role. When deciding whether to donate a kidney to a relative, for example, potential donors may evaluate effects of this action on their public image, their physical well-being, their future abilities, and their sense of self-worth (Simmons, Klein, & Simmons, 1977). Only action based on their sense of self-worth, affirming the value they themselves place on the welfare of others, entails altruistic motivation.

Karylowski (1982) has suggested that there are two types of altruistic motivation rather than the one type we propose. The first, which he calls *endocentric,* derives from the desire to conform with one's own standards and ideals and thereby to protect or enhance self-esteem. The second type of altruistic motivation, which he calls *exocentric,* is regulated by direct concern for others. Helping motivated by value affirmation may appear to be exocentric (when personal goals are generated from such values as compassion and equality) or endocentric (when the crucial values are self-respect or self-esteem).

We suggest, however, that the exocentric-endocentric distinction blurs when value affirmation is the source of altruistic motivation. Values such as compassion focus directly on others (exocentric), yet they guide our behavior because they are important for self-evaluation (endocentric). Values such as self-respect focus on our own standards (endocentric), yet they promote helping others only if we tie others' welfare to our self-evaluation (exocentric). Hence we conclude that altruistic motivation entails the joining of concern for others to self-evaluation.

Current social psychology has emphasized the influence of situational variables on helping behavior. If values also influence helping behavior, development of intervention programs designed to change values would be desirable. This is one important reason to develop approaches that examine whether and how values influence behavior. Over the past several years we have developed and refined such a model of the decision-making process presumed to underlie prosocial behavior (Schwartz, 1970a, 1973, 1977; Schwartz & Howard, 1981, 1982). Our focus on altruism leads to an emphasis on the role of internalized moral values in this decision making. This chapter will provide a brief

[1]In familiar situations requiring low cost help, however, people may skip assessment of the value implications of action and utilize plans developed in the past (scripts). People tend to acquiesce virtually automatically, for example, for trivial favors (e.g., a polite request to let someone go ahead in line and photocopy five pages in a library; Langer, 1978), relying on a script that points to the behavioral sequence and desired outcome without weighing value implications.

overview of the model and examines theoretical and operational issues in working with its central concept—feelings of moral obligation. We shall then discuss the relationship of this concept to other forms of intrinsic motivation. For full presentations of the model, see Schwartz and Howard (1981, 1982).

## 2. THE VALUE-BASED DECISION-MAKING MODEL

The model specifies five sequential stages: attention to need and awareness of potential actions, generation of value-based motivation, evaluation of the costs and benefits of potential actions, possible defense against anticipated moral costs, and overt behavior or inaction (See Figure 1). The decision maker's progress through the specific steps in each stage of this model is influenced by situation and person variables that we have sought to identify.

### 2.1. Attention

During the attention stage the person becomes aware of characteristics of a situation that determine whether any decision need be made. There are three steps in the attention stage.

1. *Awareness of a person in need.* First, a person in need must be noticed and his or her state must be defined as needy. Need may be noticed spontaneously (e.g., when an urban native notices that a perplexed tourist is lost), or it may be brought formally to the potential helper's attention (e.g., when the tourist asks the native for directions) (Pearce & Amato, 1980). Helping is more likely to be experienced as internally controlled when helpers become aware of others' needs spontaneously rather than responding to needs formally presented to them. The motivation for internally controlled helping is more readily attributed to self (cf. Batson, Coke, Jasnoski, & Hanson, 1978). Hence spontaneity in noticing need may increase the degree of value affirmation a helping act can provide both for altruistic values and for such values as independence, self-respect, and competence.

Situational salience and clarity of need as well as individual receptivity to need cues increase awareness of need. These situational and person variables are therefore conducive to helping. The impacts of salience and clarity are illustrated by the findings that bystanders are more likely to help in emergencies the closer their visual proximity to the victim (Piliavin & Piliavin, 1973), and the more clearly need is spelled out (Schwartz, 1970b). The impact of individual receptivity to need cues is illustrated by the finding that persons who tend spontaneously to become aware of the negative consequences for others of remaining in their needy state (measured by the Awareness of Consequences scale) behave more helpfully and considerately in everyday peer contacts (Schwartz, 1968a).

2. *Identification of potentially helpful actions.* Which potential actions a person perceives as relevant in a situation of need depends upon the specific situational inputs and the person's cognitive associations with these inputs. Those actions recognized as relevant determine, in turn, which values will be activated, since each action has different implications for some unique subset of the person's values. Helping by feeding a starving peasant as opposed to teaching him innovative irrigation techniques, for example, has different implications for such values as nurturance, compassion, a sense of accomplishment, and competence. Identifying which patterns of value implications are tied to given helping acts is a challenge for future research.

3. *Recognition of own ability to engage in these actions.* Once potentially helpful actions are recognized, a person considers his or her own ability to execute them. Values are relevant only for actions we feel capable of performing. A newcomer to Jerusalem who is asked directions to the Dome of the Rock, for example, will generate no feelings of moral obligation. Assuming she lacks the ability to help, she will sense that failing to provide directions does not have implications for her internalized moral values. She may, of course, feel empathic distress for the confused questioner.

In sum, the *attention* stage entails a sequence of steps that activate three types of perceptions necessary to confront a person with a decision about helping. The potential helper may not notice need or perceive need as sufficiently severe to stimulate a search for appropriate actions; relevant actions may not be recognized; or they may be perceived as missing from the person's behavioral repertoire. Unless each of these perceptions is activated in turn, the decision-making process terminates with inaction. Inaction at the attention stage is not yet connected to internalized values. Values become relevant only during the next stage in decision making.

## 2.2. Generation of Feelings of Obligation

If a person feels capable of performing those actions perceived as relevant to another's need, three types of action implications are considered: (1) physical or material implications that follow directly from the action (e.g., getting burned when rescuing a child from a fire); (2) social implications—outcomes dependent upon the reactions of others (e.g., rewards for heroism or condemnation for foolhardiness); (3) psychological, value-based implications—expression or rejection of values important to the self-concept (e.g., expressing love and rejecting comfort, attaining excitement and risking personal security).

Rokeach (1973) has suggested that values can be divided into a personal/competence subset and a social/moral subset. Although there is little empirical support for this classification, it is conceptually useful for defining altruism. The moral subset of values includes those values concerned with protecting or enhancing the welfare of others. Attempts to help can be viewed as altruistically motivated only insofar as they are guided by the person's desire to affirm or to avoid undermining such moral values as love, compassion, helping, and concern.

Each person internalizes a unique structure of values in the course of his or her history of social interactions. These values vary from person to person in their importance to self, their specificity, their interconnections, their relationships to experience, and their accessibility to activation (Bem, 1970; Rokeach, 1973; Rosenberg, 1979; Schwartz, 1977). Hence the value implications of engaging in a specific behavior vary across people. Considering the implications of action alternatives for one's moral values results in the generation of feelings of moral obligation to perform or refrain from specific action. We have labeled these feelings of obligation *personal norms.*

Personal norms include both a cognitive component of value-based expectations or goals for behavior and an emotional component of anticipatory feelings of self-(dis)satisfaction. A personal norm is constructed for each potential action perceived as relevant. People implicitly ask themselves whether they are morally responsible for these potential actions in this situation, given their own internalized moral values. Thus personal norms are situated, self-based standards for specific behavior generated from internalized values during the process of behavioral decision making. The sanctions attached to personal norms are based in the self-concept, because anticipated compliance with these behavioral expectations elicits feelings of self-satisfaction, whereas anticipated inaction elicits feelings of self-deprecation. Since the stimuli that activate the scanning of internalized values arise in the situation, however, the personal norms generated are momentary, rather than enduring standards. In contrast, values are relatively enduring preferences for general outcomes or modes of behavior. In sum, personal norms are situation-specific reflections of the cognitive and affective implications of a person's values for particular actions.

Personal norms are usually measured by confronting people with hypothetical behavior choices and asking them to describe the intensity of moral obligation to act (positive, neutral, or negative) they anticipate feeling. Note that for each of these choices, motivation also derives from anticipated material and social costs and benefits and from psychological outcomes tied to nonmoral (e.g., competence type) values. There is no guarantee that the actions specified in items used to measure personal norms are the actions that will actually be considered in the later situation of behavioral choice, when the personal norms that influence behavior are constructed. Consequently, only relatively low positive correlations between premeasured personal norms and subsequent single helping behaviors are expected. Significant but low correlations are typically observed ($\bar{r}$ = .29 across six studies; Schwartz & Howard, 1981).

The decision-making model suggests that the strength of association between personal norms and helping depends upon the moderating effects of attention conditions. Consider an example of one such moderating effect, from a study of everyday helpfulness and considerateness among peers (Schwartz, 1968a). Personal norms were correlated substantially with behavior for students who tended to notice others' need spontaneously and who were therefore likely to attend to need and construct personal norms in behavioral choice situations ($r$ = .44, high AC quartile). In contrast, for those who tended to overlook others' need, there was no correlation between answers to personal norm questions, which draw attention directly to need, and everyday interpersonal behavior in which need may remain unnoticed ($r$ = −.01, low AC quartile).

### 2.3. Anticipatory Evaluation

Having identified the material, social, and psychological outcomes implied by specific helping behaviors, the decision maker evaluates the anticipated payoffs of these outcomes. Minimal material costs of time and effort are inherent in any helping action. Socially mediated outcomes are also common, though their influence depends on who gains knowledge of behavior. Moreover, helping actions typically imply psychological costs and benefits tied to the person's value structure. If the combined set of anticipated payoffs clearly favors either action or inaction, a decision is reached. A decision to act is followed by the particular helping action evaluated. People do not help when the cost–benefit analysis clearly opposes the possible helping actions.

To illustrate how different types of costs and benefits may influence a decision, consider a study of volunteering to help elderly welfare recipients (Schwartz & Fleishman, 1978). One set of women indicated in a survey that they felt a moral obligation to help elderly welfare recipients (positive personal norms), another set indicated feelings of moral obligation to oppose such aid (negative personal norms), and a third set responded that such actions elicited no feelings of moral obligation for them (no personal norms). A subsequent telephone appeal for help described the elderly persons' need as either socially illegitimate (because of their lack of trustworthiness) or legitimate (because of arbitrary events beyond their control). Regardless of the legitimacy of need, women tended to volunteer if their premeasured personal norms were positive, and to refuse if their norms were negative; moral payoffs apparently guided the decision for those who viewed the situation as involving moral obligation. In contrast, women who had responded on the premeasure that such actions were not a moral issue for them volunteered twice as much when the need was socially legitimate rather than illegitimate. In the absence of personal norms, these women were apparently guided by socially defined payoffs.

If the various costs and benefits of available actions do not point clearly to a decision, that is, if they are relatively balanced, conflict is experienced. This conflict adds to other sources of emotional arousal such as physical danger. The decision is then delayed while the person tries to reduce decisional conflict through defense.

### 2.4. Defense

The preferred method for reducing decisional conflict is to weaken one's feelings of moral obligation through redefining one's own perceptions and interpretations of the situation. It is less possible to modify the physical and social outcomes of action merely by redefining them in one's own mind. Four types of denial can reduce feelings of moral obligation. Each is implied by one of the earlier steps in the model: denial of need, denial of effectiveness of actions, denial of ability, and denial of responsibility. Each type of denial enables the person to cycle back through part of the decision-making process and generate a new definition of the situation. The new definition may facilitate a clearer behavioral decision. Where the new cycle begins depends upon the form of denial employed (See Figure 1).

1. *Denial of need.* A person may reexamine the situation, seeking cues that permit denial of the need or at least a reduction in its perceived severity (e.g., "That's not an assault, it's a lovers' quarrel"). Total denial of the reality of need permits termination of decision making without incurring moral costs. Reducing the perceived severity of need is likely to lead to a lower estimate of the various costs of not helping, so that the new payoff ratio clearly favors inaction.

2. *Denial of effectiveness of actions.* People may conclude from reexamining the situation that the action in question would not be effective (e.g., "No point intervening, they'll start up again as soon as I leave"). Alternatively, another line of action with lower costs (e.g., reporting to

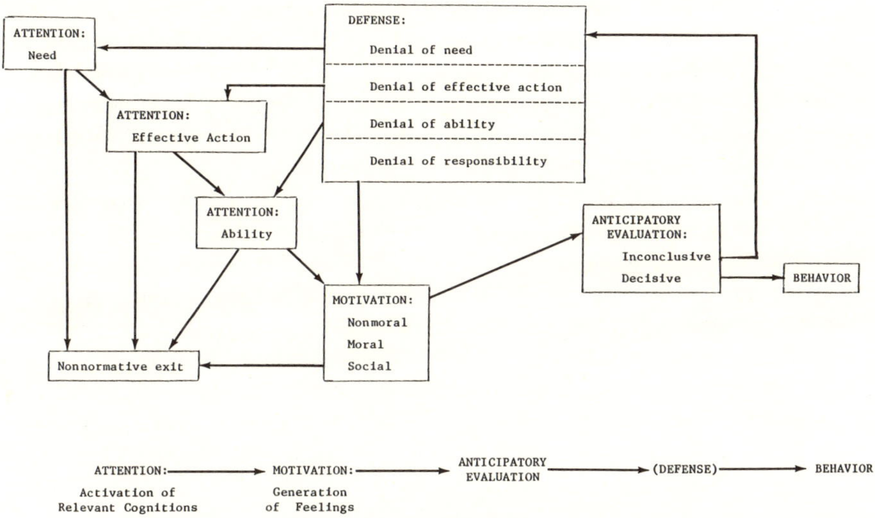


Figure 1. A value-based model of altruistic decision-making.

the policeman on the corner) may be defined as more appropriate. This new action would then be evaluated in subsequent decision-making steps.

3. *Denial of personal ability.* Upon reconsideration, people may conclude that they lack the competence to perform the original actions considered or any new actions redefined as appropriate. This mode of defense may deflect both the moral and social costs of inaction.

4. *Denial of responsibility.* Finally, people may deny their responsibility to conform with the moral or social obligations: They may claim that *under the circumstances* these personal or social norms do not reasonably apply. Denial of liability for action is justified by such extenuating circumstances as provocation, overwhelming outside pressure, job requirements, illness, and so on.

Our model thus implies several hypotheses regarding the moderation of personal norm effects of altruism by all four types of denial. In general, personal norms should affect altruistic behavior when none of these forms of denial is employed. The use of any form of denial may neutralize the impact of personal norms on behavior. Since responsibility denial has been investigated most extensively, we shall illustrate the moderation effect with work on the individual tendency to accept or deny personal responsibility for the interpersonal consequences of one's actions, measured by the Responsibility Denial Scale (Schwartz, 1968b).

Four separate studies have found that personal norms correlate substantially with altruistic behavior among people who tend not to deny responsibility, but that the correlation is near zero among people high in responsibility denial. Most striking is a correlation of .72 between personal norms and volunteering to tutor blind children in a group of Israeli undergraduates low on responsibility denial, compared with a correlation of −.03 among students high on responsibility denial (Schwartz & Howard, 1980).

In summary, decisional conflicts produced when evaluating the anticipated costs and benefits of an action elicit defenses against the feelings of moral obligation to perform that action. If these defenses succeed, actors may terminate decision making, or they may construct new personal norms and reach a behavioral decision on the basis of the reevaluated material, social, and psychological outcomes. Repeated recycling is unlikely; the passage of time leads to changes that end the process—need intensifies or dissipates, attention is focused or diverted.

### 2.5. Behavior

The decision-making process culminates in helping behavior or inact1on. The outcomes of behavioral action or inaction, in turn, influence future decision making. The responses and satisfactions obtained from helping or inaction, and the inferences drawn from them, may change the person's system of internalized values. They may also influence the person's subsequent expectations and evaluations of social and material payoffs. In addition to these changes in the person's cognitions, emotions, abilities, and even physiology, the outcomes of behavior also influence the actual external opportunities and constraints that may guide future decisions (cf. Bandura, 1978).

Our overview of the value-based decision-making model has necessarily been sketchy. Our purpose has been to set the context for discussing the central motivational concept that distinguishes our approach to understanding altruism—feelings of moral obligation as expressed in personal norms. We turn now to that discussion.

## 3. ISSUES IN THE STUDY OF FEELINGS OF MORAL OBLIGATION

### 3.1. The Relation of Personal Norms to Values

#### *3.1.1. Why Interpose Personal Norms between Values and Behavior?*

If values are indeed the basis of altruistic decisions, why interpose the concept of personal norms? First, because values are general, the implications of values for specific actions are necessarily vague. Knowing that a person values compassion highly suggests that he will aid suffering victims in general, but it does little to increase our certainty that he will adopt an Asian orphan. To determine whether and how values influence a particular act, they must be measured as they are translated into decisions about that act. As Ajzen and Fishbein (1977) have demonstrated convincingly for attitudes, success in predicting behavior (and hence inferring causality) depends upon the degree to which the attitude and the behavior are conceptualized and measured at the same level of specificity–generality. Personal norms provide the parallel conceptual link between general values and specific acts.

Second, any single act typically follows from several values and perhaps contradicts others. Rokeach (1973, 1979) explicitly recognizes this by working with the relative rankings of values in his research on civil rights behavior. Yet values are a poor predictor of behavior in this research. This is probably because of both a failure to consider sufficiently complex profiles of several values simultaneously, as well as the fact that the same feelings of obligation regarding an act may be generated from different profiles of values.[2]

The use of personal norms overcomes these difficulties because personal norms express the feelings of moral obligation toward specific acts that result from the application of each person's unique total profile of relevant values. They mediate between the activated value system and the particular actions in context. To enhance understanding of value–behavior relations, we can examine the ways complex value profiles relate to personal norms, and then how these personal norms relate in turn to behavior. What evidence is there for this sequential relationship of values to personal norms to behavior?

### 3.1.2. *Evidence for the Value–Personal Norm–Behavior Relationship*

Consider first the relationship we have postulated between values and personal norms. This relationship implies that people feel stronger personal norms regarding those actions that are especially relevant to the values central to their self-conceptions. A study of everyday considerateness among college students who shared living quarters provides data on this hypothesis.[3] The students responded to a variety of personal norm questions, including three personal norms regarding considerateness behaviors. They also ranked seven values, including considerateness,with respect to relative importance for their self-evaluation.

[2]Also problematic in some of these studies is the use of several behavioral variables that are presumed to be related, but that may actually be motivated by quite different combinations of values (e.g., joining the NAACP and switching from natural to social science majors).

[3]Previously unreported data from the study described in Schwartz (1968a,b).

The importance people attributed to the value considerateness correlated significantly with the strength of their personal norms regarding considerateness behaviors ($r = .28$, $p < .01$). The importance rankings of the other values were unrelated to personal norms for considerateness. These findings support the idea that value centrality leads to stronger personal norms.

Consider next the relationship of personal norms and of values to behavior. We would expect that any particular behavior will be correlated more strongly with the matching personal norm than it will be with even the most relevant value. This is because personal norms are the *situated* expressions of the whole relevant value profile. The data, though weak, do reflect such a trend: The average correlation of the personal norms with peer ratings of each respective considerateness behavior was .25 ($p < .01$), and the average correlation of the ranking of the considerateness value with these behaviors was .17 ($p < .05$). The relatively low values of these correlations undoubtedly reflect the fact that variables moderating the impact of values and personal norms on behavior have not been considered.

Another implication of our analysis is that personal norm items that ask about behaviors relevant to a person's more central values will measure the feelings of obligation likely to be experienced in actual choice situations better than items referring to behaviors relevant to less central values. This is because personal norm questions addressed to behavioral dimensions of low importance to the self may elicit relatively random responses. This hypothesis also received support. The correlation between personal norms and peer rankings of considerateness behavior was significantly stronger among students who ranked considerateness as one of their top two values than among those who ranked this value lower ($\bar{r} = .39 > \bar{r} = .03$, $p < .05$).

Finally, our view that personal norms are constructed in the situation from an underlying value structure implies that premeasured personal norms will predict subsequent behavior well only if the person's relevant underlying values are stable. If the underlying values are unstable, they may change between the time personal norms are first measured and the time when the personal norms that influence behavior are generated in the situation of behavioral choice. Thus, when relevant values are unstable, the premeasured personal norms and the personal norms operative in the situation are likely to be different. Data from a study of volunteering to tutor blind children (Schwartz, 1978) demonstrate this aspect of the relationship between values, personal norms, and behavior.

In this study, the general underlying altruistic values potentially relevant to a person's decision whether to tutor blind children were measured twice, separated by a 3-month interval. Instability in the underlying values was measured by the absolute differences between responses at the two times. The sample was then trichotomized on value stability to produce tertiles in which we would expect premeasured personal norms to be good, moderate, and poor predictors of subsequent behavior. Correlations between the specific personal norm regarding tutoring blind children and actual volunteering behavior 3 months later were then computed for each tertile. Consistent with the view of personal norms as situationally constructed from underlying values, the correlation was significantly higher in the tertile with the most stable versus the least stable underlying value ($r = .47 > r = -.03$, $p < .01$) and intermediate ($r = .26$) in the moderately stable tertile.

This finding suggests that the feelings of moral obligation that influence nonroutine actions are actively generated from underlying values at the time of behavioral choice. Various findings from this study contradict the view that personal norms are stored in memory and retrieved directly when the situation increases the salience of appropriate cues. This study is therefore an example of the most common situation, a situation in which personal norms are actively constructed rather than functioning as preexisting cognitive-emotional structures awaiting activation.

### 3.2. Measuring Feelings of Moral Obligation

Personal norm questions are intended to measure the feelings of moral obligation[4] a person is likely to generate in a behavioral choice situation. Although those feelings are responsive to momentary, situational inputs from the environment, memory, and physiology, we have assumed they can be approximated within limits by questionnaire self-reports of anticipated feelings. The validity of self-reported personal norms depends upon three factors—the stability of the relevant values, the detail with which the behavioral choice is portrayed in the questionnaire, and the respondents' ability to project themselves into the hypothetical situation. From the respondents' viewpoint, answering personal norm questions is an exercise in reporting the feelings elicited by a simulated behavioral choice. Respondents are not asked to explain the causes of their feelings or to predict their own behavior, both tasks they are ill-suited to perform well (Nisbett & Wilson, 1977; Wilson & Nisbett, 1978).

[4]A related discussion detailing additional aspects of this topic is found in Schwartz, 1977, pp. 235–241.

Table 1. *Examples of Personal Norm Measurement*

| Question | Response categories and distributions | | | | | | | Sample and source |
|---|---|---|---|---|---|---|---|---|
| | Strongly ought not to<br>−3 | −2 | −1 | No obligation<br>0 | 1 | 2 | Strongly ought to<br>3 | |
| 1. Assume someone favoring welfare increases asked . . . indicate whether you would feel a personal obligation to . . . give some free time to a civic organization helping welfare recipients in need. | 9% | 5% | 5% | 29% | 23% | 16% | 13% | $N$ = 382 Wisconsin females[a] |
| | Strong obligation to refuse<br>−3 | −2 | −1 | No obligation either way<br>0 | 1 | 2 | Strong obligation to agree<br>3 | |

| | | | | | | | | |
|---|---|---|---|---|---|---|---|---|
| 2. How much of a moral obligation would you feel if the State Employment Service requested you to employ a delinquent youth with a police record? | 11% | 5% | 5% | 9% | 13% | 38% | 19% | $N$ = 127 Tel Aviv male private employers[b] |
| | Obligation not to donate −1 | No obligation either way 0 | 1 | 2 | 3 | 4 | Strong obligation to donate 5 | |
| 3. If a stranger to you needed a bone marrow transplant and you were a suitable donor, would you feel a moral obligation to donate bone marrow? | 12% | 36% | 12% | 13% | 8% | 9% | 10% | $N$ = 132 Wisconsin female clerical workers[c] |

[a]Source Schwartz & Fleishman, 1978.
[b]Source Schwartz, unpublished data.
[c]Source Schwartz, 1973.

### 3.2.1. *Past Methods of Measurement*

Three examples of personal norm items are presented in Table 1. Personal norm questions usually follow the format: "In specific circumstances X, would you feel a moral (personal) obligation to perform act Y?" A paragraph preceding the personal norm items instructs respondents to report what they themselves would "feel they ought to do, regardless of what others might expect of them or of what they might actually do." The response instructions refer to a sense of *oughtness*, which constitutes a force toward action (Heider, 1958). The term *obligation* also emphasizes action, linking personal norms more closely to overt behavior than the more strictly cognitive or evaluative terms typically used in attitude measurement.

The most important implication of *obligation* is that the actions considered will lead to positive or negative sanctions. The qualifiers *moral* or *personal* are intended to indicate that the relevant obligations are to one's own values, so that respondents will see the self as the source of sanctions. Since feelings of obligation are experienced before behavior, respondents to personal norm questions can base their answers on the directly experienced feelings they have when considering a specific behavior. In contrast, guilt or pride, terms often used to refer to moral reactions, are feelings that arise following behavior. Answers to questions about these reactions would depend more upon conjecture that upon directly experienced feelings.

Note from Table 1 that response scales include a zero point of "no obligation." Choosing the zero point enables people to assert that they do not view the particular decision in terms of morality or obligation. Such a response signifies that the decision does not have implications for the person's moral values. It indicates that the person is not likely to generate feelings of moral obligation that would influence the choice of whether to enact the behavior in the actual situation.

On each sample item in Table 1, some respondents indicated feelings of obligation to oppose the action. Our research has identified two moral bases for opposition. First, opposition may derive from the perception that the act in question endangers or undermines important values (e.g., Q3: the integrity of the human body). Second, even a positively valued act may conflict with obligations to protect the welfare of one's dependents (e.g., Q2: harming co-workers). For low cost acts of helping blameless targets (e.g., reading to blind children), virtually no one expresses negative personal norms. Hence a symmetrical response format of positive and negative options is not always needed.

Contrasting our method for measuring personal norms with Fishbein's technique for measuring the ostensibly similar concept of "personal normative beliefs" points to our distinctive concern with moral values. Fishbein (e.g., Ajzen & Fishbein, 1969) asked respondents how probable it is that they should engage in behavior X. Responses were made on a probability judgment scale. This method captures a belief about the self akin to a behavioral intention; but it misses entirely the value-based sense of obligation to act that our approach aims to operationalize.

Psychoanalytic thought has emphasized guilt avoidance as the primary motivation for conformity to internalized standards (Fenichel, 1945). The avoidance of value violation may indeed play a role in altruism. But people perform many self-sacrificing acts with little sign of the drivenness or duty-boundedness one associates with guilt avoidance. We have therefore chosen to cast our approach to moral obligation more in terms of feelings arising from the desire to affirm values and less in terms of feelings arising from pressures to defend against guilt. There are, however, no clear grounds for assuming that the feelings of self-evaluation that are anticipated when considering a value-relevant action are consistently focused on the possibility either of self-enhancement (positive feelings) for value affirmation or of self-deprecation (negative feelings) for value violation. The terms *moral* or *personal obligation* used in operationalizing personal norms have the virtue of relative neutrality with respect to the positivity–negativity of the feelings implied.

Results of three studies suggest that obligation indexes of internalized motivation do capture whatever impact anticipated guilt and pride have on helping behavior, plus something more. In these studies, obligation items and anticipated guilt or pride items were positively and significantly correlated with each other. However, obligation items were more powerful predictors of the respective behaviors, blood donation (Pomazal, 1974), purchasing lead-free gasoline (Heberlein & Black, 1976), and intentions to donate a kidney to a family member or a stranger (Fellner & Schwartz, 1971). Moreover, when included as predictors, guilt or pride items explained no additional variance in these behaviors or intentions.

### 3.2.2. *Contrasting Personal Norms, Attitudes, and Social Norms*

Given the common definition of attitudinal variables as affective or evaluative responses to an object (Schuman & Johnson, 1976), personal norms may be viewed as a class of attitudes. Personal norms are conceptually distinct from other attitudinal concepts in the type of evaluation to which they refer. Whereas other attitudinal concepts refer to evaluations based on material, social, and/or psychological payoffs, personal norms focus exclusively on the evaluation of acts in terms of their moral worth to the self.

Personal norms are also related conceptually to perceived social norms. Our own values and self-expectations, typically acquired in the course of socialization, are influenced by shared social expectations. Like personal norms, social norms entail obligations and sanctions, but social norms are anchored in social groups whereas personal norms are anchored in the self. Thus personal norms influence behavior through self-evaluation and self-sanctioning, whereas compliance with social norms reflects anticipation of social sanctions.

In our emphasis on feelings of moral obligation, we are claiming that anticipated self-evaluation for actions relevant to one's internalized moral values is a distinctive source of motivation. Two types of evidence are required to support this claim. First, it must be shown that personal norms are empirically distinguishable from other attitudinal variables and from social norms. Second, it must be shown that personal norms function differently than other attitudinal variables and than social norms in their relations to morally relevant behavior.

Initial evidence on these two points is available in three studies in which personal norms toward helping acts (e.g., blood and kidney donation) were correlated with attitudes toward these acts measured by semantic differential or Likert techniques (Pomazal & Jaccard, 1976; Schwartz & Tessler, 1972; Zuckerman & Reis, 1978). The personal norm–attitude toward the act correlations were significant ($\bar{r}$ = .42, range .31–.54), but not so substantial as to suggest conceptual identity. Correlations between personal norms and perceived social norms were also significant ($\bar{r}$ = .40, range .17–.66). Again, the sizes of these correlations do not suggest that social and personal norms are interchangeable. Moreover, these studies revealed that personal norms added significantly to the variance in helping behavior accounted for by other attitudes and by social norms.

The empirical relationships among personal norms, other attitudes, and social norms were examined more rigorously in a recent study of firearm regulation, increasing welfare payments, and reinstating the death penalty (Schwartz & Fleishman, 1979). Respondents indicated agreement–disagreement with statements on each issue (attitude to the object), reported whether "many people I know would favor or oppose my acting" on each issue (social norms), and reported their personal norms regarding each of four different acts that would aid each cause. Separate factor analyses of the full set of items for each issue yielded the same three-factor solutions. Personal norms, social norms, and attitude items loaded exclusively on their own factors.

The distinctiveness of personal norms was further corroborated in this study by evidence that personal norms function differently from social norms or attitudes to the object in their relation to helping behavior. Each of the three attitudinal variables correlated with subsequently measured volunteering to join a campaign for increased welfare payments. However, only the association of personal norms with volunteering behavior was moderated by responsibility denial (RD). The less likely people were to deny responsibility, the greater the correlation between personal norms and subsequent volunteering ($r$ = .49 [lowest RD quartile] > $r$ = .07 [highest RD quartile], p. < .01). Responsibility denial had no moderating effect for attitudes to the object or for social norms. In summary, the evidence suggests that individual feelings of moral obligation play a distinctive role in motivating behavior and that they can be operationalized so as to distinguish them from related attitude and social norm concepts.

### 3.2.3. *Some Clarifications*

One problem of new theoretical approaches is the need to coin terms for new concepts. Descriptions of our approach in the published literature and discussions with students point to four recurrent misunderstanding of our new concept—*personal norms*—that are sufficiently common to warrant comment.

The term *norms* is usually understood by social psychologists as referring to social norms defined as standards for behavior, (1) backed by positive and/or negative sanctions, and (2) shared by the members of a social group. The first component of this definition applies to personal norms as well. However, personal norms may be unique to each person, rather than shared by members of a group. Personal norms refer to standards that derive from each person's own value system; hence they may vary across group members and must be measured at the individual level.

Yet another quality commonly attributed to the term *social norms* does not apply to personal norms. Social norms are often viewed as *general* prescriptions or proscriptions (e.g., the norm of reciprocity). In contrast, personal norms are often specific to the situation in which they are generated. General underlying values provide a degree of cross-situational consistency and stability to the personal norms generated from them. The personal norms themselves, however, usually entail specific expectations and are relatively impermanent.

Third, personal norms are not simply past social expectations that have been internalized and tied to self-evaluation while retaining their earlier content. Nor, finally, do personal norms commonly persist as enduring standards or expectations in the person's cognitive system from which they are retrieved when appropriate to the situation. When people repeatedly encounter the same situations, social norms may be internalized and become enduring standards that function as scripts retrievable from memory. As noted above, however, it is probably more frequently the case that we generate personal norms in the situation, because morally relevant decisions are seldom routine and trivial.

### 3.2.4. *Measurement Problems and Alternatives*

How do those who respond to personal norms questionnaires understand the terms used? Are the questions meaningful? If so, *what* do they mean? Informal discussions with college-student respondents suggest problems with two key terms, *moral* and *obligations.* A substantial minority of respondents reports that these terms connote external pressure to act rather than motivation based on their own internalized values. For such respondents, the operationalization of personal norms is apparently inappropriate.

To examine alternative ways of measuring personal norms, we undertook an investigation of the meanings of six potentially useful wordings.[5] We interviewed a sample of 60 persons, heterogeneous with respect to age, sex, and occupation, regarding norms toward one of the following: donating bone marrow, giving time to a civic organization helping welfare recipients, or signing a newspaper ad supporting reinstatement of the death penalty.

Each interviewee responded to the six different wordings of a personal norm item, counterbalanced for order across the sample. *Moral obligation* and *personal obligation* were included because they are the wordings used regularly in past research (cf. Table 1, Questions 1 & 2). Because the implications of actions for one's values is the key notion underlying our view of personal norm construction, the wordings *personal values* and *moral values* were also examined. Two terms common in psychological literature (e.g., Bandura, 1978), *self-expectations* and *personal standards,* were chosen because they too might express aspects of internalized, self-based regulation of behavior. For each of the latter four wordings, respondents were asked: "If . . . , how would you feel you ought to act based on your own *(term inserted)?*" Response scales for these wordings were labeled "strongly feel ought not to do it (−4)," "strongly feel ought to do it (+4)," and "no feelings of oughtness about this (0)."

Interviewees were told that we were "interested in getting a clearer idea of what some of the terms we have used in past questionnaire surveys mean to people." After giving a numerical response to each

[5]We thank Frank Waite for his aid in designing and conducting this study.

question, they were asked: "Could you tell me what you thought about that led you to answer that way?" Comments were recorded verbatim.

As expected, given the conceptual and measurement similarity of the items and their proximity in the questionnaire, correlations among the numerical responses to the different wordings for each issue were high. Of primary interest are the connotations of the various wordings for respondents. Each comment was coded by two judges into one or more of 15 content categories developed to encompass all recurrent ideas. Better than 80% agreement on category assignment was attained. Since the pattern of connotations was quite similar across the three issues, results are reported for the total set of comments.

The only wording to draw more than two responses as meaningless or difficult to understand was *self-expectations* (5 respondents). Responses both to this term and to *personal standards* were frequently explained as predictions based on past qualities and behavior (18 and 7 respondents, respectively), and as reflections of the impact of social and physical costs and benefits (13 and 7). Both these terms are apparently inappropriate for measuring personal norms, because we wish to tap feelings of obligation regardless of predicted behavior, and feelings based on moral evaluations, not on other costs and benefits.

The term *moral obligation* was associated with universalistic principles and values (25) derived from a suprapersonal social order (19). Several mentioned that moral obligation is experienced as an internal motivation to act (10), is acquired through socialization (9), and generates self-evaluation (7). These connotations are congruent with the personal norm concept, explaining past success in research employing this wording. Corroborating prior informal comments, however, a substantial number of respondents (primarily students) associated moral obligation with outside rather than own pressure to act (17).

*Personal obligation,* also employed in past research, generated a very different profile of associations, one not especially congruent with the personal norm concept. Although unique individual characteristics were mentioned as a source (18), there was little association with universalistic principles or values (6) or with derivation from a suprapersonal order (4). Motivational pressure was almost as frequently external (9) as internal (10). Degree of personal obligation was seen as dependent on the nature of the relationship with the target of need (18), based on free individual choice (14), and reflecting specified attitudes and opinions (14).

The major connotations of *moral values* were the same as those of moral obligation. Unlike moral obligation, however, moral values elicited very few comments about feelings of motivational pressure, whether internal (4) or external (1). Prominent in the profile of *personal values* were unique individual characteristics as a source (22) and universalistic principles and values (15), both connotations congruent with personal norms. Also congruent, but mentioned less frequently, were self-ideals (7) and internal (5) rather than external (0) motivation. On the other hand, a substantial number associated this wording with specified attitudes and opinions (14).

Overall, this heterogeneous group of respondents found the questions meaningful and mentioned a set of associations congruent with the distinctive connotations of personal norms. Not surprisingly, no single wording induced responses based on precisely the types of cognition and emotion postulated in our theory of personal norm construction. Taken alone, *moral obligation* and *moral value* come closest, but the former implies external pressure for too many people, and the latter evokes little sense of motivational force. These data suggest that the optimal strategy for measuring personal norms is to add to *moral obligation* the responses to *personal values*. The latter adds those associations with unique individual characteristics and self-ideals lacking in the former. Moreover, what little motivational force personal values measure is exclusively associated with internal pressures, strengthening this element in the combined personal norm score.

Since there is probably little subjective awareness during norm construction, one should not expect self-reported feelings and cognitions to reflect the postulated process fully. The adequacy of alternative operations must therefore be evaluated through further construct validation.

## 4. ALTRUISM, MORAL VALUES, AND INTRINSIC MOTIVATION[6]

When people derive satisfaction directly from performing an activity rather than from any external material or social rewards it brings, the motivation that underlies their action is spoken of as intrinsic (Deci, 1975; Lepper & Greene, 1978). This chapter suggests that feelings of moral obligation are the intrinsic motivation for helping acts. Ideas from the intrinsic motivation literature can be used to explain a puzzling finding in the research on helping—the occurrence of boomerangs against appeals for help under conditions originally hypothesized to be highly conducive to altruistic motivation. To view altruistic motivation as a subclass of intrinsic motivation requires some extension of intrinsic motivation theory. We turn first to this extension.

[6]Many of the ideas in this section were developed during discussions with Mary Clevenger and appear in her master's thesis (Clevenger, 1980).

## 4.1. Personal Norms as an Intrinsic Source of Motivation

Deci and Porac (1978) suggest that intrinsic motivation is an innate human characteristic that originates as a general need for competence and self-determination. Gradually, intrinsic motivation becomes differentiated into specific needs for achievement or self-actualization through socialization and interaction with the environment. In order to satisfy the general need for competence and self-determination and the specific needs into which the general need is differentiated, people seek challenges. People recognize challenges when they perceive an incongruity between a current stimulus input (a perception of reality) and an internal standard (e.g., value, adaptation level, or achievement). They pursue these challenges by acting to reduce this incongruity. When people perceive their behavior to be under their own control, their success in conquering a challenge produces enhanced feelings of self-determination, whereas their failure diminishes their sense of self-determination. When people attribute the control over their behavior to external causes (e.g., payment or other extrinsic rewards), however, performance does not offer an opportunity to affirm self-determination. Intrinsic motivation for such behavior may even be undermined by external attributions.

As people develop a system of values that guides their lives, the basic need identified by Deci is experienced as a need to live according to one's own values. It is from these values that personal norms are generated. The choice to act on moral values despite nonmoral costs—what we have defined as altruistic behavior—is an assertion both of one's self-determination and of what might be called one's competence as a moral actor. Thus behavioral affirmation of one's self-conception as a moral, concerned, social being can become a vehicle for demonstrating competence and self-determination.

If moral values are part of the person's motive structure, Deci's (1975) cognitive-evaluation model and the current value-based model of decision making closely parallel each other. These parallels will not be detailed here, but several major points of agreement can be noted: Both models begin with a cognitive assessment of the situation in which person and situation variables interact to produce a motive. This motive is generated by the comparison of the current situation with one's standards or values. In both models the motive has an affective and cognitive (purposive) component, and it points to possible self-reinforcements. The self-reinforcements are balanced against other costs and benefits in reaching a behavioral decision. Both models emphasize perceived locus of responsibility or causality as a key mediator of the implications behavior has for one's self-evaluation. Both models conceptualize decision making as processual, suggesting that recycling through the process may occur when feelings of incongruity are not satisfactorily reduced.

### 4.2. Undermining Intrinsic Motivation and Boomerangs against Helping Appeals

An intriguing finding regarding intrinsic motivation is that when people perform activities under conditions that are apparently externally controlling (e.g., payment for solving puzzles, deadlines for word games), their intrinsic motivation to perform these activities decreases. If personal norms are sources of intrinsic motivation, one might also expect to observe undermining of altruism under external constraints to help. Some evidence to this effect can be cited, though a definitive study investigating the undermining of personal norms when people are constrained to act helpfully has not been published.

Uranowitz (1975) exposed women in a shopping center to two requests for help. He found that women who agreed to help a first experimenter who offered a strong justification for his request were less likely to help a second experimenter in a subsequent low justification situation than women who had earlier agreed to help in response to a minimally justified request. Providing high initial justification (external constraint) for helping resulted in less subsequent helping presumably because it undermined later altruistic motivation, or at least weakened any enhancement of intrinsic moral motivation that might have derived from helping originally.

Zuckerman, Lazzaro, and Waldgeir (1979) found that housewives who agreed to a 5-minute telephone interview without payment were more likely to agree to a 25-minute interview than those either paid to agree to the smaller request or receiving no initial request. The external control implied by payment apparently undermined the enhancement of intrinsic moral motivation that might have derived from agreeing to the first request. There was even a hint that payment undermined the base level of altruistic motivation; those paid for helping initially tended to help less in response to the larger request than those who received no initial request.

In two experiments by Batson *et al.* (1978), undergraduates who agreed when offered payment to help an experimenter by coding data or a young woman by completing a questionnaire rated themselves as less helpful and cooperative than those who agreed without being offered payment. This finding provides direct evidence that extrinsic incentives for helping can prevent or undermine perceptions of oneself as altruistic.

Boomerangs against appeals for helping have been found in a number of studies (Schwartz, 1977, pp. 263–268). In each instance the combination of conditions and/or individual characteristics theoretically most conducive to altruism yielded the least overt helping: (1) Blood donors refused to have their blood typed for matching as a bone marrow donor more frequently under high than under low salience of consequences, when there was a fair chance of being called upon to donate. (2) Students high in spontaneous awareness of consequences pledged less time to aid Head Start when the need portrayed was high versus low. (3) The personal norms of clerical workers correlated with volunteering to donate bone marrow under all combinations of salience of need and of responsibility in an appeal except the high-high combination.

An analysis of the three boomerangs in which surprisingly little help occurred suggests that the people involved may reasonably have experienced these as situations of strong external constraint. Drawing on the conceptualization of such situations in the intrinsic motivation literature, these potential helpers would then be expected to view helping not as an altruistic affirmation of moral values, but as an extrinsically constrained behavior. Deprived of the opportunity for intrinsic, moral satisfaction from helping, these people would not be motivated to help by their moral values.

## 5. CONCLUDING REMARKS

This chapter has emphasized the role of internalized moral values as motivators of prosocial behavior. To the extent that affirmation of moral values motivates helping, we can describe such behavior as *altruism*. The processual model and the methods for measuring personal norms we have discussed justify distinguishing altruistic helping from other forms of helping and they facilitate empirical study of altruism. In practice, prosocial behavior undoubtedly stems from a mixture of motivations, all of which warrant investigation. Nonmoral motivations and those not grounded in hypothetical constructs such as internalized moral values are easier both to conceptualize and to investigate. Nevertheless, we hope the current approach, which allows us to conceptualize various types of motivation in a single context, will reassure researchers that it is not necessary to abandon altruism in the search for a scientific understanding of helping.

## 6. REFERENCES

Ajzen, I., & Fishbein, M. The prediction of behavioral intentions in a choice situation. *Journal of Experimental Social Psychology*, 1969, *5*, 400–416.

Ajzen, I., & Fishbein, M. Attitude–behavior relations: A theoretical analysis and review of empirical research. *Psychological Bulletin*, 1977, *84*, 888–918.

Bandura, A. The self-system in reciprocal determinism. *American Psychologist*, 1978, *33*, 334–358.

Batson, C. D., Coke, J. S., Jasnoski, M. L., & Hanson, M. Buying kindness: Effect of an extrinsic incentive for helping on perceived altruism. *Personality and Social Psychology Bulletin*, 1978, *4*, 86–91.

Bem, D. *Beliefs, attitudes and human affairs*. Belmont, Calif.: Brooks/Cole, 1970.

Birch, D., Atkinson, J. W., & Bongort, K. Cognitive control of action. In B. Weiner (Ed.), *Cognitive views of human motivation*. New York: Academic Press, 1974.

Blumer, H. *Symbolic interactionism: Perspective and method*. Englewood Cliffs, N.J.: Prentice-Hall, 1969.

Clevenger, M. *Personal norms as a type of intrinsic motivation*. Unpublished master's thesis, University of Wisconsin, 1980.

Deci, E. L. *Intrinsic motivation*. New York: Plenum Press, 1975.

Deci, E. L., & Porac, J. Cognitive evaluation theory and the study of human motivation. In M. Lepper & D. Greene (Eds.), *The hidden costs of reward*. Hillsdale, N.J.: Lawrence Erlbaum, 1978.

Fellner, C. H., & Schwartz, S. H. Altruism in disrepute: Medical vs. public attitudes toward the living organ donor. New England Journal of Medicine, 1971, *284*, 582–585.

Fenichel, O. *The psychoanalytic theory of neurosis*. New York: W. W. Norton, 1945.

Heberlein, T., & Black, J. S. Attitudinal specificity and the prediction of behavior in a field setting. *Journal of Personality and Social Psychology*, 1976, *33*, 474–479.

Heider, F. *The psychology of interpersonal relations*. New York: Wiley, 1958.

Karylowski, J. Two types of altruistic behavior: Doing good to feel good or to make the other feel good. In V. Derlega & J. L. Grzelak (Eds.), *Cooperation and helping behavior: Theories and research*. New York: Academic Press, 1982.

Langer, E. J. Rethinking the role of thought in social interaction. In J. M. Harvey, W. Ickes, & R. F. Kidd (Eds.), *New directions in attribution research* (Vol. 2). Hillsdale, N.J.: Lawrence Erlbaum, 1978.

Lepper, M. R., & Greene, D. (Eds.). *The hidden costs of reward*. Hillsdale, N.J.: Lawrence Erlbaum, 1978.

Mead, G. H. *Mind, self, and society*. Chicago: University of Chicago Press, 1934.

Mischel, W. Toward a cognitive social learning reconceptualization of personality. *Psychological Review*, 1973, *80*, 252–283.

Nisbett, R. E., & Wilson, T. D. Telling more than we can know: Verbal reports on mental processes. *Psychological Review*, 1977, *84*, 231–259.

Pearce, M., & Amato, P. A taxonomy of helping: A multidimensional scaling approach. *Social Psychology Quarterly*, in press.

Piliavin, J. A., & Piliavin, I. M. *Good samaritan: Why does he help?* Unpublished manuscript, University of Wisconsin, 1973.

Pomazal, R. J. *Attitudes, normative beliefs, and altruism: Help for helping behavior*. Unpublished doctoral dissertation, University of Illinois, 1974.

Pomazal, R. J., & Jaccard, J. J. An informational approach to altruistic behavior. *Journal of Personality and Social Psychology*, 1976, *33*, 317–326.

Reykowski, J. Prosocial orientation and self-structure. In J. Reykowski (Ed.), *Studies on the mechanisms of prosocial behavior*. Warsaw: Warsaw University Press, 1975.

Rokeach, M. *The nature of human values*. New York: Free Press, 1973.

Rokeach, M. Value theory and communication research. In D. Nimmo (Ed.), *Communication Yearbook* (Vol. 3). New Brunswick, N.J.: Transaction Books, 1979.

Rosenberg, M. *Conceiving the self*. New York: Basic Books, 1979.

Schuman, H., & Johnson, M. P. Attitudes and behavior. *Annual Review of Sociology*, 1976, *2*, 161–207.

Schwartz, S. H. Awareness of consequences and the influence of moral norms on interpersonal behavior. *Sociometry*, 1968, *31*, 355–369. (a)

Schwartz, S. H. Words, deeds, and the perception of consequences and responsibility in action situations. *Journal of Personality and Social Psychology*, 1968, *10*, 232–242. (b)

Schwartz, S. H. Moral decision-making and behavior. In J. Macaulay & L. Berkowitz (Eds.), *Altruism and helping behavior*. New York: Academic Press, 1970. (a)

Schwartz, S. H. Elicitation of moral obligation and self-sacrificing behavior. *Journal of Personality and Social Psychology*, 1970, *15*, 283–293. (b)

Schwartz, S. H. Normative explanations of helping behavior: A critique, proposal, and empirical test. *Journal of Experimental Social Psychology*, 1973, *9*, 349–364.

Schwartz, S. H. Normative influences on altruism. In L. Berkowitz (Ed.), *Advances in experimental social psychology* (Vol. 10). New York: Academic Press, 1977.

Schwartz, S. H. Temporal stability as a moderator of the attitude-behavior relationship. *Journal of Personality and Social Psychology*, 1978, *36*, 715–725.

Schwartz, S. H., & Fleishman, J. A. Personal norms and the mediation of legitimacy effects on helping. *Social Psychology*, 1978, *41*, 306–315.

Schwartz, S. H., & Fleishman, J. A. *Personal norms as a distinctive attitudinal variable.* Unpublished manuscript, University of Wisconsin, 1979.

Schwartz, S. H., & Howard, J. A. Explanations of the moderating effect of responsibility denial on the personal norm-behavior relationship. *Social Psychology Quarterly*, 1980, *43*, 441–446.

Schwartz, S. H., & Howard, J. A. A normative decision-making model of altruism. In J. P. Rushton & R. M. Sorrentino (Eds.), *Altruism and helping behavior*. Hillsdale, N.J.: Lawrence Erlbaum, 1981.

Schwartz, S. H., & Howard, J. A. A self-based motivational model of helping. In V. Derlega & J. Grzelak (Eds.), *Cooperation and helping behavior: Theories and research*. New York: Academic Press, 1982.

Schwartz, S. H., & Tessler, R. C. A test of a model for reducing measured attitude-behavior discrepancies. *Journal of Personality and Social Psychology*, 1972, *24*, 225–236.

Simmons, R. G., Klein, S. D., & Simmons, R. L. *The gift of life*. New York: Wiley, 1977.

Stryker, S., & Gottlieb, A. Attribution theory and symbolic interactionism: A comparison. In J. H. Harvey, W. Ickes, & R. F. Kidd (Eds.), *New directions in attribution research* (Vol. 3). Hillsdale, N.J.: Lawrence Erlbaum, 1981.

Uranowitz, S. W. Helping and self-attributions: A field experiment. *Journal of Personality and Social Psychology*, 1975, *31*, 852–854.

Wilson, T. R., & Nisbett, R. E. The accuracy of verbal reports about the effects of stimuli on evaluations and behavior. *Social Psychology*, 1978, *41*, 118–131.

Wispé, L. G. Positive forms of social behavior: An overview. *Journal of Social Issues*, 1972, *28*, 1–7.

Zuckerman, M., & Reis, H. T. Comparison of three models of predicting altruistic behavior. *Journal of Personality and Social Psychology*, 1978, *36*, 498–510.

Zuckerman, M., Lazzaro, M. M., & Waldgeir, D. Undermining effects of the foot-in-the-door technique with extrinsic rewards. *Journal of Applied Social Psychology*, 1979, *9*, 272–296.

# 12

# Freedom of Choice and Moral Behavior

Miroslaw Kofta

## 1. THEORETICAL INTRODUCTION

The relationship between freedom of choice as a psychological experience of an individual and his social behavior has attracted growing interest among psychologists during the past 20 years (Harvey & Harris, 1977; Harvey, Harris, & Lightner, 1979). First came the famous modification of dissonance theory proposed by Brehm and Cohen (1962), who ascribed a crucial role to the perceived volition (or freedom of choice) in arousing postdecisional dissonance. In a number of studies performed in the counterattitudinal paradigm (cf. Harvey & Mills, 1971; Linder, Cooper, & Jones, 1967; Sherman, 1970), it was consistently demonstrated that typical dissonance effects—consisting of a greater postdecisional attitude change under low rather than high external justification—are observed only when a person decides freely to engage in counterattitudinal behavior. As a result of these studies experimental psychologists had evidence for the first time suggesting the considerable impact of freedom of choice on an individual's social behavior in the domain of attitude change.

Whereas the dissonance approach suggested that cognitive accentuation of freedom to decide can have remarkable influence on human

MIROSLAW KOFTA • Department of Psychology, University of Warsaw, Warsaw, Poland.

conduct, the theory of psychological reactance (Brehm, 1966; Wicklund, 1974) proposed that the experience of having freedom eliminated or merely threatened with elimination can produce even stronger changes in human behavior. According to this theory, when the opportunity to choose is expected by an individual, any attempt to eliminate freedom will activate reactance motivation directed toward the reestablishment of freedom. It was in the framework of the reactance approach that the relationship between freedom of choice and moral behavior became an object of empirical research. In the realm of prosocial activity it was shown that when a request for help is perceived as a threat to freedom to refuse help, it may result in a decrease in helping behavior; this effect is presumably mediated by tbe arousal of reactance motivation (Berkowitz, 1973; Brehm & Cole, 1966; Horowitz, 1968; Jones, 1970). The same mediating process is seen as responsible for the curvilinear relationship sometimes noted between need for help perceived by a potential helper and the amount of help offered (Schwartz, 1970). There is also evidence that reactance motivation can play an important role in the regulation of aggression: Elimination of freedom was shown to arouse emotional aggression, which was directed against the freedom-eliminating agent (Wicklund, 1974).

To summarize, the reactance approach has opened a new, exciting theoretical perspective on the problem of the linkage between freedom of choice and moral behavior. Although its importance as a theoretical context in this area can hardly be denied, it seems to suffer from a rather obvious limitation. Namely, the theory of psychological reactance deals exclusively with the effects of the violation of an individual's expectancies of free choice. One may ask, alternatively, whether mere creation of the opportunity to choose freely is also influential in the domain of moral behavior.

Recently, the autonomous regulation model of freedom has been developed (Kofta, 1980, 1982; Kofta & Michalowska, 1980). This model describes some hypothetical consequences of perceived choice for behavior regulation. It is assumed that—as a consequence of the perception of explicit choice[1]—some mediating cognitive changes are evoked, affecting both the decision made and the manner in which postdecisional behavior is regulated.

[1]The terms *explicit choice, conscious choice,* and *experience of choice* will be used interchangeably to mean the kind of psychological situation where an individual has clearly articulated in his awareness the existence of at least two different options to act, the decision depending on him rather than on the external circumstances.

Taking into account a conceptual distinction proposed by Steiner (1979), one might suggest that the model to be presented is concerned with autonomous choices rather than discriminative or evaluative ones.

The first mediating process postulated by the model consists of the cognitive accentuation of the self as the origin of action.[2] On the phenomenological level it is expressed by the feeling of being the "master of one's own fortunes" and will be referred to as a sense of originship.

The second mediating process is the cognitive response of the individual to the situational demand to make a choice. In order to choose he must first stop acting and think about the consequences of the behavioral alternatives. Then, where alternatives appear to be close in attractiveness, a person reflects upon himself and considers relevant personal standards in order to define better his preferences. He finds in this way a rational basis for his future decision (the process described by choice–certainty theory is postulated here; see Mills, 1968). Thus the subject's attention is expected to shift from the alternatives to personal standards of correctness relevant to the behavior to be undertaken in a given situation.

A crucial assumption of the model is that a person is faced with a set of alternatives of comparable overall attractiveness: If the options differed markedly in this respect, one would expect neither an increased sense of originship (because subjective freedom of choice is fairly small in such circumstances; see Ajzen, 1971; Harvey, 1976; Steiner, 1970) nor an attentional shift to the self (because a person is not motivated to look for additional "internal rationale" in order to make a reasonable decision).

Assuming that the perception of explicit choice produces the cognitive changes described (i.e., arouses a sense of originship and turns the subject's attention to the situationally relevant personal standards of correctness), a number of predictions can be derived concerning the impact of perceived choice on behavior (see Kofta, 1980). Let us consider only one implication of the autonomous regulation model of freedom, namely, that for moral behavior.

Supposing that perception of freedom to choose in the situational context implying moral behavior produces an attentional shift toward the person's internal standards of proper conduct, one should expect these standards to become salient in the predecisional period. It seems reasonable to expect, furthermore, that their influence on the decision itself as well as on the course of postdecisional behavior should increase as a consequence of "free choice" experience. In other words, mere experience of freedom of choice before the decision should lead—according to the theory—to activation of personal standards of moral conduct applicable to the situation.

[2]Using DeCharms's (1968) terms, shift toward the "origin" pole on the origin–pawn dimension is expected as a consequence of choice experience.

Based on this reasoning, it is generally predicted that perception of choice between behavioral alternatives in the domain of moral behavior should (1) increase moral behavior–moral standards consistency, and (2) heighten the proportion and the intensity of morally positive forms of behavior. These predictions are founded on the assumption that, other things being equal, once an internalized moral standard is activated, it arouses a tendency to behave in accordance with the standard, the strength of this tendency being modified by the relative importance of the standard for the subject.

These predictions hold to the extent that the choice under consideration is meaningfully related to the postdecisional behavior to be measured, that is, involves a decision about its initiation or rejection, possible form, and (in the case of interpersonal conduct) about the person toward whom it is directed. For this reason one could hardly expect an act of choice between, say, different ability tests to perform, to bring any consequences for behavior emitted in response to the request for help, because personal standards of achievement, presumably activated during the decisional process, are irrelevant to prosocial behavior.

In the series of studies to be briefly reported an effort was made to verify hypotheses generated by the autonomous regulation model of freedom, in the area of moral behavior. The research strategy consisted of the following steps: (1) a measurement of personal importance of a given moral standard for each subject; (2) a creation in one group of the situation of meaningful choice (in the sense described above) with no choice given to subjects in another group (or groups); and (3) a measurement of the effects of such a manipulation upon some quantitative aspects of moral behavior and upon the consistency between behavior and the moral standard.

The object of inquiry in the first two studies was aggressive behavior and a counteraggressive standard; in the third study, helping behavior and a prosocial standard.

## 2. FREEDOM OF CHOICE AND AGGRESSION

In the first study (Kofta, Dziubak, & Stanczyk, 1980), the effects of choosing a partner for the role of "pupil," and of ego involvement, on pain-producing behavior to the partner were investigated. The Buss paradigm for studying aggression (Buss, 1961) was used. The subjects were 48 first-year female students of psychology at the University of Warsaw.

At the beginning of the study a modified version of Rokeach's Instrumental Values Survey was used, with the value "leniency," defined as "avoidance of producing pain and enforcing one's will upon other people," inserted into the list of 18. Each subject was asked to rank the values according to their importance for her. The rank order position of the value "leniency" was an index of the personal importance of a counteraggressive normative standard.

Two weeks later subjects took part in the experiment with a 2 × 2 factorial design, with freedom of choice and ego involvement as factors, and intensity and duration of aggression as the main dependent variables.

In the high ego involvement condition subjects were informed that the purpose of the study was to obtain information about their predispositions and psychological knowledge (in the domain of personality assessment). In the low ego involvement condition the alleged purpose of the study was an investigation of some rules governing the process of human learning.

Next, manipulation of the choice variable was introduced. In both groups subjects were given three personality questionnaires (composed of a set of self-descriptive rating scales) filled in seemingly by three different female college students.

In the choice condition the subject was asked to read the questionnaires and choose one of these students, allegedly waiting, for the role of "pupil" in the experiment. In the no-choice condition the subject was also asked to read all three self-descriptions and was told that one of the students was to participate in the experiment in the "pupil's" role depending on who was first to finish her work in another study run simultaneously at the institute.

Then, depending on experimental condition, the "chosen" or "fate assigned" partner was allegedly introduced into the adjacent room and the study in Buss paradigm was run.

The effect of ego involvement as well as of ego involvement × freedom of choice interaction appeared nonsignificant. In line with predictions, subjects in the choice condition engaged in a lower level of aggressive behavior directed toward the partner (the difference being significant only with respect to aggression intensity, however). As can be seen in Table 1,[3] subjects in the choice condition behaved in a manner

[3]The index of personal importance of the value "leniency" was calculated by substracting its rank order position in the individual hierarchy from 19 (the same was done with the value "helpfulness" in Experiment 3). Thus it increases numerically along with the value "importance."

Unfortunately, some of the subjects did not participate in the group measurement of values, so that cell frequencies for correlational analysis are smaller than those in the analysis of variance.

A composite index of aggression was calculated by multiplying $Z$ scores obtained by a given subject on intensity and duration of aggression. In order to avoid minus values, a value of 5 was added to each $Z$ score before the multiplication.

*Table 1. Spearman's Correlations between Personal Importance of the Value "Leniency" and Aggression*[a]

| | Intensity of aggression | Duration of aggression | Composite index of aggression |
|---|---|---|---|
| No-choice condition | .10 | .44 | .30 |
| $N = 16$ | (n.s.) | ($p < .05$) | (n.s.) |
| Choice condition | −.19 | −.58 | −.39 |
| $N = 18$ | (n.s.) | ($p < .05$) | ($p < .06$) |

[a]A one-tailed test was used.

highly consistent with their aggression-disapproving standards (which is indicated by negative correlations between personal importance of "leniency" and aggression). Conversely, subjects in the no-choice condition behaved in an inconsistent fashion, tending to be more aggressive the higher the personal importance of the aggression-disapproving standard.

One can try to explain the results by assuming that the act of choosing a partner for an unpleasant task can produce guilt feelings that cause subjects to reduce aggression.[4] Assuming additionally that the higher the position of "leniency" in the personal values hierarchy the stronger the sense of guilt should be, one could also predict the changes in moral consistency obtained in the study. There are additional data, however, that seem to contradict the guilt explanation. In the postexperimental questionnaire a five-item scale designed to measure an emotional attitude toward the study was inserted. If the guilt explanation were valid, negative emotions, and, consequently, negative evaluation of the whole experiment would be expected in the choice condition. However, an analysis of variance has revealed that subjects in the choice condition evaluated the experiment far more positively than subjects in the no-choice condition.

The next study (Kofta *et al.*, 1980) was a replication of the previous research with some modifications. The subjects were 40 female and 12 male college students, naïve in psychology.

In the first stage of the study a measure of the hierarchy of values (by means of the method used in the previous study) with the same instruction was taken. In the second phase, a few weeks later, an experiment in the Buss paradigm was performed using a 2 × 2 factorial design, with freedom of choice and importance of leniency as factors. The latter variable was obtained by splitting the sample (separately for males and

[4]It was shown in a series of studies that an experimentally produced guilt state arouses rather strong expiational behavior (Freedman, 1970).

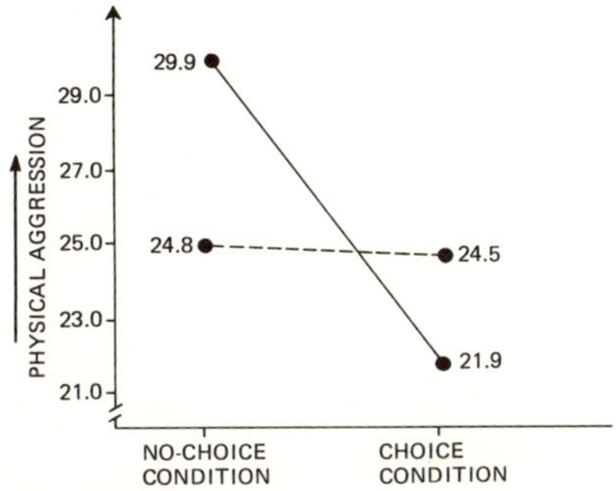


Figure 1. The effect of freedom of choice and importance of "leniency" on aggression/composite index; (●———●) high leniency group, (●- - -●) low leniency group.

females) at the median point on the distribution of the variable "personal importance of leniency."

There were two main procedural differences between the present study and the first one: (1) The ego involvement treatment was excluded (because of its weak influence on the dependent variables noted previously), and (2) in the no-choice group, because of a special procedure, in each case the preferred partner was assigned to the subject; thus the subject worked with the person "he would have chosen if he had the possibility to do so." Subjects in the Choice versus no-choice conditions differed only with respect to the "illusion of choice." In both groups, they had partners they preferred for the role of "pupils."

As in Experiment 1, after introducing the manipulation of the choice variable, the dependent variables (i.e., duration and intensity of pain-producing behavior against the partner) were measured. A significant effect of the choice variable in the predicted direction was obtained, thus replicating the results of the first study. As Figure 1 shows, the pattern of the interactional tendency is also consistent with the prediction that the difference between choice and no-choice conditions will be significant within the high leniency group, and nonsignificant within the low leniency group. It fits the theoretical expectations well: If the inhibitory influence of choice on aggression is mediated by the process of activation of the personal aggression-disapproving standard, then the higher the importance of that standard the stronger the (inhibitory) influence should be.

## 3. FREEDOM OF CHOICE AND RESPONSE TO THE REQUEST FOR HELP

In the last study to be reported (Kofta, 1982), the main research question was whether freedom to choose among different forms of helping affects willingness to help as well as consistency between helping and prosocial standards. The subjects were 57 female and 8 male students in the introductory course in psychology at the University of Warsaw.

The whole study was completed in one session in groups of 11 to 18 individuals. The alleged purpose of the investigation was the study of the values of university students. Personal values were measured first by means of the method described before: Each subject was asked to order the values in the list according to their importance for him or her. Among 18 values "helpfulness" was inserted, defined as "working for the benefit of other people." Its rank order position was assumed to express personal importance of prosocial standards for the subject.

Subjects were then asked for help in carrying out psychological research. In order to arouse prosocial motivation subjects were told that the Institute of Psychology had growing financial problems with organizing assistance in psychological research, and that recently these difficulties had become so great that it was virtually impossible to complete several important projects without some assistance.

At that point short descriptions of two different projects (with an assistant role described) were given to subjects. In the choice condition the experimenter underscored that he wanted subjects to do what they liked best, and everybody—after having acquainted themselves with projects and evaluated them—was asked to choose the task preferred. In the no-choice condition the experimenter said that assessment of these projects made by subjects would have some consequences only for future research planning and that in order to make frequencies in both groups equal, subjects would be assigned to the first or the second task. Next, a measurement of the dependent variable (time of assistance declared) was taken. After being given a task (the one chosen, in the choice condition, and the one assigned, in the No-Choice condition) subjects were asked to indicate how much time they would be willing to volunteer.

Since all subjects defined their preferences toward both projects, it was possible to identify the subjects within the no-choice group who were assigned to the preferred task versus unpreferred task condition at the moment when No-Choice treatment was introduced.

A significant effect of choice on willingness to help was noted, in the predicted direction; planned comparisons revealed that only the differences between the choice group and each of the no-choice subgroups were significant. The results of correlational analyses are shown in Table 2. A rather strong differential effect of experimental treatment in the expected direction was noted: In the choice condition subjects

*Table 2. Spearman's Correlations between Personal Importance of the Value "Helpfulness" and Helping*[a]

| Choice | No choice preferred task | No choice unpreferred task | No choice data combined |
|---|---|---|---|
| .34<br>($p < .04$)<br>$N = 28$ | −.34<br>($p < .10$)<br>$N = 16$ | −.24<br>(n.s.)<br>$N = 21$ | −.26<br>($p < .06$)<br>$N = 37$ |

[a]A one-tailed test was used.

were fairly consistent with respect to their personal prosocial standards,[5] whereas in the no-choice conditions they were inconsistent.

At first glance the results are in line with the hypotheses tested: The choice experience resulted in an increase in amount of helping as well as in helping–prosocial standard consistency. There is the possibility, however, that the theory of psychological reactance (Brehm, 1966) can provide an alternative explanation of the results. Arguably, in the no-choice conditions the mere awareness of the existence of two possibilities—being beyond the personal control of subjects—could have given rise to the reactance process, leading to the decrease in willingness to help as well as to the striking moral inconsistency observed. That is to say, the reactance process in the no-choice conditions, rather than hypothesized moral sensitization in the choice condition, would be responsible for the pattern of data obtained.

It is reasonable to assume that, if the reactance process were actually aroused, it should also have manifested itself in subjects' general attitude toward taking part in psychological research, and in the ratings of the attractiveness of the role to be performed (Questions 1 and 2 from the postexperimental questionnaire, respectively). However, in neither case was a significant effect of freedom of choice obtained. This seems to contradict the reactance explanation.

One can conclude that the opportunity to choose between different forms of help aroused prosocial motivation and made subjects far more consistent with respect to their personal standards of prosocial conduct. The effects cannot be attributed to the operation of the attractiveness variable. Subjects in the first no-choice group were given the task they preferred (i.e., the one they would have chosen had they been able to do so); in spite of this, they did not differ significantly from the no choice–unpreferred task group in amount of helping, or in helping–pro-

[5]As previously, importance of the value index was obtained by subtracting the value rank order position from 19.

social standard consistency. On the other hand, each of the no-choice groups differed substantially from the choice group. It appears that pure "illusion of choice" (i.e., perception of the power to decide) was the crucial variable.

## 4. CONCLUDING REMARKS

In general, considerable correspondence was found between the theory and the data: In the three experiments presented, the autonomous regulation model predictions were substantiated to a greater or lesser degree.

In some cases an effort was made to assess whether some alternative explanation would be appropriate. It appeared that the explanations considered could be ruled out, mainly on the ground that they accounted only for some aspects of the data but were unable to predict the whole pattern obtained in a given study.

An interesting question remains as to whether the whole pattern of data presented could be explained within different, possibly simpler theoretical frameworks. One potential candidate is objective self-awareness theory (Wicklund, 1975, 1978). The theory proposes that if some aspect of the self receives attention, attention will then shift to whatever self-related dimension is most salient. As a consequence of attentional shift, any within-self discrepancies concerning this dimension are cognitively accentuated, the result being negative affect and motivation to reduce discrepancy. Within the realm of moral behavior it follows that one should expect greater behavior–norm consistency in the objective rather than the subjective self-awareness state, provided that the relevant norm is made salient. The last prediction has received some empirical support (Karylowski, 1979; Scheier, Feningstein, & Buss, 1974; Wicklund, 1978, pp. 517–518).

Applying such a theory to the domain of freedom of choice one can assume that perception of explicit choice before decision may temporarily individuate a person, leading to self-focused attention. The content features of behavior to be undertaken, for instance, pain-producing activity (as in aggression studies reported here), can serve as situational cues making counteraggressive standards salient. Then, the objective self-awareness state, via increased motivation to reduce within-self discrepancy, would lead to a greater consistency between aggressive behavior and the standards, as we noted in our research.

Predictions generated by Wicklund's theory are thus in line with the hypotheses derived from the autonomous regulation model. However, objective self-awareness theory would additionally predict that the moral sensitization effect will happen even in the case where the choice situation is irrelevant to postdecisional behavior, whereas the theory presented here claims that the choice alternatives should be relevant in order to get the predicted results. The problem delineated is open to future research, which may throw more light on the nature of psychological processes evoked by the perception of explicit choice, and eventually eliminate one of the alternative explanations.

Another explanation may involve the assumption that perception of choice leads to heightened feelings of personal responsibility for the behavioral outcomes, a linkage assumed by many theories (cf. Collins & Hoyt, 1972; Kiesler, 1971; Zimbardo, 1969) and demonstrated empirically in some studies on self-perception as well as on attribution of freedom (Harvey, Harris, & Barnes, 1975; Kruglanski & Cohen, 1973; Wortman, 1975). According to the theory developed by Schwartz (1970; Schwartz & Howard, 1980), supported by numerous data, a person behaves in a morally consistent fashion to the extent that he feels personally responsible for the interpersonal consequences of his decision. Combining both assumptions, the effects of choice, as demonstrated in the studies presented here, could be attributed to the greater sense of personal responsibility created by the perception of explicit choice before decision.

This explanation, however, does not seem incompatible with the autonomous regulation model: In essence, the theory proposes some hypotheses about cognitive mechanisms leading to the emergence of feelings of (anticipatory) responsibility for behavioral outcomes. In addition, it permits the formulation of some theory-specific predictions about conditions of responsibility arousal not mentioned in Schwartz's model (e.g., the theory predicts that thinking before decision is an important precondition for obtaining the increased consistency effect).

On the basis of the data collected, it seems clear that cognitive attentional mechanisms as well as temporary changes of belief in personal control deserve special attention in studies on prosocial and antisocial behavior. Transitory changes in the course of internal cognitive activity, accompanying the choice experience, can strongly interact with personal standards of conduct in producing behavioral effects.

## 5. REFERENCES


Ajzen, I. Attribution of dispositions to an actor: Effects of perceived decision freedom and behavioral utilities. *Journal of Personality and Social Psychology*, 1971, *18*, 144–156.

Berkowitz, L. Reactance and the unwillingness to help others. *Psychological Bulletin*, 1973, *79*, 310–317.

Brehm, J. W. *A theory of psychological reactance*. New York: Academic Press, 1966.

Brehm, J. W., & Cohen, A. R. *Explorations in cognitive dissonance.* New York: Wiley, 1962.

Brehm, J. W., & Cole, A. Effect of favor which reduces freedom. *Journal of Personality and Social Psychology,* 1966, *3,* 420–426.

Buss, A. H. *The psychology of aggression.* New York: Wiley, 1961.

Collins, B. E., & Hoyt, M. F. Personal responsibility for consequences: An integration and extension of the "forced compliance" literature. *Journal of Experimental Social Psychology,* 1972, *8,* 558–593.

DeCharms, R. *Personal causation.* New York: Academic Press, 1968.

Freedman, J. L. Transgression, compliance and guilt. In J. R. Macauley & L. Berkowitz (Eds.), *Altruism and helping behavior.* New York: Academic Press, 1970.

Harvey, J. H. Attribution of freedom. In J. Harvey, W. J. Ickes, & R. F. Kidd (Eds.), *New directions in attribution research* (Vol. 1). Hillsdale, N.J.: Lawrence Erlbaum, 1976.

Harvey, J. H., & Harris, B. *Social psychology: An attributional approach.* St. Louis: C. V. Mosby, 1977.

Harvey, J. H., & Mills, J. Effect of a difficult opportunity to revoke a counterattitudinal action upon attitude change. *Journal of Personality and Social Psychology,* 1971, *18,* 201–209.

Harvey, J. H., Harris, B., & Barnes, R. D. Actor–observer differences in the perceptions of responsibility and freedom. *Journal of Personality and Social Psychology,* 1975, *31,* 101–106.

Harvey, J. H., Harris, B., & Lightner, J. M. Perceived freedom as a central concept in psychological theory and research. In L. C. Perlmuter & R. A. Monty (Eds.), *Choice and perceived control.* Hillsdale, N.J.: Lawrence Erlbaum, 1979.

Horowitz, J. A. Effects of choice and locus of dependence on helping behavior. *Journal of Personality and Social Psychology,* 1968, *8,* 373–376.

Jones, R. A. Volunteering to help: The effect of choice, dependence, and anticipated dependence. *Journal of Personality and Social Psychology,* 1970, *14,* 121–130.

Karylowski, J. Self-focused attention, prosocial norms and prosocial behavior. *Polish Psychological Bulletin,* 1979, *10,* 56–66.

Kiesler, C. R. *The psychology of commitment.* New York: Academic Press, 1971.

Kofta, M. Freedom of choice and autonomous regulation: Outline of a theory. *Polish Psychological Bulletin,* 1980, *11,* 13–21.

Kofta, M. Freedom to choose among modes of helping, value system, and the willingness to help. *Polish Psychological Bulletin,* 1982, *13,* 13–21.

Kofta, M., & Michalowska, K. [Freedom of a role choice and resistance to social pressure.] *Studia Psychologiczne,* 1980, *19,* 57–73.

Kofta, M., Dziubak, K., & Stanczyk, A. [*Freedom to choose a partner, value system and aggressive behavior.*] Unpublished data, Institute of Psychology, University of Warsaw, 1980.

Kruglanski, A. W., & Cohen, M. Attributed freedom and personal causation. *Journal of Personality and Social Psychology,* 1973, *26,* 245–250.

Linder, D. E., Cooper, J., & Jones, E. Decision freedom as a determinant of the role of incentive magnitude in attitude change. *Journal of Personality and Social Psychology,* 1967, *3,* 245–254.

Mills, J. Interest in supporting and discrepant information. In R. P. Abelson, E. Aronson, W. J. McGuire, T. M. Newcomb, M. J. Rosenberg, & P. J. Tannenbaum (Eds.), *Theories of cognitive consistency: A sourcebook.* Chicago: Rand McNally, 1968.

Scheier, M. F., Feningstein, A., & Buss, A. H. Self-awareness and physical aggression. *Journal of Experimental Social Psychology,* 1974, *10,* 264–273.

Schwartz, S. H. Moral decision making and behavior. In J. R. Macaulay & L. Berkowitz (Eds.), *Altruism and helping behavior.* New York: Academic Press, 1970.

Schwartz, S. H., & Howard, J. A. A normative decision-making model of altruism. In J. P. Rushton & R. M. Sorrentino (Eds.), *Altruism and helping behavior.* Hillsdale, N.J.: Lawrence Erlbaum, 1980.

Sherman, S. J. Effects of choice and incentive on attitude change in a discrepant behavior situation. *Journal of Personality and Social Psychology,* 1970, *15,* 245–252.

Steiner, I. D. Perceived freedom. In L. Berkowitz (Ed.), *Advances in experimental social psychology,* (Vol. 5). New York: Academic Press, 1970.

Steiner, I. D. Three kinds of reported choice. In L. C. Perlmuter & R. A. Monty (Eds.), Choice and perceived control. Hillsdale, N.J.: Lawrence Erlbaum, 1979.

Wicklund, R. A. *Freedom and reactance.* Hillsdale, N.J.: Lawrence Erlbaum, 1974.

Wicklund, R. A. Objective self-awareness. In L. Berkowitz (Ed.), *Advances in experimental social psychology* (Vol. 7). New York: Academic Press, 1975.

Wicklund, R. A. Three years later. In L. Berkowitz (Ed.), *Cognitive Theories in Social Psychology.* New York: Academic Press, 1978.

Wortman, C. B. Some determinants of perceived control. *Journal of Personality and Social Psychology,* 1975, *31,* 282–294.

Zimbardo, P. G. (Ed.). *The cognitive control of motivation.* Glenview, Ill.: Scott, Foresman, 1969.

# 13

# The Altruistic Personality

## Evidence from Laboratory, Naturalistic, and Self-Report Perspectives

J. Philippe Rushton

### 1. INTRODUCTION

The last few years have seen an increasing diversity of approaches to altruism and prosocial behavior. Numerous books have documented this healthy growth in both the English-speaking and non-English-speaking research communities (e.g., Bar-Tal, 1976; Eisenberg, 1982; Mussen & Eisenberg-Berg, 1977; Reykowski, 1975; Rushton, 1980; Rushton & Sorrentino, 1981; Staub, 1978, 1979; Wispé, 1978). Despite this voluminous literature there is as yet no systematic program of research into "consistent patterns of individual differences" in altruistic behavior. This is because most researchers do not believe there is a trait of altruism—or at least, not one broadly based enough to warrant major research attention. This chapter aims to correct this erroneous impression.

The chapter has three sections. The first concerns evidence for an altruistic personality from controlled (usually experimental laboratory) situations. The second concerns evidence from naturalistic studies of

J. PHILIPPE RUSHTON • Department of Psychology, University of Western Ontario, London, Ontario, Canada N6A 5C2.

community volunteers; and the third presents evidence from studies using self-report measures of altruism.

## 2. EVIDENCE FROM CONTROLLED LABORATORY INVESTIGATIONS

### 2.1. Evidence for Consistency

In recent years there has been a disenchantment with the traditional wisdom of the "trait" approach to personality. This is because critics erroneously believe that there is little consistency in the way a person behaves from situation to situation. Interestingly enough, this erroneous view derives in large part from the faulty conclusions drawn by the investigators of the first intensive empirical study ever carried out into altruism—the enormous "Character Education Inquiry" (Hartshorne & May, 1928; Hartshorne, May, & Maller, 1929; Hartshorne, May, & Shuttleworth, 1930).

These investigators gave 11,000 elementary and high school students some 33 different behavioral tests of their altruism (referred to as the "service" tests), self-control, and honesty in home, classroom, church, play, and athletic contexts. Concurrently, extensive ratings of the children's reputations with their teachers and their classmates were made in all these areas. Altogether more than 170,000 observations were collected. By intercorrelating the children's scores on all these tests it was possible to discover whether the children's behavior was specific to situations or generalizable across them. To the extent that cross-situational correlations are high, the behavior is generalizable. There is, thus, a crucial test of the trait hypothesis. This is the largest study of the question ever undertaken, raising most of the major points of interest, and has been seriously misinterpreted by many investigators, as has been noted by Rushton (1980).

Let us consider the results from their measures of altruism. The behavioral measures intercorrelated +.20 on the average, thus suggesting little support for the generality viewpoint. If the five measures were combined into a battery, however, they had a much higher correlation (+.61) with the measures of the child's altruistic reputation among teachers and classmates. Hartshorne *et al.* (1929) wrote, in this regard:

> The correlation between the total service score and the total reputation score is .61. . . . *Although this seems low, it should be borne in mind that the correlations between test scores and ratings for intelligence seldom run higher than .50.* (p. 107, italics added)

On the "Guess Who" test of reputation (e.g., "Guess who is kind to younger children?"), the teachers' perceptions of the students' altruism agreed extremely highly with that of the students' peers ($r = .81$, Hartshorne *et al.*, 1929, p. 91). Taken together these latter results indicate a considerable degree of consistency in altruistic behavior.

Virtually identical results were found for the measures of honesty and self-control as well. Any one behavioral test correlated, on the average, only +.23 with any other behavioral test. When, however, the measures were combined into more reliable batteries, higher relationships were found either with teachers' ratings of the children or with any single measure taken alone. Typically these correlations were on the order of +.50 and +.60. (See, e.g., Vol. 1, Book 2, p. 130, Table 97; Vol. 2, Book 1, p. 104, Table 20; Vol. 2, Book 2, pp. 351–352).

Not only did total scores within the battery of altruism tests and measures yield evidence of consistency, but so too did measures of self-control, persistence, honesty, and moral knowledge. Indeed there was evidence for a pervasive general factor of moral character (e.g., Hartshorne *et al.*, 1930, p. 230, Table 32). One of the first to make a point of this was Maller (1934), an author of the second volume of the character education inquiry. Using Spearman's tetrad difference technique, Maller (1934, p. 100) demonstrated a common fator throughout the intercorrelations of the character tests of honesty, altruism, self-control, and persistence. Subsequently, Burton (1963), in a reanalysis of the original Hartshorne and May data, found a large general factor that accounted for 35% to 40% of the total variance.

Oddly enough, Hartshorne and May throughout the study chose to focus on the smaller correlations of +.20 and +.30 in support of the notion of behavioral specificity. They stated:

> Neither deceit nor its opposite, "honesty," are unified character traits, but rather specific functions of life situations. Most children will deceive in certain situations and not in others. (1928, p. 411)

Their conclusions, and their data, have often been referred to in defending such a position. For example, Mischel (1968), in a highly influential review, extolled again the notion of specificity in behavior, pointing out that the average correlation between two behavioral instances of a "trait" is .20 to .30. Persons, therefore, are said to exhibit "discriminative facility" between situations.

This specificity doctrine has provided a service by emphasizing that contexts are important and that people acquire different ways of dealing with different situations. Unfortunately, some have interpreted this as meaning that consistency either does not exist or is very small. By focusing on correlations of +.20 and +.30 between any two behaviors or items, rather than the higher ones based on a battery of items, a very misleading impression can be created. A more accurate representation is obtained by examining the predictability achieved from sampling a number of behavioral exemplars. These exemplars are more reliable and hence better predictors, a point following directly from the work of Spearman and Brown. Although Hartshorne and May employed the Spearman-Brown formula, they failed to realize its implications in interpreting their data.

"Situationism" is a pervasive view in current social-personality psychology, and has led to a general disenchantment with the traditional trait approach. It is based on a belief that a correlation of +.20 and +.30 is representative of the degree of cross-situational generality of behavior. One can, however, point to a major error of interpretation. The error is to believe that correlations between two items or behavioral events are stable and representative. They very rarely are. Predictive validity usually occurs only when scores are summed over a number of items. This greater predictability occurs because the inevitable randomness found in behavior observed in a particular situation is usually large compared with the nonrandom component of interest. By combining and summing over situations the randomness ("error variance") tends to average out because it is not cumulative, whereas behavioral consistencies ("true score variance") do accumulate. These expectations are made explicit in psychometric theory in one of its oldest and most frequently confirmed formulations, namely, that reliability increases as a function of the number of observations. Imagine how inappropriate it would be for professors to assess the knowledge of the students in their courses on the basis of one or two multiple-choice items. The intercorrelations of such items are typically around +.20 or lower. By employing a larger number of items, one obtains a far more reliable (and fairer) assessment. This is also true in measuring personality (see Rushton, Jackson, & Paunonen, 1981; Rushton, Brainerd, & Pressley, 1983, for more extended discussions of this point).

Since the pioneering work of Hartshorne and May many other studies have provided data that relate directly to the issue of the specificity versus generality of altruism. The typical correlation between any two behavioral indexes is about +.30. Combining measures, on the other hand, typically leads to greater predictability. Let us consider very briefly some of this additional evidence. Dlugokinski and Firestone (1973) took from 164 children age 10 to 13: a pencil-and-paper measure of how one understood the meanings of kindness; a pencil-and-paper measure of the relative importance of altruistic as opposed to selfish values; judgments from their classmates of how considerate or selfish they were viewed to be; and a behavioral measure concerned with donating money to a charity. The six possible correlations were all positive and ranged from +.19 to +.38. Further multiple correlations of any three variables as predictors of the fourth ranged from +.42 to +.51. In a later article,

Dlugokinski and Firestone (1974) replicated these relationships. Other studies have examined the relations among children's naturally occurring altruism. For example, in a study of children's free play behavior in a university preschool, Strayer, Wareing, and Rushton (1979) studied 26 children over a 30-hour period. These authors found relationships of +.50 and +.60 between such coded altruism as donating and sharing objects, cooperation, and helping.

On the basis of a great deal of additional evidence (see Rushton, 1980), it would seem that there is a "trait" of altruism. Some people are consistently more generous, helping, and kind than others. Furthermore, such people are readily *perceived* as more altruistic, as is demonstrated by the several studies showing positive relationships among behavioral altruism and peers' and teachers' ratings of how altruistic a person seems (Dlugokinski & Firestone, 1973, 1974; Hartshorne *et al.*, 1929; Krebs & Sturrup, 1974; Rushton & Wheelwright, 1980).

There is, therefore, more consistency to altruistic behavior than is often supposed. The typical coefficient of consistency is +.50 and +.60, somewhat more substantial than the often cited figures of +.20 and +.30. Correlations of +.20 and +.30 can be found between individual "items," which is in fact quite high given the error variance involved in single-item tests. However, it is no more sensible to measure the trait of altruism by one task than it is to assess students' ability in a subject by asking them only one question. Students' abilities tend to be quite stable and consistent when adequately assessed—so also is their altruism.

## 2.2. Motivations for Altruism

If there are consistent patterns of individual differences in altruistic behavior, one question that arises is: What are the motivations for altruism? Rushton (1980) proposes that much of the research literature on altruism could be usefully ordered in terms of (1) a person's empathy, and/or (2) a person's internalized rules of appropriate behavior.

### 2.2.1. *Empathy*

Empathy may be defined as experiencing the emotional state of another. A state of empathy is said to exist between A and B when A matches his or her feelings with those of B. This matching of emotion can result from either (1) cues given off *directly* by B, or (2) A's conscious knowledge of B's situation. Both animals and extremely young infants experience empathy on the basis of direct cues. Furthermore, direct cues undoubtedly will continue to be important in eliciting altruism throughout the life span. Among humans, however, cognitive abilities come into play as age increases, which vastly extend the capacity for empathic responding. Role-taking abilities—that is, the focusing of A's attention on B's situation and the attempt to imagine what that situation is like—provide the capacity to empathize, even with individuals who lived thousands of years ago or who are still to be born.

### 2.2.2. *Personal Rules, Standards, or Norms of Appropriate Behavior*

A rule may be defined as a standard by which events are judged and on that basis approved or disapproved. An individual might apply such standards to distinguish good from bad, right from wrong, appropriate from inappropriate, beauty from ugliness, or truth from falsehood. Standards vary in the degree to which they are internalized. Those that are held strongly enough to be considered "oughts" are called moral principles. Those held more abstractly are referred to as values; those held tentatively, and found arbitrary, may be called social conventions. For present purposes, personal rules will encompass all constructs such as goals, norms, principles, standards, and values.

There are many rules concerned with prosocial behavior. For example, there are (1) norms of social responsibility, (2) norms of equity, and (3) norms of reciprocity. These have in common the fact that they are all internal standards against which events are judged. If one's own behavior does not match up, one censures oneself which produces an aversive state requiring redress.

It must be recognized that empathy and rules are properties of individuals. This brings us directly back to the "altruistic personality." If there is an altruistic personality, and if these motivations are the important ones, then we should expect to find consistent patterns of individual differences in empathy and personal standards. We should, therefore, expect to find that some people are more empathic and/or have more internalized moral rules than others. This allows us a direct test of the adequacy of these motivational constructs. Compared to people who are relatively low in empathy, for example, people who are highly empathic should (1) register more physiological distress at the sight of another's suffering, (2) perceive themselves as more empathic, (3) be perceived by others as more empathic, and (4) behave more to reduce the unhappiness or the suffering of another. Similarly, persons who have high moral standards should (1) endorse statements based on those standards more than individuals who have not internalized the same high standards, (2) behave more in accordance with those standards than other people, (3) be able and willing to verbalize rules based on those standards to others, and (4) apply sanctions to individuals who violate the rules. Let us examine the two motivation systems from the perspective of individual differences.

### 2.2.3. *Measures of Empathy*

Several studies have supported the view that paper-and-pencil measures of empathy predict situational altruism (e.g., Eisenberg-Berg & Mussen, 1978; House & Milligan, 1976; Liebhart, 1972; Mehrabian & Epstein, 1972). To discuss but one of these, Mehrabian and Epstein (1972) found that university students' empathy scores predicted both a refusal to administer high levels of shock to another person and agreement to volunteer time to help an emotionally upset confederate of the experimenter. Empathy was assessed by a 33-item questionnaire with such positively keyed items as "It makes me sad to see a lonely stranger in a group" and "I really get involved with the feelings of the character in a novel," and such negatively keyed items as "I find it silly for people to cry out of happiness" and "I often find that I can remain cool in spite of the excitement around me."

### 2.2.4. *Personal Rules*

A wide range of studies have demonstrated that individuals with higher scores on paper-and-pencil or verbal measures of social responsibility, other-oriented values, or moral reasoning tasks are more likely to engage in prosocial behavior than those with lower scores on the same tests (see Rushton, 1980, for a review). A few of these studies will be discussed very briefly here.

Berkowitz and Daniels (1964) found that high scorers on a measure of "social" responsibility" behaved more altruistically than low scorers did. Their measure of altruism consisted of the number of cardboard boxes made for another person who was allegedly dependent on the subject for his or her help. Social responsibility was measured by such items as "I am the kind of person people can count on." Staub (1974) had students fill out a large number of scales, including (1) the measure of "social responsibility" just discussed, (2) a measure of social *irresponsibility*, Machiavellianism, which included endorsing such items as "Anyone who completely trusts anyone else is asking for trouble" and disagreement with "Most men are brave," (3) a measure of how high such values as "helpful" and "equality" were ranked in a long list of alternative values, and (4) a measure of moral reasoning based on Kohlberg's dilemmas. In a test of whether any of these measures predicted helping behavior, Staub gave all the subjects the opportunity to intervene in an emergency situation some weeks after completing all the questionnaires. The results of this study demonstrated that all the measures, that is, social responsibility, Machiavellianism, moral reasoning ability, and having helpful values, grouped significantly together on a single factor in a factor analysis, along with measures of helping behavior. Thus a broad, prosocial orientation emerged that manifested itself in a variety of ways.

Of interest in Staub's (1974) study was the finding that an individual's level of moral reasoning correlated both with the more traditional questionnaires of moral attitudes and with measures of altruistic behavior. Several other studies have also found that individuals with "high" levels of moral judgment as assessed on either Piagetian or Kohlbergian moral reasoning tasks behave more altruistically than those who are low (Rushton, 1980). These studies differed considerably from each other in the age range tested, the measure of moral judgment used, and the indexes of altruistic behavior assessed. Taken together they strongly support the notion of an altruistic personality based on internalized personal rules. We shall consider just a few of the studies.

Emler and Rushton (1974) used two moral judgment stories from Piaget and found that better than chance predictions of 60 7- to 13-year-old children's anonymous donations to a charity could be made from knowledge of the children's level of moral judgment. In a subsequent study, Rushton (1975) replicated this with 140 7- to 11-year-olds and, furthermore, showed that the relation between moral judgment and altruism held up over a 2-month retest. The findings are not limited to laboratory measures, for Harris, Mussen, and Rutherford (1976) used peer ratings of the children's prosocial disposition and found that these correlated with indexes of the children's moral judgment. Other studies have been carried out with adults. Krebs and Rosenwald (1977), for example, demonstrated a significant, positive relationship between the moral development of university students assessed on Kohlberg's tests and their altruism. The test of altruism was whether students would mail a questionnaire back to the experimenter at some minor inconvenience to themselves. Although over 90% of those at Kohlberg's Stages 4 and 5 helped in this way, only 40% of those at Stages 2 and 3 did so.

### 2.3. Summary

It would seem that there is an altruistic personality and that he or she can be described as follows: The person is more motivated to engage in altruistic acts. He or she is more empathic to the feelings and sufferings of others and able to see the world from their emotional perspective, and/or he or she has internalized personal rules of justice, social responsibility, and modes of moral reasoning, judgment, and knowledge. On the basis of such motivations, this person is likely to value, and to engage in, a great variety of altruistic behaviors—from giving to people more needy than oneself, to comforting others, to rescuing others from aversive situations. Altruists also behave consistently more honestly, persistently, and with greater self-control than do non-altruists. As a result of his or her altruistic activity, this person will have a reputation for being altruistic among his or her peers and colleagues. Furthermore, although not described here, the consistently altruistic person is likely to have an integrated personality, strong feelings of personal efficacy and well-being, and what might generally be called "integrity" (Rushton, 1980).

## 3. EVIDENCE FROM NATURALISTIC STUDIES OF COMMUNITY VOLUNTEERS

The evidence supporting the existence of the altruistic personality has so far been based on laboratory research conducted with either schoolchildren or university students. We now examine whether the "altruistic personality" can be found in a naturally occurring group of altruists such as community volunteers. Community volunteers provide assistance to a variety of client populations; indeed, without the efforts of these individuals many services (particularly in the mental health field) would either be greatly reduced or become unavailable altogether. An examination of the personalities of these altruists, therefore, should provide an additional test of the hypothesis that there is an "altruistic personality."

Allen and Rushton (1983) reviewed the published literature on the personality characteristics of community mental health volunteers who had been compared with nonvolunteers on a variety of paper-and-pencil measures of personality. The findings are very briefly reviewed here in regard to empathy and personal rules that, as was demonstrated in the previous section, help to organize the literature on the motivations to be altruistic. If the hypothesis of the altruistic personality is correct, then we should find that community mental health volunteers, in contrast to control groups, are either more empathic and/or have internalized higher personal standards.

### 3.1. Empathy

At least seven separate studies have found community volunteers to be more empathic than matched controls on a variety of paper-and-pencil measures of empathy and nurturance.

In an early study, Knapp and Holzberg (1964) found volunteers to have a higher "need to give nurturance" than nonvolunteers. Beckman (1972) found that volunteers view mental health patients and expatients in more positive terms than do nonvolunteers. Turner (1973) discovered volunteer telephone counselors to be more nurturant than either nonvolunteers or potential volunteers. In addition, volunteers expressed more supportive attitudes toward recipients of the telephone service than did controls. Adler and Graubert (1975) observed that, in contrast to nonvolunteers, volunteers placed less projected social distance between "themselves" and stimuli relating to mental illness, thus suggesting that volunteers are more understanding of, and feel closer to, this client population. Jamison and Johnson (1975) report crisis telephone personnel to have higher scores on a scale measuring empathy than a control group of undergraduate students. Schneider (1977) observed that individuals who volunteered to read to a blind student exhibited more "thoughtfulness" than nonvolunteers. Finally, Crandall (1980) found that volunteers scored significantlv higher than nonvolunteers on a scale measuring both empathy and altruism.

### 3.2. Internal Moral Standards

The results from at least five separate studies support the view that community mental health volunteers have internalized "higher" and more prosocial standards than nonvolunteers.

In one earlier study, Knapp and Holzberg (1964) observed that, compared with nonvolunteers, those who volunteered to be companions to hospitalized mental patients were concerned more with societal and religious values than with economic ones. Tapp and Spanier (1973) noted that telephone crisis and counseling service volunteers perceived themselves as more ethical, and more concerned with religion, morality, honesty, and the "rightness or wrongness" of behavior, than a control group perceived themselves. Smith and Nelson (1975) report that volunteers were more conscientious, and had greater "superego strength," than nonvolunteers. Howarth (1976), using quite different assessment techniques, found similar results. Finally, Benson, Dehority, Garman, Hanson, Hochschwender, Lebold, Rohr, and Sullivan (1980) demonstrated that the overall amount of volunteering in numerous self-report categories was positively correlated with subjects' scores on a variety of self-report measures including social responsibility and having religious values.

### 3.3. Summary

It would appear that evidence does support the hypothesis that community mental health volunteers both are more empathic and have higher, more internalized standards of social responsibility than nonvolunteers. Although not discussed here, several other characteristics of the altruistic personality that were observed from the literature derived from the experimental laboratory were also found among the community volunteers. These included general positive attitudes and moods both to self and others, feelings of self-efficacy, and good emotional adjustment (Allen & Rushton, 1983).

## 4. EVIDENCE FROM STUDIES USING A SELF-REPORT MEASURE OF ALTRUISM

If there are consistent patterns to the individual differences in altruistic behavior, then it should be possible to demonstrate this by measuring them directly through self-reports. With this in mind Rushton, Chrisjohn, and Fekken (1981) constructed the Self-Report Altruism (SRA) Scale. This has an easy-to-administer, self-report format and consists of the 20 items shown in Table 1. Respondents are instructed to rate the frequency with which they have engaged in the altruistic behaviors using the categories "never," "once," "more than once," "often," and "very often."

Initial analyses demonstrated the SRA Scale to be psychometrically stable, to have high internal consistency, and to have good discriminant validity. Of particular note was the correlation between the SRA Scale and a measure of social desirability ($r$ = .05), suggesting that the SRA Scale is not merely measuring the tendency to answer in a socially desirable fashion. Several additional studies were carried out to examine whether those who reported themselves as engaging more frequently in altruistic behavior were also the ones who were perceived by others to be altruistic, and who responded altruistically in other assessment tasks.

### 4.1. The Peer Rating Study

If the SRA Scale is validly measuring altruism, then scores on the SRA Scale should correlate with peer ratings of altruism. To examine this, 118 undergraduates at the University of Western Ontario initially filled out the SRA Scale during class time. Subsequently they were given eight peer rating forms and eight prestamped and addressed envelopes and were asked to give these forms to eight people who knew them well. Raters were to be asked to complete the forms anonymously and mail them back to the authors.

The peer rating forms were divided into two sections. One section asked the judges to assess how frequently the subject engaged in the 20 different behaviors comprising the items of the SRA Scale. Another section asked for four global ratings of the subject's altruism—how car-

*Table 1. The Self-Report Altruism Scale*

| *Instructions*: Tick the category on the right that conforms to the frequency with which you have carried out the following acts. | Never | Once | More than once | Often | Very often |
|---|---|---|---|---|---|
| 1. I have helped push a stranger's car out of the snow. | | | | | |
| 2. I have given directions to a stranger. | | | | | |
| 3. I have made change for a stranger. | | | | | |
| 4. I have given money to a charity. | | | | | |
| 5. I have given money to a stranger who needed it (or asked me for it). | | | | | |
| 6. I have donated goods or clothes to a charity. | | | | | |
| 7. I have done volunteer work for a charity. | | | | | |
| 8. I have donated blood. | | | | | |
| 9. I have helped carry a stranger's belongings (books, parcels, etc.). | | | | | |
| 10. I have delayed an elevator and held the door open for a stranger. | | | | | |
| 11. I have allowed someone to go ahead of me in a lineup (at a xerox machine, in the supermarket). | | | | | |
| 12. I have given a stranger a lift in my car. | | | | | |
| 13. I have pointed out a clerk's error (in a bank, at the supermarket) in undercharging me for an item. | | | | | |
| 14. I have let a neighbor whom I didn't know too well borrow an item of some value to me (e.g., a dish, tools, etc.) | | | | | |
| 15. I have bought "charity" Christmas cards deliberately because I knew it was a good cause. | | | | | |
| 16. I have helped a classmate whom I did not know that well with a homework assignment when my knowledge was greater than his or hers. | | | | | |
| 17. I have before being asked, voluntarily looked after a neighbor's pets or children without being paid for it. | | | | | |
| 18. I have offered to help a handicapped or elderly stranger across a street. | | | | | |
| 19. I have offered my seat on a bus or train to a stranger who was standing. | | | | | |
| 20. I have helped an acquaintance to move households. | | | | | |

ing, how helpful, how considerate of others' feelings, and how willing to make a sacrifice. Each of these ratings was to be made on a 7-point scale.

There were 968 peer rating forms distributed to the 118 subjects who initially completed the SRA Scale. Approximately 45% of the peer rating forms were returned ($N = 416$) and 88 subjects (75% of the subjects in the original sample) had one or more raters.

A peer rating score on the 20-item scale was found by summing across the 20 items for each rater, adding these totals, and then dividing by the number of raters (peer-rated SRA Scale altruism). A peer rating score was also calculated on the four-item global test by summing across the four items for each rater, adding these totals, and dividing by the number of raters (peer-rated global altruism).

The validity of the SRA Scale was assessed by correlating it with the peer ratings. The correlations between the SRA Scale and peer-rated SRA Scale altruism and peer-rated global altruism were $r(86) = .35$ ($p < .001$) and $r(86) = .21$ ($p < .05$), respectively. These correlations were recomputed correcting for attenuation due to unreliability of measurement. Using Spearman's correction formula and substituting coefficient alpha as the reliability of the SRA Scale, and the interrater correlations as the reliabilities of the peer ratings, the correlations of the SRA Scale with peer-rated SRA Scale altruism and peer-rated global altruism were raised to $r(78) = .56$ and $r(78) = .69$, respectively.

Thus this study demonstrates that those persons who report themselves as engaging in a high frequency of altruistic behavior are also reported by their families and friends as engaging in a high frequency of such behavior, as well as being judged overall to be caring, considerate, and helpful.

## 4.2. The Predicting Altruistic Responses Study

In this study, carried out with 146 undergraduates over three testing sessions, the SRA Scale was correlated with eight "altruistic" responses. These included (1) volunteering to read to blind persons in response to a telephone solicitation; (2) volunteering to participate in experiments for a needy experimenter; (3) whether they had ever taken a first aid course; (4) whether they had completed a medical organ donor card which is attached to all Ontario driver's licenses; (5) a questionnaire measuring "sensitive attitudes" compiled by the Educational Testing Service (ETS); (6) the nurturance scale of the Personality Research Form (PRF, Jackson, 1974); (7) paper-and-pencil measures of helping in emergency simulations; and (8) having helping interests on the Jackson Vocational Interest Survey (JVIS, Jackson, 1977).

The SRA Scale was found to be positively and significantly related to four measures: having filled out the organ donation card, the ETS paper-and-pencil measure of sensitive attitude, the PRF nurturance scale, and the responses to the altruism simulations. The SRA Scale was also found to predict a linear combination of the eight measures at $r = +.40$ ($p < .01$). When corrections were made for the unreliability of the measures, the multiple correlation rose to $r = +.59$. Furthermore, the results were demonstrated not to be attributable to social desirability response bias.

## 4.3. The Convergent Validity Study

In order to examine the relationship between the SRA Scale and existing measures of social responsibility, empathy, moral judgment, and prosocial values, a variety of scales were given to some 200 university students. These included: the Social Responsibility Scale (Berkowitz & Daniels, 1964); the Emotional Empathy Scale (Mehrabian & Epstein, 1972); the Social Interest Scale (Crandall, 1980); the Fantasy–Empathy Scale (Stotland, Mathews, Sherman, Hansson, & Richardson, 1978); the Machiavellianism Scale (Christie & Geis, 1970); the Rokeach Value Survey (Form C, Rokeach, 1973); the nurturance scale of the Personality Research Form (PRF, Jackson, 1974); and the Defining Issues Test of moral reasoning (Rest, 1979). The social desirability scale of the Personality Research Form (Jackson, 1974) was also administered.

The intercorrelations of these tests can be seen in Table 2. Self-report altruism correlated positively with measures of social responsibility, empathy, nurturance, having equality and helpfulness as personal values, having "high" levels of moral reasoning, and negatively with Machiavellianism. Thus knowledge of how people endorse such items as "I am the kind of person that people can count on" and "I really get involved with the feelings of the character in a novel" allows a greater than chance prediction of whether they will report having engaged in such diverse behaviors as making change for a stranger and allowing someone to go first on a xerox machine or at a supermarket checkout counter. The SRA Scale also predicted an aggregated composite of the nine other measures of prosocial value at $r$ (135) = +0.44 ($p < .001$).

For a subsample of 93 of the original 200, PRF social desirability scores were available. Low but significantly positive relationships were found between social desirability and all the questionnaire measures of prosocial orientation. Nevertheless, when social desirability was covaried, the relationships in Table 2, and that between the SRA Scale and the composite, remained intact.

*Table 2. Intercorrelations of Self-Report Altruism with Other Paper-and-Pencil Indexes of Prosocial Orientation*[a]

| | 1 | 2 | 3 | 4 | 5 | 6 | 7 | 8 | 9 | 10 |
|---|---|---|---|---|---|---|---|---|---|---|
| 1. Self-report altruism | 1.00 | | | | | | | | | |
| 2. Social responsibility | .15[b] | 1.00 | | | | | | | | |
| 3. Emotional empathy | .17[b] | .25[b] | 1.00 | | | | | | | |
| 4. Social interest | .07 | .16[c] | .29[b] | 1.00 | | | | | | |
| 5. Fantasy-empathy | .20[b] | .17[b] | .28[b] | .09 | 1.00 | | | | | |
| 6. PRF—nuturance | .28[b] | .35[b] | .49[b] | .30[b] | .12 | 1.00 | | | | |
| 7. Machiavellianism | −.13[c] | −.52[b] | −.34[b] | −.15[c] | −.09 | −.37[b] | 1.00 | | | |
| 8. Rokeach's equality | .12 | .17[b] | .15[c] | .09 | .06 | .21[b] | −.17[b] | 1.00 | | |
| 9. Rokeach's helpful | .14[c] | .05 | .26[b] | .19[b] | .09 | .40[b] | −.19[b] | .24[b] | 1.00 | |
| 10. Rest's moral judgments | .16[b] | .18[b] | .11 | −.08 | −.08 | .04 | −.22[b] | .11 | −.05 | 1.00 |

[a]Correlations and significance levels are based on differing numbers of subjects depending on the usability of individual records.
[b]$p < .01$.
[c]$p < .05$.

### 4.4. Summary

Three studies using the SRA Scale provide additional evidence that there is a broad-based trait of altruism. Knowing a person's score on one item of the self-report questionnaire allows better than chance prediction of that person's behavior in other test situations. The SRA Scale, for example, correlated significantly positively with peer ratings of altruism, whether respondents had completed the medical organ donor card which is attached to all Ontario driver's licenses, and a variety of paper-and-pencil measures of moral reasoning, nurturance, sensitive attitude, social responsibility, empathy, and prosocial values. Although all of these correlations are low, taken together they support the idea of a broad-based prosocial disposition. People high in prosocial disposition are expected to behave prosocially over a diverse range of situations. Although any two measures intercorrelated, on average, only a modest +.20, higher correlations typically occur if the principle of aggregation is adhered to.

Although the SRA Scale has been useful for demonstrating the broad base of the prosocial behavior trait, it is probably not a maximally effective way of measuring this trait. It may be too specific. The more usual format of personality inventories is to ask respondents to make general inferences about themselves. By requiring respondents to make highly specific statements as to their past behavior ("I have donated blood—never, once, more than once, often, and very often"), their answers were constrained. This was a deliberate policy for we wished to measure something behaviorally concrete. Subsequently such concrete and specific behavioral items were found to be predictive of each other, as well as of more global measures. However, to tap maximally into the broad-based trait of prosocialness, it might be more useful to employ a general and global response format than the one used here. One alternative is to ask respondents to imagine that they are in a situation where they could engage in the sort of items on the SRA Scale, and then to estimate the probability that they would do so. Or, researchers may prefer to employ a combination of the nurturance, social responsibility, and empathy scales described above.

## 5. CONCLUSIONS

This chapter has attempted to demonstrate that, from a number of different research perspectives, there is a broadly based trait of altruism on which stable individual differences occur. This viewpoint has been supported from a review of the literature of the experimental-laboratory research, from a study of community mental health volunteer workers, and from studies using the Self-Report Altruism Scale. All three areas provide data that support the hypothesis of the altruistic personality. It is also worth noting that all three areas of research also provide evidence that empathy and personal standards are useful motivational constructs with which to understand individual differences in altruism.

One very important question now arises: From where do such traits arise? A large literature on the socialization of altruism has emerged, and summaries of it now abound (e.g., Rushton, 1980; Staub, 1979). In addition, as ideas emerging out of sociobiology might suggest, perhaps heredity also makes a contribution to the consistent patterns of individual differences in human altruism that have been found (Wilson, 1975). Support for this hypothesis has recently been found in comparative studies on monozygotic (identical) and dizygotic (fraternal) twins on measures of kindness (Loehlin & Nichols, 1976), empathy (Matthews, Batson, Horn, & Rosenman, 1981), and altruism, empathy, and nurturance (Rushton, 1983). In my own study of over 500 pairs of twins, approximately 50% of the variance of the SRA scale was attributable to genetic factors. I found similar results for the measures of empathy and nurturance. Thus, it appears that the altruistic personality is partly "born" and partly "made"; both genes and social learning have influence. Additional support for this conclusion is found in reviews of the literature on the heritability of other personality traits suggesting that genetic factors exert influence on individual differences in aggression, anxiety, criminality, dominance, emotionality, intelligence, political attitudes, sexuality, and sociability (Plomin, DeFries, & McClearn, 1980; Rushton, in press). These findings provide exciting additions to current theorizing in social–personality–developmental psychology.

## 6. REFERENCES

Adler, L. L., & Graubert, J. G. Projected social distances from mental patient related items by male and female volunteers and nonvolunteers. *Psychological Reports*, 1975, *37*, 515–521.

Allen, N., & Rushton, J. P. The personality of community volunteers: A review. *Journal of Voluntary Action Research*, 1983, *12*, 36–49.

Bar-Tal, D. *Prosocial behavior: Theory and research*. Washington, D.C.: Hemisphere, 1976.

Beckman, L. Locus of control and attitudes toward mental illness among mental health volunteers. *Journal of Consulting and Clinical Psychology*, 1972, *38*, 84–89.

Benson, P. L., Dehority, J., Garman, L., Hanson, E., Hochschwender, M., Lebold, C., Rohr, R., & Sullivan, J. Intrapersonal correlates of nonspontaneous helping behavior. *Journal of Social Psychology*, 1980, *110*, 87–95.

Berkowitz, L., & Daniels, L. R. Affecting the salience of the social responsibility norm:

Effects of past help on the response to dependency relationships. *Journal of Abnormal and Social Psychology*, 1964, *68*, 275–281.

Burton, R. V. Generality of honesty reconsidered. *Psychological Review*, 1963, *70*, 481–499.

Christie, R., & Geis, G. (Eds.). *Studies in Machiavellianism*. New York: Academic Press, 1968.

Crandall, J. E. Adler's concept of social interest: Theory, measurement, and implications for adjustment. *Journal of Personality and Social Psychology*, 1980, *39*, 481–495.

Dlugokinski, E. L., & Firestone, I. J. Congruence among four methods of measuring other-centeredness. *Child Development*, 1973, *44*, 304–308.

Dlugokinski, E. L., & Firestone, I. J. Other centeredness and susceptibility to charitable appeals: Effects of perceived discipline. *Developmental Psychology*, 1974, *10*, 21–28.

Eisenberg, N. *The development of prosocial behavior*. New York: Academic Press, 1982.

Eisenberg-Berg, N., & Mussen, P. Empathy and moral development in adolescence. *Developmental Psychology*, 1978, *14*, 185–186.

Emler, N. P., & Rushton, J. P. Cognitive-developmental factors in children's generosity. *British Journal of Social and Clinical Psychology*, 1974, *13*, 277–281.

Harris, S., Mussen, P., & Rutherford, E. Some cognitive, behavioral and personality correlates of maturity of moral judgment. *Journal of Genetic Psychology*, 1976, *128*, 123–135.

Hartshorne, H., & May, M. A. *Studies in the nature of character*. Vol. 1. *Studies in deceit*. New York: Macmillan, 1928.

Hartshorne, H., May, M. A., & Maller, J. B. *Studies in the nature of character*. Vol. 2. *Studies in self-control*. New York: Macmillan, 1929.

Hartshorne, H., May, M. A., & Shuttleworth, F. K. *Studies in the nature of character*. Vol. 3. *Studies in the organization of character*. New York: Macmillan, 1930.

House, T. H., & Milligan, W. L. Autonomic responses to modeled distress in prison psychopaths. *Journal of Personality and Social Psychology*, 1976, *34*, 556–560.

Howarth, E. Personality characteristics of volunteers. *Psychological Reports*, 1976, *38*, 855–858.

Jackson, D. N. *Personality Research Form Manual* (Rev. ed.). Port Huron, Mich.: Research Psychologists Press, 1974.

Jackson, D. N. *Jackson Vocational Interest Survey Manual*. London, Canada: Research Psychologists Press, 1977.

Jamison, R., & Johnson, J. E. Empathy and therapeutic orientation in paid and volunteer crisis phone workers, professional therapists and undergraduate college students. *Journal of Community Psychology*, 1975, *3*, 269–274.

Knapp, R. H., & Holzberg, J. D. Characteristics of college students volunteering for service to mental patients. *Journal of Consulting Psychology*, 1964, *28*, 82–85.

Krebs, D. L., & Rosenwald, A. Moral reasoning and moral behavior in conventional adults. *Merrill-Palmer Quarterly of Behavior and Development*, 1977, *23*, 77–87.

Krebs, D. L., & Sturrup, B. Role-taking ability and altruistic behavior in elementary school children. *Personality and Social Psychology Bulletin*, 1974, *1*, 407–409.

Liebhart, E. H. Empathy and emergency helping: The effects of personality, self-concern, and acquaintance. *Journal of Experimental Social Psychology*, 1972, *8*, 404–411.

Loehlin, J. C., & Nichols, R. C. *Heredity, environment, and personality: A study of 850 sets of twins*. Austin: University of Texas Press, 1976.

Maller, J. B. General and specific factors in character. *Journal of Social Psychology*, 1934, *5*, 97–102.

Matthews, K. A., Batson, C. D., Horn, J., & Rosenman, R. H. "Principles in his nature which interest him in the fortune of others . . .": The heritability of empathic concern for others. *Journal of Personality*, 1981, *49*, 237–247.

Mehrabian, A., & Epstein, N. A measure of emotional empathy. *Journal of Personality*, 1972, *50*, 525–543.

Mischel, W. *Personality and assessment*. New York: Wiley, 1968.

Mussen, P., & Eisenberg-Berg, N. *Roots of caring, sharing, and helping: The development of prosocial behavior in children*. San Francisco: W. H. Freeman, 1977.

Plomin, R., DeFries, J. C., & McClearn, G. E. *Behavioral genetics: A primer*. San Francisco, Calif.: Freeman, 1980.

Rest, J. R. *Development in judging moral issues*. Minneapolis: University of Minnesota Press, 1979.

Reykowski, J. (Ed.). *Studies in the mechanisms of prosocial behavior*. Warsaw: Warsaw University Press, 1975.

Rokeach, M. *The nature of human values*. New York: Free Press, 1973.

Rushton, J. P. Generosity in children: Immediate and long-term effects of modeling, preaching, and moral judgment. *Journal of Personality and Social Psychology*, 1975, *31*, 459–466.

Rushton, J. P. *Altruism, socialization, and society*. Englewood Cliffs, N.J.: Prentice-Hall, 1980.

Rushton, J. P. *Altruism and genetics*. Paper presented at the meeting of the Fourth International Congress on Twin Studies, London, England, July 1, 1983.

Rushton, J. P. Sociobiology: Toward a theory of individual and group differences in personality and social behavior. In J. R. Royce and L. P. Mos (Eds.), *Annals of theoretical psychology* (Vol. 2). New York: Plenum Press, in press.

Rushton, J. P., & Sorrentino, R. M. (Eds.). *Altruism and helping behavior: Social, personality, and developmental perspectives*. Hillsdale, N.J.: Lawrence Erlbaum, 1981.

Rushton, J. P., & Wheelwright, M. Validation of donating to charity as a measure of children's altruism. *Psychological Reports*, 1980, *47*, 803–806.

Rushton, J. P., Chrisjohn, R. D., & Fekken, G. C. The altruistic personality and the Self-Report Altruism Scale. *Personality and Individual Differences*, 1981, *2*, 293–302.

Rushton, J. P., Jackson, D. N., & Paunonen, S. V. Personality: Nomothetic or idiographic? A response to Kenrick and Stringfield. *Psychological Review*, 1981, *88*, 582–589.

Rushton, J. P., Brainerd, C. J., & Pressley, M. Behavioral development and construct validity: The principle of aggregation. *Psychological Bulletin*, 1983, *94*, 18–38.

Schneider, K. S. Personality correlates of altruistic behavior under four experimental conditions. *Journal of Social Psychology*, 1977, *102*, 113–116.

Smith, B. M. M., & Nelson, L. D. Personality correlates of helping behavior. *Psychological Reports*, 1975, *37*, 307–310.

Staub, E. Helping a distressed person: Social, personality, and stimulus determinants. In L. Berkowitz (Ed.), *Advances in experimental social psychology* (Vol. 7). New York: Academic Press, 1974.

Staub, E. *Positive social behavior and morality*. Vol. 1. *Social and personal influences*. New York: Academic Press, 1978.

Staub, E. *Positive social behavior and morality* Vol. 2. *Socialization and development*. New York: Academic Press, 1979.

Stotland, E., Mathews, K. E., Sherman, S. E., Hansson, R. O., & Richardson, B. Z. *Empathy, fantasy and helping*. Beverly Hills, Calif.: Sage, 1978.

Strayer, F. F., Wareing, S., & Rushton, J. P. Social constraints on naturally occurring preschool altruism. *Ethology and Sociobiology*, 1979, *1*, 3–11.

Tapp, J. T., & Spanier, D. Personal characteristics of volunteer phone counselors. *Journal of Consulting and Clinical Psychology*, 1973, *41*, 245–250.

Turner, J. R. Personal and situational determinants of volunteer recruitment for a campus "hotline" program. *Journal of the American College Health Association*, 1973, *21*, 353–357.

Wilson, E. O. *Sociobiology: The new synthesis.* Cambridge, Mass.: Harvard University Press, 1975.

Wispé, L. G. (Ed.). *Altruism, sympathy, and helping: Psychological and sociological principles.* New York: Academic Press, 1978.

# 14

# Competence and Helping

## Notes toward a Model

Elizabeth Midlarsky

## 1. INTRODUCTION

Although the literature on helping has burgeoned in the past several years, it has primarily emphasized questions regarding motives or activating mechanisms (cf. Hornstein, 1978; Midlarsky & Suda, 1978; Piliavin, Dovidio, Gaertner, & Clark, 1981; Staub, 1978). Yet, like other interpersonal transactions, helping consists of three analytically distinct components: (1) a motive or goal, (2) the behavior, and (3) the consequence(s) (Barton, 1969; Ossorio, 1966). Hence, in addition to the need to investigate the motivational basis of helping acts, one must also bear in mind that altruistic or helpful behaviors may vary in nature, duration, and extensity, and that the consequences of altruistic behavior for both the recipient(s) and the actor may vary as well. In contrast to other efforts, it is proposed here that at a minimum, a model of helping should include all three of the components designated—the motivational antecedents, the behavioral component, and the consequences.

The primary thesis of this chapter is that although helping may have a variety of personal and situational antecedents, helping that is altruistic is limited, by definition, to behaviors in which the expectation of gratification by the actor is outweighed by costs (Dressel & Midlarsky, 1978; Midlarsky, 1968; Midlarsky & Bryan, 1967, 1972; Midlarsky, Bryan, & Brickman, 1973), and where any anticipated rewards are intrinsic in

ELIZABETH MIDLARSKY • Department of Psychology, University of Detroit, Detroit, Michigan 48221.

nature—such as the enhancement of positive attributions to the self, or pleasure in doing a good deed (Karylowski, 1977). Of the possible sources of intrinsic motivation, competence or effectance motivation, the motive to *effectively* intervene, is seen as a critical determinant of the consequences both for the actor and for the recipient. It is the actor who is competent in all senses of the term—both actual and perceived competence, whether specific or general in nature—who is most likely to engage in aiding behavior, and whose efforts are most likely to benefit the recipient, thus resulting in the sense of satisfaction that is likely to be contingent on positive outcomes. The purpose of this chapter is therefore to propose some of the conceptual links between competence and helping, to present an initial version of a conceptual model depicting some of the proposed relationships, and to briefly outline some of the empirical data that bear upon the resulting formulations. Although an empirical test of the complete model has not yet been made, an initial effort is currently being undertaken to assess several of the links in the model (Midlarsky & Kahana, 1981a,b, 1983).

## 2. MODEL OF COMPETENCE AND HELPING

The proposed relationship between competence and helping is illustrated in Figure 1. In this model, the individual whose goal is to help and/or to enhance the self-concept, and who is also competent and self-confident, engages in helping behavior. When all other factors, particularly situational exigencies, are held constant the outcome of helping by a competent individual is likely to be successful. The consequences of successful helping will consist of benefits to the recipient in the form of increased resources for the recipient, or the amelioration of negative conditions. Benefits to the helper may, in turn, consist of such positive psychosocial outcomes as an increased sense of well-being and an enhanced perception of "we-ness," or social integration. These consequences may then lead to increases in the competence motivation and in self-confidence that are likely to promote further helping acts.

But why should the capable person want to give help, however capable he or she believes him or herself to be? Midlarsky and Midlarsky (1973) have suggested several possibilities: (1) A competent individual with a self-perception of high competence relative to others may desire to help out of a sense of *noblesse oblige;* (2) the individual with a self-perception of high competence may have come to expect positive outcomes from his or her efforts; and (3) lower costs may be anticipated, as a result of helping, because if one views oneself as potent the world is likely to be seen as a relatively nonthreatening place.

In addition to the personal factors that promote helping, the model

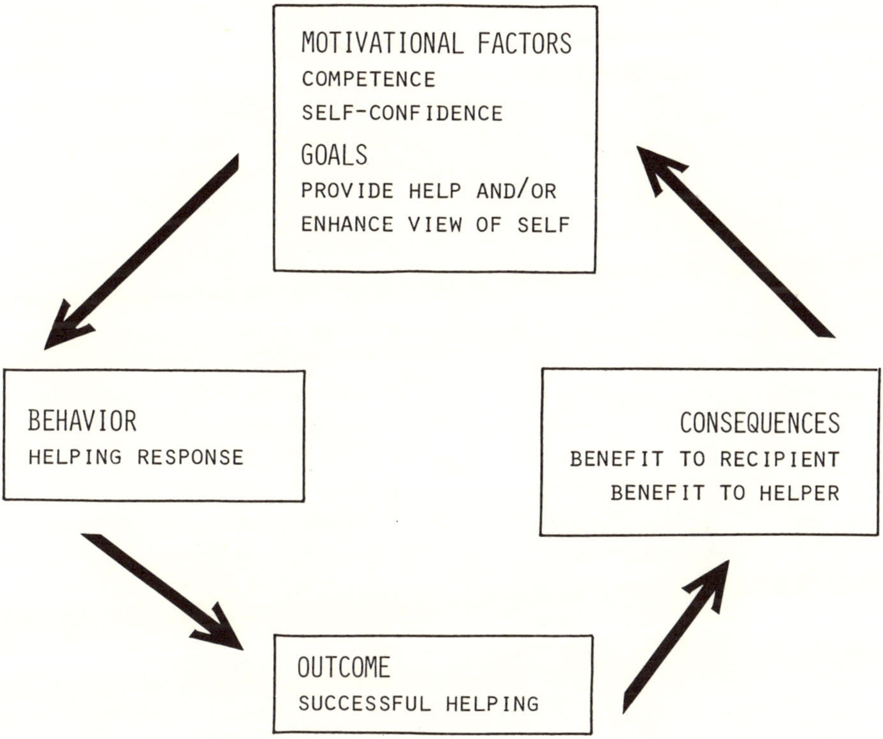


Figure 1. The competence–helping cycle.

would be incomplete without at least noting the role of situational or environmental factors. Like "The Little Train That Could," in order to be of service, we need to feel that we are responsible for providing help and/or that we wish to help, and that we *can* help—but ultimately, we must be able to find the resources within ourselves to help *relative to the demands of the situation*. In Heider's classic analysis of interpersonal relations, any behavioral outcome is viewed as a function of the person and the environment (Heider, 1958, pp. 87–89).

$$x = f\,(ff \text{ person}, ff \text{ environment}) \tag{1}$$

The "person" elements consist of two components, effort and power:

$$x = f\,(\text{trying, power}, ff \text{ environmental force}) \tag{2}$$

or,

$$x = f\,(\overbrace{\text{trying, power [e.g., abilities]}}^{ff \text{ personal force}}, ff \text{ environmental force}) \tag{3}$$

with "can" set below "abilities], *ff* environmental force".

In this formulation, it is not sufficient to *want* to help and to *try* to help. One must be *able* to help as well.

On the other hand, both trying and power may be a function, at least in part, of one's power and abilities (i.e., competence). This perception, which may be viewed as a form of self-confidence or self-esteem, may be based on the actual outcomes of one's performance and/or the attributions by others. Because as in (3) above the outcome, $x$, is based in part on environmental factors, success is not an entirely accurate source of confidence. For example, success can occur because the task was easy, and failure can occur because it was difficult. Furthermore, success may be a typical or atypical outcome for individuals such as ourselves. It is, perhaps, in part because success is less than a perfect indicator of competence that we rely on others' evaluations of our performance.

The opinions, attributions, and evaluations by others may be based on: (1) the difficulty (or costliness) of the task; (2) the abilities of the actor, based on (a) assessments of competence ("John always does well in arithmetic; thus, he is high in quantitative ability"), (b) attributions based on sex ("Boys are good at math. Therefore, John is good at math"), (c) attributions based on age ("A 10-year-old surely won't be able to divide fractions"), and (d) attributions based on seemingly irrelevant, "out of skin" concepts such as our status as veterans or homeowners ("A person of his stature must surely have the ability"). The resulting attributions and expectations may, in turn, affect our motives and abilities to act in subsequent situations.

Heider's (1958) analysis bears certain similarities to elements of self-esteem theory (Coopersmith, 1967). That is, the individual who optimistically *tries*, and achieves success, is likely to have a positive self-image. The self-system, in turn, is built up from two parallel sources of input into self-esteem—feedback from the physical and social environment resulting from one's intentional acts upon it, and the reflected appraisals of others (cf. Smith, 1968). Self-esteem, or confidence in one's own competence or efficacy is of special importance because it is a factor essential in the cycle of events associated with success or with failure. The individual with high self-esteem is convinced that success will occur. This sense of competence and self-worth may serve to prompt further action. Freedom from disabling anxiety may permit the full exercise of one's competencies, which in turn raises the probability of success. Further successes serve to augment positive self-evaluation.

The individual with high perceived competence is, in this model, more likely to respond to further opportunities to act in a diversity of situations calling for competent action than one who is low in competence. As Figure 2 indicates, the competent individual may be faced with an opportunity to benefit another individual. Such action on behalf of

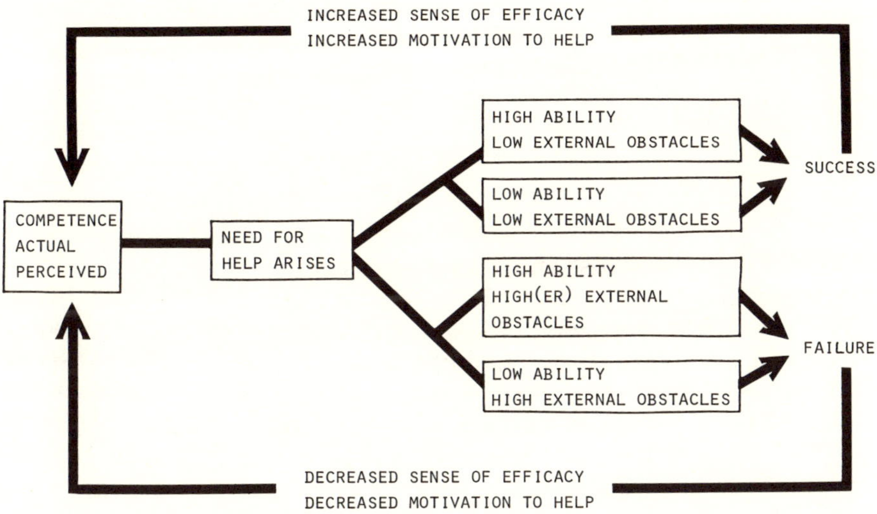


Figure 2. Personal and environmental factors in the competence–helping cycle.

the other may result in success or failure, based on an advantageous or disadvantageous combination of environmental factors and abilities. Success will lead to an increased sense of competence, and an enhanced probability that the individual will make some response to the next opportunity to be of service.

Examples of this cycle may provide clarification. An elderly widow who has successfully raised a family hears a radio announcement that foster grandparents are needed for children with learning problems. Although she has some doubts about her ability to relate to children with problems, she decides to make the attempt to help. With the support of the Foster Grandparents Program (amelioration of external obstacles) she achieves considerable success as a helper. Over several years she continues to work with children, often serving five or six at a time, and achieves considerable success with them as well as self-satisfaction. Figure 3 shows how this sequence of events could be diagramed.

On the other hand, consider the small child who sees that her

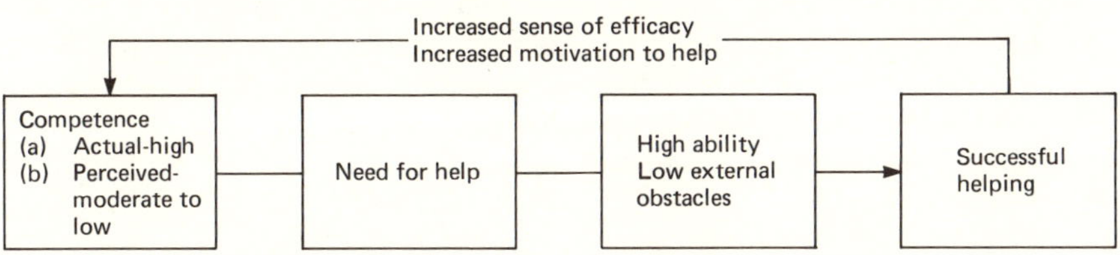


Figure 3. Example of result of successful helping.

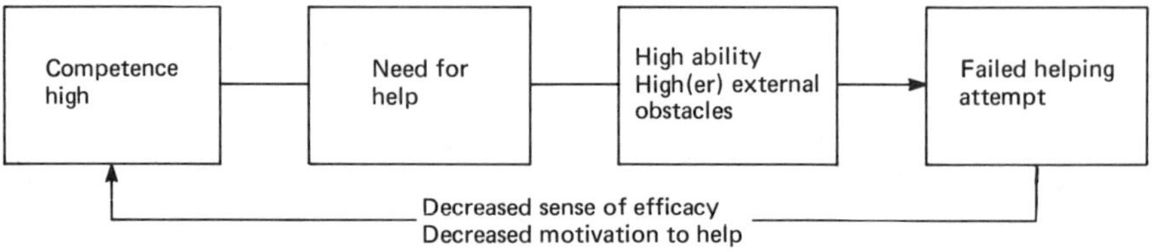


Figure 4. Example of result of unsuccessful helping.

mother is in pain because she has burned her arm. The child runs to the freezer for ice to place on the burn, because she has observed others help in this way. Her mother, however, brushes her out of the way because she assumes that a child of her daughter's age is incapable of helping her (high external obstacles). The child may be less likely to attempt to help should a similar opportunity arise.

Nothing in this version of the model (see Figure 2) provides a basis for predicting whether the competent individual will choose to be of service to himself or to another should both opportunities arise simultaneously. Presumably, such a choice would rest on a variety of additional personal and situational characteristics outside the scope of this presentation (cf. Boulding, 1974). However, this model does assume that the individual who feels competent and experiences success is less likely to take advantage of opportunities to *harm* either himself or others than is the individual who feels incompetent and experiences failure, whether in the course of helping or in activities other than helping. On the other hand, the individual who experiences failure is more likely to be frustrated, and the sense of frustration may, in turn, lead to an aggressive attitude (Dollard, Doob, Miller, Mowrer, & Sears, 1939; Midlarsky, 1975). This aggressive attitude may, in turn, lead to an enhanced willingness to hurt (Midlarsky & Midlarsky, 1976).

In summary, then, it is proposed here that there is a "benign cycle," in which competence is a precursor or antecedent of helping behavior. Competence may be general or specific in nature, and may be actual and/or perceived. Furthermore, it is recognized that there may be inconsistencies in the various competencies possessed by an individual, and that these inconsistencies in themselves may have impacts on helping (Midlarsky & Midlarsky, 1973, 1976). It is also proposed that when people contribute to the welfare of others, they also contribute, however inadvertently, to their own sense of mastery and well-being. Just as being consistently on the receiving end may have negative consequences for one's self-concept (Fisher, Nadler, & Whitcher, 1980), being a successful helper may enhance one's sense of autonomy and competence.

## 3. SUPPORTING EVIDENCE

Data from a number of investigations tend to support elements of the model presented in Figures 1 and 2. However, the emphasis on motivational antecedents of altruism has led to a preponderance of studies on the antecedents of helping, and relatively little attention has been paid to the outcomes of helping, either for the recipient or the helper. We shall now turn to the evidence that exists thus far.

### 3.1. Competence as an Antecedent of Helping

In general, competence has been found to be related to helping (Clark & Word, 1974; Harris & Huang, 1973; Kazdin & Bryan, 1971; Midlarsky, 1968, 1971; Midlarsky & Midlarsky, 1973, 1976). Findings indicate that a complex of competencies, including both a task-related skills component (Form & Nosow, 1958; Marks & Fritz, 1954) and the more general sense of personal control or "ego strength" may be related to helping (Fincham & Barling, 1978; Reykowski, 1975). Competence may also be actual or perceived, and there is a modicum of evidence that both may be related to helping.

#### *3.1.1. Actual Competence*

In regard to actual competence, a basic qualification for help giving consists of certain types of physical prowess, including health. The fact that virtually no attention has been paid to the role of physical health in the literature on altruism and helping is probably attributable to the fact that the research has primarily been conducted with healthy younger people, for whom health may not hold the same significance that it does for groups such as the elderly. Yet it is clear that there are situations in which actual health, and other physical competencies essential for giving, would be a critical determinant either in inhibiting or facilitating helping. For example, among potential blood donors, only those with actual physical competence are even *permitted* to give blood. Indeed, there are

> health criteria set for blood donors [and a] need for high standards in donor selection in the interest of the recipients because of the potentially lethal quality of human blood and the dangers of transmitting disease. (Titmuss, 1971, p. 70)

On the other hand, among eligible donors who had given blood, those with a special competence, such as a rare blood type, seemed to be particularly interested in giving, on the basis of felt responsibility to make their blood accessible to those in need of it. In a similar vein, Fellner and Marshall (1970) have reported that selection of donors is made from those with appropriate physical characteristics, including organ suitability for the recipient, among other considerations.

Actual financial resources may also be a source of actual competence to give, particularly when the giving is financial in nature. It is eminently clear that people cannot donate more money or material goods than they possess. On the other hand, the amount that one chooses to donate out of one's material possessions has the potential to vary. Among children, the actual parental income has generally been found to have little effect on donations (Madsen, 1967; Rosenhan, 1969). Children, of course, may have little sense of proprietorship over the earnings of their parents, and in many cases may be unaware of the precise level of family income. Among adults, on the other hand, actual income does appear to be a predictor of philanthropy. In a sample consisting of 402 elderly persons, Pruchno (1979) found that only those in the lowest income categories did not engage in giving, and the amount of giving increased with income level. In a national sample of 2,917 American households, Morgan, Dye, and Hybels (1979) found that the average dollar amount given per year is clearly related to income level; yearly donations ranged from $75 for families earning less than $4,000 in 1973, to $70,000 for those earning $500,000 or more.

Skills, abilities, and experiences of various kinds may also be related to helping. Among children, Fischer (1963) found that those who were more intelligent learned to share more rapidly than those who were less intelligent. In a study in which the criterion measure of altruism (rated as highest for altruism in comparison with over 200 situations) was "taking the blame to protect someone you have just met," Burley (1977) found that the best predictor of altruism was a cognitive factor, social intelligence. According to Burley, when applied to altruism, social intelligence is "the ability to sum up the precise need of the other in the situation, and to know what actions are required to best alleviate that need." Furthermore, anecdotal accounts of behavior during natural disasters indicate that the possession of particular skills or experiences seems to be related to helping (Barton, 1969; Form & Nosow, 1958).

### 3.1.2. *Perceived Competence*

Whatever the actual competence possessed by an individual, perceived competence is likely to be particularly critical. As Rogers (1959) has pointed out, the behaviors that people are most likely to exhibit tend to be consistent with their *perception* of themselves and, we may add, of their abilities. These self-perceptions are, in turn, built up from at least two sources of input: feedback from the physical and social environment resulting from one's actual impact on them, and the reflected appraisals, or attributions, by others (Midlarsky, Midlarsky, & Franks, 1974; White, 1959). In the case of altruistic behavior, there is evidence that the perceptions of competence that may spur altruistic action may be either general or specific in nature.

In regard to the sense of general competence, or self-esteem, in his interpersonal theory of psychiatry Sullivan (1953) argued that before one can turn one's attention to the needs of others, one must have inner strength, and freedom from intense personal concerns. In the empirical domain, evidence exists that self-esteem is correlated with positive character traits, and that generous and helpful children are more likely to be emotionally stable (Midlarsky, 1968).

More recently, studies have been performed to test explicitly for changes in standard measures of self-esteem—such as the Tennessee Self-Concept Scale—as a result of experimental procedures, and the degree of relationship between such changes and helping. One study (Midlarsky, Berger, & Kilpatrick, 1981) explored the effects on helping of trait self-esteem and situational competence by individuals who were "repressors" and "sensitizors" (Byrne, 1961). Results indicated that the individual most likely to help was the one who had higher predispositional self-esteem and yet was a sensitizor, and who experienced success in the experimental situation. Endurance and generalization of these effects were also found, and these results were later replicated in a different paradigm, employing a broader sample that included black males and females as well. Other investigators, such as Berkowitz and Connor (1966), Kazdin and Bryan (1971), and Ashton and Severy (1976) have also found that general perceived competence bears a significant relationship both to volunteering to help and to helping. In addition, just as higher self-esteem is related to a greater likelihood of helping, individuals with high social anxiety help less than those with low social anxiety (McGovern, 1976).

Another form of general perceived competence that has been found to be significantly related to helping is locus of control. Internal control, which has been found to be related to perceived competence (Midlarsky, 1971; Phares, 1976) and to favorable self-concepts (Kuypers, 1972), is defined as belief in one's ability to influence events and to bring about desired outcomes (Phares, 1976; Rotter, 1966); hence, it would be expected to enhance the individual's likelihood to initiate action and to actively pursue goals, including goals involving helping others.

Data from a variety of sources suggest the importance of this variable. First, Sorokin (1950) found that one of the characteristics of his "good neighbors" was a sense of mastery over future outcomes. In an early study, Gore and Rotter (1963) found that black college students who made verbal commitments to social action were more likely to be internal controllers. Also, in the domain of attitude expressions, Midlarsky and Kahana (1981b) found that personal control orientations were strongly related to the expression of altruistic sentiments among elderly persons living in a Florida retirement community. Strickland (1965) found that internal controllers were not only more apt to commit themselves to social action, but were significantly more likely to be active participants in civil rights activities in the South.

Several experimental studies explored the relationship between locus of control and helping. Midlarsky (1971) measured locus of control in a study in which male subjects could help another male manipulate small objects in a motor coordination task. The subject always completed the task first, and could help another person, the confederate, who was still working on a somewhat different task. A high correlation between locus of control scores and amount of helping was found here, and was replicated in two subsequent experiments (Midlarsky & Midlarsky, 1973, 1976). In still another experiment, Fincham and Barling (1978) found that in 9- and 10-year-old boys, locus of control orientation predicted the number of candies donated to a charity, again with internal controllers donating more.

The relationship to helping of specific, task-related perceived competence has been studied as well. Harris and Huang (1973) found that more individuals volunteered for an aesthetic judgment task from a group told earlier that they were very competent on a similar task. In a study by Schwartz and Ben David (1976), persons told that they would be readily able to handle rats had a higher likelihood of helping than those informed that they would not be as able. A series of studies conducted in my laboratory has employed a paradigm in which the experimenter met two individuals, a subject and a trained collaborator, in a waiting room outside the "test research office." Participants were told that the purpose of their participation was to go through the tests currently being developed, and to help evaluate them. Each participant would be working on a different test, and because of their newness there was as yet no way to predict the length of time needed to complete them. Therefore, if one participant finished first, he was permitted to help his partner. In all cases the collaborator timed his work so that the subject would finish first. Thus the subject had the opportunity to provide help in all cases. One of the tests was then described as a test of "motor coordination," and the second as a test of "manual dexterity." They were described as instruments designed to simulate performance situations in which skilled workers, such as pilots, might be exposed to stress in the course of their work. Helping was operationally defined as the proportion of electrified test items with which the subject helped his "partner."

In the first study using this paradigm (Midlarsky, 1971), before taking the test, subjects in the high competence condition were shown GSR (galvanic skin response) readings indicating that they were "low reactors" whereas those in the low competence condition were shown that they were "high reactors." During the experiment, the level of stress was controlled so that subjects in the high competence condition received a constant, moderate level; as they readily adapted to that level, they received further confirmation of their competence. In the low competence condition, the amount of stress was gradually increased from a low to a high level, in which the average was equal to that received by subjects under high competence. The subjective experience of these latter subjects was found to be that of a fairly constant level to which they never seemed to adapt. As predicted, the relationship between competence and helping was significant ($p < .001$) and accounted for 34% of the variance.

Although the results of Study 1 indicated a strong positive relationship between competence and helping, there was a limitation on the interpretation of the finding. This came from the procedure for eliciting perceptions of competence, wherein subjects in the high competence condition were actually experiencing somewhat less stress immediately before the helping opportunity than were those in the low competence condition. Study 2 (Midlarsky & Midlarsky, 1973) was therefore designed to investigate the relationship to helping of task-relevant competence unconfounded by costs. The cost of helping, defined as the magnitude of stress received, was independently varied in order to determine the separate relationship between this variable and helping.

In this study the concept of competence was more closely examined. Both here and in subsequent investigations (Midlarsky & McKnight, 1980; Midlarsky & Midlarsky, 1976) a distinction was made between competence attributed to individuals by the experimenter, and the sense of competence based on one's achievement in the situation. The theoretical basis for anticipating that these two forms of evaluative feedback may have both separate and interactive effects on helping was that self-esteem or competence is based both on direct feedback on the efficacy of our actions, that is, the direct experience of competence (White, 1959), and on the appraisals of our actions by others (Midlarsky *et al.*, 1974; Smith, 1968). Although these two forms of competence are generally confounded in research investigations, two studies in my laboratory have indeed indicated that they do have separate effects (Midlarsky & McKnight, 1980; Pelc & Midlarsky, 1977).

Procedures in Study 2 were similar to those in Study 1. The competence (achieved status) induction was modified by setting the amount of stress at the beginning of the test and leaving it unchanged. In the high status condition, the subject was given a statement indicating the importance and value of his participation in the experiment; in the low status condition, such a statement was made to the collaborator and overheard by the subject. Subjects in the high cost condition were exposed to discernibly higher stress than those in the low cost condition.

The efficacy of these procedures was found to be quite good. For example, in both this experiment and in subsequent studies of this kind (Midlarsky & Midlarsky, 1976), the only significant main effect on perceptions of competence on the postexperimental questionnaire was yielded by the experimental induction of competence, accounting for an average of 62% of the variance across studies. Significant interactive effects on helping of both perceived competence × status, and competence × status × costs, indicated that costs and status attributions tended to modify the effects of the competence variable on helping behavior.

Results indicated that even when costs are controlled, competence—or achieved status—has a very potent effect on helping ($F = 104.59$, $p < .001$). The main effects of attributed status ($F = 57.39$, $p < .001$) and costs ($F = 4.09$, $p < .05$) were also significant. Although the effects of both forms of competence were far more powerful than the effect of costs, it is certainly noteworthy that many situations may be imagined in which costs (environmental obstacles) may be sufficiently onerous that they may match or outweigh the effects of competence.

A third experimental study (Midlarsky & Midlarsky, 1976) employed a similar experimental paradigm. In this study the achieved status variable was operationalized as ability on a task similar to the experimental task, whereby the subject determined his ability by comparing his own performance with a chart representing "group norms." Ascribed status (termed "attribution") was operationalized in the same manner as in Study 2. Dependent variables included both the amount of stress that the subject was willing to undergo to help his partner, and the subject's "willingness to hurt," which was evaluated by means of items that tapped the willingness to administer the experimental stressor to others as a punitive measure, and the amount of stress that the subject would be willing to administer.

Results of this study indicated that the forms of competence studied here were all significantly related to helping ($p < .001$), and accounted for large amounts of the variance. Analyses of the postexperimental questionnaire indicated that the experimental inductions of achievement and attribution were both valid and independent of one another. Other studies have provided still further support regarding both the validity of this conceptualization of the two forms of competence/status and the operational definitions used. For example, if the means for inducing attributed status is correct, then attributions of importance should work only when made by a high status source, whereas achievement should work whatever the experimenter's status. This was indeed a finding within a fourth experimental study. Also of interest was the finding in that fourth experiment that the induced states of competence may be relatively enduring and may generalize across situations. That is, in Study 4, subjects in both the high achievement and the high attribution conditions were significantly more likely than others to volunteer their services in a community help program (which seemed entirely separate from the psychology laboratory) and to follow through by providing arduous and competent help for the project some 2 to 4 weeks after their experimental participation. Thus evidence exists that (1) these operations were valid, (2) they were independent of one another, and (3) they tended to endure and generalize.

### 3.2. Competence and Effective Helping

In addition to the prediction that competence may evoke helping behavior, the model presented above predicts that helping attempts will be more *successful* when the helper is higher in competence and self-confidence. On an intuitive level, this should certainly be the case, particularly in regard to competencies relevant to the task at hand. The skilled, sensitive, and confident psychotherapist certainly appears to be more helpful than one who is less experienced and skilled (Midlarsky, 1981), and the potential philanthropist will be unable to help if he or she is currently out of funds. It is likely that a wide range of competencies, from role-taking ability (Hoffman, 1976) to the ability to postpone gratification (Mischel & Mischel, 1976) to knowledge of what constitutes appropriate help (Schwartz, 1974), may be related to effective helping.

The key point here is that helping acts not only be emitted by well-meaning persons, but that these acts have consequences that are effective and safe for all concerned, rather than being impulsive and misguided. As Bergin (1963) has pointed out in regard to professional helping, if we genuinely believe that psychotherapy is powerful enough to bring about positive change, we must also acknowledge that it is powerful enough to be toxic under certain circumstances. Fisher *et al.* (1980) remind us of the potential damage to self-esteem of the recipient of miscalculated helping, and Vinacke (1980) speculates that the competent altruist realizes that not helping is sometimes the best way to be socially constructive (e.g., as in refusing to give a child excessive "help" with homework).

The role of competence as an antecedent to effective helping is quite notable in the largely anecdotal accounts of sudden natural disasters. When such disasters occur, there is typically an appearance of high motivation to help the victims, resulting in sympathy and comfort as well as material goods. However, despite the strong motivation to help, ineffective helping is more frequent than effective helping. Indeed, the literature on disasters is replete with such examples as the delivery of shipments of brassieres to flooded areas, and the mass convergence of untrained persons wishing to help, which may impede the efforts of those who are actually capable of being useful (cf. Barton, 1969). In one of the few experiments that have been performed, Clark and Word (1974) found that whereas "electrically sophisticated" individuals intervened in an electrical emergency both quickly and carefully, those who were not sophisticated acted in ways that were potentially both ineffective and quite harmful. As Marx requested in *Das Kapital*, "The road to hell is paved with good intentions." Conversely, "The road to helping may be paved with competence."

### 3.3. Psychosocial Outcomes of Helping

There is a paucity of systematic research on the psychosocial outcomes of helping. However, it seems quite apparent that the outcomes will be quite different for the effective helper than for the ineffective helper. The ineffective helper is an individual who has given time, money, or effort, or who has incurred possible danger or discomfort, all to no avail. Should this individual become aware of the ineffective outcome, the result may be decrements in self-esteem or morale, possibly self-blame, and, in extreme cases, even prosecution (Ratcliffe, 1966). Furthermore, as Barton (1969) has noted, the rate of "psychological casualties" among helpers is likely to be greatest among those for whom there is the greatest discrepancy between the strength of the motivation to help, and the capacity for effectiveness in the helping role.

In sharp constrast to the likelihood of adverse outcomes for ineffective helpers, the effective helper is predicted to experience psychosocial benefits. Now, altruistic behavior is, by definition, a form of behavior intended to help others and not expected to bring extrinsic rewards. On the other hand, helping others effectively may lead, albeit unintentionally, to the development and maintenance of satisfying social bonds (Eibl-Eibesfeldt, 1972; Troll, Miller, & Atchley, 1975). There is also some evidence that helping may be related to a sense of well-being, and even to physical survival (e.g., Havighurst, 1961; Midlarsky, 1968; Midlarsky & Suda, 1978). Furthermore, studies of survivors of natural and man-made disasters indicate that the individual responsible for others appears to maintain a higher level of physical and psychological integrity than one who is helped and protected by others. For example, Rachman (1978) notes that individuals who are most active in a socially responsible way during stressful times appear to experience less fear and stress than those who are less active on behalf of others.

One of the major expected outcomes of effective helping is seen as enhanced self-esteem. Fellner and Marshall (1970) report that although kidney donors have been viewed as persons who "give up something and get nothing in return," all of the donors in their investigation reported feeling "'good,' 'noble,' 'bigger,' 'happier,' and [the experience] generally increased their self-esteem." The increase in self-esteem as the consequence of helping may, however, be greatest in groups such as the elderly, for which other avenues to active participation in society may be blocked (Midlarsky & Kahana, 1981a,b, 1983). Press and McKool (1972) list, as one of the four primary determinants of status in old age, the extent to which one can contribute to the well-being of others. Although the fostering of dependency through thoughtless "helping" often appears to lead to self-blame and depression (Midlarsky & Kahana, 1983). a converse may well be provided by giving opportunities for older persons to be helpful to others. In contrast to the recipient's implied lack of competence, the prevailing image and self-concept of the helper is as a powerful and active figure (Frank, 1963). Hence it is quite likely that especially for persons such as the elderly, the handicapped, and other members of "recipient groups," should the opportunity be provided for them to be effective helpers, then this strategy may enhance mental health and generally lead to positive psychosocial outcomes as well as benefits for society.

## 4. CONCLUSION

This chapter has presented notes toward a model depicting the relationships among competence, helping behavior, and the outcomes of helping. Although elements of this model have received a fair amount of support from empirical data thus far available, considerable additional work is needed. For example, the preponderance of research in the literature on altruism and helping has been directed to the study of the motivational and situational antecedents of prosocial behavior, under the apparent assumption that helping is beneficial for potential recipients. However, the conditions under which helping may have beneficial or adverse effects have rarely been systematically considered. Furthermore, few investigations have been directed at the psychosocial effects of helping on the helper. Future research may well be directed to the study of links in the causal model that was presented in an initial form here. In addition, it is proposed that the armamentarium of research strategies for altruism researchers should include simultaneous investigations of the antecedents, nature, and outcomes of helping acts, in addition to the more limited experimental designs heretofore employed.

## 5. REFERENCES


Ashton, N., & Severy, L. Arousal and costs in bystander intervention. *Personality and Social Psychology Bulletin*, 1976, *2*, 268–272.

Barton, A. H. *Communities in disaster*. Garden City, N.Y.: Doubleday, 1969.

Bergin, A. E. The effects of psychotherapy. *Journal of Counseling Psychology*, 1963, *10* 244–250.

Berkowitz, L., & Connor, W. H. Success, failure, and social responsibility. *Journal of Personality and Social Psychology*, 1966, *4*, 664–669.

Boulding, E. The child and non-violent social change. In C. Wulf (Ed.), *Handbook on peace education*. Frankfurt-am-Main/Oslo: International Peace Research Association, 1974.

Burley, P. *A model for the prediction of altruistic behavior*. Unpublished manuscript, University of Oxford, 1977.

Byrne, D. The Repression-Sensitization Scale. *Journal of Personality*, 1961, *29*, 334–349.

Clark, R., & Word, L. Where is the apathetic bystander? *Journal of Personality and Social Psychology*, 1974, *29*, 279–288.

Coopersmith, S. *Antecedents of self-esteem*. San Francisco: W. H. Freeman, 1967.

Dollard, J., Doob, L., Miller, N. E., Mowrer, O., & Sears, R. R. *Frustration and aggression*. New Haven: Yale University Press, 1939.

Dressel, S., & Midlarsky, E. The effects of models' exhortations, demands and practices on children's donation behavior. *Journal of Genetic Psychology*, 1978, *132*, 211–223.

Eibl-Eibesfeldt, I. *Love and hate*. New York: Holt, Rinehart & Winston, 1972.

Fellner, C., & Marshall, J. Kidney donors. In J. Macaulay & L. Berkowitz (Eds.), *Altruism and helping behavior*. New York: Academic Press, 1970.

Fincham, R., & Barling, J. Locus of control and generosity in learning disabled, normal achieving, and gifted children. *Child Development*, 1978, *49*, 530–533.

Fischer, W. Sharing in preschool children as a function of amount and type of reinforcement. *Genetic Psychology Monographs*, 1963, *68*, 215–245.

Fisher, J., Nadler, A., & Whitcher, S. *Recipient reactions to aid*. Unpublished manuscript, University of Connecticut, 1980.

Form, W., & Nosow, S. *Community in disaster*. New York: Harper & Row, 1968.

Frank, J. D. *Persuasion and healing*. New York: Schocken, 1963.

Gore, P., & Rotter, J. B. A personality correlate of social action. *Journal of Personality*, 1963, *31*, 58–64.

Harris, M., & Huang, L. Competence and helping. *Journal of Social Psychology*, 1973, *89*, 203–210.

Havighurst, R. The nature and value of meaningful free-time activity. In R. Kleemeier (Ed.), *Aging and leisure*. New York: Oxford University Press, 1961.

Heider, F. *The psychology of interpersonal relations*. New York: Wiley, 1958.

Hoffman, M. Empathy, role-taking, guilt, and the development of altruistic motives. In T. Lickona (Ed.), *Moral development and behavior*. New York: Holt, Rinehart & Winston, 1976.

Homans, G. *Social behavior: Its elementary forms*. New York: Harcourt, Brace, 1961.

Hornstein, H. Promotive tension and prosocial behavior. In L. Wispé (Ed.), *Altruism, sympathy and helping*. New York: Academic Press, 1978.

Karylowski, J. Explaining altruistic behavior: A review. *Polish Psychological Bulletin*, 1977, *8*, 27–34.

Kazdin, A., & Bryan, J. H. Competence and volunteering. *Journal of Experimental Social Psychology*, 1971, *7*, 87–97.

Kuypers, J. Internal-external locus of control, ego functioning and personality characteristics in old age. *The Gerontologist*, 1972, *12*, 168–173.

Madsen, M. Cooperative and competitive motivation of children in three Mexican subcultures. *Psychological Reports*, 1967, *20*, 1307–1320.

Marks, E., & Fritz, C. *Human reactions in disaster situations*. Unpublished manuscript, University of Chicago, 1954.

McGovern, L. Dispositional social anxiety and helping under three conditions of threat. *Journal of Personality*, 1976, *44*, 84–97.

Midlarsky, E. Aiding responses. *Merrill-Palmer Quarterly*, 1968, *14*, 229–260.

Midlarsky, E. Aiding under stress. *Journal of Personality*, 1971, *39*, 132–149.

Midlarsky, E. *Competence, affect, and helping: The Wounded Knee caper*. Unpublished manuscript, University of Detroit, 1980.

Midlarsky, E. Family therapy: Two case studies. *Journal of Psychiatric Treatment and Evaluation*, 1981, *3*(4), 349–353.

Midlarsky, E., & Bryan, J. H. Training charity in children. *Journal of Personality and Social Psychology*, 1967, *5*, 409–415.

Midlarsky, E., & Bryan, J. H. Affect expressions and children's imitative altruism. *Journal of Experimental Research in Personality*, 1972, *6*, 195–203.

Midlarsky, E., & Kahana, E. *Altruism and helping among the elderly*. Paper presented at the meeting of the American Psychological Association, Los Angeles, California, August 1981. (a)

Midlarsky, E., & Kahana, E. *Altruism in the aged*. Paper presented at the meeting of the Gerontological Society of America, Toronto, Canada, November 1981. (b)

Midlarsky, E., & Kahana, E. Helping by the elderly: Conceptual and empirical considerations. In M. Kleiman (Ed.), *Interdisciplinary topics in gerontology* (Vol. 17),. Basel, Switzerland: S. Karger, 1983.

Midlarsky, E., & McKnight, L. Effects of achievement, evaluative feedback, and locus of control on children's expectations. *Journal of Genetic Psychology*, 1980, *136*, 203–212.

Midlarsky, E., & Midlarsky, M. Some determinants of aiding under experimentally-induced stress. *Journal of Personality*, 1973, *41*, 305–327.

Midlarsky, E., & Suda, W. Some antecedents of altruism in children. *Psychological Reports*, 1978, *43*, 187–208.

Midlarsky, E., Bryan, J. H., & Brickman, P. Aversive approval. *Child Development*, 1973, *44*, 321–328.

Midlarsky, E., Midlarsky, M., & Franks, D. *The comparative effects of socially-derived self-image and self-assessment of competency behavior through the generalized other on subsequent helping in an experimental situation*. Paper presented at the meeting of the Rocky Mountain Social Sciences Association, El Paso, Texas, September 1974.

Midlarsky, E., Berger, M., & Kilpatrick, D. Predispositional and situational influences on changes in self-esteem and helping. *Academic Psychology Bulletin*, 1981, *3*, 395–399.

Midlarsky, M. *On war*. New York: Free Press, 1975.

Midlarsky, M., & Midlarsky, E. Status inconsistency, aggressive attitude, and helping behavior. *Journal of Personality*, 1976, *44*, 371–391.

Mischel, W., & Mischel, H. A cognitive social learning approach to morality and self-regulation. In T. Lickona (Ed.), *Moral development and behavior*. New York: Holt, Rinehart & Winston, 1976.

Morgan, J., Dye, R., & Hybels, J. *Results from two national surveys of philanthropic activity.* Ann Arbor, Mich.: Institute for Social Research, 1979.

Ossorio, P. *Persons.* Los Angeles: Linguistic Research Institute, 1966.

Pelc, R., & Midlarsky, E. Effects of evaluative feedback on the subjective probability of success. *Journal of Psychology,* 1977, *76,* 191–196.

Phares, E. J. *Locus of control in personality.* Morristown, N.J.: General Learning Press, 1976.

Piliavin, J., Dovidio, J., Gaertner, S., & Clark, R. *Emergency intervention.* New York: Academic Press, 1981.

Press, I., & McKool, M. Social structure and status of aging. *Aging and Human Development,* 1972, *3,* 297–306.

Pruchno, R. *Social networks of the elderly,.* Unpublished master's thesis, Oakland University, 1979.

Rachman, S. *Fear and courage.* San Francisco: W. H. Freeman, 1978.

Ratcliffe, J. *The Good Samaritan and the law.* New York: Anchor Books, 1966.

Reykowski, J. Introduction. In J. Reykowski (Ed.), *Studies in the mechanisms of prosocial behavior.* Warsaw: Wydaevnictiva Universytetu, 1975.

Rogers, C. A theory of therapy, personality and interpersonal relationships as developed in the client-centered framework. In S. Koch (Ed.), *Psychology: A study of science.* New York: McGraw-Hill, 1959.

Rosenhan, D. *Determinants of altruism.* Paper presented at the meeting of the American Psychological Association, Washington, D.C., August 1969.

Rotter, J. Generalized expectancies for internal versus external control of reinforcement. *Psychological Monographs,* 1966, *80* (1, Whole No. 609).

Schwartz, S. H. Awareness of interpersonal consequences, responsibility, denial, and volunteering. *Journal of Personality and Social Psychology,* 1974, *30,* 57–63.

Schwartz, S. H., & Ben David, T. Responsibility and helping in an emergency. *Sociometry,* 1976, *39,* 406–415.

Smith, M. B. Competence and socialization. In J. Clausen (Ed.), *Socialization and society.* Boston: Little, Brown, 1968.

Sorokin, P. A. *Altruistic love.* Boston: Beacon Press, 1950.

Staub, E. *Positive social behavior and morality.* Vol. 1. *Social and personal influences.* New York: Academic Press, 1978.

Strickland, B. R. The prediction of social action from a dimension of internal-external control. *Journal of Social Psychology,* 1965, *66,* 353–358.

Sullivan, H. S. *The interpersonal theory of psychiatry.* New York: W. W. Norton, 1953.

Titmuss, R. M. *The gift relationship.* New York: Pantheon Books, 1971.

Troll, L., Miller, S., & Atchley, R. *Families in later life.* Belmont, Calif.: Wadsworth, 1975.

Vinacke, W. E. Prosocial behavior. *Academic Psychology Bulletin,* 1980, *2,* 259–286.

White, R. W. Motivation reconsidered. *Psychological Review,* 1959, *66,* 297–333.

# 15

# Altruism and Patterns of Social Interaction

Hans Werner Bierhoff

## 1. INTRODUCTION

Prosocial behavior implies an interaction of at least two persons: the helper (A) and the recipient of help (B). Therefore, prosocial responses have to be understood in the context of social interaction in general.

According to this view, it is important to make a distinction between behavioral plans of the individuals and contingencies among their social responses. Each person approaches the interaction with a set of goals or intentions. Moreover, each response is determined by social influence produced by the other person. If so, it would follow that four patterns of social interactions can be identified that vary in the weights to be attached to goals/plans and social influence/contingency (E. E. Jones & Gerard, 1967):

In *pseudocontingency*, the interaction situation is basically noncontingent. Very little consideration to the other person is necessary. Despite these limitations, a "simple synchronization of responses" (E. E. Jones & Thibaut, 1958, p. 155) is achieved. An illustration of this process is provided by such simple requests for assistance as "Excuse me, I wonder if you could tell me how to get to Times Square?" (Darley & Latané, 1970, p. 89). Although the prosocial response benefits another, this response plays a minor role in the benefactor's social behavior.

---

HANS WERNER BIERHOFF • Department of Psychology, Philipps-University Marburg, 3550 Marburg, West Germany.

In *asymmetrical contingency*, the behavior of one person (A) is contingent on the behavior of the other (B), but B's behavior is not contingent on A. An example is provided by the norm of social responsibility: People should help those who are dependent upon them (Berkowitz & Daniels, 1963).

In *reactive contingency*, the question is whether bystanders will intervene to help another person in an emergency. If the emergency is not dealt with immediately the situation will deteriorate within a few minutes.

In *mutual contingency*, the behavior of A is partially dependent on the responses of B and vice versa. In addition, goals and behavioral plans are important causes of A's and B's behavior. That is, the exchange of prosocial responses is reciprocal. This reciprocity induces trust. Prosocial responses are strong evidence of trust and trustworthiness.

If, as is suggested, the interaction contingencies may be important for helping behavior, then A's decision to give or withhold help from B is likely to depend on the variations in contingency and related aspects of the interaction. Therefore, let us look at the crucial features of the four classes of social interaction and explore further what may happen phenomenologically in the interaction.

## 2. INCIDENTAL HELPING

Pseudocontingent interactions can be found in many real-life situations, for example, the encounter of several persons on a bus, in an elevator, or in a restaurant. We might begin our analysis by specifying the crucial features that are inherent in pseudocontingent relationships:

- The actors are—independent of each other—concerned with certain (primary) goals. Here, then, the actors are involved in independent action sequences, rather than in using the preceding actions of the other as information about the appropriate response.
- In addition to concern with a primary goal, elements of a coordination between A and B emerge, and a "simple synchronization" (E. E. Jones & Thibaut, 1958) is achieved.

The conceptual distinction that we have been drawing between primary goals and secondary contingencies appears to be useful for an understanding of nonemergency helping behavior. In many real-life situations A's help is an incidental event, because A fulfills other and more important obligations at the same time. If so, it would follow that salient features of the requester as well as appeals based on different types of justifications will affect helping behavior differently. An example may clarify these issues:

> A and B are waiting for the arrival of their train. B asks A to take care of the suitcase while he or she buys a drink on the other platform. In the meantime A continues to study the timetable. B returns, takes the suitcase, thanks for the help, and leaves.

It appears from this example that the appeal of the requester is a crucial factor in producing coordination of the response sequences in pseudocontingent interactions. The request suggests a specific definition of the situation (Langer & Abelson, 1972).

In two field experiments Moriarty (1975) found that a request for help had a dramatic effect on a bystander's response to a simulated theft. Confederates initiated a brief dialogue with another person at Jones Beach in New York. He or she either said, "Excuse me, I'm here alone and have no matches . . . do you have a light?" or "Excuse me, I'm going up to the boardwalk for a few minutes . . . would you watch my things?" Whereas—in both experiments—27 out of 28 persons prevented the theft in the second condition, only 5 out of 28 intervened in the first condition. Similar results were obtained in a study by Shaffer, Rogel, and Hendrick (1975).

The results of these experiments support the hypothesis that the establishment of a minimal coordination breaks down the bystander's apathy and elicits prosocial responses, in this case, intervention in order to stop the thief. Therefore, it seems most likely that an adequate explanation will be found in an analysis of the interaction processes. On the assumption that coordination results from requests, it is expected that without a request bystanders would be significantly less helpful and more passive. Data from the studies tend to support this prediction. An additional issue in these studies was the pseudocontingent–reactive contingent distinction regarding the interactions. That is, the pseudocontingency of A and B opens up the willingness of A to enter into a reactive contingency with the thief.

In the typical pseudocontingent situation A and B are strangers. Moreover, A is forced to infer the relevant information for his or her decision to give or withhold help from B on the basis of B's request. If so, it is obvious that the phrasing of the appeal influences A's definition of the situation and willingness to help. Langer and Abelson (1972) suggest that "victim oriented" phrases and "target oriented" phrases should be distinguished. In the appeal "My knee is killing me, I think I sprained it. Would you do something for me? Please do me a favor and call my husband and ask him to pick me up," the first part is an example of phrases with victim-oriented properties and the second part ("Would you do something . . .") is an example of phrases with target-oriented properties. Any appeal that describes the state of the victim is referred to as victim oriented. Alternatively, if emphasis is placed on prosocial responses of target persons, the appeal is referred to as target oriented.

Depending on the type of appeal, Langer and Abelson (1972) obtained differences in response to legitimate or illegitimate requests for a person to make a telephone call, or post an envelope. The likelihood of a prosocial response was greater when the opening phrases of the *legitimate* request were victim oriented (rather than target oriented) and when the opening phrases of the *illegitimate* request were target oriented (rather than victim oriented).

Mikula (1977) obtained the same pattern of results in four studies. When prosocial responses were unlikely (as in the case of illegitimate appeals, unattractive requesters, or an effortful response), the target-oriented appeal evoked more compliance than the victim-oriented appeal. By way of contrast, when prosocial responses were likely, the victim-oriented appeal was more successful than the target-oriented appeal. (As Innes & Gilroy, 1980, point out, this pattern of results has considerable cross-cultural stability.)

The victim-oriented appeal emphasized the victim's state of need and gave a justification for the request. In another study, when the person making the request explained that he or she needed to make a telephone call, he or she was helped two-thirds of the time. When no explanation was given for the appeal, 34% complied (Darley & Latané, 1970).

If persons are responding to simple requests for assistance on the basis of a script that goes something like "favor $X$ + reason $Y \rightarrow$ comply," then the structure of the request is an important determinant of compliance (Langer, 1978, pp. 46–50; Langer, Blank, & Chanowitz, 1978). This prediction is qualified by the assumption that people should not behave on the basis of a script when the interaction requires an effortful response.

Langer *et al.* (1978, Experiment 1) have provided support for the script hypothesis by demonstrating the "mindlessness" of certain prosocial responses. A person about to use a copying machine was asked by a confederate to use the machine first. The request was made in one of the following ways:

1. Request only: Excuse me, I have 5 (20) pages. May I use the xerox machine?
2. Meaningless justification: Excuse me, I have 5 (20) pages. May I use the xerox machine, because I have to make copies?
3. Sufficient justification: Excuse me, I have 5 (20) pages. May I use the xerox machine, because I'm in a rush?

The prediction was that the likelihood of help should be equivalent in Conditions 2 and 3 and greater than in Condition 1. The results provide support for this hypothesis. The proportion of persons who agreed did not show any systematic effect of the plausibility of the justifications. In addition, fewer persons in the request-only condition complied than in Conditions 2 and 3. Therefore, violations of the structure of one's past experience (deviations from the script) seem to reduce compliance. This pattern of results was not obtained when the prosocial response was effortful (in the 20-pages conditions). Rather, more persons in the sufficient justification condition complied than in Conditions 1 and 2.

"Mindlessness" is defined as ignorance of relevant information (Langer *et al.*, 1978). Mindlessness can be understood as a phenomenon similar to cue control. Cue control is defined by E. E. Jones and Gerard (1967, p. 710) as "the use of information about previously learned contingencies to trigger certain responses in the other." Much as Langer *et al.* (1978) do, Jones and Gerard (1967) argue that one person can elicit preestablished habit patterns in another.

## 3. ASYMMETRICAL CONTINGENCIES: NORMATIVE EXPLANATIONS

> Asymmetrical contingency suggests a type of interaction in which the behavior of one actor is fully contingent on the behavior of another, but the other's behavior is independently determined. (E. E. Jones & Thibaut, 1958, p. 155)

Norms can be thought of as prescriptions: "Norms say more or less specifically what should or should not be done by particular types of actors in given circumstances" (Schwartz, 1977, p. 232). As can be seen from this definition of norms, normative influence makes the behavior of an actor contingent on given circumstances. An essential part of these circumstances is other persons. If so, the perception of the plight of another person may activate a "norm of giving" (Leeds, 1963).

Schwartz (1977, pp. 235–237) has proposed a number of questions for the measurement of norms, for example, "If the School for the Blind asked you to read schoolbooks to blind children a few times a week in the afternoon or evening, would you feel a moral obligation?" One way of explaining the success of such a question is to consider the appeal as a cue for arousing the pervasive norm of social responsibility. On the one hand, the power of the School for the Blind (B) is small. On the other hand, the normative appeal exerts an additional influence on the potential helper. Thus the existence of the norm adds another social influence, other than that of the School for the Blind, which will influence the target person's (A's) behavior. In summary:

- B's normative appeal is a cue for arousing normative influence. A could presumably ignore the appeal. The range of outcomes that B can directly administer to A is extremely narrow.
- By adding the norm of social responsibility to the direct influence of the requester, B's influence over A is extended (Schopler & Bateson, 1965), and an asymmetrical contingency is established: A's behavior is contingent on the normative appeal, but B's behavior is "independently determined."

People appear to be strongly committed to the norm of social responsibility (Berkowitz & Daniels, 1963), the norm of giving (Leeds, 1963), and norms of fairness and justice (Lerner, Miller, & Holmes, 1976). To say that many persons recognize the existence of prosocial norms does not mean, however, that these norms will govern their behavior to an equal extent in all situations. The adherence to the norm depends on the awareness of the normative standard at a given time and the motivation to act in accordance with the norm (Berkowitz & Connor, 1966). Normative appeals on the basis of the norm of social responsibility may restrict A's freedom of choice (Berkowitz, 1973). Norm pressures can elicit feelings of resentment, and, as a result, the willingness to act in accordance with normative standards of conduct is reduced.

The normative appeal arouses feelings of obligation to help. In addition, the appeal may also arouse another type of motive: a desire not to get involved with someone else because the involvement reduces one's freedom of choice (Wicklund, 1974). The person could save himself from these consequences by passing the responsibility to others or by employing other techniques of denial of responsibility (Schwartz, 1977).

The restriction of independence and the resulting resentment should be dependent on at least two conditions: (1) B exaggerates the normative pressure (as in Schwartz, 1970), and (2) the normative appeal implies far-reaching duties and obligations (R. A. Jones, 1970).

Although it is clear that helping can be inhibited if the normative appeal elicits resentment, many situations minimize the potential restriction of independence. First and most obviously, the resentment is reduced if an interference with A's plans and intentions is avoided. For example, normative considerations affect the person's self-esteem. Helping behavior would be normative and would be rewarded by feelings of well-being. Therefore, the link between helpfulness and self-esteem should be emphasized. Second, the resentment is reduced if B requires assistance because of factors beyond his or her control rather than because of his or her own deficiencies (Berkowitz, 1969; Schopler & Matthews, 1965). For example, in one study helpfulness was lowest when the cause of the need was internal to the requester and controllable (Weiner, 1980). In another study (Meyer & Mulherin, 1980), controllability of cause exerted the greatest influence on willingness to help.

Finally, the resentment may be reduced if the helpfulness is based on moral convictions positively calling for prosocial responses. For example, children are influenced by simple prohibitions although they are completely irrelevant (Staub, 1971). Prosocial rules of moral conduct and prosocial moral reasoning should be emphasized more strongly, in practice as well as in theory (cf. Eisenberg-Berg, 1979; Eisenberg-Berg & Hand, 1979).

## 4. SUDDEN EMERGENCIES

An important feature of an emergency is that it requires immediate action (Latané & Darley, 1970). Therefore, the potential helper is prevented from considering the possible alternatives. A's attention is completely absorbed by the emergency. B is in a similar situation. The emergency involves threat of harm, and B is prevented from considering his or her alternatives. Under these circumstances, if A intervenes to help B, the interaction pattern can be described as a reactive contingency. The requirement for immediate action prevents both persons from planning their course of action. In summary, the following features of reactive helping are important:

- B's situation involves a threat of harm.
- The emergency is an unforeseen and rare event.
- The requirement for immediate action prevents A from planning an appropriate intervention.

The following (from Schwartz & Ben David, 1976) illustrates the basic characteristics of sudden emergencies:

> Person A participates in an experiment with an experimenter (B). B administers shocks to a rat which is described as particularly wild and uncontrollable. B is in an adjoining room near the cage of the rat. During the second series of shocks the rat escapes and attacks B.

Very rapid helping has been designated as "impulsive helping" (J. A. Piliavin, 1976). Impulsive helping is related to low ambiguousness of the emergency. A simple procedure that demonstrates the importance of unequivocal cues was used by Solomon, Solomon, and Stone (1978). These investigators compared the frequency of intervention in an audio condition with an audio plus visual condition. Ambiguity was defined as audio plus visual (low) versus audio-only (high) presentation of an emergency. More help was found in the audio plus visual condition (67%) than in the audio-only condition (30%).

One of the clearest results obtained within simulations of emergencies is that a bystander is more likely to intervene if alone than if in the presence of others who might also respond to the emergency (Latané & Darley, 1970). Later studies (Latané & Darley, 1976; Schwartz & Gottlieb, 1976) have showed that three social influence processes have independent effects: diffusion of responsibility, pluralistic ignorance, and evaluation apprehension. Diffusion of responsibility requires that A thinks that others who could also intervene are present. Pluralistic ignorance requires that A is aware of the responses of other bystanders. Finally, evaluation apprehension requires that A believes others are aware of his or her responses.

In a number of studies only an audio channel connected the victim with the bystander. Therefore, the emergency was not defined unambiguously. Depending on the ambiguity of the emergency situation, bystanders seem to inhibit each other's responsiveness. Solomon *et al.* (1978) found such an inhibition of prosocial responses only in their audio condition. Moreover, J. A. Piliavin and Piliavin (1972), I. M. Piliavin, Piliavin, and Rodin (1975), and I. M. Piliavin, Rodin, and Piliavin (1969) found no indications of an inhibition of prosocial responses as a function of the number of people present. In their field experiments, emergencies were simulated in a face-to-face public situation of a subway car. Presumably, this audio plus visual condition (Solomon *et al.*, 1978) permitted the bystanders to infer unambiguously an emergency.

In summary, the influence of social inhibitions seems to depend on the ambiguity of the emergency situation. As was demonstrated in a study by Yakimovich and Saltz (1971), the frequency of intervention in an audio-only condition can be increased by a simple device: a cry for help. Moreover, the cry for help has an additional consequence: The social inhibition of prosocial responses vanishes (Clark & Word, 1972). The more ambiguous emergency elicited less helping than the unambiguous emergency, and was also the typical situation to show a social inhibition of prosocial responses.

## 5. MUTUALITY OF PROSOCIAL RESPONSES

Reciprocity is an important feature of social interactions (Bierhoff, 1981; Gouldner, 1960; Triandis, 1978). The principle suggests that people should reciprocate whatever positive or negative consequences accrue from others. For example, one can easily imagine an ever increasing cycle of prosocial responses and trust (cf. Rubin, 1973). The reciprocity principle introduces the time dimension into social interactions:

> Once interaction is seen as taking place over time, we may note that the norm of reciprocity so structures social relations that, between the time of Ego's provision of the gratification and the time of Alter's repayment, falls the shadow of indebtedness. (Gouldner, 1960, p. 174)

Mutual contingencies are "reciprocally contingent interactions" (E. E. Jones and Thibaut, 1958). E. E. Jones and Gerard (1967, p. 715) define mutual contingency as

> a type of dyadic interaction in which the responses of each person are jointly determined by the responses of the other and by his own motivated plans. That is, the actions of both parties are to an important extent purposeful and self-determined, but each is responsive to the other.

The reciprocity principle has a fairly large impact on social behavior, for example, on aggression, self-disclosure, and prosocial responses.

What are the distinctive features of "reciprocally contingent interactions"?

- Person A cannot attain his or her goal without assistance from B, and vice versa. The attainment of their primary goals is facilitated by coordinated social responses.
- The reciprocity principle establishes a set of reciprocal demands and obligations.
- The reciprocity principle provides stability to a social relationship, and a long-range coordination of response sequences can be achieved.

That the reciprocity norm is a determinant of prosocial as well as aggressive behavior is of special significance. According to Gouldner's view, altruism and aggression are interrelated. Gouldner (1960, p. 171) states that the norm of reciprocity "makes two interrelated, minimal demands: (1) people should help those who have helped them, and (2) people should not injure those who have helped them." Although the first assumption seems to be empirically valid, the second is questionable. An interesting experimental effort to study this second assumption was undertaken by Nacci, Stapleton, and Tedeschi (1973). They found that persons who received benefits provided as many shocks to the other person as did persons who were not given benefits. The authors conclude that there were two norms of reciprocity that were important determinants of whether a person would reciprocate a prosocial or an aggressive response. The first of these, which they called the positive norm of reciprocity, refers only to obligations to return favors. The second was called the negative reciprocity norm and refers only to the right of a person to harm those who have attacked him or her.

Mutual interactions are—in sharp contrast to asymmetrical contingencies—advantageous to both persons. From a general perspective, the advantages are as follows:

1. The likelihood of boomerang effects as a result of unilateral norm pressure and restriction of freedom is minimized. A and B have no special obligations beyond reciprocity, and such negative feelings as resentment and hostility are not likely to be aroused.

2. The recipient of help is not seen as weak or vulnerable. The recipient's response to help, of course, is not always positive. Fisher and Nadler (1974) demonstrated that the recipient of unilateral help may experience self-esteem problems. Perceived similarity of donor and recipient emphasizes the negative implications of the benefit. B's social comparison with the benefactor accentuates personal weakness, inferiority, and perceived dependency. The recipient's self-concept influences how the positive and negative features of the benefit are weighted (Nadler, Fisher, & Streufert, 1976; Nadler, Altman, & Fisher, 1979).

## 6. SUMMARY AND CONCLUSIONS

According to E. E. Jones and Gerard (1967), four patterns of social interaction can be distinguished: pseudocontingency, asymmetrical contingency, reactive contingency, and mutual contingency. This conceptual framework should serve two major functions in the social psychology of prosocial behavior:

1. It can provide an outline of the necessary conditions of helping behavior. For example, to explain prosocial behavior in pseudocontingencies we must refer to the "simple synchronization of responses." As we have previously seen, this situation calls for appropriate cues, especially requests, that elicit the notice of the potential benefactor. On the other hand, given the features of the requirement for immediate action and low predictability, prosocial responses in reactive contingencies are influenced by such determinants as the ambiguity of the emergency and training.

2. It can provide a useful bridge between theories of prosocial behavior and of classes of social interaction (Bierhoff, 1980). For example, the theory of promotive tension (Hornstein, 1972) can explain actions that involve pseudocontingent relationships. The simple coordination between victim and benefactor is simulated by the lost-letter technique. On the other hand, equity and reciprocity arise from a symbolic representation of the self and the other person. The actors impute reciprocal trust and obligations to themselves and to the other actor. Finally, normative appeals in terms of the norm of giving or the norm of social

responsibility focus primarily on asymmetrical relationships. People act within a normative structure and conform to widely shared standards of conduct.

These considerations are intended to be heuristic rather than neatly derivable from a general theory of prosocial behavior. The four classes of interaction provide one useful way of organizing what is a vast amount of data and minitheories. They are best seen as tools for analyzing the field and for describing a number of essential features.

ACKNOWLEDGMENTS

I wish to thank Janusz Reykowski for his helpful comments on this chapter.

## 7. REFERENCES

Berkowitz, L. Resistance to improper dependency relationships. *Journal of Experimental Social Psychology*, 1969, *5*, 283–294.

Berkowitz, L. Reactance and the unwillingness to help others. *Psychological Bulletin*, 1973, *79*, 310–317.

Berkowitz, L., & Connor, W. H. Success, failure, and social responsibility. *Journal of Personality and Social Psychology*, 1966, *4*, 664–669.

Berkowitz, L., & Daniels, L. R. Responsibility and dependency. *Journal of Abnormal and Social Psychology*, 1963, *66*, 429–436.

Bierhoff, H. W. *Prosocial behavior*. Darmstadt: UTB, 1980.

Bierhoff, H. W. Exchange theory. In H. Werbik & H. J. Kaiser (Eds.), *Key-words in social psychology*. Munich: Fink, 1981.

Clark, R. D., & Word, L. E. Why don't bystanders help? Because of ambiguity? *Journal of Personality and Social Psychology*, 1972, *24*, 392–400.

Darley, J. M., & Latané, B. Norms and normative behavior: Field studies of social interdependence. In J. Macaulay & L. Berkowitz (Eds.), *Altruism and helping behavior*. New York: Academic Press, 1970.

Eisenberg-Berg, N. Development of children's prosocial moral judgment. *Developmental Psychology*, 1979, *15*, 128–137.

Eisenberg-Berg, N., & Hand, M. The relationship of preschoolers' reasoning about prosocial moral conflicts to prosocial behavior. *Child Development*, 1979, *50*, 356–363.

Fisher, J. D., & Nadler, A. The effect of similarity between donor and recipient on recipient's reaction to help. *Journal of Applied Social Psychology*, 1974, *4*, 230–243.

Gouldner, A. W. The norm of reciprocity: A preliminary statement. *American Sociological Review*, 1960, *25*, 161–178.

Hornstein, H. A. Promotive tension: The basis of prosocial behavior from a Lewinian perspective. *Journal of Social Issues*, 1972, *28*(3), 191–218.

Innes, J. M., & Gilroy, S. The semantics of asking a favor: Asking for help in three countries. *Journal of Social Psychology*, 1980, *110*, 3–7.

Jones, E. E., & Gerard, H. B. *Foundations of social psychology*. New York: Wiley, 1967.

Jones, E. E., & Thibaut, J. W. Interaction goals as bases of inference in interpersonal perception. In R. Tagiuri & L. Petrullo (Eds.), *Person perception and interpersonal behavior*. Stanford, Calif.: Stanford University Press, 1958.

Jones, R. A. Volunteering to help: The effects of choice, dependency, and anticipated dependency. *Journal of Personality and Social Psychology*, 1970, *14*, 121–129.

Langer, E. J. Rethinking the role of thought in social interaction. In J. H. Harvey, W. Ickes, & R. F. Kidd (Eds.), *New directions in attribution research* (Vol. 2). Hillsdale, N.J.: Lawrence Erlbaum, 1978.

Langer, E. J., & Abelson, R. P. The semantics of asking a favor: How to succeed in getting help without really dying. *Journal of Personality and Social Psychology*, 1972, *24*, 26–32.

Langer, E. J., Blank, A., & Chanowitz, B. The mindlessness of ostensibly thoughtful action: The role of "placebic" information in interpersonal interaction. *Journal of Personality and Social Psychology*, 1978, *36*, 635–642.

Latané, B., & Darley, J. M. *The unresponsive bystander: Why doesn't he help?* New York: Appleton-Century-Crofts, 1970.

Latané, B., & Darley, J. M. *Help in a crisis: Bystander response to an emergency*. Morristown, N.J.: General Learning Press, 1976.

Leeds, R. Altruism and the norm of giving. *Merrill-Palmer Quarterly*, 1963, *9*, 229–240.

Lerner, M. J., Miller, D. T., & Holmes, J. G. Deserving and the emergence of forms of justice. In L. Berkowitz & E. Walster (Eds.), *Advances in experimental social psychology* (Vol. 9). New York: Academic Press, 1976.

Meyer, J. P., & Mulherin, A. From attribution to helping: An analysis of the mediating effects of affect and expectancy. *Journal of Personality and Social Psychology*, 1980, *39*, 201–210.

Mikula, G. *The semantics of asking a favor and prosocial behavior*. Reports from the Department of Psychology, University of Graz, 1977.

Moriarty, T. Crime, commitment, and the responsive bystander: Two field experiments. *Journal of Personality and Social Psychology*, 1975, *31*, 370–376.

Nacci, P., Stapleton, R. E., & Tedeschi, J. T. An empirical restatement of the reciprocity norm. *Journal of Social Psychology*, 1973, *91*, 263–271.

Nadler, A., Fisher, J. D., & Streufert, S. When helping hurts: Effects of donor-recipient similarity and recipient self-esteem on reactions to aid. *Journal of Personality*, 1976, *44*, 392–409.

Nadler, A., Altman, A., & Fisher, J. D. Helping is not enough: Recipient's reactions to aid as a function of positive and negative information about the self. *Journal of Personality*, 1979, *47*, 615–628.

Piliavin, I. M., Rodin, J., & Piliavin, J. A. Good samaritanism: An underground phenomenon? *Journal of Personality and Social Psychology*, 1969, *13*, 289–299.

Piliavin, I. M., Piliavin, J. A., & Rodin, J. Costs, diffusion, and the stigmatized victim. *Journal of Personality and Social Psychology*, 1975, *32*, 429–438.

Piliavin, J. A. *Impulsive helping, arousal, and diffusion of responsibility*. Paper presented at the meeting of the International Congress of Psychology, Paris, July 1976.

Piliavin, J. A., & Piliavin, I. M. Effect of blood on reactions to a victim. *Journal of Personality and Social Psychology*, 1972, *23*, 353–361.

Rubin, Z. *Liking and loving: An invitation to social psychology*. New York: Holt, Rinehart & Winston, 1973.

Schopler, J., & Bateson, N. The power of dependence. *Journal of Personality and Social Psychology*, 1965, *2*, 247–254.

Schopler, J., & Matthews, M. W. The influence of the perceived causal locus of partner's dependency on the use of interpersonal power. *Journal of Personality and Social Psychology*, 1965, *2*, 609–612.

Schwartz, S. H. Elicitation of moral obligation and self-sacrificing behavior: An experimental study of volunteering to be a bone marrow donor. *Journal of Personality and Social Psychology*, 1970, *15*, 283–293.

Schwartz, S. H. Normative influences on altruism. In L. Berkowitz (Ed.), *Advances in experimental social psychology* (Vol. 10). New York: Academic Press, 1977.

Schwartz, S. H., & Ben David, A. Responsibility and helping in an emergency: Effects of blame, ability and denial of responsibility. *Sociometry*, 1976, *39*, 406–415.

Schwartz, S. H., & Gottlieb, A. Bystander reactions to a violent theft: Crime in Jerusalem. *Journal of Personality and Social Psychology*, 1976, *34*, 1188–1199.

Shaffer, D. R., Rogel, M., & Hendrick, C. Intervention in the library: The effect of increased responsibility on bystander's willingness to prevent a theft. *Journal of Applied Social Psychology*, 1975, *5*, 303–319.

Solomon, L. Z., Solomon, H., & Stone, R. Helping as a function of number of bystanders and ambiguity of emergency. *Personality and Social Psychology Bulletin*, 1978, *4*, 318–321.

Staub, E. Helping a person in distress: The influence of implicit and explicit "rules" of conduct on children and adults. *Journal of Personality and Social Psychology*, 1971, *17*, 137–144.

Triandis, H. C. Some universals of social behavior. *Personality and Social Psychology Bulletin*, 1978, *4*, 1–16.

Weiner, B. A cognitive (attribution)-emotion-action model of motivated behavior: An analysis of judgments of help-giving. *Journal of Personality and Social Psychology*, 1980, *39*, 186–200.

Wicklund, R. A. *Freedom and reactance*. Potomac, Md.: Lawrence Erlbaum, 1974.

Yakimovich, D., & Saltz, E. Helping behavior: The cry for help. *Psychonomic Science*, 1971, *23*, 427–428.

# 16

# The Helpfulness of Urban Villagers

Charles Korte

## 1. INTRODUCTION

The failure of people in urban settings to lend assistance to strangers who need help has provoked consideration of many factors that have proved useful in the explanation of helping behavior, for example, diffusion of responsibility, environmental overload, and time pressures. This suggests that there might be equally valuable lessons to be learned if we could find and analyze settings where helpfulness toward strangers occurred to a high degree. This would be particularly interesting if such settings could be found within an urban environment. One of the most intriguing accounts of a helpful place is Jane Jacobs's description of the North End of Boston, a working-class Italian neighborhood that figured prominently in her now-classic book *The Death and Life of Great American Cities* (Jacobs, 1961). Jacobs tells of the high level of personal safety experienced by persons in this neighborhood, both residents and outside visitors alike, because of the virtual absence of street crime. Local residents attributed this safety to the readiness of shopkeepers, passersby, and window kibitzers to intervene on behalf of persons threatened with any kind of street danger, whether mugging, harassment, or car accidents.

This particular neighborhood quality has been noted in other urban communities by different observers (e.g., Gans, 1962; Newman, 1973) and can perhaps best be termed an *urban village* quality. An urban village

CHARLES KORTE • Division of University Studies, North Carolina State University, Raleigh, North Carolina 27650.

appears to be distinctive on environmental, geographical, and social, as well as behavioral, criteria. Typically it is a distinctive enclave within the city, forming a geographical area that is clearly demarcated as a neighborhood. The physical design of these settings is commonly characterized by small-scale features (short streets, low-rise buildings, high density of units) together with an active street life. Identification with the neighborhood seems to be at a high level among the residents. Socially, urban villages are regarded as having a high level of familiarity and social contact among residents and a high level of residential stability (e.g., many residents having lived there a long time). For our purposes here, the interesting behavioral characteristic of an urban village is its helpfulness, toward strangers as well as among the residents themselves. This reputation of helpfulness has been attributed to various features of the urban village. Jacobs (1961) saw the physical design and the diversity of activity in an urban village as critical. People use space more when there is a small-scale physical layout and this, together with the diverse, round-the-clock activity of an urban village, means there is more street life in an urban village and more of a feeling of responsibility among residents for what happens on the street. Thus the stranger who needs assistance finds numerous bystanders with feelings of responsibility for what goes on within this enclave. Newman (1973) has developed a similar analysis, focusing more on specific architectural features that enhance territorial responsibility.

Gans (1962), on the other hand, traces social behavior in the urban village to the social backgrounds of the residents. Often the inhabitants of these urban villages have rural origins and are bound together within the social traditions and public norms of a particular ethnic subculture, which often stresses responsibility for one another's well-being as well as for the well-being of strangers who need assistance. These neighborhoods are also seen as somewhat insulated from the disintegrating forces of the surrounding urban environment (e.g., high residential mobility and population heterogeneity) and hence able to maintain a social atmosphere that supports helpfulness and intimacy.

What is of course immediately striking about this picture of urban districts with higher helpfulness is that it runs counter to the view that various forms of helpfulness, for example, helpfulness toward strangers who need assistance, suffer a decline in urban environments. There is at this point good evidence, documented elsewhere (Korte, 1978, 1981), that in North America the likelihood of helping a stranger is lower in cities than it is in small towns. Yet, although this basic city–town comparison in helpfulness is informative, it tells us little about the within-city variations, which may be significant and, if significant, should illuminate considerably our understanding of the determinants of naturalistic occurrences of helpfulness. Perhaps we will discover after all these years that Kitty Genovese's main misfortune was not that she lived in a city, but that she lived in the wrong neighborhood of that city!

Data to evaluate the idea that there are particular districts of cities that show higher levels of helpfulness are extremely scarce. There are a few studies that have compared helpfulness in suburbs with center-city areas (e.g., Rushton, 1978), but the only systematic comparison among a number of different districts within the same city is a study carried out in Amsterdam by Korte, Ypma, and Toppen (1975), plus a very recent study carried out by Ayvalioglu and Korte in Philadelphia and Pittsburgh. The Amsterdam study involved, first, a social survey of Amsterdam residents to identify those neighborhoods that might be regarded as urban villages: Survey respondents were asked to rate a list of Amsterdam neighborhoods in terms of how friendly and helpful the inhabitants were toward each other and toward outsiders. This resulted in the identification of two neighborhoods, the Jordaan and Kinkerbuurt, with very high ratings on this variable. Both of these neighborhoods are old, stable, working-class districts located near the center of Amsterdam; in many respects they would appear to fit the picture of urban villages. The actual helpfulness shown toward strangers in these neighborhoods was then compared with the helpfulness shown in the two neighborhoods in Amsterdam that ranked lowest on helpfulness in the survey study, Buitenveldert and Apollolaanbuurt. Helpfulness was assessed using three different naturalistic measures: the response to a request for cooperation in a street interview, the response to the sight of another pedestrian dropping a key without seeming to notice it, and the response to a bewildered pedestrian scrutinizing a map in an effort to get oriented.

The results of this study lent no support to the expectation that higher levels of helpfulness would be found in particular districts of the city that were seen as having urban village social patterns; none of the four neighborhoods was different from any of the others on any of the three measures. These results were equally surprising to Amsterdam residents, who found it hard to believe that there were not striking differences between these two groups of "helpful" and "unhelpful" neighborhoods. In addition, a more recent repeat of this study carried out by Ayvalioglu and Korte in Philadelphia and Pittsburgh produced essentially identical results. Three helpfulness measures were administered in four districts in each of these cities, with again no indication of any differences among districts in terms of the helpfulness shown toward a stranger.

These two studies bring into question the idea that helpfulness is influenced by overall neighborhood qualities that relate to the urban village stereotypes; perhaps the "helpfulness" of urban villagers is nothing but a stereotype. On the other hand, there are several reasons for believing that "helpful" urban villages might still be a genuine phenomenon. First, it may be that helpfulness is expressed in ways other than those picked up by the measures used so far. Perhaps helpfulness is directed only toward the more familiar figures of the local scene, for example, neighbors, friends, and relatives. If urban villagers are more genuinely helpful in this way, it is easy to imagine how the impression of this trait could be generalized, perhaps without justification, to include helpfulness toward strangers. Second, the previous studies may not have located instances of "genuine" urban villages. It may be that urban villages are a rather short-lived phenomenon, depending upon the sometimes temporary circumstances of rural-to-urban migration and the resulting stable, homogeneous, ethnic enclaves. The present-day versions of urban villages may in fact be best found within the cities of the developing nations, which are presently undergoing extraordinary population growth swelled by significant rural-to-urban migration. These new urban residents frequently settle into "squatter" neighborhoods, which remain quite stable and are composed of lower- and working-class persons with rural origins.

In light of these considerations, a study was recently carried out by Korte and Ayvalioglu (for a partial report see Korte & Ayvalioglu, 1981) to see whether "helpful" urban villages could be found in the cities of a developing nation, Turkey, and whether the social behavior of these urban villagers was distinctive in a variety of different types of social relationships, including those involving neighbors and relatives as well as strangers. Such a test should resolve many of the present uncertainties surrounding the reality of "helpful" districts within an urban environment and may also offer some insights into the factors that foster helpfulness in an urban setting.

## 2. HELPFULNESS IN TURKISH URBAN VILLAGES

The squatter settlements, or urban villages, of Istanbul and Ankara bear a close resemblance to those in other major cities within developing nations (Karpat, 1976; Levine, 1973; Suzuki, 1964; Yasa, 1966; Yavuz, Keles, & Geray, 1978). The settlements can best be described as districts of low quality housing erected illegally on unused land by migrants to the city who find, with their limited economic means, no other viable alternative for housing. Once erected, these settlements are quite stable, with several in Turkey having persisted now into the third generation of inhabitants. Residence within the settlement is often organized according to the particular village or rural district from which the settlers originate. New migrants from a particular village in rural Turkey will commonly seek out fellow villagers who preceded them in their migration to Istanbul or Ankara and join them in that part of the settlement. The squatter settlements form a significant part of the urban population in these two cities; at present, 59% of the total population of Ankara and 45% of the Istanbul population reside in these settlements.

Accounts of the social patterns within the squatter settlements (Karpat, 1976; Yasa, 1966) suggest that the forms of social behavior usually associated with urban villages are attributed to Turkish settlements as well. The residents have been depicted as helpful, supportive of one another, and engaged in extensive mutual aid networks involving friends, family, and neighbors. There is good reason to expect, then, that measures of helpfulness will show these Istanbul and Ankara urban villagers to be distinctively different from their nonsquatter urban counterparts. There is little mention of social behavior toward strangers, except that these squatter residents are seen as strong adherents to traditional Islamic norms, which stress the importance of assisting strangers.

The basic design of the study consisted of a comparison of different residential groups in Istanbul and Ankara on various measures of helpfulness. There were four different samples of squatter residents, representing two squatter neighborhoods in Istanbul (Zeytinburnu and Gaziosmanpasa) and two in Ankara (Kaleici-Yenidogan and Sentepe). These were selected in consultation with municipal housing officials in the two cities who were asked to name the two squatter settlements that were most representative of this settlement type; the neighborhoods selected were those most frequently cited by the officials. Eight nonsquatter neighborhoods were also selected for study, four from each of the two cities. These were selected on the basis of a social survey that presented respondents, 173 randomly selected sidewalk pedestrians in Istanbul and Ankara, with descriptions (in Turkish) of four different types of neighborhoods and asked them, for each type, to pick from a list of city neighborhoods the one that best illustrated that type. The four neighborhoods most cited as illustrating each type in the two cities (center-city upperclass residential area; centrally located, mixed commercial and apartment district; mixed commercial and working-class neighborhood; and suburban neighborhood) became the eight nonsquatter neighborhoods in the study.

Helpfulness was assessed by means of a set of naturalistic measures of helpfulness toward strangers as well as an interview study that measured the level of helpfulness among neighbors, friends, and relatives. The set of naturalistic measures consisted of three different helpfulness measures administered by two Turkish researchers, one male and the other female. The response to each measure was rated on a 3-point scale. The first measure was a request for change (squatter sample, $n$ = 110; nonsquatter sample, $n$ = 236). The second was a request for cooperation in responding to a short questionnaire ($n$ = 109 and 228, respectively). The third measure was a staged mishap, consisting of the researcher dropping the top box of an awkward load and proceeding with ineffectual efforts to retrieve it ($n$ = 110 and 239, respectively). With each measure, subjects were randomly selected pedestrians from the different sample neighborhoods. Multiple visitations to each neighborhood for data collection and counterbalancing of the order of data collection were done to maximize the comparability of the data from the different neighborhoods.

The interview study was carried out with a nonsystematic sample of 101 squatter residents and 89 nonsquatter residents in Istanbul and Ankara. Efforts at obtaining a random sample of respondents for the interview study were defeated by innumerable practical difficulties in Turkey; the researchers simply used informal procedures to obtain as wide a cross-section of respondents as possible within the different neighborhoods. The response rate of persons asked to complete the interview was in fact very high, approaching 100%. Included in the interview were three items related to helpfulness. Respondents were asked to report how many different types of help they had exchanged with neighbors, friends, and then relatives in the past 6 months. This was indicated by having respondents check, from a list of 16 types of everyday help (e.g., borrowing household items, looking after children, helping with jobs), those that had occurred in the last 6 months.

With these data, it was then possible to evaluate whether Turkish urban villagers give evidence of greater involvement in helpful deeds with friends, relatives, neighbors, and strangers. Of additional interest, though not of central concern to the intraurban focus of this chapter, was the presence in this study of a nonurban sample, drawn from four different towns in Turkey quite remote from metropolitan centers. Each of the helpfulness measures described above was administered in these four towns, thus creating a nonurban sample to serve as a basis for comparison.

The results from these different measures were strikingly consistent, for on each of the measures used the Turkish urban villagers showed significantly greater helpfulness than those urbanites living in nonsquatter neighborhoods. First, on the naturalistic measures, the urban villagers showed significantly more helpfulness toward strangers on each of the three measures used: assisting with a request for change (89% helpful vs. 55% in the rest of the city), cooperating with an interview request (94% vs. 77%), and helping with a dropped box (92% vs. 54%). Second, on the self-report measures from the interview study, the urban villagers showed a greater exchange of help in each of the three relationships that were examined: with their neighbors, with their friends, and with their relatives. All differences were significant at the .05 level.

With results showing such a clear differentiation of this one segment of the urban population on a variety of different types of helpfulness, it is interesting to examine other and more detailed neighborhood comparisons. The results from the sample of the four Turkish towns showed virtually no differences in the level of helpfulness on any of the different measures between squatter settlements and the towns. These two groups were significantly different only on the extent of helpfulness occurring between friends, with the squatters reporting the higher levels. In addition, helpfulness in the towns exceeded that in the nonsquatter urban neighborhoods of Istanbul and Ankara to a significant degree on all measures.

Comparisons among the four different squatter settlements, using only the naturalistic measures (in view of the relative scarcity of data from the interview study), showed some consistent differences though not of a large order. What is interesting is that for each of the three measures of helpfulness toward strangers, the highest levels of helpfulness always occurred in the same settlement (Sentepe, in Ankara), whereas another settlement (Zeytinburn, in Istanbul) was the least helpful squatter neighborhood on two of the measures and next to last on the third measure. Finally, comparison of the different nonsquatter urban neighborhoods also showed a consistent ranking of these areas in terms of their level of helpfulness toward strangers, though again these differences did not reach statistical significance. For each of the three measures, the most helpful nonsquatter area, in both Istanbul and Ankara, was the working-class neighborhood; the least helpful one was the suburban neighborhood, followed by the center-city area. The level of helpfulness obtained in the working-class neighborhoods was in fact not much different from that obtained in the squatter neighborhoods; for each of the three measures of helpfulness toward strangers, helpfulness was higher in squatter versus working-class neighborhoods, but this difference was significant only for the dropped-box measure. Overall, then, the urban villager thesis was strongly supported by the Turkish data: In these neighborhoods, helpfulness toward strangers and among neighbors, friends, and relatives was indeed higher than what was found in the other parts of these cities.

## 3. CONCLUSIONS

The results of this study appear to be unique in that they do show empirical verification of significant *within*-city variations in several types of helpfulness. The differences in helpfulness among different districts within the city even exceeded those obtained in the overall urban-non-urban comparison. What seems particularly striking about the results is that the Turkish urban villagers were not only more helpful than the urbanites in other parts of Istanbul and Ankara in their interaction with neighbors, friends, and relatives, but also more helpful toward strangers. These squatter settlements are indeed areas of the city where a stranger needing assistance finds his needs readily met by the people there, ranging from a low of 89% helpfulness on the request-for-change measure to a high of 94% helpfulness on the request-for-interview measure.

How might we account for the high level of helpfulness obtained in these Turkish urban villages? It is clear that this study can only suggest factors that might have led to the high levels of helpfulness; it was not designed to evaluate the influence of any single factor. It also seems highly probable that the types of helpfulness examined in this study are influenced by a multiplicity of factors. One promising explanation for the high level of helpfulness shown toward *strangers* in these Turkish urban villages is that it might have resulted from the combined presence of two factors: an active street life, and the residential character of the area. It may be that neither of these two factors alone leads to increased helpfulness but that in combination they do enhance the level of helpfulness. Indirect support for this hypothesis can be found in the data from the other areas of Ankara and Istanbul. As we have seen, helpfulness was much lower in the suburban neighborhoods and the center-city districts. The former are residential but lack an active street life, the latter have an active street life but lack a residential character. Where both these factors were present, that is, the squatter settlements and working-class neighborhoods, helpfulness was higher. That a residential area with an active street leads to greater helpfulness toward strangers is consistent with Jacobs's (1961) explanation that in such settings there are greater feelings of territoriality and an accompanying feeling of responsibility toward local events that require assistance. Impressions of these helpful areas did suggest that interacting with a stranger was a rather natural and easy extension of the ongoing public interaction among people in these areas, a feature that was clearly absent in the suburban and center-city areas.

It is also possible to interpret the helpfulness in the urban villages in terms of the lower socioeconomic status of the residents. For example, social norms of the urban villagers, in contrast to those that prevail in higher socioeconomic areas of the city, may facilitate responding in public to a stranger who needs assistance. The same contrast between the helpfulness of the squatter settlements and working-class neighborhoods versus the suburbs and center-city areas supports a social class interpretation of the results. Further research by Ayvalioglu and Korte is under way that will evaluate the variation in social norms among some of these different districts of Istanbul and Ankara.

It is also interesting to consider the applicability of environmental explanations for the squatters' helpfulness. Substantial support has accumulated for the view that helpfulness declines in situations of high environmental demand and stimulation (Korte, 1978, 1981); yet the results of this study seem to suggest that any negative effects of environmental "overload" in the squatter settlements were more than offset by some of the other factors mentioned above. The squatter settlements are indeed noisy, busy, complex environments that may overload the people living there. Yet helpfulness was high, whereas the least helpful urban districts were the quiet and sedate suburbs where residents and pedestrians should be least overloaded.

There seems good reason to relate the helpfulness shown by the urban villagers toward relatives, friends, and neighbors to the social and cultural factors present within those areas. As was mentioned earlier, many of the residents are long-time residents, quite familiar with each other, and share a common rural, and ethnic, background. It is easy to see how these factors could foster greater helpful involvement among friends, neighbors, and relatives, and there is evidence elsewhere to show the links among some of these features, for example, between length of residence and social contact among neighbors (Kasarda & Janowitz, 1974). In the Turkish squatter settlements, it seems likely that much of this helpfulness reflects the social patterns of the settlement culture—traditional, Islamic, and rural background—which stresses the importance of generosity and responsibility toward other people (Karpat, 1976). In addition, a high degree of need and interdependence is generated by the low economic status of these people and their precarious position vis-à-vis the legality of their residential status. Extensive mutual aid is clearly demanded by the often difficult circumstances of these Turkish urban villagers. In fact, it is encouraging to see that these people are particularly helpful as well toward strangers in their areas, when there are clearly grounds for a more uncharitable response toward strangers especially if they are regarded as outsiders.

This study has shown that significant intraurban variations in helpfulness do exist and has supported the view that urban villages in particular are areas where strangers, as well as friends, relatives, and neighbors, are assisted to a high degree. What remains are the questions whether such results are specific to Turkish and other cities of the developing world, and whether the helpfulness within urban villages can be exploited to advance our understanding of helping behavior.

## 4. REFERENCES

Gans, H. *The urban villagers.* New York: Free Press, 1962.

Jacobs, J. *The death and life of great American cities.* New York: Vintage Books, 1961.

Karpat, K. *The Gecekondu, rural migration and urbanization.* London: Cambridge University Press, 1976.

Kasarda, J., & Janowitz, M. Community attachment in mass society. *American Sociological Review,* 1974, *39,* 328–339.

Korte, C. Helpfulness in the urban environment. In A. Baum, J. Singer, & S. Valins (Eds.), *Advances in environmental psychology* (Vol. 1). Hillsdale, N.J.: Lawrence Erlbaum, 1978.

Korte, C. Constraints on helping behavior in an urban environment. In J. P. Rushton & R. Sorrentino (Eds.), *Altruism and helping behavior.* Hillsdale, N.J.: Lawrence Erlbaum, 1981.

Korte, C., & Ayvalioglu, N. Helpfulness in Turkey: Cities, towns, and urban villages. *Journal of Cross-Cultural Psychology,* 1981, *12,* 123–141.

Korte, C., Ypma, I., & Toppen, A. Helpfulness in Dutch society as a function of urbanization and environmental input level. *Journal of Personality and Social Psychology,* 1975, *32,* 996–1003.

Levine, N. Old culture, new culture: A study of migrants in Ankara, Turkey. *Social Forces,* 1973, *51,* 355–368.

Newman, O. *Defensible space.* New York: Collier Books, 1973.

Rushton, J. P. Urban density and altruism: Helping strangers in a Canadian city, suburb, and small town. *Psychological Reports,* 1978, *43,* 987–990.

Suzuki, P. Encounters with Istanbul: Urban peasants and rural peasants. *International Journal of Comparative Sociology,* 1964, *5,* 208–216.

Yasa, I. *Ankara squatter families.* Ankara, Turkey: Ministry of Health and Social Welfare, 1966.

Yavuz, E., Keles, R., & Geray, C. *Urbanism: Problems, applications, and policy.* Ankara, Turkey: Ankara University Press, 1978.

# IV
# HELP SEEKING AND HELP RECEIVING

# Introduction

Daniel Bar-Tal

To focus only on help giving while studying interactions involving helping behavior can be compared to watching only a half-court during a basketball game. In order to understand the dynamics of helping interactions, it is necessary to study all the parts of the helping sequence—*help seeking, help giving,* and *help receiving.* The sequence involves acts and reactions. That is, a behavior of one person functions as a stimulus for the other person, and in turn the reaction of the latter person functions as a stimulus for the former person, and so it may continue. The dynamism and mutual influence are the essence of any interpersonal interaction, including helping interactions.

*Help giving* often comes as a result of help seeking. *Help seeking* indicates that a person realizes he has a need and cannot satisfy it alone, but only with others' help. It therefore involves identifying one's own needs, and deciding whether and how to seek help from another person. Help seeking depends on various skills and can take different forms. For example, it depends on the ability to identify one's own needs, to recognize a potential helper, and to emit signals indicating the need. Also, the signaling of help seeking can take the form of directly approaching the potential helper, indirectly approaching, or signaling passively.

Social and developmental psychologists have largely neglected the investigation of help seeking. Future study of helping interactions, however, will have to focus more on this part of the sequence since help seeking is a very important behavior in human life. Individuals constantly seek help, starting as infants and finishing as old people. Too, they look for different forms of help ranging from psychotherapeutic or welfare help to aid from friends or neighbors.

Help seeking can be negative, reflecting dependence and maladjustment, or positive, reflecting adaptation and intelligent use of resources. The evaluation of help seeking as adaptive or maladaptive depends on when, for what, and how individuals seek help. And there are cultural as well as individual differences in the performance and evaluation of help seeking behavior.

The chapter by DePaulo, Leiphart, and Dull analyzes aspects of help seeking behavior and describes several studies that investigated this behavior. The authors demonstrate that help seeking behavior is determined by personal variables as well as by situational factors. This chapter is one of the few written contributions to the understanding of how people seek help.

While studying help giving, it is also necessary to investigate the consequences of this act. Whereas little attention has been given to the helper's reaction, much more has been directed at the recipient's. One interesting finding from the latter line of research is that recipients of help do not necessarily react positively to help receiving. Investigators have focused especially on the negative consequences for the recipient, and it has been suggested that the recipient may experience an aversive state of indebtedness, reactance, loss of power, loss of self-esteem, or loss of status.

*Help receiving* is frequent among individuals, groups, and nations. The study of help receiving has important implications for both the helper and the recipient. Helpers are often surprised by the recipient's negative reaction, and recipients often decide to avoid receiving help because of aversive feelings. Help giving and help receiving, however, need not be negative experiences. The study of when, how, and whom to help is an important future direction of research that can clarify the recipient's reactions.

Three chapters by Rosen, by Worchel, and by Nadler and Fisher shed light on the consequences of helping behavior. Rosen and also Worchel discuss possible outcomes of helping acts for the helper and recipient. Whereas Rosen, however, focuses on status differentiation, Worchel considers reallocation of power. Rosen suggests that helping behavior may promote helper–recipient status differences, and that whether this outcome occurs depends on situational and personal variables. Discussing power differences, only one aspect of status differentiation, Worchel suggests that individuals gain power by giving help and lose power by receiving it. Nadler and Fisher focus on the negative outcomes of help receiving for the recipient; they suggest that receiving help may be a self-threatening experience for the recipient. They also delineate the conditions that foster negative reaction by the recipient.

# 17

# Help Seeking and Social Interaction

## Person, Situation, and Process Considerations

Bella M. DePaulo, Vicki Leiphart, and W. R. Dull

## 1. INTRODUCTION

By the hundreds of studies they have already conducted on altruism, psychologists have amply demonstrated their concern that people in need of help should obtain the necessary and appropriate resources. However, this research has focused almost exclusively on help that is initiated by someone else. In contrast, the process whereby people actively seek the help that they themselves want or need, despite its clear importance in medical, psychiatric, and educational settings, and in everyday life situations, is only now beginning to receive substantial research attention (DePaulo, 1983; DePaulo, Nadler, & Fisher, 1983).

Broadly conceived, instances of help seeking might include requests for financial and material assistance (e.g., applying for loans and for food stamps); attempts to secure medical aid; the seeking of socioemotional counsel and support; probes for problem-solving hints in academic and occupational settings; and more mundane transactions such as asking for directions, borrowing trivial sums of money, and asking for small favors. With this degree of diversity at hand, it is probably best to

---

BELLA M. DEPAULO, VICKI LEIPHART, and W. R. DULL • Department of Psychology, Gilmer Hall, University of Virginia, Charlottesville, Virginia 22901.

start with the assumption that help seeking is not likely to be a unidimensional psychological phenomenon. Different factors (e.g., concerns about imposition or about indebtedness; feelings of inadequacy or of shyness; the need to achieve; and the desire to initiate and maintain interpersonal relationships) are differentially salient in different types of helping interactions. These factors can be conceptualized as situational parameters (i.e., in certain situations, issues of indebtedness might be especially important, whereas in other situations, concerns about competence might be much more central); or, alternatively, these factors can be considered as individual difference variables, that is, as personal orientations toward asking for help. Presumably, people vary systematically in the kinds of concerns that are most important to them in helping interactions. For some, considerations of indebtedness might be foremost. Others perhaps worry more about the possibility that their help request might be an imposition upon the help giver. For other people feelings about inadequacy might be the focal point of helping transactions—these people perceive the need to ask for help as an indicator of inadequacy, incompetence, or inferiority. Issues of competence are also salient to achievement-oriented people, but their resistance to asking for help is best characterized not as a fear of appearing incompetent or inferior but rather as a more positive preoccupation with meeting internal standards completely independently. For people with a shyness orientation toward help seeking, difficulty with asking for help is just one manifestation of a much more generalized interpersonal timidity. Alternatively, some people might approach help-seeking interactions with a much more positive orientation; for example, they might perceive helping transactions as opportunities to develop and maintain satisfying interpersonal relationships.

The research to be described in this chapter was guided by a process model of helping interactions. It is assumed that help seekers come to a helping interaction with a certain orientation (as described above), a set of expectations about the probable nature and outcomes of the interaction, as well as a set of traits, skills, and sensitivities. These individual differences, in addition to many situational factors, are important determinants of the conditions under which they ask for help, the frequency with which they ask for help, the amount of help they request, and the specific ways in which they request it. The manner in which help is requested (or the helper's perceptions thereof) and the kind of help that is requested in turn affect the helper's reaction to the help request. (The helper's reaction is, of course, also determined by the helper's characteristics, expectations, and situational "presses"—e.g., is the helper already preoccupied at the time of the request?) Help seekers' perceptions of the helper's reaction—which are determined in part by their interpersonal sensitivities and skills—influence their readiness to request help again in the future, and the manner in which they request any subsequent aid (cf. DePaulo, Brittingham, & Kaiser, 1983).

The research described in this chapter illustrates several of the hypothesized links in the help-seeking process, focusing primarily on research related to helping interactions in which imposition is likely to be an important consideration. Needy individuals who are trying not to impose will probably ask for help (if at all) only with tasks that are not particularly demanding of the helper's time or effort, and not particularly aversive for the helper to deal with. Most often they will have a legitimate reason for needing the help. Imposition-oriented help seekers will probably also ask for help in a polite way, and at times when the helper is not already preoccupied.

Compared to, for example, individuals whose reluctance to seek help is based primarily upon their embarrassment at admitting personal inadequacies, imposition-oriented help seekers appear to be characterized by concerns that are much more helper oriented. That is, their help-seeking strategies and inclinations seem to be importantly affected by considerations of the costs and rewards that might accrue to their potential helpers. Perhaps help seekers who seem to be attuned to the helper's costs and rewards are those who empathize with helpers' distress at being disturbed.

However, the reluctance to ask for help that appears to be helper focused might just as plausibly be motivated by self-centered concerns in addition to (or instead of) helper-oriented concerns. Self-centered concerns that might inhibit individuals from making imposing requests include the following:

1. Requests that are imposing to the helper may be more likely to be refused than requests that are not an imposition.

2. Even if the helper does not refuse the request, he or she may agree inamicably. Help that is given grudgingly may be distressing to the help seeker.

3. Even if the helper agrees to help, and shows no outward signs of reluctance, resentment, or annoyance, the help seeker might still be concerned that the helper has evaluated him or her negatively as a result of the help request. This perceived negative evaluation could in turn affect the help seeker's self-concept as well as the quality of his or her future relationships with the helper. For example, a helper who has been the target of an imposing request might perceive the help seeker as a burdensome person to be avoided in the future.

4. Regardless of the affective quality (actual or perceived) of the helper's response, the help seeker might suffer a decrement in self-esteem as a result of having made an imposing request.

5. Finally, the help seeker might become especially indebted to the helper who agrees to an imposing request. As Greenberg (1980) has pointed out, indebtedness can be aversive in that it is often associated with decrements in status and power, the anticipation of costly repayment, and restrictions on one's behavioral freedoms (in that the indebted individual is normatively obliged to repay in some way).

The question whether (or to what extent) help-seeking reluctance is governed by self-oriented, as opposed to helper-oriented, costs and rewards is likely to be just as problematic as the often debated issue of whether any behavior can ever be truly altruistic. We shall not attempt to answer such questions here. However, we shall address the related issue of whether help seekers behave in ways that are likely to be particularly effective in light of what is already known about the conditions under which helpers are more or less likely to comply with help requests.

Documented facilitators and inhibitors of helping are by now innumerable; here we shall briefly review representative research on three factors that are particularly relevant to the imposition theme. These factors are the cost to the helper of giving help, the reason for the help seeker's dependence or need for help, and the manner in which help is requested.

Imposing requests are costly requests—costly in terms of the helper's time, effort, and emotional or physical well-being. Research on help giving provides strong support for the intuitively compelling hypothesis that costly requests are less likely to elicit compliance than requests that are not costly to the helper. Midlarsky and Midlarsky (1973), for example, manipulated the amount of physical pain that subjects would have to endure if they chose to help. They found that subjects who suffered more intense shocks in the helping act helped less than those who experienced less intense shocks. Allen's study (described in Darley & Latané, 1970) of subway misinformants can also be construed as a manipulation of threat to the potential helper: In that study, a subway rider who was given incorrect directions was less often given corrected directions by a bystander when the misinformant established himself as a bully than when he did not. The "Good Samaritan" study (Darley & Batson, 1973) involved a manipulation of time pressure: Seminarians who were led to believe that they were late for their next appointment were less likely to help a distressed individual whom they passed en route to their appointment than were seminarians who were told that they had plenty of time.

Studies involving various manipulations of convenience to the helper have also demonstrated that helpers are less likely to agree to inconvenient (high cost) requests than to convenient ones. For example,

Gross, Wallston, and Pilivian (1975) found that more subjects agreed to complete a questionnaire if they could take it home with them and return it by mail than if they had to complete it at the laboratory. Also, Weyant (1978) reports that subjects volunteered more time to solicit donations if they were asked to sit at a donation desk than if they were requested to solicit donations door-to-door. In a study in which subjects were asked to donate their own money (Wagner & Wheeler, 1969), they were more willing to do so if they could give a small amount each month than if they were asked to give the entire amount in one sum. Finally, when potential helpers were forewarned that one request might lead to another, they were less helpful than they were when they believed that the first request would be the only request (Jones, 1970).

People's decisions about giving help are also importantly determined by the reason for the recipient's dependency or need. Initially, these reasons were classified as either internal or external. Staub (1978) describes internally caused dependency as occurring when "a person intentionally creates circumstances under which another's help is needed to satisfy some need or reach a goal" or when "the person [chooses] to rely on others' help when such help is not truly necessary" (pp. 235–236). By this definition, research provided strong support for the hypothesis that people are more helpful toward help seekers whose dependency is externally caused than toward help seekers whose dependency is internally caused. For example, Schopler and Matthews (1968) showed that subjects who could have obtained needed resources from an impersonal source but instead chose to seek it from their partner in the experiment were less often aided than subjects who could only obtain help from their partner. In a subsequent study by Berkowitz (1969), subjects who had fallen behind on a task because they initially "took it easy" (internal) received less help from a fellow-subject than those who fell behind because of an error by the experimenter (external). Horowitz (1968), however, reports that subjects were less resistant to helping a graduate student whose need to finish a project quickly was because of poor planning (internal) when they felt that they had a choice about whether or not to help. When subjects were told that they *had* to give at least some minimal amount of help, they helped the internally dependent graduate student much less than the externally dependent student (whose need to finish quickly was caused by an unforeseeable change in the adviser's schedule).

More recently, it has been argued that helpers' responses to requests can be more precisely predicted by classifying the causes of dependency as either controllable or uncontrollable rather than as internal or external (Ickes & Kidd, 1976; Meyer & Mulherin, 1980; see also Weiner, 1980). For example, Barnes, Ickes, and Kidd (1979) showed that students were less likely to lend notes to a classmate who simply did not make the effort to take good notes than to one who lacked the ability to do so. Although both effort and ability are internal factors, effort is usually perceived as the more controllable one. Meyer and Mulherin (1980) also found that more help was given to a person whose need arose from an uncontrollable cause (illness) than to one whose need was the result of something more controllable (lack of effort). Descriptive results from a nonexperimental study are also consistent with the controllability formulation: Bryan and Davenport (described in Berkowitz, 1972) found that the greatest number of contributions to the *New York Times 100 Neediest Cases* was elicited by victims whose need for help arose from circumstances beyond their control.

Even when the cause of a person's dependency or need and the costs involved in helping are held constant, helpers vary markedly in their willingness to give help according to the way in which help is requested. In one of the earliest studies of the manner of requesting help, Darley and Latané (1970) found that help seekers who volunteered some information about themselves (e.g., why they needed help) received more help in response to their simple requests (for the time, directions, a dime) than did more abrupt help seekers. Langer and Abelson (1972) add that calling immediate attention to one's need for help (a "victim oriented" request) is especially effective in obtaining help only when one's help request is legitimate. When one's request is of questionable legitimacy, a "target oriented" request, which begins by stressing the target's responsibility to give help, is relatively more effective. Cunningham, Steinberg, and Grev (1980) also used a responsibility-oriented request ("You owe it to the children—give to the World Children's Fund"), which they called a negative request, and contrasted it with a positive request ("Keep the children smiling—give to the World Children's Fund"). Subjects who were in a good mood responded most helpfully to the positive request, whereas subjects who felt guilty responded more helpfully to the negative request. Finally, in a study involving the wrong-number technique, more help was given to help seekers who made a simple request ("would you please call my garage for me?") or a positive request ("If you help me, I'd appreciate it and you'd know you helped someone out of a really tough spot") than to those whose request was more negative ("Look, think how you would feel if you were in a similar situation and you were not helped") (Kriss, Indenbaum, & Tesch, 1974).

In summary, people are especially helpful when the costs of giving help are low; when the help seeker is in need of help for reasons beyond his or her control; and when help is requested in a way that is appropriate to the type of need and the state (e.g., mood) of the helper. The studies to be described in this chapter begin to address the following questions:

1. Are people especially willing to ask for help in the kinds of situations in which others are especially likely to give help? For example, do people ask for more help when the helper is not already preoccupied with an important task?

2. Do people ask for help differently when their request is more imposing to the helper? Also, are certain variations in help-seeking styles particularly characteristic of people who are especially sensitive to the possibility of interpersonal rejection (e.g., people who are shy)?

3. Although it is clear that people often respond less helpfully to more imposing requests, there are many everyday situations in which compliance with simple requests is extremely high. When helpers comply with requests that they secretly resent, does their resentment become apparent in the manner in which they give help? Is their resentment differentially reflected in different verbal and nonverbal channels? The vast literature on helping has had a great deal to say about the conditions under which people will give help, but very little to say about the way in which help is given.

4. What is the relationship between interpersonal sensitivity and willingness to ask for help? Is it possible that people who are especially reluctant to ask for help are overly sensitive to subtle signs of helper resentment?

Four studies will be reported. Study 1 documents some of the ways in which the rate of help seeking and the types of problems for which help is sought are affected by the costs to the helper of giving aid. Study 2 describes the ways in which people who are high or low in shyness ask for help in several different situations, including one in which, over time, the help request becomes increasingly burdensome to the helper. In Study 3, helpers' reactions to different kinds of help requests are examined. Half of the help requests constituted an imposition upon the helper either because the requests were illegitimate, because the help was requested in a rude way, or because the helper was working under a time deadline at the time of the request. Study 4 cycles back to the help seeker and examines the role of nonverbal sensitivity in asking for help.

## 2. STUDY 1: THE RELUCTANCE TO IMPOSE

Probably the first and most basic step in understanding the role of imposition in help seeking is to show that people are less willing to ask for help when their help request is likely to be an imposition upon the helper. Previous research has shown that people sometimes seek less help when helping entails more work (Gross & Somerson, 1974) or a greater sacrifice (Castro, 1974; Shapiro, 1980) on the part of the helper. This study tests whether subjects also ask for less help when the helper is already preoccupied with another task.

To begin to study the dynamics of imposition, we recruited 62 undergraduate women for an experiment described as a study of the factors that influence people's accuracy at understanding interpersonal communications (DePaulo & Fisher, 1980). One of the questions of interest was said to be whether people would be more or less accurate at interpreting an ambiguous interpersonal message when they had the opportunity to seek the advice of an expert (but fallible) helper.

Subjects were to attempt to identify the emotions communicated in 30 photographs of the face or body of a young woman. For each photograph, subjects chose from among a set of five emotion labels, only one of which correctly described the expression in the photograph. Subjects were told to indicate, for each item, which answer they believed to be correct, and also to circle those items for which they would like to receive help from the (bogus) expert helper. They were told that they would be allowed to consult with the helper after indicating their own preferred responses to each item. They were informed that if they got an answer right, using either their answer or the helper's answer, they would get credit for it. However, if they got it wrong, they would receive no credit.

After administering the instructions to the subjects, and immediately before leaving them to work alone on the tasks, the experimenter handed the subjects a handwritten note from the helper indicating her schedule for the day. The schedule indicated that at certain times the helper was in the computer center, in class (not available for consultation), or at lunch. During the time period when the subject was to ask for help, the helper's schedule always indicated that she was in her office (a specific office number was given on the schedule) and available for consultation. For half of the subjects (high cost to helper) the schedule indicated that she would be working on her dissertation at that time; for the other half (low cost to helper) it indicated that she had "no special plans." The primary dependent measure was the number of items that subjects circled (indicating their desire to consult with the helper on that item).

As predicted, subjects who believed that the helper was busy working on her dissertation asked for less help than subjects who believed that she had no special plans at the time. Moreover, those subjects who asked for more than the median amount of help (compared to those who asked for less help) expected the helper to view them as less competent, and they also reported feeling more nervous and more uncomfortable about approaching her for help.

The photographs that subjects were trying to interpret varied in difficulty in two different ways. First, the photographs of the faces, in this study and in previous studies employing the same stimulus materials, are always easier to judge than the pictures of the bodies. Second, the response alternatives provided to the subject varied such that for some of the items, the alternatives described very similar emotions (thereby rendering the selection of the one exactly correct answer particularly difficult), whereas for other items, the alternatives described very different emotions (thereby making the subjects' task much easier).

Overall, subjects asked for more help with the difficult items than with the easy ones. More interestingly, subjects planned to seek help with different kinds of problems depending on whether they expected their helper to be busy or free. Subjects who expected the helper to be busy were especially reluctant to ask her for help with problems that were either easy along both dimensions (i.e., pictures of faces described by very dissimilar response alternatives) or difficult along both dimensions. These results suggest that individuals deciding whether to seek help sometimes take into account not only their own costs and rewards, but also the costs and rewards that would accrue to their helper. Specifically, subjects may feel that the problem is simply too easy to warrant bothering a preoccupied helper when both the content of the pictures and the structure of the response alternatives facilitate performance. When both content and form render the problem particularly difficult, subjects may feel that it would take an especially long time to solve, and hence may hesitate to seek aid from someone who has important alternative ways of spending her time. If this interpretation is correct, the findings suggest that the dynamics of imposition are sometimes intriguingly intricate.

## 3. STUDY 2: THE SOUNDS OF SHYNESS

There are times when a help-request that starts out as a small imposition or perhaps no imposition at all ("Can I talk to you for a few minutes?" "Can you take 5 minutes to answer this questionnaire?") becomes very imposing as the talk drags on and on, and the questionnaire is only partially completed long after the first 5 minutes have passed. A help seeker who is especially apprehensive about imposing upon others—or even about merely interacting with others, as is true of someone who is shy (e.g., Leary & Schlenker, 1981)—should be particularly interesting to study when trapped in this type of help-seeking situation. The shy person's manner of interacting with the helper should be most markedly different from the nonshy person's under these kinds of imposing circumstances.

To study the help-seeking styles of shy and nonshy people in situations varying in intrusiveness, we (DePaulo & Dull, 1984) administered Pilkonis's (1977) shortened form of the Stanford Shyness Survey to a large sample of undergraduates. Eight males and eight females with shyness scores in the upper third of the sample and eight males and eight females scoring in the lower third were invited to participate for course credit. When they arrived at the laboratory, they were told that they were participating in a study of the psychological factors related to heart disease. The experimenters were said to be engaged in a long-term project on that topic, and to further their study of it, they needed to design more effective recruitment strategies. The subject's task was to contact two males and two females by telephone and to persuade them to complete the researchers' three-page questionnaire dealing with the psychological and physical aspects of health. The questionnaire included approximately 70 items altogether, dealing with the respondent's history of heart disease, perceptions of physical symptoms, aspects of life style (smoking, drinking, etc.), and various psychological attributes (achievement motivation, energy level, etc.). Subjects were to ask one male and one female to fill out the questionnaire (which would be mailed to them) and return it in the enclosed envelope; they were to persuade the other male and female to answer the entire questionnaire right then and there over the phone. Subjects were given a list of names drawn randomly from the university directory and told to start with the first name that was not already crossed out. (Subjects made their four calls in one of four different orders.) To further motivate them to do well, subjects were also told that they would be required to continue phoning until they had convinced two males and two females to complete the questionnaire.

Before making any of their calls, subjects were asked how persuasive they thought they were and how they expected each of the four respondents to react to their help request. After each call, they were asked how nervous they felt during the call, how they thought the respondent had reacted to their request, and (in the "mail" condition) whether they thought that the respondent really would return the questionnaire.

The subjects' parts of the calls were tape-recorded, with their knowledge and permission. Each subject's initial request for help from each respondent (e.g., "Would you fill out this questionnaire if I mail it to you?") was rerecorded onto a master tape, and in the "phone" conditions, subjects' readings of two of the first items of the questionnaire, two of the middle items, and two of the last items were also recorded onto the master tape.[1] Additional subjects were recruited to judge, on 9-point scales, the degree of warmth, friendliness, confidence, dominance, persuasiveness, and nervousness that seemed to characterize each segment. (They were not told that the callers differed in shyness.) Two factors emerged from these ratings—a warmth factor (warm, friendly) and a confidence factor (confident, dominant, persuasive, relaxed).

The design allows for the study of differences in help-seeking styles by different kinds of people (males and females, high and low in shyness) in different kinds of situations (more or less imposing to the helper). In addition, individual differences in initial expectations and attitudes about asking for help can be identified and related to differences in help-seeking styles and to variations in the successfulness of the help-seeking attempt (i.e., how many respondents actually did return the questionnaire). Furthermore, differences in subjects' manner of asking for help can be related to their success at obtaining help.

High and low shyness subjects varied significantly in their initial perceptions of their own persuasiveness: The former perceived themselves as being much less persuasive people than the latter. High and low shyness subjects did not differ in their predictions about how the respondents would react to their help requests. Instead, subjects overall tended to expect more positive responses from female respondents than from males. This result accords well with a finding from an earlier survey study involving over 300 subjects at four different age levels who were asked to predict help seekers' reactions to 22 different helping situations (DePaulo, 1982). In that study, too, subjects indicated that they expected much more positive responses when asking females for help than when asking males. An even stronger result in the present study was an expectation of more positive reactions from respondents of the opposite sex than from same-sex others. Finally, respondents overall were expected to respond more negatively when asked to answer the questionnaire over the phone than when asked to return it by mail.

Subjects differed notably in the ways that they asked for help depending on whether they were delivering an imposing request (answer the questionnaire right now over the phone) or a nonimposing request (return it by mail). Callers sounded warmer and more confident when delivering their "phone" pleas than their "mail" requests. Thus, in the condition in which subjects expected the most negative reaction (the

[1]A typewritten transcript of the master tape was also made, and judges were randomly assigned to make their ratings from either the transcripts or the audiotape. Results presented in this report are collapsed over the transcript and the audiotape conditions.

imposing "phone" condition), subjects appeared especially confident and warm. Perhaps subjects put on their warmest and most convincing performance when they believe that the extra affective effort is especially necessary.

We also examined the degree of warmth and confidence conveyed by the callers as they read the early, middle, and late items to the respondents who answered the questionnaire over the phone. We expected the subjects—particularly the shy subjects—to have an especially difficult time during the middle of the questionnaire when (usually) at least 5 minutes had already passed and the questionnaire was still far from being completed. We expected the subjects to sound more in control when they first began to read the questionnaire, and we also expected to find evidence of an end spurt, with subjects sounding more in control at the end of the questionnaire, when they knew that they were on the verge of successfully completing their task and could honestly assure the respondent that this was the last group of items he or she would have to put up with. This is exactly what we did find. Subjects sounded most confident when they read the early and late items, and least confident when they read the middle items (*M*s = 5.2, 5.0, 5.2, respectively, for the early, middle, and late items).

Also as predicted, the "middle lag" described the shy callers especially well. Subjects who were not shy maintained their level of confidence over the course of the questionnaire (*M*s = 5.2, 5.2, 5.3 for the early, middle, and late items). Shy subjects, however, became especially insecure and unconvincing halfway through the task (*M*s = 5.1, 4.7, 5.0).

The results presented so far tell how the callers were perceived by a group of judges. But how did the callers feel about themselves and about their effect on the respondents after making their calls? First, shy subjects reported feeling much more nervous while asking for help than nonshy subjects did. However, this difference was not readily apparent to the judges, who did not perceive a significant difference in confidence between the shy and the nonshy subjects.

Also, actually talking to respondents over the phone did not appreciably alter callers' initial convictions that females would react more positively than males to their help requests. Subjects tended to believe that more of the females who said they would return the questionnaire actually would do so, and they believed that those females who answered the questionnaire over the phone found the experience less objectionable than did the males.

In fact, however, the female respondents were not any more likely actually to return the questionnaire than the males were. Nor were they any more likely to agree to answer the questionnaire items over the phone. In both the mail and phone conditions, the response rate was surprisingly high (86% of the mailed questionnaires were returned, and 89% of the respondents who were asked to answer the questionnaire over the phone actually did so). Even with this extremely high level of cooperation, response rate for the mailed questionnaires was sensitive to the subject shyness, subject sex, and respondent sex variables: non-shy subjects had more questionnaires returned to them by respondents of the opposite sex, whereas shy subjects were more successful in eliciting help from same-sex respondents. Subjects' manner of requesting help appeared to importantly mediate these results. For example, even though shy subjects were less successful overall in eliciting help from opposite-sex respondents, those shy subjects who sounded more confident when requesting help from the opposite sex were somewhat more successful in obtaining help than were the shy subjects who sounded less confident.

## 4. STUDY 3: VERBAL AND NONVERBAL "BUSY SIGNALS"

There are many different ways in which a help request can be an imposition upon the person asked for help. The wrong kind of request (e.g., an illegitimate one rather than a legitimate one) or a request made in the wrong way (e.g., rudely rather than politely) or at the wrong time (e.g., when the helper is working under time pressure on some other task) all might put off a helper who might otherwise comply amicably. A help request that occurs at an inopportune time for the helper is an imposition with a locus that is internal to the helper. That is, the request represents an imposition because of something about the helper him or herself (e.g., his or her schedule). When a helper is preoccupied, even the most polite and most legitimate of requests can be an imposition. Illegitimate requests and rude requests, on the other hand, are external impositions in that it is something about the request, or about the way that it is made, that constitutes an intrusion, rather than something about the helper.

In this experiment, we studied the reactions of helpers to these different kinds of impositions. Helpers working on a timed task, or faced with illegitimate or rude help requests, are trapped in an interesting conflict situation. In the case of the busy helper, working on a task under a time deadline, there is the problem of somehow getting the intruder to leave quickly, without at the same time being too overtly unfriendly to this perhaps innocent invader. The helper faced with a rude intruder or a help seeker bearing an illegitimate request is in a slightly different dilemma: These intruders perhaps deserve an unfriendly response, but how unfriendly can the helper be and still remain within the bounds of decency and courtesy in social interaction?

The study of the differential use of verbal and nonverbal behaviors seems particularly appropriate to the analysis of these kinds of interpersonal dilemmas. For a variety of reasons, people are probably quite adept at controlling their verbal communications; they have much practice in choosing just the right words to express what they feel, and they get plenty of feedback from others on their success at doing so. By contrast, nonverbal aspects of communication, such as facial expression and particularly tone of voice, are less skillfully and less readily controlled, and the person "sending" these cues is held less responsible for them (cf. DePaulo, Zuckerman, & Rosenthal, 1980; Ekman & Friesen, 1969). Thus the interplay of these various verbal and nonverbal cues might be especially revealing in the conflict situations into which helpers are sometimes thrust.

To study helpers' verbal and nonverbal reactions to different kinds of help requests, we (Leiphart & DePaulo, 1980) recruited 32 male and 32 female undergraduate subjects to take part in what we described as a study of the thought process involved in problem solving. Subjects were given a difficult logic problem to work on, and were told to think out loud, into the microphone, as they attempted to solve the problem. Another subject (actually a confederate), who arrived at about the same time as the subject, was ostensibly listening to the same instructions (via an intercom) in a different room. The instructions delivered over the intercom either informed the subjects that they had 10 minutes to complete the task (timed condition; 10 minutes was an inadequate amount of time) or no time limit was mentioned (untimed). After the subject had been working on the task for several minutes, he or she was interrupted by the confederate who asked the subject to repeat the instructions either because his or her intercom faded out (legitimate request) or because he or she "wasn't really paying attention" (illegitimate request). These requests were made either rudely or politely.

Subject-helpers were surreptitiously videotaped as they responded to these help requests, starting immediately after the last word of the confederate's request. New samples of male and female judges were randomly assigned to rate the helpers' reactions from (1) the full videotape with sound; (2) only the audiotape; (3) a typed transcript, or (4) only the visual portion of the videotapes. They rated each helper's response for its degree of friendliness, informativeness, annoyance, and abruptness. Judges were not told about any of the experimental manipulations.

Female helpers overall responded in a noticeably friendlier way to all help seekers than did male helpers. This finding accords well with the results of the survey research discussed earlier in which respondents reported expecting more positive responses from female helpers than from males. It is also consistent with the results of Study 2, in which the callers expected more positive results from female respondents before they made their calls, and believed that the women did respond more positively than the men after they had actually talked to them.

Both male and female helpers responded in a much friendlier way when they were working on an untimed task than when they had a strict deadline for completing their task. Thus their verbal and nonverbal "busy signals" were quite apparent even to naïve judges. This tendency for the helpers to be more friendly when they were not working under time pressure than when they were was particularly striking when the help seeker was someone of the same sex. Helpers were only slightly less friendly to opposite-sex help seekers when they were busy than when they were not busy. The same tended to be true of helpers' signs of annoyance. Helpers' annoyance was noticeably more evident on timed than on untimed tasks only when the intruder was of the same sex.

Helper's reactions to rude requests were more apparent from the abruptness ratings. Helpers were slightly more abrupt with people who asked for help rudely than with those who asked politely. Male helpers, compared to female helpers, were most unfriendly and most uninformative when asked for help in a rude way while working on a timed task; female helpers were most friendly and most informative when working on an untimed task and asked for help in a polite way. Men, then, who generally react in a less friendly way than women, are especially unfriendly when faced with a rude intruder during a busy time; women, who are generally more friendly, react to a polite request when they are not preoccupied with even more friendliness than usual.

As we expected, helpers did express their reactions differently in different verbal and nonverbal ways. The first section of Table 1 shows the friendliness expressed visually, through words, by audiotape, and via all audiovisual cues by helpers working on timed or untimed tasks. The bottom row is of difference scores, which show the extent to which helpers working on an untimed task seemed friendlier than those working on a timed task. These difference scores show that in the most readily controlled channel—the words-only channel, or transcript condition—helpers did not show a difference in friendliness. By the words that they chose, helpers did not appear any less friendly (and in fact appeared a tiny bit more friendly) in the timed than in the untimed condition. However, in all other conditions, in which nonverbal cues (visual and/or tone of voice) were present, helpers were clearly less friendly when every minute counted. When working under time pres-

*Table 1. Helper's Verbal and Nonverbal Reactions to Different Types of Help Requests*

| | Visual only | Words only | Audio | Audiovisual |
|---|---|---|---|---|
| Friendliness | | | | |
| Untimed | 21.72 | 18.08 | 23.00 | 20.70 |
| Timed | 18.22 | 18.80 | 19.89 | 18.39 |
| Untimed minus timed | 3.50 | −.72 | 3.11 | 2.31 |
| Friendliness | | | | |
| Polite | 18.67 | 18.89 | 21.72 | 20.02 |
| Rude | 21.27 | 17.98 | 21.17 | 19.08 |
| Polite minus rude | −2.60 | .91 | .55 | .94 |
| Informativeness | | | | |
| Polite | 17.92 | 13.39 | 16.62 | 15.25 |
| Rude | 18.30 | 11.64 | 14.22 | 13.44 |
| Polite minus rude | −.38 | 1.75 | 2.40 | 1.81 |
| Annoyed | | | | |
| Polite | 19.56 | 18.91 | 18.03 | 19.55 |
| Rude | 18.20 | 20.27 | 19.22 | 20.58 |
| Polite minus rude | 1.36 | −1.36 | −1.19 | −1.03 |
| Abrupt | | | | |
| Polite | 17.56 | 20.88 | 22.02 | 20.28 |
| Rude | 17.11 | 23.66 | 24.27 | 22.19 |
| Polite minus rude | .45 | −2.78 | −2.25 | −1.91 |
| Informativeness | | | | |
| Legitimate | 17.22 | 13.05 | 16.03 | 14.72 |
| Illegitimate | 19.00 | 11.98 | 14.81 | 13.97 |
| Legitimate minus illegitimate | −1.78 | 1.07 | 1.22 | .75 |

sure (compared to conditions of no time pressure), helpers did not express their displeasure in the channel that they would be held most accountable for (i.e., their words); the difference in friendliness between time-pressured and unconstrained helpers was evident only when nonverbal cues were present.[2]

In the external locus of imposition conditions, in which the help seekers were intruding with an illegitimate or a rude request, it was probably more justifiable for the helpers to express their displeasure. Hence, they did express this displeasure even in the most controllable channels—those involving words. In every channel that contained words (words only, audio, audiovisual), helpers were less friendly, less informative, more annoyed, and more abrupt to the rude intruders than to the polite ones. They were also less informative in these channels to

[2]Although the results of this study are generally consistent with the literature on verbal and nonverbal communication, the complexity of the findings, and the fact that it is perhaps the only study of helpers' differential verbal and nonverbal reactions to different help requests, suggest the need for replication.

the help seekers with illegitimate requests than to those with legitimate requests. In the purely visual channel, however, something quite different occurred. Helpers were actually a tiny bit *more* positive (i.e., more friendly and informative and less annoyed and abrupt) to the rude and illegitimate intruders than to the polite and legitimate ones (see Table 1). This might be a phenomenon of "visual overcontrol"—in trying hard *not* to be unpleasant to the rude intruder, the helpers send visual cues that are actually more pleasant to these rude intruders than to the polite ones. Alternatively, the visual pleasantness displayed in response to the rude and illegitimate requests might be a kind of submissiveness or appeasement gesture, as is sometimes displayed by victims of aggression.

It could also be hypothesized that the pleasant visual display is intended sarcastically, as when a person says something insulting and smiles at the same time. If this were true, however, we would expect the impact of the total message (audiovisual condition) to be extremely negative and this was not always true in these data.

Inspection of the overall impact of the channels (collapsed across all conditions) shows, in terms of a rank ordering, that the visual channel appears to judges to be the least abrupt, the most informative, the second most friendly, and the next-to-least annoyed. A person asking for help, then, might do well to attend most closely to the helper's visual cues, for it is from this sometimes "overcontrolled" source of cues that the help seeker is likely to perceive the most positive helper response.

## 5. STUDY 4: SELECTIVE NONVERBAL SENSITIVITY—A FACILITATOR OF HELP SEEKING

In Study 4 we examined the relationship between skill at understanding face and body cues of emotion and willingness to ask for help (DePaulo & Fisher, 1981). In addition to the suggestive evidence in Study 3, a large literature in nonverbal communication also suggests that the face is a source of "controlled" affect. Particularly in comparison with the body, it communicates what a person intends to express and does not communicate what a person intends to hide (e.g., DePaulo *et al.*, 1980; Ekman & Friesen, 1969). In the context of helping interactions, a person who is asked for help may facially express polite compliance, while bodily "leaking" feelings of resentment or annoyance. People who chronically pick up these covert cues communicated by body movements and postures and who fail to read the more overt cues expressed by the face may be deterred from initiating very many help requests. In keeping with this formulation, we predicted that individuals who were more willing to ask for help would be relatively more sensitive to the more polite and controlled facial cues and relatively less sensitive to the leakier body cues than individuals who were more reluctant to seek help.

Data collected in Study 1 were useful in testing this hypothesis. Subjects from that study were divided into low and high help seekers according to whether they had asked for more or less than the median amount of help. Since the faces and bodies in the photographs that subjects judged were posing specific emotions, there were right and wrong answers. Hence subjects' accuracy at understanding facial and body cues of emotion could be assessed by their judgments of the photographs. As predicted, high help seekers were significantly more accurate than low help seekers at understanding facial cues ($M$ = 52.6% for high help seekers, 45.9% for low ones), and slightly less accurate at reading body cues ($M$ = 32.3%, 36.2%). When a self-report scale of willingness to ask for help (DePaulo, 1978) was used to identify high and low help seekers, along with a measure of sensitivity to face and body cues similar to the one used in this study, the same results were obtained (see DePaulo & Rosenthal, 1979).

In helping interactions, facial cues might convey a helper's polite compliance with the request, whereas body cues might "leak" his or her true feelings of annoyance or resentment. People who are especially insensitive to helpers' polite and accommodating facial cues may frequently be deterred from initiating help requests (as when they fail to see that the helper welcomes the opportunity to be of assistance). Moreover, in those cases in which they do ask for help, they may feel especially badly about having done so (as when they overlook the helper's congenial reactions to the help request) and therefore especially reluctant to do so again.

## 6. SUMMARY AND CONCLUSIONS

We started our research with the assumption that help seeking is not a unidimension psychological phenomenon. Different factors (e.g., concerns about imposition or about indebtedness; feelings of inadequacy or of shyness; the need to achieve; and the desire to initiate and maintain interpersonal relationships) are differentially salient in different types of helping interactions. In the studies reported in this chapter we focused primarily on help-seeking situations in which imposition was likely to be an important consideration. The studies were guided by an interactive, process model of help seeking.

In Study 1 we showed that people are especially reluctant to ask for help when they know that their request might be an imposition upon the helper. Furthermore, their choice of the kinds of problems to seek help with seems to take into account the helper's costs and rewards as well as their own. Study 2 demonstrates that shy people differ from nonshy people in their initial expectations about helping interactions, in the ways that they actually do ask for help, and in their success at obtaining help from different kinds of helpers. The shy person's manner of requesting help differed most notably from the nonshy person's style when obtaining the necessary help required that the help seeker maintain contact with the helper over an extended period. Study 3 documents helpers' verbal and nonverbal reactions to help seekers who, half the time, were asking for the wrong kind of help, in the wrong way, or at the wrong time. Helpers were especially unfriendly when intrusions occurred at the "wrong time"—when they were busy working on a timed task. Their unfriendly reactions to untimely intruders were particularly apparent in their nonverbal (compared to their verbal) reactions. In responding to rude help seekers, on the other hand, helpers seemed to be "overcontrolling" their facial reactions, responding visually in a slightly more positive way to the rude than to the polite intruders. Their verbal reactions, however, were less friendly when the help seekers were rude than when they were polite. Study 4 shows that people who are high help seekers (compared to people who are more reluctant to ask for help) are especially adept at reading the well-controlled and polite facial cues but somewhat less skilled at reading the less controlled (and probably less polite) body cues.

It is interesting that the literature on individual differences in giving help does not include programmatic studies of helpers' sensitivity to interpersonal cues. This is especially perplexing in view of the fact that one of the most influential conceptualizations of prosocial behavior, Latané and Darley's (1970) model of bystander intervention, suggests that people's perceptions of the reactions of other bystanders is a key factor in determining their own willingness to initiate help attempts.

## 7. REFERENCES

Barnes, R. D., Ickes, W., & Kidd, R. F. Effects of the perceived intentionality and stability of another's dependency on helping behavior. *Personality and Social Psychology Bulletin*, 1979, *5*, 367–372.

Berkowitz, L. Reactance to improper dependency relationships. *Journal of Experimental Social Psychology*, 1969, *5*, 283–294.

Berkowitz, L. Social norms, feelings, and other factors affecting helping behavior and altruism. In L. Berkowitz (Ed.), *Advances in experimental social psychology* (Vol. 6). New York: Academic Press, 1972.

Castro, M. A. Reactions to aid as a function of cost to donor and opportunity to repay. *Journal of Applied Social Psychology*, 1974, *4*, 194–209.

Cunningham, M. R., Steinberg, J., & Grev, R. Wanting to and having to help: Separate motivations for positive mood and guilt-induced helping. *Journal of Personality and Social Psychology*, 1980, *38*, 181–192.

Darley, J., & Batson, C. From Jerusalem to Jericho: A study of situational and dispositional variables in helping behavior. *Journal of Personality and Social Psychology*, 1973, *27*, 100–108.

Darley, J. M., & Latané, B. Norms and normative behavior: Field studies of social interdependence. In J. Macauley & L. Berkowitz (Eds.), *Altruism and helping behavior*. New York: Academic Press, 1970.

DePaulo, B. M. Help-seeking from the recipient's point of view. JSAS *Catalog of Selected Documents in Psychology*, 1978, *8*, 62. (Ms. No. 1721)

DePaulo, B. M. Social psychological processes in informal help-seeking. In T. A. Wills (Ed.), *Basic processes in helping relationships*. New York: Academic Press, 1982.

DePaulo, B. M. Perspectives on help-seeking. In B. M. DePaulo, A. Nadler, & J. D. Fisher (Eds.), *New directions in helping* (Vol. 2): *Help-seeking*. New York: Academic Press, 1983.

DePaulo, B. M., & Dull, W. R. *Shyness and help-seeking*. Manuscript in preparation, University of Virginia, 1984.

DePaulo, B. M., & Fisher, J. D. The costs of asking for help. *Basic and Applied Social Psychology*, 1980, *1*, 23–35.

DePaulo, B. M., & Fisher, J. D. Too tuned-out to take: The role of nonverbal sensitivity in help-seeking. *Personality and Social Psychology Bulletin*, 1981, *7*, 201–205.

DePaulo, B. M., & Rosenthal, R. Ambivalence, discrepancy, and deception in nonverbal communication. In R. Rosenthal (Ed.), *Skill in nonverbal communication*. Cambridge, Mass.: Oelgeschlager, Gunn & Hain, 1979.

DePaulo, B. M., Zuckerman, M., & Rosenthal, R. Detecting deception: Modality effects. In L. Wheeler (Ed.), *The review of personality and social psychology* (Vol. 1). Beverly Hills, Calif.: Sage, 1980.

DePaulo, B. M., Nadler, A., & Fisher, J. D. (Eds.). *New directions in helping* (Vol. 2): *Help-seeking*. New York: Academic Press, 1983.

DePaulo, B. M., Brittingham, G. L., & Kaiser, M. K. Receiving competence-relevant help: Effects on reciprocity, affect, and sensitivity to the helper's nonverbally-expressed needs. *Journal of Personality and Social Psychology*, 1983, *45*, 1045–1060.

Ekman, P., & Friesen, W. V. Nonverbal leakage and clues to deception. *Psychiatry*, 1969, *32*, 88–106.

Greenberg, M. S. A theory of indebtedness. In K. J. Gergen, M. S. Greenberg, & R. H. Willis (Eds.), *Social exchange: Advances in theory and research*. New York: Plenum Press, 1980.

Gross, A. E., & Somerson, S. *Helper effort as an inhibitor of help-seeking*. Paper presented at the meeting of the Psychonomic Society, Boston, 1974.

Gross, A. E., Wallston, B. S., & Piliavin, I. M. Beneficiary attractiveness and cost as determinants of responses to routine requests for help. *Sociometry*, 1975, *38*, 131–140.

Horowitz, I. Effect of choice and locus of dependence on helping behavior. *Journal of Personality and Social Psychology*, 1968, *8*, 373–376.

Ickes, W. J., & Kidd, R. F. An attributional analysis of helping behavior. In J. H. Harvey, W. J. Ickes, & R. F. Kidd (Eds.), *New directions in attribution research* (Vol. 1). Hillsdale, N.J.: Lawrence Erlbaum, 1976.

Jones, R. A. Volunteering to help: The effects of choice, dependence, and anticipated dependence. *Journal of Personality and Social Psychology*, 1970, *14*, 121–129.

Kriss, M., Indenbaum, E., & Tesch, F. Message type and status of interactants as determinants of telephone helping behavior. *Journal of Personality and Social Psychology*, 1974, *30*, 856–859.

Langer, E. J., & Abelson, R. P. The semantics of asking a favor: How to succeed in getting help without really dying. *Journal of Personality and Social Psychology*, 1972, *24*, 26–32.

Latané, B., & Darley, J. M. *The unresponsive bystander: Why doesn't he help?* New York: Appleton-Century-Crofts, 1970.

Leary, M. R., & Schlenker, B. R. The social psychology of shyness: A self-presentation model. In J. T. Tedeschi (Ed.), *Impression–management theory and social psychological research*. New York: Academic Press, 1981.

Leiphart, V., & DePaulo, B. M. *Helpers' verbal and nonverbal reactions to rude, untimely, and illegitimate help-requests*. Unpublished data, University of Virginia, 198O.

Meyer, J. P., & Mulherin, A. From attribution to helping: An analysis of the mediating effects of affect and expectancy. *Journal of Personality and Social Psychology*, 1980, *39*, 201–210.

Midlarsky, E., & Midlarsky, M. Some determinants of aiding under experimentally induced stress. *Journal of Personality*, 1973, *41*, 305–327.

Pilkonis, P. A. Shyness, public and private, and its relationship to other measures of social behavior. *Journal of Personality*, 1977, *45*, 585–595.

Schopler, J., & Matthews, M. W. The influence of the perceived causal locus of partner's dependence on the use of interpersonal power. *Journal of Personality and Social Psychology*, 1965, *2*, 609–612.

Shapiro, E. G. Is seeking help from a friend like seeking help from a stranger? *Social Psychology Quarterly*, 1980, *43*, 259–263.

Staub, E. *Positive social behavior and morality: Social and interpersonal influences*. New York: Academic Press, 1978.

Wagner, C., & Wheeler, L. Model, need, and cost effects in helping behavior. *Journal of Personality and Social Psychology*, 1969, *12*, 111–116.

Weiner, B. A cognitive (attribution) -emotion-action model of motivated behavior: An analysis of judgments of help-giving. *Journal of Personality and Social Psychology*, 1980, *39*, 186–200.

Weyant, J. M. Effects of mood states, costs, and benefits on helping. *Journal of Personality and Social Psychology*, 1978, *36*, 1169–1176.

# 18

# Some Paradoxical Status Implications of Helping and Being Helped

Sidney Rosen

## 1. INTRODUCTION

A prosocial act, on the surface, may appear as a redistribution of resources in the direction of equalizing the worth of donor and recipient. Yet we are told that the act may well promote inequality in a direction favoring the donor. We seem, then, to be confronted by a paradox. Since paradoxes have little currency in our empirical world, how do we resolve it?

Let us consider the "inequality" alternative. Blau (1964) proposes that the reciprocation of benefits is conducive to social bonds in a relationship of peers, whereas nonreciprocation promotes status differentiation, and probably power differentiation, by validating the initial donor's claim to superior status (see also Homans, 1960). Moreover, recipients are obliged to reciprocate, if possible, lest they be sanctioned (Gouldner, 1960). If reciprocation is unfeasible, the obligation is said to be discharged by according superior status to the donor.

Before inquiring about the evidence, we should note that although

SIDNEY ROSEN • Institute for Behavioral Research and Department of Psychology, University of Georgia, Athens, Georgia 30602. This work was funded in part by the Graduate School, the Department of Psychology, and the Institute for Behavioral Research of the University of Georgia.

Blau mentions different kinds of status, his theorizing has nothing to say about those differences. Here, we too shall assume that different kinds of help imply different resource dimensions (e.g. Foa & Foa, 1974; French & Raven, 1959; Rosen, Levinger, & Lippitt, 1961), and although the pattern of status differentiation based on some dimensions (e.g., likeability) may differ from that based on others (e.g., expertness), for the time being we shall not pursue these distinctions. Note also that the primary social unit in Blau's treatment appears to be the face-to-face, informal group, including informal groups that evolve in work settings. Our focus, too, will be on the informal group.

What empirical support is there for Blau's theorizing? Virtually the sole source of relevant support is his often cited field study (1963) of consultative patterns in one department of a federal agency. That department consisted of 16 agents, a clerk, and their supervisor. Each agent had the responsibility of deciding whether certain assigned business firms were violating any of a large set of complex regulations, and to submit written reports recommending actions. If an agent encountered difficulties, official policy dictated that he seek the supervisor's advice, and forbade consultation with fellow-agents. In actuality, agents often avoided seeking the supervisor's advice for fear that they would appear indecisive, if not given to inaccuracies, impressions that would prompt the supervisor to enter low ratings in their personnel record. Instead, there arose informal patterns of consultation with fellow-agents,. Those few agents who were recognized as clearly more competent than the rest and were cooperative were often consulted unilaterally. In return, the recipients would defer to the views that these "experts" expressed at formal group meetings; furthermore, the "experts" were free to assume a dominant role in dealing with outside officials. There also evolved *mutual* consultation pairs, in which each agent consulted the other. The advice that one pair member received from his partner may have been of lesser quality than that which the "expert" agents could have given, but then he could avoid the high social psychological costs of being perceived as dependent on, and of possibly being rebuffed by, those experts.

Unfortunately, *direct* experimental support is lacking for the hypothesis that nonreciprocation may promote status (and power) differentiation. There is substantial experimental support (with important exceptions, e.g., Clark, Gotay, & Mills, 1974) for the proposition that needy people are loath to accept help if they anticipate no future opportunity to reciprocate (for early evidence, see Greenberg & Shapiro, 1971; Morris & Rosen, 1973), and that people tend to reciprocate help, given the resources to do so (e.g., Lanzetta & Wilke, 1971).

Let us assume, nevertheless, that the alleged status-differentiating effect of helping is valid, but that its occurrence is moderated by certain factors. A person × situation approach suggests itself, in principle, as a strategy for identifying such moderators. Since the number of possible moderators seems endless, I shall limit myself here to the exploration of only a few likely candidates. First, I shall focus on one possible situational moderator, namely, the nature of the preexisting relationship. Next I shall turn to one personal moderator, self-esteem. Then I shall report on two exploratory studies that include situational and personal moderators. Finally, we shall suggest further avenues for exploration.

## 2. THE PREEXISTING RELATIONSHIP AS A SITUATIONAL MODERATOR

### 2.1. Preexisting Relationships among Nonpeers

There is converging evidence that in a heterogeneous group where members are distinguishable in terms of *diffuse status characteristics,* such as sex or race, those preexisting status differences generalize to determine the social structure of that group. The most widely cited theoretical accounting for this phenomenon is called *expectation states theory* by its sociological propounders (e.g., Berger, Cohen, & Zelditch, 1972; Cohen, 1979; Meeker & Weitzel-O'Neill, 1977; Webster & Driskell, 1978). In essence, members with the more desirable characteristics (e.g., the males and whites) expect and are expected by their counterparts (e.g., the females and blacks) to perform relatively better in task-oriented groups, in the absence of *perceived* information to the contrary. These shared expectations legitimate the taking of more active roles, as in initiating ideas, by such more "competent" members, and leads to their being relatively more influential and being attributed with relatively greater status and power by other members.

It is particularly notable that such status generalization can occur even when these diffuse status characteristics are task irrelevant. For example, Moore (1969) led junior college females to believe they would be interacting with either a Stanford University or a high school female. Half were told that former subjects with the same educational status had performed either better or less well on the forthcoming task; the other half were given no such explicit information. Subject resistance to the alleged partner's judgments on "disagree" trials was charted. Of greatest interest was the gradual "erosion" in such differential resistance when task relevance was left implicit, but the striking *divergence* over time in the differential resistance of high versus low status subjects when task relevance was made explicit.

Apparently, it takes extraordinary measures, such as providing those with lower diffuse status with an initial advantage (e.g., via special training) on a task-specific dimension, to produce status equalization (Aronson & Bridgeman, 1979; Cohen, 1979; Webster & Driskell, 1978). Making them equally task competent is insufficient. The burden of proof is said to be on those with low diffuse status to convince their counterparts that their task-specific competence, *not* the diffuse status characteristic, is relevant.

What does all this have to do with helping and being helped? It suggests that the same benefit may be valued more by both parties if it came from someone with higher than with lower diffuse status. Moreover, people with subordinate status who wish to help their counterparts face the dilemma (Blau, 1964) of needing to advertise their wares if they are to improve their status level, but risk cheapening their resources if they persist in offering help frequently (Crosbie, 1972). Furthermore, generous acts from a high status donor are likely to be seen as internally caused, whereas those from a low status donor might be attributed to external prompting, viewed as ingratiation attempts (cf. Brickman, Coates, Rabinowitz, & Cohn, 1977; Thibaut & Riecken, 1955), or seen as "tribute" (Blau, 1964).

A well-differentiated status structure is not inevitable (Freese, 1974; Rosen, 1959): Some small groups fail to show clear-cut status differentiation (Fisek & Ofshe, 1970). To the extent, however, that a differentiated status (and power) structure does develop, another seeming paradox occurs. Those lower in the social hierarchy may well seek help from peers wbo ostensibly possess fewer resources or are less able to provide help effectively (Blau, 1963; Rosen, 1959). This, by the way, does not contradict the well-documented findings that high status individuals generally receive more communications from lower status persons than they initiate to the latter (e.g., Barnlund & Harland, 1963; Hurwitz, Zander, & Hymovitch, 1953); there are far fewer constraints against the upward communication of pleasantries and task-irrelevant comments than of hostile remarks (cf. Kelley, 1951) and direct influence attempts.

It may be, as Blau suggests, that inferior help from a peer of similarly low status is perceived to be less costly or easier to reciprocate. Or, it may be that obtaining help outside the group is even costlier. Direct, experimental evidence is needed, however, not only that such perceptions exist but that they steer behavior. We know that help seekers do expect to be viewed as being less competent (DePaulo & Fisher, 1980), and that their expectations are well founded (Wills, 1976, 1978).

Members who see themselves as having relatively high status or power also tend to be more resistant to attempted influence by other members (Levinger, 1959; Lippitt, Polansky, & Rosen, 1952; Moore, 1969). If the attempted influence entails an offer of help, it might be viewed as hazardous by those lower in the hierarchy to refuse the offer from someone higher. Blau (1964) suggests that one loses even more status by rejecting help from someone of higher status, since the refusal may be interpreted as concealing an inability to reciprocate. If this reasoning is correct, there is a distinct possibility that would-be donor versus recipient attributions concerning the refusal of help may well depend on the relative status of the parties. Blau also maintains that the consequences of refusing help from donors of lower status are enmity, not status loss. This, however, would not explain why older people, that is, people with higher diffuse status, refuse help from younger people (DePaulo, 1978; Druian & DePaulo, 1977).

It is probable that certain recipients (e.g., wards of the state, pensioners) acknowledge their lesser status, whether out of principle or expedience, in order to justify being exempted from having to reciprocate (cf. Lipman & Sterne, 1962). There is experimental evidence that handicapped persons (paraplegics) who acknowledge their handicap to the nonhandicapped are preferred as future partners by the latter to those who do not make such an acknowledgment. The investigators (Hastorf, Wildfogel, & Cassman, 1979) suggest that such acknowledgment may be a useful social tactic, since it reduces discomfort and uncertainty in the nonhandicapped concerning how to interact. It is a moot question, however, whether the same level of positive regard would be induced if the acknowledgment were coupled with a request for help, particularly help that is handicap irrelevant. In the latter case, a more effective tactic might be to have the help requested by third parties in behalf of the handicapped person.

### 2.2. Preexisting Peer and Close Relationships

Blau (1964), among others, distinguishes between social and economic exchange. Obligations incurred by being benefited in a social rather than in an economic exchange are left unspecified, and their discharge is said to depend on trust. If the benefit is reciprocated, the relationship becomes characterized by social bonds between peers. In the case of mutual attraction and love, explicit bargaining or open allusion to reciprocation is taboo. Note that the obligation to reciprocate does not disappear, except as a topic of conversation.

A more extreme view is taken by Clark and Mills (1979), who prefer the terms "exchange relationship" to "economic relationship" and "communal relationship" to "social relationship." They insist that the essence of a communal relationship (e.g., a friendship or kinship) is mutual responsiveness to one another's needs, and that explicit or prompt reciprocation can threaten the viability of the relationship. Although Clark and Mills present experimental data suggesting that partners who reciprocate in a communal context are less liked, and those who do so in an exchange context are more liked, than those who do not reciprocate, the role of reciprocation in intimate relationships is still unresolved.

In this connection, a study by Bar-Tal, Bar-Zohar, Greenberg, and Hermon (1977) is instructive. Students were asked to voice their expectations of, and felt gratitude for, receiving help that they supposedly had requested from a parent, sibling, close friend, acquaintance, or stranger, respectively. The more intimate the relationship, the more they expected that the help *should* be forthcoming, the less gratitude they felt on getting it, and the more resentment they felt when they were refused the help. It appears that an intimate relationship constitutes a limiting condition in which being helped, in the short run, does not enhance the status difference between donor and recipient, since the latter feels *entitled* to the help. One wonders, however, what the *donors* feel is their due after complying or how they justify refusing help. Would parents believe that they are entitled to deference from offspring? If so, might not this suggest a desire to at least maintain the status difference? Conceivably, a parent might insist on maintaining surveillance to ensure that the child used a benefit "wisely." Might not this attempt to control the use of the benefit reinforce the status difference (cf. Brickman *et al.*, 1977)?

To summarize, it appears that the status differences in preexisting relationships of nonpeers have a self-perpetuating quality. Those of lower status defer to the wishes of those of higher status, including presumably overt acceptance of unwanted "help" from the latter. It is also the case that high status members are resistant to influence attempts from lower status members, and that the latter often tend to direct most of their influence attempts to same-status members. We do not know, however, to what extent the resistance of higher status members reflects an intent by such members to discourage reciprocation, and if it is perceived as such by their low status counterparts. With regard to preexisting peer and close relationships, even if we accept that in the short run the "squaring of accounts" through reciprocation is a tactless act, we lack hard evidence as to how long a communal relationship would continue in the absence of reciprocation, whether a status difference would be an inevitable consequence of repeated nonreciprocation, and whether a recipient's claim of entitlement serves to inhibit status differentiation.

## 3. SELF-ESTEEM AS A PERSONAL MODERATOR

One particularly important personal factor that affects the readiness to seek or accept help is self-esteem. By and large, people with high (manipulated) self-esteem are more willing to seek help than those with low self-esteem, even if they anticipate no future opportunity to reciprocate (Morris & Rosen, 1973), unless important attributes are threatened (Gergen, Morse, & Kristeller, 1973; Tessler & Schwartz, 1972). There are also indications that acceptance of help does come to reflect adversely on self-esteem (Fisher, Harrison, & Nadler, 1978; Nadler, Altman, & Fisher, 1979) and on the donor's inferred esteem for the recipient (DePaulo & Fisher, 1980). It should be noted, too, that *some* people with high self-esteem (Morris & Rosen, 1973) or high need achievement (Tessler & Schwartz, 1972) may be so bent on mastering a task through their own efforts that they do not seek help on it. Perhaps it is because the task poses a compelling personal challenge for them, rather than because accepting help would cast them into an inferior status relationship, that they do not seek help. We might view these findings as indicating that people who view themselves favorably on a sufficient number of other status attributes may be relatively less concerned about acknowledging a donor's superior status on an isolated attribute, unless that particular attribute is of signal importance, or they view the particular task as a challenge to their mettle.

Less is known about the impact of self-esteem on giving help. As Midlarsky indicates both in Chapter 14 and elsewhere (Midlarsky, 1971; Midlarsky & Midlarsky, 1973, 1976), high self-esteem is conducive to extending help, and successful helping serves to reinforce one's self-esteem. Still to be determined, however, is whether either effect relates to status differentiation, and is affected by the prospect of reciprocation.

## 4. SOME EFFECTS OF EFFICACY- VERSUS EMPATHY-BASED HELPING ON SELF–OTHER EVALUATIONS

Central, perhaps, to the notion of self-esteem is a construct variously labeled *efficacy* (e.g., White, 1965), self-efficacy, personal control, or competence. This construct has been conceptualized by social learning theorists (Bandura, 1977; Kanfer, 1979; Midlarsky, Chapter 14, this volume) as an instigator of helping. What makes the construct especially interesting here is that it appears to have drastically different implications for status differentiation than does that personal instigator of helping known as *empathy*. Note that the contrast to be drawn is not between altruism and self-interest, since self-interest is too broadly construed for our purposes. In principle, self-interest could be promoted either through self-enhancement or self-maintenance. In practice, it has often been equated with the latter, as when donors are said to help in order to avoid pain (Batson, Duncan, Ackerman, Buckley, & Birch, 1981).

The Kanfer (1979) and Feshbach (1978) approaches to efficacy and empathy, respectively, are especially pertinent. According to Kanfer, an implicit objective in all societies is to develop in the individual a sense of personal control over the environment. But the unbridled encouragement of individuality and self-determination may threaten a group's stability and survival. The "dialectic" solution is training in self-control such that persons come to act for the benefit of another because successful help will make the donor feel more efficacious. The initial step requires external incentives such as approval or recognition for prosocial acts, at low cost to the trainee. Costs would be gradually increased. In time, as the trainee discovers that he or she can *effectively* benefit another, the external incentives can give way to self-generated incentives for such behavior.

Feshbach's cognitive-affective-empathy training stresses, instead, learning to discriminate and match affective cues in others, learning to take the perspective of others (decentering), and emotional responsiveness (cf. Coke, Batson, & McDavis, 1978). Such training has as its broad objective the reduction of aggression and the fostering of prosocial values, and is said to promote social understanding, compassion, and communication skills. (See Crandall, 1980, on the related construct of "social interest.")

The most striking implication is that Kanfer's efficacy seems more likely than Feshbach's empathy approach to promote status differentiation following a prosocial act. This is because the motive in the former case is an enhanced feeling of competence. In contrast, empathic concern seems conducive to cognitive-affective *unit formation,* not differentiation, between donor and recipient.

Assuming these interpretations of the two motive bases are correct, certain differential consequences suggest themselves: Unlike the empathy-motivated potential helper, the efficacy-motivated counterpart might be more inclined to process the relevance of a prosocial act for promoting self-efficacy in deciding whether to help. If so, one might expect relatively greater temporizing or response latency by the "efficacious" donor; greater selectivity (see also Phares & Lamiell, 1975) in choice of recipient (helping a young child on a simple task would do little for an adult's sense of efficacy); greater likelihood of helping when the recipient or an audience (Midlarsky, 1971) is present (since external incentives might be needed more, occasionally); and less attention to the recipient's wishes as to when (and if) the help should begin and end.

Since empathizing increases the likelihood of generating situational rather than dispositional explanations (e.g., incompetence) for the recipient's state (Regan & Totten, 1975), it seems plausible, too, that empathy-based helping would be relatively less likely to validate a donor's claims to superior status.

Suppose, however, that both the "efficacious" and the "empathic" persons did extend help. How might this affect status differentiation? Might actual reciprocation interact with the motive base for helping in influencing status differentiation? These questions were explored in our laboratory (Rosen, Tomarelli, & Kidda, 1981). It seemed plausible that after successfully extending help, the efficacious helper would exhibit greater self-enhancement than would the empathic helper. The literature provides no clear-cut guidelines on the role that reciprocity might play here. According to some (Blau, 1964; Homans, 1960), donors may prefer that reciprocation not be complete, since the superior status engendered by helping could be maintained if not enhanced by incomplete reciprocation. Schwartz (1967) speculates that people "maintain ascendancy by regulating the indebtedness of others"—as when leaders ensure that the favors they render are never fully repaid (Whyte, 1964). This suggests that greater self-enhancement or devaluation of the recipient would occur under nonreciprocation than under reciprocation. However, for our study, such expectations seemed more applicable to the efficacious helper.

The role of gender in this context must also be considered. A variety of studies and minitheories suggest a greater affinity of males for efficacy and females for empathy (Austin, 1979; Austin & McGinn, 1977; Hoffman, 1977; Leventhal, 1973). Motive base would therefore interact with gender to produce more favorable self-enhancement by males under efficacy, and by females under empathy. Concerning gender and reciprocity, two experiments failed to find sex differences in the impact of opportunity to reciprocate on help seeking (Greenberg & Shapiro, 1971; Morris & Rosen, 1973), thus suggesting that gender would *not* interact with reciprocity. On the other hand, two lines of evidence suggested greater responsiveness by male than female helpers to variation in reciprocity: the favoring of equalitarian relationships by females but equitable relationships by males (Leventhal, 1973), and a finding that male recipients were relatively less likely than females to reciprocate when the donor had undeservedly come by his or her resources (Schubot & Rosen, 1978).

In the present study, subjects were asked to imagine that while walking to class they had stopped to help a same-sex motorist with car trouble. Motivational bases for helping were varied by systematic cues that accentuated either the efficacious or empathic orientation. In the former case, the helper recalls an earlier model who had shown pleasure on hearing the helper's car respond properly after demonstrating how to make the appropriate repair. The helper then reacts similarly in the present situation, and also remembers parental advice that you really know you are "somebody" when you succeed in helping someone. In the empathy condition, the helper recalls the helping model's reaction of pleasure on seeing his or her expression of relief once the car began to function properly. The helper now exhibits positive affect-matching with the present recipient when the repair is completed, and also recalls parental advice to take the perspective of persons in need, feel as they do, and render assistance. Reciprocation was varied by having the helper either accept or refuse the recipient's offer of a ride to class. Subsequently, participants rated both themselves (as helper) and the driver (the recipient) on 16 7-point bipolar evaluative scales (some culled from Dion, Berscheid, & Walster, 1972).

Since the rating scales suggested the presence of more than one evaluative factor, the data were factor analyzed. As expected, varimax rotation yielded (1) a factor we labeled "sociability," on which sensitivity, altruism, kindness, likability, modesty, and sympathy loaded highly; and (2) a factor we called "competence," on which strength, capability, sophistication, poise, skill, and competence loaded highly. Two pairs of weighted factor scores were then constructed, the weights being the respective factor loadings. Each pair consisted of a self (i.e., helper) score and a recipient score on a given factor. Since evaluating the self more favorably than the recipient seems to capture a status-differentiating or *perceived superiority* effect most directly, each pair of same-factor scores was further reduced to a difference, or superiority, score.

What were some of the findings relative to perceived superiority? Motive base interacted with reciprocation and gender in the case of *competence:* The females produced larger treatment differences. Specifically, empathic females judged their own competence as more superior under reciprocation than under nonreciprocation, whereas efficacious females judged their own competence to be less superior under reciprocation than under nonreciprocation. It was also noteworthy that although helpers generally rated themselves as superior on competence rather than on sociability, only on sociability did the magnitude of perceived superiority of empathic helpers exceed the comparable judgments of the efficacious helpers.

Certain methodological shortcomings in this study make interpretation of these complex results problematic. For instance, a largely female sample was confronted with a largely "masculine" helping task. Furthermore, since the helper's skill was acquired from a model who had helped similarly, this may have suggested that the present help constituted an indebtedness-reducing or equity-restoring (Austin & Walster, 1974) act, and therefore that reciprocation by the present recipient would only serve to reestablish inequity.

A follow-up study was therefore conducted (Rosen, Tomarelli, & Kidda, 1981) that varied not only motive base (empathy vs. efficacy) and reciprocation (acceptance vs. nonacceptance of a car ride), but also the helping context (helping with the car vs. helping an adult pacify a crying infant). Furthermore, the study eliminated mention of the helping model from the basic scenario, and employed relatively equal numbers of each gender. Since the two factors of sociability and competence again emerged, the same kinds of scores were again constructed.

Once again, helpers generally saw themselves as superior on competence, not on sociability. This was more the case in the baby context than in the car context. Although context made more of a difference for females than for males, it is clear that males more than females saw themselves as having superior competence with the car, whereas the reverse was the case with the baby, as expected. Closer examination revealed that this disordinal interaction of gender and context was confined to the efficacious helpers; the empathic helpers of both sexes produced greater superiority scores on competence in the baby than in the car situation.

The factor of reciprocation exerted some interesting effects on sociability. Although females generally expressed greater superiority on sociability than did males, the perceived superiority of females was higher under reciprocation than nonreciprocation, whereas that for males was relatively higher under nonreciprocation than under reciprocation. Of interest, too, is that superior sociability was expressed, by and large, under nonreciprocation than under reciprocation.

What have we learned? It becomes clear that our initial theorizing was rather simplistic. Furthermore, we may have muddied the waters by labeling one factor "competence" and the other "sociability" but failing to specify whether both were equally relevant indicators of status differentiation. In retrospect, we feel that more appropriate labels would have been "technical competence" and "interpersonal competence," respectively (cf. Elder, 1968; White, 1965), and that both should be examined.

Efficacy-based helping is not necessarily more conducive to status differentiation than is empathy-based helping. If we regard the results of the second study as more representative and generalizable than those of the first, we are led to the proposition that where *technical* competence is concerned, the efficacy-motivated helper's perceived superiority is partly dependent on whether the helping task is sex-role relevant. Thus males are more likely to see themselves as relatively superior than are females on the "masculine" (i.e., car) task, whereas the converse is the case on the "feminine" (i.e., baby) task. This is consistent with the view (Hoffman, 1977) that empathy is a relatively feminine outlook, at least in the present culture. (An isolated finding in the first study might be cited here: Efficacious males portrayed themselves as more self-respecting than did empathic males; this difference was reversed in the case of females.) Note, however, that although motive base did interact with gender, the specific prediction of greater perceived superiority of males under efficacy than under empathy, and of females under empathy than efficacy, was not supported.

Concerning the impact of reciprocation, the results are consistent with the thesis that nonreciprocation does promote status differences (Blau, 1964; Schwartz, 1967). That is especially true for males, regardless of motive base, but in the limited context of *interpersonal* competence. It should be borne in mind, though, that the recipient was only permitted to attempt reciprocation through an offer of a car ride, an act that may reflect more on the interpersonal competence than technical competence of the recipient. This constraint may partly explain why helpers generally saw themselves as having technical superiority rather than interpersonal superiority.

## 5. FURTHER AVENUES FOR NEEDED RESEARCH

Not only should gender-specific or gender-irrelevant types of tasks be employed in the future, but it is also advisable to consider to what extent competence of a particular sort is critically relevant for the kind of help required. Contributing one's labors on an additive task that does not require technical skill would seem to reflect less on self-efficacy than would assistance or advice on a difficult, disjunctive task, as Midlarsky's chapter implies. An expert's failure to help on a difficult task might be expected to elicit radically different attributions than failure to help on an easy task.

Translating these considerations into terms of status, we might propose that the status implications of helping and being helped are especially applicable, if not peculiar, to status dimensions that directly involve perceived competence. Whether this is as applicable to interpersonal as to technical competence remains to be seen. Since technical competence is probably easier to objectify and less dependent on social comparison, it might be easier to demonstrate the applicability of technical competence.

Thus far we have begged the question of what a helper's evaluations of self and recipient have to do with status. As sociologists use the term, status connotes value consensus by group members regarding a particular location on a given attribute dimension, and consensus as to what member, if any, occupies that position (cf. Berger *et al.*, 1972; Webster & Driskell, 1978). Can one afford to rely, then, only on the donor's or only on the recipient's views of status differences? If helpers engage in uniformly self-enhancing attributions or other "attribution errors" after extending help, could those attributions enable us to predict successfully the further relationship between donor and recipient? Obviously our confidence would be strengthened if we knew which views both parties *share*, and which they do not share, about their joint futures and what they believe each party can contribute towards that future.

It is noteworthy that M. Midlarsky and Midlarsky (1973, 1976) report a *direct* effect of status consistency (high achieved and high ascribed status) on willingness to help a partner, at some cost to the self (electric shock), but an *inverse* effect of status inconsistency (high achieved, low ascribed status) on helping. *Ascribed* status was manipulated by having the experimenter publicly state that the subject (or partner) was astute, pleasant to work with, and so on. *Achieved* status was manipulated by having the subjects "discover" that one of the pair was better at the eye–hand coordination task than was the average college student. Numerous other investigators would, instead, have made no allusion to the term "status," but would have claimed to have performed successfully two orthogonal manipulations of esteem or competence.

Several field experiments employing a same-age peer-tutoring paradigm were also conceptualized in terms of status level and status congruence (Rosen, Powell, & Schubot, 1977; Rosen, Powell, Schubot, & Rollins, 1978). Each student in several classrooms was paired with a same-sex classmate who was described to *both* parties as having performed better, about the same as, or worse than the partner in mathematics (achieved status). One member of each pair was randomly assigned to the more prestigious role of tutor, the other to the lesser role of tutee (ascribed status). Tutors received daily training, then tutored their respective partners daily. All took weekly performance tests and completed weekly evaluative questionnaires. After 2 weeks the partners exchanged roles, then carried out a similar 2-week sequence.

Not only did tutors rate their anticipated and actual performance higher than did tutees, they rated themselves as *more* important, valuable, and powerful (i.e., "like the boss"). Furthermore, tutors were *less* desirous of exchanging roles than were tutees. These differences were reversed after the partners were made to exchange roles. Decrements in performance and self-regard, and increments in desire to exchange roles, were especially forthcoming from those former tutors who were initially more competent than their partner and were now cast in the lesser role of tutee.

Although these tutoring studies bring self-evaluations somewhat closer to the notions of status used by sociologists, they only employed outcome measures. More complete understanding of the impact of status variables might have been obtained had we been in a position to observe the actual tutoring process. What might one look for in observing such interaction? Some possible candidates are the air of confidence and authority that the helper subsequently shows, and in the case of the recipient, verbal expressions of appreciation, accorded status (e.g., remarks by the recipient that acknowledge or imply superior knowledge or skill in the helper; Lippitt *et al.*, 1952), and nonverbal indicators of deference (e.g., eye gaze, posture, proxemic measures, etc.). The importance of distinguishing between "spontaneous" and "asked for" help (compliance) has been documented by Eisenberg-Berg, Cameron, and Tryon (see Chapter 5). It might also be useful to distinguish acts of compliance that constitute reciprocation from compliant acts that do not (Kaplowitz, 1978).

Earlier we drew attention to the thesis by some sociologists that, in order to maintain superior status, donors may prefer not to be fully repaid. Our exploratory studies, however, treated reciprocity in all-or-none terms. This equation of nonreciprocation with incomplete reciprocation may have been ill advised. Perhaps a donor's reactions to subsequent reciprocation are some *nonlinear* function of reciprocation magnitude. It may also be that the likelihood of *extending* help is some nonlinear function of the expected magnitude of reciprocation. Simmel (1950) believed that a spontaneous gift gave the donor a sense of moral superiority over the recipient, since it could never be fully repaid (reciprocation requires premeditation). It is unclear, though, how such a vicarious form of self-reward translates readily into a practical claim for superior status, since calling attention to the spontaneity might suggest that one's gift was premeditated. Besides, applying for sainthood is in bad form.

Our discussion of alternative socialization paradigms of prosocial behavior has focused only on the donor. The question arises as to the possible existence of alternative socialization practices addressed to the *recipient's* role—what to accept or reject, from whom, under what circumstances, and in what manner. Clearly, the problem has received little systematic attention. The preceding chapter represents a good beginning in this direction. One seeming paradox is that some investigators view the acceptance of help as activating an aversive drive state of "indebtedness" (Greenberg & Shapiro, 1971; Shumaker & Jackson, 1979). Others see it as inducing a positive feeling of gratitude or at least a pleasant state (Batson, Harris, McCaul, Davis, & Schmidt, 1979; Cunningham, Steinberg, & Grev, 1980; Tesser, Gatewood, & Driver, 1968). It is conceivable that each is more relevant for some rather than other kinds of help and/or relationship. Perhaps felt indebtedness, in contrast to gratitude, is more likely when accepting help under conditions that appear conducive to status differentiation and to reflect negatively on the recipient's competence.

The final issue to be addressed concerns status differences in ongoing, intimate relationships. Clark and Mills (1979) hold that elements of both exchange and communality may be present in any intimate relationship, but that when the partners begin dickering at length about who is doing or has done what and how much for the other, the relationship may be degenerating into one of exchange. It might be useful to investigate whether open allusions to status differences or status incongruence occur in long-term relationships, and if so, in association with what critical events. Other clues might be sought in the comparative rates of giving and receiving help. An experiment by Lanzetta and Wilke (1971) is suggestive of what to look for. They found support for a "credit" hypothesis when aid by one party decreased, but for an "unconditional reciprocity" hypothesis when aid increased. Just how long a partner in an intimate relationship who has grown less responsive can draw on past credit, and what attributional processes by the "disadvantaged" partner sustain that credit, is a challenging empirical question. It is also important to determine to what extent the communal elements remain prepotent, when because of external circumstances beyond one partner's control that partner is no longer able to minister adequately to the needs of the other partner.

## 6. CONCLUSIONS

This conceptual analysis of the allegation that prosocial behavior may promote donor–recipient status differences has raised many, one hopes provocative, questions. If it has uncovered few definitive answers, this is probably because those of us who are aware of the allegation have been content up to now merely to cite it in passing, perhaps to accept it as a given, but in any case not to pursue it directly as an important enough problem for systematic, empirical research. One might even go so far as to say that this failure is an inevitable outcome of our almost exclusive preoccupation with individual psychological variables.

A social order can be both an important source of forces for, as well as an important consequent of, prosocial action. So much is implicit in our person × situation analysis of the possible linkage between helping behavior and status differentiation. In that analysis I have proposed that the assertion needs to be qualified by multiple moderator variables. Thus I have suggested, for illustrative purposes, that the linkage is probably influenced by such situational moderators as the nature of the preexisting relationship; entitlement, or the perceived right to receive certain benefits; and the prospect of reciprocal helping. It was also suggested that it is probably influenced by such personal moderators as self-esteem or perceived competence, achievement motivation, and the particular motivational basis for helping—as, for example, whether we are prompted by an empathic concern for the recipient, or by the belief that helping someone would enhance our sense of efficacy. There is much to be done here.

## 7. REFERENCES


Aronson, E., & Bridgeman, D. Jigsaw groups and the desegregated classroom: In pursuit of common goals. *Personality and Social Psychology Bulletin,* 1979, *5,* 438–446.

Austin, W. Sex differences in bystander intervention in a theft. *Journal of Personality and Social Psychology,* 1979, *37,* 2110–2120.

Austin, W., & McGinn, N. C. Sex differences in choice of distribution rules. *Journal of Personality,* 1977, *45,* 379–394.

Austin, W., & Walster, E. Participants' reactions to "Equity with the world." *Journal of Experimental Social Psychology,* 1974, *10,* 528–548.

Bandura, A. Self-efficacy: Toward a unifying theory of behavioral change. *Psychological Review,* 1977, *84,* 191–215.

Barnlund, D. C., & Harland, C. Propinquity and prestige as determinants of communication networks. *Sociometry,* 1963, *26,* 467–479.

Bar-Tal, D., Bar-Zohar, Y., Greenberg, M. S., & Hermon, M. Reciprocity behavior in the relationship between donor and recipient and between harm-doer and victim. *Sociometry,* 1977, *40,* 293–298.

Batson, C. D., Harris, A. C., McCaul, K. D., Davis, M., & Schmidt, T. Compassion or compliance: Alternative dispositional attributions for one's helping behavior. *Social Psychology Quarterly,* 1979, *42,* 405–409.

Batson, C. D., Duncan, B. D., Ackerman, P., Buckley, T., & Birch, K. Is empathic emotion a source of altruistic motivation? *Journal of Personality and Social Psychology,* 1981, *40,* 290–302.

Berger, J., Cohen, B. P., & Zelditch, M., Jr. Status characteristics and social interaction. *American Sociological Review,* 1972, *37,* 241–255.

Blau, P. M. *The dynamics of bureaucracy: A study in interpersonal relations in two governmental agencies* (Rev. ed.) Chicago: University of Chicago Press, 1963.

Blau, P. M. *Exchange and power in social life.* New York: Wiley, 1964.

Brickman, P., Coates, D., Rabinowitz, V. C., & Cohn, E. *Dilemmas of helping.* Unpublished manuscript, Northwestern University, 1977.

Clark, M. S., & Mills, J. Interpersonal attraction in exchange and communal relationships. *Journal of Personality and Social Psychology,* 1979, *37,* 12–24.

Clark, M. S., Gotay, C. C., & Mills, J. Acceptance of help as a function of similarity of the potential helper and opportunity to repay. *Journal of Applied Social Psychology*, 1974, *4*, 224–229.

Cohen, E. G. *The desegregated school: Problems in status power and interracial climate.* Paper presented at the meeting of the American Psychological Association, New York, September 1979.

Coke, J. S., Batson, C. D., & McDavis, K. Empathic mediation of helping: A two-stage model. *Journal of Personality and Social Psychology*, 1978, *36*, 752–766.

Crandall, J. E. Adler's concept of social interest: Theory, measurement, and implications for adjustment. *Journal of Personality and Social Psychology*, 1980, *39*, 481–495.

Crosbie, P. V. Social exchange and power compliance: A test of Homans' propositions. *Sociometry*, 1972, *35*, 203–222.

Cunningham, M. R., Steinberg, J., & Grev, R. Wanting to and having to help: Separate motivations for positive mood and guilt-induced helping. *Journal of Personality and Social Psychology*, 1980, *38*, 181–192.

DePaulo, B. M. Accepting help from teachers—when the teachers are children. *Human Relations*, 1978, *31*, 459–474.

DePaulo, B. M., & Fisher, J. D. The costs of asking for help. *Basic and Applied Social Psychology*, 1980, *1*, 23–35.

Dion, K., Berscheid, E., & Walster, E. What is beautiful is good. *Journal of Personality and Social Psychology*, 1972, *24*, 285–290.

Druian, P. R., & DePaulo, B. M. Asking a child for help. *Social Behavior and Personality*, 1977, *5*, 33–39.

Elder, G. H., Jr. Adolescent socialization and development. In E. F. Borgotta & W. W. Lambert (Eds.), *Handbook of personality theory and research.* Chicago: Rand, McNally, 1968.

Feshbach, N. D. *Empathy training: A field study in affective education.* Address presented at the meeting of the American Educational Research Association, Toronto, March 1978.

Fisek, M. H., & Ofshe, R. The process of status evolution. *Sociometry*, 1970, *33*, 327–346.

Fisher, J. D., Harrison, C. L., & Nadler, A. Exploring the generalizability of donor-recipient similarity effects. *Personality and Social Psychology Bulletin*, 1978, *4*, 627–630.

Foa, U. G., & Foa, E. B. *Societal structures of the mind.* Springfield, Ill.: Charles C. Thomas, 1974.

Freese, L. Conditions for status equality in informal task groups. *Sociometry*, 1974, *37*, 174–188.

French, J. R. P., Jr., & Raven, B. The bases of social power. In D. Cartwright (Ed.), *Studies in social power.* Ann Arbor: University of Michigan Press, 1959.

Gergen, K. J., Morse, S. J., & Kristeller, J. L. The manner of giving: Cross-national continuities in reactions to aid. *Psychologia*, 1973, *16*, 121–131.

Gouldner, A. W. The norm of reciprocity: A preliminary statement. *American Sociological Review*, 1960, *25*, 161–178.

Greenberg, M. S., & Shapiro, S. P. Indebtedness: An adverse aspect of asking for and receiving help. *Sociometry*, 1971, *34*, 290–301.

Hastorf, A. H., Wildfogel, J., & Cassman, T. Acknowledgment of handicap as a tactic in social interaction. *Journal of Personality and Social Psychology*, 1979, *37*, 1790–1797.

Hoffman, M. L. Sex differences in empathy and related behaviors. *Psychological Bulletin*, 1977, *84*, 712–722.

Homans, G. C. *The human group.* New York: Harcourt, Brace & World, 1960.

Hurwitz, J. E., Zander, A. F., & Hymovitch, B. Some effects of power on the relations among group members. In D. Cartwright & A. Zander (Eds.), *Group dynamics: Research and theory.* Evanston, Ill.: Row, Peterson, 1953.

Kanfer, F. H. Personal control, social control, and altruism: Can society survive the age of individualism? *American Psychologist*, 1979, *34*, 231–239.

Kaplowitz, S. A. Towards a systematic theory of power attribution. *Social Psychology,* 1978, *41,* 131–148.

Kelley, H. H. Communication in experimentally created hierarchies. *Human Relations,* 1951, *4,* 39–56.

Lanzetta, J. T., & Wilke, H. The obligation to help: The effects of levels of prior help on subsequent helping. *European Journal of Social Psychology,* 1971, *1,* 97–106.

Leventhal, G. S. *Reward allocation by males and females.* Paper presented at the meeting of the American Psychological Association, Montreal, August 1973.

Levinger, G. The development of perceptions and behavior in newly formed social power relationships. In D. Cartwright (Ed.), *Studies in social power.* Ann Arbor: University of Michigan Press, 1959.

Lipman, A., & Sterne, R. Aging in the United States: Ascription of a terminal sick role. *Sociology and Social Research,* 1962, *53,* 194–203.

Lippitt, R., Polansky, N., & Rosen, S. The dynamics of power. *Human Relations,* 1952, *5,* 37–64.

Meeker, B. F., & Weitzel-O'Neill, P. A. Sex roles and interpersonal behavior in task-oriented groups. *American Sociological Review,* 1977, *42,* 91–105.

Midlarsky, E. Aiding under stress: The effects of competence, dependency, visibility, and fatalism. *Journal of Personality,* 1971, *39,* 132–149.

Midlarsky, M., & Midlarsky, E. Some determinants of aiding under experimentally induced stress. *Journal of Personality,* 1973, *41,* 305–327.

Midlarsky, M., & Midlarsky, E. Status inconsistency, aggressive attitude, and helping behavior. *Journal of Personality,* 1976, *44,* 371–391.

Moore, J. C., Jr. Social status and social influence: Process considerations. *Sociometry,* 1969, *32,* 145–158.

Morris, S. C., III, & Rosen, S. Effects of felt adequacy and opportunity to reciprocate on help seeking. *Journal of Experimental Social Psychology,* 1973, *9,* 265–276.

Nadler, A., Altman, A., & Fisher, J. D. Helping is not enough: Recipient's reactions to aid as a function of positive and negative information about the self. *Journal of Personality,* 1979, *47,* 615–628.

Phares, E. J., & Lamiell, J. T. Internal-external control, interpersonal judgments of others in need, and attributions of responsibility. *Journal of Personality,* 1975, *43,* 23–38.

Regan, D. T., & Totten, J. Empathy and attribution: Turning observers into actors. *Journal of Personality and Social Psychology,* 1975, *32,* 850–856.

Rosen, S. Effects of adjustment on the perception and exertion of social power. In D. Cartwright (Ed.), *Studies in social power.* Ann Arbor: University of Michigan Press, 1959.

Rosen, S., Levinger, G., & Lippitt, R. Perceived sources of social power. *Journal of Abnormal and Social Psychology,* 1961, *63,* 188–190.

Rosen, S., Powell, E. R., & Schubot, D. B. Peer-tutoring outcomes as influenced by the equity and type of role assignment. *Journal of Educational Psychology,* 1977, *69,* 244–252.

Rosen, S., Powell, E. R., Schubot, D. B., & Rollins, P. Competence and tutorial role as status variables affecting peer-tutoring outcomes in public school settings. *Journal of Educational Psychology,* 1978, *70,* 602–612.

Rosen, S., Tomarelli, M. M., & Kidda, M. L., Jr. *Some consequences of empathic versus efficacy-seeking motivation for helping.* Paper presented at the meeting of the Southeastern Psychological Association, Atlanta, March 1981.

Schubot, D., & Rosen, S. *The effect of resource deservedness and opportunity to reciprocate on help seeking.* Paper presented at the meeting of the Southeastern Psychological Association, Atlanta, March 1978.

Schwartz, B. The social psychology of the gift. *American Journal of Sociology,* 1967, *73,* 1–11.

Shumaker, S. A., & Jackson, J. S. The aversive effects of nonreciprocated benefits. *Social Psychology Quarterly*, 1979, *42*, 148–158.

Simmel, G. Faithfulness and gratitude. In K. H. Wolff (Ed.), *The sociology of George Simmel*. Glencoe, Ill.: Free Press, 1950.

Tesser, A., Gatewood, R., & Driver, M. Some determinants of gratitude. *Journal of Personality and Social Psychology*, 1968, *9*, 233–236.

Tessler, R. C., & Schwartz, S. H. Help seeking, self-esteem, and achievement motivation: An attributional analysis. *Journal of Personality and Social Psychology*, 1972, *21*, 318–326.

Thibaut, J. W., & Riecken, H. W. Some determinants and consequences of the perception of social causality. *Journal of Personality*, 1955, *24*, 113–133.

Webster, M., Jr., & Driskell, J. E., Jr. Status generalization: A review and some new data. *American Sociological Review*, 1978, *43*, 220–236.

White, R. The experience of efficacy in schizophrenia. *Psychiatry*, 1965, *28*, 199–211.

Whyte, W. F. *Street corner society*. Chicago: University of Chicago Press, 1964.

Wills, T. A. *Perceptual consequences of helping another person*. Paper presented at the meeting of the American Psychological Association, Washington, D.C., September 1976.

Wills, T. A. Perceptions of clients by professional helpers. *Psychological Bulletin*, 1978, *85*, 968–1000.

# 19

# The Darker Side of Helping

## The Social Dynamics of Helping and Cooperation

Stephen Worchel

## 1. INTRODUCTION

I have always looked forward to discussing the literature on helping behavior in my social psychology classes. Students' attention can be captivated instantly and tears brought to their eyes by recounting examples such as the Kitty Genovese case where help was needed but was not forthcoming. This introduction increases the students' receptiveness to examining the theories and research in the area. Then the coup de grace is usually supplied by the students who clamor for additional work on helping behavior, reasoning that if "we" knew the factors that motivate such behavior, "we" could increase its frequency and thereby make the world better.

This notion probably lurks in the minds of researchers in this area. Indeed, many of the studies (Darley & Latané, 1968; Latané & Darley, 1968; Piliavin, Piliavin, & Rodin, 1975) are designed so that the help giver saves the day and is presented in a positive light. Even the terminology (prosocial behavior, charity, helping) used to describe the giving of aid suggests that the help giver should incur admiration.

Although the donor is regarded warmly by most investigators and

---

STEPHEN WORCHEL • Department of Psychology, Texas A & M University, College Station, Texas 77840. Parts of this chapter were prepared while the author was a Senior Fulbright Research Scholar in Athens, Greece. The research was partially supported by grants from the National Science Foundation (BNS77-04892) and the National Institute of Mental Health (MH33468-01).

readers of helping literature, there is still the question of how the recipients of aid respond to these heroic donors. And, embedded in the answer to this question may be additional information about why people help or do not help. Indeed, there are theoretical grounds to predict that the donor should be valued and liked, especially by the recipient of the help. One of the basic models of interpersonal attraction (Lott & Lott, 1968; see also Byrne & Clore, 1970) posits that individuals like those who reward them. Norms that govern society espouse the virtues of helping others (Berkowitz, 1972). And theories of moral development equate altruistic behavior with the highest morals (Rubin & Schneider, 1973).

There is, however, another side of the coin that suggests that the rendering of aid may not be such a direct road winning the hearts of recipients and improving interpersonal relationships. Jones and his colleagues (Jones, 1964; Jones & Wortman, 1973) point out that the giving of aid or other rewards will not be reciprocated if such actions are interpreted as efforts to ingratiate the recipient. Suspected ingratiators are often the target of hostility and aggression.

More recent research has found that the risks faced by a donor extend far beyond the possibility of having his or her behavior attributed (or misattributed) to ingratiation. These studies, which focus on the recipient's reaction, indicate that receiving aid can lead to discomfort because recipients may feel indebted to the help giver (Greenberg, 1980). Indebtedness is an unpleasant arousal state that motivates the individual to seek means for reducing his or her obligation. Although the theory of indebtedness argues that recipients are motivated to reciprocate help, other investigators have found that helping can have the opposite effect on recipients; namely, helping may result in reactance and a determination not to reciprocate. Worchel and Andreoli (1974) and Brehm and Cole (1966) found that being the recipient of help may cause individuals to feel that their freedom not to reciprocate help is threatened. As a result of this reactance, they feel hostile toward the donor and refuse opportunities to reciprocate. Fisher and Nadler (1974, 1976) found that receiving aid, especially from a very similar donor, has negative effects on the recipient's self-esteem and self-confidence. In fact, these investigators found that placing individuals in the position where help might be forthcoming was sufficient to motivate them to help themselves. These efforts lessened the need for help and protected their self-esteem.

The studies on recipients' reactions demonstrate the complexity and wide-ranging effects of helping behavior. Helping is not simply an act in which one person gives something to another; help giving involves an interpersonal relationship between donor and recipient which is characterized by actions and feelings on the part of each.

## 2. THE INTERPERSONAL DYNAMICS OF HELPING

The act of helping can have two very different effects on the relationship between the helper and recipient. On the positive side, help giving can be seen as the first overture in a positive social exchange. The helper has taken a risk and given up a valuable resource in a situation that neither required the altruistic act nor demanded reciprocation. According to Schlenker, Helm, and Tedeschi (1973) and Swinth (1967), these conditions should promote the establishment of trust and attraction between donor and recipient. Clearly, there are numerous cases in which helping facilitates social interaction and brings the participants closer together (e.g., Huesmann & Levinger, 1976).

There is, however, another approach to examining helping behavior; this approach identifies social dynamics inherent in the helping exchange that may separate and alienate the participants. Taking this perspective, help giving is seen as *drawing boundaries* between the two parties involved; on the one hand, there is the donor, and on the other, the recipient. Distinguishing between the donor and recipient not only labels each party, but also separates them in terms of psychological distance. Simply making clear distinctions may damage the relationship between the help giver and recipient. Tajfel and his associates (Tajfel, 1970; 1974; Tajfel & Turner, 1979) have shown repeatedly that placing individuals into different groups, even when the assignments are based on arbitrary issues, may result in intergroup hostility. Byrne and his associates (e.g., Byrne, 1971) report that similarity between individuals is one of the major determinants of interpersonal attraction. The force toward interpersonal separation that is inherent in helping should work against mutual attraction.

Helping behavior not only draws a clear distinction between the donor and the recipient, it also defines a *power hierarchy;* the donor is cast in the role of a powerful figure whereas the recipient is relegated to a position of low power. Helping allows the donor to demonstrate that he or she has useful abilities and resources and can influence the behavior of others. Receiving help, on the other hand, forces the recipient to acknowledge needs and to demonstrate some degree of dependence on the donor.

Thus the present position is that there is a *yin* and a *yang* to helping. Since most previous theories and research have focused on the positive, integrating forces of helping, here I shall examine its darker side. This examination begins from the premise that there are indigenous forces in the helping relationship that separate donor and recipient and bestow power upon the donor and powerlessness upon the recipient.

## 3. POWER: A MOTIVE FOR HELPING

Examining the helping relationship in this manner suggests a possible motive for helping that has largely been overlooked by previous theories. According to a "wise saying" generally traced to ancient Chinese philosophy (although I recently found a similar statement inside a fortune cookie at a very American restaurant), an individual's true worth (or power) is measured not by what he has, but by what he gives away to others. This principle is also embodied in the potlach ceremony practiced by the Plains Indians. According to this practice an individual demonstrates his power by giving his personal possessions to other members of the tribe; the more that is given, the greater the power that accrues to the donor. In these ceremonies, great fortunes may be distributed to the tribe. According to our present analysis, there may be a great deal of application in the wise saying and in the potlach ceremony. If, as hypothesized, the act of rendering aid gives the donor power, then it may well be that *one* of the motives behind the help giving is the quest for power.

Power is generally equated with the ability to influence others (Michner & Suchner, 1972). Given this definition, there are a number of ways by which a donor can augment his or her power through helping. When the donor and recipient are in direct contact, the rendering of aid exercises an immediate influence on the recipient's behavior. In the simplest case, this relationship can be seen when an individual helps another across the street; the direction and speed of the recipient's travel are under the control of the helper. Another type of influence that accrues to the donor is that he or she may ask for the return of the favor in future settings. This might be seen as the "loaded pistol" position since the donor can choose the time and place when he or she desires the reciprocation. However, even when the donor and recipient are not in direct contact, helping behavior allows the donor to broadcast his or her superiority over the situation and demonstrate the capacity to influence. For example, the message, often explicit, in charity drives is that "powerful" and fortunate people should support the less powerful and unfortunate others. Donating to such a charity, therefore, implies that the donor is to be counted among the powerful.

This view of helping is clearly related to social exchange theories (e.g., Blau, 1964; Homans, 1961; Thibaut & Kelley, 1959). As with these theories, the present position suggests a "profit" motive behind helping behavior. However, the traditional approach suggests that the "profit" results largely because the recipient becomes obliged to return the favor at some later date. The reciprocation can be in the form of future favors or even simple friendship, but, regardless of the nature, the profit is based largely on the recipient's response. In the present model, this is not the case. Rather, it argues that power and powerlessness are intrinsic to helping. The donor gains power simply because he or she has helped, not because the recipient is obligated to return the favor. In essence, the recipient reciprocates by accepting the help. Although the donor may receive additional reward (and power) if the recipient returns the favor at some later date, this reciprocation is not necessary for the donor to gain power through helping.

Schopler (1970) has also examined the relationship between power and helping behavior, but using a somewhat different approach. Schopler focuses on the fact that donors often relinquish power by giving up information or some commodity that will enhance the position of the recipient vis-à-vis *that of the donor.* Schopler argues that the loss of power is a major factor that makes individuals reluctant to help. It is consistent with the present position to argue that individuals will refuse to help if they perceive that they will sacrifice more power than they receive by helping. The present position, however, stresses that helping involves more than the donor giving something to the recipient. Rather, the donor gains power by rendering aid and this augmentation of power is one factor that motivates helping behavior.

## 4. LEARNING TO HELP

How is the helping–power relationship learned? A quick glance at the world reveals that it is full of models suggesting that helping and power are closely related. As young children become aware of their surroundings, one of the first principles they learn is that their comfort and survival are dependent on receiving help from their parents. The parents' assistance is necessary to secure food, clothing, shelter, and to perform basic activities such as tying shoelaces or brushing teeth. The parent–child relationship is clearly one of unequal power; the parent is associated with power and the child is equated with powerlessness and dependence. The parent's power (and the child's powerlessness) is reaffirmed each time the parent helps the child. Thus in the parent–child relationship there is a clear model that power is associated with the act of helping.

The helping–power relationship is further personified in the basic teaching of most of the world's religions. A common theme is of a high, powerful deity extending help and protection to the needy, powerless masses. That the deity can and does exercise forgiveness and extend help is one root of the deity's power.

Many more examples could be cited. The world is filled with models that relate helping and power. In many cases, these lessons show that powerful people help because they are powerful, not because they hope to receive future favors from the people whom they help. Given these models, it is a short jump to the reasoning that power can be achieved by imitating helping behavior. Bandura, Ross, and Ross (1961) found children very willing to imitate the behavior of powerful and successful models.

It is also likely that the helping–power relationship is learned through reinforcement. A donor may quickly learn that a little bit of kindness goes a long way in influencing the behavior of others. Not only can a donor determine the course of the recipient's actions, but he or she may also be the recipient of praise from observers of the helping behavior. Although there may be direct utility in these responses, there is also additional confirmation of the belief that from helping comes power.

## 5. THE PSYCHOLOGY OF RECEIVING HELP

If power seeking is one currency that motivates help giving, then according to the present model, the act of accepting help involves relinquishing power. People accept help for many reasons. In some cases, they may use receiving help as the basis of an interpersonal relationship. In other cases, individuals may see themselves as deserving of help for their past actions. Although there are many reasons to accept help, the present model offers one reason why individuals may be reluctant to accept help. Namely, accepting an offer of aid may imply that the individual is unable (powerless) to handle the situation by his or her own efforts. Also involved in accepting help is the allowance for the donor to control, at least to some degree, the behavior of the recipient. The ills of helping behavior are highlighted in the Chinese proverb: "Why do you hate me? I have never helped you."[1]

If we view the recipient's position in this light, we can make a number of predictions about reactions to help. Some of these predictions can also be based on other theories of helping. However, these predictions are relevant to the present model and can be derived from the

[1]Thanks are due Leonard Berkowitz who supplied this information.

helping–power model. For example, an individual who relinquishes power by accepting help in one situation should be motivated to recapture this power by offering help in another situation. This prediction is similar to Greenberg's hypothesis (1980) that accepting help leads to the desire to return help. However, whereas Greenberg reasons that indebtedness results from a norm of reciprocity that help *should* be reciprocated, the present position is that the recipient wishes to reciprocate as a means of restoring power.

The helping–power analysis also suggests that the desire to reciprocate help should be strongest when the issue of power between the donor and recipient is salient. For example, help that is rendered by a high status donor should be less threatening than help rendered by a donor of equal or lower status than the recipient. The donor's status is important because it influences the recipient's attributions about the reasons for help. A high status donor is unlikely to gain much power by helping a lower status recipient. In such cases, power acquisition is an unlikely motive for the helping. Furthermore, the issue of power should not be salient since the clear differences along this dimension should reduce tendencies of social comparison (Festinger, 1954). However, a person of equal or lower status may be seeking to enhance his power by offering help. In support of this position, Thibaut and Riecken (1955) found that help is more willingly accepted from a high power person than a lower status donor.

Similarly, the locus of causality for the helping behavior may influence the salience of power and, thereby, determine the recipient's response. If the donor's actions are seen as guided by some external restraint, it is less likely that the recipient will see the helping as motivated by the desire for power enhancement. However, if the donor's actions are viewed as being under his or her voluntary control, the recipient may view power enhancement as being a motivating force behind the actions. Based on this reasoning, two predictions can be made. First, the recipient should be more anxious to reciprocate helping when it is seen as being internally caused by the donor than when it is viewed as being caused by environmental constraints.[2] Second, given an ambiguous situation, recipients should be motivated to attribute external causes for helping behavior. Such attributions should reduce the salience of power in the donor–recipient relationship and, thereby, reduce the motivation to reciprocate.

Both predictions have received support in previous research.

[2]The helping–power model is not the only position from which this prediction can be derived. It is also possible to argue that the internal locus of causality suggests that the donor's actions were intentional. Therefore, the recipient may feel more indebted to return the help in this case than if the helping were given unintentionally.

Greenberg and Frisch (1972) found that recipients were more likely to reciprocate help when the donor was perceived as acting voluntarily rather than as guided by situational constraints. Worchel, Andreoli, and Archer (1976) found that, when given the opportunity, recipients tended to make situational attributions for the cause of a donor's actions. The tendency toward situational attributions was most strong when the power relationship between the donor and recipient had previously been made salient. Nadler, Fisher, and Streufert (1974) found that aid from a friendly donor was reacted to more positively than aid from an unfriendly donor. According to Nadler *et al.*, the issue of motives and power is more salient between antagonists than between friends.

Finally, viewing the helping relationship in terms of power allows us to address the issue raised at the start of this chapter: Is rendering aid an effective way to win the admiration and gratitude of others? The present model suggests that, at least in some cases, it is not. Regardless of the motives of the donor, help giving enhances the donor's power and reduces that of the recipient. This argument may be extended to predict that the larger the favor, the greater the exchange of power. Certainly the recipient's loss of power must be weighed against the gains he or she receives through the help giving. Although it is difficult to compare the value of power against the direct gains accrued from receiving help, we can focus on some of the factors that will determine the outcome of this comparison. One of the most important factors is the salience of power for the recipient. As pointed out, in cases where power is salient (e.g., receiving help from an adversary), help giving is likely to elicit hostility rather than gratitude. A related issue involves the need of the recipient. In situations where help is a necessity for the recipient's well-being, the donor is likely to elicit attraction; the direct gain from the aid will be a more important issue than the exchange of power. However, when help is given in a situation where the recipient's need is ambiguous, gratitude is unlikely to be exchanged for aid. Along these lines, it is interesting to note that Latané and Darley (1968) found that individuals are reluctant to help in emergencies where needs of the victim are unclear. It is possible that the donor weighs these considerations before offering help.

## 6. POWER, HELPING, AND INTERGROUP RELATIONS

The research and theorizing on helping behavior has concentrated almost exclusively on the interpersonal level. Clearly, many of the examples of helping behavior that occur in everyday life are found in dyadic interactions. However, many other incidents of helping behavior are found at the intergroup level or are motivated by an individual's membership in a particular group. For example, a member of the International Red Cross may give food and clothing to the victims of a flood. Although this interaction may take place between two individuals, the underlying cause for the behavior is the actor's membership in the group; the donor helps because he or she is a member of the Red Cross and the recipient receives aid because he or she is a flood victim.

In addition to the fact that helping behavior often occurs at the intergroup level, there are theoretical reasons for examining the effects of intergroup help giving. First, many investigators (Levine & Campbell, 1972; Tajfel & Turner, 1979; Worchel & Norvell, 1980; Worchel, Axsom, Ferris, Samaha, & Schweitzer, 1978) have argued that there is a positive relationship between the salience of group boundaries and intergroup hostility. These investigators suggest that events that discriminate between groups increase ingroup favoritism. The present model argues that one of the consequences of helping is to separate the donor and recipient and increase the salience of interpersonal and intergroup distinctions.

Second, the model's focus on power is also central to the study of intergroup behavior. According to Shaw (1976), one of the major reasons that individuals join groups is to augment their power and status. Individuals actively seek to join groups that can afford them protection and increase their ability to influence others. Hence, a group is attractive to the extent that it has power and can fulfill its members' needs. Therefore, the issues of power may be inherently more important in intergroup interactions than in interpersonal interactions. And any action that threatens a group's power should be met with swift retaliation. There are numerous examples of this reaction in international diplomacy where offers of aid by one country are either directly rebuffed or accepted with reluctance and, at times, hostility. Taking note of this fact, a conservative senator from North Carolina recently called for drastic cuts in the foreign aid program arguing that history has shown that the United States has bought more enemies than friends through international aid.

There are a number of factors that influence the salience of group boundaries and the importance of power in intergroup relations. Worchel *et al.* (1978) found that group boundaries became most prominent when groups competed, or when previously hostile groups cooperated on a task that resulted in an unsuccessful outcome. Group boundaries diminished in importance when the cooperative efforts of the group members were rewarded with success. Turning to the issue of power, Sherif, Harvey, White, Hood, and Sherif (1961) found that competition led not only to intergroup hostility, but also to a tendency to view outgroup members with suspicion. Actions, even seemingly benign ones, by outgroup members were frequently interpreted as being aimed at usurping power and gaining advantages.

Thus the present model suggests that helping at the intergroup level may lead to a deterioration in intergroup relationships. This effect should be most evident when distinctive group boundaries exist and power is salient. Specifically, help giving should have a negative effect when it does not lead to an immediately successful outcome for the recipient and/or when the groups have previously experienced or expect to have competitive interactions.

## 7. COOPERATION: AN ALTERNATIVE TO HELPING

I have painted a rather bleak picture of the results of help giving. However, it must be remembered that the villain in this model is not in the substance of the aid; rather, it is in the process by which the aid is given. It is the dynamics of the helping interaction that separates the two parties and creates the power hierarchy. An important consideration is whether there is another means by which aid can be exchanged without rupturing the relationship of the parties involved.

In a series of studies on intergroup relations, Sherif and his colleagues (Sherif & Sherif, 1979; Sherif *et al.*, 1961) collected data showing that cooperation between members of different groups leads to intergroup attraction. This finding has been replicated numerous times (Blake & Mouton, 1971, 1979; Blanchard, Adelman, & Cook, 1975; Worchel *et al.*, 1976, 1978) in both field and laboratory settings. Unlike the helping relationship, individuals or groups involved in a cooperative interaction participate in a mutual exchange of effort, information, or materials. It is also clear, implicitly if not explicitly, that the parties are working for a similar goal and will share the outcome of their mutual effort. Cooperation should have a different effect than helping in many situations. Rather than separating the parties, cooperation brings the participants closer together. There is no distinction made between donor and recipient; each party is contributing to the exchange. The goal of cooperation is to reduce the boundaries between the parties. Because of these mutual efforts, the issue of power or a power hierarchy should not be salient in a cooperative relationship. Certainly some question may arise regarding the contribution of the various parties, but the power to influence is not central to the relationship.

Cooperation should not give rise to feelings of indebtedness (Greenberg, 1980) as does helping. It was postulated earlier that one cause of indebtedness is the recipient's desire to restore power through reciprocation. Since cooperative ventures do not entail acknowledging powerlessness vis à vis the other party, there is little reason why the feeling of indebtedness can arise. Also, because cooperation does not separate the parties and classify them in terms of power, engaging in cooperation should increase interpersonal or intergroup attraction. Helping, on the other hand, may strain the relationship and even lead to hostility between the participants.

## 8. HELPING, COOPERATION, AND INTERGROUP RELATIONS: AN EXPERIMENTAL EXAMINATION

One prediction derivable from the present analysis is that cooperation facilitates intergroup relations to a greater degree than does helping. It can also be predicted that differences in the effects of cooperation and helping should be particularly strong when the two groups have a history of competitive or antagonistic relationships. This prediction is based on the hypothesis that competition will sensitize members of the two groups to actions that threaten their power.

In order to examine these predictions, an experiment was designed to manipulate the history of interaction between two groups and then to have the two groups meet in either a helping, cooperative, or independent relationship. Intergroup attraction was measured both before and after the last interaction. It was expected that cooperation would lead to the greatest increase in intergroup attraction and that this effect would be strongest when the two groups had a history of competition. Helping, on the other hand, should be most damaging to intergroup relations after competition.

After subjects arrived at the experimental room they were given time to get acquainted before being divided into two three-man groups. The division into groups, which seemed random to subjects, was planned so that one group consisted of naïve subjects whereas the second was comprised of experimental confederates. The subjects were then told that the study would examine various methods for solving human relations problems that might be encountered in an organizational setting. In half the conditions, subjects were told that the two groups would be given the same information and their task was to develop the best solution. Their solutions would then be compared and the "winning group" would be announced after the study. It was made clear that the two groups would be competing for the best solution. In the noncompetitive conditions, subjects were told that the two groups would receive different information regarding the situation. The task of each group was to develop the best solution based on the available information. After they had completed their task, the two responses would be combined to obtain an overall solution to the problem. Following these instructions, the two groups were separated and given the problems on which to work—adapted cases from exercises in industrial relations (Maier, 1978). After subjects had worked on the problems, they were asked to rate how much they enjoyed the tasks and how well they liked each member of their group and the other group.

The experimenter then explained that it would take some time to examine the responses and asked the subjects to wait in their separate rooms. While he was talking to the group of naïve subjects there was a knock on the door and the experimenter went into the hall and engaged in a conversation. When he returned, he announced that another experimenter was in need of subjects to work on an anagram task. It would take only a short time but subjects would be rewarded with an hour of experimental credit if they achieved the criterion. The experimenter stated that at least three people would be needed, and he arranged a drawing to see which group would participate in the extra-credit exercise. In all cases the group of naïve subjects was chosen.

The second experimenter entered the room. In the *helping condition* he stated that he was authorized to give only 3 additional hours of credit and, hence, only the chosen group of three could work for credit. He did say that the other three subjects could help the chosen group by counting the anagrams and eliminating duplicates. This aid would increase the likelihood that the group would reach criterion and get their credit. The experimenter then left the room to explain the situation to the second group. When he returned, he informed the subjects that the second group "would be glad to help." In the *cooperation condition,* the second experimenter returned to announce that he could use all six subjects to work on the anagrams. By coordinating their efforts, it was more likely that they would reach criterion and all subjects could receive extra credit. After discussing this with the second group of subjects, the experimenter announced that the second group "would be glad to work together on the tasks." The instructions in the *no-interaction* group were similar to those in the cooperation group, except that it was clear that the two groups would not work together. Instead, each group would work on separate tasks; the tasks were unrelated and the responses of one group would not affect those of the other group.

The groups were then combined and the experimenter stated that he was interested in finding out how fast groups of people could work on this type of task. Before beginning the task, he asked all subjects to complete a questionnaire that "would assess their psychological state immediately before working on the time-pressure task." The questionnaire asked subjects to describe their mood using adjective pairs, rate how attracted they were to each individual in the room (including the experimenter), and answer a number of "filler" questions. This concluded the experiment and subjects were debriefed about the purposes and predictions of the study.

## 9. RESULTS

The inter- and intragroup attraction scores after the first phase of the study were similar to those found in previous research. Subjects who competed were significantly less attracted to outgroup members than were subjects who worked interdependently ($F = 27.82$, $df = 1{,}54$, $p < .001$). There was, however, greater attraction for ingroup members in the competition condition than in the interdependent conditions ($F = 5.32$, $df = 1{,}54$, $p < .05$). These were the only significant effects found on the questionnaire given after the first phase of the study.

The major concern of the study was how helping and cooperation affected attraction for outgroup members. This effect can be examined most directly by comparing the differences in attraction rating on the first and second questionnaires. As can be seen from the results presented in Table 1, when the groups had a history of competition, cooperation in the second phase led to a significant ($p < .05$) increase in attraction for the outgroup (cooperation vs. no interaction). Helping, on the other hand, served to make the outgroup members significantly ($p < .05$) less attractive (helping vs. no interaction). However, when the groups had previously worked independently, helping resulted in a significant ($p < .05$) increase in attraction for the outgroup (helping vs. no interaction). Although not significant, this effect was stronger than the one created by cooperation. It is somewhat difficult to estimate the true magnitude of this effect since attraction in these conditions was already very positive.

*Table 1. Mean Change Score in Attraction for Outgroup Member's Relationship in Second Phase*

| | Present work relationship | | |
|---|---|---|---|
| | Helping | Cooperation | No interaction |
| Competitive | −.72[a] | 1.52 | .60 |
| Independent | .52 | .32 | −.27 |

[a]The rating scale asked each subject to indicate how attracted he was to each outgroup member on a 7-point scale (1 = like very much, 7 = dislike very much). The above scores represent change from two phases on average attraction for outgroup members. A positive score represents increased attraction in the second phase.

Another interesting effect occurred in the mood ratings. When the subjects had previously competed, subjects in the helping condition (received help) reported feeling significantly ($p < .05$) more angry, tense, and ill-at-ease than subjects in the cooperation and no-interaction conditions. No significant effects were found on mood ratings when the groups had previously worked interdependently.

## 10. THE HELPING DILEMMA: SOME CONCLUDING REMARKS

It is important to reiterate the point that individuals help others for a variety of reasons; many of these are positive and reflect only the purest of intentions. The present model identifies one of the not-so-positive motives of helping behavior. It does not suggest that individuals or groups help only to gain power or that power is an explicit goal in many helping relationships. It does argue that the exchange of power is a necessary by-product of many helping interactions. Furthermore, the model suggests that this exchange of power may be one of the reasons that helping is not always received with gratitude and warmth. The reported study demonstrated that recipients of help may not only be unappreciative of the aid, but may respond by disliking the donor. These reactions are most likely to occur when the donor and recipient have previously competed.

These results can be readily understood from the position that the helping relationship involves a give-and-take of power; the donor augments his or her power whereas the recipient forfeits power. It has been suggested that the quest for power may be one of the factors that motivates helping. It should, however, be pointed out that even if help is offered with the purest of altruistic motives, the accompanying exchange of power may tarnish the relationship.

A similar line of reasoning offered by Nadler, Altman, and Fisher (1979) can also be used to explicate the present results. These investigators suggest that under some conditions, the recipient may forfeit self-esteem by receiving help. Self-esteem, like power, is likely to be a particularly sensitive issue between individuals who have engaged in a competitive relationship. Therefore, subjects in the experiment may have been reacting to the diminished self-esteem they felt in the competitive–helping condition. Although feelings of self-worth and power are closely related, future research should examine how both of these influence reactions to receiving help.

Interestingly, the present research suggests that a relationship that is already positive may flourish on exchanges of help, whereas a weak relationship may be further damaged by helping. We may also speculate that aid giving is unlikely to lead to the development of a positive and close relationship when competition may occur in the future.

On the other hand, the research suggests that aid exchanged in the form of cooperation will have a positive effect on even a weak relationship. Cooperation is a case where both parties contribute efforts to achieve a common goal and share the outcome of their efforts. Cooperation is mutual helping that brings the parties together rather than separating them.

One interesting prediction from the present model is that receiving help should motivate the recipient to extend help. The most preferred target of this help should be the original donor, since helping him or her should be the most effective route for reestablishing power. However, the recipient can also augment his or her own power by helping others. Although this domino effect has a positive result in that it perpetuates helping behavior, the model also suggests a negative side. That is, the chain reaction of helping behavior may have a detrimental effect on interpersonal relationships.

Admittedly, much of this theorizing is based on speculation. The theory needs fleshing out, and such terms as "power" and "helping" need more operational precision. Future research must demonstrate more directly that issues of power motivate both helping and the reluctance to receive help.

Finally, helping occurs in the context of an interpersonal or intergroup relationship. In order to completely understand helping behavior, it is necessary to examine the psychology of both the donor and recipient and of the effects that helping has on the relationship. Whether the focus is norms, social exchange, or power, the answer to the question of why people help (or do not help) will most likely be found only by focusing on the donor, the recipient, and the dynamics of their relationship.

### Acknowledgments

I should like to thank Daniel Bar-Tal, Bella DePaulo, and Frances Worchel for suggesting ideas that were incorporated in this chapter.

## 11. REFERENCES

Bandura, A., Ross, D., & Ross, S. Transmission of aggression through imitation of aggressive models. *Journal of Abnormal and Social Psychology*, 1961, *63*, 575–582.

Berkowitz, L. Social norms, feelings and other factors affecting helping and altruism. In L. Berkowitz (Ed.), *Advances in experimental social psychology* (Vol. 6). New York: Academic Press, 1972.

Blake, R., & Mouton, J. Reactions to intergroup competition under win–lose conditions. *Management Science,* 1961, *7,* 420–435.

Blake, R., & Mouton, J. Intergroup problem solving in organizations: From theory to practice. In W. Austin & S. Worchel (Eds.), *The social psychology of intergroup relations.* Monterey, Calif.: Brooks/Cole, 1979.

Blanchard, F., Adelman, L., & Cook, S. The effect of group success and failure upon interpersonal attraction in cooperating interracial groups. *Journal of Personality and Social Psychology,* 1975, *31,* 1020–1030.

Blau, P. *Exchange and power in social life.* New York: Wiley, 1964.

Brehm, J., & Cole, A. Effect of a favor which reduces freedom. *Journal of Personality and Social Psychology,* 1966, *3,* 420–426.

Byrne, D. *The attraction paradigm.* New York: Academic Press, 1971.

Byrne, D., & Clore, G. A reinforcement model of evaluative responses. *Personality: An International Journal,* 1970, *1,* 103–128.

Darley, J., & Latané, B. Bystander intervention in emergencies: Diffusion of responsibility. *Journal of Personality and Social Psychology,* 1968, *8,* 377–383.

Festinger, L. A theory of social comparison processes. *Human Relations,* 1954, *7,* 117–140.

Fisher, J., & Nadler, A. The effect of similarity between donor and recipient on reactions to aid. *Journal of Applied Social Psychology,* 1974, *4,* 230–243.

Fisher, J., & Nadler, A. The effect of donor resources on recipient self-esteem and self-help. *Journal of Experimental Social Psychology,* 1976, *12,* 139–150.

Greenberg, M. A theory of indebtedness. In K. Gergen, M. Greenberg, & R. Willis (Eds.), *Social exchange: Advances in theory and research.* New York: Plenum Press, 198O.

Greenberg, M., & Frisch, D. Effect of intentionality on willingness to reciprocate a favor. *Journal of Experimental Social Psychology,* 1972, *8,* 99–111.

Homans, G. *Social behavior: Its elementary forms.* New York: Harcourt, Brace, 1961.

Huesmann, R., & Levinger, G. Incremental exchange theory: A formal model for progression in dyadic interaction. In L. Berkowitz & E. Walster (Eds.), *Advances in experimental social psychology* (Vol. 9). New York: Academic Press, 1976.

Jones, E. *Ingratiation.* New York: Appleton-Century-Crofts, 1964.

Jones, E., & Wortman, C. *Ingratiation: An attributional approach.* Morristown, N.J.: General Learning Press, 1973.

Kelman, H. Compliance, identification, and internalization: Three processes of opinion change. *Journal of Conflict Resolution,* 1958, *2,* 51–60.

Latané, B., & Darley, J. *The unresponsive bystander: Why doesn't he help?* Englewood Cliffs, N.J.: Prentice-Hall, 1968.

Levine, R., & Campbell, D. *Ethnocentrism: Theories of conflict, ethnic attitudes and group behavior.* New York: Wiley, 1972.

Lott, A., & Lott, B. A learning theory approach to interpersonal attitudes. In A. Greenwald, T. Brock, & T. Ostrom (Eds.), *Psychological foundations of attitudes.* New York: Academic Press, 1968.

Maier, N. *Psychology in industrial organizations.* New York: Houghton Mifflin, 1978.

Michner, A., & Suchner, R. The tactical use of social power. In J. Tedeschi (Ed.), *The social influence process.* Chicago: Aldine, 1972.

Nadler, A., Fisher, J., & Streufert, S. The donor's dilemma: Recipients' reaction to aid from a friend or foe. *Journal of Applied Social Psychology,* 1974, *4,* 275–285.

Nadler, A., Altman, A., & Fisher, J. D. Effects of positive and negative information about the self on recipient's reactions to aid. *Journal of Personality,* 1979, *47,* 616–629.

Piliavin, I., Piliavin, J., & Rodin, J. Costs, diffusion, and the stigmatized victim. *Journal of Personality and Social Psychology,* 1975, *32,* 429–438.

Rubin, K. H., & Schneider, S. W. The relationship between moral judgment, egocentrism, and altruistic behavior. *Child Development,* 1973, *44,* 661–665.

Schlenker, B., Helm, B., & Tedeschi, J. The effects of personality and situational variables on behavioral trust. *Journal of Personality and Social Psychology,* 1973, *25,* 419–427.

Schopler, J. An attribution analysis of some determinants of reciprocating a benefit. In J. Macaulay & L. Berkowitz (Eds.), *Altruism and helping behavior.* New York: Academic Press, 1970.

Shaw, M. *Group dynamics: The psychology of small group behavior.* New York: McGraw-Hill, 1976.

Sherif, M., & Sherif, C. Research in intergroup relations. In W. Austin & S. Worchel (Eds.), *The social psychology of intergroup relations.* Monterey, Calif.: Brooks/Cole, 1979.

Sherif, M., Harvey, O., White, B., Hood, W., & Sherif, C. *Intergroup conflict and cooperation: The robber's love experiment.* Norman: University of Oklahoma Press, 1961.

Swinth, R. The establishment of the trust relationship. *Journal of Conflict Resolution,* 1967, *11,* 335–344.

Tajfel, H. Experiments in intergroup discrimination. *Scientific American,* 1970, *223*(5), 96–102.

Tajfel, H. Social identity and intergroup behavior. *Social Science Information,* 1974, *13*(2), 65–93.

Tajfel, H., & Turner, J. An integrative theory of intergroup conflict. In W. Austin & S. Worchel (Eds.), *The social psychology of intergroup relations.* Monterey, Calif.: Brooks/Cole, 1979.

Thibaut, J., & Kelley, H. *The social psychology of groups.* New York: Wiley, 1959.

Thibaut, J., & Riecken, H. Some determinants and consequences of the perception of social causality. *Journal of Personality,* 1955, *24,* 113–133.

Worchel, S., & Andreoli, V. Attribution of causality as a means of restoring behavioral freedom. *Journal of Personality and Social Psychology,* 1974, *9,* 237–245.

Worchel, S., & Norvell, N. Effect of perceived environmental conditions during cooperation on intergroup attraction. *Journal of Personality and Social Psychology,* 1980, *38,* 764–772.

Worchel, S., Andreoli, V., & Archer, R. When is a favor a threat to freedom?: The effects of attribution and importance of freedom on reciprocity. *Journal of Personality,* 1976, *44,* 294–310.

Worchel, S., Axsom, D., Ferris, F., Samaha, G., & Schweitzer, S. Determinants of the effects of intergroup cooperation on intergroup attraction. *Journal of Conflict Resolution,* 1978, *12,* 429–439.

# 20

# Effects of Donor–Recipient Relationships on Recipients' Reactions to Aid

Arie Nadler and Jeffrey D. Fisher

## 1. INTRODUCTION

In every interpersonal helping encounter there is a helper and a recipient of help, and social psychologists working in the area may focus their research on the helper, the recipient, or both. Yet, as the contents of this volume indicate, the majority of past research in the area of prosocial behavior has dealt with the psychology of help-giving behavior. Over the past 15 years questions have been raised regarding situational, personality, and socialization factors that determine willingness to help. The other side of the helping paradigm, the recipient's reaction to receiving help, remains relatively unexplored.

What accounts for this disproportional research emphasis? One likely reason is the common assumption that receiving help is a uniformly positive experience for the recipient and therefore merits no special research attention. Also, since the research on help giving has often been seen as responding to acute social needs, devising ways to pro-

---

ARIE NADLER • Department of Psychology, Tel Aviv University, Ramat-Aviv, Israel. JEFFREY D. FISHER • Department of Psychology, University of Connecticut, Storrs, Connecticut 06268. Research reported in this chapter was supported by a grant from the Israeli Academy of Science to the first author, and by a grant (2290) from the Bi-National Science Foundation (U.S.–Israel) to both authors. The preparation of the manuscript was also supported by the grant (2290) from the Bi-National Science Foundation.

mote help giving may have seemed especially important in times of deteriorating systems of social control (cf. Kanfer, 1979).

A closer examination of reports by professional helpers indicates that the assumption about the uniform positivity of receiving help is not valid. The potential degrading and stigmatizing effects of receiving help have been amplified in discussions of the reactions of disabled war veterans (e.g., Ladieu, Hanfman, & Dembo, 1947; Nadler, Sheinberg, & Jaffe, 1981), the aged (e.g., Kalish, 1967; Lipman & Sterne, 1962), and welfare recipients (Briar, 1966). Recent social psychological experimentation indicates that receiving help is a mixed blessing at best and can be a negative, self-threatening experience for the recipient (see Fisher, Nadler, & Whitcher-Alagna, 1982, for a review).

Receiving help may be an aversive experience for the recipient because of the implied inferiority and dependency that are associated with being helped. These elements are inconsistent with deeply ingrained values of self-reliance and individual achievement (cf. Merton, 1968). In addition to affecting the recipient's view of self, conditions associated with receiving help may determine the recipient's perceptions of his or her benefactor, and of the aid itself. Such perceptions are not always favorable, and gratitude and goodwill are not always the rule in helping encounters. As we shall see, anecdotal as well as more systematic research efforts clearly show that the recipient may bite the hand that feeds. The recipient of aid may attribute ulterior, self-serving motives to the donor and downgrade the value of the aid. Thus, at times, receiving help may inhibit rather than promote an atmosphere of goodwill between the two parties to a helping interaction.

The task of the social psychologist is to explain how situational, personal, and interpersonal variables that surround the helping interaction relate to (1) the recipient's feelings and view of self; (2) his or her external perceptions and evaluations (i.e., of donor and aid); and (3) his or her relevant behaviors (e.g., reciprocity, self-help, further request for help).[1]

## 2. RECIPIENTS' REACTIONS TO AID: THEORY AND RESEARCH

Since recipients' reactions to aid represent a set of attitudinal and behavioral phenomena that relate to a single interpersonal event (i.e.,

[1]Our discussion of recipients' reactions to help does not include cases of either extremely light or extremely severe states of need. In the first case, the effects of receiving help may be minute and inconsequential. In the second, an acute need for help (e.g., a starving person asking for food) is likely to dominate the scene, and little variance in the recipient's reaction is expected.

receiving help), most of the theoretical concepts used in this context have been borrowed from other areas in social psychology. In extant investigation, four theoretical orientations have been employed to predict and explain recipients' reactions to aid. We shall first briefly discuss the implications of each theoretical approach to the issue at hand (for a more thorough discussion, cf. Fisher *et al.*, 1982; Gross, Wallston, & Piliavin, 1979).

## 2.1. Equity

The concepts embedded in equity theory in its different formulations (e.g., Adams, 1963; Hatfield & Sprecher, 1983; Pritchard, 1969; Walster, Walster, & Berscheid, 1978) imply that receiving help is a potentially inequitable situation (i.e., as a consequence of receiving help the recipient has a more favorable ratio of inputs to outcomes than the donor); therefore, a receipt of help should often elicit tension in the recipient. In a related conception, Greenberg (1980) has suggested that receiving aid arouses a state of indebtedness, which he describes as

> a state of obligation to repay another. The state of indebtedness is assumed to have motivational properties, such that the greater its magnitude, the greater the resultant arousal and discomfort, and hence, the stronger the ensuing attempts to deal with or reduce it. (p. 4)

Past studies within this theoretical tradition have shown that to avoid indebtedness, individuals who do not foresee an opportunity to reciprocate refrain from seeking help (e.g., Morris & Rosen, 1973). If aid has been received, recipients invest efforts in order to reciprocate the aid and restore equity, and if direct opportunity to reciprocate does not exist, the recipient restores equity via psychological means (e.g., devaluating the aid).

## 2.2. Reactance

One likely consequence of receiving aid is the recipient's loss of freedom for action. In fact, after the receipt of help the recipient may feel obligated to act in a certain manner toward his or her benefactor (e.g., follow his or her advice, act thankful). A more explicit case of loss in freedom associated with receiving help is when aid is given with "strings attached." In whatever case, reactance theory, which states that people wish to maximize their freedom of choice and react negatively to the perceived source of freedom limitation, implies that recipients of aid will respond negatively to aid that is seen as restricting their behavioral choices (cf. Gross *et al.*, 1979).

### 2.3. Attribution Theories

It seems that since the introduction of attribution theories into social psychology (Jones & Davis, 1965; Kelley, 1967), no area has failed to note their implications. The area of recipients' reactions to aid is no exception. First, research has explored the attributions of intent the recipient makes for the helper's benevolence (e.g., Nadler, Fisher, & Streufert, 1974). Second, research has dealt with recipients' locus of attribution for their need in help (i.e., internal or external attribution of need, e.g., Tessler & Schwartz, 1972). Although heuristic and useful, these theoretical orientations tend to focus on the cognitive-evaluative reactions of the recipient, and give less attention to the affective consequences of receiving help. The final theoretical orientation, that is, threat to recipient's self-esteem, amends this shortcoming.

### 2.4. Threat to Self-Esteem

This approach views the receipt of help as a mixture of self-supporting (e.g., donor's concern and liking for the recipient) and self-threatening psychological elements (e.g., relative inferiority and dependency). It suggests that aid-related variables determine the relative weight of the self-supporting and self-threatening elements, thereby making aid an overall positive-supporting or negative-threatening event. If receiving aid is a relatively self-supporting experience, a cluster of "positive" reactions are expected (favorable affect, positive evaluations of self and helper, willingness to seek more help). If, however, receiving aid is relatively self-threatening, a cluster of "negative" reactions are expected (unfavorable affect, negative evaluations of self and other, unwillingness to seek help). Research has generally supported these predictions (e.g., Fisher & Nadler, 1974, 1976; Nadler, Fisher, & Streufert, 1976; Nadler, Altman, & Fisher, 1979; Tessler & Schwartz, 1972), and the reader is referred elsewhere for a more thorough discussion of this theoretical orientation and its links with other formulations in this research context (Fisher *et al.*, 1982).

## 3. DONOR–RECIPIENT RELATIONS AND RECIPIENTS' REACTIONS TO AID

The research on recipients' reactions to aid falls into three major categories that correspond with the view of helping as an interaction in which a certain *recipient* is given *help* by a specific *helper*. Thus one line of research has explored how the *characteristics of the recipient* (e.g., level of self-esteem, Nadler *et al.*, 1979; age, DePaulo, 1978a) influence his or her responses to the receipt of help. A second group of studies had investigated the way in which *characteristics of the help* (e.g., amount of aid given, Freeman, 1977) determine the recipient's reaction. Finally, a third research direction has explored how the *characteristics of the helper* (e.g., helper's quality of relationships with the recipient, Gergen & Gergen, 1974) affect the recipient's reactions to help. Our focus of concern here is with the third line of research.

Both intuition and formal observations (e.g., Weiss, 1969) suggest that one's reactions to a receipt of help depend, among other things, on the identity of the helper. Studies in social psychology that have explored the effects of the helper's identity on the recipient's reactions have proceeded in two major directions. One line of investigation has been concerned with the effects of the *overall quality* of donor–recipient relations on the recipient's reactions. This research has explored such issues as the differential reactions to a receipt of help from an enemy versus an ally (Nadler *et al.*, 1974) or from a friend versus a stranger (e.g., Bar-Tal, Zohar, Greenberg, & Hermon, 1977). The second line of investigation has been concerned with the effects of donor–recipient similarity on the recipient's reactions. This research has explored such issues as whether recipients respond differently to a receipt of help from helpers with similar versus dissimilar degrees of task-relevant knowledge (e.g., Fisher, Harrison, & Nadler, 1978).

Although both groups of investigations deal with the same general issue, that is, effects of helper's identity on recipient reactions, they differ from each other in several important respects. First, the research on overall quality of donor–recipient relationships deals with a generic variable (e.g., friendship) that encompasses many other variables, and refers to an ongoing and relatively long-term relationship. On the other hand, research on donor–recipient similarity has focused on a narrower and more tightly defined slice of the interpersonal helping arena, that is, donor–recipient similarity on a specific dimension (e.g., attitudes: Fisher & Nadler, 1974; Nadler *et al.*, 1976; task-relevant knowledge: Fisher *et al.*, 1978).

Second, these two research directions differ in their choice of dependent variables. Whereas the research on overall quality of donor–recipient relations has centered on recipients' external perceptions (e.g., evaluations of help and helper) and externally directed behaviors (e.g., reciprocity toward the donor), the research on donor–recipient similarity has looked at the effects of help on recipients' evaluations of self, and on self-directed behaviors (e.g., self-help efforts). Finally, the two research directions have relied on different conceptual backgrounds. Whereas the first has employed concepts from attribution theory (e.g., Nadler *et al.*, 1974), role theory (e.g., Bar-Tal *et al.*, 1977) and Goffmanian analysis of interpersonal behavior (e.g., Clark & Mills, 1979), the second has been more homogeneous in its conceptual approach and is anchored in the threat to self-esteem model of reactions to help. Thus these two lines of research differ in their (1) operationalization of the independent variable, (2) choice of dependent variables, and (3) conceptual underpinnings. These differences call for a separate description of each line of study before an overall outlook can be offered.

## 3.1. Overall Quality of Donor–Recipient Relations

### 3.1.1. *Perceived Favorability of Preexisting Relations*

In a pioneering series of investigations in this area, Gergen and his colleagues explored the reactions of foreign aid officials in several countries to American foreign aid. In general, it was observed that, contrary to expectations, American foreign aid often failed to secure goodwill toward the donor nation (Gergen & Gergen, 1971). Thus, although the donor may have viewed the giving of help as an unselfish and humanitarian way to promote goodwill, the recipient did not always share this outlook.

In an attempt to explain such phenomena, Gergen and Gergen (1971, 1974) conducted surveys and interviews with foreign aid officials in over 20 recipient countries. They identified several major factors that can explain the mixed effects of receiving help. For example, they noted that receiving aid can precipitate negative evaluations of the helper if stipulations are put on the way it is to be used, or if the donor country is perceived as making a relatively minor sacrifice in donating.

Yet a major determinant of recipients' reactions in this context seems to be their preexisting conceptions about the helper. In fact, it has been noted that if the recipient country has an unfavorable view of the donor country, the experience of receiving aid seems to be colored by these negative opinions. Thus the donor's generosity does not lead to an improvement in the recipient's evaluations of the donor, and the aid itself is seen as minor and unimportant. Furthermore, the recipient in such a case is likely to see the donor's actions as motivated by ulterior, self-serving, rather than altruistic, motives (Gergen & Gergen, 1971). In contrast, when the preexisting conception of the donor is favorable, and the donor is viewed as an ally, receiving aid has positive effects (enhanced attraction, constructive use of aid) and the helping interactions can be viewed as improving relations that are already at least moderately favorable.

Further support for these findings has been obtained in a study we conducted using an experimental simulation (Nadler *et al.*, 1974). In this study subjects participated in a highly involving international conflict simulation (the Tactical and Negotiation Game; cf. Streufert, Kliger, Castore, & Driver, 1967) in which they played the role of military/political decision makers. The course of this simulation was determined by the experimenter such that subjects were facing failure because of an unexpected need state. Subsequently, half the subjects received an offer of aid from another party that was predefined throughout the simulation as an ally, and the other half received the same offer from another party that was predefined as a foe. Subjects' perceptions of the donor and the aid were then collected. The findings support the general patterns observed by Gergen and Gergen (1971) in their field studies. Help given by an "enemy" donor was seen as motivated by ulterior self-serving motivations, whereas that of an "ally" donor was perceived as motivated by the donor's true concern for the recipient. In line with the different attributions, the ally donor was more favorably evaluated as a consequence of helping whereas the negative evaluations of the enemy donor were not attenuated by the help. Furthermore, recipients who had received the help from an ally donor saw it as beneficial and instrumental, whereas those who received it from an enemy donor saw it as relatively unimportant and noninstrumental.

These findings give a rather gloomy picture regarding the possible use of aid as a vehicle to promote goodwill and ease tensions between conflicting parties. This contrasts with the idea endorsed by some social psychologists that a unilateral manifestation of goodwill of one party toward its adversary may lead to a reduction of tensions (Osgood, 1962). The data presented here suggest that at least in the short run this may not be the case. In fact, these data indicate that the recipient responds to the receipt of help in ways that are consistent with preconceptions of the donor. Whether a more prolonged helping effort may break this vicious circle is a question that has still not been addressed by the research to date.

Moving from intergroup helping to interpersonal helping, DePaulo (1978b) found that individuals who were asked to state their preference for a socially close or a socially distant helper (i.e., friend vs. stranger) preferred to receive help from someone with whom they enjoyed mutual attraction. Similarly, Nadler, Bar-Tal, and Drukman (1982) found that quality of interpersonal relations associated with different degrees of density of living conditions also affects receptiveness to help. Thus students living in socially cohesive residential environments were more receptive to help than those living in colder and more formal residential environments. These studies, too, lend support to the conclusion that the receipt of help from a socially close helper is an overall more positive experience for the recipient than the receipt of help from a socially distant other.

### 3.1.2. *Communal and Exchange Relationships*

A second line of investigation that dealt with the effects of the overall quality of donor–recipient relationships is Clark and Mills's (1979) recent work on the distinction between "communal" and "exchange" relations, as it applies to helping interactions.

Based on Goffman's (1961) distinction between social and economic exchange, Clark and Mills suggest that individuals' reactions to a receipt of a benefit are dependent on whether they are in a communal or exchange relationship with their benefactor. In essence, communal relationships involve a high degree of psychological proximity and are characteristic of relationships between close friends, relatives, and romantic partners. Exchange relationships involve a low degree of psychological proximity and are characteristic of relationships between coworkers and business partners. The communal-exchange distinction has several implications for the understanding of interpersonal helping interactions (cf. Clark, 1983). In communal relationships giving is assumed to be determined by the recipient's need. Also, the giver is thought to be motivated by a desire to make the other feel good. In exchange relations, one gives because one has received help from the other in the past, or expects that the other will reciprocate in the future. Thus it seems that whereas giving in an exchange relationship is governed by the norm of reciprocity, giving in a communal relationship is governed by the norm of social responsibility.

Having made this distinction, Clark and Mills (1979) proceeded to test its implications. It was predicted that since in a communal relationship giving is seen as the donor's response to the recipient's need, the recipient's offer to reciprocate immediately after help had been given would be considered inappropriate. In contrast, since in exchange relationships giving is seen as determined by principles of reciprocity, the recipient's failure to offer reciprocity would be considered inappropriate. To test this prediction the investigators created an experimental situation where half the subjects expected an exchange relationship and the other half a communal relationship with another individual. Later, subjects were offered reciprocal help from the individual whom they had helped before. In line with the hypotheses, in exchange conditions subjects liked the other better if she offered to reciprocate, but in communal conditions they liked the other better if she did not offer reciprocity. In the same line, Clark and Wadell (in Clark, 1983) report that in exchange but not in communal relationships subjects liked and felt less exploited by a person who aided them in return than by a person who did not.

Finally, employing role theory as an explanatory framework, Bar-Tal *et al.* (1977) suggest that we feel relatively less indebted toward helpful relatives or friends because we view their benevolence as part of their role requirement as intimate others.

### 3.1.3. *Effects of Quality of Donor–Recipient Relations: An Overall View*

Taken together, the findings described in the previous two sections indicate that the quality of the relationship between the donor and the recipient affects a series of recipient reactions to aid. When the quality of preexisting relations is positive the giving of aid is seen by the recipient as (1) motivated by the donor's concern for the recipient's well-being; (2) placing the donor in a more favorable light; and (3) beneficial and instrumental. In contrast, if the quality of preexisting relations is negative, the recipient is (1) likely to attribute ulterior self-serving motivations to the donor; (2) not likely to change his or her unfavorable evaluations of the donor; and (3) likely to view the help itself as relatively noninstrumental and unimportant. Finally, the quality of preexisting relations between the donor and the recipient affects the recipient's felt need to reciprocate. In relatively distant (i.e., exchange) or unfavorable donor–recipient relations, the recipient feels a stronger need for an immediate reciprocity than in closer, more favorable (i.e., communal) relations.

## 3.2. Donor–Recipient Similarity: The Comparison Stress in Aid

Parallel to developments in the research on the effects of quality of donor–recipient relationships, several studies have explored the effects of similarity between donor and recipient on recipient reactions to the receipt of help. The links between interpersonal similarity and quality of interpersonal relations have been well documented by past research and theory (e.g., Byrne, 1971; Suls & Miller, 1977; Tesser, 1980). Yet, as noted before, important differences between the research on quality of donor–recipient relationships and the research on donor–recipient similarity necessitate a separate examination of each line of investigation before an overall view can be provided.

The research on effects of donor–recipient similarity has centered on the self-implications inherent in the receipt of aid. It proceeded from the assumption that a major question that the recipient may ask him or herself is: "what does the fact that I received help and am now dependent on others say about *myself?*" Furthermore, it has suggested that an immediately available clue to answer this question is the donor's similarity or dissimilarity from the recipient. In line with conceptual approaches that highlight the greater informational value which is inherent in the lot of a similar other relative to that of a dissimilar other (cf. Festinger, 1954; Tesser, 1980), we have reasoned that the message of "I failed to the point of needing" whereas "my partner succeeded to the point of providing" should be more self-threatening and aversive when the helper is a similar other (cf. Nadler, Jazwinski, Lau, & Miller, 1980). Put otherwise, we have suggested that in line with social comparison theory (Festinger, 1954) and more recent conceptual developments (e.g., Brickman & Bulman, 1977), the *comparison stress* inherent in a receipt of aid from a similar other is psychologically significant, and therefore such aid should be relatively self-threatening.

To test this possibility, we ran an experiment (Fisher & Nadler, 1974) in which male subjects played a stock market simulation that was said to reflect on their investment abilities. At the end of the first part of the simulation all subjects were in a losing position, and faced the prospect of being eliminated from the game. At that point some subjects received financial help from a bogus partner who had been presented earlier as attitudinally similar or attitudinally dissimilar. This help ensured their future participation in the game. Subjects in the control conditions underwent the same procedures except that they did not receive help. Thus the experiment was a 2 (attitudinally similar vs. dissimilar other) × 2 (aid vs. no aid) between-subjects design.

The results lend support to our prediction. Subjects who received aid from a similar other had less favorable affect and lower self-ratings than individuals who did not receive help from a similar other. An opposite tendency was observed in the dissimilar conditions. Thus, in line with our proposed logic, the comparison stress inherent in help from a similar other seems to have made the receipt of such help a self-threatening experience for the recipient.

At this point a major question presented itself. Although past research indicates that individuals are more likely to compare themselves with attitudinally similar than dissimilar others (Castore & DeNinno, 1977), the question whether the effects that we had found were unique to *attitude* similarity, with its associated consequences (e.g., liking), remained open.

To explore this issue we next defined similarity in terms of task-relevant knowledge (Fisher *et al.*, 1978). In that experiment the donor was said to have similar or differential amounts of task-relevant knowledge. The results of this study are in accordance with our initial findings. Thus, relative to a control group, individuals who received aid (advice on a pattern recognition task) from another with a similar degree of task-relevant knowledge had lower self-evaluations than individuals in a control group who did not receive such aid. This was not the case in the different task-relevant knowledge conditions.

Taken together, the data from these two experiments establish a *base relationship* concerning the effects of donor–recipient similarity on the recipient's affect and self-evaluations. Specifically, support is provided for the idea that the unfavorable comparison that is forced on the recipient during helping can lead to self-threat. Furthermore, in line with other theoretical orientations in social psychology (e.g., Festinger, 1954; Reykowski, Chapter 3, this volume) this comparison stress is amplified by an overall similarity between the donor and the recipient. Corroborative evidence is also available from the observations of Weiss (1969) that welfare recipients report being more "bothered" when interviewed by a similar than a dissimilar interviewer, and from the findings of Clark, Gotay, and Mills (1974) that less aid is accepted from a similar than a dissimilar other when no opportunity for reciprocity is envisioned.

The next step we took was to identify relevant personality and situational variables that moderate donor–recipient similarity effects. We began by looking at relevant personality characteristics and reasoned that since threat to recipient's self-esteem was suggested as the major intervening variable between donor–recipient similarity and recipient reactions, recipient's level of persistent self-esteem should moderate this relationship. To test this, we employed similar procedures and design to those we had used before (i.e., Fisher & Nadler, 1974), and added the recipient's level of self-esteem as a third experimental factor. Thus this experiment (Nadler *et al.*, 1976) consisted of a 2 (attitudinally similar vs. dissimilar) × 2 (aid vs. no aid) × 2 (high vs. low self-esteem individuals) between-subjects design.

The results of this study (see Figure 1) replicate and extend the findings from the earlier studies. Thus recipients who had received help from an overall similar donor had lower affect and self-evaluations than recipients in a control condition who did not receive aid. More important, however, this was true only for high self-esteem recipients. Low self-esteem individuals reacted relatively favorably to a receipt of help from a similar *or* a dissimilar other.

The finding that recipient's level of self-esteem moderates the effects of donor–recipient similarity supports our interpretation that these effects are because of differential degrees of self-threat in aid (cf. Underwood, 1975). The pattern of the data is congruent with a consistency explanation in this context (cf. Bramel, 1968). In effect, the comparison stress inherent in the receipt of aid from a similar other is more inconsistent with the self-cognitions of the high than the low self-esteem recipient, and is therefore a more aversive experience for the former. Before

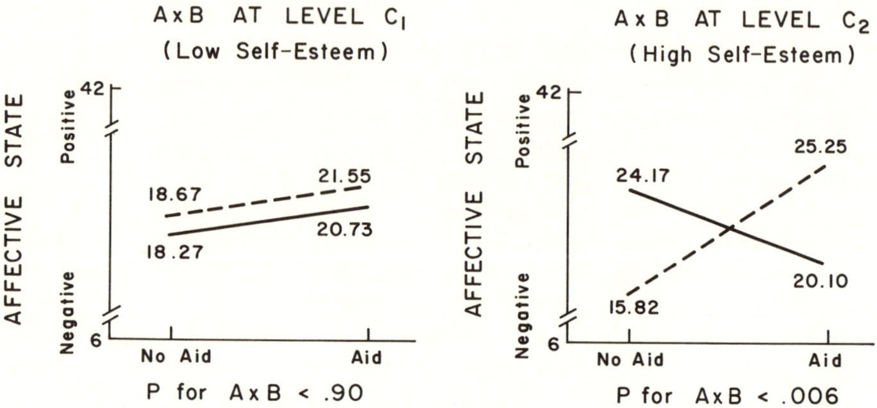


Figure 1. Similarity by aid interaction (A × B) for affective state at each level of self-esteem ($C_1$ and $C_2$): (——) similar-pair mate ($A_1$); (- - -) dissimilar-pair mate ($A_2$). (Adapted from Nadler *et al.*, 1976.)

continuing it should be noted that in accordance with these findings, several studies have shown that high self-esteem individuals are more sensitive than low self-esteem individuals to the self-threat (i.e., elements of relative dependency and inferiority) inherent in a receipt of aid (DePaulo, Brown, Ishii, & Fisher, 1891; Nadler, Altman, & Fisher, 1979). The reader is referred elsewhere for a more complete discussion of this fascinating issue (Nadler & Mayseless, 1983).

After we had identified self-esteem as a conceptually relevant personality moderator in this context, our attention was drawn to the fact that our use of the term "help" had thus far been very general. In fact, receiving help may refer to getting psychological counseling or to being helped by a passerby to change a flat tire. It seems both intuitively compelling and empirically valid (cf. Tessler & Schwartz, 1972) that the type of aid one gets may importantly affect one's reactions.

An important task characteristic which is relevant in this context is the egocentrality of the task on which one receives help. Help may reflect inferiority on a task that is central (e.g., intelligence) or noncentral to self-esteem (e.g., manual dexterity). Our previous discussion implies that receiving help is potentially self-threatening only if it reflects inferiority on a psychologically *central* dimension (cf. also Tessler & Schwartz, 1972). Consequently, only under such conditions can we expect donor–recipient similarity to generate comparison stress that will make the receipt of help a negative, threatening experience. When help reflects on noncentral dimensions, its receipt should not be self-threatening regardless of donor–recipient similarity.

To test this, we have conducted several experiments at the laborato-

*Table 1. Ratings of Situational Self-Esteem by Recipients of Central and Noncentral Aid from an Attitudinally Similar/Dissimilar Other (N = 40)*

| | Attitudinally similar | Attitudinally dissimilar |
|---|---|---|
| Central task | 10.1 | 11.8 |
| Noncentral task | 11.1 | 10.8 |

ries of Tel Aviv University. In the first such experiment we ran a 2 (similar vs. dissimilar) × 2 (central vs. noncentral task) × 2 (aid vs. no aid) between-subjects design (Nadler & Altman, 1981). In this experiment subjects were to work on a complex and ambiguous problem-solving task. Half were told that performance was related to intelligence and creativity (central dimensions), whereas the other half were told that no such relations existed (noncentral dimensions). Afterward, subjects received help from a similar or dissimilar partner. As can be seen in Table 1, donor–recipient similarity effects like those observed previously (i.e., aid from a similar other being self-threatening) were evident for the *central* but not the *noncentral* task.

Further support for the important role of task centrality in this context comes from two studies that examined the joint effect of donor–recipient similarity and task centrality on the recipient's behavior. Specifically, Nadler and Kolker (1981) found that individuals sought the least help when the helper was similar and the help reflected inadequacy on a central task. In another study we looked at self-help behavior as a function of donor–recipient similarity and task centrality (Nadler & Fisher, 1981). We reasoned that relative to individuals for whom receiving help is not self-threatening, those who find it self-threatening will invest greater efforts to terminate the uneasy dependency. We tested this prediction by giving subjects who received help in a 2 (attitudinally similar vs. dissimilar helper) × 2 (central vs. noncentral task) experiment an opportunity to prepare themselves for an upcoming task. We then measured the amount of effort that each subject invested in such a preparation.

In line with our prediction we found a similarity × task centrality interaction on the measure of self-help, $F(1.44) = 3.9$, $p < .05$. An examination of cell means involved in this interaction shows that most self-help efforts were made by individuals who received help from a similar other on a central task (means are 16.9 and 6.2 for the central and noncentral aid, respectively, with a similar donor; and 11.3 and 13.8 for central and noncentral aid with a dissimilar donor).

What conclusions can be drawn from our research thus far on donor–recipient similarity? At this point we believe that different levels of donor–recipient similarity induce differential degrees of comparison stress thereby ameliorating the relative amount of self-threat in aid. Receiving help from a similar other is a relatively unpleasant and self-threatening experience for the recipient and this self-threat precipitates affective, evaluative, and behavioral responses.

Furthermore, in line with our conceptual logic we found that relevant characteristics of the recipient and the situation moderate these effects. These are (1) characteristic of *high self-esteem* individuals, and (2) occur only when the need for help reflects on a psychologically *central* dimension.

## 4. DONOR–RECIPIENT SIMILARITY AND OVERALL QUALITY OF RELATIONS

### 4.1. An Overall View

In the preceding sections we have reviewed two lines of research that addressed the issue of the effects of the helper's identity on the recipient's reactions (i.e., quality of donor–recipient relations, and donor–recipient similarity). The links between these two concepts are many. We tend to use others whom we like as frames of reference for self-judgments, and we express more liking toward similar than dissimilar others (Byrne, 1971). Yet, in spite of the conceptual affinity, the two lines of research differ in theoretical orientation, choice of dependent variables, and overall conclusions.

If we were to look at the two concepts as two facets of the same interpersonal coin, namely, social proximity, than we would be forced to derive incongruent conclusions regarding the effects of social proximity between the donor and recipient on the recipient's reactions to help. On the one hand, the research on the effects of overall quality of donor–recipient relations indicates that receiving help from another with whom we have good relations is an overall positive interpersonal event. The recipient attributes positive intentions to the helper, appreciates the helping effort, and evaluates the help itself quite positively. On the other hand, the research on donor–recipient similarity indicates that the comparison stress inherent in social proximity renders the receipt of help from a socially close other a relatively negative/threatening interpersonal event for the recipient.

### 4.2. Toward Integration

How is the conflict between these two lines of research to be resolved? An integrated outlook is possible on the basis of the following assumptions: (1) Receiving help from a socially close other contains positive (a sign of concern from a psychologically significant other) *and* negative (comparison stress) psychological elements; but (2) one can identify the major conditions that affect the relative weight of each, thus determining whether the receipt of aid from a socially close other is an overall positive or negative experience. As for (1), it is congruent with other related statements in this regard. In fact, such a dual perspective is not unique to the area of recipients' reactions to aid. In line with the foregoing discussion, the idea that social proximity contains the potential for both greater "pain" *and* "pleasure" has recently been voiced in several theoretical-empirical endeavors (Brickman & Bulman, 1977; Mette & Riskind, 1974; Nadler *et al.*, 1980; Tesser, 1980).

What then may be major determinants of the relative weight of "pain" and "pleasure" in interpersonal helping relations? The research reviewed in the previous sections suggests such a variable. We believe that the concept of centrality of aid may do much to provide a clearer perspective. Thus we suggest that only help that reflects inferiority on a central dimension carries with it the potential to be an aversive and self-threatening experience for the recipient. Whether the receipt of help from a socially close other will be colored by the darker and self-threatening hues of the comparison stress or the brighter rays of other's caring will depend on the relative absence or existence of elements of inferiority *on a psychologically relevant dimension* (e.g., intelligence).

In order to test this proposition, it is necessary to examine how people respond to a receipt of help from a friend or a stranger (psychologically close or distant others) when help reflects inferiority on a psychologically central or peripheral dimension. Furthermore, to offer a unified and integrative outlook on the two parallel lines of past research in this area, an assessment of a broad spectrum of dependent measures is needed. Specifically, since one line of research (that on quality of preexisting relations) has looked at the effects of aid on the recipient's *external* perceptions, whereas the other has centered on recipient's self-perceptions, a unified outlook calls for assessment of the two clusters of responses.

We have recently completed such an effort at Tel Aviv University (Nadler, Fisher, & Ben-Itzhak, 1983). In this experiment we invited subjects to come to the laboratory with a good same-sex friend. Half the subjects were under the impression that they were in a team with their friend, whereas the other half thought that the other with whom they would team up was a stranger. Also, half the subjects were told that performance on the task reflected on psychologically central qualities (e.g., intelligence), whereas the other half were told that performance on the task had no relationship to central qualities (i.e., it reflected the operation of chance factors).

Later, subjects worked on the experimental task (identifying the murderer in a detective story) but were unable to complete the task on their own and were helped to do so by their partner. Finally, since we have reasoned that the intensity of the comparison stress inherent in help may depend on whether it is given repeatedly or only once, half of our subjects received help once, and the other half twice, before filling out the dependent measures. We expected that *repeated* instances of self-threatening help (from a friend on a central task) would intensify the negative feelings associated with its receipt. In all, the experiment was a 2 (good friend vs. stranger as helper) × 2 (central vs. noncentral task) × 2 (subject helped once vs. twice) between-subjects design.

It should be noted that this experiment is unique in several respects. Most important for the present discussion, it is a first attempt to integrate two lines of parallel past research by investigating the elements of comparison stress that may exist in receiving aid from a friend. Furthermore, this study attempts to assess the effect of this stress on self-perceptions as well as on the recipient's external perceptions (of donor and aid).

The data lent support to our major assertion that the effects of donor–recipient relations on recipient's reactions depend on the centrality of the task. Specifically, a 2 (friend vs. stranger) × 2 (central vs. noncentral aid) × 2 (help given once vs. twice) interaction $F(1.88) = 3.81$, $p < .05$, indicates that subjects who were helped twice by a good friend on a *central* task had the lowest affect score, whereas subjects who were helped twice by a good friend on a *noncentral* task had the highest affect score (means are 12.8 and 17.2, respectively). The same pattern was observed on the self-evaluation scale. The marginally significant, $F(2.88) = 3.45$, $p. < .07$, three-way interaction indicates that subjects who were helped twice by a good friend on a central task evaluated themselves significantly less favorably than subjects who were helped twice by a good friend on a noncentral task (means are 9.2 and 11.0, respectively).

As for the recipient's external perceptions, parallel, marginally significant three-way interactions for the Interpersonal Judgment Scale measure of liking (cf. Byrne, 1971), $F(1.88) = 3.17$, $p < .08$, and for the measure of expected quality of future relations with the donor, $F(1.88)$

$= 2.3$, $p < .12$, yield a similar pattern of findings. In fact, the donor was least liked and worst relations were expected with him when he was a good friend who helped twice on a central task.

On the whole, the data indicate that being helped repeatedly by a good friend to accomplish a task that reflected on a central quality was the most self-threatening in comparison to the other experimental cells. This supports our analysis that the *interaction* between characteristics of the aid (i.e., centrality) *and* the characteristics of the helper (i.e., social proximity) provide a more solid base for understanding and prediction in the context.

Based on these findings and the data reviewed in earlier sections, a more formal statement of the effects of receiving help from socially close others can be made. We shall attempt to subsume in a unified framework the conclusions that emerged from the research on overall quality of donor–recipient relations and on donor–recipient similarity.

1. Receiving help from a socially close other is a more psychologically meaningful and intense experience than receiving help from a socially distant other (i.e., a dissimilar other, or an other with whom one does not enjoy social proximity). Yet it is a mixed blessing. On the one hand, it carries with it the positive implications of concern from a psychologically relevant other. On the other hand, it contains the comparison stress that may be induced by the receipt of help from a psychologically close other.

2. Whether the receipt of help from a psychologically close other constitutes a positive message of other's caring or a negative message of other's superiority and one's own inferiority (comparison stress) depends on the psychological centrality of the help. If help is not indicative of the recipient's inferiority on a psychologically central dimension, receiving aid from a socially close other will constitute an overall positive experience for the recipient. If, however, help *is* indicative of the recipient's inferiority on a psychologically central dimension, receiving help from a socially close other will constitute an overall negative experience for the recipient.

3. Other situational and personality characteristics may act to catalyze these processes. On the basis of the study we have reviewed in this section and of other research, two such conditions can be identified: (1) the recipient's level of persistent self-esteem, and (2) the duration of the aid relationship. Thus when the recipient has high self-esteem and the help is given repeatedly, these psychological processes may be catalyzed and the predicted effects would be more intense.

4. In line with a recent threat to self-esteem conceptualization in this context (Fisher, Nadler, & Witcher-Alagna, 1982), the resulting self-sup-

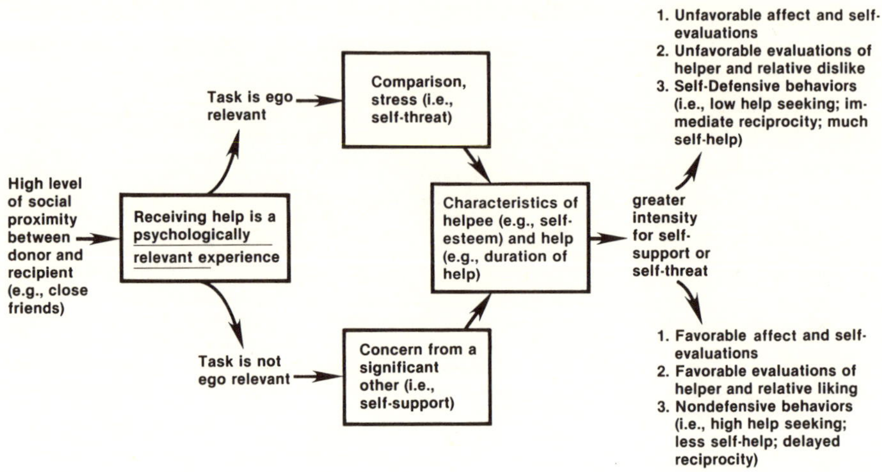


Figure 2. Effects of donor–recipient relationships on the recipient's reactions to aid. (From Nadler, Fisher, & Ben-Itzhak, 1983.)

port or self-threat should be reflected in affective reactions, self-evaluations, external evaluations, and relevant behaviors (e.g., help seeking, self-help efforts).

The link among social proximity between the donor and the recipient, centrality of task, and the recipient's reactions to aid is shown paradigmatically in Figure 2.

### 4.3. Links with Past Research and Theory

A more thorough examination of the studies reviewed earlier lends support to our analysis. In fact, it seems that studies on the quality of donor–recipient relations that have found that receiving help from a socially close other is a relatively positive experience for the recipient have studied situations that did not involve recipients' inferiority on ego-central dimensions. Clark and Mills (1979) examined situations in which receipt of help was not indicative of inferiority on a psychological dimension. In fact, subjects were helped by a partner *after* they had outperformed and helped him or her earlier. Clark and Wadell (in Clark, 1983) asked subjects to imagine to themselves mundane helping transactions that were not at all central to their self-esteem (helping to syphon gas from one car to another; borrowing charcoal for a barbecue).

The other related studies also used nonego-involving situations. Bar-Tal *et al.* (1977), DePaulo (1978b), and Nadler *et al.* (1982) all used role-playing procedures where subjects imagined to themselves that they were being helped. These procedures cannot be regarded as creating ego-central helping interactions (cf. DePaulo, 1982). Finally, the state of need that was experimentally created by Nadler *et al.* (1974) in their study of international conflict stimulation was associated with chance factors and was not reflective of any ego-central inferiority of the recipients. The case for the noncentrality of help in the studies by Gergen and Gergen (1971, 1974) on responses to international aid is less clear. Possibly, a country that receives help from another country resorts to noncentral explanations in order to disarm the self-threat that may otherwise be inherent in the receipt of help. Thus, for example, people in the receiving country may attribute their need for help to harsh weather or lack of natural resources rather than to their own lack of resourcefulness.

In contrast, in studies that have demonstrated the arousal of comparison stress in aid (i.e., studies on donor–recipient similarity), the receipt of aid reflected inferiority on a central dimension (e.g., investment abilities of young male subjects) (Fisher & Nadler, 1974, 1976; Nadler & Fisher, 1981; Nadler *et al.*, 1976; Nadler *et al.*, 1979). Moreover, in studies where centrality was actively manipulated, comparison stress effects were apparent only under central aid conditions (Nadler & Altman, 1981; Nadler & Fisher, 1981; Nadler and Kolker, 1981).

## 5. CONCLUDING REMARKS

In summary, we propose that the emerging contradiction between the two lines of research (one group of studies concluding that help from a socially close other is overall positive, and the other concluding that it is overall negative and self-threatening) is apparent rather than real. It reflects the fact that one group of studies (on donor–recipient similarity) has dealt with help that reflects inferiority on psychologically central dimensions, whereas the second group (on overall quality of donor–recipient relations) has studied helping interactions that do not reflect such inferiority.

In addition to its integrative function, the model outlined earlier has important empirical implications. For example, based on this logic we would suggest that contrary to predictions made by existing theory (Clark, 1983), recipients in communal relations may under certain conditions have a stronger need for an immediate reciprocity than those in exchange relations. More specifically, our analysis implies that if help reflects inferiority on a psychologically central dimension, the recipient may feel a greater need to return it and regain independence when the helper is a close friend than when he or she is a stranger. However, this and other implications await further research.

Finally, the idea that close interpersonal relations involve a higher intensity of both "pleasure" and "pain" is in agreement with research and theory in social psychology (e.g., Brickman & Bulman, 1977; Klages, 1928; Mettee & Riskind, 1974; Morse & Gergen, 1970; Nadler *et al.*, 1980). Furthermore, the role of task centrality as a determinant of whether the close relations will yield "pain" or "pleasure" has also received recent empirical and conceptual support (Tesser, 1980). Finally, the notion that (1) receiving help is a mixed blessing and that (2) person and situation variables determine the relative weight of the "positive" and "negative" elements in aid, thereby (3) precipitating either of two clusters of recipient reactions, lends support to our recent threat to self-esteem model of recipients' reactions (Fisher *et al.*, 1982).

## 6. REFERENCES

Adams, J. S. Toward an understanding of inequity. *Journal of Abnormal and Social Psychology*, 1963, *67*, 422–436.

Bar-Tal, D., Zohar, Y. B., Greenberg, M. S., & Hermon, M. Reciprocity in relationship between donor and recipient and between harm-doer and victim. *Sociometry*, 1977, *40*, 293–298.

Bramel, D. Dissonance, expectation and the self. In R. Abelson, E. Aronson, T. M. Newcomb, W. J. McQuire, M. J. Rosenberg, & P. H. Tannenbaum (Eds.), *Sourcebook of cognitive consistency*. Chicago: Rand McNally, 1968.

Briar, S. Welfare from below: Recipient's view of the public welfare system. In J. Brock (Ed.), *The law of the poor*. San Francisco: Chandler, 1966.

Brickman, P., & Bulman, R. J. Pleasure and pain in social comparison. In J. M. Suls & R. L. Miller (Eds.), *Social comparison processes: Theoretical and empirical perspectives*. Washington, D.C.: Hemisphere, 1977.

Byrne, D. *The attraction paradigm*. New York: Academic Press, 1971.

Castore, C. H., & DeNinno, J. A. Investigations in the social comparison of attitudes. In J. M. Suls & R. L. Miller (Eds.), *Social comparison processes: Theoretical and empirical perspectives*. Washington, D.C.: Hemisphere, 1977.

Clark, M. S. Communal-exchange relations and reactions to receiving help. In J. D. Fisher, A. Nadler, & B. M. DePaulo (Eds.), *New directions in helping*. Vol. 1. *Recipient reactions to aid*. New York: Academic Press, 1983.

Clark, M. S., & Mills, J. Interpersonal attraction in exchange and communal relationships. *Journal of Personality and Social Psychology*, 1979, *37*, 12–24.

Clark, M. S., Gotay, C. C., & Mills, J. Acceptance of help as a function of similarity of the potential helper and opportunity to repay. *Journal of Applied Social Psychology*, 1974, *4*, 224–229.

DePaulo, B. M. Accepting help from teachers—when the teachers are children. *Human Relations*, 1978, *31*, 459–474. (a)

DePaulo, B. M. Help-seeking from the recipient's point of view. *JSAS Catalog of Selected Documents in Psychology*, 1978, *8*, 62. (b)

DePaulo, B. M. Social psychological processes in asking for help. In H. Wills (Ed.), *Basic processes in helping relationships*. New York: Academic Press, 1982.

DePaulo, B. M., Brown, P. L., Ishii, S. H., & Fisher, J. D. Recipient reactions to kindly and unkindly bestowed help. *Journal of Personality and Social Psychology*, 1981, *41*, 478–487.

Festinger, L. A theory of social comparison processes. *Human Relations*, 1954, *1*, 117–140.

Fisher, J. D., & Nadler, A. The effect of similarity between donor and recipient on reactions to aid. *Journal of Applied Social Psychology*, 1974, *4*, 230–243.

Fisher, J. D., & Nadler, A. Effect of donor resources on recipient self-esteem and self-help. *Journal of Experimental Social Psychology*, 1976, *12*, 139–150.

Fisher, J. D., Harrison, C., & Nadler, A. Exploring the generalizability of donor–recipient similarity effects. *Personality and Social Psychology Bulletin*, 1978, *4*, 627–630.

Fisher, J. D., Nadler, A., & Whitcher-Alagna, S. Recipient reactions to aid: A conceptual review. *Psychological Bulletin*, 1982, *91*, 27–54.

Freeman, H. R. Reward vs. reciprocity as related to attraction. *Journal of Applied Social Psychology*, 1977, *1*, 57–66.

Gergen, K. J., & Gergen, M. International assistance from a psychological perspective. *Yearbook of world affairs* (Vol. 25). London: Institute of World Affairs, 1971.

Gergen, K. J., & Gergen, M. Foreign aid that works. *Psychology Today*, 1974, *8*, 54–58.

Goffman, E. *Asylums.* Garden City, N.Y.: Doubleday, 1961.

Greenberg, M. S. A theory of indebtedness. In K. Gergen, M. S. Greenberg, & R. Willis (Eds.), *Social exchange: Advances in theory and research.* New York: Plenum Press, 1980.

Gross, A. E., Wallston, B. S., & Piliavin, I. Reactance, attribution, equity, and the help recipient. *Journal of Applied Social Psychology*, 1979, *9*, 297–313.

Hatfield, E., & Sprecher, S. Equity theory and recipient reactions to aid. In J. D. Fisher, A. Nadler, & B. M. DePaulo (Eds.), *New directions in helping* Vol. 1. *Recipient reactions to aid.* New York: Academic Press, 1983.

Jones, E. E., & Davis, K. E. From acts to dispositions: The attribution process in person perception. In L. Berkowitz (Ed.), *Advances in experimental social psychology* (Vol. 2). New York: Academic Press, 1965.

Kalish, R. A. Of children and grandfathers: A speculative essay on dependency. *The Gerontologist*, 1967, *7*, 185ff.

Kanfer, F. H. Personal control, social control and altruism. *American Psychologist*, 1979, *34*, 231–239.

Kelley, H. H. Attribution theory in social psychology. In D. Levine (Ed.), *Nebraska Symposium on Motivation.* Lincoln: University of Nebraska Press, 1967.

Klages, L. *Die Grundlugen der characterkunde.* Leipzig: Barth, 1928.

Ladieu, G., Hanfman, E., & Dembo, T. Studies in adjustment to visible injuries: Evaluation of help by the injured. *Journal of Abnormal and Social Psychology*, 1947, *42*, 169–192.

Lipman, A., & Sterne, R. Aging in the United States: Ascription of a terminal sick role. *Sociology and Social Research*, 1962, *53*, 194–203.

Merton, R. K. *Social theory and social structure.* New York: Free Press, 1968.

Mettee, D. R., & Riskind, J. Size of defeat and liking of superior and inferior ability competitors. *Journal of Experimental Social Psychology*, 1974, *10*, 333–351.

Morris, S. C., III, & Rosen, S. Effects of felt adequacy and opportunity to reciprocate on help-seeking. *Journal of Experimental Social Psychology*, 1973, *9*, 265–276.

Morse, S., & Gergen, K. Material aid and social attraction. *Journal of Applied Social Psychology*, 1971, *1*, 150–212.

Nadler, A., & Altman, A. *Similarity, centrality and reactions to aid.* Unpublished manuscript, Tel Aviv University, 1981.

Nadler, A., & Fisher, J. D. *Self-help as a function of aid centrality and donor–recipient similarity.* Unpublished manuscript, Tel Aviv University, 1981.

Nadler, A., & Kolker, S. *Donor–recipient attitude similarity, self-esteem and help seeking behavior.* Unpublished manuscript, Tel Aviv University, 1981.

Nadler, A., & Mayseless, O. Recipient's self-esteem and reactions to aid. In J. D. Fisher, A. Nadler, & B. M. DePaulo (Eds.), *New directions in helping.* Vol. 1. *Recipient reactions to aid.* New York: Academic Press, 1983.

Nadler, A., Fisher, J. D., & Streufert, S. The donor's dilemma: Recipient's reaction to aid from friend or foe. *Journal of Applied Social Psychology*, 1974, *4*, 272–285.

Nadler, A., Fisher, J. D., & Streufert, S. When helping hurts: The effects of donor–recipient similarity and recipient self-esteem on reactions to aid. *Journal of Personality*, 1976, *44*, 392–409.

Nadler, A., Altman, A., & Fisher, J. D. Helping is not enough: Recipient's reactions to aid as a function of positive and negative self-regard. *Journal of Personality*, 1979, *47*, 615–628.

Nadler, A., Jazwinski, C., Lau, S., & Miller, A. The cold glow of success: Responses to social rejection as affected by attitude similarity between chosen and rejected individuals. *European Journal of Social Psychology*, 1980, *10*, 279–289.

Nadler, A., Sheinberg, O., & Jaffe, Y. Coping with stress in male paraplegics through help seeking: The role of acceptance of physical disability in help seeking. In C. D. Spielberger, I. G. Sarason, & N. A. Milgram (Eds.), *Stress and anxiety* (Vol. 8). Washington, D.C.: Hemisphere, 1981.

Nadler, A., Bar-Tal, D., & Drukman, O. Density does not help: Help giving, seeking and reciprocating of students living in high-rise and lower dormitories. *Population and Environment: Behavioral and Social Issues*, 1982, *5*, 26–42.

Nadler, A. Fisher, J. D., & Ben-Itzhak, S. With a little help from my friend: Reaction to receiving prolonged vs. one-act help from a friend or stranger, as a function of the centrality. *Journal of Personality and Social Psychology*, 1983, *44*, 310–321.

Osgood, C. E. *An alternative to war or surrender*. Urbana: University of Illinois Press, 1962.

Pritchard, R. D. Equity theory: A review and critique. *Organizational Behavior and Human Performance*, 1969, *4*, 176–211.

Streufert, S., Kliger, S. C., Castore, C. H., & Driver, M. J. Tactical and negotiations game for analysis of decision integration across decision areas. *Psychological Reports*, 1967, *20*, 155–157.

Suls, J. M., & Miller, R. L. (Eds.). *Social comparison processes: Theoretical and empirical perspectives*. Washington, D.C.: Hemisphere, 1977.

Tesser, A. Self-esteem maintenance in family dynamics. *Journal of Personality and Social Psychology*, 1980, *39*, 77–91.

Tessler, R. C., & Schwartz, S. H. Help-seeking, self-esteem, and achievement motivation: An attributional analysis. *Journal of Personality and Social Psychology*, 1972, *21*, 318–326.

Underwood, B. J. Individual differences as a crucible in theory construction. *American Psychologist*, 1975, *30*, 128–134.

Walster, E., Walster, G. W., & Berscheid, E. *Equity: Theory and research*. Boston: Allyn & Bacon, 1978.

Weiss, C. H. Validity of welfare mothers' responses. *Public Opinion Quarterly*, 1969, *32*, 622–633.

# V

# APPLICATIONS OF KNOWLEDGE ABOUT PROSOCIAL BEHAVIOR

# Introduction

Jerzy Karylowski and Daniel Bar-Tal

Prosocial behavior is a real-life phenomenon. It takes place in various human frameworks. For example, prosocial behavior occurs in interpersonal relations between strangers as well as between friends; in intergroup relations when one group helps another group; in institutional frameworks when formal organizations help either individuals or groups; and in international frameworks when a state provides aid to another state or an international organization gives economical or other aid to a nation. Human beings establish professions and institutions, whose main objective is to provide help to individuals, groups, and nations who are in need. Sometimes the help is provided as part of an exchange process, and sometimes it originates as a consequence of self-interest or as a result of social responsibility.

Prosocial behavior is considered a positive form of human behavior. Societies teach this behavior and encourage its practice. But research and experience have shown that prosocial behavior can also be mishandled and produce negative effects. In this respect, psychologists have an opportunity not only to contribute their knowledge in order to facilitate its development among children and to maintain its performance among adults, but also to indicate how to carry it out, for whom, and when on personal as well as institutional levels.

However, although the study of prosocial behavior has become of great interest for psychologists in the past 15 years, only recently have they begun to study applied problems of prosocial behavior. Until now most of the research was restricted to investigations of determinants and correlates of prosocial behavior between strangers in simulated situations either in the laboratory or the field. The increasing emphasis on applied problems of prosocial behavior reflects the growing interest of psychologists in being useful and relevant. At a time when social problems increasingly involve and preoccupy public interest, there is increasing pressure on psychology to engage in applied and relevant studies of these problems. Another reason for the emergence of applied research is the development of theoretical models. In the late seventies, a number of general theoretical models of prosocial behavior have been proposed that attempt to go beyond laboratory experiments to a study of applied problems.

The four chapters in this section reflect the trend of application. Each of the chapters deals with a different social problem and each approaches the problem from a different perspective. Hertz-Lazarowitz and Sharan discuss the possibility of enhancing prosocial behavior through cooperative learning in the classroom. The authors developed a teaching method (small-group teaching) in which students learn in small groups via such processes as mutual communication, division of labor, cooperation, and mutual assistance. The program was implemented in several schools and the results showed that the formulated social objectives to enhance prosocial behavior were largely achieved. The success of the project seems encouraging, suggesting that schools may play important functions in enhancing various forms of prosocial behavior both among students and among their teachers.

Bickman's contribution brings us close to the issue of unresponsive bystanders. He reviews psychological research on bystander intervention that simulated an emergency and compares the results with operating programs in various states of the United States that are designed to increase the probability of bystander intervention in crimes (Citizen Crime Reporting projects). On the basis of the comparison, the author proposes new lines of research that may provide important information for these programs.

Piliavin, Evans, and Callero deal with another specific area of application, blood donation. Blood donation systems based on volunteering have an advantage over the system based on paid donors. Therefore, the question how to develop and maintain motivation for regular blood donation is important. The authors present an elaborated model of the commitment process to regular blood donation that is based on extensive research on blood donation.

Finally, in contrast to the other three chapters which deal with specific applications of the study of prosocial behavior, Sinha raises a general issue with regard to application research. He points out that any application has to take into consideration the sociocultural context of the environment in which the application is done. Specifically, he is concerned with the study of prosocial behavior in communities in India. In this case, research must relate prosocial behavior to the sociocultural and economic context of an Indian community.

# 21

# Enhancing Prosocial Behavior through Cooperative Learning in the Classroom

Rachel Hertz-Lazarowitz and Shlomo Sharan

## 1. INTRODUCTION

One of the primary institutions for socialization in society is the school. The entire school and classroom system can be viewed as a critical arena for the study and development of prosocial behavior. However, to date, a substantial amount of research and theoretical writing has accumulated concerning how parental childrearing at home, and other adult influences outside the school system, contribute to the development of positive behavior in children (Staub, 1978, 1979). In recent publications, several attempts have been made to apply theoretical concepts and laboratory findings to other social settings, especially to schools (Bar-Tal, 1978; Bar-Tal & Raviv, 1982; Harris, Eisenberg, & Carroll, 1982; Staub, 1981). The assumption is that a "teacher" replaces the "parent" in the socialization sequence and thus the same processes that enhance prosocial behavior in general are applicable to teacher–student relationships in the classroom. However, since there are very few research findings to support such an assumption, one may question its validity especially in light of the vast differences between "life in the classroom" (Jackson, 1968) and in the home environment.

RACHEL HERTZ-LAZAROWITZ • School of Education, Haifa University, Haifa, Israel.
SHLOMO SHARAN • School of Education, Tel Aviv University, Tel Aviv, Israel.

We see the classroom as a unique social world. Our main principle is that a classroom is a *peer society,* and the nature and quality of peer interactions in the classroom are the critical variables that facilitate prosocial behavior among children. We shall look at the Small Group Teaching (SGT) Project, where classrooms were experimentally restructured toward a peer-cooperation mode of learning. The main goal of the SGT Project was to test the effects of cooperative learning on prosocial behavior. In order to change the classroom from an individualistic-competitive goal structure (Johnson, 1981; Johnson & Johnson, 1974, 1978) to a cooperative–prosocial goal structure, changes had to be made in many dimensions of the classroom. The social-organizational structure was a "group of groups" with interaction and cooperation within and between groups. The role of the teacher, communication patterns among students, and between teacher and students had to become friendly, warm, and nurturing. Learning tasks had to be restructured in order to create interdependence, coordination, cooperation, exchange, and helping. The students' role had to be drastically changed so that they would be important and necessary. The notion of a "source" and not an "origin" (DeCharms, 1976) best defines this conception. Hence, students had to hold a different set of personal goals in the classroom (Staub, 1981).

In the sequence of the SGT Project a vast number of variables were studied, and the project is fully reported elsewhere (Sharan & Hertz-Lazarowitz, 1981, 1982; Sharan, Hertz-Lazarowitz, & Reiner, 1978). Here we shall briefly discuss the classroom as the most significant social world of childhood (Hartup, 1979) and analyze the very few long-term studies available to support our claim that different types of schools do make a difference in prosocial development. Next, we shall briefly discuss the conceptual framework of the group investigation model in cooperative learning.

The bulk of this chapter will present our research findings in Israel and discuss the effect of cooperative learning on prosocial development, awareness, and behavior. Finally, we shall suggest avenues of research on the role of peers as facilitators of prosocial behavior. The cooperative classroom seems to be a significant environment for utilizing prosocial behavior via natural socialization, participation, and active implementation of prosocial deeds. Social-developmental psychologists need to examine more closely and understand better the peer society in a classroom. Thus child–child interactions and not only adult–child interactions must become a focus of future research.

### 1.1. The Classroom: A Social World of Childhood

There is more than a kernel of truth in the often-repeated observation that the classroom is the child's social universe. Indeed, when children emerge from the relatively limited circle of family and neighborhood friends and enter the school and classroom, their social environment, for many hours each day for 12 years, becomes enormously expanded and complex. In many critical ways the social-psychological complexity of the classroom and school compares with that of the macrosocial world of the adult: Schoolchildren and adults alike must cope with sets of tasks within a multidimensional network of social relationships. The school presents children with the continuing need to relate to many levels of social structure: to peers in a one-to-one relationship, to the almost ever present social unit of the classroom with its formal and informal groupings, and to the multiage population of the entire school. One may even argue that few adults are constrained by their daily working environment to maintain such a complex set of social interactions with such a wide range of individuals and groups as are schoolchildren.

Given these conditions, the school presents a unique setting for socializing children into the patterns of thought and behavior that society deems worthy of transmitting. Socialization can be promoted at all levels of the school society so that children learn how to live in harmony with other individuals old and young, with groups and within a large social organization. This includes relating to members of the other sex and of other cultural groups as well. Since children display a high level of emotional involvement in the social relations they experience in school, they are particularly susceptible to influence by figures and groups with whom they interact and identify there. Such influence may become a permanent part of children's personality and behavior.

Despite this prominent role of school in socializing almost 100% of our children, perusal of the research literature on socialization in schools reveals that remarkably little is known about this process. How do peer relations in schools affect children's social behavior? How do schools mold children's interactions with people of different ages or groups? There are very few answers to such questions.

Our knowledge is especially limited concerning the acquisition of prosocial behaviors in the classroom. Most adult observers of the classroom claim that social interactions in school are distinctly competitive, fiercely individualistic, at times asocial or antisocial. Moreover, these behavioral patterns are supported by prevailing school and classroom organization and regulations (Dreeban, 1968; Jackson, 1968). Jackson (1968) affords a sobering glimpse into daily life in schools. School life as described by Jackson approximates more the drama of the survival of the fittest described by advocates of a superficial social Darwinism than a pursuit of the goals of social responsibility and continuity proclaimed by school functionaries. Schools highlight social comparison and the distinction between the "weak" and the "strong." The latter terms are the single most widespread adjectives used by teachers for "classifying" pupils in schools and classroom, revealing that school is perceived as a perpetual contest. The second most common pair of descriptive terms, "good" or "bad" students, concerns the extent to which pupils conform to teachers' wishes, that is, to a largely impersonal power in order to be evaluated as "good."

### 1.2. How Do Schools Make a Difference?

School experience is never a value vacuum or a behavioral vacuum in the social sense (Friere, 1974). Yet one of the most significant socializing factors in schools—the students themselves—is not yet a "respected" variable for research. Johnson (1981) describes nine significant areas where he claims peers have the most crucial impact on the development and socialization processes of others. Yet "student-student interaction [is] the neglected variable in education."

Social scientists and educators should be interested in the central processes of socialization in different types of schooling. We should ask whether schools make a difference. One of the most extensive and pioneering studies of the effects of schooling on children was conducted by a team of investigators from the Bank Street College of Education (Minuchin, Biber, Shapiro, & Zimiles, 1969). They documented the differential effects on a host of dependent variables of two different kinds of educational philosophies, progressive versus traditional forms of schooling. Evidence supports the contention that progressive schooling fostered a higher level of moral reasoning, where pupils used basic principles as guidelines more than did pupils with traditional schooling.

Early in this massive text, the authors contrast the two styles of interaction patterns among pupils in the two kinds of schools (see in particular Table 3–2, p, 39). Under the category of "Use of Peer Groups in Organization of Children's Work," we note that classroom learning included much experience in peer groups: activities encouraging democratic ways of social functioning; use of discussion techniques; engaging the class in problem-solving techniques; and opinion formation involving codes of social behavior as well as study content. What the Bank Street study shows is that progressive schools fostering higher levels of social conduct embedded prosocial norms for behavior in the self-determined group processes that transpired as an essential part of classroom learning. In this fashion, the social and academic aspects of school experience were integrated. By contrast, in the traditional schools classes were organized as whole units treated uniformly according to principles of "universalism," and pupils engaged in individual question-and-answer exchanges with the teacher as the primary method of intellectual discourse in the classroom. Thus student interaction was not fostered. A lower level of social conduct and moral development was found in those classrooms.

We are not aware of another long-term research project dealing with this type of schooling and its effects on *social*-cognitive variables. Many studies, however, use children as subjects in studies of moral development, social-cognitive skills, and prosocial behavior. Investigators frequently refer to them in terms of their school grades, but use this information merely to index the children's chronological status. These researchers frequently ignore the elementary fact that a large portion of social-cognitive skills and behaviors are influenced by the specific school setting in which those subjects are functioning. Thus psychologists frequently study the social-cognitive behavior of children who go to school, but not the effect of schooling on this behavior.

### 1.3. Conceptual Overview of the Group Investigation Model in Cooperative Learning

The various cooperative learning methods continue the tradition of Deweyian progressivism in education. The Deweyian philosophy (1916) asserted that regular classroom learning is a primary socializing agent, and that democratic processes of organization and interaction in the classroom socialize children into democratic and humanistic forms of conduct. Staub (1981) claims, on a similar line of thought, that one of the most effective ways to promote prosocial behavior in children is through their actual participation in positive behavior (Staub, 1979, Chapter 6). This form of positive behavior might be enhanced only in a classroom where both the teachers and students may participate and practice certain behaviors. Without creating such a positive social world in the classroom, it is impossible to socialize children toward prosocial behavior. The past decade saw a revival of interest in continuing the tradition of Deweyian progressivism. One of the most significant outcomes of this is the development of cooperative learning methods in small groups, and their implementation in classrooms. The new methods benefited in conception and implementation from recent advances in social psychology, organizational development, and the human relations movement. Moreover, these methods have been subjected to a remarkable series of experimental field studies (for review, see Johnson, Maruyama, Johnson, Nelson, & Skon, 1981; Sharan, 1980; Sharan, Webb, Hare, & Hertz-Lazarowitz, 1980; Slavin, 1980a).

The first period of the cooperative learning movement was strongly influenced by general social problems in schools, mainly interracial relations in the heterogeneous junior high school classrooms. Aronson's

Jigsaw Method and Slavin's Cooperative Methods were mainly addressed to achieving social integration with positive effects on academic achievements (Aronson & Goode, 1980; Slavin, 1980b, 1983).

Of interest here is that some of the recent studies using various versions of small group learning in the classroom made initial attempts to evaluate students' reactions to their experiences in these groups from the point of view of prosocial behavior. Reports of this research suggest that pupils involved in small cooperative groups tended to prefer cooperative learning situations to competitive ones, that they preferred to help each other rather than work alone or without the opportunity to share their ideas, and that cooperative learning promoted increased ability of students to take the perspective of others in evaluating affective and intellectual situations and in creating interracial friendships (Aronson, Bridgeman, & Geffner, 1978; Hansell & Slavin, 1981; Johnson & Johnson, 1978). Only very recently has the research in cooperative learning begun to address itself specifically to the enhancement of prosocial behavior. Definition of cooperation within a learning task in a classroom is provided by Sharan and Hertz-Lazarowitz (1978) and by Bar-Tal and Geser (1980). The group-investigation model developed in the Israeli project goes beyond the structured equal interdependence found in the Jigsaw or the Student-Team-Achievement Division (STAD) (Slavin, 1980b). The unique feature of the group investigation model is the theoretical concept of *planned prosocial peer interaction,* where the students themselves serve as models, reward givers, reinforcers, role players, and a challenging support system for each other. Indeed, in this conceptualization children themselves can utilize various ways to facilitate the development of high quality helping behavior, which was reserved only for teachers and adults in a previous work (Bar-Tal & Raviv, 1982). In the group investigation project, practical training strategies and activities were developed to train teachers and students (Sharan & Hertz-Lazarowitz, 1978, Chapter 5, 1980).

In order to clarify how the Small Group Teaching (SGT) project relates to helping behavior, we wish to state our conception of this domain and its relation to school experience. For contrast, let us recall the social conditions that prevail in the typical traditional classroom. The teacher is the central figure in the class, exercising control over and mediating all communication. Pupils compete for the teacher's attention and praise, which affords them status in the class, in the eyes of peers and of the teacher. A large percentage of the pupils (some studies claim up to 70%) remain outside the circle of teacher–pupil interaction, and direct communication among peers is largely discouraged (Flanders, 1970; Hunter, 1972; Sommer, 1967). Social relations among pupils in the traditional classroom involve a considerable amount of conflict fanned by constant competition, all of which has a decidedly negative effect on classroom social climate. Pupils with low status are stigmatized as underprivileged, culturally deprived, educationally handicapped, and so on and occupy a peripheral place in the classroom's social network. Such conditions of favoritism or even discrimination, common in many traditionally taught classrooms, foster low group cohesiveness and the atomization of the class into rivalrous or closed cliques.

In the group investigation model, the classroom functions as a "group-of-groups" (Weick, 1969) with multilateral communication and cooperation within each of the several (up to eight) small groups in the class. There is also coordination among the groups so that the class remains an integral social unit. Thus the classroom operates as a *peer society* organized into subunits each concentrated on some aspect of a broad learning task. These subunits provide its members with mutual help and support, collaboration on task-related activities, exchange of ideas and other resources, and mutual acceptance. Children from different ethnic groups, socioeconomic levels, with differing levels of academic achievement or personal traits, all have an opportunity to contribute to achieving a collective group goal. The sequence of the group investigation model is structured in six stages, elaborating the early model proposed by Thelen (1954, 1960): (1) identifying the topic and organizing pupils into research groups; (2) planning the learning task; (3) carrying out the investigation; (4) preparing a final report; (5) presenting the final report to the classroom; and (6) evaluation (peer evaluation and teacher evaluation).

In order to facilitate the effective functioning of these groups, teachers must assist pupils in acquiring sets of social skills, including: active listening to peers, utilizing others' ideas, sharing one's own thoughts and resources with others, respecting the speaking privileges of others, allowing the spontaneous emergence of informal leadership behaviors in the group, counteracting tendencies for power relations and concentration of dominance, and accepting responsibility for performing one's part in a division-of-labor structure (Schmuck & Schmuck, 1974; 1979). When these conditions prevail, they foster the emergence of role taking, empathy, friendship and close personal relations, and acceptance of others without regard for stereotyped attributions. In short, classroom learning in this kind of social structure and social dynamics exerts a multidimensional influence on children: on their social behavior, social-affective attitudes, moral perceptions and thinking, and on their motivation to learn and work together with their peers.

From an organizational and procedural perspective, our ultimate aim in the SGT Project was the implementation and assessment of a group investigation model of classroom learning where pupils are able to perform the following kinds of procedures: cooperative planning of study projects; self-directed planning of study procedures including use of various informational resources; division of labor among group members; mutual assistance in carrying out the group's study plan; collaboration with group members in clarifying ideas, problems, and goals; group planning of a collective product to emerge from the sharing of all members' contributions to the group project; and construction of a group product in some interesting form that is presented in an appropriate fashion to members of the class as a whole (Sharan & Hertz-Lazarowitz, 1978, 1980).

Given that all of the schools participating in the SGT Project were accustomed exclusively to traditional whole-class instructional methods, implementation of the group investigation model required extensive retraining of the teachers as well as imparting new skills to the pupils themselves. The group investigation model was implemented in Israel from second grade to eighth grade. The implementation of cooperative learning methods and the developmental sequence of students into cooperative and helping behaviors in the classroom is relatively new and not yet researched. Later in this chapter we shall present findings based on students' self-report on their experiences in a cooperative classroom. These will give us a glimpse into developmental aspects of being a student in a prosocial classroom.

## 2. THE SMALL GROUP TEACHING PROJECT IN ISRAEL

### 2.1. Research Design

Three elementary schools in the greater Tel Aviv area were the experimental cooperative schools. Two elementary schools in the same area, and with similar characteristics, were matched to serve as the control traditional schools. All the schools were in low socioeconomic neighborhoods, and were defined by the Ministry of Education and Culture in Israel as "disadvantaged" schools. About 1,400 pupils, grades 2–8, and 80 teachers participated in the research.

The SGT Project had several phases. In the first year the researchers and Israeli Instructional Television prepared packages of videotapes and instructional materials to train groups of teachers for cooperative instruction in the group investigation mode (Sharan & Sharan, 1976). A full description of this stage is presented elsewhere (Sharan, Hertz-Lazarowitz, & Reiner, 1978). In the second phase of the project, in-service experiential-learning workshops were designed for the teachers of the experimental schools. During the 2 years of implementation, the experimental teachers participated in 20 workshops (each 3 hours in duration) and were exposed to consultation and collegial support within their schools. The teachers from the control schools continued their traditional teaching methods and received in-service training for improving their instruction (see also Sharan & Hertz-Lazarowitz, 1982). Gradually, the teachers trained their students to learn the group investigation methods, and implemented the change in their classrooms. It is important to note that only part of the instruction and learning became cooperative. Observations conducted during the 2 years of implementation indicated that about 30% to 40% of classroom instructional time was conducted in the group investigation methods. However, other instructional methods were practiced in the classroom. This variety of instructional modes was encouraged.

Two general questions were of primary interest to the researchers: (1) What are the effects of cooperative learning on teachers?; and (2) What are the effects of cooperative learning on students? In the teacher sample we investigated the following variables: personality, various attitudinal dimensions, and instructional behavior in the classroom. In the student sample the following variables were investigated: students' self-esteem, locus of control, academic achievement, prosocial awareness, prosocial behavior, and classroom social climate. A variety of research strategies were used: pretest and posttest measures in teachers' attitudes; repeated measures on students' self-esteem and locus of control; repeated measures of classroom social climate; comparison of academic achievement in a structured program within the project; and experimentation to test for prosocial behavior. All this research was conducted in an experimental versus control comparison. In addition, such open-ended techniques as interviews and letters were used to obtain insight into teachers' and students' experiences in the cooperative classroom.

The emphasis in the following section is on prosocial aspects of the SGT Project. However, the reader is referred to the articles that report each inquiry fully.

### 2.2. Results

#### 2.2.1. *Teachers' Behavior and Attitudes*

As mentioned earlier, the role of the teacher in the group investigation classroom is very significant. He has to restructure many of the learning tasks from their competitive or individualistic goal structure to a cooperative and prosocial goal structure. The teacher trains his students to practice various social and learning skills needed in this kind of schooling. Thus the teacher has to promote a positive classroom climate where warmth and respect for child autonomy are an explicit set of norms. In order to become the "cooperative classroom teacher," every teacher had to learn gradually to relinquish his total control over student behavior in order to allow for direct interaction and communication among students. Teachers also had to undergo basic changes in attitudes toward competition and cooperation in the classroom. Many studies have demonstrated that teachers tend to maintain a competitive atmosphere in the classroom, and that this competition stimulates hostility among students and reduces chances for cultivating helping behavior—even though teachers may believe that competition stimulates achievement motivation (Crockenberg & Bryant, 1978; Henry, 1972).

In a questionnaire assessing teachers' need to control their students' behavior in the classroom (Willower, Eidell, & Hoy 1973), the elementary school teachers participating in our study initially expressed a control ideology closer to the end of the scale reflecting a "custodial" orientation to their role in the classroom. This custodial attitude contrasts with an orientation that accords decisive significance to the cultivation of students' sense of autonomy in learning and in the classroom situation. The custodial perception of the teacher's role and the development of mutual assistance and prosocial behavior among students in the class are virtually mutually exclusive. Hence, education for prosocial behavior among peers and the decentralization of control processes in the class through marked changes in teacher behavior and attitudes are profoundly intertwined. Methods for promoting helping behavior among children through school experiences cannot exclude explicit plans for changing teacher behavior in the classroom. We might add that, upon conclusion of our study, those teachers who actually adopted small group teaching methods (and there were those who did not) evidenced a change of 1 standard deviation in their scores on the Pupil Control Ideology Scale and moved in the direction of granting students greater autonomy, so that their scores compared favorably with liberal-minded elementary school teachers in the United States. Of interest is that teachers in the control group actually expressed a more intense custodial orientation at the conclusion of the study than they had a year and a half earlier when the study began. The instructional behavior of the teachers also changed significantly. Independent observers in the classroom indicated that as much as 40% of total instruction time was in the cooperative, group investigation mode. In the interviews at the end of the project, teachers reported on professional and personal changes they experienced as a result of the project (Sharan & Hertz-Lazarowitz, 1982; Sharan, Darom, & Hertz-Lazarowitz, 1979; Sharan, Hertz-Lazarowitz, & Lichtenson, 1981).

### 2.2.2. *Students' Academic Achievement*

Several recent publications review academic achievement of elementary and junior high school students in cooperative classrooms. The extensive survey by Johnson *et al.* (1981) uses metaanalysis techniques to evaluate almost 200 studies, comparing cooperative, competitive, and individualistic goal structure methods and their effects on academic achievement. The results of this research strongly support cooperative methods in the classroom. However, most of these studies dealt with academic achievements that measured basic skills in mathematics and language arts. The Israeli study was the first to test the effect of cooperative learning on three levels of academic achievement: (1) low level thinking skills such as recall and understanding of simple content, (2) high level thinking skills such as evaluation, comparison, and analysis of complex content, and (3) creativity (in composing a conclusion to a story). Five classrooms in the experimental schools and five classrooms in the control school (grades 2–6) spent 3 weeks studying identical curriculum content in the social sciences. The curriculum, activities, worksheets, and tests were all composed by all of the teachers and a researcher who was not on the regular project staff. In the control schools the teacher presented the topics in the traditional expository way, using question-and-answer, individual work, and so on. In the experimental school, groups of students studied the topic according to the stages of the group investigation method presented earlier. At the end of the experiment all the children were tested with the same tests. Findings indicated that in low level thinking there were no significant differences between the two methods. However, significant differences were found in high level thinking skills and in creativity, in favor of the experimental cooperative classrooms (Sharan, Ackerman, & Hertz-Lazarowitz, 1979–1980).

In a second study, conducted in a different school, three eighth-grade classes were exposed to (1) traditional method, (2) cooperative Jigsaw Method, and (3) group investigation method. Significant gains in academic achievement were found in the two types of cooperative methods as compared to the traditional methods. In this study, many positive social-personal effects were also found in students who studied in the cooperative methods (Hertz-Lazarowitz, Sharan, & Sapir, 1982). Although in the group investigation method each group is responsible for *one different* part of the curriculum, the test represents all the material. The achievements of the students in the group investigation classroom also reflect the excellent work each group did in instructing other groups.

### 2.2.3. *Classroom Social Climate*

The social climate of all the classes in the experimental and control schools was measured four times during the 2 years of the project. The My-Class Questionnaire (Walberg & Anderson, 1968) was pretested before the project and adapted to the Israeli sample (Hertz-Lazarowitz & Sharan, 1979). In its final form the questionnaire included 14 items in the following subscales: satisfaction from the classroom, conflict in the classroom, competition, cohesiveness, and helping. The results obtained from 523 children tested in grades 4 and 5, 5 and 6 indicated that, in general, students reported a more positive social classroom climate in the experimental cooperative classes. This finding contrasted with a significant decline in social climate in the traditional classrooms. Generally, research on classroom social climate displays a decline in satisfaction as students progress in school grades, but in the SGT Project a significant positive increase in the social climate of the classroom was evident (Sharan & Hertz-Lazarowitz, 1981, Chapter 8). Self-esteem increased with age. Likewise, locus of control became more intrinsic with age in both traditional and cooperative classrooms; thus the instructional mode did not significantly affect these variables.

### 2.2.4. *Prosocial Awareness*

The cooperative classroom strives to alter the social environment, the quality of social learning experiences and interactions. One way to determine whether egocentric personal goals are indeed changing to more altruistic goals is to investigate the thoughts and feelings of students after being members of a classroom with a strong prosocial orientation. We decided to ask the children, in a very direct way, for their thoughts about life in the cooperative classroom. Importantly, most of the children had experienced both types of classrooms: the traditional type before the project began, and the cooperative classroom during the 2 school years (from September to July) of the project. We asked all students to send an open-ended letter to the Israel Educational Television Center (under whose auspices this study was conducted) about their experiences during the 2 years they studied in small groups. Students were not given any further instructions, and they were asked to mail their letters directly to the Television Center so that no one in school would read what they wrote. We received over 400 letters, which we content analyzed. We identified 692 separate statements, which were then categorized and counted by independent judges (Hertz-Lazarowitz, Sharan, & Shachar, 1981). These letters afforded considerable insight into the students' perceptions of everyday life in the classrooms.

The 692 statements were clearly related to four dimensions of classroom experience: (1) formal academic learning; (2) social-affective relations; (3) motivation and satisfaction; and (4) comparison between the traditional and the experimental classroom. Of the statements, 30% dealt with academic learning, 20% discussed social-affective topics, 20% were about students' motivations and satisfaction, and 30% concerned the comparison between the traditional and the small group classroom. Children from all grade levels, that is, first to eighth, supplied these responses. Research thus far conducted on classroom life has rarely asked children how they feel about the various features of classroom experience (Jackson, 1968). Of particular interest here is that the subcategory to appear with the highest frequency in the children's statements was that of helping each other. Fully 41% of the statements appearing in the social-affective category (57 of 139) indicated that it was best to study in small groups, giving such reasons as "If somebody doesn't understand, or doesn't know how to do something, another child in the group will help him," or "We can help anyone who needs help," or "In the group you can be sure that you'll be helped and you're not afraid that you'll fail." Other statements included, "You can relate to other children's opinions," "You can understand better others' ideas," "It helps to improve relationships with other children." Thus helping each other was the most salient subcategory of statements to emerge from the content analysis of these letters.

In the dimension of statements comparing traditional with small group learning, children emphasized the social benefits of the cooperative classroom as contrasted with the traditional class. In the latter, children are afraid or ashamed to fail, they fear the teacher, they struggle among each other. These were all typical assertions made by many children. Significantly, only 10% of the total number of statements made contained some negative content regarding small group learning, primarily in the statements by the youngest children in the sample, who felt that the noise as well as the requirement to work independently were somewhat distressing. Ninety percent of all the statements favored cooperative learning in the classroom. This finding is consistent with reports by other investigators (Aronson *et al.*, 1978; Johnson, Johnson, & Bryant, 1973) who also found that students tended to define traditionally taught classrooms as competitive and expressed preference for studying in cooperative small groups because the latter are more pleasant, interesting, and more fun. The text of one letter by a fourth-grade child in the SGT Project illustrates these points vividly. This letter actually contains 13 different statements.

> In my opinion, we should study in groups next year too because the work is more interesting and nicer that way. When there are more children in the group there are more ideas. When you work in a small group, it's easy and there aren't many problems. Sometimes there are problems and the children in the group explain things much better. Everyone in the group can correct the other person. It will be much harder if you don't work in a group. In the group each child feels that he has friends. Working in the group helped me a lot. When I work in a group I get all kinds of ideas and I imagine all kinds of things. It's easier for me in a group to write a story or a poem because I have more imagination, and from other [children's] poems I can write my own rhymes. When some child in the group is not my friend, and when we work together in the group, all of a sudden we get to be friends and we visit each other. Most of the time the hard-working kids in the group help the lazier ones so they should feel they're like everyone else and they can become good students too. When the teacher asks us to write a story, everyone writes a story and reads it to the others, and that helps everyone a lot.

When the statements were analyzed by grades, an interesting developmental trend was found. Younger children (grades 2 and 3) were somewhat distressed by the noise in the classroom and by within-group conflicts. Students in higher grades, however, valued the intellectual stimulation they experienced in the groups.

### 2.2.5. *Prosocial Behavior*

Before the SGT Project began, several first grades in a school implemented small group teaching in their classes. The teachers in those classes reported that as a result of cooperative teaching, they observed a tremendous change in the helping behavior of young children. The teachers reported that naturalistic helping behavior increased significantly in their classes and many conflicts disappeared. Those teachers were indeed the first to bring to our attention the fact that cooperative learning enhances and facilitates prosocial behavior.

A seminaturalistic study was then conducted to document the phenomenon (Hertz-Lazarowitz & Yaakobi, 1975). Each child from both traditional and small group classrooms was asked to complete a given task, and when it was completed he was to hand in his work to the teacher. The teacher then told the child he could choose one of two tasks to work on, one of them an individual task and the other requiring that the child help another child in the class who had not yet completed the first task. In the traditionally taught classroom, 19 out of 21 children decided to pursue the individual task that was offered to them; in the small group classrooms 13 out of the 19 who completed the first task chose to help another child, and 6 preferred to work on the individual task (a highly significant difference statistically). Following this experiment, each child was interviewed to determine the reasons for the choice made, that is, whether the reason was related to a normative or to a motivational dimension. In a preexperiment questionnaire the children responded to five questions about the "need to help," for example, "If a child in your class is sick, would you visit him and buy him a present?" or "If you see a child crying in the street, would you approach him?" The hypothetical normative questions did not differentiate between traditional and small group classes. Most of the children in both classes evidenced a high degree of readiness to help, at least in their responses to the normative questions. In the postexperiment interview each child was asked about his motives in helping a friend instead of choosing to perform an individual task. It could be argued that children from the small group classroom simply did not like the individual task, and thus chose to help another child who had not yet completed his work. However, 11 of the 13 children from the small group classroom stated unequivocally that their motive for helping another child was based on considerations of reciprocity. In the words of one, "Children help me a lot so I wanted to help others." Even at this early age, during the first grade, classroom organization and patterns of peer interaction have their distinct effect on children's helping behavior, particularly on their overt behavior and on their motivation. This influence is less evident on young children's hypothetical prosocial thinking in terms of normative modes of functioning.

In the SGT Project, the researchers and other staff of the project were closely involved in daily life in the schools. Thus it was natural for us to anticipate that students from the cooperative small group classrooms would display a higher level of concern for others, in both their judgment and their interpersonal behavior, than would their peers in traditionally taught classrooms. More to the point, we sought to learn whether students would transfer their prosocial skills from interaction with members of their immediate study groups in the classroom to interaction on nonacademic tasks led by someone other than the teacher and with peers who were not members of their study groups.

After observing that teachers were, in fact, implementing small group learning in the classroom along the lines suggested by the group investigation model, we conducted two experiments with the students, grades 3–7, to study their helping behavior and judgment (Hertz-Lazarowitz, Sharan, & Steinberg, 1980). In the first experiment, subjects were 243 children from nine classrooms in the experimental (cooperative) group and 150 children from parallel grades in a nearby school serving the same population and conducted in the traditional whole-class method of teaching. An experimenter not identified with our project tested children in groups of four to five at a time. These children were called out of their classrooms at random so that they would not be members of groups who studied together during classroom time in the small group classrooms. These children were given an expanded version of Madsen's marbel game (Kagan & Madsen, 1972), in which 14 matrices are printed on a sheet of paper and the child is asked to decide which portion of the matrix he would take for himself and which portion he would distribute to the children in his group. Selection of the particular sections of the matrices was categorized into five types: altruistic, cooperative, competitive, equal, and vengeful. Analysis of variance of the data in a design including two treatments (small group vs. whole-class), five grade levels (3–7), and two levels of religious status (religious children vs. those in secular schools) yielded main effects for treatment on four out of five of these scales. Students from small group classrooms were more altruistic and cooperative and less competitive and vengeful (i.e., would take less for themselves as long as the others also got less) than were students from the whole-class setting. There were no differences on the equality scale, nor were there any effects for religious status or for age except on the vengeance scale, where younger children were more vengeful than older children.

A second experiment was conducted a week later with children from the same 18 classrooms. Fifty-four groups of five children each were selected at random from these classrooms, and an equal number of groups from the experimental and control classrooms ($N = 270$). About 50% of these children had participated in the first experiment. The experimenter asked each group of five children to construct new words from the letters appearing in an epigram. There was a 15-minute time limit. At the start and in the middle of their work the pupils were told to try and work together on the task. Detailed protocols were kept of the children's behavior.

Judges were asked to evaluate these protocols in terms of six indicators of helping behavior (announcing new words to groupmates, having new words accepted by groupmates, consulting with others about new words, requesting help, offering help, accepting help) and five indicators of competition (rejecting new words, comparing the quantity of words created, hiding one's page from others' view, rejecting others' requests for help, rejecting suggestions by others). The total number of words created by each group of five children was also recorded as a measure of group productivity, as was the total amount of time children worked together in pairs, in small groups, or individually. Judges were also asked to evaluate the protocols in terms of their general social climate. They were asked to judge each group of five children on two 6-point scales in terms of the degree of cooperativeness and helpfulness expressed in each group and the extent of tension in the relationships in each group according to the material recorded in the protocols. On all indicators of helping behavior and on indicators of competition, that is, judges' evaluations of helpfulness and of tension in the group, the groups from the small group classroom emerged as significantly more helpful, less competitive, and less tense than did the groups from the traditional classrooms. Furthermore, in three out of five grade levels (4, 6 and 7), groups from the small group classes produced more new words than did their peers from the control classes, indicating that greater helpfulness in the groups led to superior group products.

Finally, we found that children from small group classes spent significantly more time working together in small groups and much less time working as individuals than did their peers from the whole-class schools, but there was no difference between the two groups in the amount of time they spent working together in pairs.

## 3. CONCLUSIONS AND THOUGHTS ABOUT FUTURE RESEARCH

The SGT Project had some unique features. First, it was a relatively long-term project designed and implemented in several elementary schools and exposing teachers and pupils to educational practices markedly different from those to which they were accustomed. These practices involved cognitive learning patterns, social-interactive patterns, and organizational features of the staff and the classroom. Second, teachers and children were trained, through group-centered experiences, to acquire and practice new social skills with prosocial components. Third, the implementation of prosocial behavior on both the teacher and the peer levels was achieved without direct teaching of moral or prosocial principles, but rather through experiential learning and participation involving both social and cognitive elements (Staub, 1981). The restructuring of all dimensions of classroom life, including patterns of peer communication and teacher–student communication, task–goal structure in order to facilitate cooperative study projects, and classroom peer organization created the social environment needed to support, reinforce, and internalize prosocial behavior. Finally, the data collected with a wide range of methods and measures, including teachers' and students' own perceptions of their experiences in the project, support the contention that school experience can enhance prosocial behavior among children in all grades of elementary school as well as among their teachers.

Progressive educators, theoreticians of moral education, and researchers studying small group cooperative learning are all making the same claim, and there is evidence available today to give this position substantial support. Schools can be organized, both on the staff level and on the classroom-instructional level, to support the development of helping behavior among both teachers and students. Students of school organization agree that teachers are generally isolated from each other in most schools and that this isolation has many negative consequences for their personal and professional functioning (Lortie, 1975). Teacher centers have recently sprung up in several countries where teachers can come to help each other in ways related to their work; but what is needed are work norms that promote mutual assistance among teachers who are part of the same institution and who meet daily over long periods. Practitioners of organization development in schools (Schmuck & Schmuck, 1974; Schmuck, Runkel, Arends, & Arends, 1977) have proposed establishment of mutual assistance procedures as an inherent part of school organization.

The various groups of theoreticians also concur that helping behavior can be cultivated among schoolchildren, and that progressive education stemming from the Dewey tradition did in fact create the conditions for promoting prosocial behavior. Recent work with cooperative small group teaching in the classroom highlights the position that helping behavior can be learned by children when it forms an integral part of the learning process itself, not just an appendage to the curriculum. To achieve this goal probably entails a serious investment in in-service teacher training.

Much past research on helping behavior in general and among children in particular focused on chance situations. Personal behavior in institutional settings where people meet under particular, organizational conditions over long periods, sometimes many years, has hardly been studied. The humane design of the settings, particularly schools, where children spend such a large portion of their time and under such unique and influential conditions which regulate their behavior by socially legitimated means, provides a vast potential for enhancing prosocial patterns of thought and action. Schools pose a major challenge to researchers to engage in experimental studies that may make a lasting contribution to society at large.

Future research should address itself to the following questions.

1. Is the teacher the main figure affecting prosocial behavior in the classroom? Our research suggests that peers are significant socialization agents in prosocial development. The role of the teacher and of peers demands rethinking and more research.

2. What are the specific social processes in which peer interaction may facilitate prosocial behavior? Why, how, and when do children behave prosocially in the classroom?

3. What structural and social conditions in the classroom might stimulate prosocial behavior? In a recent observational study, we found,

in all elementary grades, very little naturalistic occurrence of helping behavior among the children (Hertz-Lazarowitz, 1983). This finding contradicts findings of much naturalistic helping behavior in young children (Zahn-Waxler & Radke-Yarrow, 1982). It seems that the existing social structure in many classrooms may adversely affect prosocial behaviors.

By addressing ourselves to these factors, by viewing them as independent variables of experiments to be conducted in schools, we can learn how better to fulfill the potential that schools hold for facilitating prosocial aspects of children's development.

## 4. REFERENCES


Aronson, E., & Goode, E. Training teachers to implement jigsaw learning: A manual for teachers. In S. Sharan, C. Webb, P. Hare, & R. Hertz-Lazarowitz (Eds.), *Cooperation in education*. Provo, Utah: Brigham Young University Press, 1980.

Aronson, E., Bridgeman, D., & Geffner, R. Interdependent interactions and prosocial behavior. *Journal of Research and Development in Education*, 1978, *12*, 16–27.

Bar-Tal, D. Social outcomes of the schooling process and their taxonomy. In D. Bar-Tal & L. Saxe (Eds.), *Social Psychology of education: Theory and research*. New York: Halsted Press, 1978.

Bar-Tal, D., & Geser, D. Observing cooperation in the classroom group. In S. Sharan, C. Webb, P. Hare, & R. Hertz-Lazarowitz (Eds.), *Cooperation in education*. Provo, Utah: Brigham Young University Press, 1980.

Bar-Tal, D., & Raviv, A. A cognitive-learning model of helping behavior development: Possible implications and applications. In N. Eisenberg-Berg (Ed.), *The development of prosocial behavior*. New York: Academic Press, 1982.

Crockenberg, S., & Bryant, B. Socialization: The "implicit curriculum" of learning environments. *Journal of Research and Development in Education*, 1978, *12*, 69–78.

DeCharms, R. *Enhancing motivation: Change in the classroom*. New York: Irvington, 1976.

Dewey, J. *Democracy and education*. New York: Macmillan, 1916.

Dreeban, R. *On what is learned in school*. Reading, Mass.: Addison-Wesley, 1968.

Flanders, N. *Analyzing teacher behavior*. Reading, Mass.: Addison-Wesley, 1970.

Friere, P. *Education for critical consciousness*. New York: Seabury Press, 1974.

Hansell, S., & Slavin, R. E. Cooperative learning and the structure of interracial friendship. *Sociology of Education*, 1981, *54*, 98–106.

Harris, J. D., Eisenberg, N., & Carroll, J. L. Facilitation of prosocial behavior in children. In T. R. Kratochwill (Ed.), *Advances in school psychology*. Hillsdale, N.J.: Lawrence Erlbaum, 1982.

Hartup, W. W. The social worlds of childhood. *American Psychologist*, 1979, *34*, 994–950.

Henry, J. *On education*. New York: Vintage Books, 1972.

Hertz-Lazarowitz, R. Prosocial behavior in the classroom. *Academic Psychology Bulletin*, 1983, *5*, 319–338.

Hertz-Lazarowitz, R., & Sharan, S. Self-esteem, locus of control and perception of classroom social climate: A developmental perspective. *Contemporary Educational Psychology*, 1979, *4*, 154–161.

Hertz-Lazarowitz, R., & Yaakobi, S. [*Helping behavior of first-grade children in small-group and traditional classrooms.*] Unpublished manuscript, School of Education, Haifa University, 1975.

Hertz-Lazarowitz, R., Sharan, S., & Steinberg, R. Classroom learning style and cooperative behavior of elementary school children. *Journal of Educational Psychology*, 1980, *72*, 99–106.

Hertz-Lazarowitz, R., Sharan, S., & Shachar, H. What children think about small-group teaching. In S. Sharan & R. Hertz-Lazarowitz (Eds.), [*Changing schools: The small-group teaching (SGT) project in Israel.*] Tel Aviv: Ramot Educational System Ltd., Tel Aviv University, 1981.

Hertz-Lazarowitz, R., Sharan, S., & Sapir, C. *The effects of two methods of small-group learning on academic achievement and ethnic relations in Israeli junior high school students.* Paper presented at the meeting of the American Educational Research Association conference, New York, April 1982.

Hunter, E. *Encounter in the classroom: New ways of teaching.* New York: Holt, Rinehart & Winston, 1972.

Jackson, P. *Life in classrooms.* New York: Holt, Rinehart & Winston, 1968.

Johnson, D. W. Student–student interaction: The neglected variable in education. *Educational Researcher*, 1981, *10*(1), 5–10.

Johnson, D. W., & Johnson, R. Instructional goal structure: Cooperative, competitive and individualistic. *Review of Educational Research*, 1974, *44*, 213–240.

Johnson, D. W., & Johnson, R. Cooperative, competitive and individualistic learning. *Journal of Research and Development in Education*, 1978, *12*, 3–15.

Johnson, D. W., Johnson, R., & Bryant, D. Cooperation and competition in the classroom. *Elementary School Journal*, 1973, *74*, 172–181.

Johnson, D. W., Maruyama, G., Johnson, R., Nelson, D., & Skon, L. The effects of cooperative, competitive and individualistic goal structures on achievement: A meta analysis. *Psychological Bulletin*, 1981, *89*, 47–62.

Kagan, S., & Madsen, M. Experimental analyses of cooperation and competition of Anglo-American and Mexican children. *Developmental Psychology*, 1972, *6*, 49–59.

Lortie, D. *Schoolteacher.* Chicago: University of Chicago Press, 1975.

Minuchin, P., Biber, E., Shapiro, E., & Zimiles, H. *The psychological impact of school experience.* New York: Basic Books, 1969.

Schmuck, R., & Schmuck, P. *A humanistic psychology of education.* Palo Alto, Calif.: National Press Books, 1974.

Schmuck, R., & Schmuck, P. *Group processes in the classroom* (3rd ed.). Dubuque, Ia.: Brown, 1979.

Schmuck, R., Runkel, P., Arends, J., & Arends, R. *The second handbook of organization development in schools.* Palo Alto, Calif.: Mayfield, 1977.

Sharan, S. Cooperative learning in small groups: Recent methods and effects on achievement, attitudes and ethnic relations. *Review of Educational Research*, 1980, *50*, 241–271.

Sharan, S., & Hertz-Lazarowitz, R. [*Cooperation and communication in schools.*] Tel Aviv: Schocken, 1978.

Sharan, S., & Hertz-Lazarowitz, R. A group-investigation method of cooperative learning in the classroom. In S. Sharan, P. Hare, C. Webb, & R. Hertz-Lazarowitz (Eds.), *Cooperation in education.* Provo, Utah: Brigham Young University Press, 1980.

Sharan, S., & Hertz-Lazarowitz, R. [*Changing schools: The small-group teaching (SGT) project in Israel.*] Tel Aviv: Ramot Educational System Ltd., Tel Aviv University, 1981.

Sharan, S., & Hertz-Lazarowitz, R. Effects of an instructional change program on teachers' behavior, attitudes and perceptions. *Journal of Applied Behavioral Science*, 1982, *18*(2), 185–201.

Sharan, S., & Sharan, Y. *Small-group teaching.* Englewood Cliffs, N.J.: Educational Technology Publications, 1976.

Sharan, S., Hertz-Lazarowitz, R., & Reiner, T. Television for changing teacher behavior. *Journal of Educational Technology Systems*, 1978, *7*, 119–131.

Sharan, S., Darom, E., & Hertz-Lazarowitz, R. What teachers think about small group teaching. *British Journal of Teacher Education,* 1979, *5,* 49–62.

Sharan, S., Ackerman, Z., & Hertz-Lazarowitz, R. Academic achievement of elementary school children in small-group versus whole-class instruction. *Journal of Experimental Education,* 1979–1980, *40,* 2, 125–129.

Sharan, S., Webb, C., Hare, P., & Hertz-Lazarowitz, R. (Eds.). *Cooperation in education.* Provo, Utah: Brigham Young University Press, 1980.

Sharan, S., Hertz-Lazarowitz, R., & Lichtenson, Y. Teachers in the process of change. In S. Sharan & R. Hertz-Lazarowitz, [*Changing schools: The small-group teaching (SGT) project in Israel.*] Tel Aviv: Ramot Educational System Ltd., Tel Aviv University, 1981.

Slavin, R. E. Cooperative learning. *Review of Education Research,* 1980, *50,* 315–342. (a)

Slavin, R. E. Student team learning: A manual for teachers. In S. Sharan, C. Webb, P. Hare, & R. Hertz-Lazarowitz (Eds.), *Cooperation in education.* Provo, Utah: Brigham Young University Press, 198O. (b)

Slavin, R. E. *Cooperative learning.* United Kingdom: Longman, 1983.

Slommer, R. Classroom ecology. *Journal of Applied Behavioral Science,* 1967, *3,* 489–503.

Staub, E. *Positive social behavior and morality.* Vol. 1. *Personal and social influences.* New York: Academic Press, 1978.

Staub, E. *Positive social behavior and morality.* Vol. 2. *Socialization and development.* New York: Academic Press, 1979.

Staub, E. Promoting positive behavior in schools, in other educational settings, and in the home. In J. P. Rushton & R. M. Sorrentino (Eds.), *Altruism and helping behavior.* Hillsdale, N.J.: Lawrence Erlbaum, 1981.

Thelen, H. *Dynamics of groups at work.* Chicago: University of Chicago Press, 1954.

Thelen, H. *Education and the human quest.* New York: Harper & Row, 1960.

Walberg, H., & Anderson, G. Classroom climate and individual learning. *Journal of Educational Psychology,* 1968, *59,* 414–419.

Weick, K. *The social psychology of organizing.* Reading, Mass.: Addison-Wesley, 1969.

Willower, D., Eidell, T., & Hoy, W. *The school and pupil control ideology.* University Park: Pennsylvania State University Press, 1973.

Zahn-Waxler, C., & Radke-Yarrow, M. The development of altruism: Alternative research strategies. In N. Eisenberg-Berg (Ed.), *The development of prosocial behavior.* New York: Academic Press, 1982.

# 22

# Community as Target

## A New Perspective to Research on Prosocial Behavior

Durganand Sinha

## 1. WESTERN PERSPECTIVE

Helping others and doing service for the good of mankind are regarded as cardinal virtues almost all over the world. As the anthropologist Bohannan (1963) has pointed out, the most basic tenet of all major religions is that "unselfishness is the primary virtue and that selfishness lies at the root of the world's ills." Although this unselfishness is regarded as a virtue in different degrees in almost all cultures, psychological study of factors associated with helping behavior and altruism has long remained neglected. It is only in the last two decades that there has been a shift in research emphasis from more negative to more positive or prosocial forms of social behavior.

As generally studied, altruism or prosocial behavior has usually been conceived in terms of person-to-person relations in which a benefactor helps or does a positive act toward a recipient. It is generally defined as a voluntary behavior carried out to benefit others without any anticipation of external rewards and performed as an end in itself or as an act of restitution (Bar-Tal, 1976, p. 4). Four sets of associated variables have been analyzed, namely, (1) situational or state variables, that is, characteristics of the benefactor and the recipient, (2) trait variables, (3) social roles and demographic variables, and (4) social norms (Krebs,

DURGANAND SINHA • A.N.S. Institute of Social Studies, Patna, India.

1970). These studies have largely been individual centered and microcosmic. The main focus has been on the psychological and demographic characteristics of the individual giver or the individual recipient; the sociocultural and historical matrix that operates on the individual benefactors and recipients has been investigated only in a casual way. There are, of course, the normative and cultural approaches to the phenomenon of prosocial behaviour. I contend, however, that in these studies there is no adequate cognizance of sociocultural factors.

Campbell (1965) has suggested a kind of survival theory of altruism in which ingroup sacrifice and solidarity to combat outgroup threat gives a functional significance to prosocial behavior in sociocultural evolution. It is also suggested that altruism is likely to have genetic determinants because of the survival value of ingroup identification and outgroup hostility. Disposition for ethnocentric and altruistic behavior became inborn as a result of biological and sociocultural evolution. Later on Campbell (1972) modifies his theory, regarding self-sacrificial disposition as a product of social indoctrination rather than of genetic endowment. Altruism, in other words, helps in the survival of the group. Condition of external threat increases ingroup cooperation, loyalty, and helping others in one's group because these are necessary for the survival of the group. In still another formulation, Campbell (1975) contends that genetic competition among the cooperators places great limitations on the socially useful, individual self-sacrificial altruism that biological evolution can produce. Urban humanity, for which altruism is an essential element, is a product of both biological and social evolution. In a similar vein, Cohen (1972) has also theorized that though man is hedonistic and reward oriented as an organism, it is the culture that fosters the evolution of altruistic values as a survival mechanism.

These theories have many weaknesses and have been strongly criticized. Even without subscribing to them, one may go along with Campbell (1965) to the extent that "altruism is developed only in certain sociocultural realities in which individuals find themselves." In other words, to understand the factors that reward and sustain empathy, self-sacrifice, helping others, and other forms of prosocial behavior, it is essential to take due cognizance of the sociocultural setting in which the individual operates.

Among studies that recognize the importance of social factors, the normative approach stresses the importance of societal norms in prosocial behavior and in a way is complementary to the theories such as Campbell's and Cohen's which connect it with survival mechanism. Norms constitute a set of expectations that members of a group hold concerning how one ought to behave (Homans, 1961) and are passed from generation to generation as a part of one's cultural heritage. Conceived in this way, there is a norm of giving and thus prosocial behavior receives general approval, whereas deviation elicits disapproval. In other words, one should give not because of any anticipated returns but for its own value (Leeds, 1963). Individuals who follow the norm are socially rewarded. This formulation does not go against the definition of prosocial behavior because the norm of giving is followed not necessarily under external pressure, and the individual has the choice not to give. Furthermore, he gives and helps others not because of any anticipated gain but because giving is an end in itself. Such a norm becomes a part of one's ego-system in the course of socialization; it is internalized. Once that happens, norms are followed without external pressure.

A related concept suggested by Berkowitz and his associates (Berkowitz & Connor, 1966; Berkowitz & Daniels, 1963; Berkowitz & Friedman, 1967) is that of the social responsibility norm, that is, acting on behalf of others, not for material gain or social approval, but for one's own self-approval, for the self-administered rewards arising from doing what is right (Goranson & Berkowitz, 1966). Thus, as Bar-Tal (1976) has put it, an individual who learns that somebody is dependent on his help feels an obligation to aid that person, even though he can anticipate no direct return benefits. Related to this is the reciprocity norm (Gouldner, 1960), which is often regarded as a moral principle. A person who obtains benefit from his associates is obliged to repay them in some way. The strength of the obligation and the form in which it is manifested are likely to be affected by the norms prevailing in a given society.

In a comparative analysis of helpful, cooperative, and civil behavior toward strangers in urban and nonurban locales, Korte and Kern (1975) observed that the likelihood of help was much greater in the latter than in the former settings. The authors emphasize certain characteristics of the urban social environment as determining the development of uncivility in urban residents.

Sociocultural factors play an important role in prosocial behavior. A number of cross-cultural studies have tried to analyze a few of these factors. Feldman (1968) examined the differential treatment of foreign and compatriot strangers by Parisians, Athenians, and Bostonians in different social contexts. Although certain interesting differences among these three cultural groups were observed, firm conclusions about the effect of underlying cultural factors on these differences were not possible. Berkowitz (1966) compared altruistic behavior among American and British undergraduates. The results show similarity in helping behavior, bureaucratic middle-class boys being more helpful in both groups irrespective of the level of help received earlier. The American boys from the entrepreneurial middle class and British boys from the working class were helpful only to boys from whom they had previously received help. A comparison of altruistic behavior among Indian and American subjects revealed the latter to be more altruistic (L'Armand & Pepitone, 1975). However, their altruism was limited to situations in which no cost was involved in being helpful. Varying obligation attached to the aid along with subjects' perceptions of donors' resources, Gergen, Ellsworth, Maslach, and Seipel (1975) observed that in samples drawn from three different cultural groups of Americans, Swedish, and Japanese, subjects' attraction for donors, desire for coalition, and repayment were similar. In all three groups subjects were more attracted to a donor who obliged them to return the resources than to one who asked nothing in return. Greater attraction was also expressed for a poor as opposed to a wealthy donor. Desires for coalition were unrelated to attraction for the donor. By and large, although the wealthy rather than the poor donors were preferred for coalition, more resources were returned to the poor than to the wealthy donors. The findings indicate behavioral similarity across cultures. That all three groups were similar in having shared in material prosperity is likely to have colored their reactions to economic aid, and it is not possible to conclude that similar patterns of behavior would be found in poor and less technologically advanced cultures.

These studies point to the importance of the sociocultural matrix of helping behavior. Yet, in the fast accumulating literature in the area, due cognizance has still not been given to sociocultural variables, or at least they have not been carefully analyzed as determinants of prosocial behavior. As Krebs (1970) rightly observes, little psychological research has examined the norm of giving, even though it may have been antecedent to many altruistic situations. An individual resorts to giving and helping others because it is pious, virtuous, and the culture in which he lives enjoins him to do so. As Staub (1978) observes, certain cultures may have strong prescriptive norms of positive conduct or may foster empathy or a positive orientation toward others in the culture. One would thus expect greater uniformity in the behavior of people in such cultures—indicating a need for cross-cultural comparisons of helping behavior. But in most cross-cultural studies on prosocial behavior, the cultural, philosophical, and historical matrix in which the individual benefactor or recipient operates has been only generally taken into account. When different cultural groups have been compared with regard to different aspects of helping behavior, cultural factors have been considered more or less in a blanket fashion without analysis of discrete aspects of a given culture that are directly related to altruistic behavior. In comparisons of different samples drawn from diverse cultures, only certain similarities and differences have been highlighted with very little effort to interrelate them with the cultural, philosophical, and religious traditions of these societies. Observed similarities and differences in altruistic behavior in different cultural groups should be related to their specific sociocultural characteristics. Real insight into the dynamics of altruistic behavior cannot be gained without analyzing cross-culturally the socialization processes underlying it, the value attached to the giving and sharing of resources in different societies. These are important antecedents of prosocial behavior and their analysis is integral to our understanding of why one helps others, who constitutes the target of helping, and the manner in which altruism manifests itself in our activities.

A good strategy of study would be to analyze a particular culture in terms of prescribed norms, values, and socialization processes and then draw out specific hypotheses regarding prosocial behavior in that culture as against other cultures with different norms and practices. As anthropological studies have indicated, cultures vary with regard to the emphasis put on cooperation and competition (Mead, 1939), and any understanding of behavior reflecting one or the other requires knowledge of how the children have been socialized with regard to these activities and the value attached to them in the particular culture. Similarly, it would be advisable to analyze cultures with regard to the relative emphasis placed on aiding, helping, and sacrificing one's own good for the sake of others or of the community, and then identify the pattern of prosocial behavior in that culture and compare it with patterns from cultures with different or somewhat contrasting norms. Since cultures may vary in the extent to which they emphasize interrelatedness and mutuality among human beings and thereby foster concern and obligation toward others, it is essential to ascertain that factor in designing one's studies. As Staub (1978) suggests, classification of cultures in terms of dimensions that identify dominant characteristics relevant to positive behavior would be useful in understanding the development of prosocial behavior in specific cultures and the influences operating upon the individual in the socialization process.

All people may have certain commonalities, but differences in cultural emphasis bring about differences in development of particular behavior in the sociocultural and historical contexts. Culture creates the environment and the context in which behavior takes place. Personality characteristics and traits, the sociodemographic factors and situational variables of the benefactor and the recipient interact in the general setting provided by the cultural context, and all these influences interacting together produce the specific kind of prosocial behavior. Thus some of the specific factors in a culture that require careful analysis and on which cross-cultural comparisons are needed are the pattern of socialization of altruistic behavior, the specific norms regulating sharing of resources, and the form in which helping behavior manifests itself. Analyzing a culture in terms of religious-philosophical traditions bearing on altruism, reinforcements provided for it, and the norms regulating it would enable the formulation of specific hypotheses concerning prosocial activities of the individual that can be tested both in field and laboratory settings. A study of samples drawn from contrasting cultures would help to reveal the amount of influence these factors exercise on the behavior of the individual donor and recipient on different aspects of altruistic activities.

## 2. INDIAN PERSPECTIVE

Indian culture differs significantly from Western societies concerning attitudes toward prosocial behavior. According to the traditional Indian approach, the existence of the individual cannot be conceived as separate from the society. The model of man that is suggested is not of "man *in* society" or "man *and* society" but of "man–society"; that is, the two are in a symbiotic state of inseparable relationship (D. Sinha, 1980). In terms of individual action, concern for the good of others and the welfare of the community is regarded as a cardinal virtue. In one adage, the entire universe is to be regarded as one's kin. This attitude is deeply rooted in Indian culture. Almost all Indian philosophical and religious texts emphasize dedication to the service of others (*sarvabhuta hite rata*) for achieving the ultimate good. The interrelatedness of the whole of humanity is stressed not only when one is enjoined to do good to others and regard the universe as one's relation (*basudhaib kutumbkam*), but in the Upanisadic doctrine of ever expanding ego or self, where one begins with concern for one's self and gradually expands one's ego to encompass one's community and ultimately even the entire world. Similarly, one of the verses of the ancient epic *Mahabharat* states that for the sake of the clan one gives up the individual (person), for the sake of the village one gives up the clan, for the sake of the country (*janpada*) one gives up the village, and for the highest good one even gives up the earth. In these sources, concern for others has been given the highest place and the target is a larger group.

The famous story of Raja Harishchandra is known to children and adults all over India. It is a story of supreme sacrifice for the sake of others in which a king gives up all his material possessions including his son and wife. Through such a sacrifice he is blessed by God and ultimately everything is returned to him; and he becomes great, all-powerful, and attains the supreme reality. Not only mythology but history also records many cases of altruism where the target is the entire community. It is said that in Prayag (now called Allahabad) the great king of ancient India, Harshvardhan, used to organize a festival every 5 years in which he gave up his entire national possession for the welfare of the community and retained only his loincloth. Roland (1980), in his psychoanalytic treatment of the Indian sociocultural context, points to "affective reciprocity" as characteristic of the Indian social system. The ego boundaries are much more open to others and there is little psychological space around the self. As a result, the Hindu experienced self is more structured around "we," "our," and "us" than around "I," "mine," or "me." There is an impulse to belong to a collectivity and to undermine autonomy, initiative, and individualism. This collective belongingness is probably a social transformation of the idea of the individual striving to merge with the ultimate reality which is all-pervasive, and which is considered the ultimate goal of each individual.

Again, succorance of those who need help, security, and shelter is regarded as a fundamental developmental goal in Indian culture. Analyzing the *guru–chela* (preceptor–student) relationship, which according to Neki (1976) epitomizes the typical pattern of interpersonal transaction between the teacher and the taught, father and son, superior and subordinate, and so on, Neki analyzes the developmental sequence of dependence that characterizes these relationships. From initial dependence on teachers and parents, the individual is expected to forgo some of his dependence and develop a more mature and culturally approved pattern of transaction which is one of interdependence or even, as it has been termed, "dependability." The latter has been defined as

> altruistic purposiveness which manifests itself as a praiseworthy intention to provide support, reliance and refuge to the helpless who, by virtue of their natural or socially determined state of dependence, crave for shelter, security, affection or communication. (Neki, 1976)

In all the *pauranic* literature, two adages of the saint Vyasa are important: that doing good to others is a virtue (*paropkarah punyaya*), and that giving pain to others is a sin (*papaya parapiritam*). In the ethical and philosophical texts of India, besides truth and nonviolence, doing good or service to others is regarded as the highest virtue.

These religious-philosophical bases of prosocial behavior have been stressed because they suggest the strong social or community orientation of Indian culture, which any inquiry into the phenomenon of prosocial behavior in the Indian context can ill afford to ignore. The studies on prosocial behavior so far conducted in the West, however, have been too individualistic in their approach and have not taken this sociocultural aspect adequately into account. Seen from a collective orientation, these studies ignore a vital element of altruism and are thus somewhat unconvincing. A conceptualization of prosocial behavior has to take into account the basic concern of the individual for the good of the community which is enjoined in the culture and which is passed on from generation to generation through the process of socialization.

Finally, in most of the studies on prosocial behavior conducted so far, the benefactor and the recipient are the actors. They have been conceived in terms of person-to-person interaction with an individual as the benefactor and also as the target. Yet prosocial behavior must also be conceived in terms of the entire community or society as the referent. In certain conceptualizations of helping behavior in the Indian tradition, it is not any particular individual but the entire village or community—the group—that is the target of the benefactor. Under certain circumstances, it is enjoined that help be given in the form of alms to a particular community. In recent years we have witnessed a unique phenomenon in which people have donated an entire village for the good of the community. Various manifestations of the *Bhoodan* (land-donation) movement are well known. Similarly, some individuals have displayed altruism in the form of adopting an entire village to bring about the welfare of the people and successful development. It is also well known that in some cases not only one individual but an entire community behaves altruistically. Such instances indicate that the conceptualization of prosocial behavior in terms of individual recipients and benefactors needs to be widened and conceived in more macrocosmic terms to comprise larger social entities.

Prosocial behavior with the community or society as the referent is important because there is some evidence, though somewhat indirect, that persons showing higher levels of concern for such larger social entities as the village, community, or nation belong to groups that have achieved greater socioeconomic development. My own studies (D. Sinha, 1969a,b), conducted in villages matched for certain geographical and demographic features but differing sharply in terms of the extent of agroeconomic development, have indicated that farmers from villages which in recent years had responded well to intensive development programs were characterized by a stronger sense of concern for village, community, and country compared to those who were from poorly developed areas. Farmers from undeveloped villages were comparatively more individualistic and egocentric in their orientation, whereas those from developed villages displayed stronger orientation toward the community. In fact, it is interesting to observe that farmers from undeveloped villages were unable even to conceptualize properly the needs of the community or nation except, if at all, in egoistic terms. When conceptualizing the needs of such larger entities as village or country, they tended to project their own personal needs and seldom could conceive of the general needs of the community or country as such. On the other hand, farmers from highly developed villages could project themselves to the level of the community and the nation and were able to enumerate a few of the general needs of these collectivities.

Thus the community orientation of farmers from villages with very low agroeconomic growth was found to be weaker in comparison to those from well-developed areas. One wonders whether such a difference in orientation would also be reflected in the frequency and forms of prosocial behavior.

Of related interest are a few recent formulations about altruistic orientation as related to socioeconomic development. J. B. P. Sinha (1968) and J. B. P. Sinha and Pandey (1970), in their experiments on *nAch* (McClelland's "need for achievement") have pointed out the importance of altruistic orientation in the context of development. They found that under the condition of limited resources, individuals high on need for achievement resorted to cutthroat competition and hoarding if they had egoistic orientation. When resources were unlimited, *nAch* was found to yield maximum output. But with limited resources, not only the total output suffered but there was a marked deterioration in interpersonal and group liking as well as self-perception. However, it is significant that under altruistic orientation such ill effects were not observed. Although it is somewhat risky to transfer these results to the global problem of socioeconomic development in countries with very limited resources, the implications are revealing with respect to altruistic orientation and development. In fact, Pareek (1968) has considered altruistic orientation as an integral part of the motivational component of development. In his paradigm of development, apart from need for achievement, he has emphasized the need for *extension*—a need to extend the self or ego and relate to a larger group and its goals. As he puts it, "increasing achievement motivation (concern for excellence) and extension motivation (concern for others) are important for general socioeconomic development." These studies of the motivational variables underlying socioeconomic development indicate strongly the close association of concern for others and community orientation with the extent of development.

These studies point to a connection between prosocial orientation and socioeconomic development and to the importance of community as the target of altruistic behavior. Most studies conducted so far have ignored these aspects. In fact, the studies have been largely experimental and have generally been carried out in the laboratory. Extending the research to real-life situations by taking due regard of sociocultural variables and connecting them to such vital problems as national development would not only provide a new perspective but would have important social implications. Achieving that may require methodological "extension" including content analysis, real-life observation, and field studies. Such a perspective would not only be useful in itself but would generate many hypotheses for designing further experimental studies.

## 3. REFERENCES

Bar-Tal, D. *Prosocial behavior: Theory and research.* New York: Wiley, 1976.

Berkowitz, L. A laboratory investigation of social class and national differences in helping behaviour. *International Journal of Psychology,* 1966, *1,* 231–242.

Berkowitz, L., & Connor, W. H. Success, failure and social responsibility. *Journal of Personality and Social Psychology,* 1966, *4,* 664–669.

Berkowitz, L., & Daniels, L. Responsibility and dependency. *Journal of Abnormal and Social Psychology,* 1963, *66,* 429–436.

Berkowitz, L., & Friedman, P. Some social class differences in helping behavior. *Journal of Personality and Social Psychology,* 1967, *5,* 217–225.

Bohannan, P. *Social anthropology.* New York: Holt, Rinehart & Winston, 1963.

Campbell, D. T. Ethnocentric and other altruistic motives. In D. Levine (Ed.), *Nebraska Symposium on Motivation* (Vol. 13). Lincoln: University of Nebraska Press, 1965.

Campbell, D. T. On the genetics of altruism and the counter-hedonic components of human culture. *Journal of Social Issues,* 1972, *28,* 21–37.

Campbell, D. T. On the conflicts between biological and social evolution and between psychology and moral tradition. *American Psychologist,* 1975, *30,* 1103–1126.

Cohen, R. Altruism: Human, cultural, or what? *Journal of Social Issues,* 1972, *28,* 39–57.

Feldman, R. E. Response to compatriot and foreigner who seek assistance. *Journal of Personality and Social Psychology,* 1968, *10,* 202–214.

Gergen, K. J., Ellsworth, P., Maslach, C., & Seipel, M. Obligation, donor resources, and reactions to aid in three cultures. *Journal of Personality and Social Psychology,* 1975, *31,* 390–400.

Goranson, R. E., & Berkowitz, L. Reciprocity and responsibility reactions to prior help. *Journal of Personality and Social Psychology,* 1966, *3,* 227–232.

Gouldner, A. A norm of reciprocity: A preliminary statement. *American Sociological Review,* 1960, *25,* 161–178.

Homans, G. C. *Social behavior: Its elementary forms.* New York: Harcourt, Brace & World, 1961.

Korte, C., & Kern, N. Response to altruistic opportunities in urban and non-urban settings. *Journal of Social Psychology,* 1975, *95,* 183–184.

Krebs, D. Altruism: An examination of the concept and a review of the literature. *Psychological Bulletin,* 1970, *73,* 258–302.

L'Armand, K., & Pepitone, A. Helping to reward another person: A cross-cultural analysis. *Journal of Personality and Social Psychology,* 1975, *31,* 189–198.

Leeds, R. Altruism and the norm of giving. *Merrill-Palmer Quarterly,* 1963, *9,* 229–240.

Mead, M. *Cooperation and competition among primitive people.* New York: McGraw-Hill, 1939.

Neki, J. S. An examination of the cultural relativism of dependence as a dynamic of social and therapeutic relationships. *British Journal of Medical Psychology,* 1976, *49,* 1–10.

Pareek, U. A motivational paradigm of development. *Journal of Social Issues,* 1968, *24,* 115–122.

Roland, A. *The self in India and America: Towards a psychoanalysis of socio-cultural contexts.* Paper presented at the meeting of the Center for Psychosocial Research, Chicago, March 1980.

Sinha, D. *Indian villages in transition: A motivational analysis.* New Delhi: Associated Publishers, 1969. (a)

Sinha, D. Study of motivation in a developing country: Concept of happy-life among Indian farmers. *Journal of Social Psychology,* 1969, *79,* 89–97. (b)

Sinha, D. Social psychology in India: A historical perspective. *Psychological Studies,* 1980, *25,* 157–163.

Sinha, J. B. P. The nAch/nCooperation under limited/unlimited resource conditions. *Journal of Experimental Social Psychology,* 1968, *4,* 233–246.

Sinha, J. B. P., & Pandey, J. Strategies of high nAch persons. *Psychologia,* 1970, *13,* 210–216.

Staub, E. *Positive social behavior and morality.* Vol. 1. *Personal and social influences.* New York: Academic Press, 1978.

# 23

# Bystander Intervention in Crimes

## Research and Application

Leonard Bickman

## 1. INTRODUCTION

On his way home from work, a man sees an unfamiliar car cruising his block. Before entering his house, he notices that the driver is sitting parked in front of a neighbor's house. He thinks it is strange behavior, but does not think the police would want to be bothered with it. The next day, he learns that his neighbor's house was burglarized.

A radio-dispatched taxi driver working the midnight shift drops off a customer in a desolate, poorly lighted section of town. As he drives away, he notices a woman struggling with a man on the sidewalk. The driver slows down, and it becomes obvious from the woman's screams that the man is overpowering her. He calls over his radio to his dispatcher: "Woman in trouble. Corner of Maple and Hudson. Call the police." "Are you involved?" the dispatcher asks. "No." "Sorry, can't help you out," replies the dispatcher.

A housewife finds out, by accident, that a specific person is selling drugs to adolescents in her neighborhood. Infuriated, she considers calling the police but thinks, "They probably won't do anything about it unless I give them my name. What if the pusher found out who I was?" Instead of calling, she does nothing.

Although these situations are not as dramatic as the Kitty Genovese

LEONARD BICKMAN • Department of Psychology and Human Development, Peabody College of Vanderbilt University, Nashville, Tennessee 37203.

incident over a decade ago, in which 38 citizens witnessed the brutal murder of a young woman but did not call the police, they represent typical situations in which a citizen could have helped the victim. If the citizen-witnesses in these instances had notified the police, these crimes may have been prevented or halted in progress. The offenders may even have been apprehended.

Most criminal justice efforts, from reporting of the crime to the prosecution of the offender, depend on citizens. The initiation of almost all activity in this complex and massive system is a report to the police that a crime has been committed. Crimes are usually reported either by bystanders who witness or have indirect knowledge of the crime or by those who have been victimized. The police directly encounter only a small proportion of criminal incidents and must rely heavily upon the reports of witnesses and/or victims for their information. If taken to court, witness reporting and testimony are often critical elements of the case before trial. However, as indicated from surveys of victims, many crimes are not reported. Not only does this preclude official action toward apprehension, it also weakens the effectiveness of crime control strategies.

The last decade has seen the emergence of projects directed toward improved witness reporting of suspicious/criminal activity to law enforcement agencies in the United States. Often sponsored by police and civic community groups, these Citizen Crime Reporting Projects (CCRPs) have been studied nationally (Bickman, Lavrakas, Green, North-Walker, Edwards, Borkowski, Shane-DuBow, & Wuerth, 1976). This chapter presents a review of these programs as well as applications relevant to the problems of witness reporting.

The social scientific research on crime-reporting behavior is relatively recent and few studies are available. However, directly related are those that deal with helping behavior, describing conditions in which one individual comes to the aid of others. The assistance typically requires direct bystander involvement with a victim. Thus, although major differences between helping situations and criminal incidents (e.g., the presence of the criminal) are acknowledged, the bases for involvement are similar and the studies of witnesses to noncriminal events may be tentatively considered generalizable to the crime situation.

Cross-disciplinary examination of the research reveals three emergent strategies used to explore why people report or do not report crime.

### 1.1. Victimization Surveys

Studies of victims employ comparatively large samples of respondents representative of various population subgroups, for example, by race, sex, age (Ennis, 1967; Skogan, 1981). Basically, three types of information are acquired: (1) self-reports of criminal victimization; (2) self-reports on the absence or occurrence of incidents reported to the police; and (3) demographic and attitudinal data. Several possible sources of error have been noted in research of this type: For example, persons may forget the incident or the reasons for their reporting behavior; an event may have been misinterpreted; they may not be aware of the actual reasons behind their reporting behavior; or they may respond/rationalize their actions in a socially acceptable or otherwise satisfying manner to the interviewer.

### 1.2. Experimentation

Some knowledge of why witnesses directly intervene or report suspicious events to authorities (Bickman, 1975; Bickman & Helwig, 1979; Bickman & Rosenbaum, 1977; Huston & Korte, 1975; Latané & Darley, 1970) has emerged from social-psychological field and laboratory experimentation, whereby individuals are exposed to contrived crime. Such "witnesses" are relatively few in number and not necessarily representative of the general population. Furthermore, it is not known whether the situations studied and the variables manipulated are representative of real events. However, these situations allow the observation of actual behavior in response to various experimental conditions so that the experimenter can infer causal relationships between variables.

### 1.3. Hypothetical Events

The third methodology involves presenting a hypothetical event to various individuals and asking how they and/or others would respond in the situation. Such role playing may provide insight into some of the reasons for reporting suspicious events. However, "intentions" are weak predictors of reality (Deutscher, 1973; Liska, 1975) and the responses have been shown to be affected by slight variations in the situational descriptions.

The research literature on bystander intervention is substantial (Bar-Tal, 1976; Bryan & London, 1970; Krebs, 1970; Latané & Darley, 1970; Macaulay & Berkowitz, 1970; Midlarsky, 1968; Staub, 1974; Wispé, 1972). Almost all researchers agree that nonresponsive bystanders are not uncaring or apathetic but rather are unable to act for a variety of reasons. These findings are summarized elsewhere in this book. The focus of research in this area is on the causal explanations for intervention and nonintervention rather than on descriptive or normative data collection. As will be shown later, the findings from this body of research can be utilized to understand the bases of CCRPs.

The next part of the chapter provides a review of relevant programs developed to deal with the citizen nonreporting problem. This review is based upon a national study I conducted for the United States National Institute of Law Enforcement and Criminal Justice. The project involved a national survey of police departments and citizen groups to determine what types of activities they were conducting in this field.

The last section of this chapter will attempt to integrate the research with the programs actually operating in the field. This review will compare research results with operating programs to determine the degree of conceptual support for the programs. Moreover, suggestions will be made concerning new directions that research should take if research on bystander intervention is to be practically applied.

## 2. CITIZEN CRIME REPORTING PROJECTS (CCRPs)

This study of CCRPs was sponsored by the United States National Institute of Law Enforcement and Criminal Justice (NILECJ) as part of its National Evaluation Program (NEP). The NEP consists of a series of evaluation studies of current approaches to solving crime and criminal justice problems. The objectives of NEP research were: (1) to assess the type, quantity, and quality of information available about CCRPs; (2) to devise a descriptive classification system for CCRP projects; and (3) to assess the effectiveness of the CCRPs if possible. In the case of this last objective, substantial evidence is not available on which to form a strong conclusion about the effectiveness of CCRPs. Thus most of the research findings are descriptive in nature. No new evaluations are conducted as part of the NEP program.

### 2.1. Research Methodology

A variety of sources were explored to locate projects nationwide that were potentially relevant to this study. Previously compiled files on crime-reporting projects in cities with populations larger than 50,000 were a major source. A second source was telephone interviews with criminal justice state planning agency personnel in all 50 states and with members in Law Enforcement Assistance Administration regional offices. These telephone interviews attempted to identify potentially relevant CCRPs being funded through block and discretionary grants.

In this search, a total of 318 projects were identified as potentail CCRPs and reviewed. On the basis of this review, it was determined that 108 projects did not meet our definitional criteria for inclusion. These criteria were: (1) Projects had to be in existence at least 1 year, (2) the project must have a distinct public name, and (3) the project must have focused on improving witness reporting of crimes. The remaining 210 projects were telephoned to gather more descriptive information. On the basis of these telephone interviews, 80 additional projects were judged not to meet our definitional criteria. This left 130 projects that qualified for the project survey. Of these 130 CCRPs, 100 project sites were selected to receive the CCRP project questionnaire.

The 23-page questionnaire, consisting of 62 multistage questions, was the primary data collection instrument for this project. Information was collected about projects in the following nine questionnaire categories: organization, budget and background, staff efforts, assistance, program goals, detailed program activities, crime statistics, citizen and community information, and evaluation. Of the 100 project sites, 78 returned the questionnaire.

From the data collected from questionnaires and site visits, a classification system of six CCRP project types was constructed. The types of projects included in this study can be classified into two major categories, each having three project types. The first category consists of projects that facilitate the means of reporting suspicious/criminal activity. The second category consists of projects that use an educational approach to encourage witness reporting of suspicious/criminal activity.

### 2.1.1. *Category 1: Projects That Facilitate Reporting*

*2.1.1a. WhistleStop Projects.* WhistleStop Projects facilitate the reporting of in-progress street crimes by witnesses through a whistle alert system that signals residents in their homes to call the police. The sound of the whistle also signals persons walking in the area that someone is in need of help. The WhistleStop Projects reviewed in this study were administered by nonlaw enforcement agencies.

*2.1.1b. Radio Watch Projects.* Participation in Radio Watch CCRPs is usually limited to citizens whose occupations give them access to two-way radio taxis or trucks but may also include citizen band radio clubs. Participants in the project are asked to report suspicious/criminal activity and public hazards (e.g., fire and traffic accidents) they observe on the job to their company dispatchers, who in turn report the incident to the police.

*2.1.1c. Special Telephone Line Projects.* More than a fifth of the projects surveyed offered special telephone lines to facilitate anonymous reporting of suspicious/criminal activity. The special telephone lines have a telephone number different from the regular police emergency number. Special Telephone Line Projects are often publicized through such channels as bumper stickers, newspapers, and radio and television public service announcements. Some administering agencies mention their Special Phone Line regularly at crime prevention presentations to civic, service, or school groups. This project type can be divided into two subtypes: those that offer reward incentives and those that do not.

Typically, the Special Telephone Line Projects that offer rewards pay money only for information leading to a conviction. The amount of the award is often decided by a committee of citizens. These reward projects are operated more often by civilian agencies than any other project type.

### *2.1.2. Category 2: Educational Projects*

The following three project types resemble one another in that they attempt to encourage witness reporting through a variety of educational approaches. An example of a CCRP of national scope that uses one or more of the educational approaches described below is National Neighborhood Watch, an LEAA-supported program administered nationally by the National Sheriffs Association. The descriptions of the project types below are arranged in a hierarchial fashion according to the degree of involvement required of the citizen participant. The first project type requires the least involvement for the citizen; the last type requires the most. These projects often include other crime prevention activities as well as CCRP activities.

*2.1.2a. Group Presentation Projects.* The primary educational approach employed by this project type is group presentations to civic and service groups, schools, PTAs, church groups, and other community groups. Frequently information concerning these projects is distributed to the general public at shopping centers or county fair displays. All the Group Presentation Projects surveyed in our study are administered by the community relations or crime prevention units of police or sheriff's departments. Group Presentation Projects require little involvement by the citizen other than attending a presentation. The group presentations are usually a one-time crime prevention treatment. An officer provides information concerning home security and target-hardening techniques, as well as encouragement to citizens to report all suspicious and criminal activity to the police. Some projects give instruction on what constitutes suspicious or criminal activity, what descriptive information is important, and how to report such information to the police.

*2.1.2b. Membership Projects.* These CCRPs use essentially the same educational approach as Group Presentation projects, except that they go further in requiring greater commitment from the citizen than merely attending a presentation. Participants in membership projects usually sign up to become a member of the CCRP at a presentation given by the administrating agency. Participants in the membership projects use anonymity as an incentive for membership, and some give citizen participants a code number to use in reporting suspicious/criminal activity. The agencies that administer membership projects usually maintain a list of the names, addresses, and telephone numbers of participants.

*2.1.2c. Home Presentation Projects.* The highest priority activity of these CCRPs is presentations to neighborhood groups in a resident's home; in addition, many Home Presentation Projects also give group presentations and have a form of membership for participants. The Home Presentation Projects constituted about 30% of the projects surveyed. Nearly all use some form of publicity to inform the target population of the project's existence. Group presentations and publicity are used mainly to obtain requests for home presentations. Some Home Presentation Projects also use door-to-door canvassing to actively solicit neighbors to host home presentations. About 70% of the Home Presentation Projects surveyed were administered by law enforcement agencies. The remaining 30% were administered by the community groups or civilian-run city agencies. The Home Presentation Projects surveyed were implemented by full-time staffs ranging from 1 to 16 persons.

## 2.2. Analysis of Project Treatment of Nonreporting

The various project types can be examined to illustrate how they relate to the reasons why people may not help crime victims. Table 1 shows the assumed reasons why citizens do not report crimes that they witness and the ways these programs deal with these reasons. The reasons for nonreporting listed in Table 1 represent an integration of information received from project operators, telephone interviews of experts, and the literature review. The purpose of this table is to show how the particular structures of CCRP project types deal with the assumed factors for not reporting crimes or suspicious events. The treatments for not reporting were derived from interviews with program experts, questionnaire responses from project directors, and relevant social science research. Not all projects within a project type actually use the treatment techniques listed. It is my intention, however, to show the major focus of each of the project types.

In order to present a more comprehensive explanation of Table 1, each project type will be discussed in terms of how it deals with each treatment.

### *2.2.1. Category 1: Projects That Facilitate Reporting*

*2.2.1a. WhistleStop Projects.* Basically, WhistleStop Projects do not encourage citizen surveillance or educate citizens about how to identify crimes. Instead, these programs tend to focus on how to report a crime.

*Table 1. Reason for Not Reporting and Potential Counterstrategies by Each Project Type*

| | | Project type[a] | | | | | | | |
|---|---|---|---|---|---|---|---|---|---|
| | | Category 1 | | | | Category 2 | | | |
| | | A | B | C | D | E | F | G | H |
| Reason | Counterstrategies | | | Phone lines | | | | Home presents | |
| 1. Did not see it happen | Encourage heightened surveillance | X[b] | X | | | X | X | X | X |
| 2. Saw it but does not think it was a crime | Educate to identify crimes | X | X | | | | | X | X |
| 3. Does not know how to report | Educate on how to report | X | X | X | X | X | X | X | X |
| 4. Thinks others will report (diffusion of responsibility) | Educate about phenomenon | X | X | | | | | X | X |
| 5. Too inconvenient to report | Make reporting easier | X | X | X | X | | | | |
| 6. Fear of consequences of | Provide anonymity; provide | X | X | X | X | X | X | X | X |

| | | A | B | C | D | E | F | G | H |
|---|---|---|---|---|---|---|---|---|---|
| reporting (e.g., retaliation, embarrassment, others may disapprove) | protection; present evidence on community's norms | | | | | | | | |
| 7. Feels police would not want to be bothered (not serious enough) | Inform citizens about police willingness to respond | | X | | | X | X | X | X |
| 8. Distrusts police (anticipate poor treatment by police) | Improve police performance; change attitude toward police | | X | | | X | X | X | X |
| 9. Feels it would not matter if reported (ineffective criminal justice system) | Improve system; demonstrate system effectiveness | | X | | | X | X | X | X |
| 10. Apathy 1 (does not care about consequences to victim) | Build community cohesiveness; develop empathy | | | | | | | | X |
| 11. Apathy 2 (does not want to report for other reasons, e.g., other costs, does not feel need) | Provide incentives, e.g., awards and rewards; foster commitment to report | X | X | X | | | X | X | X |

[a] *Code:* A = Whistlestop; B = Radio watch; C = Reward; D = Nonreward; E = Group presentation; F = Membership; G = Unorganized block; H = Organized block.
[b] An X identifies a project type that is structured to imply a specific counterstrategy.

The response to witnessing a crime is twofold. One response is to blow a whistle if an individual is an eyewitness or does not have immediate access to a telephone and hears another whistle. The second response is to call the police if an individual hears a whistle being blown while having access to a telephone. Citizens are instructed that they are to assume the responsibility to call the police and not to depend upon others. The use of whistles makes it easier for a witness to report the crime insofar as others can be made aware of it. In addition, the whistle identifies that a crime is being committed and thus bystanders should call the police. Although WhistleStop Projects do not provide protection to people reporting crime, they do assure some anonymity in that the person who calls the police does not have to give his or her name. However, the act of blowing a whistle in public is certain to draw attention to an individual. Fear of embarrassment, more than anything else, may make people reluctant to blow a whistle when they witness a suspicious event. The visibility of persons carrying whistles in the neighborhood, however, could lead to the perception of community support for reporting of crime.

WhistleStop, by itself, does not deal directly with police–community relations and thus does not use treatments that depend on police performance or on informing citizens of police willingness to respond. Nor does WhistleStop deal with improving the criminal justice system or demonstrating the system's effectiveness. Similarly, WhistleStop by itself does not build community cohesiveness. However, WhistleStop does deal with developing a commitment to report crimes. The behavioral act of purchasing the whistle is assumed to lead to more reporting.

*2.2.1b. Radio Watch Projects.* Radio Watch Projects, as seen in Table 1, appear to use most of the treatments in dealing with why people do not report crimes. This is so because of the rather intensive educational sessions possible given the limited number of persons to be educated. Coupled with this advantage is the fact that many individuals driving cars equipped with two-way radios are, to some extent, trained observers. This is especially so for cab drivers.

During the educational training session, increased surveillance and better definitions of suspicious/criminal incidents are often stressed. In addition, proper radio procedure in reporting the incident to the company dispatcher is stressed. Company dispatchers are also trained on how to report to the police department. The existence of a radio in a vehicle certainly makes it more convenient to report a crime than searching for a telephone. In addition, the system allows for a great deal of anonymity.

Since Radio Watch participants are told to stay at the scene of the incident while awaiting police response, feedback concerning police response time and behavior is immediate and direct. If the police do not properly respond, participants may complain to the police officer in charge of the project who would then, it is hoped, initiate some remedial action. Thus the system's effectiveness is both monitored and demonstrated. Radio Watch does not in any general sense build community cohesiveness. However, it does deal with other factors that might be labeled apathy. A commitment to report is reinforced by posting a decal on the vehicle and going through the training sessions. In addition, many projects offer such awards as plaques and money to outstanding Radio Watch participants.

*2.2.1c. Special Phone Lines (Reward).* Special phone lines that offer rewards do not attempt to educate citizens about the importance of surveillance or how to identify crimes. They do very explicitly instruct people how to report an incident. In this sense they make reporting easier since there is a special number that is called. All projects emphasize that reports can be taken anonymously, and in some cases the citizen does not actually speak to an officer but instead to a phone answering device. These programs do not deal with the citizen's relationship with the police department, improve the criminal justice system, nor demonstrate its effectiveness. In addition, these CCRPs do not attempt community development. They do, however, provide incentives for reporting by offering rewards for convictions.

*2.2.1d. Special Phone Lines (Nonreward).* Nonreward special phone lines are similar to the reward lines except that there is no monetary reward for the information leading to conviction.

### *2.2.2. Category 2: Educational Programs*

*2.2.2a. Group Presentations.* Group Presentation Projects do attempt to encourage heightened surveillance. However, they tend not to emphasize educating individuals in identifying crimes. There is some emphasis on how to report a crime but few presentations include defining of responsibility. None of these CCRPs provides easier means for reporting but all of them do provide discussion of community norms (e.g., crime reporting is the "right" thing to do). In addition, citizens are informed about police willingness to respond to calls concerning suspicious activities. Many Group Presentation Projects conducted by police agencies use presentations to develop better community relations. Some projects, in addition, attempt to demonstrate system effectiveness by describing how police prioritize their calls, that is, citizens are informed that police may be responding to a higher priority call and that this is why some responses may take longer. However, there is little attempt to organize citizens to institute changes in the criminal justice system. The only evidence of this is the development of other projects associated with some of these CCRPs, for example, Court Watchers.

*2.2.2b. Membership Projects.* The activities of membership projects differ from Group Presentations only in providing a greater incentive for reporting. It is assumed that "joining" a group that pledges itself to reporting suspicious/criminal activities fosters a greater commitment to report.

*2.2.2c. Home Presentations (Unorganized Block).* These projects, in addition to the activities of the Membership Projects, usually educate citizens concerning how to define crimes and suspicious activities. Because the meetings are held in the participants' neighborhood, it is likely that project personnel will point out how to recognize unusual events. Additionally, it is more likely in this type of group that diffusion of responsibility (assuming that others will report) will be discouraged. Finally, attendance at such a meeting should encourage a commitment to report.

*2.2.2d. Home Presentations (Organized Block).* These projects usually maintain the same type of activities found in the previously described educational projects. This is the only type of project, however, that attempts to build community cohesiveness. The development of concern for neighbors is assumed to lead to an impact on reporting behavior. Yet initiating and maintaining some degree of organization is probably one of the most difficult activities for a CCRP to undertake.

### 2.3. Conclusions

I have described a number of programs that encourage bystander intervention in crimes and that implicitly assume a variety of explanations for why people do not intervene. All of these reasons find support in the research literature. That is, one can point to specific research findings that support the bases of these projects. Thus there seems to be a convergence between research findings and the structure of projects. However, I believe this convergence to be more apparent than actual.

- From interviews with program developers, it is extremely clear that these programs were developed *without* any research input. Program developers in this area did not base the structure of their programs on the literature on helping behavior or bystander intervention. More often their own intuition or common sense was the guiding factor. It is clear that the research findings in this area, by and large, are not known to individuals who must deal with bystander intervention as a social problem.
- Almost all the programs investigated were not scientifically evaluated. Therefore, there is a lack of strong empirical data to support

the efficacy of the programs or the correctness of the assumptions underlying the programs and thus the generalizability of research related to these assumptions.

- From the researcher's perspective, it is also clear that research in this area has been aimed at understanding the social psychological processes underlying bystander intervention, with little or no appreciation of applications. The research has not been directed at bystander intervention as a social problem but rather as a social phenomenon. This perspective has led to ignoring basic questions concerning change mechanisms. That is, how does a society increase bystander intervention in such situations as crimes? Most research has not been directed at developing change mechanisms useful in this area. For example, how does one develop an effective educational program in this area? How effective are various mass media techniques? Moreover, social science research in this area has, by and large, dealt with variables that cannot be easily manipulated in a practical and applied sense. Thus research on personality characteristics, demographic characteristics, and the number of other bystanders present does not provide program developers with useful information concerning the structure of their programs.
- Finally, there is little or no descriptive research in this area. This has drawbacks for both basic research and applications. For example, from the basic research perspective, the overreliance on experimental methods has left us with a literature concerning specific variables but not with a knowledge of how frequently the variables manipulated in the experiments occur in the real world. My own research on interpersonal influence, for example, indicates that it is a very powerful factor in encouraging bystanders to report a crime. However, I have no idea how frequently one bystander will attempt to verbally influence another bystander. Thus the ecological validity of the research is basically unknown. From the applied-policy perspective, the program developer does not have the relevant information he or she needs in order to develop a program based upon research findings. For example, the reasons for nonreporting listed in Table 1 are not accompanied by a frequency table that would indicate which are the most frequent or most serious of the reasons. Clearly, developing a counterstrategy for a reason that occurs very rarely would not be productive. Thus descriptive research would appear to be helpful not only to basic researchers, but to individuals interested in applications as well.

## 3. REFERENCES


Bar-Tal, D. Social norms, feelings, and other factors affecting helping and altruism. In L. Berkowitz (Ed.), *Advances in experimental social psychology* (Vol. 6). New York: Academic Press, 1972.

Bar-Tal, D. *Prosocial behavior: Theory and research.* Washington, D.C.: Hemisphere, 1976.

Bickman, L. Bystander intervention in a crime: The effect of a mass media campaign. *Journal of Applied Social Psychology,* 1975, *5,* 296–302.

Bickman, L., & Helwig, H. The effects of incentives on the inhibition of shoplifting. *Criminology,* 1979, *17,* 283–300.

Bickman, L., & Rosenbaum, D. Crime reporting as a function of bystander encouragement, surveillance, and credibility. *Journal of Personality and Social Psychology,* 1977, *35,* 577–586.

Bickman, L., Lavrakas, P. J., Green, S. K., North-Walker, N. N., Edwards, J., Borkowski, S., Shane-DuBow, S. S., & Wuerth, J. *Citizen crime reporting projects: A phase I national evaluation program summary report.* Washington, D.C.: U.S. Government Printing Office, 1976.

Bryan, H. H., & London, P. Altruistic behavior by children. *Psychological Bulletin,* 1970, *73,* 200–211.

Deutscher, I. *Why do they say one thing, do another?* Morristown, N.J.: General Learning Press, 1973.

Ennis, P. H. *Criminal victimization in the United States: A report of a National Survey, U.S. President's Commission on Law Enforcement and Administration of Criminal Justice.* Washington, D.C.: U.S. Government Printing Office, 1967.

Huston, T. L., & Korte, C. The responsive bystander: Why he helps. In T. Kickona (Ed.), *Morality: A handbook of moral development and behavior.* New York: Holt, Rinehart & Winston, 1975.

Krebs, D. L. Altruism: An examination of the concept and a review of the literature. *Psychological Bulletin,* 1970, *73,* 258–302.

Latané, B., & Darley, J. M. *The unresponsive bystander: Why doesn't he help?* New York: Appleton-Century-Crofts, 1970.

Liska, A. E. *The consistency controversy.* Cambridge, Mass.: Schenkman, 1975.

Macaulay, J. R., & Berkowitz, L. (Eds.). *Altruism and helping behavior.* New York: Academic Press, 1970.

Midlarsky, E. Aiding responses: An analysis and review. *Merrill-Palmer Quarterly,* 1968, *14,* 229–260.

Skogan, W. G. Issues in the measurement of victimization. *U.S. Bureau of Justice Statistics Reports,* June 1981.

Staub, E. Helping a distressed person: Social, personality, and stimulus determinants. In L. Berkowitz (Ed.), *Advances in experimental social psychology* (Vol. 7). New York: Academic Press, 1974.

Wispé, L. (Ed.). Positive forms of social behavior. *Journal of Social Issues,* 1972, *28,* 1–19.

# 24

# Learning to "Give to Unnamed Strangers"

## The Process of Commitment to Regular Blood Donation

Jane Allyn Piliavin, Dorcas E. Evans, and Peter Callero

### 1. INTRODUCTION

In 1971, Richard Titmuss published a book called *The Gift Relationship* in which he compared the British and American blood collection and distribution systems. Speaking of the British system, which is based entirely on the voluntary community donor, he described such donation as "a free gift of blood to unnamed strangers" (p. 239). In this chapter, we shall describe several aspects of a large-scale research project in which we are trying to understand how individuals in Madison, Wisconsin (where the donation system is also based on the voluntary community

---

JANE ALLYN PILIAVIN • Department of Sociology, University of Wisconsin, Madison, Wisconsin 53706. DORCAS E. EVANS • Stanford Heart Disease Prevention Program, Stanford University, Stanford, California 94305. PETER CALLERO • Department of Sociology, University of California at Riverside, Riverside, California 92502. Funds have been received from the following sources: a National Institutes of Health Biomedical Sciences Support Grant to the University of Wisconsin Graduate School, a Graduate School grant for summer salary support to the first author, and extensive support from the American National Red Cross and the Badger Blood Region through the Red Cross matching grants program, and a three-year research grant from the Heart, Lung, and Blood Institute of the NIH, Grant No. HL 24425.

donor) develop and maintain the motivations and habits underlying sustained, repeated, regular blood donation. Again, quoting Titmuss, "How can they and how do they learn to give—and to give to unnamed strangers, irrespective of race, religion, or colour?" (p. 12).

### 1.1. A General Framework for the Analysis of Action

Triandis (1977) presents a general model of the determinants of action that we have found useful in organizing our thinking about the process of developing commitment to regular blood donation. He proposes that actions are determined by a combination of behavioral intentions and habit strength. Behavioral intentions, in turn, are determined by the actor's perception of relevant social norms, his or her preferences and attitudes toward the action, and the perceived consequences of the action.

Prosocial behaviors such as blood donation can be viewed within this broad framework, as can any other type of behavior. The questions to be raised concerning the determinants of blood donation, then, can be grouped as are the levels in the general model:

1. How do potential donors come to develop the motives underlying behavioral intentions to donate? That is, how do they come to accept social norms, develop preferences for and positive attitudes toward the action of giving blood, and come to understand the consequences of their behavior, for themselves and others?
2. How do these and other factors combine to crystallize behavioral intentions to continue donating in the future?
3. How is a habit of donation developed?
4. How do intentions and habits combine to determine donation decisions on any given occasion?

We shall use this framework loosely to present our research in this chapter. First we shall discuss the nature of the motives (attitudes, perceived norms, perceived consequences) we see as relevant to blood donation. Then we shall present data on the process by which these motives, behavioral intentions, and donation habits appear to be developed. Finally, we shall attempt to show how individuals who begin their donation "careers" motivated somewhat differently develop their motives, intentions, and habits through somewhat different processes.

Before we begin our discussion we want to raise two points. First, we expect any act—including prosocial acts—to be multiply motivated: by external social pressures, by personal moral norms, by the expectation of intrinsic rewards, even by unconscious conditioning. Some of these motives will be more available to awareness than others. This does not, however, make the unconscious ones the "real" ones; self-based, conscious motives are just as real as unconscious processes. Second, with regard to acts that are repeated over time, we believe that there is a natural developmental progression by which the controls over or reinforcement for the behavior change from being *primarily* external to being *primarily* internal.

## 1.2. Development of Motives That Promote Donation

We propose that there are five rough categories of motivation that underlie voluntary "altruistic" blood donation: (1) external social motives, (2) community or social group responsibility, (3) personal moral obligation, (4) self-based humanitarian or altruistic concern, and (5) hedonic motives, involving either conscious pleasure in the activity or unconscious affective "addiction" to the act. These can be mapped onto Triandis's groupings of social norms and attitudes and preferences. It appears that, *in general*, in the developmental process through which donors move they add to their initial external "push" factors first internal "push" motives and then new internal "pull" motives. We need to make two qualifications of this statement, however. First, by far the most salient conscious motivation for donors at all levels of commitment is humanitarian or altruistic concern, often expressed as a disposition to enjoy helping others. It may be that some level of such altruistic motivation is necessary before the impact of any other factors can be felt. Nevertheless, there is also evidence for an increasing role for this type of motivation over the stages of the commitment process. Second, when we suggest that new internal motives are *added to* more external ones as socialization to the role of committed donor progresses, we do not mean to imply that external motives lose their absolute importance.[1] They lose their relative importance; total motivation to give increases as new motives are added.

The typical "rookie" donor comes to the first donation experience both encouraged by and accompanied by a friend. At Youngblood (the permanent Red Cross donation center on the University of Wisconsin–Madison campus where much of our research has been done), there is often considerable coercion involved because of competitive blood

[1]In part this is obvious. Those who do not enjoy an activity, or who cannot convince themselves that there are good moral or society-based reasons for doing it, will stop doing it. The process by which it occurs, and how the various types of internal motives are developed, is what is of interest. There will be exceptions as well. The best example is that of members of the armed forces, who are coerced to give blood, both by threats of negative sanctions and by offers of rewards (e.g., leave, time off unpleasant duties). One would not expect such individuals to develop other motives to support and justify their actions.

drives and various promotions (free ice cream, T-shirts, etc.). At mobile community drives and at places of business, there is also considerable social pressure to do one's part. At high school drives there tend to be teasing, dares, and appeals to not being "chicken." Thus external social motivations are often strongly present at the outset. The second type of motivation, community responsibility, is also present early in the process but becomes more personally relevant with time. Donors come to see donation as something any good citizen should do. This community responsibility then shades into a personal moral responsibility such that the donor will see him or herself as a less good person if he or she does not perform this act (see Schwartz, 1977). All of these motivations are largely "pushes"; the person is motivated to the act in order to avoid (1) social sanctions, (2) the image of self as not a responsible member of society, or (3) feelings of low self-worth associated with not living up to moral standards. All relate to Triandis's category of "social norms."

There are also self-based intrinsic motivations that develop (perhaps in parallel, perhaps later) that have more of a "pull" quality. That is, the donor is positively attracted to the act rather than pushed to it. These can be seen as examples of Triandis's category of attitudes and preferences. We feel (with little hard evidence) that there are probably two different kinds: (1) enjoyment of helping for its own sake, and (2) mastery. That is, part of the motivation for donation appears to be a positive sense of self-affirmation as a good, altruistic person who *likes* to help, who does it willingly, and who enjoys thinking that he or she is doing good. The other type of motivation has little to do with the manifest purpose of donation; rather, the person has a need to master the fear donation engenders and finds reward in successfully negotiating the experience *as an experience.*

The final type of motivation we believe to be involved in donation is, essentially, addiction to the emotional experience of donation *per se,* such as that described by opponent–process theory (Hoffman & Solomon, 1974; Solomon, 1980; Solomon and Corbit, 1974). This type of motivation can be developed in the context of strong emotion; in the case of blood donation, the initial negative feeling state is anxiety or fear. When this is replaced, after donation, by relief, relaxation, and a warm positive feeling about the self, the basis has been established for "addiction" to the act. The feeling of mastery discussed above could also contribute to the development of hedonic motives. Such motivation is likely to remain unconscious and to contribute mainly to the habit strength component of the model.

### 1.3. Neutralization of Constraints against Donation

In addition to considering the reasons why people donate, one must also consider the reasons why they do not. There are a number of costs attendant upon blood donation: taking time away from work, waiting in lines, finding transportation to the donation center, temporary interference with one's life style (e.g., because of prohibitions against smoking, drinking, or exercising for a time after donations), pain, and the fear of needles. Chief among these are fears about the pain of donation (Oswalt, 1977).

Kessler (1975), who studied a group of rare blood "on call" donors in New York, claims that

> Their habit seemed to grow from an inability to answer the negative question, "Why not?" People who cannot acquire the habit differ from those who can less in the positive conception of the act than in the negative one. . . . In the process of giving, certain meanings and expectations are developed, the positive component becomes clearer, new "why nots" are created possibly leading the donor to drop out after giving only a few times. . . . Only after three or four . . . donations can a donor be said to have developed a habit.

Using Triandis's framework, we can categorize these as perceived negative consequences of donation. In order to develop and sustain behavioral intentions (and a habit of donation, as Kessler points out) these negative consequences must come to be neutralized. Leading donors to attend to the importance of each individual donation for the maintenance of the blood supply can counteract natural tendencies to "free ride" on the contributions of others to avoid these costs. Simple experience with donation also tends to lead to decreased concern with the pain and other physical aftereffects.[2]

[2]Although we see blood donation as an example of the general category of prosocial behavior, it is also clear to us that there are some very specific characteristics of blood donation that may make generalization of our findings to other types of prosocial behavior difficult. First, blood donation as an instance of helping behavior always involves submitting to a physical insult to the body. Inherent in the act are the costs associated with venipuncutre and bloodletting: pain as well as loss of hemoglobin and other vital substances in the blood. A significant proportion of donors experience a range of other unpleasant effects, including fear before donation, weakness or bruising afterward, and occasionally fainting, nausea, or even convulsions during the donation process. Second, there is powerful symbolism associated with blood: religious significance, association of warfare, death symbolism, even menstrual associations that can elicit powerful emotional effects in some individuals. A third specific feature of blood donation is the constraint on the frequency with which it can be performed. The most committed of donors is not permitted to "give the gift" more than five times a year, because red blood cells regenerate relatively slowly. Pheresis programs allow some donors to give more often, since in pheresis only fractions of the blood that regenerate rapidly are extracted (e.g., white blood cells, platelets). However, pheresis donation differs from regular donation in many other ways, most importantly that it is *not* a gift to the collectivity; it is a gift to a specific, *known* stranger. Thus its motivational basis is likely to be quite different. A final difference from many other types of helping is that blood donation is indeed an anonymous gift. One receives no direct thanks or appreciation from the recipient, and never knows whether one's act had any positive effects. One is thus making a symbolic gesture of giving to the collectivity, of contributing anonymously for the use of any member of the

## 2. THE "BLOOD, SWEAT, AND FEARS" RESEARCH PROJECT

### 2.1. Empirical and Theoretical Foundations

We began this research in the spring of 1977 with a period of participant observation and open-ended discussions with nurses and donors at Youngblood. From these we developed a formal unstructured interview schedule that we administered to 22 self-defined regular donors who had given from 4 to over 12 units of blood. These regular donors suggested other important variables in the developmental process.

We also drew on three theoretical approaches to guide in the selection of variables in the donor and the donation setting that should be important for the development of commitment. First, we have relied on Becker's (1963) model of commitment to a deviant career for understanding how a donor negotiates the early stages of commitment. He posits that a positive first experience with some activity leads to self-labeling as "a person for whom the activity is possible," continued activity leads to self-definition as a member of the group (e.g., of blood donors), and commitment follows from the recognition by other members of the group that you are one of them. All of these processes take place in a group context and are dependent upon it. The motives we have discussed that reflect the outcomes of this process include community responsibility and feelings of personal moral obligation, internalized in the self-concept.

We have used attribution theory and related approaches to the development of intrinsic motivation (Csikszentmihalyi, 1978; Deci, 1975; Heider, 1958; Kelley, 1967; Kruglanski, 1978) for understanding the factors within the first few donation experiences that lead donors (1) to perceive and focus on their internal motives as contrasted to their external ones, and (2) to develop a positive attitude toward the act as an end in itself. Deployment of attention in the setting, the definition of self heard from others or developed inside one's head, and interpretations of locus of control are important factors here.

Finally, opponent–process theory (Hoffman & Solomon, 1974; Solomon, 1980; Solomon & Corbit, 1974) is most useful in our understanding of the decreasing importance of pain and fear and the increasing importance of positive affect over time for maintaining the *habit* of donating. Becker's model helps most in understanding the cognitive and social motives for giving, attributions and intrinsic motivation models in understanding self-based and attitudinal factors, and opponent-process

community. Charitable donations also have this character; emergency intervention, volunteer activities, and many other helping acts do not.

theory in understanding unconscious emotional factors. Our approach has not been to attempt to "prove" one theory or the other but rather to utilize all of them in an attempt to understand the development of the multiple motives we believe underlie commitment to regular donation.

We also consulted the literature on blood donation for clues regarding the development of commitment. This literature generally lacks evidence regarding motivational differences between rookie and return donors. Condie and Maxwell (1970) report that rookies were more influenced by friends, said they felt more reluctance to give, and experienced more pain. Paulhus, Shaffer, and Downing (1977) also found that rookies were more bothered by the pain, but that regulars were more annoyed by other cost factors such as having to wait a long time. Regulars also rated themselves as more motivated to give and more likely to give in the future. These authors also performed an experimental manipulation in which they made salient either altruistic reasons for giving, self-interest reasons, both, or neither. These manipulations had no effect on rookies; being exposed to the altruistic reasons increased veterans' estimates of the likelihood that they would donate in the future.

What evidence there is, then, suggests that regular donors are less affected by outside influences, are more motivated by an internal, altruistic desire to give, and tolerate pain more easily than do rookies. These findings could be because of selection, socialization, or both.

## 2.2. The Development of Motives for Donation and the Neutralization of Costs

### *2.2.1. Restrospective Data Regarding Initial Motivations*

Using the three theoretical frameworks discussed above, insights gathered from our unstructured interviews, and the few clues in the literature, we designed a mailed questionnaire, which was sent first to a pretest sample of regular donors and then, in April 1978, to everyone who had given blood for the first time at Youngblood from September to April of the 1977–1978 school year ($N$ = 400). We also followed their donation records through June 1979. In the questionnaire, we included a number of items tapping motives for donation. In the three columns of Table 1, we present a comparison among (1) the group of these rookies who had not yet returned for a second donation in the 13 to 22 months since their initial donation ($N$ = 197), (2) those who had returned once ($N$ = 98), and (3) those who had given three or more times, combined with the "regulars" used in the pretest ($N$ = 65). These results are probably attributable to a combination of selection and socialization.

Additional information was obtained from a second questionnaire

*Table 1. Items on Which There are Differences between "Rookies" and Returning Donors: 1977–1978 Youngblood Sample (spring 1978 mailing, with pretest)*

| Item | 1 donation ($N$ = 197) | 2 donations ($N$ = 98) | Pretest & 3+ donations ($N$ = 65) | $p$ level[a] |
|---|---|---|---|---|
| Reasons for donation:[c] | | | | |
| Enjoy helping | 1.54a | 1.39b | 1.37b | .075 |
| Obligation to group | 2.91a | 3.03ab | 3.26b | .11 |
| Not disappoint people | 2.91a | 3.08a | 3.48b | .001 |
| Curious | 2.21a | 1.96a | 2.52b | .006 |
| Moral obligation to give blood for general use[d] | 4.74a | 4.92ab | 5.23b | .10 |
| How strongly motivated?[e] | 5.23a | 5.40a | 5.93b | .003 |
| Think less of self if refused to give if able?[f] | 2.15a | 2.11a | 1.78b | .01 |
| Scales: | | | | |
| Altruism[g] | 5.05a | 4.59b | 4.69b | .02 |
| Intention to donate[h] | 3.53a | 3.22b | 3.19b | .0001 |
| Open-end answers to reasons for giving again: | ($N$ = 190) | ($N$ = 99) | ($N$ = 32)[b] | |
| "Good citizen" reasons | 48%a | 56%a | 72%b | .04 |
| "Why not?" reasons | 24%a | 35%b | 38%b | .075 |

[a]Derived from one-way ANOVAs and contrasts using SPSS, except for the open-end answers, for which $\chi^2$ with 2 df, followed by 2 × 2 $\chi^2$'s for contrasts, was used. Within each item, means (percentages) sharing the same letter subscript do not differ from each other at $p < .05$.

[b]Pretest subjects were not scored for open-end reasons for giving again. Thus $N$ in that group is decreased.

[c]1 = Sure it is a reason to 4 = Sure it is not a reason.

[d]−1 = Obligation *not* to give to 0 = No obligation to 7 = Strong obligation to give.

[e]1 = Not very important to 7 = Very important.

[f]1 = Agree strongly to 4 = Disagree strongly.

[g]Scale made up of: easy way to help, rather not be paid, enjoy helping (1 = Agree or sure it is a reason to 4 = Disagree or sure it is not a reason).

[h]Scale made up of: After donation, intend to give again? and Plan to give again in the future? (1 = Yes, 2 = All other answers) and How did you think of self after donation? (1 = Can give without difficulty, 2 = All other answers).

sent to all of the original "rookies" (but not the the pretest sample) in spring 1979. Table 2 presents responses to several questions asked in that survey.[3]

What do these data suggest about our central interest, namely, the *process* by which commitment occurs? How do individuals (1) cope with

[3]The return rate on the first questionnaire, corrected for unreachables, was about 80%. The return on the 1979 questionnaire was only about 60%, with a skew toward multiple donors.

*Table 2. Items on Which Differences between "Rookies" and Returning Donors Appear: 1977–1978 Youngblood Sample (spring 1979 mailing)*[a]

| Item | Number of donations (as of June 1979) 1 (70) | 2 (63) | 3 (31) | 4+ (68) | *p* level[b] |
|---|---|---|---|---|---|
| 1. Pain a factor in choice of activities? (1) | 4.63a | 4.97ab | 5.35bc | 5.28bc | .04 |
| 2. Mean probability of return | 84.6a | 90.1b | 97.4c | 96.9c | .0003 |
| 95% confidence interval for mean probability | 78.6–90.1 | 86.2–90.5 | 90.5–99.7 | 90.3–99.9 | |
| 3. Attention paid to body response during donation[c] | 2.63a | 3.47ab | 3.73bc | 4.21c | .01 |
| 4. Perceived self-change if stopped giving[d] | 14.95a | 16.05a | 17.20a | 18.63a | .16 |
| 5. Percentage seeing self-change on at least one quality | 55% | 53% | 70% | 72% | .05 |
| 6. Self disappointed: affect self-concept? (% yes) | 11% | 9% | 23% | 20% | .05 |
| 7. Significant others disappointed if stop (% yes) | 5% | 7% | 26% | 13% | .05 |
| 8. Percentage defining self as regular donor: | | | | | |
| Yes, regular donor | 26% | 5% | 35% | 76% | .0001 |
| Not sure | 21% | 26% | 26% | 9% | |
| No, not regular donor | 53%ab | 69%a | 39%b | 15%c | |
| 9. Ever try to recruit other donors? (% yes) | 60% | 62% | 71% | 78% | .05 |
| 10. Ever recognized by staff at Youngblood (1 = yes, 2 = no) | 1.79ab | 1.76a | 1.84a | 1.57b | .05 |

[a] *N*'s given at top of table hold only to the first line. The 1 and 2 donation groups are reduced to $N = 19$ and $N = 57$, respectively, for the remainder of the table. Those questions were in a part of the questionnaire supposed to be answered only by 2+ donors. Thus the single-donation group is peculiar.

[b] *P* values are derived from one-way ANOVAs for Items 1–4 and 10; from $\chi^2$ with appropriate degrees of freedom for Items 5–9. All contrasts were done with SPSS for the ANOVAs. Item 8 was done using a series of 2 × 3 $X^2$'s. Within each item, means (percentages) sharing the same letter subscript do not differ from each other at $p < .05$.

[c] 1 = Big factor or a great deal to 7 = No influence or no attention.

[d] Sum of perceived change in responsible, unselfish, and sympathetic self-evaluations. Larger numbers indicate greater negative impact.

the "why nots?" or negative features of donation, (2) develop the appropriate motives and incorporate the role of "blood donor" into their self-concept, (3) come to perceive themselves as likely to continue with the activity, and (4) develop a behavioral commitment to the activity? The data here suggest that all of these processes are going on among our donors, but not at the same rate.

There seem to be, from these data, three "decision points" in the process of commitment to donation. *After the first donation,* some donors can think of reasons "why not." They define themselves as people who can give with difficulty and are uncertain about their commitment to continue (intention scale). They appear to be people who attended closely to their body during donation and to have been less than completely convinced that enjoying helping was an important reason why they donated. Those who remain begin to develop a sense of moral obligation to the collectivity, to incorporate the activity into their self-concept, and to lose their concern with their obligations to particular groups. However, curiosity and not wanting to disappoint those who ask remain important reasons for a second donation. Most who return for a second donation, then, are still not committed donors. *After the second donation,* donors who return appear to have decided that they will continue as donors. They are beginning to believe that significant others will be disappointed if they stop, that they themselves will be disappointed, that they would think less of themselves if they refused, and they are strongly motivated to give. The moral obligation that has been developing now breaks through into citing "good citizen" reasons for continuation—nearly three-quarters of the three-time donors do so. Finally, *after the third donation,* the majority (76%) of returning donors define themselves as "regular donors" when specifically asked. This point corresponds to the point at which nearly half of them claim that the staff at Youngblood recognize them. We see the data in Tables 1 and 2 as consistent with the model of commitment presented by Becker.

### 2.2.2. *Time of Donation Data: Cross-Sectional Sample*

During the 1978–1979 academic year we collected a second set of data that can be brought to bear on these questions. Whereas the 1977–1978 study sampled only first-time donors and asked retrospective questions, the 1978–1979 questionnaire was filled out on the spot directly before and after donation by Youngblood rookies and regulars alike.[4] Because the emphasis in the second year's research was on affec-

[4]We continued with the same questionnaire, for "rookies" only, during the following year. From fall 1978 to April 1980, we also interviewed as many of these first-time donors

tive responses to donation, we asked very few questions concerning motives for donation. We did ask how strongly motivated they were to give overall. We also posed five reasons why people might give blood: enjoyment of helping, moral obligation, not disappointing people who asked, responsibility for helping in the community, and curiosity. Finally, we asked for an estimate of the probability that they would donate again.

In this sample, although the median number of donations was five, the range was from rookies to over 40-liter donors. The differences across donation categories are highly significant on probability of return. All of the differences on the conscious reasons for donation are also significant, except for "enjoy helping." Rookies are more likely to cite curiosity and not disappointing people who asked and less likely to say moral obligation and responsibility.

### 2.2.3. *Time of Donation Data: The Longitudinal Sample*

We also looked at the responses of a subsample for whom we have two or more questionnaires filled out over the year. For all groups, up through eight donations, there are increases in the extent to which donors say "moral obligation" and "community responsibility" are reasons. In general, these differences are not significant statistically (*N*'s are small). For the very small group of rookies for whom we have two questionnaires, however, the mean change score is significant for both the "community responsibility" question ($N = 19$, $P < .025$, one-tailed) and the "moral obligation" question ($N = 19$, $p < .05$, one-tailed). On the "strength of motivation" question, the increase in expressed desire to donate is nearly significant ($N = 35$, $p = .07$, one-tailed).[5] Although this is a small piece of evidence by itself, this longitudinal change suggests that some of the cross-sectional differences we have observed are probably because of a developmental process. (A parallel analysis comparing one-, two-, and three-or-more-time donors at the time of answering our 1977–1978 mailed questionnaire shows an identical borderline relationship, $p = .07$, to reported strength of motivation to give.)

---

as possible, given staff and donor availability. In the 1980–1981 academic year, we did follow-up telephone interviews and mailed questionnaires with this sample of about 700. Preliminary analysis of these data indicate similarities to those reported here. High school donors were also asked to fill out before and after questionnaires during the 1978–1979 and 1979–1980 school years. We then followed the donation histories of all these first-time donors to predict commitment. Since collection of the dependent variable took such a long time, we can report predictively only on the 1977–1978 sample in this chapter.

[5]The "reasons for donation" questions were added to the questionnaire about halfway through the year. The difference in *N*'s does not reflect refusal to answer.

### 2.3. Predicting Behavioral Commitment

Our previous analyses have suggested that at least four processes are going on in the development of commitment to blood donation: (1) neutralization of the perceived negative consequences of donation, (2) developing internal motives and integrating them into the self-concept, (3) making a conscious decision to continue donating, and (4) behavioral commitment, in the sense of developing a self-sustaining habit. We shall now turn to regression analyses predicting intention to continue donating[6] and three behavioral measures: (1) speed of returning for a second donation (among those who return), (2) log donation record rate through spring 1979,[7] and (3) log donation record following the first questionnaire mailing (e.g., donations during the second year of the study).

Ideally we would perform a path analysis, using initial motives and aspects of the first experience to predict developing motives, and then using both motives and prior variables to predict behavioral commitment. Unfortunately, both the "predictor" variables and the motives were obtained "midstream." That is, they both were measured midway between the initial experience and the end point of the collection of the donation record. Since we do not know to what extent the motives just discussed (e.g., strength of motivation and reasons for donation) are cause or consequence of the number of donations up to that time, we have decided to deal only with items directly referring to the initial donation, which can be more securely categorized in the time sequence.

#### 2.3.1. *Regression Analyses: Total Group*

The left panel of Table 3 presents the results of regression analyses in which we included the following categories of variables as predictors: background factors (e.g., parental donation history), factors related to

[6]The measure of intention is an index based on responses to three questions: one on self-definition as a donor and two on intention (recalled intention immediately postdonation and intention at the time of answering the questionnaire). Its range is from 3 to 6.

[7]Since our 1977–1978 sample could begin its donation history as early as September or as late as April, we had to develop a dependent measure that would control for differential opportunity to give. The log record rate measure, therefore, is calculated as the log to the base 10 of the quantity (number of donations divided by the number of days between date of first donation and last day of data collection). We use logs for this measure as well as for the last measure because donation records are highly skewed. Both measures are analyzed only for donors still residing in the Badger Blood Region through June 1979. The region covers 43 of Wisconsin's 72 counties (approximately 57% of the state's population), four counties in the upper peninsula of Michigan, Dubuque County, Iowa, and Jo Daviess County, Illinois. Slightly over two-thirds of the 330 rookies who returned the April 1978 questionnaire still lived in the area in June 1979.

| Predictors | Total sample |  |  |  | Externally motivated donors |  |  |  | Internally motivated donors |  |  |  |
|---|---|---|---|---|---|---|---|---|---|---|---|---|
|  | Intention | Speed of return | Log ARC record rate | Log 1978–1979 ARC record | Intention | Speed of return | Log ARC record rate | Log 1978–1979 ARC record | Intention | Speed of return | Log ARC record rate | Log 1978–1979 ARC record |
| 1. Predonation factors |  |  |  |  |  |  |  |  |  |  |  |  |
| Internal-external | +.17[e] | +.34[e] | +.12[b] |  |  |  |  |  |  |  |  |  |
| Come in alone |  | (.11) | +.17[d] | +.12[b] |  |  |  |  |  | +.26[c] | +.23[d] | +.15[b] |
| Motivation strength | +.20[e] | (.12) |  |  | +.26[c] | (+.16) |  |  | +.18[c] |  |  |  |
| 2. Donation experience factors |  |  |  |  |  |  |  |  |  |  |  |  |
| Donor density |  | +.16[c] |  |  |  | +.31[c] | +.21[c] |  |  |  |  |  |
| Waiting time |  |  | −.19[d] | −.19[d] | (+.11) |  | (−.15) | −.18[b] |  |  | −.24[d] | −.22[c] |
| Nervousness | −.23[e] |  |  |  | −.25[c] | (−.18) |  |  | −.21[c] | +.20[c] | (+.10) |  |
| Concentration |  |  |  |  | −.16[b] |  | +.26[c] | +.25[c] |  |  |  | (−.13) |
| Warm feelings | +.26[c] |  | (.10) |  | +.21[b] |  |  |  | +.27[d] |  | +.16[b] | +.18[c] |
| "Good deed" |  |  |  |  | (+.10) | (+.14) | (+.16) |  |  |  |  |  |
| 3. Physical effects | −.12[c] |  |  |  | (−.11) |  |  |  |  | (−.12) |  |  |
| 4. Intention (for other outcomes) | --------- |  | +.20[d] | +.12[b] | ----------- |  | +.30[d] | +.26[c] | ---------- |  | (+.13) |  |
| 5. Number of donations, 1977–1978 (for 1978–1979 record only) | --------- | ------------ | ---------- | +.17[c] | ----------- | ------------- | ----------- |  | ---------- | ------------- | ----------- | +.24[d] |
| Predictive power ($R^2$) | 23%[e] | 16%[d] | 15%[e] | 14%[d] | 27%[e] | 19% n.s. | 23%[d] | 15% n.s. | 15%[b] | 12% n.s. | 16%[c] | 20%[d] |
| Degrees of freedom | (10/219) | (11/151) | (11/215) | (12/213) | (9/89) | (9/59) | (10/86) | (11/85) | (9/120) | (10/82) | (10/119) | (11/118) |

[a]Figures in the table are standardized beta weights, the equivalent of a correlation with all other predictors held constant. Larger figures (either positive or negative) indicate stronger relationships.
[b]$p < .10$.
[c]$p < .05$.
[d]$p < .01$.
[e]$p < .001$.
[f]Figures in parentheses did not reach $p < .10$ but are suggestive.

donors' entrance into the situation (coming alone or with others, initial impetus to donation, initial perceived strength of motivation for donation), various donation experience factors, and the postdonation experiencing of physical aftereffects. Only variables with significant or suggestive relationships to the dependent variables are displayed (note that background factors were insignificant). Entries in the table are standardized beta weights. The same predictors were used in all equations, except as noted.

A critical feature of this set of regressions is that different predictors affect intentions than speed of return, and that log record rate and the 1978–1979 record are also affected by a somewhat different set of factors than those that influence intentions and speed. The important predictors of *intention* to give again are, in order, warm feelings after donation, lack of nervousness before donation, recalled strength of motives to give before donation, having an internal rather than an external impetus for first donation,[8] and not having negative physical effects during or after donation.

In contrast, only one of the predictors of intention, internal-external impetus to donation, relates to any of the measures of actual return. A new variable, donor density (the number of people who donated on the same day as the donor's rookie donation), predicts speed of return; coming in alone and waiting time are strong predictors of overall record. None of these factors relates to consciously expressed intentions to return. The effect of the presence of numerous other people could operate through mood contagion, by providing behavioral models, or by "normalizing" the activity. Waiting time (as recalled), which is frequently cited as a problem in the descriptive blood donation literature, is clearly shown here to affect return negatively.

Although four of the five predictors of intention do not relate to behavior directly, intention itself is a strong predictor of overall donation record rate. Our interpretation is that the effects of nervousness, warm feelings, motive strength, and physical aftereffects are mediated through intention; they affect intention and intention affects behavior. Figure 1 illustrates these proposed relationships. Note that the effect of intention on the later record (1978–1979) is weaker than its effect on the overall record. Again, this appears to be because of the mediation of the 1977–1978 record. It seems that intention affects early donation behavior; early donation then affects later donations.

[8]"Internal" donors are those who report coming in at the suggestion of a friend, in response to an ad or poster, "because they had always wanted to," or to replace blood used by someone (there are no nonreplacement fees in Wisconsin, so donors are not considered pressured). External donors are those who report coming in for a drive or a promotion.

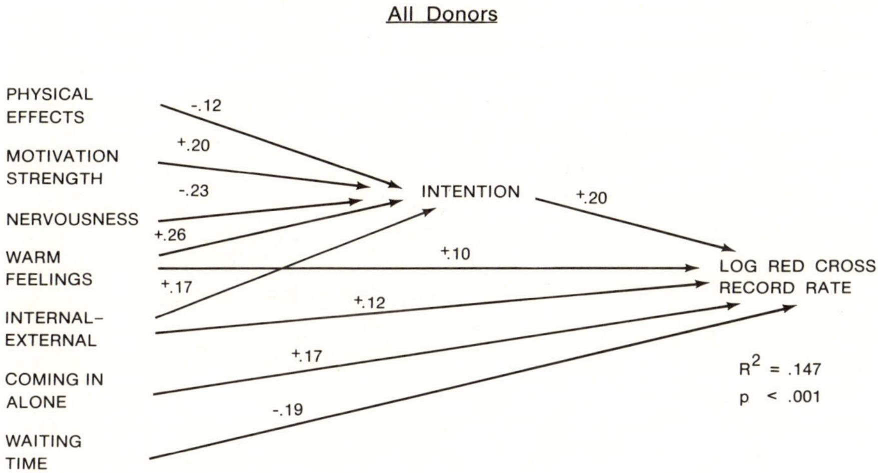


Figure 1. Relationships among predictor variables, intention, and Log Red Cross record rate (best summary indicator of commitment to donation).

### 2.3.2. *Comparative Analyses of Internal and External Impetus Donors*

The extremely strong effect of the variable "Internal-External," which reflects the nature of the initial impetus to donation, led us to carry out separate analyses on the Internals (those who came as a result of their own personal decision or at the simple suggestion of friends) and on the Externals (those who came in because of strong social pressures related to drives or other external reasons such as promotions). It seems reasonable to assume that the Internals may already be partially socialized to the role of committed donor and thus that they may already have passed through some of the stages discussed by Becker: the impact of the first experience (possibly though talking with others) and self and other labeling. Panels 2 and 3 of Table 3 present the results of comparable regression analyses performed separately on the External and Internal impetus donors, respectively.

The major points at which the regressions for the Internal and External donors differ are in the effects of donor density, waiting time, concentration, nervousness, warm feelings, and coming in alone. (An ombudsman test for equivalence of the overall regression models for the two subsamples failed to detect significant differences, although some variables are significantly predictive in one, but not both models.) Our interpretation of the apparent differences is that the externally motivated donor views the first donation in a social context. Donor density is therefore a positive factor, whereas waiting time is more or less irrelevant since it is filled with social activity. Nervousness and concentration on the procedures are negative in their effect on conscious motives—intention to return—as are negative aftereffects, since there are no strong internal motives to counter these costs.

For Externals, intentions developed as a result of donation have a strong effect on later record. Also, in regard to predicting donation record, concentration on the procedures has a positive effect, as does the factor of someone in the setting having mentioned donation in a morally self-affirming context (e.g., what a good person one is to give). (The indicator of this is called "good deed" in the table.) These factors also carry over to the prediction of the record in the second year.

Our interpretation here is that self and other labeling and the integration of the experience with the self-concept are indexed by this cluster of "concentration–good deed–intention." It is in this process that we view the applicability of attribution theory and recent work in intrinsic motivation. We suggest that concentration on the ongoing behavior—a characteristic of endogenously motivated acts—in combination with someone in the setting drawing the donor's attention to how good a person one is to give leads to a reattribution of the cause of the behavior to the self. Such an attribution is likely to lead to continued behavior consistent with the self-attribution.

Among internally motivated donors, only motivation strength, nervousness, and warm feelings relate to intention. These donors have come in more highly motivated, perhaps committed to becoming regular donors before they begin. Intention has almost no variance in this group and does not predict donation record. The social aspects indexed by donor density have no effect; on the contrary, coming in to donate *alone* predicts strongly to rapid and frequent return. External labeling ("good deed") is unrelated to donation record. Only the emotional aspects of the donation experience appear to affect these "precommitted" donors. "Warm feelings" afterward, which affected only intentions for the Externals, affect both intentions and record rate. Waiting time, which presumably engenders annoyance when the setting is not seen as a social occasion, is strongly negatively related to record rate for Internals.

Finally, whereas nervousness has the same negative relationship to the *consciously experienced* intention to continue donating, as it did for Externals, it is significantly positively related to speed of return for Internals. It is this result that suggests the relevance of opponent–process theory to the commitment process, since a negative emotion is necessary for the generation of positive aftereffects in that model. Also intriguing, although not in relationship to any theoretical model, is the fact that our ability to predict donation record *increases* for the internally motivated over time, whereas it *decreases* for the externally motivated (as indexed by the $R^2$ for total record rate as compared to 1978–1979 record). This suggests to us that an unmeasured external factor, such as continued social pressure, is helping to maintain the behavior of those Externals who do continue.

### 2.4. Internal-External Impetus Donors and Reported Motives at First Donation

The regression results reported above led us to reexamine the motive data reported earlier for both the 1977–1978 and the 1978–1979 data to discern whether Internals do indeed enter the first donation setting already partially committed.[9] It is clear from Table 4 that the Internals are more like multiple donation donors than are the rookies in the other two groups (Friend, Externals) on strength of motivation, coming in alone, and subjective probability of return. They are also more like multiple donation donors on the following reported reasons for donating in at least one of the years: "enjoy helping" and "concern for supply," on which Internals are most likely to say this was a reason, and "curious," "thought it would be exciting," "not disappoint people who asked," and "obligation to a membership group," on which Internals are usually least likely to say this was a reason. On the whole, the results are the same for the two samples, although the 1978–1979 data were gathered on the spot whereas the 1977–1978 data are retrospective, and not all of the questions asked in one year are asked in the other.

The reasons for donation questions on which Internals and Externals *do not* differ are "personal moral obligation" (both samples), "community responsibility" (1978–1979 only), and "can deal with pain easily" (1977–1978 only). Within the 1977–1978 sample, on both the "obligation" question and the question regarding pain tolerance, both Internal and External donors—but not friend donors—do show effects in the expected direction with number of donation. That is, those who have given more than once report a higher feeling of moral obligation and less concern with pain as reasons for first donation (interactions significant at $p < .05$).

We have a highly tentative interpretation which is, however, consistent both with the longitudinal results presented earlier and with attribution theory. Internal donors, as well as some External donors, tend to come in alone. Thus, *if* they return, they cannot attribute their *second* donation to social pressure or not disappointing someone. Thus they are more likely to make an *internal* attribution, to personal obliga-

[9]Table 4 presents the means for not two but three types of first donation impetus. We realized when doing the regressions reported earlier that "friend" donors were unlike "Internals" in some ways. We combined them there because of the problem of small sample size occasioned by the necessity to restrict those analyses to donors still in the Badger Blood Region.

*Table 4. The Relationship between Internal-External Initial Impetus to Donation and Reported Reasons for Donation, Strength of Motivation, and Probability of Return, in Two Samples of First-Time Donors*[a]

| | 1978–1979 sample | | | 1977–1978 sample | | |
|---|---|---|---|---|---|---|
| | Externals (41) | "Friend" (39) | Internals (43) | Externals (128) | "Friend" (89) | Internals (104) |
| Reasons given for donation | | | | | | |
| Community responsibility[b,d] | 1.88 | 1.69 | 1.95 | — | — | — |
| Enjoy helping[b] | 1.67 | 1.48 | 1.54 | 1.62 | 1.42 | 1.37[h] |
| Not disappoint people who asked[b] | 2.05 | 2.76 | 3.37[i] | 2.53 | 2.90 | 3.68[i] |
| Curious what donation would be like[b] | 2.56 | 2.10 | 2.35 | 1.98 | 1.96 | 2.41[i] |
| Personal moral obligation[b] | 2.10 | 2.10 | 2.18 | 2.05 | 2.05 | 2.11[f] |
| Felt an obligation to a membership group[b,d] | — | — | — | 2.11 | 3.48 | 3.54[h] |
| Concern for blood supply[b,d] | — | — | — | 1.98 | 1.91 | 1.67 |
| Can deal with pain easily[b,d] | — | — | — | 2.93 | 2.79 | 2.86 |
| Thought it would be exciting[b,d] | — | — | — | 2.54 | 2.66 | 3.11[f] |
| Other items | (74) | (62) | (81) | | | |
| Came in alone?[c] | 1.88 | 1.92 | 1.31[i] | 1.71 | 1.92 | 1.25[f] |
| How strongly motivated? | 4.81 | 4.92 | 5.43[g] | 5.12 | 5.22 | 5.76[h] |
| Subjective probability of return donation[e] | 8.85 | 9.05 | 9.53[i] | — | — | — |

[a]In the 1978–1979 sample, the data are obtained at the time of first donation; in the 1977–1978 sample, they are retrospective.
[b]Code: 1 = Sure it was a reason (for giving blood) to 4 = Sure it was not a reason.
[c]Code: 1 = Came alone, 2 = Came with one other, 3 = Came in a group.
[d]These questions were not asked in 1 of the 2 years.
[e]This question was not asked in 1977–1978; there an index of "intention" was calculated and related strongly to the internal-external variable, as shown in the regression results already reported. The coding of the subjective probability question runs from 0 = No chance of return to 11 = 100% likelihood of return. The distribution is highly skewed.
[f]$p = .10$.
[g]$p < .02$.
[h]$p < .01$.
[i]$p < .001$.

tion or a strong constitution. Friend donors can continue to believe they are doing it for their friend. If we assume that people are not too good at separating current motives from past motives (see Nisbett & Wilson, 1977), the answers to our question about "Time 1" may reflect their feelings at "Time 2."

## 3. SUMMARY

In summary, we see the process of commitment to donation as involving several interrelated processes that appear to be under the control of somewhat different factors and that seem to develop at somewhat different rates: (1) coping with the "why nots," (2) developing motives for donation not tied to external social pressures, (3) developing a behavioral intention, and (4) developing a self-sustaining habit of donation. We see the three theoretical models discussed early in the chapter—Becker's model of developing an identity, the attributional framework, and opponent–process theory—as having contributed to the understanding of different aspects of this process.

Some donors, and our External impetus designation is a rough means for identifying them, come in prepared *not* to continue, attentive to the reasons not to, and perceiving their motives as largely externally, socially based. They must not only learn that there are no good reasons not to donate, but they must also learn why there might be other reasons for donation than curiosity, social obligations, and a vague desire to help. They must, that is, develop "a vocabulary of motives" (Mills, 1940). They must also, in the face of all these reasons *not* to continue, develop a self-sustaining habit of donation. Small wonder that few of them do.

The Internals appear to come in unable to think of reasons for not donating, with strong internal motives to give, and without external social motivations. They seem already to think of themselves as potential regular donors. Thus they need only to be helped to make explicit their internal motives and to develop a self-sustaining, internalized habit.

Becker's model seems most applicable to the external donor. Its explicit use of the social group as an intervening mechanism between taking that first somewhat reluctant step and self-definition seems to fit the behavior of the external and friend-based donors. These donors tend to come in with others, and their continuation is positively related to the number of other donors who gave on the same day. The suggestive relationship between someone making salient the importance of their identity as a donor and their continued donation is also consistent with the importance of social factors for this group. The outcome, then, is to lead them to see themselves in relationship to both the activity and a group that engages in it. Internals already come in with the potential identity, and thus do not need the social setting.

Developing the "vocabulary of motives," first the sense of community responsibility and then a personal moral obligation, seems to happen within the first two donations. From what the fragmentary data show, it may occur more rapidly for Internals and most slowly for "friend" donors who continue to donate with another person. Self-definition as a "regular" occurs by the third or fourth donation. It is in understanding these processes that attribution theory is most useful; the absence of obvious external reasons for performing an action, especially one with clear costs, leads more rapidly to a "biased search" for internal motives and consistency with one's self as perceived.[10]

Finally, developing a habit of regular donation at frequent intervals appears to be under the control of yet other factors. Coming in alone, waiting a short time, and having positive feelings afterward are predictors of frequent return. A straightforward reinforcement theory involving little in the way of cognitive variables seems most applicable to these effects. For Internals only, however, there is the suggestion of a *positive* effect of nervousness at first donation on speed of return for the second donation. This apparent positive effect of initial negative feelings suggests the relevance of opponent–process theory. That is, the initial negative feelings may generate "relief," which adds to other positive feelings the strength of a potentially addictive opponent–process (the "It feels so good when I stop" effect).[11]

In conclusion, we are encouraged by the consistency among our various sources of data and by their conformity to the suggested additive motivational model presented earlier. We look forward to our coming analyses of the far more extensive data sets currently being assembled, from which more definitive answers to questions regarding the process by which these motives and habits develop will be available.

[10]For a more complete discussion of the relevance of attribution and intrinsic motivation theories to blood donation, see Evans (1981).

[11]Much of Solomon's work has been directed precisely at the phenomenon of addiction, covering behaviors ranging from eating to cigarette smoking and drug dependence. Just as no one suggests that addiction is the only motivation behind the behaviors, we are not suggesting that "addiction" explains all of motivation behind blood donation. In fact, because of constraints on the frequency of blood donation, as well as the mildness of the initial A process, one would expect the effects to be rather weak. For more compelling evidence of the relevance of opponent–process theory to commitment to blood donation, see Piliavin, Callero, and Evans (1982).

ACKNOWLEDGMENTS

The authors want to thank a large number of people who have been and continue to be supportive of this research. They include Gary Becker, M.D., director of the Badger Blood Region, Brian Koski, director of Donor Recruitment, and Mac Walker, R.N., director of Youngblood. Innumerable nurses (including Mac and especially Jane, Fran, and Ruthie) have shared their insights with us and helped in many other ways. Joan Hale has put up with our snooping in her records with extremely good grace. Mary Kalscheuer, Kathy Adams, Diane Knott, and Colleen Orsburn have contributed both hard work and insights.

## 4. REFERENCES

Becker, H. *Outsiders: Studies in the sociology of deviance.* New York: Free Press, 1963.

Callero, P., and Piliavin, J. A. Developing a commitment to blood donation: The impact of one's first experience. *Journal of Applied Social Psychology,* 1983, *13,* 1–16.

Condie, S., & Maxwell, N. Social psychology of blood donors. *Transfusion,* 1970, *10,* 79–83.

Csikszentmihalyi, M. Intrinsic rewards and emergent motivation. In M. R. Lepper & D. Greene (Eds.), *The hidden costs of reward.* Hillsdale, N.J.: Lawrence Erlbaum, 1978.

Deci, E. L. *Intrinsic motivation.* New York: Plenum Press, 1975.

Evans, D. *Development of intrinsic motivation for voluntary blood donation among first-time donors.* Unpublished doctoral dissertation, University of Wisconsin-Madison, 1981.

Heider, F. *The psychology of interpersonal relations.* New York: Wiley, 1958.

Hoffman, H. S., & Solomon, R. L. An opponent-process theory of motivation. III. Some affective dynamics in imprinting. *Learning and Motivation,* 1974, *5,* 149–164.

Kelley, H. H. Attribution theory in social psychology. In D. Levins (Ed.), *Nebraska Symposium on Motivation.* Lincoln: University of Nebraska Press, 1967.

Kessler, R. *The meaning of giving: A study of voluntary blood donation.* Unpublished doctoral dissertation, New York University, 1975.

Kruglanski, A. W. Issues in cognitive and social psychology. In M. R. Lepper & D. Greene (Eds.), *The hidden costs of reward.* Hillsdale, N.J.: Lawrence Erlbaum, 1978.

Mills, C. W. Situated actions and vocabularies of motive. *American Sociological Review,* 1940, *5,* 904–913.

Nisbett, R. E., & Wilson, T. D. Telling more than we can know: Verbal reports on mental processes. *Psychological Review,* 1977, *84,* 231–259.

Oswalt, R. M. A review of blood donor motivation and recruitment. *Transfusion,* 1977, *17,* 123–135.

Paulhus, D. L., Shaffer, D. R., & Downing, L. L. Effects of making blood donor motives salient upon donor retention: A field experiment. *Personality and Social Psychology Bulletin,* 1977, *3,* 99–102.

Piliavin, J. A., Callero, P., & Evans, D. E. Addiction to altruism? Opponent–process theory and habitual blood donation. *Journal of Personality and Social Psychology,* 1982, *43,* 1200–1213.

Schwartz, S. H. Normative influences on altruism. In L. Berkowitz (Ed.), *Advances in experimental social psychology* (Vol. 10). New York: Academic Press, 1977.

Solomon, R. L. The opponent process theory of acquired motivation: The costs of pleasure and the benefits of pain. *American Psychologist,* 1980, *35,* 691–712.

Solomon, R. L., & Corbit, J. D. An opponent-process theory of motivation. I. Temporal dynamics of affect. *Psychological Review*, 1974, *81*, 119–145.

Titmuss, R. M. *The gift relationship: From human blood to social policy*. New York: Vantage, 1971.

Triandis, H. C. *Interpersonal behavior*. Monterey, Calif.: Brooks/Cole, 1977.

# Author Index

# Subject Index